BEACON
BIBLE COMMENTARY

LIBRARY OF CONGRESS
CARD NUMBER 64-22906
ISBN: 0-8341-0307-9

Printed in the United States of America

BEACON
BIBLE COMMENTARY

In Ten Volumes

Volume VIII

ROMANS
William M. Greathouse, M.A., D.D.

I CORINTHIANS
Donald S. Metz, B.D., M.A., D.R.E., Ph.D.

II CORINTHIANS
Frank G. Carver, B.D., Th.M., Ph.D.

BEACON HILL PRESS OF KANSAS CITY
Kansas City, Missouri

BEACON BIBLE COMMENTARY

In Ten Volumes

Preface

"All scripture is given by inspiration of God, and is profitable for doctrine, for reproof, for correction, for instruction in righteousness: that the man of God may be perfect, throughly furnished unto all good works" (II Tim. 3:16-17).

We believe in the plenary inspiration of the Bible. God speaks to men through His Word. He hath spoken unto us by His Son. But without the inscripted Word how would we know the Word which was made flesh? He does speak to us by His Spirit, but the Spirit uses the written Word as the vehicle of His revelation for He is the true Author of the Holy Scriptures. What the Spirit reveals is in agreement with the Word.

The Christian faith derives from the Bible. It is the Foundation for faith, for salvation, and sanctification. It is the Guide for Christian character and conduct. "Thy word is a lamp unto my feet, and a light unto my path" (Ps. 119:105).

The revelation of God and His will for men is adequate and complete in the Bible. The great task of the Church, therefore, is to communicate the knowledge of the Word, to enlighten the eyes of their understanding, and to awaken and to illuminate the conscience that men may learn "to live soberly, righteously, and godly, in this present world." This leads to the possession of that "inheritance [that is] incorruptible, and undefiled, and that fadeth not away, reserved in heaven."

When we consider the translation and interpretation of the Bible, we admit we are guided by men who are not inspired. Human limitation, as well as the plain fact that no scripture is of private or single interpretation, allows variation in the exegesis and exposition of the Bible.

Beacon Bible Commentary is offered in ten volumes with becoming modesty. It does not supplant others. Neither does it purport to be exhaustive or final. The task is colossal. Assignments have been made to thirty-nine of the ablest writers available. They are trained men with serious purpose, deep dedication, and supreme devotion. The sponsors and publishers, as well as the contributors, earnestly pray that this new offering among Bible commentaries will be helpful to preachers, teachers, and laymen in discovering the deeper meaning of God's Word and in unfolding its message to all who hear them.

—G. B. WILLIAMSON

Quotations and References

Boldface type in the exposition indicates a quotation from the King James Version of the passage under discussion. Readings from other versions are put in quotation marks and the version is indicated.

In scripture references a letter (*a, b,* etc.) indicates a clause within a verse. When no book is named, the book under discussion is understood.

Bibliographical data on a work cited by a writer may be found by consulting the first reference to the work by that writer, or by turning to the bibliography.

The bibliographies are not intended to be exhaustive but are included to provide complete publication data for volumes cited in the text.

References to authors in the text, or inclusion of their books in the bibliography, does not constitute an endorsement of their views. All reading in the field of biblical interpretation should be discriminating and thoughtful.

Acknowledgments

Scripture quotations have been used from the following sources:

The Amplified New Testament. Copyright 1958 by The Lockman Foundation, La Habra, Calif.

The Berkeley Version in Modern English. Copyright 1958, 1959 by Zondervan Publishing House, Grand Rapids, Mich.

The Bible: A New Translation, James Moffatt. Copyright 1950, 1952, 1953, 1954 by James A. R. Moffatt. Used by permission of Harper and Row, New York.

The Bible: An American Translation, J. M. Powis Smith and Edgar J. Goodspeed. Copyright 1923, 1927, 1948 by the University of Chicago Press.

The Jerusalem Bible, edited by Alexander Jones. Copyright 1966 by Doubleday and Co., Inc., New York.

New American Standard Bible. Copyright 1960, 1962, 1963 by The Lockman Foundation, La Habra, Calif.

Living Letters, Kenneth N. Taylor. © 1962 by Tyndale House, Publishers, Wheaton, Ill.

The New English Bible. © The Delegates of the Oxford University Press and the Syndics of the Cambridge University Press, 1961.

The New Testament, R. A. Knox. © 1944 by Sheed and Ward.

The New Testament in Modern English. © J. B. Phillips, 1958. Used by permission of The Macmillan Company.

The New Testament in the Language of the People, Charles B. Williams. Copyright 1937 by Bruce Humphries, Inc., assigned 1949 to Moody Bible Institute, Chicago.

The New Testament: Today's English Version. Copyright 1966 by The American Bible Society, New York.

Revised Standard Version of the Holy Bible. Copyright 1946, 1952 by the Division of Christian Education of the National Council of Churches.

The Weymouth New Testament in Modern Speech. Copyright 1929 by Harper and Brothers, New York.

How to Use "Beacon Bible Commentary"

The Bible is a Book to be read, to be understood, to be obeyed, and to be shared with others. *Beacon Bible Commentary* is planned to help at the points of understanding and sharing.

For the most part, the Bible is its own best interpreter. He who reads it with an open mind and receptive spirit will again and again become aware that through its pages God is speaking *to him*. A commentary serves as a valuable resource when the meaning of a passage is not clear even to the thoughtful reader. Also after one has seen his own meaning in a passage from the Bible, it is rewarding to discover what truth others have found in the same place. Sometimes, too, this will correct possible misconceptions the reader may have formed.

Beacon Bible Commentary has been written to be used with your Bible in hand. Most major commentaries print the text of the Bible at the top of the commentary page. The editors decided against this practice, believing that the average user comes to his commentary from his Bible and hence has in mind the passage in which he is interested. He also has his Bible at his elbow for any necessary reference to the text. To have printed the full text of the Bible in a work of this size would have occupied approximately one-third of the space available. The planners decided to give this space to additional resources for the reader. At the same time, writers have woven into their comments sufficient quotations from the passages under discussion that the reader maintains easy and constant thought contact with the words of the Bible. These quoted words are printed in boldface type for quick identification.

ILLUMINATION FROM RELATED PASSAGES

The Bible is its own best interpreter when a given chapter or a longer section is read to find out what it says. This Book is also its own best interpreter when the reader knows what the Bible says in other places about the subject under consideration. The writers and editors of *Beacon Bible Commentary* have constantly striven to give maximum help at this point. Related and carefully chosen cross-references have been included in order that the reader may thus find the Bible interpreted and illustrated by the Bible itself.

PARAGRAPH TREATMENT

The truth of the Bible is best understood when we grasp the thought of the writer in its sequence and connections. The verse divisions with which we are familiar came into the Bible late (the sixteenth century for the New Testament and the seventeenth century for the Old). They were done hurriedly and sometimes missed the thought pattern of the inspired writers. The same is true of the chapter divisions. Most translations today arrange the words of the sacred writers under our more familiar paragraph structure.

It is under this paragraph arrangement that our commentary writers have approached their task. They have tried always to answer the question, What was the inspired writer saying in this passage? Verse numbers have been retained for easy identification but basic meanings have been outlined and interpreted in the larger and more complete thought forms.

INTRODUCTION TO BIBLE BOOKS

The Bible is an open Book to him who reads it thoughtfully. But it opens wider when we gain increased understanding of its human origins. Who wrote this book? Where was it written? When did the writer live? What were the circumstances that caused him to write? Answers to these questions always throw added light on the words of the Scripture.

These answers are given in the Introductions. There also you will find an outline of each book. The Introduction has been written to give an overview of the whole book; to provide you with a dependable road map before you start your trip—and to give you a place of reference when you are uncertain as to which way to turn. Don't ignore the flagman when he waves his warning sign, "See Introduction." At the close of the commentary on each book you will find a bibliography for further study.

MAPS AND CHARTS

The Bible was written about people who lived in lands that are foreign and strange to most English-speaking readers. Often better understanding of the Bible depends on better knowledge of Bible geography. When the flagman waves his other sign, "See map," you should turn to the map for a clearer understanding of the locations, distances, and related timing of the experiences of the men with whom God was dealing.

This knowledge of Bible geography will help you to be a better Bible preacher and teacher. Even in the more formal presentation of the sermon it helps the congregation to know that the flight into Egypt was "a journey on foot, some 200 miles to the southwest." In the less formal and small groups such as Sunday school classes and prayer meeting Bible study, a large classroom map enables the group to see the locations as well as to hear them mentioned. When you have seen these places on your commentary maps, you are better prepared to share the information with those whom you lead in Bible study.

Charts which list Bible facts in tabular form often make clear historical relationships in the same way that maps help with understanding geography. To see listed in order the kings of Judah or the Resurrection appearances of Jesus often gives clearer understanding of a particular item in the series. These charts are a part of the resources offered in this set.

Beacon Bible Commentary has been written for the newcomer to Bible study and also for those long familiar with the written Word. The writers and editors have probed each chapter, each verse, every clause, phrase, and word in the familiar King James Version. We have probed with the question, What do these words mean? If the answer is not self-evident we have charged ourselves to give the best explanation known to us. How well we have succeeded the reader must judge, but we invite you to explore the explanation of these words or passages that may puzzle you when you are reading God's written Word.

EXEGESIS AND EXPOSITION

Bible commentators often use these words to describe two ways of making clear the meaning of a passage in the Scriptures. *Exegesis* is a study of the original Greek or Hebrew words to understand what meanings those words had when they were used by men and women in Bible times. To know the meaning of the separate words, as well as their grammatical relationship to each other, is one way to understand more clearly what the inspired writer meant to say. You will often find this kind of enriching help in the commentary. But word studies alone do not always give true meaning.

Exposition is a commentator's effort to point out the meaning of a passage as it is affected by any one of several facts known to the writer but perhaps not familiar to the reader. These facts may be (1) the context (the surrounding verses or chapters), (2) the historical background, (3) the related teaching from other parts of the Bible, (4) the significance of these messages from God as they relate to universal facts of human life, (5) the relevance of these truths to unique contemporary human situations. The commentator thus seeks to explain the full meaning of a Bible passage in the light of his own best understanding of God, man, and the world in which we live.

Some commentaries separate the exegesis from this broader basis of explanation. In *Beacon Bible Commentary* writers have combined the exegesis and exposition. Accurate word studies are indispensable to a correct understanding of the Bible. But such careful studies are today so thoroughly reflected in a number of modern English translations that they are often not necessary except to enhance the understanding of the theological meaning of a passage. The writers and editors seek to reflect a true and accurate exegesis at every point, but specific exegetical discussions are introduced chiefly to throw added light on the meaning of a passage, rather than to engage in scholarly discussion.

The Bible is a practical Book. We believe that God inspired holy men of old to declare these truths in order that the readers might better understand and do the will of God. *Beacon Bible Commentary* has been undertaken only for the purpose of helping men to find more effectively God's will for them as revealed in the Scripture—to find that will and to act upon that knowledge.

HELPS FOR BIBLE PREACHING AND TEACHING

We have said that the Bible is a Book to be shared. Christian preachers and teachers since the first century have sought to convey the gospel message by reading and explaining selected passages of Scripture. *Beacon Bible Commentary* seeks to encourage this kind of expository preaching and teaching. The set contains more than 1,000 brief expository outlines that have been used by outstanding Bible teachers and preachers. Both writers and editors have assisted in contributing or selecting these homiletical suggestions. It is hoped that the outlines will suggest ways in which the reader will want to try to open the Word of God to his class or congregation. Some of these analyses of preachable passages have been contributed by our contemporaries. When the outlines have appeared in print, authors and references are given in order that the reader may go to the original source for further help.

In the Bible we find truth of the highest order. Here is given to us, by divine inspiration, the will of God for our lives. Here we have sure guidance in all things necessary to our relationships to God and under Him to our fellowman. Because these eternal truths come to us in human language and through human minds, they need to be put into fresh words as languages change and as thought patterns are modified. In *Beacon Bible Commentary* we have sought to help make the Bible a more effective Lamp to the paths of men who journey in the twentieth century.

A. F. HARPER

Abbreviations and Explanations

The Books of the Bible

Gen.	Job	Jonah	I or II Cor.
Exod.	Ps.	Mic.	Gal.
Lev.	Prov.	Nah.	Eph.
Num.	Eccles.	Hab.	Phil.
Deut.	Song of Sol.	Zeph.	Col.
Josh.	Isa.	Hag.	I or II Thess.
Judg.	Jer.	Zech.	I or II Tim.
Ruth	Lam.	Mal.	Titus
I or II Sam.	Ezek.	Matt.	Philem.
I or II Kings	Dan.	Mark	Heb.
I or II Chron.	Hos.	Luke	Jas.
Ezra	Joel	John	I or II Pet.
Neh.	Amos	Acts	I, II, or III John
Esther	Obad.	Rom.	Jude
			Rev.

LXX	The Septuagint
Amp. NT	Amplified New Testament
ASV	American Standard Revised Version
Berk.	The Berkeley Version
ERV	English Revised Version
LL	*Living Letters*, by Kenneth N. Taylor
NASB	New American Standard Bible
NEB	New English Bible
RSV	Revised Standard Version
TEV	The New Testament: Today's English Version
BBC	Beacon Bible Commentary
EGT	Expositor's Greek Testament
IB	Interpreter's Bible
ICC	The International Critical Commentary
IDB	The Interpreter's Dictionary of the Bible
NBC	The New Bible Commentary
TDNT	Theological Dictionary of the New Testament

c.	chapter	OT	Old Testament
cc.	chapters	NT	New Testament
v.	verse	Heb.	Hebrew
vv.	**verses**	Gk.	Greek

Table of Contents

The Epistle to the

ROMANS

William M. Greathouse

Introduction

A. Importance

Of Romans, Martin Luther wrote: "This letter is the principal part of the New Testament and the purest gospel, which surely deserves the honour that a Christian man should not merely know it by heart word for word, but that he should be occupied with it daily as the daily bread of his soul. For it can never be read too often or too well. And the more it is used the more delicious it becomes and the better it tastes."[1]

Scholars have disputed the claim that Romans is "the principal part of the New Testament." There are strong reasons for maintaining that the Gospels hold this distinction since they constitute the primary historical witness to Christ, but we must agree with the judgment that "what the gospel is, what the content of the Christian faith is, one learns to know in the Epistle to the Romans as in no other place in the New Testament."[2]

Throughout the centuries this Epistle has in a peculiar way been able to furnish the impulse for spiritual renewal. When the Church has drifted away from the gospel, a deep study of Romans has repeatedly been the means by which the loss has been recovered.

One summer day in the year A.D. 386 the brilliant Augustine, professor of rhetoric at Milan, sat weeping in the garden of his friend Alypius. Having fled the prayers of his godly mother, Monica, he had come under the influence of Bishop Ambrose' ministry in Milan. As he sat that day in the garden, almost persuaded to break with his old life of sin, he heard the voices of children at play. He thought he caught the words, *Tolle lege! Tolle lege!* ("Take up and read! Take up and read!" Receiving this as a voice from God, he took up the scroll which lay at his friend's side and let his eyes rest on the words: "Not in rioting and drunkenness, not in chambering and wantonness, not in strife and envying. But put ye on the Lord Jesus Christ, and make not provision for the flesh, to fulfil the lusts thereof" (Rom. 13: 13-14). "Nor further would I read," he tells us, "nor needed I; for

[1]From the preface of his translation of the Epistle; quoted by Brunner, *The Letter to the Romans,* trans. by H. A. Kennedy (Philadelphia: The Westminster Press, 1959), p. 9.

[2]Anders Nygren, *Commentary on Romans,* trans. by Carl C. Rasmussen (Philadelphia: Fortress Press, 1949), p. 3.

instantly at the end of this sentence, by a light as it were of serenity infused into my heart, all the darkness of doubt vanished away."[3] Who can estimate the far-reaching effects upon the Church and the world of this illumination of Augustine's heart and mind?

In November, 1515, Martin Luther, Augustinian monk and doctor of sacred theology at the University of Wittenberg, began his expositions of Romans. As he prepared his lectures he came to see more and more clearly the meaning of Paul's gospel of justification by faith. "Certainly I had been possessed by an unusually ardent desire to understand Paul in his Epistle to the Romans," he wrote. "Nevertheless, in spite of the ardour of my heart I was hindered by the unique word in the first chapter: 'The righteousness of God is revealed in it.' I hated that word 'righteousness of God', because in accordance with the usage and custom of the doctors I had been taught to understand it philosophically as meaning, as they put it, the formal or active righteousness according to which God is righteous and punishes sinners and the unjust. . . . Day and night I tried to meditate upon the significance of these words. . . . Then, finally, God had mercy on me, and I began to understand that the righteousness of God is that gift of God by which a righteous man lives, namely, faith. . . . Now I felt as though I had been reborn altogether and had entered Paradise."[4] The consequences of this new insight the world knows.

Under the date of May 24, 1738, John Wesley notes in his *Journal:* "In the evening I went very unwillingly to a society in Aldersgate Street, where one was reading Luther's preface to the Epistle to the Romans. About a quarter before nine, while he was describing the change which God works in the heart through faith in Christ, I felt my heart strangely warmed. I felt I did trust in Christ, Christ alone for salvation: And an assurance was given me, that he had taken away *my* sins, even *mine,* and saved *me* from the law of sin and death."[5] That was the moment the Evangelical Revival of the eighteenth century was born.

What happened to Augustine, Luther, and Wesley turned the tide of Western civilization. On a smaller scale similar things

---

[3]*Confessions of St. Augustine,* trans. by Edward B. Pusey (New York: Random House, 1949), VIII, 167.

[4]Quoted by Hans J. Hillerbrand, *The Reformation* (New York: Harper & Row, 1964), p. 27.

[5]*The Works of John Wesley,* I (Kansas City: Nazarene Publishing House, n.d.), 103.

may happen to us if we will let the words of this Epistle come alive to our minds and hearts in the power of the Holy Spirit.

B. PLACE AND DATE OF WRITING

In none of Paul's other letters are the place and time of writing so clearly indicated in the letter itself as in the case of Romans. In 15:19-32 the apostle makes it clear that he is nearing the culmination of his ministry in the East. He has preached the gospel "from Jerusalem, and round about Illyricum," and goes on to say that he feels he has completed his mission in that vast region. Now he plans to go to Spain, and since Rome is already evangelized, to visit the Roman church on his way. But first he must perform a special task at Jerusalem. For some time he has been engaged in gathering a collection among the churches of Macedonia and Greece for "the poor saints which are at Jerusalem." That offering is now virtually complete, and Paul is awaiting only the opportunity of delivering it.

Since in I Cor. 16:3-4 Paul indicates that he plans to end his work on the collection in Corinth and to depart from that city to Jerusalem, and since at the time of writing II Corinthians (see 9:3-5) he is carrying out that plan and is on his way to Corinth, it is reasonable to suppose that he wrote Romans in Corinth. This position finds further support in the fact that the Epistle was delivered by the deaconess Phoebe, who was from Cenchrea, the eastern port of Corinth (16:1). This would have been the apostle's last visit to that city, since it was in Jerusalem just after this that his long imprisonment began (cf. Acts 20:2-3). The letter was dictated to a certain Tertius (16:22).

Scholars have been unable to establish with any degree of certainty the exact time of this final visit to Corinth. The date depends upon the entire chronology of Paul's ministry which one adopts. The earliest date suggested is January—March, A.D. 53, and the latest, January—March in 59.

C. OCCASION FOR WRITING

For a long time Paul had planned to visit the Roman church (1:8-15; 15:22). Now the prospect is at last in sight, as soon as he has delivered his sacramental gift to the mother church in Jerusalem. "When therefore I have performed this, and have sealed to them this fruit," he writes, "I will come by you into Spain" (15:28). "No statement of the apostle could more eloquently proclaim what he conceives his work to be. He is an evangelist, not a pastor. His calling, as he conceives it, is to plant, not to water. He not only does not wish to build on other men's

21

foundations; he does not really enjoy *building* on his own."[6] He hopes his offering—so important he intends to deliver it even in the face of threatened death—will heal the breach and bring peace to the Church. With the presentation of this gift the work he began from Antioch (Acts 13:1-4) will be culminated and he will then be free to move westward with the gospel.

But why did Paul write this kind of letter to the Romans? For one thing, he had for years been in controversy with the Pharisaical element in the Church which put great store by the Mosaic law. He had written Galatians and II Corinthians in the heat of this controversy. Now at Corinth he had leisure and quiet. It was his opportunity to set forth systematically the conclusions to which the Spirit had guided him with reference to the problem of Christ and the law. In a certain sense Romans is a systematized expansion of Galatians, but the ethical section of the Epistle shows definite affinities to I Corinthians.

Furthermore, Paul wished to clear up any misunderstandings about the gospel he preached. Since he hoped the Roman church would support his plan for evangelizing Spain, this was very important. False rumors had filtered into Rome concerning Paul's message. A careful statement of his position is therefore presented with the prayer that the Romans would give him a warm welcome when he should arrive and be in a mood to help him with his work in the westward half of the Empire.

D. The Church at Rome

We have no direct information about the origin of Christianity in Rome. Its beginnings are clouded in obscurity. The tradition that Peter was its founder has no historical support, although it is generally agreed that Peter did eventually go to Rome and that he was martyred there.[7] A reference is made to "strangers of Rome" being present in Jerusalem on the Day of Pentecost (Acts 2:10). It is possible that these converts first

[6]John Knox, *Interpreter's Bible,* IX (New York: Abingdon Press, 1954), 358-59. Subsequently referred to as IB.

[7]I Clement 5:3-7 (A.D. 95-97) associates both Peter and Paul with the Roman church. In the earliest form of tradition Peter and Paul are always named as the joint founders of Roman Christianity—i.e., Peter is no more regarded as founder than Paul. They both labored in Rome, and the form which Roman Christianity took shows the effects of their joint influence. Peter was still in Jerusalem, however, as late as A.D. 49 (Gal. 1:18), but there are no references in Acts or any of Paul's letters to Peter's presence in Rome.

took the new faith back to the Eternal City. We know that travel was widespread at this time and that there was a steady migration to the capital from all over the empire. Chapter 16 bears testimony to the fact that many of the Christians in the Roman congregation had come to the capital from other areas, especially from Asia Minor.

The fourth-century writer Ambrosiaster gives what is the most probable account of Christian beginnings in Rome. "It is established that there were Jews living in Rome in the times of the apostles, and that those Jews who had believed passed on to the Romans the tradition that they ought to profess Christ and keep the law. . . . One ought not condemn the Romans, but to praise their faith; because without seeing any signs or miracles and without seeing any of the apostles, they nevertheless accepted faith in Christ, although according to a Jewish rite."[8]

This seems to accord with the evidence we gather from Suetonius' *Life of Claudius:* "He expelled the Jews from Rome because they kept rioting at the instigation of Chrestus" (*impulsore Chresto*). We know nothing more of this Chrestus. The name was common among slaves, and possibly Chrestus was a servile agitator. But the majority of scholars incline to the view that *Chrestus* is a misspelling of *Christus* (the pronunciation of *e* and *i* hardly differed in the Greek of this period). It appears that the general public, to whom the Jewish and Christian religious term Christus would have been unintelligible, understood it as the familiar Chrestus. Thus it would be quite possible, if not probable, that Suetonius' statement is a reference to trouble which arose in the synagogues of Rome when Christianity was introduced. In any event, Christian Jews as well as unbelievers were banished from Rome by Claudius' edict in A.D. 49. This is referred to in Acts 18:2 as the reason for the presence in Corinth of Aquila and Priscilla.

We may take it, therefore, that by A.D. 49 Christianity had been introduced into the city. If Ambriosater's account is to be regarded as trustworthy, we still must account for the fact that by the time Paul wrote this Epistle the Church was predominantly Gentile (cf. 1:13; 11:13-25). We do not know exactly how events developed, but it seems likely that the edict of Claudius had the result of bringing about a modification, perhaps a profound one, in the Christian Church which was deprived of its Jewish elements. Apparently in the interval following A.D. 49 the faith spread rapidly among the Gentiles of Rome. Later the inter-

[8]Cited by Knox, IB., p. 362.

dict against the Jews was softened, and finally revoked, but by this time the Church seems to have been well on its way to separating completely from the synagogues of the city. It is obvious, however, that Roman Christianity retained a "soberer, more conservative cast than Pauline Christianity."[9] This resulted not only from the early Jewish influence we have mentioned but also, no doubt, reflected the legal Roman temperament (see 1:11, with comments).

E. The Text

Although it is not a crucial matter, we should observe two facts with regard to the text of this Epistle. (1) In the Early Church (at least after A.D. 200) Romans circulated in two forms, the shorter of which lacked cc. 15—16, except the doxology (16: 25-27). Hardly anyone doubts that Paul wrote 15:1—16:24 (the authenticity of the entire Epistle is virtually unquestionable). The question arises, however, whether the apostle wrote the short recension and later expanded it into its present form or wrote the long version, which was subsequently cut down (perhaps by another hand). (2) The second problem relates to c. 16. It has been suggested by modern critics that this chapter was originally not a part of Romans but was incorporated into the Epistle by an early editor. Most of those who subscribe to this theory think c. 16 is probably part of a lost letter to the Ephesian church.

1. The Two Forms of Romans

It is known that there were Latin translations of Romans around A.D. 200 which ended with 14:23, but which included the doxology (16:25-27), and numbers of Greek MSS in this short form have come down to us. The famous heretic Marcion claimed he knew the Epistle only in this form. Some of the MSS also lack the phrase "in Rome" in 1:7, 15. This would suggest that the short form may have made its rounds as a circular letter.

A glance at c. 15 reveals that it is a continuation of the theme of 14:1-23. Indeed, without 15:1-6 the discussion would be incomplete. Moreover, the plan of the Epistle calls for some such conclusion as we find in 15:7-13. The most probable theory, and the one held by practically all responsible scholars, is that Paul wrote the long version and that it was later cut down. Many scholars believe that it was Marcion who created the shorter recension, since it is known that he freely and drastically cut Jew-

[9]*Ibid.*

ish elements from the books he included in his NT Canon.[10] The doxology is thought by some to be Marcion's work.

2. *The Problem of Chapter 16*

In addressing this problem we should bear in mind that there is no MS evidence whatever for separating c. 16 from c. 15. Those who question whether c. 16 belongs to the original Epistle do so on the grounds that (1) it seems improbable that Paul should send such a large number of greetings to individuals in a church to which he is a stranger; (2) the exhortations of 16:17-20 are out of keeping with the content and tone of the rest of Romans; and (3) the apostle places a benediction at 15:33, apparently concluding the Epistle at that point.

Admittedly these are problems, but no one has been able to demonstrate from these objections that Paul did not write this portion of Romans. Scholarship has not gone beyond speculation on these points, and any proposed solution is open to criticism.

Concerning the first objection, we may point out that in none of Paul's letters to churches where he is personally known does he single out individual members for special greetings. (Apparently this was to avoid the show of favoritism.) This is perhaps the strongest argument against the theory that c. 16 is a fragment of an otherwise lost letter to the Ephesians. On the other hand, Paul had reasons for wishing to establish personal contacts with the Roman church and may have decided for that reason to send greetings to any members he might have known. It is not improbable that this many of his friends had moved to Rome. All roads led to the Eternal City, and there was an astonishing amount of travel in those days, especially by tradesmen such as Priscilla and Aquila (16:3). It is likely also that some, perhaps many, of the friends the apostle greets were Jewish believers he had met after Claudius' edict had scattered them from Rome in A.D. 49 (see p. 23). Other names in Paul's list are known to have been prominently identified with the Roman church (see comments on 16:3-15).

The difficulty of accounting for the warning against "divisions and offences contrary to the doctrine" that the Romans had learned (16:17) is not imaginary. But Dodd writes: "As for its contents, it would not be true to say that the *only* danger Paul apprehended for the Roman church arose from the extreme

---

[10]Marcion was the first Christian teacher to form a NT Canon (A.D. 140). He was later expelled from the Roman church for teaching that the OT God is not the God and Father of Jesus Christ.

Jewish party. He clearly has in mind, from time to time, unethical interpretations of Christianity such as later found expression in some of the gnostic heresies, and directs against them his emphatic teaching about the ethical demands of the Gospel (e.g. vi. 1-14, viii. 5-13, xii. 2). Although he does not in the body of the epistle definitely indicate such tendencies as a peril to the unity of the Church, he may have felt impelled to give a warning against such a peril before closing."[11]

The problem occasioned by the introduction of the benediction at 15:33 is not major. This can be taken simply as a brief prayer which rounds out the main body of the Epistle before the introduction of personal greetings (cf. 16:20, 24).

"We are in good company," Barth remarks, "if we notice this problem but leave it open and apply ourselves to the text as it is presented to us by the overwhelming majority of textual evidence, and as it has in fact always been read by the Christian Church."[12]

[11]C. H. Dodd, *The Epistle to the Romans*, "The Moffatt New Testament Commentary" (New York: Harper and Brothers, 1932), pp. xxiii-xxiv.

[12]Karl Barth, *A Shorter Commentary on Romans* (Richmond, Va.: John Knox Press, 1949), p. 14.

Outline

I. Paul's Introduction, 1:1-17
   A. The Apostolic Greeting, 1:1-7
   B. Paul's Interest in the Roman Church, 1:8-15
   C. The Theme of the Epistle, 1:16-17

II. The Gospel of God's Righteousness, 1:18—11:36
   A. God's Righteousness Needed, 1:18—3:20
   B. God's Righteousness Provided, 3:21—8:39
   C. God's Righteousness in History, 9:1—11:36

III. The Fruits of God's Righteousness, 12:1—15:13
   A. The Basis of Christian Ethics, 12:1-2
   B. Christian Love Within the Church, 12:3-13
   C. Christian Love Outside the Church, 12:14—13:14
   D. Christian Tolerance and Responsibility, 14:1—15:13

IV. Personal Conclusion, 15:14—16:27
   A. Paul's Apology for His Admonitions, 15:14-21
   B. Paul's Proposed Plans, 15:22-33
   C. Introduction of Phoebe, Greetings and Warnings, 16:1-24
   D. Final Doxology, 16:25-27

Section I *Paul's Introduction*

A. The Apostolic Greeting, 1:1-7

Ancient letters all opened according to a certain pattern: "Gaius to Junius, greeting." Paul uses the customary form—**Paul ... to all that be in Rome**—but he expands and gives a Christian emphasis to each part of the formula. The length of the salutation is explained by the fact that Paul had not founded nor yet visited the Roman church. Also at the very outset the apostle felt the necessity of setting forth the salient points of the polemic which was to follow.[1] This fact gives unusual weight to his opening words. "They are much more than a formal introduction. Again and again the tremendous theme of the letter appears in them. The great issue is at hand from the beginning."[2]

Paul introduces himself as a **servant** (*doulos*, bond servant or slave) **of Jesus Christ** (1). This is more than an expression of humility; Paul is completely at his Master's disposal. "The man who is now speaking is an emissary, bound to perform his duty; the minister of his King; a servant, not a master. However great and important a man Paul may have been, the essential theme of his mission is not within him but above him."[3] Abraham (Gen. 26:24; Ps. 105:6, 42), Moses (Num. 12:7-8), David (II Sam. 7:5, 8), and the prophets (Amos 3:7; Isa. 20:3; Jer. 7:25) were called servants of the Lord. This is the first instance of a similar use in the NT, and "it is noticeable how quietly St. Paul steps into the place of the prophets and leaders of the Old Covenant, and how quietly he substitutes the name of his own Master in a connexion hitherto reserved for that of Jehovah."[4]

---

[1]John Murray, *The Epistle to the Romans*, I ("New International Commentary"; Grand Rapids: Wm. B. Eerdmans Publishing Co., 1959), 1.

[2]Anders Nygren, *op. cit.*, p. 43.

[3]Karl Barth, *The Epistle to the Romans* (London: Oxford University Press, 1933), p. 27.

[4]W. Sanday and A. C. Headlam, *The Epistle to the Romans* ("The International Critical Commentary"; New York: Charles Scribner's Sons, 1929), p. 3. Hereafter cited as ICC.

He further identifies himself as one **called to be an apostle.**
The Greek phrase (*kletos apostolos*) means literally "a called
apostle." Godet explains that this signifies "an apostle *by way
of call.*"[5] *Kletos* also has its roots in the OT. Abraham (Gen. 12:
1-3), Moses (Exod. 3:10), and the prophets (Isa. 6:8-9; Jer. 1:4-5;
Amos 7:14-15) were God's servants by a divine summons. So
was Paul. *Apostolos* means literally "a messenger" ("one sent
forth"); it is the Greek equivalent of "missionary," which derives
from the Latin *missus.* **Apostle** has two meanings. In the narrower
sense it is applicable to the original Twelve (Mark 3:14; Luke 6:
13), but in a wider sense it is used to include Barnabas (Acts
14:4, 14), perhaps James the brother of Jesus (Gal. 1:19) and
others (Rom. 16:7). Paul was an apostle in the broader accepta-
tion of the term, but in referring to himself as *kletos apostolos* he
is stressing the fact that he is not merely an apostle by virtue of
possessing the qualifications described in Acts 1:21-22, but
through a personal encounter with the risen Christ (cf. I Cor.
15:8; Gal. 1:1, 15-16). "His summons to be an apostle, a special
commissioner of Christ, came directly, he claims, from 'Jesus
Christ, and God the Father' (Gal. 1:1), who laid on him the
responsibility of proclaiming the gospel in the Gentile world
(Gal. 1:16)."[6]

Separated unto the gospel thus parallels *kletos apostolos.*
Separated (*aphorismenos*) has the same root meaning as *Pharisee* (*pharisaios*). "Paul, who had set himself apart from the law,
is set apart by God for the Gospel."[7] "Are we then to name him
a Pharisee?" Barth asks. "Yes, a Pharisee—'separated', isolated,
and distinct. But he is a Pharisee of a higher order."[8] He is separated **unto the gospel of God.** Dedication is the human response
to the divine act of separation. God separates His servants, who
in turn dedicate themselves to Him.[9] The human acceptance of
the divine act of separation shows the place of free moral agency

[5]*St. Paul's Epistle to the Romans* (New York: Funk and Wagnalls, 1883),
p. 74.

[6]F. F. Bruce, *The Epistle of Paul to the Romans* ("The Tyndale Bible
Commentaries"; Grand Rapids: Wm. B. Eerdmans Publishing Co., 1963),
p. 71.

[7]Nygren, *op. cit.,* p. 46.

[8]*The Epistle to the Romans,* p. 37.

[9]G. T. Thomson and F. Davidson, "The Epistle to the Romans" (*New
Bible Commentary;* Grand Rapids: Wm. B. Eerdmans Publishing Co., 1953),
p. 942.

in the outworking of the preordained plan of God (cf. I Cor.
9:27). **The gospel of God** is "His joyful proclamation of the victory and exaltation of His Son, and the consequent amnesty and
liberation which we may enjoy through faith in Him."[10]

Paul next proceeds to show the continuity of the gospel dispensation with the old covenant. The good news had been **promised afore by his prophets in the holy scriptures (2)**. The gospel
represents, not a break with the past, but a consummation of it.
Thus Paul writes in I Cor. 15:3-4 that "Christ died for our sins
according to the scriptures . . . and that he rose again the third
day according to the scriptures." The repeated insistence that
these things happened in accordance with scripture shows how
vital this fact was for Paul. "The words of the prophets, long
fastened under lock and key, are now set free . . . Now we can
see and understand what was written, for we have an 'entrance
into the Old Testament' (Luther)."[11]

Although the gospel has its source in God, the good news is
concerning his Son (3), in whom all the OT promises are fulfilled (II Cor. 1:20) and the saving acts of God performed (II Cor.
5:18-19). "The gospel has one center around which it all re-
volves. From beginning to end it treats of the Son of God."[12] A
brief (probably credal) formula expounds the nature of the Son
of God. He was **made of the seed of David according to the flesh;
and declared to be the Son of God with power, according to the
spirit of holiness, by the resurrection from the dead (3-4)**. Various NT passages affirm the Davidic descent of Jesus (e.g., Matt.
1:1; Acts 2:30; Rev. 5:5); however, this is the only undoubted
Pauline reference (but cf. 15:12). C. K. Barrett writes, "It is the
probable view that he mentions the latter because he is quoting
a formula which he did not himself compose; and not impossible
that he quotes in order to commend his orthodoxy to persons he
knew would recognize the formula."[13] There seems to be con-
sensus among modern scholars at this point. Franz J. Leenhardt
makes the further observation that the formula was probably of
Palestinian origin, as is suggested by the concern to connect the

[10]Bruce, *loc. cit.*, p. 71.

[11]Barth, *The Epistle to the Romans*, p. 28. Cf. II Cor. 3:14-16.

[12]Nygren, *op. cit.*, p. 47.

[13]*The Commentary on the Epistle to the Romans* ("Harper's New Testament Commentaries"; New York: Harper & Brothers, Publishers, 1957),
pp. 18-19.

Messiah with the lineage of David and similarly with the preaching of Peter in the Acts.[14]

The key to understanding this Christological formula is to grasp its antithetical character. **According to the flesh,** Jesus was descended from David, in harmony with the OT promise which calls the Messiah the Son of David. But Christ not only shares our common humanity. **According to the spirit of holiness,** He who in His human existence belonged to the seed of David was **declared to be Son of God with power . . . by the resurrection from the dead.** "It is implied that there are two things to be said about Christ, not indeed contradictory but complementary to and different from each other. Christ belongs to two spheres or orders of existence, denoted respectively by flesh and Spirit."[15]

An even more basic truth, however, underlies the formula. It was He who was *from the beginning* Son of God who was manifested first in weakness, then in power. It was the preexistent Son who was incarnate, whom God "sent" in the flesh (8:3; cf. 8:32; Gal. 4:4). The participle **made** (*genomenou*) properly denotes "transition from one state or mode of subsistence to another." "It is rightly paraphrased '[Who] was born' and is practically equivalent to the Johannine *'elthontos eis ton kosmon'* ('coming into the world')."[16]

Jesus, then, as a man was **of the seed of David,** but was **declared to be the Son of God with power** by the Resurrection. **Declared** (*horisthentos*) is elsewhere translated "determined," "ordained," or "limited" (Luke 22:22; Acts 11:29; 17:26, 31; Heb. 4:7). John Murray says flatly, "There is neither need nor warrant to resort to any other rendering than that provided by the other New Testament instances, namely, that Jesus was 'appointed' or 'constituted' Son of God with power and points therefore to an investiture which had an historical beginning parallel to the historical beginning mentioned in verse 3."[17] The truth is similar to that expressed in Hebrews 1:5, on which Wiley comments:

> The words, "This day have I begotten thee," (1:5a) are applied by St. Paul to the Resurrection in Acts 13:33, and by St. John in Rev. 1:5. The Son was indeed the "only begotten of the Father" before all worlds, and the deity of the Son necessarily underlies the Incarnation and the Resurrection; otherwise, it would exclude His

[14]*The Epistle to the Romans* (Cleveland and New York: The World Publishing Co., 1957), p. 36.

[15]Barrett, *op. cit.,* p. 19.   [16]ICC, p. 6.   [17]*Op. cit.,* p. 9.

work as Mediator. *But the Son was also begotten again in the Resurrection, which marked the full out-birth of the humanity of Jesus from its state of humiliation to that of its glorification and exaltation.*[18]

Whether, therefore, we translate *horisthentos* **declared,** or "designated" (RSV), or "appointed," we are not threatening the doctrine of Christ's essential deity. The important phrase is **with power.** Paul does not say that Jesus was appointed Son of God but that He was appointed **Son of God with power.** Nor must we forget that already in v. 3 the Son of God is viewed not simply as the eternal Son but as the incarnate Son, subject to historical conditions—the human conditions of being born **of the seed of David.** Nygren brings all these ideas into focus: "To be sure, from the beginning He was Son of God, but in weakness and lowliness. The divine glory, which formerly was hidden, was manifest after the resurrection. From that hour He is the Son of God in a new sense: He is Son of God 'in power,' Son of God in glory and fullness of power."[19]

Three other phrases in this formula require comment. The most difficult is that which is rendered literally and accurately by **the spirit of holiness.** Is this a reference to Jesus' human spirit or to the Holy Spirit? Is it a contrast between Jesus' flesh and spirit; or is it between His human nature ("the sphere of the flesh") on the one hand and His heavenly nature ("the sphere of the Holy Spirit") on the other? By capitalizing "Spirit of holiness" the RSV identifies the phrase with the Holy Spirit. It is true that Paul nowhere else refers to the Holy Spirit by this phrase (*pneuma hagiosynes*), which is probably of Semitic origin; but the problem is explained if we accept the thesis that the apostle is quoting a Palestinian formula.

A second phrase which may appear surprising to those who know Greek is that translated in the KJV **by the resurrection from the dead.** Literally the phrase means "resurrection of those who are dead." Paul says actually that Christ was designated the Son of God with power "by a resurrection of dead ones." Nygren understands Paul to mean: "Through Christ the resurrection age has burst upon us. He who believes in the Son of God 'has passed

---

[18]*The Epistle to the Hebrews* (Kansas City: Beacon Hill Press, 1959), pp. 52-53 (italics mine). Wiley quotes Rom. 1:3-4 as a passage parallel to Heb. 1:5.

[19]*Op. cit.,* p. 48.

from death to life' (John 5:24)."[20] In Eph. 1:19—2:7 we find an expansion of this same truth. The very power which raised Christ from the dead has resurrected us from the death of sin. And the final meaning is given in I Cor. 15:19-58. *"So the resurrection is the turning point in the existence of the Son of God. Before that He was the Son of God in weakness and lowliness. Through the resurrection He became the Son of God in power. But the resurrection is also the turning point in humanity's existence.* Before this the whole race was under the sovereign sway of death; but in the resurrection of Christ life burst forth victoriously, and a new aeon began, the aeon of the resurrection and life."[21]

Finally, there is the phrase **Jesus Christ our Lord** (3).[22] The primitive Christian confession was simply, "Jesus is Lord" (I Cor. 12:3; Phil. 2:11). God designated Jesus Son of God with power by the Resurrection and gave Him the name which is above every name, the name **Lord.** The name **Jesus** identifies a remembered Person, the incarnate Son. **Christ** speaks of this One as the promised Messiah of Israel. **Lord** identifies Him with the ineffable name of God in the OT—Yahweh—translated in the Septuagint by the very word here ascribed to Jesus, *Kyrios.* When God exalted Jesus Christ as Lord and gave Him the name which is above every name, it was in order that every knee should bow and every tongue confess that He is Lord.

The revelation of the lordship of Jesus rounds out the Christological formula Paul quotes and also amplifies and explains the nature of the apostle's commission to preach the gospel in Rome. From the exalted and glorified Lord Paul **received grace and apostleship** (5).[23] Not everyone who receives grace is made an apostle. But for Paul the two were inseparable. He was not first converted and then later called to be an apostle. Rather, he received the double call on the Damascus Road (cf. Acts 9:15; Gal. 1:15-16). He was commissioned at his conversion to bear the gospel to the Gentiles, **among all nations, for his name.**

---

[20]*Op. cit.,* p. 50.   [21]*Ibid.,* p. 51.

[22]In the Greek this phrase comes at the conclusion of v. 4.

[23]*Elabomen,* translated **we have received** in the KJV, is in the aorist tense and should be rendered "we received." The categorical plural refers to Paul, and does not include the other apostles, since the succeeding phrase, **among all nations,** points to himself alone as the apostle to the Gentiles (Marvin R. Vincent, *Word Studies in the New Testament* [New York: Charles Scribner's Sons, 1905], III, 4).

Since Jesus Christ is Lord of all, every knee must bow to Him and every tongue confess His name. The phrase translated **for obedience to the faith** (*eis hupakoen pisteos*) is given its literal meaning in the KJV marginal reading, "to the obedience of faith." The context makes this meaning clear. Lordship and obedience are correlative terms. J. A. Beet comments aptly: "The act of faith is submission to God."[24] Since sin means making self the end and rule of life, faith means the abdication of self and the exaltation of Jesus Christ as Lord. Paul's objective is to bring every human being "to the obedience of faith."

The apostle has now come to the point where he can address himself directly to the Roman church. The phrase **among whom are ye also** (6) identifies the Roman congregation as predominantly Gentile. As the apostle to the Gentiles, Paul has the right to address this Epistle to them and to preach the gospel among them. However, he addresses them, not as Gentiles, but as Christians. They have been **called of Jesus Christ.** Moreover, they are **beloved of God, called to be saints** (7).

The phrase **called of Jesus Christ** is more correctly rendered "called to belong to Jesus Christ" (RSV). The NEB reads: "You who have heard the call and belong to Jesus Christ." How do we come to belong to Christ? We are prone to refer to our voluntary choice of Him. The NT refers to the call of God. For this reason Paul addresses the Romans as *kletoi,* **the called.** Sanday and Headlam point out that there is a difference between the use of this term in the Gospels and in the Epistles. "In the Gospels *kletoi* are all who are invited to enter Christ's kingdom, whether or not they accept the invitation; the *eklektoi* [the chosen or elect] are a smaller group, selected to special honour (Matt. xxii 14). In St. Paul both words are applied to the same persons; *kletos* implies that the call has been not only given but obeyed."[25] In referring to believers as **the called,** the NT keeps before us the all-important truth of the divine initiative in salvation, which is

---

[24]*A Commentary on St. Paul's Epistle to the Romans* (London: Hodder and Stoughton, 1885), p. 33. On this verse Leenhardt says: "The question of faith will be taken up again in Ch. 4 where it will be seen that faith is always obedience . . . The expression here used by Paul defines admirably the goal at which Christian apostleship aims; to bring men back into a state of obedience, since the present state is essentially one of disobedience (5:19)" (*op. cit.*, pp. 39-40). F. F. Bruce paraphrases the expression, "The obedience that is based on faith in Christ" (*op. cit.*, p. 74).

[25]ICC, p. 4.

wholly by grace, "not of works, lest any man should boast" (Eph. 2:8-9).

The Roman Christians are also **beloved of God** (*agapetois theou*, 7). Here Paul employs the great NT word for love—*agape*. This *agape* is God's own love revealed supremely in the Cross, where Christ died for us "while we were yet sinners" (5:8), even "when we were enemies" (5:10). It has been poured into the hearts of Christians by the Holy Spirit (5:5). "That love now encompasses their entire life. Henceforth no power whatever can separate them from the love of God in Christ Jesus (8:35-39). When Paul addresses the Christians as 'God's beloved,' he uses that word in its deepest and most inclusive sense. That name characterizes their entire existence as Christians."[26]

Finally, they are **called to be saints** (*kletois hagiois*). Godet has noted that "called saints has quite another meaning from **called to be saints** (which would assume that they are *not* so). The meaning is, *saints by way of call*, which implies that they are so in reality."[27] All believers are "saints," or "holy ones" (*hagioi*), in the NT (15:25-26, 31; 16:2, 15).

The basic idea of sainthood is separation. The saints are the people of God who have been separated "from among all the people of the earth, to be . . . [His] inheritance" (Deut. 7:6; I Kings 8:53; I Pet. 2:9-10). In this sense the Roman Christians were holy. They were no longer simply Gentiles; they had been "called to belong to Jesus Christ." "They were men whom God had claimed for Himself. They might be carnal like the Corinthians, I Cor. iii. 3: like the Corinthians they were still sanctified in Christ, I Cor. i. 2."[28]

The saints are not only the *separated;* they are also the *purified.* "Since all sin is the erection of self into the end and rule of life, sin is utterly opposed to holiness. God's holiness makes Him intolerant of sin, because sin robs Him of that which His holiness demands. Only the holy are pure, and only the pure are holy."[29] This purification begins in conversion. Commenting on I Cor. 6:9-11, John Wesley makes this illuminating observation: " 'Ye are washed,' says the apostle, 'ye are sanctified;' namely cleansed from 'fornication, idolatry, drunkenness,' and all other *outward* sin; and yet at the same time, in another sense of the word they were unsanctified, they were not washed, not *inwardly* cleansed

[26]Nygren, *op. cit.*, p. 57.   [27]*Op. cit.*, p. 74.
[28]Beet, *op. cit.*, p. 34.   [29]*Ibid.*, p. 39.

from envy, evil surmising, partiality."[30] All saints have been purified from sin in the sense that God's claims upon them have broken the *reign* of sin in their lives; and having received the sanctifying Spirit, they yearn to be cleansed from the *root* of sin which remains within. The entirely sanctified are those who have fully yielded themselves to God in decisive consecration and are being "transformed by the renewing of their minds" (6:13; 12: 1-2; cf. I Cor. 7:1; I Thess. 5:23-24).

We come now to Paul's word of greeting: **Grace to you and peace from God our Father, and the Lord Jesus Christ** (7). The usual salutation of an ancient Greek letter was simply the word *chairein* (greeting). Paul uses a similar word *charis* **(grace)**, which means the free, undeserved favor of God, and adds *eirene* **(peace)**, the inner serenity and sense of well-being men enjoy through God's grace. Since **peace** (Heb., *shalom*) was the common Jewish salutation, Paul's **grace . . . and peace**, the salutation in all his letters, combines the Greek and Hebrew forms of greeting.[31]

From God our Father, and the Lord Jesus Christ is a significant phrase, suggesting the close union in Paul's mind of the Father and Jesus Christ. Grace comes from the Father through Christ (3:24).

B. PAUL'S INTEREST IN THE ROMAN CHURCH, 1:8-15

Since Paul has never been to Rome and has had no part in the founding of the Roman church, he feels he must disarm their suspicions. Before he can do anything else he must "get alongside them so that the barriers of strangeness and suspicion may be broken down."[32]

He begins with a sincere compliment, **I thank my God through Jesus Christ for you all, that your faith is spoken of throughout the whole world** (8). "Paul knows nothing of a faith which is so concealed nothing of it is visible. The whole world speaks of the

[30]Sermon XIII, "Sin in Believers," *The Works of John Wesley* (Kansas City: Nazarene Publishing House, n.d.), V, 150.

[31]John Knox, "The Epistle to the Romans" (Exegesis), *The Interpreter's Bible,* ed. George A. Buttrick *et al,* IX (New York: Abingdon-Cokesbury Press, 1954), 385.

[32]William Barclay, *The Letter to the Romans* ("The Daily Study Bible"; Philadelphia: The Westminster Press, 1957), p. 5.

35

faith of the Roman brethren, and this calls for gratitude."[33] **My God** bespeaks the intimacy and reality of Paul's religious faith. Yet he addresses God **through Jesus Christ.** Wesley observes, "The gifts of God all pass through Christ to us and all our petitions and thanksgivings pass through Christ to God."[34] **Throughout the whole world** is probably best understood as "throughout the Christian Church and wherever people know of your faith."

Paul goes on to add, as in all his introductions, that he prays for them. Bishop Charles Gore remarks that it makes a profound difference in the feelings of others toward us if they have reason to believe that we have prayed for them.[35] Paul gives himself this advantage. **For God is my witness,** he writes, **that without ceasing I make mention of you always in my prayers (9).** His specific request is that he may **have a prosperous journey by the will of God (10)** to visit with them. **For I long to see you, that I may impart unto you some spiritual gift** (*charisma pneumatikon,* 11). Evidently the Romans will miss this endowment if they remain personally unacquainted with the apostle.

The character of this *charisma* is best understood by reading the descriptions found in other Pauline letters. Within it are both the "fruit" of divine love (I Corinthians 13; Gal. 5:16, 22-25) and the "gifts" of service to the body of Christ (I Cor. 12:4-31; 14:1-40). "Paul probably felt that Roman Christianity lacked the 'charismatic' quality which for him was so highly significant. The bestowal of this 'gift' would be the chief interest of his visit, but hardly of a letter."[36] Karl Barth believes, however, that "this particular gift of the Spirit is simply the Gospel, which according to i.5 has been entrusted to him. Other men have other gifts . . . This particular gift, the proclamation of the Gospel, is the gift of the apostolic office bestowed on him."[37] If this is what Paul means, the Romans would receive the Spirit by hearing the gospel in faith and thereby experience the *charisma* (cf. Acts 19:1-6; Gal. 3:2).

[33]Emil Brunner, *The Letter to the Romans* (Philadelphia: The Westminster Press, 1959), p. 15.

[34]*Explanatory Notes upon the New Testament* (London: The Epworth Press, 1950 [reprint]), p. 517.

[35]*St. Paul's Epistle to the Romans,* I (London: John Murray, 1902), 54.

[36]Albert E. Barnett, *The New Testament, Its Making and Meaning* (New York: Abingdon-Cokesbury Press, 1946), p. 63.

[37]*A Shorter Commentary on Romans* (Richmond: John Knox Press, 1959), p. 18.

After this forthright beginning Paul expresses the reason for his desire to visit them, **to the end ye may be established.** He does not say, "that I may establish you." The modest use of the passive omits Paul's personal part. So he continues, "That we may be mutually encouraged by each other's faith, both yours and mine" (12, RSV). The stress falls on the mutuality of what will take place when he visits them. The Roman Christians will have something to give him too. Paul here exemplifies the spirit of a person who is genuinely spiritual. He has no airs of religious superiority (cf. Gal. 6:1).

Paul may be a stranger in Rome, and the church founded by another man, yet as the apostle to the Gentiles he can write, "I want you to know, brethren, that I have often intended to come to you . . . in order that I may reap some harvest among you as well as among the rest of the Gentiles" (13, RSV).[38] There is no question of his right, or his desire, to preach in Rome. The reason he has not already visited them is that he **was let hitherto,** i.e., "Thus far I have been prevented." "Paul does not here (as at I Thess. 2:18) speak of a hindering by Satan; indeed the use of the passive may (in Semitic fashion) conceal a reference to God— it had not been God's will that Paul should come (cf. Acts 16:6 f. and perhaps I Cor. xvi. 12). This should probably be understood to mean that urgent tasks (only recently completed, xv. 18 f., 22 f.) had kept him in the East."[39]

Paul wants to make it clear that the reason for his longed-for visit is greater than his own wish; it is his inescapable duty. Accordingly his introduction reaches its culmination in the declaration, **I am debtor both to the Greeks, and to the Barbarians; both to the wise, and to the unwise. So, as much as in me is, I am ready to preach the gospel to you that are at Rome also** (14-15). The **Greeks** and the **Barbarians** mean practically "the cultured and the uncultured." Similarly, **the wise** and **the unwise** signify "the educated and the uneducated."[40] Paul means simply to acknowledge the inclusive character of his debt. His task as an apostle is to bring all men under the lordship of Jesus Christ and "into the obedience of faith."

---

[38]Cf. 11:13, 25-28; 15:15-16. These passages certainly indicate the Gentile character of the Roman church.

[39]Barrett, *op. cit.,* p. 26.

[40]C. H. Dodd, *The Epistle of Paul to the Romans* ("The Moffatt New Testament Commentary"; New York: Harper and Brothers, 1932), p. 8.

C. The Theme of the Epistle, 1:16-17

These last two verses of the introductory section give a definition in Paul's own terms of the gospel he has just said he intends to preach in Rome.[41] Here the apostle begins to present the cause for which the Epistle is being written. The transition from what precedes, however, is hardly noticeable.

He begins by assuring the Romans that he is **not ashamed of the gospel** (16).[42] He means them to understand that his delay betrays no misgivings on his part about the gospel. "No one should think that he could not or would not come because he shunned the challenge which Rome especially, as the impressive centre of the Gentile world, would mean to his message. He is not afraid that the Gospel might not be equal to its encounter with the accumulated culture and vulgarity of the metropolis, that the spiritual and unspiritual powers, the culture and banality prevailing there might confound the Gospel and stultify him as well."[43] But this shamelessness is not based on any reliance in his own spiritual resources, or his eloquence, or anything else of this kind. His confidence rests solely upon the power of the gospel (cf. I Cor. 2:1-5).

Barth points out that Paul does not say the gospel *has* such power, but that it *is* the power of God—God's own power, unique, incomparable, omnipotent. When the gospel is proclaimed in the Holy Spirit, God's power (*dynamis*) is at work. Paul might have used *energeia* here, but his choice of *dynamis* puts the stress upon the Source rather than the process of the gospel's power.[44] God is is the Source of salvation but He saves through the message of the gospel (cf. I Cor. 1:18-21). "And the implication is that God's power as it is operative unto salvation is through the gospel alone. It is the *gospel* which is God's power unto salvation. The message is God's word, and the word of God is living and powerful (cf. Heb. 4:12)."[45]

Salvation (*soterian*) is the effect of the gospel. *Soteria* means deliverance, "both in the negative aspect of a rescuing from the

---

[41]In 1:3-4, Paul employs an earlier credal formula of the gospel known to the Romans, as an entree to the minds and hearts of his readers.

[42]The phrase **of Christ** is not attested by the most ancient MSS, but since the person of Christ is the content of the gospel the interpolation is no real alteration.

[43]Barth, *A Shorter Commentary on Romans*, p. 20.

[44]ICC, p. 23.   [45]Murray, *op. cit.*, p. 27.

Wrath under which the whole world is lying (v. 18 ff.) and in its positive aspect as the imparting of eternal life (Mark x. 10; John iii. 15, 16; etc.)."[46] The possession of these two privileges is man's health (*soteria*, from *sos*, safe and sound). The salvation which the gospel produces is Messianic—that is, it was inaugurated, though not consummated, in the ministry, death, resurrection, and ascension of Christ, "and from the beginning it was marked by power: in the miracles, in the resurrection, and subsequently in the work of the Holy Spirit. It was in virtue of this power that the Gospel preached by Paul . . . had its effect among those who heard it, and experienced the 'powers of the age to come' (Heb. vi. 5)."[47]

It is this anticipatory enjoyment of salvation in the power of the gospel which is the key to Paul's thought. **The power of God unto salvation** is at work in **every one that believeth.** In the strict sense of the Greek terms believers are not saved but are in process of being saved. Paul bases his certitude of final salvation on the fact that "Christ died for us" (5:9-10). Meanwhile believers groan and travail while awaiting the redemption of their bodies, since they are "saved by hope" (8:23). But they have the help of the Spirit (8:26-27) until the final consummation of the work of salvation (13:11).

While salvation is certainly *oriented to the end,* when Christ shall return, it is not improper to think of it as threefold, in relation to the past, the present, and the future. As to the past, the believer can say, "I have been saved." He has been delivered from the penalty and death of sin (Eph. 2:1-10). As to the present, he can say, "I am being saved" (I Cor. 1:18, RSV). With the gracious assistance of the Holy Spirit he is "working out" his salvation (Phil. 2:12-13). As to the future, he can say, "I shall be saved" (5:9-10; 13:11). He is anticipating the final resurrection and the consummation of all things (I Cor. 15:19-26). "Sal-

---

[46]ICC, p. 24. The roots of the Pauline doctrine of salvation are in the OT. There the word has at least three meanings. (1) It signifies deliverance from physical peril (Judg. 15:18; I Sam. 11:9, 13). In this sense Paul himself speaks of salvation in Phil. 1:19. (2) Salvation also describes the deliverance of the people of God (*a*) at the Red Sea (Exod. 14:13; 15:2) and (*b*) from the Captivity (Isa. 45:17; 46:13; 52:10; etc.). (3) The OT also prophesies Messianic salvation (Jer. 31:31-34; Ezek. 36:25-27; Joel 2:28-32). It is this view of salvation which becomes the basis of the NT doctrine (Matt. 1:21; Luke 1:69, 71, 77; 7:50; etc.)

[47]Barrett, *op. cit.,* p. 28.

vation is from the penalty, the power, the presence of sin. It is
Justification, Sanctification, Glorification."[48] It is in this comprehensive sense that Paul here speaks of **the gospel** as **the power of
God unto salvation.** Paul knows a work has been set in motion
that will remain in motion. "Being confident of this very thing,"
he wrote the Philippians, "that he which hath begun a good work
in you will perform it until the day of Jesus Christ" (Phil. 1:6).

To every one that believeth points to the one condition under
which the gospel becomes **the power of God unto salvation.** When
Paul writes **to every one** he is expressing the *universality* of God's
offer; the expression **that believeth** points to the *freeness* of that
offer. Godet explains, "The *faith* of which the apostle speaks is
nothing else than the simple acceptance of the salvation offered in
preaching." He continues:

> God says: I give thee; the heart answers: I accept; such is faith.
> The act is thus a receptivity, but an active receptivity. It brings
> nothing, but it takes what God gives; as was admirably said by a
> poor Bechuana: "It is the hand of the heart." In this act the en-
> tire human personality takes part: the understanding discerning the
> blessing offered in the divine promise, the will aspiring after it,
> and the confidence of the heart giving itself up to the promise, and
> so securing the promised blessing. The preaching of free salvation
> is the act by which God lays hold of man, faith is the act by which
> man lets himself be laid hold of.[49]

To the Jew first, and also to the Greek underscores the truth
that God's salvation is entirely a free gift. Both **Jew** and **Greek**
must meet the same terms. No one must think that the gospel is
only for the Greeks, while the Jews should find their salvation
through the law. "Even Abraham was not justified by the law
(chap. 4). Now that the promise is fulfilled in Christ, it does
apply 'to the Jew first.' But this is not to say it is in any way to
mean less to the Gentiles . . . The Jew, indeed 'the Jew first,' is
called through the promise to receive the new righteousness which
God proffers through Christ. But the Gentile is just as truly
called. Neither is preferred to the other."[50]

"The Good News" is the theme of 1:14-16. The gospel is good
news about (1) The purpose of God, **salvation**, 16; (2) The **power
of God**, 16; (3) The plan of God, **to every one that believeth**, 16
(W. T. Purkiser).

---

[48]W. H. Griffith Thomas, *St. Paul's Epistle to the Romans* (Grand Rapids:
Wm. B. Eerdmans Publishing Company, 1947 [reprint]), p. 61.

[49]*Op. cit.,* p. 92.   [50]Nygren, *op. cit.,* pp. 73-74. Cf. 3:28-30.

Paul now comes to what we may call the thematic topic of the Epistle—**the righteousness of God** (17). The gospel is God's power to salvation *because* **therein**—that is, in the gospel—**is the righteousness of God revealed.** It was the discovery of the *scriptural* meaning of this phrase which made Luther the Reformer of Christendom. Formerly he had understood the phrase scholastically to mean "the formal or active righteousness according to which God is righteous and punishes sinners and the unjust."[51]

> Day and night I tried to meditate upon the significance of these words: "The righteousness of God revealed in it, as it is written: The righteous shall live by faith." Then, finally, God had mercy on me, and I began to understand that the righteousness of God is that gift of God by which a righteous man lives, namely, faith, and that this sentence—The righteousness of God revealed in the Gospel—is passive, indicating that the merciful God justifies us by faith, as it is written: 'The righteous shall live by faith.' Now I felt as though I had been reborn altogether and had entered Paradise. In the same moment the face of the whole of Scripture became apparent to me.[52]

The understanding of "God's righteousness" is the key not only to this Epistle but to the gospel itself.

There has been much discussion whether **the righteousness of God** (*dikaiosyne theou*) is here (1) a divine attribute and activity or (2) a gift bestowed by God upon man ("a righteousness of which God is the author and man the recipient"). No doubt it is both of these. Sanday and Headlam wisely remark, "The 'righteousness of God' is a great and comprehensive idea which embraces in its range both God and man; and in this fundamental passage of the Epistle neither side must be lost sight of."[53]

As evidence that the term means the righteousness of God himself several considerations may be urged. (1) This is the consistent meaning in the OT, especially in those passages which form the immediate background of this verse. Thus we read in Isa. 51:5, "My righteousness is near; my salvation is gone forth" (cf. Ps. 71:15-16; Isa. 45:21-25; 46:13). One verse in Psalms closely resembles our text: "The Lord hath made known his salvation: his righteousness hath he openly shewed [mar., re-

---

[51]Quoted by Brunner, *op. cit.*, p. 16.

[52]*D. Martin Luther's Werke* (Weimar, 1883 ff.), 54, 183 f. Cited by Hans J. Hillerbrand, *The Reformation* (New York: Harper & Row, Publishers, 1964), p. 27.

[53]ICC, p. 24.

vealed] in the sight of the heathen" (Ps. 98:2).[54] (2) Elsewhere in Romans *dikaiosyne* has the meaning of "the righteousness of God himself." In 3:21-22 and 10:3 the phrase has the comprehensive meaning of 1:17. In 2:5 it means the punishment which God will mete out upon sin in the day of judgment. In 3:5 it is seen as the fidelity with which God fulfills His promises. In 3:25-26 it describes the culminating exhibition of divine resentment against sin. The death of Christ is the final proof of God's displeasure with sin but at the same time the means by which His righteousness "goes forth" to justify the person who believes in Christ. *In the death of His Son, God's righteousness becomes His saving mercy extended to all mankind.* (3) Finally, the way in which Paul speaks of the wrath of God being revealed (*apokalyptetai*) in v. 18 is precisely the way in which he says the righteousness of God is revealed (*apokalyptetai*) in v. 17. This requires that the genitive *theou* (of God) be taken in the same sense in both verses.

But at the same time those who insist that **the righteousness of God** means "a gift bestowed upon man by God," "a righteousness not so much '*of* God' as '*from* God,'" have strong support for their position also. (1) The righteousness in question is described as being **revealed from faith to faith** (*ek pisteos eis pistin*), and in the parallel passage, 3:22, it is qualified as "the righteousness of God which is by faith [*dia pisteos*] of Jesus Christ unto all and upon all them that believe [*eis pantas tous pisteuontas*]." That is, God's righteousness is a gift to be received through faith. (2) Furthermore, in the quotation from Habakkuk which Paul cites to show the OT support for his teaching, the word *dikaios* is applied, not to God, but to the man who has faith: "He who through faith is righteous shall live" (16, RSV). (3) Finally, in the parallel Phil. 3:9 the thought of Paul is made unmistakably clear: "And be found in him, not having mine own righteousness, which is of the law, but that which is through

---

[54]G. Martin has thus defined the righteousness of God in the OT: "Righteousness is attributed to the holy God who commits no iniquity; it is attributed to the holy God who cannot leave wickedness unpunished nor the good unrecognized; it is attributed to the God who is merciful and slow to anger who, according to Ezekiel's phrase, does not desire the death of the sinner but that he should repent and live. It is attributed to the God of love who communicates his righteousness to the sinner and justifies him." Cited by Edmond Jacob, *Theology of the Old Testament* (New York: Harper and Brothers, Publishers, 1958), p. 96.

the faith of Christ [*ten dia pisteos Christou*], the righteousness which is of God by faith [*ten ek theou dikaiosynen epite pistei*]." Sanday and Headlam comment, "The insertion of the preposition *ek* transfers the righteousness from God to man, or we may say traces the process of extension by which it passes from its source to its object."[55]

The two foregoing positions must be understood not as exclusive but rather as inclusive of each other. The righteousness of which Paul speaks not only is a gift of God but *is* God's own righteousness. He combines both ideas in 3:26—"that he might be just [*dikaion*], and the justifier [*dikaiounta ton*] of him which believeth in Jesus." God is both just in himself *and* the Justifier. This is the grand disclosure of the gospel, and it is this glorious revelation which makes the gospel the power of God unto salvation.[56] "For," says Luther, "God does not want to save us by our own but by an extraneous righteousness which does not originate in ourselves but comes to us from beyond ourselves, which does not arise on our earth but comes from heaven."[57]

Thus, the gospel is the revelation of a righteousness which is **from faith to faith** (*ek pisteos eis pistin*). This phrase modifies **the righteousness of God** rather than the verb **revealed**. The sentence might be written thus, "In it is the righteousness of God revealed—and that from faith to faith." The Greek phrase may be rendered "through faith for faith." The gospel discloses a righteousness which is "based on faith and addressed to faith,"[58] a righteousness which is by "faith from start to finish."[59] Nygren sees the phrase as suggesting something like the Protestant formula *sola fide* ("by faith alone"). "When the righteousness of God is revealed in the gospel, it is to faith and faith alone."[60] The Gospels speak often of repentance and faith; Paul says little about repentance. This is probably because, "as he understands it, the word 'faith' (or 'to believe') includes also the equivalent of repentance. Faith is an attitude toward God which involves an attitude toward self—all trust in one's own deserving is shut

[55]ICC, p. 25.

[56]The preceding treatment follows rather closely the analysis of Sanday and Headlam, ICC, pp. 24-25.

[57]*Lectures on Romans,* translated and edited by Wilhelm Pauck ("The Library of Christian Classics"; Philadelphia: The Westminster Press, 1961), XV, 4.

[58]NEB, marginal reading.   [59]So Dodd, Nygren, Knox, and others.

[60]Nygren, *op. cit.,* pp. 78-79.

out. This attitude of faith, Paul is going to insist in this letter, is the sole condition of salvation."[61] To support this thesis he quotes Hab. 2:4, **The just shall live by faith.**

The quotation from Habakkuk has been variously understood. The word translated **faith** (Heb., *emunah*) comes from a verb meaning "to be firm" and has the meaning of steadfastness or fidelity. In the Hebrew it is *"his* faith" (*emunatho*), but the Septuagint renders it as if it had been *emunathi, "my* faith" (that of God or the Messiah). The prophet's reference, however, is not to God or to the Messiah who is to prove His identity by courageous fidelity to His commission, "but to the believing soul who in 'faith' has the touchstone of perseverance" (cf. Heb. 10: 38-39).[62] "Faithfulness" rather than "faith" is in the forefront of Habakkuk's thinking, but, as Kirkpatrick observes, "this faithfulness must spring from faith."[63] Since the *pistis* means both "fidelity" and "faith," Paul correctly translates Hab. 2:4, *Ho dikaios ek pisteos zesetai.*

A second question must be answered. Does the phrase **by faith** (*ek pisteos*) go with the predicate **shall live** (*zesetai*) or with the subject **the just** or "righteous" (*ho dikaios*)? Does Paul quote Habakkuk to mean, "The righteous shall live by faith," or "The righteous by faith shall live"? Certainly the righteous person shall live by his faith, but is this what Paul is setting out to prove by the quotation? Is he not rather citing Habakkuk to support his thesis that the righteousness of God is a righteousness which comes through faith (*ek pisteos*)? J. B. Lightfoot in his *Notes on the Epistles of St. Paul* insists that *"ek pisteos* here corresponds to *ek pisteos* in the former part of the verse, where it belongs, not to the predicate, but to the subject. It is here separated from *ho dikaios* as it is there separated from *dikaiosyne."*[64] The Greek should then read, *ho dikaios ek pisteos, zesetai.*[65] To translate literally, this means, "The righteous by

[61]John Knox (Exegesis), IB, X, 392.

[62]L. E. H. Stephens-Hodge, NBC, p. 734.   [63]*Ibid.* (quoted).

[64]Quoted by John Murray, *op. cit.,* p. 33.

[65]Adam Clarke, *The New Testament of Our Lord and Saviour Jesus Christ* (New York: Abingdon-Cokesbury Press, n.d.), VI, 42. Cf. Nygren, pp. 84-90, for a vigorous defense of this position. He shows how the first phrase, "The righteous by faith," summarizes cc. 1—4, while the verb "shall live" epitomizes cc. 5—8. "Faith" occurs 25 times in cc. 1—4 and only twice in cc. 5—8. It is just the opposite with "live" and its correlatives, which are found 25 times in cc. 5—8, but not counting 1:17, only twice in cc. 1—4.

faith, shall live." The NEB renders it, "He shall gain life who is justified through faith." In Gal. 3:11, where Paul also quotes Hab. 2:4, the context is still more decisive. There, in deep conflict with the Judaizers who were attacking his gospel of justification by faith alone, he quotes Habakkuk specifically to make the point that righteousness comes, not through law observance, but simply through faith in Christ.

In the light which Christ sheds upon the prophet's statement Paul understands Habakkuk to be speaking about a righteousness by faith. "And the scripture, foreseeing that God would justify the heathen through faith, preached before the gospel unto Abraham, saying, In thee shall all nations be blessed" (Gal. 3:8). When the promise was first made, its deeper meaning was not apparent. But the veil which had formerly concealed the Old Testament's profounder meaning has been removed by Christ (II Cor. 3:14). Now we see the deeper significance of Habakkuk's statement. Even if the prophet himself did not apprehend the full truth about the faith of which he wrote, it was God's purpose to speak of justifying faith.[66]

As Paul views the religious world, it is divided into two classes: (1) those who, being ignorant of God's righteousness, go about seeking to establish their own righteousness, and (2) those who receive the righteousness of God through faith in Jesus Christ (cf. 10:3-4). His quotation from Habakkuk is intended to establish his central thesis that the gospel reveals the righteousness of God through faith. Either we can achieve perfect obedience, and thereby earn the favor of God, or we cannot. If we can, then the whole gospel is overthrown and Christ's sacrifice is meaningless. If we cannot, then all depends upon the mercy and grace of God in Christ. It is Paul's purpose in this Epistle to show that we can neither justify nor sanctify ourselves. First, the law shows us our guilt before God and therefore our need for justification (1:18—3:20). Secondly, the law reveals to us the inward sinfulness of our hearts and therefore our need for sanctification (7:7-25). When Paul triumphantly declares the gospel to be God's power **unto salvation,** He is assuring us that what the law can never do for us God's grace in Christ can do. Through faith we may be justified—*made righteous before God* (cc. 1—4). Through faith we may be sanctified and live "in righteousness and true holiness" (cc. 5—8). This life is climaxed in

---

[66]Nygren, *op. cit.*, p. 83. Cf. I Pet. 1:10-11.

true glory (5:2; 8:30). The life which begins in justification issues in sanctification, and is consummated in glorification.

In vv. 14-17 we find "The Christian and the Gospel." (1) The obligation of the gospel, **I am debtor,** 14; (2) The dedication of the gospel, **I am ready,** 15; (3) The inspiration of the gospel, **I am not ashamed,** 16 (John Allan Knight).

Section **II** *The Gospel of God's Righteousness*

Romans 1:18—11:36

A. GOD'S RIGHTEOUSNESS NEEDED, 1:18—3:20

This first major subdivision of Romans is basic to the development of Paul's main theme. Men have no claim to divine favor; the whole race of unbelieving men exist under the wrath of God —all men in general, because they have turned from the Creator to the creature and have become morally depraved; the Jews in particular, because they have disobeyed the higher revelation of God in the law. "There is none righteous, no, not one" (3:10). The consequence is that every mouth is stopped and all the world becomes guilty before God (3:19-20). "Paul's aim is to show that the whole of humanity is morally bankrupt, unable to claim a favourable verdict at the judgment bar of God, desperately in need of His mercy and pardon."[1]

1. *The Human Predicament* (1:18-32)

It is possible to understand this passage merely as a description of the contemporary Gentile world in its idolatry and gross iniquity. But to limit this penetrating discussion to one period or one segment of mankind is to miss in it God's word to us. Paul here speaks of the **unrighteousness of men** (*anthropon*, 18) in every age and culture. His purpose is not simply to inform the Roman Christians about many of their contemporaries but more deeply to show the sinful predicament of fallen man. He is describing the human situation apart from the redemptive power of God. "Humanity, as a result of its disobedience to God, has involved itself in a desperate and morally sick situation."[2]

a. Introduction: The wrath of God (1:18). Man's situation in sin is an existence under **the wrath of God,** which **is revealed from heaven.** The repetition of the verb **revealed** (*apokalyptetai*) is proof of a double revelation—of "righteousness" (17) and of **wrath** (18). Just as "the righteousness of God" means "the whole situation which exists where man is in right relation with God," so **the wrath of God** means man's total situation where he has turned away from the Creator.[3] This perspective must be widened to embrace all humanity. Every person without excep-

[1]Bruce, *op. cit.,* pp. 81–82.   [2]Leenhardt, *op. cit.,* p. 60.
[3]Nygren, *op. cit.,* p. 98.

tion knows either God's righteousness or God's wrath—His love or His displeasure, His saving power or His judgment. "In Christ," Luther once remarked, " 'God is love.' Outside Christ, 'Our God is a consuming fire.' "

God's wrath is thus no incidental truth. It is part and parcel of the divine self-disclosure associated with the gospel. This **wrath . . . is** (now being) **revealed,** just as is "the righteousness of God." The tense is the continuous present, so that Paul is describing a process which is going on before our very eyes.[4] But as salvation anticipates the final manifestation of the righteousness of God, so wrath anticipates the final judgment of the sinner in "the day of wrath and revelation of the righteous judgment of God" (2:5).

What is **the wrath of God** (*orge theou*)? In only two other places does Paul add to the word **wrath** the genitive **of God** (Eph. 5:6; Col. 3:6), and he never uses the verb "to be angry" with God as the subject. This has led many interpreters to define wrath in a wholly impersonal sense. Dodd claims that "to Paul, 'the Wrath' meant, not a certain feeling or attitude of God towards us but some process or effect in the realm of objective facts."[5] In other passages the apostle warns that "whatsoever a man soweth, that shall he also reap" (Gal. 6:7), and that "the wages of sin is death" (6:23). God has created a moral order in which sin is its own punishment and destruction, and in this chapter the divine wrath means that God gives men up to the consequences of their rebellion and misdeeds (1:24-32).

Calvin comments here that "the word *wrath*, referring to God in human terms as is usual in scripture . . . implies no emotion in God, but has reference only to the feelings of the sinner who is punished."[6] But is Calvin correct? No doubt we should be cautious in speaking of divine emotion. Nonetheless, the manner in which Paul places **the wrath of God** against His "righteousness" in v. 17 and uses the dynamic term **revealed** in both cases suggests that **wrath** represents something in the attitude and purpose of God. As there is a positive outgoing of divine love and mercy in providing salvation for men, just so there is a positive outgoing of divine displeasure at sin. P. T. Forsyth asks: "When a man piles up his sin and rejoices in iniquity, is God

---

[4]Dodd, *op. cit.*, p. 20.   [5]*Ibid.*, p. 22.

[6]*The Epistles of Paul to the Romans and to the Thessalonians,* trans. by Ross Mackenzie (Grand Rapids: Wm. B. Eerdmans Pub. Co., 1961), p. 30.

simply a bystander and spectator of the process? Does not God's pressure on the man blind him, urge him, stiffen him, shut him up into sin, if only that he might be shut up to mercy alone? Is it enough to say that this is but the action of a process which God simply watches in a permissive way? Is He but passive and not positive to the situation? Can the Absolute be passive to anything? If so, where is the inner action of the personal God whose immanence in things is one of His great modern revelations?"[7] When Paul goes on to say "God gave them up" (24, 26, 28), this surely describes personal activity.

John Murray sees wrath as "the holy revulsion of God's being against that which is a contradiction of his holiness."[8] Alan Richardson defines it as "God's righteous and implacable condemnation of sin in every form."[9] A. M. Hunter gives a comprehensive definition of God's wrath as "his holy love reacting against evil—the 'adverse wind' of the divine will blowing against the sinner, not only on the Judgment Day, but now, and resulting in the degeneration and debasement of the sinner."[10] Because God is God, His wrath is a terrible reality. But wrath is not hate. "Hate opposes love; wrath is the form love takes with those who oppose it. Hate is unjust; wrath is just. Hate seeks to destroy; wrath forgives. So when Paul says that the wrath of God is being disclosed along with His righteousness, he is saying that God is offering acquittal, but that those who refuse to accept it are condemned."[11]

---

[7]Quoted by Leon Morris, *The Apostolic Preaching of the Cross* (Grand Rapids: Wm. B. Eerdmans Pub. Co., 1956), p. 165.

[8]*Op. cit.*, p. 35.

[9]*An Introduction to the Theology of the New Testament* (New York: Harper and Brothers, 1958), p. 224.

[10]*Interpreting Paul's Gospel* (Philadelphia: The Westminster Press, 1954), pp. 69-70.

[11]Burton H. Throckmorton, Jr., *Romans for the Layman* (Philadelphia: The Westminster Press, 1961), p. 24. In the OT, God's wrath has a special reference to His covenant with Israel; it is an expression of Yahweh's jealousy, of that exclusive love which will tolerate no infidelity (Lev. 10: 1-2; Num. 16:33, 46). In the prophets the infliction of wrath is gradually concentrated on "the great and terrible day of the Lord" (Joel 2:31; cf. Isa. 2:10-22; Jer. 3:7-8; etc.). The NT use is this eschatological prophetic view (Matt. 3:7; Rom. 2:5; I Thess. 1:10; Rev. 6:16-17; etc.). Wrath is one aspect of the day of the Lord, namely, the destruction of those who resist God's sovereign purpose. Christians are delivered from this wrath both now and in that day (Rom. 5:9).

The **ungodliness** (*asebeia*) **and unrighteousness** (*adikia*) against which the divine wrath is revealed should be distinguished but not separated from each other, since they both spring from the refusal to glorify God as God (1:20). *Asebeia* describes an offense in the religious realm and expresses itself as idolatry, the worship of the creature rather than the Creator (1:19-23). *Adikia* means moral perversity, and is illustrated by immorality and wickedness (1:24-32). Both of these sins are the expression of human willfulness on the part **of men, who hold** ("restrain," RSV; "stifle," NEB) **the truth in unrighteousness.** The verb is used here in the same sense as in II Thess. 2:6-7. It carries the idea of "holding back" and is therefore well-suited to express their reaction to the truth thus manifested. This implies, as Paul will show, that all men have the truth, and that by their unrighteousness they prevent it from attaining its purpose. Thus all sin is positive resistance to God.

By opening this section with an announcement of God's outpoured wrath upon sinners, Paul is laying the groundwork for the declaration of God's righteousness which follows in 3:21—8:39. In order to seek divine help, it is not enough to know that such help is available; man must be convinced that he desperately needs it. "The existential anguish of man is what incites him to seek God; but his anguish must be so deep and far-reaching that it ceases to be satisfied by fallacious responses."[12] Paul therefore begins here to describe man's sinful predicament, before setting forth the plan by which God comes to his rescue in Christ. "Before being saved, man is condemned; but he is condemned in order to be saved; his condemnation is the first phase of his salvation, for only he who knows he is lost, has recourse to grace and is able to appreciate its utter gratuity. That is why the 'good news' itself implies as a prerequisite the proclamation of 'the wrath of God.' "[13]

b. *Man's original sin* (1:19-23). Paul now tells us why God's wrath is outpoured on wicked men. The reason is that men have refused the knowledge of God offered them by the Creator. The wickedness of men is but a symptom of a more basic fault. "All the perversions of life [Paul will show] can be traced back to one fundamental cause, and this original sin is not to be found in the field of morals but in the soil of religion: perversion of life arises

[12]Leenhardt, *op. cit.,* p. 60.   [13]*Ibid.*

from perversion of faith."[14] We have violated divine truth. Paul begins, "For all that may be known of God by men lies plain before their eyes, indeed God himself has disclosed it to them" (NEB). The KJV translates the first phrase (*en autois*) is **manifest in them.** The expression means simply that any revelation must pass through human consciousness.[15] But notice that God **may be known** because He *makes himself* known. Human discovery must be understood within the framework of divine disclosure.

The **invisible** God has made himself known **from the creation of the world** (20). Although the phrase *apo ktiseos kosmou* may be rendered "from the created universe," it is generally agreed that Paul's thought is temporal: *"since the creation of the universe."* Ever since its origin creation has spoken to the reflective mind about God. Although God cannot be known directly through reason (I Cor. 1:21), He is knowable. This knowledge, however, is not thrust upon a passive subject; to learn about God we must adopt a positive and receptive attitude. Creation exists as an invitation to dialogue with God. Certain things may be **clearly seen,** but only if we are willing to see.

Man's contemplation of the world considered as a work of God has two objects: (1) **his eternal power,** and (2) His **Godhead.** Man is aware of his dependence upon a Power (*dynamis*) which presides over his existence. Through it he comes into being, and in the face of it he knows his nothingness. Moreover, when he considers the temporality of his own existence, this power he perceives to be **eternal.**

Secondly, we see **Godhead** or deity (*theiotes*). The universe is not moved by blind power, but power that is divine in character—*it is God.* "That is, what is clearly seen is that God is God and not man. Observation of created life is sufficient to show that creation does not provide the key to its own existence.[16] Nevertheless, we miss the point entirely if we interpret Paul as attempting to "prove" God's existence. In fact, the sins Paul castigates later in this chapter are not those of men who do not believe in God, but of those who *refuse to honor God as God.* This is why sinners and unbelievers are **without excuse.** "God may rightly visit men with wrath because, though they may not

---

[14]Walter Luthi, *The Letter to the Romans* (Richmond, Virginia: John Knox Press, 1961), p. 22.

[15]ICC, "Romans," p. 42.   [16]Barrett, *op. cit.,* p. 35.

have had the advantage of hearing the Gospel, they have rejected the rudimentary knowledge of God which was open to them."[17]

The root of men's sinful predicament is that, although **they knew God, they glorified him not as God, neither were thankful** (21). As a creature, man owed his Creator glory and thanksgiving. This means not merely to acknowledge God's existence, but to recognize His lordship and to live in grateful obedience. What is required is that man joyfully and thankfully *acknowledge his creaturehood* in faithful service to God. Centuries before Paul, Isaiah voiced the divine complaint, "The ox knoweth his owner, and the ass his master's crib: but Israel doth not know, my people doth not consider" (Isa. 1:3). In the pride of his heart man refuses to glorify God as God. In the preoccupation with himself he turns away from God as the Center of his being and source of his happiness—from divine love to self-love. He is unwilling to recognize the Lord of his being; he chooses to be lord himself and to glorify himself. This setting up of self as the false end of life is man's original sin and the source of all his misery.[18]

The immediate consequence of man's self-idolatry is the darkening of his reasoning power. Because men turned away from God they **became vain in their imaginations** (*dialogismois,* reasonings), **and their foolish heart was darkened.** *Dialogismos* is almost always used in both the Septuagint and the NT in a bad sense as "perverse, self-willed reasonings and speculations."[19] The NASB translates, "Became futile in their speculations."

---

[17]*Ibid.,* p. 36.

[18]"Man was created looking directly to God, as his last end; but, falling into sin, he fell off from God, and turned into himself. Now, this infers a total apostasy and universal corruption in man; for where the last end is changed, there can be no real goodness. And this is the case of all men in their natural state: They seek not God, but themselves. Hence though many fair shreds of morality are among them, yet 'there is none that doeth good, no, not one.' For though some of them 'run well,' they are still off the way; they never aim at the right mark. Whithersoever they move, they cannot move beyond the circle of self. They seek themselves, they act for themselves; their natural, civil, and religious actions, from whatever spring they come, do all run into, and meet in, this dead sea" (John Wesley; quoted by Colin W. Williams, *John Wesley's Theology Today* [New York: Abingdon Press, 1960], p. 50).

[19]ICC, p. 44. Sanday and Headlam cite as a parallel Enoch 99:8-9, "And they will become godless by reason of the foolishness of their hearts, and their eyes will be blinded through the fear of their hearts and through visions of their dreams. Through these they will become godless and fearful, because they work all their works in a lie and they worship a stone."

52

Heart (*kardia*) has a wide range of use. It is the organ of feeling (9:2), thought (10:6), and will (I Cor. 4:5; 7:37), the inward, hidden self (2:29; 8:27). Paul's meaning here is that the heart as the center of man's affections, intellect, and volition is **darkened** and senseless because of his self-idolatry: **Professing themselves to be wise, they became fools** (22). Out of touch with reality, men's pretentious speculations are senseless folly.

Because men have lost the true God they have invented human "religion." They have **changed** ("exchanged," NASB) **the glory of the uncorruptible God into an image made like to corruptible man, and to birds, and fourfooted beasts, and creeping things** (23). This illustrates the depths of folly to which men's reasoning sinks when they reject God's truth. "They got God down on two legs, then down on all fours, then down on the belly!"[20] All the while they were "claiming to be wise" (RSV)!

c. *Man's moral depravity* (1:24-32). Paul now describes the moral consequences of man's rebellion against God. If the *root* of man's sin is religious perversity, the *fruit* is moral corruption. Cut off from God as the Source of his life and happiness, man sought satisfaction in the creature. But in so doing he became subject to the creature. "Rebellion against God has created a vacuum in human nature," D. R. Davies writes. "That vacuum must be filled, if not by God, then by the devil of self. All the lusts and excesses of human behaviour are attempts to satisfy that 'aching void the world can never fill.' Man, as a result of his fall from Divine Grace, is cursed by an infinite craving."[21] It is this divine curse upon mankind which Paul depicts in the remainder of this chapter. Three times he repeats the phrase, **God gave them up** (vv. 24, 26, 28), expressing with horrifying emphasis the consequences of man's revolt. God has abandoned sinners to sensuality (24-25), sex perversion (26-27), and antisocial living (28-32).

(1) *Sensuality* (1:24-25). The conjunction **Wherefore** (24) indicates that the retribution Paul is about to describe finds its ground in the antecedent sin and is a just infliction for man's rebellion. Because men have revolted against God, the Creator

---

[20]Chester Warren Quimby, *The Great Redemption* (New York: The Macmillan Company, 1950), pp. 45-46.

[21]*Down Peacock's Feathers* (New York: The Macmillan Company, 1944), p. 70.

has abandoned them **to uncleanness through the lusts of their
own hearts, to dishonour their own bodies.** "They sinned by
degrading God, **wherefore also** God degraded them."[22] In Wesley's
words, "If a man will not worship God as God, he is so left to
himself that he throws away his very manhood."[23] In the same
vein Barth observes, "When God has been deprived of His glory,
men are also deprived of theirs. Desecrated within their souls,
they are also desecrated in their bodies, for men are one."[24]

Such men have **changed the truth of God into a lie** (*to
pseudei,* "the lie"). **The truth** is that God is God; the **lie** is the
exaltation of **the creature** above **the Creator, who is blessed for
ever** (25). While the apostle's immediate reference in this passage is to pagan idolatry, his ultimate reference is to the sinful
pride of the human heart. The **lie** is the creature's idolatrous
usurpation of the divine glory. It had its origin with Satan, whom
Jesus called the father of the lie (John 8:44-45). In the Garden,
Satan lied to the first pair, promising that if they should assert
their independence of their Creator they would be "like God"
(Gen. 3:4-5, RSV) in power and wisdom. The unspeakable and
irreparable conclusion of sin is to refuse to love **the truth** and to
believe the **lie** (II Thess. 2:9-12). This is to be damned forever.
Such apostasy is the end of moral capacity; it brings total moral
and spiritual disintegration. Such is the incurable religiousness
of the human heart that, if man does not worship **the Creator,** he
inevitably serves **the creature.**

(2) *Perversion* (1:26-27). **For this cause,** we read, **God gave
them up unto vile affections** (26). "Being life's most explosive
urge, when released from mental control, sex breaks loose in wild
perversions."[25] The obvious reference here is to homosexuality,
which exchanges the natural use of sex into that which is **against
nature.** Sex is God's gift to mankind for the procreation of the
race (Gen. 1:27-28, 31) and for personal fulfillment in monog-
amous marriage (Gen. 2:18-24; cf. I Cor. 7:1-7). Homosexuality
is a nauseating and pitiful perversion of this sacred and beautiful
gift (cf. I Cor. 6:9-10).[26] **Burned in their lust one toward another**
(27) is a reference to the intensity of this unnatural passion and

[22]Godet, *op. cit.,* p. 107.

[23]*Explanatory Notes upon the New Testament,* p. 521.

[24]*The Epistle to the Romans,* p. 51.   [25]Quimby, *op. cit.,* p. 46.

[26]It is cause for concern that this ancient sin of Sodom is being increasingly countenanced today.

is not to be confused with the burning of I Cor. 7:9, which finds an outlet in marriage. Here it is "the burning of an insatiable lust that has no natural or legitimate desire of which the lust is a perversion or distortion. It is lust directed to something that is essentially and under all circumstances illegitimate."[27]

The words **receiving in themselves that recompence of their error which was meet** refer to the thought expressed in vv. 24-26; abandonment to immorality is the judicial consequence of man's rebellion. The **error** being recompensed is the sin of idolatry described in 21-23. The **recompence** consists in "the growing unsatisfied lust itself, together with the dreadful physical and moral consequences of debauchery."[28] This description of the moral squalor of sinful mankind prepares us for the further analysis of God's judicial abandonment in the verse which follows.

(3) *Antisocial living* (1:28-32). Paul has described the "ungodliness" of the world—rebellion and idolatry. Its punishment is sensuality and perversion. He now describes the other aspect of the world's sin—"unrighteousness"—and its punishment, "hardboiled and disruptive living"[29] (cf. 1:18).

The apostle writes, **And even as they did not like to retain God in their knowledge, God gave them over to a reprobate mind** (28). The term **reprobate** (*adokimon*) is literally "not standing the test." There is a wordplay here: "As they did not *approve*, God gave them up to a mind *disapproved*."[30] Barrett attempts to represent the play on words in the original: "And as they did not *see fit* to take cognizance of God, God handed them over to an *unfit* mind."[31] By rejecting God from their minds, their mentality was rejected. The evidence of this **reprobate mind** is the practice of **those things which are not convenient.** This phrase is a technical term employed by Stoic writers and is better rendered "things which are not proper" (NASB) or simply "improper conduct" (RSV).[32]

In the catalogue of vices which follows we need not look for a rigorously systematic order, but in this apparent disorder Godet detects a certain grouping, "a connection through the association of ideas." The first four, **unrighteousness . . . wickedness, covet-**

---

[27]Murray, *op. cit.*, p. 48.
[28]William G. T. Shedd; quoted by Murray, *ibid.*
[29]Quimby, *op. cit.*, p. 48. [30]Vincent, *op. cit.*, p. 21.
[31]*Op. cit.*, p. 39. [32]Dodd, *op. cit.*, pp. 27-28.

ousness, **maliciousness** (29a), refer to injustices with respect to the well-being and properties of others. The next five, **envy, murder, debate, deceit, malignity** (29b), are injustices in which we harm the person of our neighbor. Then comes an allusion to six dispositions of the mind centering in pride, **whisperers, backbiters, haters of God, despiteful, proud, boasters** (29c-30a). Finally, the last seven terms, **inventors of evil things, disobedient to parents, without understanding, covenantbreakers, without natural affection, implacable, unmerciful** (30b-31), relate to the destruction of all natural sentiments and affections.[33] By thus drawing up an inventory of the evil deeds of man, Paul was conforming to a widespread custom among both Jews and pagan moralists, namely, that of making lists of virtues and vices for pedagogic purposes.[34]

In the first list, **fornication** (29a, *porneia*) is lacking in the best attested MSS and should be omitted. This presents no problem since the subject has been exhausted in the preceding section. **All unrighteousness** (*adikia*) is a comprehensive term (cf. 1:18), including all the vices which follow. **Wickedness** (*poneria*) contains the idea of "*active* mischief."[35] **Covetousness** (*pleonexia*) has a long history in Greek ethical writing. "Its general connotation is that of ruthless, aggressive self-assertion. In Plato, for example, it is the characteristic vice of the tyrant; and all through Greek literature it describes the man who will pursue his own interests with complete disregard for the rights of others and for all consideration of humanity."[36] Such ruthlessness may express itself in the sphere of sexual relations but it is never simply lust. **Maliciousness** (*kakia*) denotes "inward viciousness of disposition."[37]

The terms of 29b form a natural grouping which embraces the injustices whereby the *person* of our neighbor is injured. The adjective **full of** (*mestous*) means literally "stuffed."[38] **Envy** (*phthonou*) was often combined by classical writers with **murder** (*phonou*) because of the similarity of sound in both words; "besides, envy leads to murder, as is shown by the example of

---

[33]*Op. cit.*, pp. 110-11.

[34]Leenhardt, *op. cit.*, p. 70. Cf. 13:13; I Cor. 5:10-11; 6:9-10; II Cor. 12:20; Gal. 5:19-21; Eph. 4:31; Col. 3:8; I Tim. 1:9-10; II Tim. 3:2-5.

[35]ICC, p. 47.   [36]Dodd, *op. cit.*, p. 27.

[37]ICC, p. 47.   [38]Godet, *op. cit.*, p. 110.

Cain."[39] If envy does not go so far as to destroy another, it always leads at least to **debate** (*eridos*, "strife," RSV; or "quarrelsomeness," Phillips). The NEB translates it "rivalry." Finally, in this course one seeks to injure his neighbor by **deceit** (*dolos*) or to render his life miserable by **malignity** (*kakoetheias*, "spite," Phillips).

Whisperers, backbiters, haters of God, despiteful, proud, boasters (29c-30a) represent vices all of which center in pride. **Whisperers** (*psithyristas*) pour poison against their neighbor into a listening ear; **backbiters** (*katalalous*) blacken reputations publicly. **Haters of God** (*theostygeis*) are "those who see that His justice stands in the way of their wickedness."[40] Although *theostygeis* may be translated "hated of God," the context favors the active rendering adopted by practically all translators. **Despiteful** (*hybristas*) is from *hybris*, the cruelest of all sins in the eyes of the Greeks. It is mingled pride and cruelty. "*Hybris* is the pride which makes a man defy God, and the arrogant contempt which makes him trample on the hearts of his fellow man."[41] Such arrogant persons are inevitably **boasters** (*alazonas*), for they seek to attract admiration by claiming advantages they do not really possess.

The last group includes **inventors of evil things, disobedient to parents, without understanding, covenantbreakers, without natural affection, implacable, unmerciful** (30b-31). This group "refers to the extinction of all the natural feelings of humanity, filial affection, loyalty, tenderness and pity."[42] **Inventors of evil things** are those who spend their lives thinking of the evil to be done to others. "So Antiochus Epiphanes is called by the author of 2 Macc. (vii. 31)."[43] People of this stripe have become such because in their homes they were **disobedient to parents.** The phrase **without understanding** (*asynetos*) describes a person who refuses to listen to counsel or heed advice; thus understood, it has a natural connection with the preceding term (cf. Ps. 32:8-9). **Covenantbreakers** (*asynthetous*) are the "faithless" (RSV) and the "untrustworthy" (NASB). **Without natural affection** (*astorgous*) is the negative from *stergein*, which means to cherish, foster, or caress. *Astorgous* denotes the destruction of all feelings

---

[39]*Ibid.*   [40]Calvin, *op. cit.*, p. 38.

[41]William Barclay, *More New Testament Words* (London: SCM Press Ltd., 1958), pp. 84-85.

[42]Godet, *op. cit.*, p. 111.   [43]*Ibid.*

of natural tenderness, as is seen by the mother who exposes or kills her child, a father who abandons his family, or children who neglect their aged parents. **Implacable** (*aspondous*) is not in the best attested MSS and should be omitted here. **Unmerciful** (*aneleemonas*) means "without pity" (NEB) and is closely connected with *astorgous*, but the meaning is more general. It refers not only to a lack of tender feelings within the family circle but also to the kind of hardness of heart which applauds the flow of human blood in a gladiatorial contest. It is also the callousness which is unmoved by the spectacle of human calamity or misery.

Men such as Paul has described, while **knowing the judgment of God, that they which commit such things are worthy of death, not only do the same, but have pleasure in them that do them** (32). **Death** here denotes "death as God only can inflict it, the pains of Hades, which the Gentiles also recognized."[44] The final clause of this verse has been variously understood. It may mean that encouraging others to commit such sins is worse than doing them oneself. To Godet it suggests "the mind deprived of discernment, to which God has given up men, in its most monstrous manifestation; not only doing evil, but applauding those who do it!"[45] John Knox thinks Paul may be pointing to a general breakdown of principle in the pagan world, as though he would say: "Not only are these terrible things done, but they are done with the tacit if not the expressed approval of the whole society."[46] This would suggest that God has withdrawn himself from that society, leaving it not only in sin, but in the darkness it has perversely chosen. Barrett thinks the difficulty can be solved only by looking forward to 2:1-3, where Paul deals with those who do *not* approve of the sinful actions just described. Before doing so he deals with those who *do* approve.[47]

> Here is the final vacuity and disintegration. Chaos has found itself, and anything may happen. The atoms swirl, the struggle for existence rages. Even reason becomes irrational. Ideas of duty and of fellowship become wholly unstable. The world is full of personal caprice and social unrighteousness—this is not a picture merely of Rome under the Caesars! The true nature of our unbroken existence is here unrolled before us. Our ungodliness and unrighteousness stand under the wrath of God.[48]

[44]*Ibid.*, p. 112.   [45]*Ibid.*
[46]IB (Exposition), IX, 404.   [47]*Op. cit.*, p. 41.
[48]Barth, *The Epistle to the Romans*, p. 53.

In this passage Paul was not attempting a complete and exact portrait of pagan society or of the natural man. He was aware that some pagans fulfilled many of the prescriptions of the law (2:14), and that Greek and Roman philosophers condemned many of the forms of depravity he had described. No one individual embodies all the depravities Paul enumerates. But this is not the point. His purpose is rather to bring the reader to examine his heart and to ask himself whether he finds in his own character any of the features of this portrait of a man without God.

"Such a self-examination is intended to bring him to the realization that he too is in solidarity with a humanity which is thus ravaged to its depths by its rejection of God. . . . Paul writes not as a moralist but as a preacher of the gospel and in order to make us realize that all men . . . stand under the 'wrath' of God. No one is guilty of so many sins in their totality, but no one is altogether innocent and no one can claim that what is said here does not concern him at all."[49]

In 1:18-32 may be seen "The Nature and Progress of Sin." (1) Ingratitude, 21; (2) Idolatry, 25; (3) Moral Degradation, 26-32.

2. The Failure of the Jews, 2:1—3:8

So far, Paul has argued the visible degradation of men who have rejected the truth; God's wrath is now working its terrible havoc in those who do not see fit to acknowledge Him as God. But Paul knew there were those who joined in his condemnation of human wickedness. He imagines one of these critics objecting, "Yes, that's what the heathen and the worldly are like. But surely you don't class us with this riffraff? They are lost, but as for us, we are neither lost, nor do we need this Saviour you are proclaiming."[50] At first it is not clear, but it soon becomes apparent that this healthy man who needs no physician is primarily (but not exclusively) the Jew.[51]

a. God's judgment and the critic (2:1-16). Therefore thou art inexcusable, O man, whosoever thou art that judgest: for wherein thou judgest another, thou condemnest thyself; for

---

[49]Leenhardt, *op. cit.*, p. 72.   [50]Luthi, *op. cit.*, p. 29.

[51]The moral Gentile is probably included.

thou that judgest doest the same things (1). Paul is here addressing his readers in the ancient diatribe style. Throughout the Epistle it will be easier to follow his argument if we imagine the apostle face-to-face with a heckler who interrupts his argument from time to time with an objection which he proceeds to answer, first rebuking with a "God forbid!" ("Perish the thought!") and then demolishing it with a reasoned answer.[52]

Therefore (1) marks the beginning of a transition from the Gentiles to the Jews.[53] It is not until v. 17 that Paul turns specifically to the problem of the Jews; here, as in vv. 9-10, 12-16, his thought is equally applicable to Gentiles and Jews. While he is undoubtedly thinking primarily of the Jews, he frames his argument in terms that are general enough to include others who are also critical of the wicked practices delineated in the preceding section. In bringing home the guilt of the Jew, Paul establishes first the general principles of judgment, which he proceeds to apply with telling effect to the Jew in vv. 17-29.

F. F. Bruce sees the Stoic moralist Seneca, contemporary of Paul and tutor of Nero, as representative of another side of the pagan world of the first century. Seneca could write so effectively on the good life that Tertullian called him affectionately "our own Seneca."[54] He not only exalted moral virtues but also exposed hypocrisy and saw the pervasive character of evil. "All vices," he wrote, "exist in all men, though all vices do not stand out prominently in each man." He taught and practiced daily self-examination, ridiculed vulgar idolatry, and assumed the role of a moral guide. Yet he often tolerated vices in himself not so different from those he condemned in others—the most flagrant instance being his complicity in Nero's murder of his mother, Agrippina.[55]

That Paul is thinking primarily of the Jew even in this section, however, is evident from his repetition of the phrase, **to the Jew first, and also to the Gentile (9-10)**. Murray argues convincingly for identifying the objector as a Jew. (1) The propensity to judge the Gentiles for their religious and moral

[52]Cf. 3:5; 4:1; 6:1; 7:7; 8:31; 9:14, 30. See also 9:19; 11:19.

[53]Wesley, *Explanatory Notes upon the New Testament*, p. 523.

[54]Bruce, *op. cit.*, p. 87.

[55]*Ibid.*

perversity was a peculiar characteristic of the Jew, who was intensely conscious of his high privilege and prerogative as a member of the chosen community of Israel.[56] (2) The person being addressed enjoys in a special way **the riches of** God's **goodness and forbearance and longsuffering** (4), as a covenant privilege. (3) Paul's argument is to the effect that special privilege or advantage does not exempt from the judgment of God (vv. 3, 6-11). (4) Finally, "the express address to the Jew in verse 17 would be rather abrupt if now for the first time the Jew is directly in view, whereas if the Jew is the person in view in the preceding verses then the more express identification in verse 17 is natural."[57]

Therefore (*dio*) connects Paul's argument with 1:32a, "Who knowing the judgment of God." "Men know God's verdict on such sinners as are described in 1:29 ff.; *therefore* the man who judges proves himself to be without excuse, for he sins [also], and in the act of judging proves that he knows what is right."[58] **Inexcusable** harks back to 1:20. Just as the man who suppresses "the truth in unrighteousness" (1:18) is "without excuse" (1:20), so is the man who **judgest another** and yet **doest the same things**. The judge is without excuse if he commits wrong, because as a judge he knows the law—he of all men cannot plead ignorance. Here is the fact of conscience, which will be discussed more fully in vv. 14-15. The perversity of the human heart is revealed in its tendency to condemn others for what it permits in itself. The clue to c. 2 is the last clause of v. 1. The self-appointed judge is doing the same things as the one he condemns; that is, he refuses to honor God or to give thanks, and claims to be wise (cf. 1:21-22).[59] Behind all the sins in the previous catalog lies the sin of idolatry, which reveals the human ambition to put self in the

---

[56]"Weigh in the balances our iniquities and those of other nations and it will be seen on which side the scale dips. When have the inhabitants of other lands not sinned against you? And what nation, like ourselves, has kept your commandments?" (4 Ezra 3:34-35) Not only were all heathen consigned to Gehenna (Sanh. 13:2; Sifre Deut. 32:8; 2 Bar. 85:9), but they were regarded not as men but as beasts (Yeb. 61b).

[57]Murray, *op. cit.*, pp. 55-56.

[58]Barrett, *op. cit.*, p. 43.

[59]Paul S. Minear, "The Truth About Sin and Death," *Interpretation*, VII (April, 1953), 148.

place of God. This is precisely what the judge does when he assumes the right of condemning his fellow creature.[60]

With characteristic insight Karl Barth observes, "There emerges from the righteousness of the God of the Prophets the human righteousness of the Pharisees, which is as such ungodliness and unrighteousness."[61] But also, from the righteousness of God revealed in the gospel the selfsame human righteousness may emerge. The Pharisee lurks in each of us: "God, I thank thee, that I am not as other men" (Luke 18:11). "Pride in all its forms, vanity, egotism, spiritual complacency, a self-centered religion, the Pharisaism which is goodness, and yet a false goodness—all these forms of moral evil are most likely to appear in those whose lives are disciplined and virtuous."[62] This is the elder-brother spirit condemned by our Lord in the parable of the two sons (Luke 15:25-32). Spiritual pride and censoriousness cut us off from the love of God as surely as adultery or theft. So Jesus taught and so Paul here warns. The only antidote to such self-righteousness is the recognition that our "hope is built on nothing less than Jesus' blood and righteousness," and that whatever good may be found in us is wholly by the grace of God and not of our own doing (I Cor. 15:10; Eph. 2:8-9; Phil. 2:12).

Verse 2 should be understood as an objector's remark. Moffatt therefore places the statement in quotation marks: " 'We know the doom of God falls justly upon those who practise such vices.' " That is, God's judgment is impartial (cf. 11). In v. 3, Paul agrees: "Very well; and do you imagine that you will escape God's doom, O man, you who judge those who practise such vices and do the same yourself?" (Moffatt) The second "you" is emphatic: Do you suppose that *you* of all men will escape?[63] The objector doubtless did suppose this, since he had not been handed over "to a reprobate mind" (cf. 1:28-32), the sign of God's wrath upon the Gentiles. "He was rather the object of God's

---

[60]Barrett, *op. cit.*, p. 44. "The selfish principle," J. B. Mozley writes, "does not require vice as its instrument; so long as it can get behind an erected set of virtues, can dominate the situation, and dictate the motive, it is enough. It retreats then behind the last ground gained, whether of truth or morals, and uses the latest virtues as its fulcrum and leverage" (quoted by R. Newton Flew, *The Idea of Perfection* [London: The Oxford University Press, 1934], p. 333).

[61]*The Epistle to the Romans*, p. 60.   [62]Flew, *op. cit.*, p. 333.

[63]Sanday and Headlam paraphrase, "Thou, of all men" (ICC, p. 55).

kindness. But this was a privilege he had misunderstood. He is now to be enlightened."[64]

Or despisest thou the riches of his goodness and forbearance and longsuffering? (4) The Jewish tendency was to accept all this as a proof of divine partiality to the Chosen People. The Book of Wisdom, which Paul seems to be following closely as he pens this entire section, helps us to feel the full force of his accusation. At the end of Wisdom 14 we find a list of pagan vices similar to Paul's catalog in 1:29-31. The writer continues: "But Thou our God art gracious and true, longsuffering, and in mercy ordering all things. For even if we sin, we are thine, knowing thy dominion; but we shall not sin, knowing that we are accounted thine: for to know thee is perfect righteousness, yea, to know thy dominion is the root of immortality. For neither did any evil device of man lead us astray, nor yet the painters' fruitless labour, a form stained with various colours [idols]" (Wisdom 15: 1-4). This passage describes the critic Paul has in mind. He considers himself superior to the idolator. Even if he does sin, he shuns the fundamental sin of idolatry; he belongs to the Chosen People, and is thereby assured of salvation.[65] But, Paul is saying, this is "misinterpreting God's generosity and patient mercy" (4, Phillips). Such spiritual complacency misses the whole point of the divine forbearance. "Don't you realize that God's kindness is meant to lead you to repentance?" (Phillips) We have been given the power of moral judgment, not to censure our fellow creatures, but to judge ourselves and thus be brought **to repentance** and a turning back to God. "To know the good does not furnish us with a claim to divine indulgence. The fact that the hour of divine judgment has not yet struck does not by any means show that God judges us favorably. Knowledge of the good is one of the conditions of repentance; the second is the time of respite granted by the patience of God."[66]

The Jew, then, knows that God is kind and merciful. But in the face of divine kindness he exhibits **hardness** and an **impenitent heart** (5). This "removes him out of the sphere of divine grace, as surely as does the sin of idolatry among the pagans."[67] To despise the riches of divine mercy is to store up **wrath against the day of wrath and revelation of the righteous**

[64]Barrett, *op. cit.*, p. 44.   [65]*Ibid.*, p. 45.
[66]Leenhardt, *op. cit.*, p. 75.   [67]Dodd, *op. cit.*, p. 33.

judgment of God. Wrath is here invoked upon the Jewish critic as it had been upon mankind in general in 1:18. The two passages are parallel. There is only one difference between them—against the Gentiles the wrath is now being revealed, while the storm is gathering for the Jews. The time when it will burst upon them Paul calls **the day of wrath.**[68] This phrase goes back to the OT prophets. "That day is a day of wrath, a day of trouble and distress, a day of wasteness and desolation, a day of darkness and gloominess, a day of clouds and thick darkness" (Zeph. 1:15; cf. Joel 2:2 and Amos 5:18). By adding the word **revelation** Paul intimates what this **day of wrath** will be: the manifestation of God's justice.

In vv. 4-6 we see "The Long-suffering of God." (1) The gracious fact, 4a; (2) The abuse, 4-5; (3) The exhaustion of mercy, 6; (4) The purpose, 4b.

The difference between the revelation of wrath in c. 1, where it is a process observable in the experience of mankind, and the **day of wrath** here, which is an end-time event in the future, is not as great as it seems. They are only two ways of looking at the same fact. As salvation anticipates the final manifestation of the righteousness of God (see comments on 1:16-17), so the present manifestation of God's wrath among the Gentiles anticipates the final day of judgment (see comments on 1:18). "The main point that Paul wishes to urge is that, however the Wrath is revealed, there is no substantial difference between Jew and pagan when it is revealed. The moral order is one; its laws operate consistently."[69] It shall be **tribulation and anguish, upon every soul of man that doeth evil, of the Jew first, and also of the Gentile; but glory, honour, and peace, to every man that worketh good, to the Jew first, and also to the Gentile: for there is no respect of persons with God** (9-11). When the judgment is held, membership in the Chosen People and assumed moral superiority will be irrelevant. **The judgment of God is according to truth** (2), or reality.

God **will render to every man according to his deeds** (6). Although Paul makes no direct quotation from the OT, he assumes his readers will understand this statement as such (cf. Ps. 62:12; Prov. 24:12; Jer. 17:10; 32:19; Job 34:11).[70] "Not

[68]Godet, *op. cit.*, p. 116.   [69]Dodd, *op. cit.*, p. 33.

[70]In the NT cf. Matt. 16:27; II Cor. 5:10; II Tim. 4:14; I Pet. 1:17; Rev. 2:23; 20:12; 22:12.

hearing the law, being the proud and privileged possessor of it, but doing it is what matters."[71] Nor is this to imply any contradiction of Paul's doctrine of free justification "by faith without the deeds of the law" (3:28). The faith which justifies is a "faith which worketh by love" (Gal. 5:6). Here Paul's teaching closely parallels the thought of James: "Faith without works is dead" (cf. Jas. 2:14-26). Unless our faith is a living and loving faith which has produced a harvest of righteousness, it is not justifying faith (cf. Phil. 1:9-11). Verses 7 and 8, which form a balanced couplet, make this idea clear.

Paul deals first with those who hope for **eternal life** (7). "This is the opposite of corruption (Gal. vi. 8), and describes not the blessedness of the Christian life in this world but the greater blessedness of life beyond the final judgment."[72] It will be bestowed upon those **who by patient continuance in well doing seek for glory and honour and immortality.** The term **patient continuance** (*hypomonen*) is better rendered "patient endurance." It is closely related to hope (cf. 8:24-25; I Cor. 13:7; I Thess. 1:3). "It suggests a readiness to look beyond the present moment, to see the full meaning of the present, and, in particular, of the things men do in the present, not in themselves but in the future, that is (for one who looks upon the future in the biblical manner), in God."[73] They work with patient endurance who hope in God for the reward of their labors. **Glory and honour and immortality** are eschatological terms, and as such are exclusively God's gifts.[74] "The reward of eternal life, then, is promised to those who do not regard their good works as an end in themselves, but see them as marks not of human achievement but of hope in God. Their trust is not in their good works, but in God, the only source of glory, honour, and incorruption."[75]

The second half of this couplet deals with those whose recompense is **indignation** (*orge*) **and wrath** (*thymos*, 8).[76] Who are these persons? They who are **contentious** (*eritheia*), **and do not**

---

[71]Barrett, *op. cit.*, p. 46.   [72]*Ibid.*   [73]*Ibid.*

[74]**For glory,** see 8:18, 21; 9:23; I Cor. 14:43; for *incorruption*, see I Cor. 15:42, 50, 53-54.

[75]Barrett, *loc. cit.*

[76]"*Orge* is a settled feeling; *thymos* the outward manifestation" (ICC, p. 57). These words should be in the accusative case; Paul has apparently forgotten the construction of the two previous verses and writes as if he were beginning a new sentence.

obey the truth. The rendering of KJV, as also that of ASV ("them that are factious") and RSV ("those who are factious"), assumes the false derivation of *eritheia* from *eris* ("strife"). Sanday and Headlam rightly see *eritheia* as deriving rather from *erithos* ("a hired laborer"), from which we get *eritheuein* ("to act as a hireling, to work for pay, to behave as, show the spirit of, a hireling").[77] The rendering of NASB ("those who are selfishly ambitious") and NEB ("those who are governed by selfish ambition") recognizes the true derivation of *eritheia*.[78] Bruce paraphrases, "Those who have no aim beyond self-interest."[79] Those who shall experience divine **wrath** and **indignation** are they who look upon their good works as achievements of their own by which they expect to claim the favor of God. This makes them as disobedient to the truth (of God's sovereign lordship) and as prone to **unrighteousness** (rebellion against the Creator, 8b) as the persons of 1:18, against whom the wrath of God is revealed. They too will be the objects of God's **indignation and wrath.**

Barrett gives a helpful summation of Paul's position:

> The analysis of works presupposed by vv. 7 f. has the important consequence of dissolving the barrier between Jew and Gentile. The former no longer possesses the exclusive privilege of performing good works done in obedience to the revealed law. The "good" which God will reward does not consist in "works of law," but in patient seeking, in looking beyond human activity to its divine complement; the "bad" which he punishes may include good deeds, "works of law," done in a servile spirit with a view to profit.[80]

In vv. 12-16, Paul deals with an objection which might justly be raised to his conclusion that Jew and Gentile are equal before God. The difference between Jew and Gentile is more than a matter of race; it is a matter of revelation. God through Moses gave the law to Israel; this privilege the Gentile never had. The objection, however, cannot stand. In 1:19-32, Paul showed that the Gentile without benefit of *special* revelation is guilty of a responsible act of rebellion against the Creator in view of God's *general* revelation in nature. In the same way, the lack of a

[77]ICC, p. 57.

[78]There can be no doubt, however, that the usage of *eritheia* has been affected by its close association with *eris* (cf. II Cor. 12:20; Gal. 5:20), even though there is no real connection between the two words.

[79]*The Letters of Paul, an Expanded Paraphrase* (Grand Rapids: Wm. B. Eerdmans Publishing Co., 1965), p. 187.

[80]*The Epistle to the Romans*, p. 48.

revealed law in no way excuses the Gentile from judgment. **For as many as have sinned without law shall also perish without law** (12). The Jew would agree with this. But Paul proceeds, **And as many as have sinned in the law shall be judged by the law.** "The mere possession of the law gives the Jew no position of advantage; it only determines the standard by which he shall be judged."[81] **For not the hearers of the law are just before God, but the doers of the law shall be justified** (13). It is important to observe the sense in which Paul is thinking of being **justified** here. "The present passage refers only to the sentence, whether of condemnation or acquittal, pronounced at the last judgment."[82] This John Wesley calls *final* justification, in distinction from *evangelical* justification, which is by faith alone (cf. 3:24-28).

Paul now returns to his opening statement in v. 12, which, as it stands, appears open to objection. How can judgment take place **without law?** The fact is that the Gentiles are *not* without law. **For when the Gentiles, which have not the law, do by nature the things contained in the law, these, having not the law, are a law unto themselves** (14); hence the possibility of sin and judgment. The expression **law unto themselves** does not mean what we suggest when we say a man is a law to himself. In reality it means exactly the opposite, that they themselves, by reason of what is implanted in their nature, are morally responsible creatures. As Meyer expresses it, "Their moral nature, with the voice of conscience commanding and forbidding, supplies to their own Ego the place of the revealed law possessed by the Jews."[83]

The construction implies that **Gentiles** sometimes[84] do "the things of the Law" (NASB). **By nature** (*physei*) means that "spontaneously they have sufficient knowledge of what God wills or forbids" to do occasionally what the law requires.[85] Here Paul comes close to the Greek moralists. Plutarch asks, "Who shall govern the governor?" and replies, "Law, the king of all mortals and immortals, as Pindar called it; which is not written on papyrus rolls or wooden tablets, but is his own reason within the soul."[86] Similarly, Aristotle writes, "The cultivated and free-

---

[81]Dodd, *op. cit.,* p. 34.   [82]Barrett, *op. cit.,* p. 50.

[83]Quoted by Murray, *op. cit.,* pp. 73-74.

[84]**When** (*hotan*) suggests what is occasional; **Gentiles** (*ethne*) means some Gentiles; *ta ethne* would mean all or most Gentiles.

[85]Leenhardt, *op. cit.,* pp. 80-81.   [86]Quoted by Dodd, *op. cit.,* p. 36.

minded man will so behave as being a law to himself."[87] The Stoics spoke of this inner law as the "law of nature." Their teaching was that, as the universe is itself rational, each individual partakes of the universal *logos* or reason. Thus, for man, right and wrong are determined by the law of human nature. Man, being himself rational, is capable of discerning this law and living by it. What is "natural" in this sense is right. A man's conscience recognizes the immanent law of his nature and judges his actions by this standard.

Paul's thought is certainly close to this when he writes, **Which shew the work of the law written in their hearts, their conscience also bearing witness, and their thoughts the mean while accusing or else excusing one another (15)**. Paul does not say that the law itself is written in men's hearts, but **the work of the law** (*to ergon tou nomou*), or "the effect of the law." "The law has, as it were, left its stamp upon their minds; this stamp is their conscience."[88]

Conscience (*syneideseos*) means literally "co-knowledge" or "knowing with." It is "the knowledge or reflective judgment which a man has *by the side of* or *in conjunction with* the original consciousness of the act."[89] It implies man's ability to rise above himself and to view his actions and character more or less objectively. He is thus able to act as a witness for or against himself. Man's **thoughts . . . accusing or else excusing one another** denotes the inner arguments which a man has within himself as he struggles to determine the course of action he should take. "When Gentiles, after such inner debates, accomplish the things of the law, their deeds are moral in character."[90] We must avoid supposing, however, that Paul wishes to show "how the Gentiles can be saved in spite of their not having received the law." Such interpretation is against the whole argument of this section of the Epistle, which is to show the universal guilt of mankind and the worldwide need for the righteousness of God. "There is no basis for deducing the power of the will from the present passage, as if Paul had said that the keeping of the law is within our power, for he does not speak of our power to fulfill the law, but of our knowledge of it."[91]

---

[87]*Nichomachean Ethics*, 1128A; quoted by Dodd, *ibid.*
[88]Barrett, *op. cit.*, p. 53.
[89]ICC, p. 60.
[90]Leenhardt, *op. cit.*, p. 82.
[91]Calvin, *op. cit.*, p. 48; cf. 7:14-25.

It seems best to join v. 16 to the end of 13: **The doers of the law shall be justified . . . in the day when God shall judge the secrets of men.** Verses 13-15 are thus a parenthesis as in KJV and Moffatt. Moffatt transposes v. 16, placing it before 14-15, but there is no MSS support for this. If Paul were writing today, he would make vv. 13-15 a footnote "to show that the Gentiles also would be entitled to believe themselves justified, if all that was necessary for this end were to possess and hear a law without doing it."[92] Having rejected this false idea, Paul resumes the thread of his discourse at v. 16.

On the day of judgment **God shall judge the secrets of men.** "None of those fine externals of piety or morality will deceive the eye of God in that day of truth. He will demand holiness of heart."[93] He shall judge men **by Jesus Christ.** This recalls Jesus' own claim that He will return as the Judge of mankind.[94] "If it is really He who is to preside in the great act of final judgment, it is plain that, being such as He has made Himself known to us, He will not be satisfied with a parade of external righteousness, and that He will demand a holiness like that which He realized Himself, which, taking its origin in consecration of the heart, extends over the whole life."[95] **According to my gospel** is at first glance surprising, since, as we have seen, the expectation that Christ shall be the final Judge belonged to apostolic teaching in general. Nevertheless it was Paul who, in consequence of his personal experience, saw most clearly the contrast between the *works of the law,* which are legal and external, and the *fruits of faith* working by love (Gal. 5:6; Eph. 2:9-10; Phil. 3:9). This antithesis was one of the foundations of the apostle's preaching.

In 2:1-16 we see "The Judgment of God." (1) According to truth, 1-3; (2) According to works, 4-11; (3) According to light, 12-16.

b. *The guilt of the Jews* (2:17-29). Returning to the diatribe (see comment on 2:1), Paul addresses the Jew directly. What he has said in 1-16 is applicable to both Jews and Gentiles, but verse by verse the relevance of his argument to the Jew has become

[92]Godet, *op. cit.,* p. 126.

[93]*Ibid.* Godet compares v. 16 with v. 29, where Paul speaks of "a Jew, which is one inwardly" and of the "circumcision . . . of the heart."

[94]Matt. 7:21-23; 25:31-46; cf. Acts 17:31; II Cor. 5:10.

[95]Godet, *op. cit.,* pp. 126-27.

increasingly apparent. Now he turns directly to the man who is proudly conscious of his membership in the Chosen People: **Be-hold,**[96] **thou art called** (*eponomaze*)[97] **a Jew** (17).[98] The term **Jew** first occurred in the OT in II Kings 16:6. "Paul's use of it here and in verses 28, 29 as well as other evidence (Gal. 2:15; Rev. 2:9; 3:9; cf. Zech. 8:23) indicates it was a name associated in the mind of the Jew with all on which he prided himself."[99] The following enumeration of advantages accruing from the gift of the law is somewhat satirical, for Paul shows how the Jew has perverted his privileges. **Thou . . . restest** (*epanapaue*) **in the law** suggests "supine assurance."[100] "The Jew was chosen of God, and the gift of the Torah was proof of the fact. Hence possession was considered enough without worrying about practice."[101] He reposed in the law and relied upon it to give him a secure standing before God. In the same way he made his **boast** (*kauchasai*) **of God**—better, "gloried in God"—not humbly, according to Jer. 9:24, but arrogantly. "Without any knowledge of the goodness of God," Calvin says of the Jews, "they made Him peculiarly their own, although they did not inwardly possess Him, and assumed that they were His people, for the sake of

----

[96]**Behold** translates *ide*, but all the oldest MSS, as well as the leading versions, favor *ei de*, "But if" (ASV, RSV, NASB).

[97]"Thou bearest the name" (ASV).

[98]"Paul evidently speaks now to the man to whom he spoke in vv. 3, 4. But the word **Jew** was kept back, because others besides Jews might cherish the fallacious hope there expressed; and because this hope, whether in Jew or Greek, was dispelled by one universal principle, that God has no respect of persons. In the present case, Paul's reasoning applies to Jews only" (Beet, *op. cit.*, p. 78).

[99]Murray, *op. cit.*, p. 81. "Hebrew" implies origin and language; "Israel-ite" recalls their covenant relation to God. " 'Jew' is the man of Jewish blood bound to the Law. Since this is the essential hallmark of the Jew, Paul can no longer refer to himself as a Jew after his conversion without qualification; he is only a 'Jew by birth' (Gal. 2:15). He can become 'as a Jew' to the Jews, namely, 'to those under the law as one under the law' (I Cor. 9:20). However, even as a Christian he can still continue to call himself a 'Hebrew' (Phil. 3:5; 2 Cor. 11:22) as a child of a Jewish-Pales-tinian family, and an 'Israelite' (2 Cor. 11:22; Rom. 11:1; cf. Phil. 3:5) as a member of the nation standing within God's covenant and called to God's salvation (Eph. 2:12)" (Leonhard Goppelt, *Jesus, Paul and Judaism* [New York: Thomas Nelson & Sons, 1964], p. 135).

[100]Gerald R. Cragg, IB (Exposition), IX, 413.

[101]NBC, p. 904.

empty ostentation before their fellow men. This, then, was not the glorying of the heart, but the boasting of the tongue."[102]

Paul now concedes to the Jew a knowledge of **his will** (18, *to thelema*) —lit. "the will"[103]—and approval of those **things that are more excellent** (*ta diapheronta*), which he had gained from **being instructed out of the law.** *Ta diapheronta* may be translated "things which differ." The NEB reads, "You are aware of moral distinctions because you receive instruction from the law." "The meaning is that the Jew claims to be able to discern right and wrong and the shades of moral value between lesser and greater good (cf. Phil. i:10)."[104] Because of all these advantages of the law he prides himself upon his ability to guide, teach, and judge others. **A guide of the blind** (19; cf. Matt. 15:14; 23:16, 24) was probably a proverbial saying. **An instructor of the foolish** and **a teacher of babes** (20) are phrases which suggest how the Gentiles appeared to the Jews—as infants in religious knowledge. These proud claims all rested upon the possession of **the form of knowledge and of the truth in the law.** The word for **form** (*morphosin*) here may mean the outline, delineation, "the full embodiment" of the essential form (*morphe*; Phil. 2:6-7). Sanday and Headlam observe, "The Law was a true expression of the Divine truth, so far as it went."[105] However, as Thomson and Davidson point out, Paul may be employing *morphosis* here in the same sense as he uses the word in II Tim. 3:5, where it is put in contrast to *dynamis*, "power." "Certainly the gift of revelation was real; but the point is that the Jew, by his obedience, could have had a fuller insight into it, and, in spite of his boast, was in fact but a poor guide, light, corrector and teacher of the heathen."[106]

Arising from these advantages there follows in vv. 21-24 a scathing exposure of the inconsistency of the Jew. It is phrased in "a series of pungent questions, founded on these admissions . . . and put in startling contrast with them."[107] **Thou therefore which teachest another, teachest thou not thyself? thou that**

---

[102]*Op. cit.*, p. 51.

[103]"*To thelema* is the divine will. . . . This word *thelema* came to be so appropriated to the divine will that it is sometimes used in this sense even without the definite article" (J. B. Lightfoot, *On a Fresh Revision of the English New Testament* [New York, 1873]; quoted by Murray, *op. cit.*, p. 82).

[104]NBC, p. 945.   [105]ICC, pp. 65-66. Cf. 7:12.

[106]NBC, p. 945.   [107]Gifford; cited by Murray, *op. cit.*, p. 83.

preachest (*ho kerysson*)[108] a man should not steal, dost thou
steal? thou that sayest a man should not commit adultery, dost
thou commit adultery? thou that abhorrest idols, dost thou commit sacrilege? (21-22) The last question is generally translated,
"Thou that abhorrest idols, dost thou rob temples?" (ERV)
Godet thinks the meaning is, "Thy horror of idolatry does not go
the length of preventing thee from hailing as a good prize the
precious objects which have been used in idolatrous worship,
when thou canst make them thine own."[109] The Jews themselves
probably did not pillage the Gentile temples but they no doubt
profited from such theft (cf. Acts 19:37). "The dishonor done to
God arises from their greed of gain, their deceits and hypocrisy,
which were thoroughly known to the Gentile populations among
whom they lived."[110] Perhaps this kind of sacrilege was justified
by the Jews with the argument that they were thus destroying
the objects of idolatrous worship. Actually, by such miscon-
duct the Jew was causing **the name of God** to be **blasphemed
among the Gentiles** (24).

While instances of all these abuses can undoubtedly be adduced, Paul's argument is weakened if he must rely on these
unusual events, and it is simply not true that the average Jewish
missionary behaved in this way. It was the purity of Jewish
morals, together with Jewish monotheism, which made the deepest impression upon the Roman world. Almost every synagogue
had attracted to itself a company of Gentile God-fearers and
proselytes, as the Book of Acts makes clear. The fact that the
actual crimes were occasionally committed makes Paul's argument more vivid, and such criminals involved the nation in guilt;
but the nation was inwardly guilty already. When theft, adultery,
and sacrilege are radically understood, there is no one who is not
guilty of all three.[111] Paul is giving these words the same kind
of interpretation Jesus gave in Matt. 5:21-48.

For theft, compare Mal. 3:8-9. "Will a man rob God? Yet ye
have robbed me. But ye say, Wherein have we robbed thee? In
tithes and offerings. . . ." "Israel as a whole has robbed God of

---

[108]From *keryssein,* which means to herald or proclaim, a technical term
for Christian proclamation (*kerygma*), perhaps borrowed from Jewish usage.
"The Jews looked upon themselves as the heralds of God. The man before us
does that which, as herald, he forbids others to do" (Beet, *op. cit.,* p. 80).

[109]*Op. cit.,* p. 129.   [110]*Ibid.*

[111]Barrett, *op. cit.,* pp. 56-57.

the honour due to him; even their boasting in God (v. 17) is a
subtle arrogance which gives to man what is due to God."[112] As
to **adultery,** Jesus said that the man who looks upon a woman
with a lustful intent has already committed adultery with her in
his heart (Matt. 5:28). But adultery in the OT also had a spiritual sense (Hosea 1—3; Jer. 3:8; etc.); and as the bride of God,
Israel could not escape the charge of harlotry. The word **sacrilege** "is conclusively proved by inscriptions and papyri to have a
wider meaning."[113] Calvin writes, "Sacrilege is simply a pro-
fanation of the divine majesty."[114] Wesley interprets the word as
"robbing Him 'who is God over all' of the glory which is due to
Him."[115] In exalting himself as a judge and lord over his fellow
creatures man usurps this glory to himself.

Verse 23 may be taken as a question (KJV) or as a statement
summing up the position that has now been reached: "While you
take pride in the law, you dishonour God by breaking it" (NEB).
This is more than Paul's opinion; it is the verdict of Scripture
itself. "For, as Scripture says, 'Because of you the name of God
is dishonoured among the Gentiles'" (24, NEB). This is a quotation from Isa. 52:5 in the Septuagint (see also Ezek. 36:20).
Calvin comments, "Every transgressor of the law dishonours God,
since we are all born in order to worship Him in holiness and
righteousness. Paul, however, justly charges the Jews in this
respect with special guilt, for when they proclaimed God as law-
giver, without being over-anxious to regulate their lives according to His rule, they clearly proved that they paid little regard to
the Majesty of God, which they so easily despised. In the same
way at the present time, those who argue wildly about the doctrine of Christ, while trampling on it by their unrestrained and
wanton life, dishonour Christ by transgressing His Gospel."[116]

In v. 25 the apostle "pursues the Jew into his last retreat"
and proceeds to strip him of the last refuge, his illusive trust in
the possession of circumcision.[117] He also anticipates 3:1-2,
where he is careful to indicate the advantage of circumcision—
For circumcision verily profiteth, if thou keep (*prasses*) **the law.**
This sentence throws light on what Paul means by keeping, or

---

[112]*Ibid.,* p. 57.   [113]*Ibid.*

[114]*Op. cit.,* p. 53.

[115]*Explanatory Notes upon the New Testament,* p. 526.

[116]*Op. cit.,* p. 53.   [117]Murray, *op. cit.,* p. 85.

practicing, the law. For the apostle, to **keep the law** or to **fulfil the law** (27) does not mean carrying out the detailed precepts written in the Torah, *but fulfilling that relation with God to which the law points—a relation not of legalism but of faith* (3:31; 10:6-11). "Circumcision was the sign and seal of the covenant dispensed to Abraham which was a covenant of promise and of grace. Hence it had relevance only in the context of grace and not at all in the context of law and works in opposition to grace. The practicing of the law, therefore, which makes circumcision profitable is the fulfilment of the conditions of faith and obedience apart from which the claim to the promises and grace and privileges of the covenant was presumption and mockery. The keeping of the law is thus equivalent to the keeping of the covenant."[118] By the same token to be a **breaker of the law** is to be unfaithful to the covenant obligations, which is called in the OT the breaking of the covenant. Thus, in this passage the apostle is not laying down the stipulations of a legalistic system but the obligations of that covenant of grace signified and sealed by the rite of circumcision.

The Jew, of course, would challenge the contrast Paul makes between circumcision and keeping the law; circumcision is part of the law, and you cannot possibly keep the law without being circumcised.

Paul now considers the man who keeps **the righteousness of the law** even though he is of **the uncircumcision** (26). **The righteousness of the law** (*ta dikaiomata tou nomou*) is literally "the ordinances" or "the righteous requirements" **of the law.** These ordinances, as noted above (cf. v. 25), are the requirements of the covenant of grace symbolized by circumcision. Who are the Gentiles who thus keep "the precepts of the law" (RSV)? The apostle is referring, in Godet's words, "to those many Gentiles converted to the gospel who, all uncircumcised as they were, nevertheless fulfil the law in virtue of the spirit of Christ, and thus become the true Israel, the Israel of God, Gal. vi. 16."[119] Keeping the ordinances or precepts of the law is therefore to be interpreted in terms of that faith and obedience which, in v. 25,

---

[118]*Ibid.*

[119]*Op. cit.*, p. 130. "This *true* Jew, even according to the Old Testament, was not a historical reality but a *prophecy*" (Goppelt, *op. cit.*, p. 138). See Jer. 31:31-34; Ezek. 36:25-27.

we found to be the import of keeping the law. This is identical with "the obedience of faith" of which Paul writes in 1:5.

Verse 27 is to be regarded as continuous with 26. To keep the ordinances or precepts of the law is to **fulfil the law** (*ton nomon telousa*). Godet speaks of this as "a phrase expressing real and persevering fulfilment. The love which the gospel puts into the believer's heart is in fact the fulfilment of the law, Rom. xiii. 10."[120] The Christian believer **shall . . . judge the Jew, who by the letter and circumcision dost transgress the law.** The expression **shall . . . judge** does not mean "shall sit in judgment" but refers to "the judgment of comparison and contrast" (cf. Matt. 12:41-42).[121] **Letter** refers to the law written on tables of stone or in the OT (cf. 7:6; II Cor. 3:6-7). Living by the letter rather than by the Spirit, the Jew actually transgresses the law.

Verses 28-29 explain why the rite of circumcision can avail so little. God looks upon the heart and does not regard externalities. Verse 28 contains the negative and 29 the affirmative statement of this general truth. **He is not a Jew, which is one outwardly** (*en to phanero*, in appearance); **neither is that circumcision, which is outward** (same Gk. phrase) **in the flesh (28).** Charles Hodge paraphrases, "He is not one of the people of God who is such externally."[122] Nothing external or visible secures this special relation to God. The affirmative statement is, **But he is a Jew, which is one inwardly; and circumcision is that of the heart, in the spirit, and not in the letter (29).**

A true Jew is one who is such **inwardly** (*en to krypto*, in the secret), i.e., in that which is hidden from external observation (cf. 2:16; I Cor. 4:5; 14:25). "The hidden man of the heart" (I Pet. 3:4) signifies what a man is in the recesses of his heart in distinction from any external profession. True **circumcision is that of the heart, in the spirit, and not in the letter.** The phrase

---

[120]*Op cit.*, p. 130. The phrase **by nature** (*ek physeos*) must not be confused with the same phrase in v. 14, where it is said that "the Gentiles . . . do by nature [*ek physeos*] the things contained in the law." In v. 27, *ek physeos* is connected with *he akrobystia* and not *telousa*. Furthermore, the law the apostle has in mind here is not the law of nature but specifically revealed law. Men do not "by nature" fulfill the law; this fulfillment is possible only by the Holy Spirit (cf. v. 29).

[121]Murray, *op. cit.*, p. 87.

[122]*The Epistle to the Romans* (Grand Rapids: Wm. B. Eerdmans Publishing Co., 1950), p. 65.

circumcision . . . of the heart means the purification of the heart. "The Lord thy God will circumcise thine heart, and the heart of thy seed, to love the Lord thy God with all thine heart, and with all thy soul" (Deut. 30:6; cf. Deut. 10:16; Jer. 4:4; 9:25-26). The phrase **in the spirit, and not in the letter** is not immediately self-explanatory. *En pneumati ou grammati* may be translated just as correctly "by the Spirit, not by the letter" (NASB), understanding *en* as an instrumental dative. The KJV interprets **spirit** to refer to the human spirit and as therefore a further specification of the inward sphere in which true circumcision takes place. Since it is **of the heart** it is **in the spirit** of man. **Letter** by way of contrast would mean that which is **outward**—literal or physical circumcision. All of this is of course true, but there are two reasons for rejecting this interpretation. (1) It would be empty repetition for Paul to specify the sphere after he has said that **circumcision is that of the heart.** (2) In other passages where Paul contrasts *pneuma* and *gramma* (7:6; II Cor. 3:6-8; cf. vv. 17-18), the contrast is between the life-giving power of the Holy Spirit and the impotence of the law. This is the contrast which must be adopted here. Thus what Paul says is that *the circumcision which is of the heart is by the Holy Spirit and not by the law.* The word **spirit** ought therefore to have been written with a capital to indicate that the reference is to the Holy Spirit. NEB adopts this interpretation: "The true Jew is not he who is such in externals, neither is the true circumcision the external mark in the flesh. The true Jew is he who is such inwardly, and the true circumcision is of the heart, directed not by written precepts but by the Spirit."

Comparing these vv. with Col. 2:11-12, Hodge makes a significant observation. "As circumcision signifies inward purification, and was a seal of the righteousness of faith, it was, as to its import and design, identical with baptism. Hence what in Col. ii. 11, Paul expresses by saying, 'Ye are circumcised,' he expresses in ver. 12 by saying, 'Ye are buried with him in baptism.' What, therefore, he teaches of the worthlessness of external circumcision, without internal purity, and of the possibility of the external sign being received without the internal grace, is no less true of baptism."[123]

The concluding clause of 29, **whose praise is not of men, but of God,** is probably an allusion to the etymological meaning of

[123]*Ibid.*, p. 66.

the name **Jew**, which signifies "the praised one."[124] When Leah
bore her fourth son, she said, "Now will I praise the Lord: therefore she called his name Judah" (Gen. 39:35). And when Jacob
lay dying he began his blessing upon Judah in these words,
"Judah, thou art he whom thy brethren shall praise" (Gen. 49:8).
Murray sees Paul as here striking again at that which lies in the
background of the entire chapter and forms the basis of his indictment against the Jew, namely, the iniquity of relying upon
appearance and upon what impresses men. "It is the application
to the subject in hand of the word of the Lord himself: 'How can
ye believe, who receive glory one of another, and the glory that
cometh from the only God ye seek not?' (John 5:44; cf. vss.
41-43)."[125]

The apostle has concluded his indictment of the Jew who
rests in the law. The disobedient Jew finds himself in precisely
the same situation in regard to the wrath of God as the disobedient Gentile. In the sight of God, who judges the secrets of men,
the Jew who trusts in the law turns out to be a transgressor of
that law (2:17-24); for what the law requires is not legal or
ritual observance but covenant love and fidelity, symbolized by
circumcision (2:25-27). In placing his confidence in the rite of
circumcision and legal righteousness the Jew fails to recognize
that God's concern is not for such external matters but for heart
purity and loving obedience, which circumcision symbolizes
(2:28-29). *If this is the case, then what remains of the prerogative which divine election seemed to assure to him?* Before going
further and drawing the general conclusion following from the
two preceding passages (1:18-32 and 2:1-29), the apostle feels
he must answer this objection; this is the aim of the following
section.

In 2:17-29 we find "True Religion." (1) What it is not:
(*a*) Not the observance of outward forms, 25-28; (*b*) Not regulated by the praise of men, 29c; (2) What it is: (*a*) An inward
reality, 29a; (*b*) The work of the Spirit of God, 29b; (c) Expressed in moral obedience, 21-24.

c. *The advantage of the Jew* (3:1-8). What Paul has just
said seems to wipe out the advantage of the Jew. Not so, he
answers. The order of thought in this passage, one of the most
difficult in the Epistle, is as follows:

---

[124]Vincent, *op. cit.*, p. 31.   [125]Murray, *op. cit.*, pp. 89-90.

(1) If the Jew stands under the wrath of God, as do the Gentiles, what advantage has he over them? *Answer:* He possesses the oracles of God (vv. 1-2).

(2) But if this possession has not served its intended end (the faith of Israel in the Messiah), does this not annul the faithfulness of God? *Answer:* Absolutely not; it rather enhances God's faithfulness (vv. 3-4).

(3) But if God makes human sin to glorify Him, how can He make sinners the object of His wrath? *Answer:* Such an objection stands self-condemned, for it calls into question the very justice of God (vv. 5-8).

First Question. **What advantage then hath the Jew? or what profit is there of circumcision?** (1) Paraphrased, the question is: "Well then, if it is being a Jew inwardly that counts, if it is the 'circumcision of the heart' that really matters, is there any advantage to belonging to Israel or in being physically circumcised?"

Paul answers: **Much every way** (2). Of course there is an advantage to belonging to the people of God, **chiefly, because that unto them were committed the oracles of God.** The term **chiefly** (*proton*) generally means "first of all" or "in the first place" (NEB). But if this is the sense in which Paul uses the word here, his thought is deflected and broken off.[126] Godet thinks Paul is here deliberately limiting his argument. "The preceding words, **every way,** suggest: 'I might mention many things under this head; but I shall confine myself to one which is in the front rank.' This form of expression, far from indicating that he purposes to mention others, shows, on the contrary, why he will not mention them. They all flow from that which he proceeds to indicate."[127] The first and all-inclusive advantage of the Jews consists in this, that they have been entrusted with **the oracles of God.** In a Jewish context **oracles** can mean only Scripture, and it was to the Jews that the word of God was spoken. The parallel in 9:4 suggests that the entire OT is meant. "To possess the law is itself an advantage. Israel knows the mind of God (cf. ii. 18), and cannot deny the total moral claim which he makes upon his creatures (see vv. 10-18)."[128] To possess the

---

[126]Other "advantages" are listed in 9:4-5, to which the reader is referred.

[127]*Op. cit.,* p. 132.   [128]Barrett, *op. cit.,* p. 62.

revelation of God's will and purpose is a high honor indeed; but if it is a high honor, it is also a grave responsibility. As our Lord said, "For unto whomsoever much is given, of him shall be much required" (Luke 12:48).

Second Question. **For what if some did not believe? shall their unbelief make the faith of God without effect?** (3) The expression **For what** may be rendered, "What then?"[129] or, "And what of that?"[130] The question is, "What of it if some of the Jews did not receive Christ?" **Did not believe** (*epistesan*) is an aorist verb and "refers to a particular historical fact rather than a permanent state of things, such as Jewish unbelief had been under the covenant."[131] It was Israel's rejection of Jesus as the Messiah which seemed to nullify **the faith of God.**[132] The phrase **the faith of God** (*ten pistin tou theou*) could, in another context, mean "faith in God." Here the genitive must be taken as possessive, and the noun must mean "faithfulness" (RSV, NEB, NASB). The question is: Can Jewish unbelief in regard to Jesus invalidate God's faithfulness to His people?

God forbid (4; *me genoito,* "may it not be!"), Paul answers. Absolutely not, for God has given His word; and whatever men may or may not do, He will keep that word (cf. II Tim. 2:13). **Yea, let God be true, but every man a liar; as it is written, That thou mightest be justified in thy sayings, and mightest overcome when thou art judged.** "The unfaithfulness of men simply sets His truth in relief: His righteousness is always vindicated against their unrighteousness."[133] Paul here quotes Ps. 51:4, agreeing word for word with the Septuagint. We shall see the significance of this quotation as we consider the next question.

Third Question. **But if our unrighteousness commend the righteousness of God, what shall we say? Is God unrighteous who taketh vengeance? (I speak as a man)** (5). That is to say, "If my faithlessness sets God's faithfulness in bolder relief; if my unrighteousness establishes His righteousness; why should He find fault with me? His is really the gainer by my sin; why should He exact retribution for it?"[134] Here the significance of

[129]Murray, *op. cit.,* p. 93.   [130]Barrett, *op. cit.,* p. 63.
[131]Godet, *op. cit.,* p. 133.
[132]With this problem Paul will deal at length in cc. 9—11.
[133]Bruce, *The Epistle of Paul to the Romans,* p. 95.
[134]*Ibid.* Observe here that **the righteousness of God** means His fidelity to His word of promise.

Paul's quotation (Ps. 51:4) becomes apparent. David said, "Against thee, thee only, have I sinned, and done this evil in thy sight: that thou mightest be justified when thou speakest, and be clear when thou judgest." The thought seems to be that, since sin (even against one's fellowmen, as was David's) is first of all and ultimately sin against God, therefore God in His judgments upon men for sin is always just.

This then is Paul's answer. Since sin is primarily and ultimately against God, He is just in punishing all sin (6). That this is Paul's use and interpretation of Ps. 51:4 the succeeding verses indicate. For he proceeds to deal with the false inferences which his opponents would (and have) drawn from the proposition that sin vindicates the justice and judgment of God. "But if through my lie the truth of God abounded to His glory, why am I also still being judged as a sinner? And why not say (as we are slanderously reported and some affirm that we say), 'Let us do evil that good may come'?" (7-8, NASB) "If my falsehood makes God's truth shine more brightly by contrast, it redounds to His glory; why then does He insist on condemning me as a sinner?" the objector reasons. "The end—God's glory—is good; why is the means—my sin—counted wrong? Surely the end justifies the means?"[135]

This line of reasoning evokes from the apostle the observation of v. 8. The fact is, he continues, that is precisely what some of my opponents say my gospel amounts to: **Let us do evil, that good may come.** But this charge is not only slanderous; it stands self-condemned because it is such a contradiction in terms. God's truth is always within a hair's breadth of error, but the gospel of justification "by faith without the deeds of the law" (3:28) *can never mean antinomianism,* as Paul will show conclusively in c. 6. There he will demonstrate that the justified man has died to sin. At this point he is content to retort that such reasoning can come only from a twisted moral nature which makes light equivalent to darkness. For such a nature, **damnation is just.**

The apostle has vividly drawn two unforgettable pictures of the reign of God's wrath—over the Gentile world (1:18-32) and over the Jewish people (2:1-29). By way of appendix he has added a passage to the second picture, intended to sweep away the objection which might be raised by the Jewish critic—the objection that his gospel sets aside the ancient people of God and

[135]*Ibid.,* p. 96.

thereby undercuts the faithfulness of God. Now, to the judgment which follows from the preceding arguments Paul affixes the seal of Scripture, "without which he regards no proof as finally valid."[136]

3. *Scriptural Proof of the Guilt of All Mankind,* 3:9-20

What then? (9).[137] "What then is the state of things? To what result are we thus brought?"[138] The second question is: **Are we better than they?** "Are we Jews any better off?" (RSV) Phillips paraphrases, "Are we Jews then a march ahead of other men?" This appears to be the correct sense of the verb *proecho-metha.* "You have said that it is an advantage to belong to the Jewish nation. Does it not follow that we are superior to those Gentiles who have not the privileges we have?"[139] **No, in no wise,** Paul answers. "No, not at all!" (NEB) **For we have before proved both Jews and Gentiles, that they are all under sin.** By relentless logic and penetrating psychological insight Paul has just proved that the Jews are in the same sinful predicament as Gentiles, both alike are under sin. To be **under sin** signifies to be not only under the *guilt* but also under the *power* of sin. "These two meanings, sin as a trespass, and sin as a power, are both demanded by the context."[140] But far more important than any such analysis as I have made, Paul continues, is the fact that *this is the verdict of Scripture*—**As it is written, There is none righteous, no, not one (10).**

Sin is so universal as to admit *not a solitary exception.* To prove this accusation Paul adduces a series of six OT quotations in which the general sinfulness of mankind is summed up. These quotations clinch a case already established by various arguments.

a. Sin in human character (3:10-12). **There is none righteous, no, not one: there is none that understandeth, there is none that seeketh after God. They are all gone out of the way, they are together become unprofitable; there is none that doeth good, no, not one.** This is a quotation from Ps. 14:1-3 (cf. 53: 1-4). Godet observes that "this delineation applies to the moral

---

[136]Godet, *op. cit.,* p. 139.   [137]ICC, p. 76.
[138]Godet, *op. cit.,* p. 139.
[139]Bruce, *The Epistle of Paul to the Romans,* p. 97.
[140]Godet, *op. cit.,* p. 140.

character of man, so long as he remains beyond the influence of divine action."[141] Apart from divine grace, there is no understanding of God, no seeking of God, no goodness whatever. Man in himself, apart from the working of God in His prevenient grace (cf. Phil. 2:13), is totally blind, helpless, and corrupt. This is what theologians mean by the doctrine of total depravity.

b. Sin in human speech (3:13-14). **Their throat is an open sepulchre; with their tongues they have used deceit; the poison of asps is under their lips: whose mouth is full of cursing and bitterness.** We note here a reference to the different organs of speech, with each exercising its power under the control of sin. The throat is compared to a **sepulchre;** this refers, says Godet, to the brutal man who seems as if he would like to eat you. The characteristic which follows is just the opposite; "It is the sugared tongue, which charms you like a melodious instrument."[142] These two ideas are drawn from Ps. 5:9, where they describe the conduct of the Psalmist's enemies. The next proposition is drawn from Ps. 140:3, which declares that **lips** which speak such calumny and falsehood are like a serpent's tongue, infused with **poison.** The fourth idea is borrowed from Ps. 10:7, which describes the wickedness which is cast in your face by a mouth that **is full of cursing and bitterness.**

c. Sin in human conduct (3:15-17). **Their feet are swift to shed blood: destruction and misery are in their ways: and the way of peace have they not known.** These accusations are taken from Isa. 59:7-8, where the prophet indicts the nation of Israel for its terrible corruption. The **feet,** as the emblem of walking, symbolize the whole conduct. "Man acts without regard to his neighbor, without fear of compromising his welfare and even his life. He oppresses (*syntrimma*) his brother, and fills his life with misery (*talaiporia*), so that the way marked out by such a course is watered by the tears of others."[143]

d. The cause of all sin (3:18). The quotation in v. 18 is drawn from Ps. 36:1. The **fear of God** is a term descriptive of piety in the OT. "The fear of the Lord is the beginning of knowledge" (Prov. 1:7). God is sovereign Lord; man is creature. The recognition of this relationship is the basis of true religion. But sinful men have repudiated this. **There is no fear of God before**

[141]*Ibid.,* p. 141.   [142]*Ibid.*
[143]*Ibid.,* p. 142.

their eyes. This declaration shows "that it belongs to man freely
to evoke or suppress this inward view of God, on which his
moral conduct depends."[144]

> The apostle in drawing this picture, which is only a grouping
> together of strokes of the pencil, made by the hands of psalmists
> and prophets, does not certainly mean that each of those character-
> istics is found equally developed in every man. Some, even the
> most of them, may remain latent in many men; but they all exist
> in germ in the selfishness and natural pride of the *ego,* and the least
> circumstance may cause them to pass into the active state, when the
> fear of God does not govern the heart. Such is the *cause* of the
> divine condemnation which is suspended over the human race.[145]

  e. The application (3:19-20). By **we know** (19), Paul appeals to the common sense of his readers. It is obvious that the
quotations of v. 19, taken from the Jewish scriptures, are primarily applicable to Israel. **What things soever the law** (meaning
the entire OT) **saith, it saith to them who are under the law.** But
if the Jews are thus proven guilty before God, *a fortiori* so are all
other men. The whole world is brought to trial before God. The
ASV translates, "That . . . all the world may be brought under
the judgment of God." The term *hypodikos* (**guilty;** "under
judgment," ASV) occurs only here in the NT. "In classical Greek
it signifies brought to trial or liable to be tried."[146] The whole of
mankind is brought before the divine judgment bar and declared
to be **guilty before God.** In the face of both empirical evidence
and scriptural witness all arguments of the defense are silenced:
every mouth is **stopped.** Mankind stands condemned to die.

> The Jews and Greeks, those who know the revealed will of
> God from Holy Scripture and those who do not know it, the elect
> to whom has been entrusted the holy treasure of God's word, who
> from their youth have been made familiar with it, and all the rest
> who do not possess this advantage—they all live "under the power
> of sin." This is the common denominator of all, however great the
> differences may be in other respects. The differences between the
> people of God and the others is great and ought not to be denied;
> but it is nothing when the question is raised: What about the last
> and decisive thing? How will you appear then, before God's judg-
> ment? The verdict then can only run: Guilty. We have to expect
> absolute condemnation. This terrible verdict concerns all so far as
> they appeal to the Law, in so far as they wish to appear in their
> own righteousness.[147]

[144]*Ibid.*   [145]*Ibid.*
[146]Vincent, *op. cit.,* p. 36.   [147]Brunner, *op. cit.,* p. 26.

The person who wishes to place himself opposite God on the grounds of the law, as one who is to fulfill God's demand in his own strength, is foredoomed to fail. **Therefore by the deeds of the law there shall no flesh be justified in his sight** (20). By the **deeds of the law** we must understand, "not the Mosaic law in its ritual or ceremonial aspect; but the law in a deeper and more general sense, as written both in the decalogue and in the hearts of the Gentiles, and embracing the moral deeds of both Gentiles and Jews. The Mosaic law may indeed be regarded as the primary reference, but as representing a universal legislation and including all the rest."[148] Moreover, these are not good works simply, "but works done in obedience to the law and regarded as, in themselves, a means of justification."[149] In quoting Ps. 143:2, Paul substitutes **no flesh** for "no man living." **Flesh** (*sarx*) here suggests *man in his moral weakness* (cf. 8:3), and thus anticipates Paul's later elaboration of the doctrine of the flesh. Man in his fallen and corrupt state cannot possibly please God (cf. 8:9). "No man who knows what righteousness is will come into God's presence with a claim of his own to it. And if he does, so far from the claim being recognised, it will be regarded as the one disqualification for the reality to which it pretends."[150] It is the delusion of legalism or moralism that man can extricate himself from his sinful predicament, if only he treats God's commands seriously enough; the following chapters of the Epistle will destroy this delusion. Yet this does not mean that God's law is unimportant for man in his search for salvation. The law cannot make us righteous, but it can reveal to us what is wrong, **for by the law is the knowledge of sin.** The law effects, not salvation, but wrath (cf. 4:15). This is no insignificant matter. "The Law, taken seriously, breaks the arrogance of man; yes, it breaks man himself. But only as someone who is broken, as a person who is thoroughly shaken, as someone who has come to the end of his tether, can he understand what has to be said to him now as being the one and only Gospel message."[151]

Paul has made his case. If men are to be saved, they must find some way of which they have never dreamed. All mankind stands under the wrath of God.

[148]Vincent, *op. cit.*, p. 36.
[149]Barrett, *op. cit.*, p. 70.
[150]Du Bose, quoted by W. H. Griffith Thomas, *op. cit.*, p. 106.
[151]Brunner, *op. cit.*, pp. 27-28.

In vv. 19-20, J. Radford Thompson finds "The Purpose of the Law." (1) The primary purpose—to reveal God's requirements (cf. 7:12); (2) The secondary purpose—to reveal sin (cf. 7:7-13); (3) The ultimate purpose—to prepare the way for the gospel (cf. Gal. 3:24) (*Pulpit Commentary*).

B. GOD'S RIGHTEOUSNESS PROVIDED, 3:21—8:39

The apostle is now ready to take up again the theme he so boldly set forth in 1:16-17. He has demonstrated the utter failure of man to win by his own achievement or merit a rightness with God. *But now in Christ a new day has dawned in the history of man.* God has himself broken the impasse and provided a righteousness of His own as a free gift to be received by faith. This righteousness means justification, sanctification, and complete redemption.

1. *The Gospel of Man's Justification,* 3:21—5:21

a. *Justification defined* (3:21-26). Paul grandly announces, **But now the righteousness of God without the law is manifested** (21). **But now** (*nuni de*) could signify a temporal contrast ("But at this moment") or a logical contrast ("But as it is"); in reality both meanings are required by the passage.

Paul is saying that something utterly new has entered history. "The righteousness of God has been manifested" (RSV). With that the new age predicted by the ancient prophets has appeared. " 'The old has passed away, behold, the new has come.' These words from II Corinthians 5:17 apply most profoundly here, as do also those which follow immediately thereon, 'All this is from God.' "[152] This new situation is not man's own achievement; it has been brought about by God's intervention. **Now,** in the coming of Jesus Christ, the miracle has happened.

---

[152]Nygren, *op. cit.,* p. 144. Sanday and Headlam cite the following parallel passages which confirm the temporal meaning of *nuni:* Rom. 16: 25-26; Eph. 2:12-13; Col. 1:26-27; II Tim. 1:9-10; and Heb. 9:26. "It may be observed (i) that the N.T. writers constantly oppose the pre-Christian and Christian dispensations to each other as periods (comp. in addition to the passages already enumerated Acts xvii. 30; Gal. iii. 23, 25, iv. 3, 4; Heb. i. 1); and (ii) that *phanerousthai* is constantly used with expressions denoting time (add to passages above Tit. i. 3 *kairos idiois,* I Pet. i. 20 *ep eschaton ton chronon)*" (ICC, p. 82).

85

But now, however, also has a logical and moral significance. These words contrast the revelation of righteousness with that of wrath (1:18—3:20). They contrast the condemnation pronounced by the law (20) with the new righteousness acquired **without the law** (21). After men have sought God in their own way only to experience His wrath, God himself has entered into their midst and made known to them His justification and life.

This, then, is the *kerygma,* the apostolic proclamation, that **now,** in the new age which Christ has ushered in, **the righteousness of God without the law is manifested.** For a full discussion of what Paul means by **the righteousness of God** see comments on 1:17. In this crucial section three meanings are demanded. Two aspects of the term are indicated by the two clauses of v. 26, "that he might be just" and that He might be "the justifier of him which believeth in Jesus." That is, it includes (1) God's own righteousness—the quality of *being* just or righteous, and (2) the justifying *activity* of God in Christ. Finally, it means (3) the righteousness which a person enjoys as a consequence of God's justifying act, or a "righteousness *from* God." Godet defines this aspect of the term as "the state of reconciliation with God in which man is placed by the sentence which declares him just."[153] John Wesley prefers to think of it as "the manner of becoming righteous which God hath appointed."[154]

The manifestation of God's righteousness in the gospel is "apart from law" (RSV; Gk. *choris nomou*). The NEB renders it "quite independently of law." The term **law** here is used in the sense of "deeds of the law" (20). The idea is that the law *as commandment* cannot effect our justification. But Paul quickly adds a declaimer, **being witnessed by the law and prophets.** Here **law** has an entirely different meaning. "Law in one sense pronounces the opposite of justification, the law in another sense preaches justification."[155] Paul declares that **the law and the prophets** join in thus witnessing to the manifestation of God's righteousness. **Being witnessed** (*martyroumene*) implies that "the new order of things is in no way contrary to the old, but rather a de-

---

[153]*Op. cit.,* p. 146.

[154]*Explanatory Notes upon the New Testament,* p. 530.

[155]Murray, *op. cit.,* p. 110. "This illustrates the necessity in each case of determining the precise sense in which the term 'law' is used by the apostle and we must not suppose that the term has always the same denotation and connotation" (*ibid*).

velopment which was duly foreseen and provided for."[156] In speaking of **the law and the prophets** Paul is referring to the holy Scriptures of the old covenant in their own main divisions.[157] Righteousness by the law (in the sense of v. 20) is not found in the Torah or the prophets rightly interpreted.[158] Even **the law and the prophets** bear witness to **the righteousness of God,** which is now **manifested** completely in the gospel. Nygren points out that Paul took the theme of Romans from **the prophets:** "He who through faith is righteous shall live" (1:17; Hab. 2:4). And from **the law,** the Torah, he draws his illustration of Abraham as the representative and archetype of "him who through faith is righteous" (c. 4). Thus both **the law and the prophets** bear witness against law- or works-righteousness.[159]

The righteousness of God of v. 22 is the same as that of v. 21 and 1:17, and the words **by faith of Jesus Christ unto all and upon all them that believe** have the same force as "from faith to faith" in 1:17.[160] For the first time, however, Paul makes it clear that the faith which justifies is not a general faith in God but "faith in Jesus Christ" (NASB, RSV). Although some interpreters insist that the phrase *pisteos Iesou Christou* means "the faith *of* Christ" (like the "faith of Abraham" in 4:16),[161] most exegetes agree with Sanday and Headlam that this is a genitive of object and should be rendered "faith *in* Jesus Christ" (cf. Gal. 2:20). "As works belong with law, faith belongs with Christ."[162] In I Cor. 1:30 the apostle declares that Christ is presented to us as the righteousness from God. In II Cor. 5:21 he writes: "For he hath made him to be sin for us, who knew no sin; that we might be made the righteousness of God in him." When we believe in Christ with saving faith, *His righteousness becomes ours.*

This gift of God's righteousness is not restricted to a select few but is **unto all** (*eis pantas*) and **upon all** (*epi pantas*) **them**

---

[156]ICC, p. 83. Cf. Rom. 1:2; 3:31; c. 4; 9:25-33; 10:16-21; 11:1-10, 16-29; 15:8-12; 16:26; etc.

[157]The third division was called "The Writings," and began with the Psalms; for this reason it was sometimes spoken of as "The Psalms" (cf. Luke 24:44).

[158]Thus Judaism in developing the doctrine of justification by works actually perverted the OT teaching.

[159]Nygren, *op. cit.,* pp. 148-49.   [160]Murray, *loc. cit.*

[161]Cf. Karl Barth, *The Epistle to the Romans,* pp. 96-97.

[162]Nygren, *op. cit.,* p. 150.

that believe: for there is no difference (22). Scholars are inclined to regard these two phrases as "a conflation, or combination of two readings originally alternatives."[163] Thus NASB translates the phrase "for all who believe." RSV and NEB adopt the same view. Nygren, however, sees in the two phrases a Pauline characteristic of repeating a noun with different prepositions for the sake of special emphasis. He cites 1:17 as an example with its parallel use "from faith to faith" (*ek pisteos* with *eis pistin*).[164] **Unto all** would thus emphasize the universality of God's offer of justification. **Upon all** parallels 1:18, where it is said that "the wrath of God is revealed from heaven against all ungodliness and unrighteousness of men." "These two passages make precisely parallel affirmations as to the old age and the new, respectively. They are equally universal. *All* are under the wrath of God; and *all* who believe in Christ share the righteousness of God. In both cases the same preposition is used, *epi,* 'upon.' "[165] From above comes the wrath of God upon all unrighteousness; from above comes the righteousness of God upon all who believe. To **believe** is to trust in Christ as the appointed means of our reconciliation with God, to abandon our own futile effort to save ourselves and rely completely upon the mercy of God offered through Christ. The manifestation of righteousness is directed to all who have faith, **for there is no difference** (distinction), i.e., between Jew and Gentile. There is a difference between Jews and Gentiles, but in respect to sin each stands guilty before God (vv. 19-20).

For all have sinned, and (therefore) **come short of the glory of God** (23). **All have sinned** (*pantes hemarton*) is literally "all sinned" (cf. 2:12 and 5:12, where the exact form is found). Sanday and Headlam call this a "collective aorist," which may be represented in English by the perfect. "From the point of view from which the Apostle is speaking, the sin of each offender is simply a past fact, and the sin of all a series or aggregate of facts together, constituting a past fact."[166] The second verb in v. 23 is in the present tense, but the KJV obscures this fact; "fall short" is therefore better (RSV, NASB). Because **all have sinned,** they fall short of the divine glory. But what does Paul mean by **the**

---

[163]ICC, p. 84. **And upon all** is not in the oldest Greek MSS.

[164]*Op. cit., loc. cit.*   [165]*Ibid.,* pp. 151-52.

[166]ICC, pp. 58-59. This observation is made relative to *hemarton* in 2:12, but the parallel is exact (cf. ICC, p. 84).

glory of God? Godet is undoubtedly correct when he defines it as "the divine splendor which shines forth from God Himself, and which He communicates to all that live in union with Him."[167] Murray comments, "We are destitute of that perfection which is the reflection of the divine perfection and therefore of the glory of God."[168] The verb translated "fall short" (*hysterountai*, lack) expresses the general idea of deficit. This suggests that man's normal state is one of conformity to the divine image. When man sinned, he fell away from his true nature in the image of God.

Verse 24 presents a serious difficulty in grammatical construction. The participle **being justified** does not appear to stand in relation to what precedes in a way that is readily understood. Sanday and Headlam offer four proposals for solving the difficulty, but they caution that "the construction and connexion of this word are difficult, and perhaps not to be determined with certainty." Most likely, they think, v. 23 must be taken as a parenthesis; thus **being justified** (*dikaioumenoi*) refers to **all them that believe** in 22. The construction, however, would be rough and irregular, but in their opinion not too irregular for Paul.[169] Recently NT scholars have put forward the view that vv. 24-26a are "a pre-Pauline formula, a confession of faith, which was perhaps employed liturgically in Hellenistic-Jewish Christianity."[170] The break in the construction would thus be explained by the fact that Paul is here inserting a quotation. There is much to commend this view, which has the further advantage of explaining the technical use of *hilasterion* in v. 25.[171]

Verse 24 also contains the first instance in which Paul uses the verb *dikaioumenoi* directly and positively in reference to the leading theme of the Epistle.[172] The verb *dikaioo* in its evangelical

[167]*Op. cit.*, pp. 148-49.

[168]*Op. cit.*, p. 133. Cf. Murray's thorough examination of this concept on pp. 132-33. The contrast to 3:23b is II Cor. 3:18, where salvation is described as transformation into the image of God, "from glory to glory." Cf. also ICC, p. 85; Knox, IB, IX, 430.

[169]ICC, pp. 85-86.

[170]John Reumann, "The Gospel of the Righteousness of God," *Interpretation*, XX (October, 1966), 432. The entire article is a significant exegesis of 3:21-31.

[171]See comments on v. 25.

[172]The previous uses (2:13; 3:4, 20) do not relate to the evangelical doctrine of being justified by faith.

sense here (and throughout Romans) means "to make righteous" in the sense of "to make right, to clear, to acquit in God's court." Barrett insists that justification "means no legal fiction but an act of forgiveness on God's part, described in terms of proceedings of a law court. Far from being a legal fiction, this is a creative act in the field of divine-human relations."[173] **Being justified freely by his grace** means that justification is "by his grace as a gift" (RSV). **Grace** (*charis*) is the free, gracious favor of God, the love He bestows on men while they are yet sinners (5:8); but for Paul it is more specifically *love in action*, a gracious activity which provides for our **redemption** (*apolytroseos*). This word denotes "a deliverance obtained by way of a purchase (*lytron*)."[174] **In Christ Jesus** the sway of the powers which oppose God are broken once for all, and those who are in Christ are thereby free from those forces which formerly held them captive.

How did God manifest His righteousness? Paul says that it was by setting Christ forth as a **propitiation** (25) for the sins of mankind. The noun *hilasterion*, used only here and in Heb. 9:5 in the NT, means literally "mercy seat," the golden cover or lid on the ark of the covenant, which was behind the veil in the holy of holies. If Paul is quoting a Hellenistic-Jewish formula,[175] the presence of such a technical term is explained. He can assume that many of his readers understand its scriptural significance.[176] Beneath the mercy seat, within the ark, the oracles of God were deposited (Exod. 25:17-21). Above it God himself dwelt and

---

[173]*Op. cit.*, pp. 75-76. "We believe that justification is that gracious and judicial act of God, by which He grants full pardon of all guilt and complete release from the penalty of sins committed, and acceptance as righteous, to all who believe on Jesus Christ and receive Him as Lord and Saviour" (Article IX, *Manual*, Church of the Nazarene).

[174]Sanday and Headlam observe that "in view of the clear resolution of the expression in Mark x. 45 (Matt. xx. 28) . . . and in view also of the many passages in which Christians are said to be 'bought,' or 'bought with a price' (I Cor. vi. 20, vii. 23; Gal. iii. 13; 2 Pet. ii. 1; Rev. v. 9: cf. Acts xx. 28; I Pet. i. 18), we can hardly resist the conclusion that the idea of the *lytron* retains its full force. . . . The emphasis is on the cost of man's redemption. We need not press the metaphor yet a step further by asking (as the ancients did) to whom the ransom or price was paid" (ICC, p. 86).

[175]Cf. comments above on v. 24.

[176]This would also meet the objections, raised by Godet, that Romans does not move in the sphere of Levitical symbolism so characteristic of Hebrews and that Paul nowhere else employs this type to explain Christ's death (see Godet, *op. cit.*, p. 151).

manifested His presence in the midst of Israel (I Sam. 4:4; II Sam. 6:2; Ps. 80:1). It was the place from which God spoke to Moses (Exod. 25:22; Num. 7:89). Preeminently, however, it was the place where, on the great Day of Atonement, the people were reconciled to God by the sprinkling of blood (Lev. 16:14-15).

> The analogy with Jesus is especially appropriate, because the mercy seat is no more than a particular, though very significant, place. By the express counsel of God, Jesus had been appointed from eternity[177] as the place of propitiation above which God dwells and from which He speaks; now, however, He occupies a position in time, in history, and in the presence of men. The life of Jesus is the place in history fitted by God for propitiation and fraught with eternity—*God was in Christ reconciling the world unto himself* (2 Cor. 5:19). At this place the Kingdom of God is come nigh: so near is it, that here His coming and His redeeming power are recognized; so near, that here God dwells with men and His communing is unmistakable; so near, that here the pressure of faith is a commanding necessity. . . . The propitiation occurs at the place of propitiation—only by blood, whereby we are reminded that God gives life only through death. Consequently, in Jesus also atonement occurs only through the faithfulness of God, *by his blood.*[178]

Throckmorton takes a mediating position which has much to commend it. "It may well be," he writes, "that Paul's intention was, at least in part, to allude to the mercy seat . . . but it is also probably true that Paul did not intend to limit his meaning to 'mercy seat,' for most Gentiles would probably not have known what the mercy seat was."[179] We must therefore inquire further into the meaning of *hilasterion.* All scholars agree that the *general* meaning is either **a propitiation** or "an expiation" (RSV).

[177]Sanday and Headlam, who do not advocate this view of *hilasterion,* point out that the Greek verb translated **set forth** (*proetheto*) may mean "whom God proposed to Himself" or "purposed" (ICC, p. 87). Nygren, however, who adopts the same view of *hilasterion,* advocates the primary meaning of *proetheto:* "He has now put Christ forward before all the world as our *hilasterion,* our mercy seat" (*op. cit.,* p. 158).

[178]Barth, *The Epistle to the Romans,* pp. 104-5. This interpretation was advocated by Origen and was accepted by Luther and Calvin, as well as by Adam Clarke. Among modern proponents are Brunner, F. F. Bruce, and Barrett (in *Reading Through Romans* [London: The Epworth Press, 1963], p. 23). Alan Richardson argues cogently for this interpretation in his *Introduction to New Testament Theology* (p. 225).

[179]*Romans for the Layman,* p. 32. While Calvin thinks the allusion is to the mercy seat, he writes: "Since, however, the other view cannot be disproved, if the reader prefers the more simple sense, I shall leave the question open" (*op. cit.,* p. 75).

The death of Christ was thus "a propitiatory sacrifice" or "an expiatory sacrifice." The choice between the two will be determined by the interpreter's overview of the atonement. In reality, both ideas are inherent in *hilasterion*[180] and are necessary to a biblical doctrine. Richardson goes so far as to say, "In its biblical meaning 'propitiation' must be thought of as more or less synonymous with 'expiation.' "[181] Propitiation has a *Godward* reference: through the death of Christ God's wrath is overcome and His justice is demonstrated. Expiation has a *manward* reference: Christ's sacrifice removes the guilt of man's sin.

When we speak of Christ's sacrifice as a propitiation, we do so against the background teaching of this Epistle that "the wrath of God is revealed from heaven against all ungodliness and unrighteousness of men" (1:18). Of course this does not mean that God needs to be appeased like an angry man. Such a perversion of the biblical doctrine of propitiation misses the fundamental point made everywhere in the Bible, that it is God himself who puts forward the propitiatory offering for man's sin. Paul writes of Jesus, **Whom God hath set forth to be a propitiation.** See also II Cor. 5:18-21, where the apostle makes explicit that the atonement is from first to last the work of God himself: "And all things are of God, who hath reconciled us to himself by Jesus Christ."[182] Propitiation means that God has found a way to uphold the law and safeguard His justice (cf. v. 26) while He extends mercy to a guilty sinner who trusts in Christ. "Expiation" means that in Christ the guilty rebel is forgiven of his sin and cleansed from its demerit. "For our sake he made him to be sin who knew no sin, so that in him we might become the righteousness of God" (II Cor. 5:21, RSV). "God . . . puts forward the means whereby the guilt of sin is removed, by sending Christ."[183]

---

[180]Arndt and Gingrich: "that which expiates or propitiates, (concr.) a means of expiation, gift to procure expiation." Harper's *Analytical Greek Lexicon:* "propitiatory, invested with propitiatory power." Stegenga: "propitiation." Thayer: "1. the propitiatory; 2. an expiatory sacrifice; a piacular victim." (Most of these authorities also note the meaning of mercy seat.)

[181]*Op. cit.,* p. 224.

[182]Cf. I John 4:10, where God's *agape* is declared to be the motive of the atonement (John 3:16; etc.). The OT similarly ascribes the initiative in this matter of God's grace: "For the life of the flesh is in the blood; and I have given it to you upon the altar to make an atonement for your souls" (Lev. 17:11).

[183]Dodd, *op. cit.,* p. 55.

It is important to see that the idea of **propitiation** is qualified by two parallel and mutually completing phrases: (1) **through faith,** indicating the subjective condition; and (2) **in his blood** (or "by his blood," instrumental dative), setting forth the historical or objective condition of the atonement. "Propitiation does not take place except through faith on the part of the saved, and through blood on the part of the Saviour."[184] Thus we may paraphrase Paul's words: "Jesus Christ, whom God settled beforehand as the means of propitiation on the condition of faith, through the shedding of His blood."[185]

To say that Christ is our **propitiation** "by faith" (RSV) means that we associate ourselves in heart and mind with God's objective condemnation of our sin. Erdman rightly insists that "one who accepts the crucified Saviour as his Lord really submits to the divine sentence upon sin."[186] Noting the sacrificial imagery of the verse, Leenhardt comments:

> The immolation of the victim . . . symbolized the process by which the sinner, whom the animal victim represents, surrenders his former condition of life, and allows his existence in its most vital aspects to be abandoned to God in self-consecration and self-offering. The sinner associates himself with the victim by placing his hand upon it; such is the sign of a unity which the penitent wishes to affirm and effect. Moreover he recognizes that his sins have made this sacrifice necessary and he recognizes it by making confession of his sins. The communion thus realized by sacrifice gives to the believer access to the renewing and revitalizing forces released by contact with the altar, that is, with God, through this vicarious sacrifice.[187]

This is what it means for Christ to become our propitiatory or expiatory Offering. **Through faith** (*dia pisteos*) we identify ourselves with Christ's death, *accepting God's judgment upon our sins and dying to them,* while at the same time we receive God's life and salvation. Then with Paul we can confess, "I have been crucified with Christ; it is no longer I who live, but Christ who lives in me; and the life I now live in the flesh I live by faith in the Son of God, who loved me and gave himself for me" (Gal. 2:20, RSV).

---

[184]Godet, *op. cit.,* p. 153; cf. Heb. 9:22.   [185]*Ibid.*

[186]*The Epistle of Paul to the Romans* (Philadelphia: The Westminster Press, 1925), p. 53.

[187]*Op. cit.,* pp. 103-4.

The phrase **in his blood** (*en to autou haimati*) has been much debated. The order of the sentence seems to imply that the object of faith is the Blood itself. But Paul nowhere writes of believing in any inanimate object; faith is always in a Person. Thus we take the phrase as independently valid: Christ's sacrifice was through the shedding of blood, or the outpouring of His life. What the apostle means is strengthened by the remainder of the verse, **to declare his righteousness for the remission of sins that are past, through the forbearance of God.** This means that the death of Christ was the demonstration of God's judgment upon sin. The Cross was God's dramatic and conclusive condemnation of the world's sin. The word translated **to declare** (*endeixin*) means to "show forth and vindicate." It means both a simple showing forth and a proof. The Cross is the final proof that God is holy and just in spite of the fact that He has been forbearing toward the past sins of mankind. God could afford to "wink" at man's ignorance and sin in former times (cf. Acts 17:30-31) because He had *determined from the beginning* to set forth Christ *before the eyes of the whole world*[188] as a propitiatory Sacrifice.

Verse 26 concludes Paul's long sentence begun at 21. **To declare, I say, at this time his righteousness, that he might be just, and the justifier of him which believeth in Jesus.** Brunner wisely observes, "Christ's death is the sign of judging righteousness, as well as forgiving love; of God's wrath upon every kind of godlessness and unrighteousness of men as well as that of his incomprehensible mercy. The blood of Christ serves not for the removal but for the revelation of the punitive wrath on sins."[189]

We may thus reconstruct vv. 25-26 in some such way as this:

> Whom God set forth as propitiatory—through faith—in His own blood—for a display of His righteousness; because of the passing over of foregone sins in the forbearance of God with a view to the display of His righteousness at the present moment, so that He might be at once righteous (Himself) and declaring righteous him who has . . . faith in Jesus.[190]

[188]This is to understand *proetheto* (**set forth**) in its double sense of (1) purposing and (2) showing forth.

[189]*Op. cit.*, p. 30. The phrase **just, and the justifier** recalls Isa. 45:21, "a just God and a Saviour."

[190]ICC, p. 90.

"Guilt and Grace" are contrasted in 3:23-26. (1) The guilt of all, 23; (2) Grace for all, 24 (W. T. Purkiser).

b. Some inferences (3:27-31). Paul now draws three inferences from what he has just written.[191]

(1) Righteousness by faith excludes boasting (3:27-28). Paul asks, **Where is boasting then?** (27) What has become of the boasting of the Jew (cf. 2:17)? It no longer exists. **It is excluded** once for all. **By what law? of works? Nay: but by the law of faith.** When our salvation is a matter of **works,** our pride is fed, but there is no credit or merit in throwing ourselves on the mercy of God in Christ. **Law** (*nomou*) may here be paraphrased "system" or law in the sense of a "constituted order of things." "Under what kind of a system is this result obtained? Under a system the essence of which is Faith."[192] **Therefore we conclude that a man is justified by faith without the deeds of the law** (28). Here is the basis for the Protestant doctrine of *sola fide*, "by faith alone." Yet faith has no power apart from its Object. Faith is simply "the hand of the heart" which receives the gift of God's pardon through Christ.

(2) *Righteousness by faith is suited to all* (3:29-30). Paul next asks, **Is he the God of the Jews only?** (29) This was another aspect of Jewish boasting. The Jew thought of God as his special possession. But Paul continues, **Is he not also of the Gentiles? Yes,** he answers, **of the Gentiles also.** There are not two Gods, and "seeing that God is one, it is impossible for Him to have two different methods of saving mankind."[193] The **one God . . . shall justify the circumcision by faith, and uncircumcision through faith** (30). Since both Jew and Gentile alike are saved only through the mercy of God proffered in the Cross, the religious distinction between Jew and Gentile is thereby removed.[194]

In 3:22-30 we discover that "There Is No Difference." (1) In the fact of guilt—**all have sinned,** in the past; **and come short of the glory of God,** in the present, 23; (2) In the provision of redemption, 24-30; (3) In the conditions of salvation, 10:12-13.

---

[191]See Thomas, *op. cit.,* pp. 120-25.

[192]ICC, p. 95. Barrett thinks *nomos* here means "religious system" (*op. cit.,* p. 83).

[193]Thomas, *op. cit.,* p. 122.

[194]For the full development of this idea see Eph. 2:11-22.

(3) *Righteousness by faith establishes the law* (3:31). In this last verse Paul asks, **Do we then make void the law through faith?** He answers, **God forbid: yea, we establish the law.** The word **law** (*nomos*) is used by Paul in various ways in Romans. (*a*) When we are told that God's way of righteousness through faith is "witnessed by the law and the prophets" (3:21), the law clearly means the first five books of the OT, the Pentateuch. (*b*) In 3:19 we read, "Now we know that what things soever the law saith, it saith to them who are under the law." This statement applies to a group of scriptures from Psalms and the prophet Isaiah (cf. 3:10-12). If it is the law that says these things, the law can mean only the Hebrew Bible, or our OT in its entirety. (*c*) In 3:27 "law" means what we would express by some such term as "religious system" (cf. 7:21, 23). (*d*) Much more often it refers to the moral law, the commandments of God, known in some degree by the Gentiles (2:14-15), but disclosed to the Jews in a preeminent measure in the Decalogue and elsewhere in the Torah. This is the form in which Paul had come to know the law in his own experience (7:7-13). This is the sense in which he thinks of the law in 3:20; 4:15; 5:13; 7:14, 22, 25*a*; 8:3; 9:31-32; 13:8-10.[195] But sin perverts this law into Pharisaism, the false belief that fallen, sinful man can fulfill God's law by his own moral endeavor. God's law thereby becomes "the law of sin and death" (8:2).

When Paul here declares that **through faith . . . we establish the law,** he means in the immediate context that there is no contradiction between the gospel and the OT, as the example of Abraham (c. 4) will make perfectly clear. "Paul's gospel was accused of making void the law by setting aside legal works as a means of justification; and he has just proved to his adversaries that it is his teaching, on the contrary, which harmonizes with the true meaning of the law, while the opposite teaching overturns it."[196] *The law itself teaches justification by faith* (4:3-8). By creating a legalistic system the Pharisees had overlooked the undeniable fact that the old covenant was in reality a covenant of grace. (See comments on 2:25-29.)

Yet Paul is saying more, as cc. 7—8 will make clear. Through God's grace in Christ we experience the true sanctification by

[195]Cf. Bruce, *The Epistle of Paul to the Romans*, pp. 52-55; IB (Exegesis), IX, 438.

[196]Godet, *op. cit.*, p. 166.

which the law of God is fulfilled according to its original intent. "For the law of the Spirit of life in Christ Jesus hath made me free from the law of sin and death. For what the law could not do, in that it was weak through the flesh, God sending his own Son in the likeness of sinful flesh, and for sin, condemned sin in the flesh: that the righteousness of the law might be fulfilled in us, who walk not after the flesh, but after the Spirit" (8:2-4). Through Christ, God liberates us from "the law of sin and death" and establishes His law anew as the Spirit of grace and loving obedience. Through Him "the love of God is poured into our hearts" and this "love is the fulfilling of the law" (13:8-10).[197]

Thus, instead of making the law void, the gospel establishes the law by showing the permanent validity of the OT and by disclosing the only way by which its true intention can be realized. *Therefore, from the ultimate perspective, gospel and law are one.* "The law of the Spirit of life in Christ Jesus" is God's law established according to the terms of the new covenant (cf. Jer. 31:31-34; Heb. 10:14-17).

From 3:27-31, W. H. Griffith Thomas discusses "God's Righteousness." (1) Righteousness by faith excludes boasting, 27-28; (2) Righteousness by faith is equally suited to all, 29-30; (3) Righteousness by faith establishes the law, 31.

c. *Justification defended* (4:1-25). We come now to a digression in which the apostle illustrates and defends his doctrine of justification by faith apart from law. This he does by a reference to Abraham, who as the father of the Chosen People had a preeminent place in the religious thought of Judaism. Paul has just said that by the doctrine of justification through faith "we establish the law" (3:31). As we have seen, this means that the OT revelation "contains within it a conception of religion as personal trust in God, more fundamental than the legal strain in it which received one-sided emphasis in Pharisaic Judaism."[198] From this point of view Abraham, recognized by the strictest Pharisee as the ideal righteous man, was justified by faith rather than by the works of the law. In proving this point Paul makes the strongest kind of scriptural defense for his doctrine.

(1) *Abraham justified by faith, not works, 4:1-8.* In all likelihood, Paul had no choice about dealing with Abraham; his

[197]Cf. Barth, *A Shorter Commentary on Romans*, pp. 88-92.
[198]Dodd, *op. cit.*, p. 64.

Jewish opponents probably faced him with the story. "Look at Abraham, they said; there's a righteous man for you. He obeyed the law perfectly, even before it was given. He has something to boast about; what about works and faith now?"[199]

Paul picks up their question in v. 1: **What shall we say then that Abraham our father** ("forefather," NASB) **hath found?** He answers: **If Abraham were justified by works,** you are right: **he hath whereof to glory;** before men, perhaps, **but not before God** (2). Abraham has no ground of boasting before God. **For what saith the scripture?** (3) Paul's answer refers to Gen. 15:6, quoted from the Septuagint: **Abraham believed God, and it was counted unto him for righteousness.** What did Abraham believe? The promise of God: "And he brought him forth abroad, and said, Look now toward heaven, and tell the stars, if thou be able to number them: and he said unto him, So shall thy seed be" (Gen. 15:5). Then follows Paul's quotation, **Abraham believed God.** Faith does not operate in a void; it is always based on God's promise (cf. 10:17). Abraham's trust in God's promise "was reckoned to him as righteousness" (RSV). That is, Abraham was justified because he put his trust in the word of God. (In vv. 17-22, Paul gives an illuminating exposition of the nature and character of Abraham's faith.)

We must observe how Paul fastens upon the verb "to count" (*elogisthe*).[200] Evidently if faith is **counted . . . for righteousness,** it is not itself identical with, but distinguishable from, righteousness. *We must avoid the notion that faith is a refined kind of righteousness which God accepts in lieu of legal obedience.* Faith and righteousness are in different categories. The faith by which Abraham was justified derived its power from God. Faith is not relying on our trust; it is *relying upon God* (cf. vv. 20-21). We are not justified by the virtue of our faith but *by God.* Otherwise we shall have **whereof to glory; but not before God.** Justifi-

---

[199]Barrett, *Reading Through Romans*, pp. 25-26. "We find that Abraham our father had performed the whole law before it was given, for it is written, Because that Abraham obeyed my voice and kept my charge, my commandments, my statutes and my laws (Gen. xxvi.5)" (*Kiddushin*, 4:14).

[200]The same verb is rendered **counted** (3, 5), **reckoned** (4), **imputeth** (6), and **impute** (8). It is a metaphor from accounts and means "to set down" (in v. 3) "on the credit side." "The notion arises from that of the 'book of remembrance' (Mal. iii. 16) in which men's good or evil deeds, the wrongs and sufferings of the saints, are entered (Ps. lvi. 8; Is. lxv. 6)" (ICC, p. 100). Cf. Dan. 7:10; Rev. 20:12.

cation by grace through faith is wholly apart from any trace of human merit.

Paul proceeds to elaborate this truth: **Now to him that work-eth is the reward not reckoned (***logizetai***) of grace, but of debt. But to him that worketh not, but believeth on him that justifieth the ungodly, his faith is counted (***logizetai***) for righteousness (4-5).** The contrast between **of grace** and **of debt** is instructive. " 'Works' and 'due' belong together as correlatives; 'faith' and 'grace' similarly correspond, and it is to this pair that 'counting' belongs. It follows that since Abraham had righteousness **counted** to him, he cannot have done works, but must have been the recipient of grace."[201] Therefore to be justified by grace through faith is to be *given* a righteousness which is not one's deserving: God **justifieth the ungodly.** This seems to fly in the face of Scripture (Exod. 23:7; Prov. 17:15; Isa. 5:23).[202] And it scandalizes those who feel that the sinner must *do* certain things before he is worthy of justification. When we read that God **justifieth the ungodly,** we are to understand that God acquits the guilty sinner for reasons of His own mercy apart from any human worthiness or merit. Justification is an act of sheer grace on the part of God. No one saw this more clearly than John Wesley, who notes on this passage:

> We see plainly how groundless that opinion is, that holiness or sanctification is previous to our justification. For the sinner, being first convinced of his sin and danger by the Spirit of God, stands trembling before the awful tribunal of divine justice; and has nothing to plead, but his own guilt, and the merits of the Mediator. Christ here interposes; justice is satisfied; the sin is remitted, and pardon is applied to the soul, by a divine faith wrought by the Holy Ghost, who then begins the great work of inward sanctification. Thus God justifies the ungodly, and remains just, and true to all His attributes. . . . If a man could possibly be made holy before he was justified, it would entirely set his justification aside; seeing he could not, in the very nature of the thing, be justified if he were not, at that very time, ungodly.[203]

This is what Luther meant when he called the Christian's righteousness an "alien righteousness." In his *Lectures on Romans* he says, "Everything . . . is outside us and in Christ. . . . For

---

[201]Barrett, *The Epistle to the Romans*, p. 88.

[202]These passages in reality do not touch on justification by faith, but rather state the demand for justice in human affairs.

[203]*Explanatory Notes upon the New Testament*, p. 532.

God does not want to save us by our own but by an extraneous righteousness which does not originate in ourselves but comes to us from beyond ourselves, which does not arise on our earth but comes from heaven. Therefore, we must come to know this righteousness which is utterly external and foreign to us. That is why our own personal righteousness must be uprooted."[204] He goes on to point out that "virtues are often the greater and worse faults," for they tend to cause us to trust in ourselves rather than in Christ. "But now Christ wants all our feeling to be so bare that, on the one hand, we are not afraid to be cast into confusion on account of our faults, nor delight in praise and vain joy on account of our virtue, yet, on the other hand, we do not glory before men in that external righteousness which, coming from Christ, is in us, nor suffer defeat because of those sufferings and evils which befall us for his sake."[205] And this is what August Toplady saw when he penned,

> *Could my tears forever flow,*
> *Could my zeal no languor know,*
> *These for sin cannot atone;*
> *Thou must save, and Thou alone.*

In examining the doctrine of propitiation we saw that to be justified the sinner must "submit to the divine sentence upon sin"—i.e., confess his guilt and genuinely repent.[206] However, such repentance must not be regarded as a meritorious work but simply as a preparation for the faith which alone becomes the channel of God's justifying grace. For we have already seen "that a man is justified by faith without the deeds of the law" (3:28). It is "by faith alone" (*sola fide*) because it is "by grace alone" (*sola gratia*).

Nor is Abraham an isolated instance of the principle of justification by faith; another OT example lies ready to hand in the case of David. Paul now quotes the opening words of the thirty-second psalm, where, in joyful relief at the assurance of divine pardon, David exclaims: **Blessed are they whose iniquities are forgiven, and whose sins are covered. Blessed is the man to**

---

[204]Trans. and ed. by Wilhelm Paulk, "The Library of Christian Classics" (Philadelphia: The Westminster Press, 1961), XV, 4.

[205]*Ibid.*, pp. 4-5.   [206]See comments on 3:25*a*.

whom the Lord will not impute (*logizetai*) **sin** (7-8).[207] We
have observed the recurrence of the verb *logizomai* in vv. 3-8.
This word constitutes a formal link between Ps. 32:1-2 and Gen.
15:6. "In rabbinical exegesis such a link was held to encourage
the interpretation of one passage by the other, by the principle
called *gezerah shawah* ('equal category')."[208] The conclusion to
be deduced from this principle is that the "counting of righteousness" is equivalent to the "not counting of sin." It is now crystal-
clear that justification, or the counting of righteousness, does not
mean the just evaluation of human virtue (such as the Jew supposed Abraham to have), but forgiveness or acquittal. The man
is justified **whose iniquities are forgiven, and whose sins are
covered.**[209]

In this section we find a treatment of "Righteousness by
Faith." (1) The necessity of faith, 1-2; (2) The object of faith,
2-3; (3) The principle of faith, 4-5; (4) The acceptance of faith,
5; (5) The outcome of faith, 6-8.

(2) *Abraham justified by faith, not circumcision* (4:9-12).
Thus far Paul has used (1) general methods and (2) *gezerah
shawah* (see fn. 208) to interpret Gen. 15:6. He now sees an
opportunity of carrying his argument one step further by applying his *gezerah shawah*, as it were, in reverse: Gen. 15:6 can be
used to illuminate Ps. 32:1-2.[210] **Cometh this blessedness** (the forgiveness of which David speaks) **upon the circumcision only, or
upon the uncircumcision also?** (9) There is nothing in this psalm
to answer the question. Since David was a member of the Chosen
People, we might suppose **this blessedness** was a special Jewish
privilege. But applying the *gezerah shawah* yields a different
answer. It is for **the uncircumcision also, for we say that faith
was reckoned to Abraham for righteousness.** The apostle now
comes to his clinching argument. He asks, **How was it then
reckoned? when he was in circumcision, or in uncircumcision?
Not in circumcision, but in uncircumcison** (10). This is a simple
statement of fact. Abraham was not circumcised until at least

[207]Quoted in exact agreement with LXX.

[208]Bruce, *op. cit.*, p. 115. Cf. Barrett, *The Epistle to the Romans*, p. 89.

[209]The covering of sin expresses the thought of the Hebrew *kaphar*,
translated "atonement," and recalls the description of Christ crucified in
3:25. See comments there on the word "forbearance."

[210]Barrett, *The Epistle to the Romans*, pp. 89-90.

14 years later, according to Gen. 17:10-27.[211] Paul has made his point. *Abraham was a Gentile when God counted his faith as righteousness.*

The apostle then draws the inescapable conclusion. Abraham thereby became **the father of all them that believe, though they be not circumcised; that righteousness might be imputed unto them also: and the father of circumcision to them who are not of the circumcision only, but who also walk in the steps of that faith of our father Abraham, which he had being yet uncircumcised** (11*b*-12). Paul draws two inferences here, which completely reverse his early teaching and that of orthodox Judaism. (1) Abraham is the father, first of all, of believing Gentiles; (2) he is the father of the Jews, not on the grounds of their circumcision, but on the grounds of their faith. The latter point is an echo of what he has said in 2:28-29, that true "circumcision is that of the heart," "by the Spirit and not by the letter." Paul again makes his major point: For Jew and Gentile alike there is but one way to justification, the way of faith alone.

But if Abraham was already justified by faith, and if circumcision cannot justify, why then was Abraham circumcised? Paul's answer is that Abraham **received the sign of circumcision, [as] a seal of the righteousness of the faith which he had yet being uncircumcised** (11). The expression **sign of circumcision** means simply a "sign consisting of circumcision." This sign is still universally recognized as a mark of a Jew. **Seal** here means confirmation. Addressing his Corinthian converts, Paul wrote, "The seal of mine apostleship are ye in the Lord" (I Cor. 9:2). That is, the very fact that you are Christian believers confirms the fact that I am an apostle. "In a similar way, Abraham's circumcision did not confer righteousness upon him . . . but confirmed by a visible sign the fact that he had already been justified by faith."[212]

These verses have an important bearing upon a theory which has been advanced from some quarters with great confidence. The theory is that Paul taught a "sacramental religion" in the

---

[211]"Thirteen years after Ishmael's birth (Gn. xvii. 25; cf. xvii. 1, 24, with xvi. 16). And the narrative sequence of Genesis implies that the conception of Ishmael (Gn. xvi. 3 f.) was the sequel to the promise of Gn. xv. 4, that Abraham would yet have a son of his own to be his heir" (Bruce, *The Epistle of Paul to the Romans,* fn., p. 112).

[212]Barrett, *The Epistle to the Romans,* p. 92.

sense that the sacraments actually conveyed divine grace, not in the sense of strengthening faith which had already provided the sufficient condition of salvation, but actually and in themselves (*ex opere operato*) conveyed regenerating and sanctifying grace. Paul's declaration that Abraham's justification preceded his circumcision by several years, and was effected by faith and faith alone, should forever silence such an argument. C. Anderson Scott writes in this connection: "The Christian analogue to circumcision is, of course, baptism as a rite symbolizing purification and admission to the redeemed community. And there can be no doubt that all Paul had to say about circumcision he would say equally about baptism. Like circumcision, baptism 'had its value' (2:25), but, like circumcision, it had no value apart from a new creature."[213]

(3) *Abraham justified by faith, not the law* (4:13-17a). If circumcision had nothing to do with Abraham's justification, the law had even less to do with it. **For the promise, that he should be the heir of the world, was not to Abraham, or to his seed, through the law, but through the righteousness of faith** (13). As Paul had pointed out to the Galatians, the law was given 430 years later than God's promise to Abraham and could not invalidate it or restrict its scope (Gal. 3:17). **For if they which are of the law be heirs, faith is made void, and the promise made of none effect** (14). That is to say, if long after **the promise** had been given, it had been made conditional on obedience to a law which had not been mentioned at the time of the original promise, the whole basis of the promise would have been nullified. The promise was a promise of blessing, and is fulfilled in the gospel. The law does promise a blessing on those who observe it, but at the same time it invokes a curse on those who break it. And in view of the universal sway of sin, the curse is more prominent than the blessing: **The law worketh wrath** (15).[214]

A second argument is introduced parenthetically in v. 15: **For where no law is, there is no transgression** (*parabasis*). This argument interrupts the connection between vv. 14 and 16, but it fits into the pattern of Paul's thought. Its opening word, **for,** looks back to v. 13, and is further ground for the pronouncement

---

[213]"Romans," *The Abingdon Bible Commentary* (New York: The Abingdon Press, 1929), p. 1145. Cf. comments on 2:28-29.

[214]Bruce, *The Epistle of Paul to the Romans*, pp. 112-13; cf. 3:20.

of that verse.[215] The term **transgression** refers to a conscious act
of willful disobedience. A sinful tendency may indeed be present
in the absence of law, but it takes a specific commandment to
crystallize that tendency into a positive transgression or breach
of law (cf. 5:13, 20; 7:7-13, and comments on these passages).
The purpose of the law was to show how exceedingly sinful sin
is by actually showing up such **transgression,** which is of course
naturally and rightly visited with God's wrath—a very different
matter from law. Law, although good in itself (cf. 7:12, 14), is
so closely bound up with sin (cf. 7:5) and **wrath** (15a) that it is
unthinkable to consider it the basis of promise. A gracious promise such as God made to Abraham belongs to a totally different
realm than law.

Abraham's justification and its attendant blessings were not
founded in law; they were based on his faith in God; they were
not earned by effort or merit on his part but were bestowed by
God's grace. Paul declares **it is of faith, that it might be by
grace; to the end that the promise might be sure to all the seed**
(all men); **not to that only which is of the law** (the Jews), **but
to that also which is of the faith of Abraham** (all believers);
who is the father of us all (16). The principle on which God
thus dealt with Abraham applies also to his descendants—not to
his natural descendants (who are subject to the obligations of
the law), but to his spiritual descendants (those who follow the
example of Abraham's faith: "who also walk in the steps of that
faith of our father Abraham," v. 12). Paul says this is what God
meant when He gave him the name **Abraham** in place of Abram,
as he had formerly been called, and said, **I have made thee a
father of many nations** (17a). These comprise all who are justified by faith—Jews and Gentiles alike; Abraham is the father of
all believers. Here is the teaching again of the spiritual Israel
(cf. 2:28-29), as contrasted with Israel according to the flesh.[216]

(4) *Abraham's faith anticipatory of Christian faith* (4:17b-
25). Abraham is the father of Jewish and Gentile Christians, not
in virtue of any human relationship with them, but **before him
whom he believed, even God, who quickeneth the dead, and
calleth those things which be not as though they were** (17). In
this verse and the following the apostle has in mind the account

[215]Barrett, *The Epistle to the Romans,* p. 95.
[216]In cc. 9—11 Paul further develops the doctrine of the spiritual Israel.

of the birth of Isaac, the child of promise (and perhaps also the **intended sacrifice; cf. Heb. 11:19).** The God to whom Abraham directed his faith is the God "who gives life to the dead" (NASB). Abraham's was a *resurrection faith.* Furthermore, He "calls into being things which do not exist."[217] God is the Creator, and faith means reliance upon His creative power. "In hope against hope he believed, in order that he might become a father of many nations, according to that which had been spoken, 'So shall your descendants be.' And without becoming weak in faith he contemplated his own body, now as good as dead since he was about a hundred years old, and the deadness of Sarah's womb; yet, with respect to the promise of God, he did not waver in unbelief, but grew strong in faith, giving glory to God, and being fully assured that what He had promised, He was able also to perform" (18-21, NASB). The second **not** in v. 19 is omitted in NASB, as in all modern versions, since it is missing in the best MSS. Abraham **considered** the fact that **his own body** was **now dead,** and yet **he staggered not at the promise of God through unbelief** (20), giving God the glory. By thus believing Abraham was **giving glory to God**—giving Him the honor which is His due as the Creator and Life-Giver. **And therefore it was imputed to him for righteousness** (22).

Paul continues, **Now it was not written for his sake alone, that it was imputed to him; but for us also, to whom it shall be imputed, if we believe on him that raised up Jesus our Lord from the dead** (23-24). There is a precise correspondence between Abraham's faith and the faith of those who believe in Christ. Abraham believed in the "God, who quickeneth the dead" (17). Here, Paul holds, is where Abraham's faith is an example and type of the man who believes in Christ. When we believe in Jesus as **delivered for our offences, and . . . raised again for our justification** (25), we believe in the "God, who quickeneth the dead." Karl Barth writes with deep insight:

> Who was it but Jesus Christ in whom even Abraham trusted and believed when he trusted God's promise? For, indeed, Jesus Christ was the seed promised to Abraham in Isaac! In that way, and therefore in him, Abraham gave glory to the almighty power, faithfulness and constancy of God. In that way, and therefore in him, God was Abraham's righteousness. We believe no differently from Abraham, and in none other than Abraham did and all the

---

[217]Barrett's translation in *The Epistle to the Romans*, p. 97.

other faithful of the OT with him. For we simply believe in the fulfilment of the promise given to him which has now taken place.[218]

Faith in Christ is at the same time, and even more deeply, faith in **him that raised up Jesus** (24). Faith of this kind justifies "not because of its strength, quality and beauty, but only because of its object, because of Jesus Christ, because of the omnipotence, fidelity and constancy of God, continued, revealed and active in Him."[219]

We must avoid any wooden interpretation of v. 25 which would suggest that Jesus' resurrection had nothing to do with the atonement **for our offences** and His death nothing to do with **our justification.** The latter idea is ruled out by 5:9. Death and resurrection are two aspects of one divine event. Without the Resurrection, the death of Jesus would not avail as **our justification.** "If Christ be not raised, your faith is vain" (I Cor. 15:17).

Chapter 4 discusses "Saving Faith." (1) Its basis—the promise of God, 3; cf. Gen. 15:5-6; Rom. 10:17; (2) Its nature—the persuasion of the heart that God is faithful, 18-21; (3) Its outcome—justification before God, 22-25.

d. *Justification and the hope of salvation* (5:1-11). In this section Paul rounds out his doctrine of justification by putting this truth in its eschatological context. Justification means not only pardon and acquittal from the guilt of sin; it also carries within itself the **hope of the glory of God** (2) and the promise of final salvation (9-10). We have here more than the present fruits of justification; our attention is rather directed to its ultimate outcome. True enough, Paul touches lightly "the theme of the working-out of justification in moral progress (what Reformation theology described as 'sanctification')"[220] in vv. 4-5. Also in 10b the doctrine of entire sanctification is certainly implied.[221] However, the stress of this passage is upon the future glory and final salvation of those who continue in **peace with God through our Lord Jesus Christ.** Godet has put this well:

> From this point he turns his attention to the *future* which opens up to the justified soul. It is not at its goal: a career of trials and

[218]*A Shorter Commentary on Romans*, pp. 53-54.

[219]*Ibid.*, p. 54.   [220]"Dodd, *op. cit.*, p. 73.

[221]See notes on v. 10. Godet says, "The expression *be saved* denotes salvation in the full sense of the word—the final sentence which, along with justification, assumes the restoration of holiness" (*op. cit.*, p. 197).

struggles awaits it. Will its state of justification hold good till it can possess the finished salvation? The apprehension of divine wrath exists in the profound depths of man's heart. A trespass suffices to reawaken it. What justified one will not sometimes put the anxious question, Will the sentence by which my faith was reckoned to me for righteousness be still valid before the judgment seat; and *in the day of wrath* (ver. 9) will this salvation by grace, in which I now rejoice, still endure? It is the answer to this ever-reviving fear which the following piece is intended to give.[222]

Brunner entitles this section "The New Prospect."[223] Beet gives it the topic, "We Have Now a Well-Grounded Hope."[224]

Harold J. Ockenga found in these verses (1-11) "The Glorious Benefits of Being Right with God." (1) We have peace with God, 1; (2) We have access to grace, 2; (3) We rejoice in hope of glory, 2; (4) We shall be saved through His life, 9-11.

Paul begins c. 5 by saying, **Therefore being justified by faith, we have peace with God through our Lord Jesus Christ** (1). Immediately we encounter a textual problem which has puzzled interpreters. The best MSS read *echōmen* (subjunctive, "let us have") rather than *echomen* (indicative, **we have**).[225] One way out of the difficulty is to suppose that Tertius, who wrote the Epistle at Paul's dictation,[226] did not understand the apostle correctly. Since the accent is on the first syllable of the verb, the distinction between the long and the short vowel would tend to disappear, so that the two forms would sound practically the same. In the course of the dictation, therefore, Paul might have intended the one form and the scribe wrote down the other.[227]

---

[222]*Ibid.*, p. 186; see comments on v. 10.

[223]*Op. cit.*, pp. 40-43.   [224]*Op. cit.*, pp. 148-59.

[225]Beet summarizes the evidence supporting *echōmen*, and accepts it as conclusive. He writes: *"Let us have peace* was read probably by Tertullian, and is found in all, or very nearly all, the Latin MSS., which were used throughout the western church. The same reading is repeatedly quoted and commented upon by Origen; and by Chrysostom, who lived at Antioch and Constantinople, A.D. 347-407. Neither of these writers seems to have known the other reading. The same reading is found in all existing Greek MSS. earlier than the 9th century, and in some of the best cursives. Also in the oldest Syriac version, used in the Far East; and in the three other oldest versions. The earliest trace of the reading 'we have peace' is found in the Sinai MS., in a correction of the other reading made perhaps in the 4th century" (*op. cit.*, p. 149).

[226]Cf. 16:22. See Introduction and comments on c. 16 for the question of the unity of the Epistle.

[227]Bruce, *Epistle of Paul to the Romans*, p. 122.

This reconstruction appears to most interpreters to be necessary in view of the fact that the context is not hortatory, but indicative. Leitzmann takes the position which the majority of NT scholars feel compelled to adopt: "The meaning here must carry more weight than the letter. Only *echomen* gives Paul's real meaning."[228]

It should be noted, however, that all the verbs in the series may be taken as subjunctive.[229] Calvin so understands the passage and renders each as a hortatory.[230] Both the ERV and the NEB follow this interpretation. The NEB translates: "Therefore, now having been justified through faith, let us continue at peace with God through our Lord Jesus Christ, through whom we have been allowed to enter the sphere of God's grace, where we now stand. Let us exult in the hope of the divine splendour that is to be ours. More than this, let us even exult in our present sufferings." If Paul's object is to encourage the Romans to continue in the peace of God, without fear, the subjunctive would be the correct mode. We must not construe the apostle to be saying, however, "Let us *make* peace with God," but rather, "Let us keep or enjoy the peace with God which we have obtained through our Lord Jesus Christ." J. B. Phillips has given a rendering which preserves both ideas: "Let us grasp the fact that we *have* peace with God."[231] If we adopt this view, the sense is: Since we have been justified we have peace; let us therefore enjoy it. Let us never lose sight of the fact that, through the propitiatory sacrifice of Jesus Christ, we have a secure basis for our future hope. For "there is therefore now no condemnation to them which are in Christ Jesus" (8:1).

Through our Lord Jesus Christ, then, **we have peace with God. By Him also we have access by faith into this grace wherein we stand (2). By faith** (*te pistei*) is wanting in the best MSS and is omitted by RSV and NEB. **We have** (*eschekamen*) is literally "we have obtained." **Access** (*ten prosagogen*) means "our introduction." The idea is that of entrance into the presence chamber of a monarch. "The rendering 'access' is inadequate, as it leaves out of sight the fact that we do not come in our own

---

[228]Cited by Nygren, *op. cit.*, p. 194; cf. Barrett, *The Epistle to the Romans*, p. 102; ICC, "Romans," p. 120; Godet, *op. cit.*, p. 187.

[229]*Kaukometha*, "Let us rejoice" (vv. 2-3).

[230]*Op. cit.*, pp. 104-6.

[231]Italics are Phillips'.

strength but need an 'introducer'—Christ."[232] The French have a word for this: *entree*. Christ brings the justified believer into the full favor, or **grace** (*charis*) of God the Father. **This grace** means "this state of grace" of those who are in the divine favor. **We stand** translates *estekamen* and is literally "we stand fast or firm." We thus might paraphrase Paul: "It is moreover through Him also that we have gained our *entree* into this condition of divine favor where we stand firm." This thought is eloquently expanded in 8:31-39.

In view of this firm confidence, the apostle continues, Let us "rejoice in our hope of sharing the glory of God" (RSV). Calvin comments, "The reason not only for the emergence of the hope of the life to come, but also for our daring to rejoice in it, is that we rest on the sure foundations of the grace of God. Although believers are now pilgrims on earth, yet by their confidence they surmount the heavens, so that they cherish their future inheritance in their bosoms with tranquillity."[233]

"More than that," Paul goes on, "let us rejoice in our sufferings, knowing that suffering produces endurance, and endurance produces character, and character produces hope, and hope does not disappoint us, because God's love has been poured into our hearts through the Holy Spirit which has been given to us" (3-5, RSV, marg.). Since we have the hope of experiencing **the glory of God**, let us **glory in tribulations also**. Far from our being destroyed by these experiences, they should strengthen our hope. When we accept these sufferings as coming with the "all things" of 8:28, they result in **patience** (*hypomonen*), fortitude or disciplined endurance. The enduring of hardship cheerfully and patiently brings **experience**; that is, it tests and hardens character; this character in turn makes possible a more vigorous **hope** than we might otherwise have. Knox wisely cautions, however, that "it is impossible to suppose that Paul is intending to say that character is the source of our hope. That source is clearly the grace in which we stand. But the experience of tribulations properly sustained can serve to fortify the very hope they seem calculated to destroy."[234]

Returning to the main theme, Paul declares that **hope maketh not ashamed** (*ou kataischynei*), "does not prove illusory." This

---

[232]ICC, "Romans," p. 121.   [233]*Op. cit.*, p. 105.

[234]IB (Exegesis), IX, 454-55.

is a quotation of Isa. 28:16 (LXX). We are **not ashamed**—we
have no fear of being disappointed—"because God's love has been
poured into our hearts through the Holy Spirit which has been
given to us." "We hope to receive the *glory* of God, because we
have already received the *love* of God. Hope is thus more than
hope; it is hope already beginning to be realized."[235] **The love of
God** (*he agape tou theou*) is not our love for God but God's
love for us (cf. I John 4:10, 16). But this love is not simply a
fact about God which we recognize; it is the very reality of God
"poured into our hearts." Since the nature of God himself is
agape, in giving us *agape* He imparts to us something of His own
nature. Here Paul and John express themselves in almost identical language (cf. I John 4:13, 19). Dodd points out that it is at
this point that the concept of justification "enters the sphere of
moral experience."[236]

> It is interesting to note that we have here a kind of hierarchy
> of terms. The first and most important is "God's love"—also called
> "this grace" and . . . all but identified with the Holy Spirit. This
> love both manifests itself in God's act of justifying us and offers
> itself to us as the Spirit—the breath of a new life, God's own life
> imparted to us. "Faith" is our response to this love, our acceptance
> in humility and trust of what God offers us. "Peace" is the conse-
> quence of the response of faith to God's justifying act, and "hope"
> is our confident expectation that God, who has begun his good
> work in us, will complete it. Every one of these terms will appear
> again and again in the course of this part of Paul's discussion.[237]

Verse 5 shows "God's Love in Our Hearts." (1) The gift
imparted—**the love of God**; (2) The receptacle—"poured into our
hearts" (our true being); (3) The agency—**the Holy Ghost which
is given unto us** (cf. Luke 11:13; Acts 2:4).

The next three verses return to the objective meaning of
God's love. They give us the clearest possible proof that God
loves men, sinful though they are. "For God's love towards us
commends itself in this (v. 8), that Christ died for us while we
were still weak (v. 6), still sinners (v. 8), still godless (v. 6), still
enemies (v. 10). It has not waited for us, but has come to meet
us and gone before us."[238] **For when we were yet without**

---

[235]*Ibid.*, p. 455.   [236]*Op. cit.*, p. 74.

[237]IB, *loc. cit.*

[238]Karl Barth, "Christ and Adam: Man and Humanity in Romans 5"
(*Scottish Journal of Theology Occasional Papers, No. 5;* Edinburgh and
London: Oliver and Boyd, 1956), p. 2.

strength—powerless to save ourselves—**Christ died for us** (6). Our natural condition is that of moral inability; we have no **strength** in ourselves to turn and be justified. But through the cross of Christ we are given supernatural enablement to be converted. Theologians call this prevenient grace—i.e., the grace that comes before justification. The helpless sinner is further described as **ungodly** (cf. Eph. 2:12). **For scarcely for a righteous man will one die: yet peradventure for a good man some would even dare to die. But God commendeth** (*synistesin*, "sets forth" and hence "proves") **his love toward us, in that, while we were yet sinners, Christ died for us** (7-8) . . . **when we were enemies** (10). If we want to know what God's love (*agape*) is, Paul answers by pointing us to the death of Christ. Nowhere else is there a revelation of love such as we find in the Cross. There, and there alone, we discover the meaning of God's love. Again Paul's language and thought are close to John's: "Hereby perceive we the love of God, because he laid down his life for us" (I John 3:16). Through the Cross we have an aperture into the very heart of God, and we see it to be self-giving, self-sacrificing love.

Paul contrasts divine love with human love. Human love is motivated by the nature of its object—under certain conditions it may move us to die **for a good man**. Divine love is not called forth by the goodness of its object, but gives itself for **sinners**, even for its **enemies**. Divine love flows like an artesian spring from the very being of God. Its only explanation is that "God is love." It is the nature of *agape* love to pour itself out "on the evil and on the good" (see Matt. 5:43-48). It is this revelation of God as *Agape* which constitutes the uniqueness of the Christian gospel. When asked if his religion taught that God loved him, a Hindu university student answered in the affirmative. To the further question, "When does He love you?" he answered, "When I am good." The Christian message is that God loves us even in our wickedness and hostility: **God commendeth his love toward us, in that, while we were yet sinners, Christ died for us** (8). The manifestation of God's love is through a historical event—the Cross; the application of it is by the Holy Spirit (v. 5).

The fact of God's love being established, Paul returns to the main theme of the paragraph. Since God has already done so much for us, we have the expectation of final salvation. **Much more then, being now justified by his blood, we shall be saved from wrath through him** (9). We have come to the climax of the section. **Justified** recalls v. 1, with the present enjoyment of peace with God. **By his blood** is to be understood as "by means of His blood." For the thought, see comments on 3:25. **Shall be saved** points to the future. For Paul's teaching on salvation see comments on 1:16 and 13:11. Such salvation belongs essentially to the future, and the verb is here, as usual, in the future tense.[239] **Saved from wrath** refers to the final deliverance at the last judgment; such salvation is guaranteed by the fact of justification, which is an anticipation of the favorable verdict on that day. For the meaning of **wrath** see comments on 1:18 and 2:5.

The same truth is expressed differently in a descriptive parallel. **For if, when we were enemies, we were reconciled to God by the death of his Son, much more, being reconciled, we shall be saved by his life** (10). "Here it is explicitly made clear that this argument from reconciliation to salvation is logically based upon the fact that Christ has not only died but has also risen. Ahead of us lies salvation, and—since, having shared His death, we must now share His life with Him as well—we can do nothing but glory in it."[240] **Saved by his life** denotes salvation in the full and final sense—the final sense, which, with justification, assumes the restoration of holiness. The mediation **by his life** completes that begun **by his blood** and assures us of "the sanctification without which no one will see the Lord" (Heb. 12:14, NASB). Justification is thus distinct from sanctification and is indeed the gateway to it; it rests on **the death of his Son.** Sanctification flows from the **life** of Christ (Heb. 7:25) by the work of the Holy Spirit (Acts 2:33; II Thess. 2:13).[241]

Paul concludes, **And not only so, but we also joy in God** ("glory in God," Wesley) . . . **by whom we have now received the atonement** (*katallagen,* "reconciliation"; 11).[242] Christ's risen life sets a seal upon our justification effected by His death, "and because He lives, this peace, and our reconciliation, and the pouring forth of the love of God in our hearts, mark a point in our journey beyond which there is no turning back, going on from which we have only one future, and in which we can only glory"[243]—as long as we remain in Christ (cf. 11:22).

---

[239]Cf. v. 10; 9:27; 10:9, 13; 11:26; see also 13:11 and 8:24.

[240]Barth, "Christ and Adam," pp. 2-3.   [241]Cf. Godet, *op. cit.,* p. 197.

[242]At the time of the KJV **atonement** signified "reconciliation," at-one-ment.

[243]Barth, *loc. cit.*

After setting forth the *wrath of God* in the first section of
the Epistle (1:18—3:20) and the *righteousness of God* in the second (3:21—5:11), there remains nothing more than to relate
these two to their original points of departure—Adam and
Christ. This is the theme of the final paragraph of Paul's treatment of justification. He thinks of two ages. The age of Adam
is the dominion of sin and death; the age of Christ, of grace and
life. By introducing Adam and Christ the apostle is not digress-
ing; this passage is actually the high point of the Epistle, in the
light of which the whole is best understood.[244]

In vv. 6-11 our hearts are moved as we remember that "Christ
Died for Us." (1) To overcome our natural inability—**when we
were yet without strength, 6**; (2) To expiate our guilt—**while
we were yet sinners, 8**; (3) To subdue our hostility toward God—
when we were enemies, 10.

e. *The two ages: Adam and Christ* (5:12-21). The deep
certainty that in Christ we are members of God's new creation is
the underlying conviction of this crucial passage. It is essential
that we begin where Paul begins. Adam is simply **the figure**
(*typos*, type) **of him that was to come** (14; *tou mellontos*, the
coming One—the Messiah). The apostle does not move from Adam
to Christ, but from Christ to Adam. For him, this truth is so
self-evident he makes no effort to prove it by logic. Because of
his encounter with the risen Jesus he knows that "if any one is in
Christ, he is a new creation; the old has passed away, behold, the
new has come" (II Cor. 5:17, RSV). Although the old creation
has gone awry, God has made a fresh beginning in Christ.

A second Adam to the fight,
And to the rescue came.

This, for Paul, is life's deepest certainty. "The old order has
gone, and a new order has already begun" (NEB). The new age
has come upon us, and all who are in Christ have been taken out
of the dominion of death which rules Adam's race. "For He [the
Father] delivered us from the domain of darkness and transferred
us to the kingdom of His well-beloved Son" (Col. 1:13, NASB).
In His Son, He has re-created humanity (cf. 8:29). From this perspective we view all that the apostle writes in this section.

In speaking of the two ages, however, we must avoid thinking simply in terms of datable events in history. In one sense

[244]See Nygren, *op. cit.*, pp. 16-25.

the new age may be said to have begun with the death and resurrection of Jesus (ca. A.D. 30). Yet in another sense we are positing *two overlapping orders of existence.* Every person is either in Adam (by birth) or in Christ (by faith). God's justifying act removes us from the old Adamic order and places us in "the new creation" (the new race) of which Christ is the Head. In thus writing of Adam and Christ, Paul does not think of humanity as a chance gathering of individuals but as an organic unity, a single body under a single head. That head is either Christ or Adam.

Wherefore, as by one man sin entered into the world, and death by sin; and so death passed upon all men, for that all have sinned: even so by the righteousness of one the free gift came upon all men unto justification of life (12, 18b). A long parenthesis interrupts these two propositions. In it one thought after another tumbles from Paul's mind. It is difficult to establish a grammatical outline of vv. 13-18. The entire passage, however, becomes clear if we are willing to listen patiently to Paul and let him speak for himself.

Wherefore (*dia touto*) refers at least to 5:1-11 but probably reaches back to 1:18. Paul begins with a basis for a comparison, **as by one man** (Adam) **sin entered into the world** . . . Here a new term appears in Romans: *he hamartia,* "the sin." Up to this point Paul has been dealing chiefly with the problem of sin as *guilt;* now he introduces the idea of sin as *revolt.* This is indicated by the new phrase *he hamartia,* which occurs 28 times between 5:12 and 8:10.[245] In each instance it refers to "the principle of revolt whereby the human will rises against the divine will."[246] Beet comments that sin here "is not a mere act, but a living, hostile, deadly power."[247] It is almost personified. It reigns as a wicked tyrant (5:21), and taking advantage of God's commandments deceives and slays man (7:9). In 7:20 it is the "sin that dwelleth in me." From the fullest perspective *he hamartia* is sin in its entirety—a principle of revolt issuing in "many transgressions" (v. 16b, NASB). This is the sin which **entered into the world** in Eden. Adam's transgression was not something which concerned himself alone as an individual; but by his act

---

[245]5:12 (2), 20; 6:1, 2, 6 (2), 7, 10, 11, 12, 13, 17, 18, 20, 21, 22, 23; 7:7a, 9, 11, 13 (2), 14, 20, 23; 8:2, 3c. Eleven times *hamartia* is used in the same sense without the article: 5:13 (2); 6:14, 16; 7:7, 8b, 13b, 17; 8:3b (2), 10.

[246]Godet, *op. cit.,* p. 204.   [247]*Op. cit.,* p. 160.

sin was made regnant in **the world** (*eis ton kosmon*), in the human race as a whole.

And man's **death** came because of sin. Paul continues, **And so death passed upon all men, for that all have sinned** (*hemarton*, "all sinned"—Wesley, RSV, NASB). Because of Adam's disobedience "the entail of sin and death passed on to the whole human race, and no one could break it for no one was himself free from sin" (Phillips). What is the **death** (*ho thanatos*) which "spread to all men" (NASB)? Barth defines it as "the reverse side of sin." He explains by adding, "Where sin lives, death lives in sin—and we are not alive (vii. 10). Where sin reigns, it reigns in death (v. 21)—and we are dead. When sin gives orders, it pays in the currency of death (vi. 23). Sin is a bleak, lifeless, unrelated existence."[248] Paul S. Minear rightly observes that "the term death covers both the invisible alienation from God and all the visible marks of that alienation."[249] The apostle seldom refers to death as the moment a man's heart stops beating, although this tangible event is by no means excluded from the meaning (7:2-3; 8:38; 14:7). But Paul's primary concern is with the invisible state of creation to which physical death is a clue. This invisible state is *death in sin*. Sin and death are correlatives. To live in sin is living death, for one is actually a slave of death, obeying its commands (v. 17). Thus it is said that sin reigns by means of death (v. 21). But with equal force Paul can say that through sin death reigns, for the law of sin is intrinsically the law of death (7:14-24). Death is present whenever the mind of the flesh rather than the mind of the Spirit determines one's thoughts and desires (8:6-8). The apostle can say, "I died," because sin killed him through the law (7:8-12). "The act of sin embraces all the death that flows from it, and nothing flows from it but death."[250]

In the same vein Brunner declares, "When speaking of death Paul does not merely think of the physical act of dying as a natural event, so to speak, but of *corruption as a power to which human life has been forfeited*, and in connection with the wrath of God and his terrible judgment."[251] The death which follows sin is therefore (a) *physical* death, the separation of the soul from the body (II Cor. 5:8); (b) *spiritual* death, the separation of the

---

[248]*The Epistle to the Romans*, p. 170.

[249]"The Truth About Sin and Death," *Interpretation*, VII (April, 1953), 150-51.

[250]*Ibid.*   [251]*Op. cit.*, p. 44 (italics mine).

self from God by an act of disobedience (7:9); and as a final
outcome (c) *eternal* death, or the "second death" (Rev. 20:14),
the casting of both soul and body into hell (Matt. 10:28).

To recapitulate, Paul sees three things in v. 12: (1) Through
Adam's fall **sin entered into the world;** (2) as a consequence
death passed upon all men; (3) this is because **all men sinned.**
These three ideas must be kept in focus in order to grasp the
apostle's thought about sin and death. The crux of the matter
lies in the question: In what sense did all sin? (*a*) Does Paul
mean that "all sinned implicitly in the sin of Adam"? Since
Augustine, many have so understood Paul. As Levi paid tithes
in "the loins of Abraham" (Heb. 7:5, 9), so all men sinned in
Adam, "being then in the loins of their first parent, the common head and representative of them all."[252] There is no grammatical basis, however, for understanding *eph ho* to mean "in
whom," in spite of the fact that the Latin version translates this
in quo. The phrase means **for that,** or "on the ground of the fact
that." (*b*) Does the clause then mean that all men die because
they *personally* sin? Pelagius taught that all men imitate Adam's
fall and therefore die in consequence of their own sin. Even
Calvin writes, "All Adam's posterity are subject to the dominion
of death . . . because we all have sinned."[253] This idea contradicts
the very aim of the entire passage, which is to make the death of
all rest on Adam, even as the righteousness of all rests on Christ.
It has the further disadvantage of introducing the idea of personal responsibility in an argument which aims at emphasizing
the corporate nature of human sin. (*c*) Or does Paul mean that
all men sinned in Adam in the sense that Adam's transgression
had *consequences* which extend to the whole of mankind? This
appears to be the apostle's meaning.

In reality the first and the last views amount to much the
same idea if we are careful not to admit the Augustinian notion
of *imputed guilt,* which v. 13 denies. Men, after Adam, have
sinned, but under such conditions their sin was *not* imputed. *Thus
death strikes all men, but not guilt.*

Paul's thought moves within the framework of the OT concept of *solidarity.* Adam was more than an individual, the first
man; he was what his name meant in Hebrew—"mankind" (Gen.

---

[252]Wesley, *Explanatory Notes upon the New Testament,* p. 539.

[253]*Op. cit.,* p. 111; Barrett, *The Epistle to the Romans,* p. 111; and Knox,
IB, IX, 463.

5:1-2).[254] The whole of mankind is viewed as having at first existed in Adam. Because of his sin, however, Adam is seen as *mankind in alienation from God.* In the account of the Fall in Genesis 3 "all subsequent human history lies encapsuled"; its incidents are reenacted in the history of the race and indeed, to an extent, in each member of the race.[255] Because of Adam's sin **death** has spread to the whole race. As a consequence of the first man's disobedience the entire race has been corrupted. This corruption consists of men's being born out of true relation with God and condemned constantly to worsen their relationship. Elsewhere the apostle speaks of men as "having the understanding darkened, being alienated from the life of God through the ignorance that is in them, because of the blindness of their heart" (Eph. 4:18; cf. 1:18-25). The consequence of this alienation is that they are "corrupt according to the deceitful lusts" (Eph. 4:22).

As a result of his fall from divine grace, man is cursed with an infinite craving. He is *depraved* because he has been *deprived* of the sanctifying control of the Holy Spirit.[256] Whereas man's life was originally God-centered, and hence ordered and fulfilled, it is now self-centered, therefore disordered and frustrated. He *inherits* a situation of **death**—moral bankruptcy, weakness, and corruption (cf. v. 6). Sin thus lurks in wait for each new human being. Man is born free; sin is not a theoretical necessity. Practically, however, because he is a creature of "flesh," he is

---

[254]Sometimes the term "corporate personality" is employed to describe this concept. A new corporate personality is created "in Christ" (12:5; I Cor. 12:12; Eph. 1:22-23). By His death and resurrection and by the gift of the Holy Spirit, Christ now operates through "the church, which is his body." The reverse of this is found in the OT. In Isaiah 53 the Servant of the Lord, which originally was the entire nation (Isa. 44:1-2, etc.), is narrowed down to one Individual, the ideal Israel, who embodies the nation and carries out the mission of salvation which was Israel's destiny. Jesus was this "Israel encapsuled" (cf. Hosea 11 and Matt. 2:15).

[255]Bruce, *The Epistle of Paul to the Romans*, p. 126.

[256]This appears to be what Jesus meant when, in speaking of the necessity of the new birth, He said, "That which is born of the flesh is flesh" (John 3:6). In Adam man is "flesh"—i.e., he is minus the Spirit and therefore cut off from spiritual reality. This same idea is found in I Cor. 2:14, where the apostle writes of the "natural" (*psychikos*, "unspiritual," RSV) man—i.e., the man with "body" (*soma*) and "soul" (*psyche*) but without "spirit" (*pneuma*). Being cut off from a life-giving relationship with God equals being deprived of the Holy Spirit. The "last Adam," however, was a Man of the Spirit (cf. Luke 1:35) and is therefore "a quickening spirit" (I Cor. 15:45).

"weak" in the face of temptation (8:3a); sin is therefore inevitable. The more heroically he fights to throw off the tyranny of sin (7:14-23), the more pathetic his cry, "O wretched man that I am! who shall deliver me from the body of this death?" (7:24) Clearly, Paul's thought is more than speculative when he declares that "all . . . sinned" in Adam. In the profound depths of our being each of us knows that he is Adam. Our only hope is a new beginning.

A biblical doctrine of sin must recognize both the racial and the individual aspects of sin. The Hebrews had a proverb which ran, "The fathers have eaten a sour grape, and the children's teeth are set on edge." In repudiating this ancient saying both Jeremiah (31:29-30) and Ezekiel (18:1-4) were asserting the truth of personal responsibility for wrongdoing. In declaring, "The soul that sinneth, it shall die" (Ezek. 18:4), they were laying aside the primitive doctrine of the solidarity of *guilt* (cf. Joshua 7). This clear prophetic insight is our Christian heritage, and must safeguard any doctrine of racial solidarity against the doctrine of imputed guilt.[257] No man is guilty for Adam's sin; guilt and spiritual death attach only to personal transgression (7:9). Although **death** reigns as a consequence of the Fall (v. 17), it gains power over the individual only on account of his own transgression. Both truths are implied in 7:9—Paul "died" at the moment when "sin" (the indwelling sin of 7:20) became alive at the "coming" of the commandment. *Man sins because he is a sinner at heart.* A full-orbed theology of sin must revolve around the two foci of racial solidarity and personal responsibility.

Now comes Paul's extended parenthesis (vv. 13-17). He feels that his doctrine of racial solidarity in sin and death needs qualification, and this he proceeds to give in vv. 13-14. **For until the law sin was in the world: but sin is not imputed** (*ellogeitai*, "put to the account so as to bring penalty") **when there is no law** (13). Before Moses *hamartia* was in the world but not **transgression** (*parabasis*, "offense," NASB, 14). "For where no law is, there is no transgression" (*parabasis*, 4:15). We must carefully distinguish between *hamartia*, sin in general, and the other words Paul uses in this chapter. In addition to Adam's **transgression** (*parabasis*) he speaks of his **offence** (*paraptoma*; "trespass," RSV; "wrongdoing," NEB; 15-18) and his **disobedience** (*para-*

---

[257]Augustinian thought sees every man as *guilty* of Adam's sin, and this guilt as removed by baptism.

koe, 19). The NEB paraphrases Paul's use of *parabasis* by understanding him to say: "But death held sway from Adam to Moses, even over those who had not sinned as Adam did, *by disobeying a direct command*" (14). Although the heirs of Adam were not in the same situation with Adam (who sinned by violating an express command of God), they were still subject to death. **Death reigned** like a cruel tyrant because men sinned against the light of creation (1:20-21) and conscience (2:14-15). Since they had no objective law, however, the penalty on their sin was mitigated.[258] For a discussion of the last phrase of 14 see the introductory remarks which precede the exegesis of the passage, p. 113.

Up to this point Paul has showed the agreement between Adam and Christ; beginning in v. 15 he will show the differences between them. Wesley summarizes the agreement well:

> As by one man sin entered into the world, and death by sin; so by one man righteousness entered into the world, and life by righteousness. As death passed upon all men, in that all had sinned; so life passed upon all men (who are in the second Adam by faith), in that they are justified. And as death through the sin of the first Adam "reigned even over them who had not sinned after the likeness of Adam's transgression"; so through the righteousness of Christ, even those who have not obeyed, after the likeness of His obedience, shall reign in life. We may add, As the sin of Adam, without the sins which we afterwards committed, brought us death; so the righteousness of Christ, without the good works which we afterwards perform, brings us life.[259]

Now comes the contrast between Adam and Christ. The TEV gives the meaning thus: "But the two are not the same; for the free gift of God is not like Adam's sin." Paul contrasts **the offence** (15; *to paraptoma*) with **the free gift** (*to charisma*). Over against "the act of sin" (committed by Adam) stands "the act of grace" (performed by Christ). *Paraptoma* is literally "a slip or fall sideways," "a false step," "a lapse." It is appropriate that it should be used to refer to Adam's fall. *Paraptoma* describes an actualization of sin, just as *charisma* expresses an actualization

---

[258]Although the expression **from Adam to Moses** is primarily chronological, it is not strictly so. It should be given a logical sense also, alluding to categories of men in various situations. Paul is thinking theologically rather than historically; he is explaining man to himself; he is not describing merely man's past (Leenhardt, *op. cit.*, fn., p. 146).

[259]*Explanatory Notes upon the New Testament*, p. 538.

of grace (*charis*). "The two words stand in rhetorically effective juxtaposition."[260]

These two expressions, however, do not correspond to exact equivalents. "The act of grace does not balance the act of sin; it overbalances it."[261] Furthermore, Adam was a man who disobeyed God. Jesus was a Man who obeyed God, but His act was more than merely human obedience: *it was also an act of the grace of God.* **For if through the offence of one** (*tou enos*, "the one") **many** (*hoi polloi*, "the many") **be dead, much more the grace of God, and the gift by grace, which is by one man** (*tou enos anthropou*, "the one man"), **Jesus Christ, hath abounded unto many** (*eis tous pollous*, "unto the many"). "The many" who have perished because of the fall of "the one" can hardly be other than the **all men** of v. 12 (cf. I Cor. 15:22). This inclusive use of **many** is Hebraic. In the OT "many" often means "many contrasted with one or some" rather than "many contrasted with all." The effects of the Fall are *universal*. Adam's act, then, though the act of **one man**, resulted in the death of all men. Over against this, what Christ did, and the benefits it brought to mankind, can be introduced only by means of a **much more**, since these come from **the grace of God.** In a second attempt to show the actualization of that grace Paul adds the phrase **the gift by grace.** This grace, like death, is also for "the many," i.e., **all men** (cf. v. 18). It is unfortunate that the KJV ignores the article in these expressions. Paul means that the effects of redemption, like those of the Fall, are universal. Sanday and Headlam add: "to 'all,' that is potentially, if they embrace the redemption that is offered them."[262] Barrett observes that "it would be as wrong to deduce from these passages a rigid universalism as to suppose that they meant 'many and therefore not all'. The main point is that, like Adam, Christ is the progenitor of a race; only the blessings which the members of the new race derive through their Founder are far greater than the curse which Adam handed down to his children."[263]

In v. 16 we read, **And not as it was by one** (*hoi enos*, the one) **that sinned, so is the gift: for the judgment** (*to krima*, the judicial sentence) **was by one to condemnation** (*katakrima*, a condemnatory sentence), **but the free gift is of many offences unto**

---

[260]Barrett, *The Epistle to the Romans*, p. 113.   [261]*Ibid.*

[262]ICC, "Romans," p. 140.   [263]*The Epistle to the Romans*, p. 114.

justification (*dikaioma*, used here to rhyme with *katakrima*). There is no question about what Paul means. **Condemnation** and **justification** stand in opposition to each other; each is a verdict pronounced in a court of law. "After the one sin came the judgment of 'Guilty'; but after so many sins comes the undeserved gift of 'Not guilty!' " (TEV)

A third time the apostle stresses the contrast between Adam and Christ. **For if by one man's offence death reigned by one; much more they which receive abundance of grace and of the gift of righteousness shall reign in life by one, Jesus Christ** (17). The **abundance of grace** here means that grace more than undoes the ravages of sin (cf. v. 20). Through the excess of grace and the gift of righteousness the redeemed **shall reign** (*basileusousi*) **in life by** . . . **Jesus Christ.** "A new, holy, inexhaustible, and victorious vitality will pervade those receivers of righteousness, and make them so many kings. If the collective condemnation could make each of them subject to death, the conclusion therefrom should be that their individual justification will make each of them a king in life."[264]

Having now brought out the contrast between Adam and Christ, Paul changes his language for the moment and speaks of Christ as obedient Man, the true counterpart of Adam, the disobedient man. **Therefore as by the offence of one judgment came upon all men to condemnation; even so by the righteousness of one the free gift came upon all men unto justification of life** (18). The **righteousness** of Christ here is *dikaiomatos* and should be translated "act of righteousness" (NASB). Again, it is used for purposes of rhetoric; Paul needs the word *dikaiomotos* to balance with *paraptomatos*, "act of transgression." **Justification of life** means that only justification leads to life. "Paul never attempts to by-pass this step. Man must be found righteous in God's court, even though it be by the grace of the Judge."[265] **All men** corresponds to "the many" of v. 15, but this verse is so worded that it is impossible to construct from it a theory of limited atonement (cf. I Tim. 2:3-6). Paul here declares that **condemnation** and **justification** are universal possibilities. Probably the best commentary on v. 18 is found in Paul's own words later in the Epistle: "For God has shut up all in disobedience that He might show mercy to all" (11:32, NASB).

---

[264]Godet, *op. cit.*, p. 223.   [265]Barrett, *The Epistle to the Romans*, p. 116.

In v. 19 the apostle restates his position once again, in the clearest antithesis of all. **For as by one man's disobedience many were made sinners, so by the obedience of one shall many be made righteous.** Through Adam's act of **disobedience** "the many" were **made** (*katestathesan,* constituted) **sinners**; through Christ's act of **obedience** "the many" were **made** (*katastathesontai,* constituted) **righteous.** The same verb is used in Acts 7:27, "Who made thee a ruler and a judge over us?" In what sense did Adam's sin make men sinners? In what sense did Christ's obedience make us righteous? The Greek word has the same ambiguity as the English. Most interpreters see these as words of relationship rather than character. Adam's sin meant that all men were born into a race which is in revolt against God. Similarly, Christ's obedience made possible a new life-giving relationship with God. By implication, however, the ethical fruitage of these relationships is certainly brought into view. Leenhardt thus writes: "It will be noted that Christ's obedience of which our text speaks becomes also the believer's obedience, an obedience which leads to the practice of righteousness (*hypakoes eis dikaiosunen,* 6:16. . . . Christ creates a humanity of righteous men, just as Adam had created a humanity of sinners."[266]

Up to this point Paul has spoken of Adam and Christ as though there were no intervening stage in religious history. But this is to overlook a most significant event—the giving of the law (cf. v. 14). How does the law fit into the divine scheme? Paul's reply is that **the law entered** (*pareiselthen,* came in beside), **that the offence might abound** (20). Moffatt translates, "Law slipped in to aggravate the trespass." Barrett says the idea is, "The law took its subordinate place." The thought seems to be that the law came in beside what was already in position; and consequently the law is inferior to the great events with which Paul has been dealing, the fall of Adam and the redemption of Christ. Yet the law's intrusion was not without divine point—it was in-

[266]*Op. cit.,* p. 148. "Paul is thoroughly realist in his thinking here," Dodd insists. "The problem of evil is indeed something which goes beyond questions of individual responsibility, and salvation is more than a device of freeing an individual from his guilt: it must cut at the root of that corporate wrongness which underlies individual transgression. This is, according to Paul, what has actually been effected by the work of Christ. In Him men are lifted into a new order in which goodness is as powerful and dominant as was sin in the order represented by Adam; or, rather, it is far more powerful and dominant" (*op. cit.,* p. 82).

troduced to increase consciousness of wrongdoing (cf. Gal. 3:19). Men will never see their sin or feel their need of a Saviour until their sin becomes transgression (cf. 4:15). The law, said Irenaeus, is a poultice to bring sin to a head. It is therefore a precursor to grace. The accentuation of the trespass is answered by overflowing grace. For **where sin abounded, grace did much more abound.**

Three times we have encountered the significant phrase **much more** (vv. 15, 17, 20). Christ by His death has **much more** than reversed the effects of the Fall. "The benefits received from Christ, the Second Adam, are in *inverse ratio* to the disaster entailed by the first Adam."[267] Christ offers all men free pardon for all sins. But even more is promised in the gift of God's superabounding grace. In Christ we are re-created, and in God's new creation the sin which was introduced by Adam is expelled. When Christ died, the old race "in Adam" died; when He arose, the new race arose with Him. By our identification with Christ we die and rise with Him—and this means precisely death to sin (*he hamartia,* "the sin" which entered the world with Adam's defection; 6:1-14). Christ's death was thus the doom of sin (8:3), the provisional freeing of men from "the law of sin and death" in order that they may fulfill the law of God in the power of the indwelling Spirit of Christ (8:1-9). The next three chapters explore the riches of this truth, that where sin has abounded, grace may superabound. Unless the death of Christ makes for the full deliverance from indwelling sin, Adam did something to man which Christ cannot undo. Then what becomes of God's superabounding grace? Paul's answer is: "But now being made *free from sin,* and become servants to God, ye have your fruit unto holiness, and the end everlasting life" (6:22).

The discussion of Adam and Christ is thus the great divide of the Epistle from which we can look back over the glorious truth of justification by grace through faith. We can also look ahead to the promise of full sanctification and eternal life (6:1—8:17), and to the final redemption from the bodily effects of sin (8:18-39). This passage is therefore a transition section, the full implications of which are set forth in its final clause: **That as sin hath reigned unto death** (*en to thanato,* "in death" or "by means of death"), **even so might grace reign through righteous-**

---

[267]Mabie; quotation in Thomas, *op. cit.,* p. 159.

ness (*dia dikaiosynes,* "through" righteousness) **unto eternal life
by Jesus Christ our Lord** (21). Calvin observes, "As sin is said
to be the sting of death, because death has no power over men
except on account of sin, so sin executes its power by death. It
is therefore said to exercise its dominion by death."[268] The last
clause presents us with an inexact parallel, but it is a divine in-
exactitude. "If Paul had said 'in order that righteousness may
reign by Christ', his contrast would have been straightforward.
He was not, however, content to compare opposites, and adds
the word **grace,** so that he may more deeply imprint upon our
memory the truth that the whole of our righteousness does not
proceed from our own merit, but from the divine kindness."[269]
As **sin** has reigned by means of **death,** the moral weakness and
corruption which flows from the Fall, **grace** now is seeking to
establish its beautiful reign **through righteousness unto eternal
life through Jesus Christ our Lord.** "Here is pointed out the
source of all our blessings," notes Wesley, "the rich and free
grace of God. The meritorious cause: not any works of righteousness of man, but the alone merits of our Lord Jesus Christ.
The effect or end of it all: not only pardon, but life—divine life,
leading to glory."[270] It is all **through Jesus Christ our Lord.**
"And now—so this last word seems to say—Adam has passed
away; Christ alone remains."[271]

2. The Gospel of Man's Sanctification (6:1—8:39)

"Holiness and Freedom from Sin" is the subject of c. 6.
(1) The problem, 1-2; (2) The promise, 3-4; (3) The provision,
5-7; (4) The purpose, 8-10; (5) The possession, 11-14; (6) The
product, 15-19; (7) The prospect, 20-23 (W. T. Purkiser).

How does Christ bring about the new humanity which is
freed from sin? How is the universality of sin and death in Adam
replaced by the unity of the new race in Christ leading to righteousness and eternal life? If the law was not given to promote
righteousness, then what is its role? What is God's method of
setting men free from "the law of sin and death"?

Paul's underlying position is that the man who is righteous
before God through faith is also a man who has been sanctified

---

[268]*Op. cit.,* p. 120.   [269]*Ibid.*
[270]*Explanatory Notes upon the New Testament,* p. 539.
[271]Godet, *op. cit.,* p. 229.

by God.[272] The converted man has a *new existence* in Christ.
Freed from the dominion of sin through his union with the dying-
rising Saviour, he may rise to the heights of holiness through
faith and the dedication of his total self to God (6:1-14). This
new existence is also a *new order* to be respected obediently.
As he formerly abandoned himself to iniquity unto iniquity, the
new man in Christ must now abandon himself in a total obedience of righteousness. The end of this new order is sanctification
in the highest sense, issuing in eternal life (6:15-23). Death to
sin has its counterpart in death to the law as a means of salvation, for under the law man is united to sin. Man under the law
is man in the flesh (7:1-6). This, however, must not be construed to mean that the law *per se* is sinful. The law points up
man's obligation to God, but *sin* has turned God's holy and just
law into a "law of sin and death." When the commandment comes
home to man's conscience, sin springs to life, and man dies. The
law thus turns out to be God's means of showing up the exceeding
sinfulness of sin (7:7-13). The law makes claim upon man's
total devotion, but man is carnal. Because of indwelling sin, he
is spiritually impotent. The more he struggles in himself to
please God, the more pathetic his existence (7:14-25). But what
man could never do for himself God has done for him in Christ.
Sending His Son "in the likeness of sinful flesh, and for sin" God
has *doomed* sin in the flesh, so that the just requirement of the
law might be fulfilled in the man who trusts Christ and "walks
not after the flesh, but after the Spirit." In the Spirit, outpoured
in His Pentecostal fullness (cf. 5:5), man has deliverance, guidance, assurance, help, and the hope of final redemption (8:1-27).

Such is Paul's gospel of man's sanctification. God justifies
man in order that He might sanctify him. In this section of
Romans we discover the vital connection between the two grand
aspects of salvation, justification and sanctification. "Justification
by faith is the *means*," Godet rightly observes, "and sanctification
the *end*. The more precisely we distinguish between these two
divine gifts, the better we apprehend the bond which unites
them."[273] Justification is the basic reality upon which the Christian life rests. It means that the believer, through faith in Christ,
has received the new righteousness which comes from God. Sanctification properly describes the total work of the Spirit in trans-

[272]Barth, *A Shorter Commentary on Romans*, pp. 64-65.
[273]*Op. cit.*, p. 233.

forming the believer into the image of God's Son. It begins in justification, continues as growth in grace, and is made "entire" in a second crisis—after which, in what Daniel Steele called "the Wesleyan paradox," there is continued growth. As God continues to justify, sanctification proceeds, extending to the entire area of man's existence.[274]

a. *Sanctification through death to sin* (6:1-23). The closing part of c. 5—which places sin, law, and grace in juxtaposition—raises acutely a question to which Paul has already alluded in 3:7-8: "Why not indeed 'do evil that good may come,' as some libellously report me as saying?" (NEB) If justification is by faith, apart from the deeds of the law; if the law (which commands a life of virtue) serves only the purpose of bringing sin to a head; and if, when sin abounds, grace much more abounds—why should Christians strive against sin? Why not sin wholeheartedly, that grace might superabound? The fact that Paul deals at such length with this question shows how seriously his doctrine of free grace must be taken. In 3:5-8 he dealt with the question from Jewish premises: God is Judge, and the Judge of all the earth will do right. Now he feels he must give a Christian answer. Once again he resorts to the style of the diatribe (see comments on 2:1). Doubtless he is answering antinomians in some of his churches who drew the inference that sin might be indulged to the full, and also replying to adversaries who alleged that this was the logical outcome of the Pauline gospel.[275]

This dilemma presents a genuine difficulty. In times of religious revival, when fresh emphasis has been placed upon the free grace of God, there has appeared the sinister by-product of fanatical antinomianism; both Luther and Wesley had to cope with such fanaticism. Much more commonly this antinomian tendency takes the form of "a complacent acquiescence in a low or narrow moral standard combined with warm religious emotion."[276]

[274]Wesley writes: *"Justification* . . . is not the being made actually just and righteous. This is *sanctification,* which is, indeed, in some degree, the immediate fruit of justification, but nevertheless, is a distinct gift of God, and of a totally different nature. The one implies what God does for us through His Son; the other, what He works in us by His Spirit" (Sermons, I, *The Works of John Wesley* [Kansas City: Nazarene Publishing House, n.d.], V, 56).

[275]Barrett, *The Epistle to the Romans,* pp. 120-21.   [276]Dodd, *op. cit.,* p. 84.

(1) *Dying with Christ to sin* (6:1-14). In v. 1, Paul asks, What conclusions shall we draw from my preceding position? **What shall we say then? Shall we continue in sin, that grace may abound?** His object is not to draw logical consequences from his previous teaching but to reject the false inference of antinomianism. "Are we to continue [*epimenomen,* present subjunctive] in sin [*te hamartia,* the sin] that grace might increase?" (NASB) Are we to be hospitable to the sin which has reigned since Adam's fall? Are we to give this sin a home? Shall we who have been justified continue in the same relationship with "the sin" which we had before we came to Christ? Shall we continue to yield to sin and live under its dominion? Shall we sustain an attitude of cordiality with sin in order that grace may abound?[277]

The answer is a resounding **God forbid** (*me genoito,* "By no means!" RSV). **How shall we that are dead to sin** (*apethanomen te hamartia,* aorist tense—"who died to sin," NASB, RSV) **live any longer therein?** (2) Barrett reminds us that the specialized form of the pronoun *hoitines* (pronoun of quality—"people such as we") gives the sense. "We cannot as Christians go on living in sin because as Christians we have died to sin; as far as sin is concerned we are dead. The definite past tense, 'we died', points to a particular moment; conversion and (as the next verse shows) baptism must be in mind."[278]

Paul now rises above the narrow confines of human logic and opens his argument that "the nature of man's moral problems becomes clear only when you lift his life into the light of God's purpose as it has been unfolded in the great drama of Christ's death and resurrection."[279] From that perspective we can draw certain inferences as to the nature of our true life. This is logic also, but of a wider and more inclusive kind than that which prompted the question. "The passage also emphasizes one of those simple distinctions which constitute the foundation of

[277]See Kenneth S. Wuest, *Romans in the Greek New Testament* (Grand Rapids: Wm. B. Eerdmans Publishing Co., 1955), pp. 91-93. "The fundamental question," says Wuest, "is not with regard to acts of sin but with respect to the believer's relationship to the sinful nature." In v. 15, Paul raises the question of *acts* of sin in the Christian life. In fact the two questions (in vv. 1 and 15) divide the chapter into its two parts.

[278]*The Epistle to the Romans,* p. 121.

[279]Gerald R. Cragg (Exposition), IB, IX, 471-72.

all morality. 'How can we who died to sin still live in it?' There is a fundamental incompatibility between certain things, and it is as insurmountable as the difference between death and life. . . . 'To live' and 'to die' cannot be reconciled."[280] There is only one possible interpretation of Paul's words. The justified believer has been "justified from sin" (see v. 7). He is no longer tyrannized by the spirit of revolt which has plagued the race since Adam fell. Sin no longer "reigns" in his body. Barth asks: "What is forgiveness of sins (however we understand it) if it is not directly accompanied by an actual liberation from the committal of sin? . . . What is faith without obedience?"[281]

The ground for the position Paul is about to advance has already been laid in 5:12-21. "Adam was the head of the old humanity in and over which sin has won its victory and established its control; Christ is the head of the new humanity—the new man—from which sin has been excluded in shameful defeat."[282] "For as in Adam all die, even so in Christ shall all be made alive" (I Cor. 15:22). This verse gives the clue to "at least half" [283] the instances where Paul uses the phrase "in Christ." "To be 'in Christ' is to be incorporated in the newly created humanity, the new supernatural community or order of relationships, the new 'body', which has come into existence through and around Christ. The essential fact about the believer is that he is no longer 'in Adam'; he is 'in Christ.' He is no longer a 'natural man'; he is a "spiritual man.' "[284] It is to understand that the incarnate Son existed in two capacities—in His own person, and as the Representative and Head of the new humanity. Every act He wrought was performed on behalf of the new humanity which He bore in His body (cf. 8:2-4). Dietrich Bonhoeffer insists, "It is impossible to become a new man as a solitary individual. The new man means more than the individual believer after he has been justified and sanctified. It means the Church, the Body of Christ,[285] in fact it means Christ himself."[286] Our sanctifica-

---

[280]*Ibid.*, p. 472.

[281]*Church Dogmatics* (Naperville, Ill., Alec R. Allenson, Inc., 1958), IV, part 2, 505.

[282]Knox (Exegesis) IB, IX, 472.   [283]*Ibid.*, p. 473.

[284]*Ibid.*   [285]*See* Eph. 1:22-23.

[286]*The Cost of Discipleship* (New York: The Macmillan Co., 1963), p. 271. See pp. 263-76 for a penetrating analysis of the Pauline doctrine of the body of Christ.

tion is thus in Christ, in both His person (I Cor. 1:30) and in His body (Col. 2:9-12). In dying and rising with Him we are liberated from sin and become united with Him in a relationship where we may receive the Holy Spirit in Pentecostal plenitude. This is the line of truth the apostle takes in vv. 3-14.

Know ye not, that so many of us (*hosoi*, pronoun of quantity —"as many individuals as," in contrast to *hoitines* in v. 2) **as were baptized into Christ were baptized into his death?** (3) The clue to Paul's meaning of being **baptized into Christ** is furnished in I Cor. 10:1-2, where he writes of "our fathers" being "all baptized into Moses in the cloud and in the sea."[287] The same formula is applicable both to Moses and to Jesus Christ (*eis ton moysen ebaptisanto* and *ebaptisthemen eis christon iesoun*). Paul can say the children of Israel were "baptized into Moses" because he is in agreement with Stephen's sentiment that Moses was "a ruler and a deliverer" (*archonta kai lytroten*, Acts 7:35). The implications of this expression will be understood if it is compared with a formula by which Jesus himself is designated: "a Prince and a Saviour" (*archegon kai sotera*, Acts 5:31). Moses' role was of great importance and it is clear why Paul can speak of the baptism of the Israelites into him, i.e., into union with him. "Baptism in an archetypal sense is here present because the natural elements (cloud and sea) have sealed the unity of the people and their leader, enabling the people to appropriate the benefits of that saving work which God had undertaken in calling Moses: the people were virtually saved by Moses alone; Moses in his person summed up and was engaged in fulfilling the plan of God; it was necessary and it was enough for men to be united with him in order to become integrated with the movement of salvation which the prophet thrust into the historical process."[288] In the same way, except in a more profound and real sense, the person of Christ *recapitulates* the new man whom God wishes to raise up; in the thought of God He gathers into His own person all those who will be united with Him in order to share in His saving work. It is thus He initiates the new humanity, "the church, which is his body" (Eph. 1:22-23).

But to be **baptized into Jesus Christ** is to be **baptized into**

---

[287]This provides a further clue as to our relationship to sin as introduced into the race by Adam. The spiritual nature of sin and holiness is strengthened in this way.

[288]Leenhardt, *op. cit.*, p. 153.

his death. The best commentary on this latter phrase is v. 10a. When Christ died, He died to sin, once for all. His death was a complete severance from His contact with sin. Our baptism is a sign and seal of our death to sin, of our severance from the dominion of sin. We must be extremely careful here not to drag back into Paul's teaching any idea of sacramental grace, which he has already repudiated in principle (see 4:9-11 with comments). In point of fact, Paul safeguards his position against sacramentarianism by distinguishing the believer's death from his resurrection with Christ. The latter he handles cautiously, referring to it in the subjunctive mood or future tense (vv. 4-5, 8). "There is no sacramental *opus operatum* by means of which Christians can assure themselves, independently of faith and their own moral seriousness, that they have risen from death to enjoy the life of the Age to Come."[289]

On the other hand, Paul addresses the entire Roman church as a congregation of baptized believers (3a). Such was every NT congregation; there were simply no unbaptized Christians except for the catechumens who were in process of preparation for church membership. "Nor would it have been natural for Paul or any contemporary to consider the question whether faith without baptism made a man a member of Christ's Body, while the case of a person seeking baptism without faith (however rudimentary) would have seemed too abnormal to deserve notice."[290] Nevertheless, a doctrine of justification by grace through faith necessitates a distinction between initiation into the *spiritual* body of Christ (I Cor. 12:13) and identification with the *visible* body through baptism. This distinction seems to be required by the next sentence: **Therefore we are buried with him by baptism into death** (4). *Burial presupposes that death has already occurred.* Baptism dramatizes and makes objective the death to sin which has already occurred at the Cross. We therefore agree with Dodd that Paul "is not, in the present passage, expounding the nature of a sacrament as such, but exploiting the accepted significance of the sacrament for a pedagogical purpose—to bring home to the imagination a truth deeply rooted in experience, but difficult to put into purely intellectual terms."[291]

[289]Barrett, *The Epistle to the Romans*, p. 123.

[290]Dodd, *op. cit.*, p. 86.

[291]*Ibid.*, p. 87.

In v. 4 we read, **Therefore we are buried with him by baptism into death: that like as Christ was raised up from the dead by the glory of the Father, even so we also should walk in newness of life.** Godet understands Paul to be saying: " 'In consequence of this death to sin undergone in Christ, we have therefore been buried with Him . . . in order also to rise with Him,' which signifies: 'buried with Him, not with the aim of remaining in the tomb or issuing from it to return to the past life, but to penetrate into a new life, whence a return to the old is definitely precluded.' "[292] The **death** into which we are baptized is at once *His*, and *ours* included in His. This **baptism into death** is *in order that* (*hina*) we should be resurrected with Him to **walk in newness of life** (*en kainoteti zoes*). Vincent sees this as "a stronger expression than *new life*. It gives more prominence to the main idea, *newness*, than would be given by the adjective."[293] **Newness of life** follows burial with Christ, just as Christ's resurrection followed His burial; in both cases a mighty act of God is presupposed. In reality it is but one act, for the believer is indissolubly linked with Christ. This mighty act is **by the glory of the Father.** The word **glory** is an eschatological term (2:7, 10; 5:2; 8:17, 21). The Resurrection ushered in the time of fulfillment, the new age (cf. John 5:25; Eph. 2:1-7).

For if we have been planted together (*symphytoi gegonamen,* "united with Him," NASB, RSV; "become incorporate with him," NEB) **in the likeness of his death, we shall be also in the likeness of his resurrection** (5). The Greek omits the second phrase **in the likeness.** The verse therefore reads literally, "For if we have become united with Him in the likeness of His death, we shall also be of His resurrection." By baptism we imitate His death, or rather, dramatize our death to sin with Him. "Well, then," says Paul, "we shall be partakers also of His resurrection!" Our death is *like* His; our resurrection *is* His. It is His very life that He conveys to us by the Spirit when we rise with Him in **newness of life.**[294] "I have been crucified with Christ; it is no longer I who live, but Christ who lives in me" (Gal. 2:20, RSV). Phillips

[292]*Op. cit., p. 240.*

[293]*Op. cit., p. 67.*

[294]In the Early Church, baptism was related to the second epoch in Christian experience, when the believer received the Holy Spirit; yet the two events, while closely related, were not identical, as the varied patterns recounted in Acts show (see Acts 8:12, 14-17; 9:17-18; 10:44-48; 9:1-6).

has captured Paul's thought: "If we have, as it were, shared his death, let us rise and live our new lives with him!"

The use of the future tense in 5*b* is noteworthy: **We shall be . . . of his resurrection.** Is Paul speaking of the future resurrection, the bodily glorification of believers? That this is on the horizon of his thinking can hardly be doubted (cf. 8:17-23), but this is not his immediate concern. Paul is speaking here of the present participation of the believer in the life of the risen Lord. In v. 11 he makes another allusion to the new life of the believer which cannot be understood except on the basis of his sharing the life of the risen Christ.[295] "The expression, therefore, denotes only sanctification, the believer's moral resurrection. . . . We begin with union to the person of Christ by faith in that mysterious *He for me,* which forms the substance of the gospel; then this union goes forward until His whole being as the Risen One has passed *into* us."[296]

In v. 6, Paul introduces the idea of *subjective knowledge:* **Knowing this** (*touto ginoskontes*). Again in v. 9 we encounter **knowing that** (*eidotes*), and in v. 11 the verb *reckon* (*logizesthe*). The insertion of this thought is crucial to Paul's teaching; it underscores the moral significance of **we shall be** (5*b*). "Our participation in Christ's resurrection does not take place in the way of a physical and natural process. That such a result may take place, there is needed a moral cooperation on the part of the believer."[297] This moral cooperation of course presupposes a knowledge of the way and the end (v. 8) of our sanctification. **Knowing this, that our old man is crucified with him, that the body of sin might be destroyed, that henceforth we should not serve sin** (6). "The believer understands that the final object which God has in view in crucifying his old man (ver. 6) is to realize in him the life of the Risen One (vv. 8, 9), and he enters actively into the divine thought. Thereby only can this be realized."[298]

We have now come to the culmination of Paul's argument. All that has been said thus far is intended to show that the inheritance bequeathed by Adam has been provisionally counteracted in the death of the Cross, so that a new humanity might begin flowing from the risen Lord. When Christ died, it was the crucifixion of the old race in Adam. As the Son of Man, Jesus

---

[295]Leenhardt, *op. cit.*, p. 161.   [296]Godet, *op. cit.*, p. 245.
[297]Gess; quoted by Godet, *ibid.*   [298]*Ibid.*

became a Denizen of the flesh (cf. 8:3); He identified himself
with the sons of Adam absolutely, sin only excepted (Heb. 4:15).
Jesus became one with humanity, identifying himself with mankind, redeeming humanity by His entrance into it, and through
His life and death condemning and ending (potentially) sin in
humanity. When Christ died, it was therefore the death of the
old Adam. Our old man, says Godet, denotes "human nature as it
has been made by the sin of him in whom originally it was wholly
concentrated, fallen Adam reappearing in every human *ego* that
comes into the world under the sway of the preponderance of
self-love, which was determined by the primitive transgression."[299] Leenhardt comments, "This old man, this decadent
being is ourselves considered in our status as sons of Adam."[300]
It is old in the sense that it belongs to the old aeon which passed
away with Christ's death, and in contrast with the new man which
emerged with His resurrection. "This old man has been crucified
so far as the believer is concerned in the very person of Christ
crucified."[301]

Barrett writes: "The interpretation which commends itself
by its simplicity is that the 'old man' is the nature of the unconverted man, which upon conversion and baptism is replaced by a
new nature, the 'new man.' But careful reading of Col. iii, and of
the present passage, makes this interpretation impossible. In
Colossians it is Christians who are told to put off the old man,
and to put on the new. Here in Romans Christians are told that
they must *consider* themselves to be dead to sin and alive to God
(v. 11). It is much more exact to say that the 'old man' is Adam—
or rather, ourselves in union with Adam, and that the 'new man'
is Christ—or rather, ourselves in union with Christ."[302]

Christ's death was "potentially the dying of the whole human
race, just as his resurrection was potentially the re-creation of all
mankind."[303]

In Adam, that is, in their solidarity with fallen humanity in
its sinfulness, all must die; but in Christ, that is, through in-
corporation into the redeemed humanity of the body of Christ,
all are made alive (5:12—6:11). In Christ's death on Calvary
the whole human race died, because Christ is the representative
Man: "One died for all, therefore all died" (II Cor. 5:14, NASB;
the latter clause is *ara hoi pantes apethanon*). In Christ's resur-

---

[299]*Ibid.*, p. 244.   [300]*Op. cit.*, p. 161.

[301]Godet, *op. cit.*, p. 244.   [302]*The Epistle to the Romans*, p. 125.

[303]Richardson, *op. cit.*, p. 35.

rection the new man was created (Eph. 2:15; Col. 3:9-11). *The individual—through his faith, dramatized by baptism—appropriates to himself the salvation thus procured by Christ.* With Christ he dies to sin and rises to newness of life. Then with complete reality he can confess: "I have been crucified with Christ; and it is no longer I who live, but Christ lives in me" (Gal. 2:20, NASB). Baptism objectifies and ratifies our death to sin; it removes the entire experience from the realm of pure subjectivity and ties it to an event in history. As the death of Christ was an objective fact, so is our baptism. In pagan Rome the baptized man was a dead man, so far as his old life was concerned. In submitting to Christian baptism he died to his old life and was henceforth identified with Christ and the new life that He came to provide. In this entire passage the apostle is reminding the Romans of this solemn fact, which apparently they were in danger of forgetting. "Have you forgotten that all of us who were baptized into Jesus Christ were, by that very action, sharing in his death?" (v. 3, Phillips)

All of this, we should understand, is in order **that the body of sin might be destroyed, that henceforth we should not serve sin.** "The purpose of this moral execution, included in the very fact of faith, is *the destruction* of the body of sin."[304] What is **the body of sin** (*to soma tes hamartias*)? Literally, it is "sin's body" (possessive genitive): *the body of which sin has taken possession.*[305] The best commentary is probably 7:14-15. The RSV translates the phrase "the sinful body." If we call the body "sinful" we do so in the same way we speak of "filthy lucre." Out of Christ, man's body is degraded by sin. Paul is undoubtedly thinking of the physical body as an instrument of sin. Thus while *to soma tes hamartias* must be taken closely together, it is not the body as such which is to be destroyed, but *the body as sin's tool.* Set free from sin, we are then able to present our bodies as living sacrifices to God (12:1), to become "instruments of righteousness to God" (v. 13, NASB).

[304]Godet, *op. cit.,* p. 245.

[305]ICC, "Romans," p. 158. Cf. 7:24, *tou somatos tou thanatou toutou,* "the body which is given over to death"; Phil. 3:21, *to soma tes tapeinoseos,* "the body in its present state of humiliation"; Col. 2:11, *tou somatos tes sarkos,* "the body given over to fleshly impulses." Beet defines **body of sin** as "the sinner's own body, which is under the power of sin, v. 12. The importance in Paul's theology of the human body permits no other interpretation" (*op. cit.,* p. 181). It should be noted, however, that Adam Clarke (*op. cit.,* II, 77) equates the **body of sin** with **our old man.**

Some interpreters, however, think we must understand *soma* as more than the physical organism. Dodd insists that it means "the individual *self* as an organism (neither flesh nor spirit being individual, and 'soul' being merely the animating principle of the flesh, or physical structure)."[306] He therefore prefers to think of "the sinful body as a self organized out of bad and disharmonious sentiments"[307] (see 7:18). To destroy "the sinful body" would therefore be to "disintegrate these bad sentiments, and so destroy the self built out of them, in preparation for the organization of a new self about the centre supplied by Christ to the believer."[308]

Evidently Barth so understands **body** (*soma*), for he says with characteristic vigor: "This is our knowledge of Jesus Christ on which our faith is founded—that the 'old man', i.e. we ourselves, as God's enemies, have been crucified and killed in and with the crucifixion of the man Jesus at Golgotha, so that the 'body' (i.e. the subject, the person needed for the doing) of sin, the man who can sin and will and shall sin, has been removed, destroyed, done away with, is simply no longer there (and has therefore not merely been 'made powerless')."[309] The NEB translates v. 6: "We know that the man we once were has been crucified with Christ, for the destruction of the sinful self, so that we may no longer be slaves of sin." Such is the work of Christ:

[306] *Op. cit.*, p. 90. See comments on 7:18-24.

[307] *Ibid.*, p. 91. Dodd thinks Paul's "conception of the body, as the organized individual self, may be illustrated by the concept of the 'sentiment' in modern psychology. The instinctive impulses of our common human nature are conceived as organized in sentiments by reference to ends, or ideals. The individual personality is built up by means of a hierarchy of sentiments, and in proportion as they are truly harmonized with one another under a dominant sentiment, the self is unified and becomes a mature and effective personality. But each sentiment functions as a sort of sub-self, or image of the self, with its affections, ideas, and duties. If the sentiments are seriously at war with one another, we have a more or less acute case of divided personality." Leenhardt writes: "The body is not only the necessary instrument of personal existence, but the appropriate organ through which the personality expresses and realizes itself. Paul might have said, 'My body is myself, I am my body.' Hence when he speaks of the destruction of the sinful body he wishes to stress the end of the inner sinful condition" (*op. cit.*, p. 162).

[308] *Ibid.*

[309] *A Shorter Commentary on Romans*, p. 69. **Destroyed** (*katargethe*) sometimes may be rendered "made powerless." However, see I Cor. 15:26, where Paul writes, "The last enemy that shall be *destroyed* is death."

it provides a complete remedy for the sin which entered the race through Adam's transgression. By the grace of God "the sin" (cf. 5:12) may be *extirpated* from human nature. This was the purpose of Christ's death and this is the possibility which opens to every Christian. That every believer has not realized this full deliverance is the occasion for Paul's discussion here. He wants his readers to know that full salvation is a live option for the justified man.[310]

In 6:1-6, 22, J. W. Ellis sees pictured "The Sanctified Life." (1) Life questioning, 1; (2) Life answering, 2; (3) Life crucified, 3; (4) Life resurrected, 4-6; (5) Life's foundation, 6; (6) Life's superstructure, 22.

Verse 7, **For he that is dead is freed** (*dedikaiotai*, justified) **from sin,** rounds out v. 6. Sin has now lost its claim upon the man who has died with Christ. "One who is dead, he means to say, no longer having a body to put at the service of sin, is now legally exempted from carrying out the wishes of that master, who till then had freely disposed of him."[311]

Leenhardt points out that vv. 5-7 consider the baptized believer from the point of view of his participation in the *death* of Christ; vv. 8-10 will present Christ as the Bringer of *new life.* Verse 8 declares, **Now if we be dead with Christ** (*ei de apethanomen syn christo,* "if we have died with Christ," NASB), **we believe** (*pisteuomen,* we are persuaded) **that we shall also live with him.** Death with Christ is a past event; sin no longer reigns in a justified believer. But not every Christian has appropriated the full meaning of the promise that **we shall also live with him.** As in v. 5, Paul is speaking of "participation of the believer's sanctified life with the life of Christ rather than participation in future glory, which is not the point."[312] To live with Christ is to share His life as one risen and glorified. The self, having renounced its false and destructive organizing center, clings to its new and life-giving and sanctifying center—the Lord Jesus Christ. "This is our Pentecost," says Godet, "the analogue of His

---

[310]Beginning at v. 11, Paul changes to the hortatory and calls upon his readers to do two things: (1) reckon themselves by faith to be dead to sin and (2) consecrate themselves in one decisive act of self-surrender to God. In c. 8, Paul shows that the antipode to indwelling sin is the indwelling Spirit. **The body of sin is destroyed** only when we are fully indwelt by the Holy Spirit (8:9-10).

[311]Godet, *op. cit.,* p. 246.   [312]Vincent, *op. cit.,* p. 70.

resurrection."[313] Here is an echo of 5:10, where Paul spoke of our being "saved by his life." The full meaning of this concept will become clear when we come to 8:1-4. By His personal conquest of sin Christ has completely sanctified human nature and provided for us the sanctifying Spirit. As Adam pierced the dike through which the irruption of sin took place, Christ has opened the floodgates of the Holy Spirit to human nature.

Paul continues, **Knowing that Christ being raised from the dead dieth no more; death hath no more dominion over him. For in that he died, he died unto sin once** (*ephapax*, "once for all," RSV): **but in that he liveth, he liveth unto God** (9-10). The first sentence emphasizes that the resurrection of Christ was an eschatological event. Christ's resurrection, unlike that of Lazarus, precluded the possibility of His dying again. He, and He alone, has begun the resurrection life of the age to come. This is because "the death that He died, He died to sin, once for all" (NASB). "Christ died to sin because he died sinless, because he died rather than sin (by disobeying his Father), and because he died in a context of sin."[314] Therefore His death, instead of being a sign of the victory of sin over man's true nature, was a sign of "the complete rout of Sin in a decisive engagement."[315] Whereas for other men death had been the sentence of condemnation, Christ "condemned sin in the flesh" (8:3), vanquished the foe on the very battlefield where it had entrenched itself. Moreover, He was raised from the dead **by the glory of the Father** (v. 4), in order that He might continue to live **unto God** alone.

We have now arrived at what Dodd calls a "momentous conclusion."[316] Since Christ has once for all died to sin and now lives unto God, **likewise reckon ye also yourselves to be dead indeed unto sin, but alive unto God through Jesus Christ** (11).[317] This is an imperative, a hortatory challenge (*logizesthe heautous*): "Consider yourselves to be dead to sin, but alive to God in Christ Jesus" (NASB). "If in point of fact believers are partakers of the death and life of Christ; if they die with him, and live with him, then they should so regard themselves. They should receive this truth, with all its consoling and sanctifying

---

[313]*Op. cit.*, p. 247.   [314]Barrett, *The Epistle to the Romans*, p. 126.

[315]Dodd, *op. cit.*, p. 90.   [316]*Ibid.*, p. 91.

[317]The best Greek text omits **our Lord** (*to kyrio hemon*), but the meaning is not changed.

power, into their hearts, and manifest it in their lives."[318] The exhortation is: "Become actually what in Christ you are potential-ly." Enter by the reckoning of faith into the full possibilities of your new union with Christ. **Reckon** thus: "The nails which pierced His sacred hands and feet destroyed my old self. Christ and we were separated from sin by the same mysterious death; and therefore we are dead with Christ."[319]

> This implies that our separation from sin and devotion to God are God's gifts to us, and work in us. And it implies that God gives them to us in the moment we believe them to be ours. Else our reckoning, which we make at His bidding, is a mistake.
>
> We come therefore to the cross and to the empty grave of Christ. We remember the sinlessness and the devotion to God of the dead and risen Saviour. We know that He died that we, by spiritual union with Him, may be like Him. Perhaps until this moment we have been sadly alive to sin, and but partly devoted to God. But God bids us reckon ourselves to be sharers of the death and life of Christ. In view of God's purpose, and of Christ's death, we dare not hesitate. In contradiction to our past experience we say, I am dead to sin: henceforth I live only for God. What we say we reckon, at God's bidding, to be true. And God realises in us by union with Christ, His own word and our faith. Henceforth, so long as we maintain our confidence, we find by happy experience that, by the grace and power of God, in a measure unknown to us before, we are separated from sin and living for God.[320]

In 12-13, Paul writes, **Let not sin therefore reign in your mortal body, that ye should obey it in the lusts thereof. Neither yield ye** (*mede paristanete,* present imperative, "do not go on presenting," NASB) **your members as instruments of unrigh-teousness unto sin: but yield yourselves** (*parastesate,* aorist im-perative, "present yourselves 'by one decisive act' ")[321] **unto God, as those that are alive from the dead** (*hosei ek nekron zontas,* "as men who have been brought from death to life," RSV), **and your members as instruments of righteousness unto God.** Although the reign of sin is broken in justification, yet it is possible that, though sin *need* no longer reign, the justified man may nevertheless lapse from grace (v. 16) and allow it to reign.[322] It is possible for this man to "go on presenting" the members of his body as weapons for sin to use. "The very word, 'Let not sin *reign,*' assumes that it *is* still there. But it ought no

---

[318]Hodge, *op. cit.,* p. 201.   [319]Beet, *op. cit.,* p. 181.

[320]*Ibid.,* p. 187.   [321]ICC, "Romans," p. 161.

[322]Dodd, *op. cit.,* p. 93.

longer to be there as *sovereign:* for it has lost its powerful instrument and auxiliary, the body; the latter has become in Christ the instrument of God."[323] This is why the Christian, and the Christian alone, can present his **members as instruments of righteousness unto God.** He has been liberated from sin's grasp upon his personality; he is a free man in Christ. The question he now faces is: *What shall I do with my new freedom?* Shall I use it "for an occasion to the flesh," or shall I employ it to serve God and my neighbor in love? (Cf. Gal. 5:13.) Shall I put myself at the disposal of wickedness, or shall I present myself to God in an act of total consecration?

It is instructive to note Paul's exact language here. First, he urges, Present **yourselves** to God as those . . . **alive from the dead.** That is, **Yield** your inmost heart to Him, saying, "Not my will, but Thine, be done." Secondly, Present **your members as instruments of righteousness unto God.** Put every organ of your body and every power of your redeemed personality at the disposal of God. This is man's part—consecration. God's part is sanctification. This is made clear in v. 22: "But now that you have been set free from sin and have become slaves of God, the return you get is sanctification and its end, eternal life" (RSV). See 12:1-2, where the two aspects are brought together in one whole. It is ours to consecrate, God's to sanctify. It is ours to present, God's to transform.

"Three Analogies of Consecration" are suggested in this section and in what follows. (1) The analogy of slavery, 6:13, 15-22; cf. Exod. 21:1-6; (2) The analogy of marriage, 7:1-6; (3) The analogy of sacrifice, 12:1.

Paul concludes this section on dying with Christ with a final word of encouragement. **For sin shall not have dominion over you: for ye are not under the law, but under grace** (14). John Calvin writes, "We have here, I think, an encouragement for the comfort of believers, lest they should fail in their attempts to attain to holiness through a sense of their own weakness. He had exhorted them to apply all their powers in obedience to righteousness, but since they carry about the remains of the flesh, they cannot do other than walk with uncertainty."[324] This is

---

[323]Godet, *op. cit.*, p. 250. That is, sin no longer reigns even though it remains as a residual bias to self (cf. I Cor. 3:1-4).

[324]*Op. cit.*, p. 130.

the dilemma of the justified man who has not yet experienced
the divinely intended scope of sanctification in his life. He finds
himself at times overcome by sin, so that he must build again the
foundations of repentance and faith. Let this man not lose heart,
for "there is therefore now no condemnation to them which are
in Christ Jesus" (8:1). As a justified believer seeking to walk in
the full light of God, he is **not under the law, but under grace.**
God does not count his remaining sin against him (cf. I John 1:7)
so long as, turning from sin with deepest personal rejection and
turning to God in deepest personal commitment, he seeks the full
release of the Spirit in his life. Let him therefore rejoice in the
smile of God and live in the joyful expectancy of full deliverance
by the power of Christ. Although sin *remains,* it does not *reign.*
Therefore he may take encouragement and comfort in Christ.
Since we are **under grace,** too, we are not held accountable for
our inadvertent and unconscious transgressions of the law of God.
The Christian has been transferred from the legal order of works
into the evangelical order of "faith which worketh by love."[325]
But let him never forget the word of promise: "Faithful is he
that calleth you, who also will do it" (I Thess. 5:23-24).[326]

One question remains. Speaking as a new man in Christ, I
must ask, "When did I die with Christ to sin?" Paul's answer is
fourfold:

(a) You died with Christ in *provision* when He died on
Calvary. His death was potentially and provisionally your death;
His resurrection, your rising to newness of life. The Cross meant
more than propitiation, with the consequent blessing of justification (3:21-28); Christ's death was the doom of sin, its extirpation

---

[325]Cf. Colin W. Williams, *John Wesley's Theology Today* (New York:
Abingdon Press, 1960), pp. 70-71.

[326]In his sermon on "The Scripture Way of Salvation," Wesley asks:
"But what is the faith whereby we are sanctified—saved from sin and perfected in love? It is a divine evidence and conviction, First, that God hath
promised it in the Holy Scriptures. Till we are thoroughly satisfied of this,
there is no moving one step further. . . . It is a divine evidence and conviction, Secondly, that what God hath promised he is able to perform. . . .
It is, Thirdly, a divine evidence and conviction that he is able and willing
to do it now. . . . To this confidence, that God is both able and willing to
sanctify us now, there needs to be added one thing more—a divine evidence
and conviction that he doeth it. In that hour it is done: God says to the
inmost soul, 'According to thy faith be it unto thee!' " (Sermons, II, *The
Works of John Wesley* (Kansas City: Nazarene Publishing House, n.d.),
VI, 52-53.

from human nature (8:3), and therefore your sanctification (v. 6; 8:1-4; cf. I Cor. 1:30; Eph. 5:25-27).

(b) You died with Christ *in purpose* when you were justified. At the Cross you submitted to God's judgment upon your sin; so far as your intent and consent were concerned, you gave up your sinful self to die when you embraced His death in penitent faith (see Gal. 5:24). Moreover, your old existence in Adam ceased when by faith you became a new creation in Christ (see II Cor. 5:17). By God's action you were transferred to the domain of His well-beloved Son (see Col. 1:13). In Christ you were "justified from sin" (v. 7), set free from sin's grasp and sin's claims—sin no longer reigned.

(c) You died with Christ *in profession* when you submitted to Christian baptism (vv. 3-4). Descending into the waters of baptism, you were buried with Him into His death (cf. v. 10), you were cut off from your sinful past; you arose from baptism as Christ's man with a new future and a new name.

(d) Finally, you die with Christ *in present experience* when (i) in the reckoning of faith you embrace the full provisions of Calvary (v. 11) and (ii) yield yourself to God in an act of total consecration (v. 13). In this act of consecration and faith your mortal body ceases to be an instrument of sin and becomes the temple of the Holy Spirit. While we are sanctified "by faith" (Acts 26:18), God gives the Holy Spirit only to "them that obey him" (Acts 5:32). Faith and obedience are two sides of one coin.

> *Holiness by faith in Jesus,*
>   *Not by effort of thine own,*
> *Sin's dominion crushed and broken*
>   *By the power of grace alone.*
> *God's own holiness within thee,*
>   *His own beauty on thy brow;*
> *This shall be thy pilgrim brightness,*
>   *This thy blessed portion now.*
>
> —Quoted by Skevington Wood

"When God bids us reckon ourselves dead to sin, and henceforth living only for Him, we remember our moral weakness, and say, How can these things be? But when we learn that henceforth the Spirit of God will dwell within us, in order that by His power He may protect us from all sin, and by His holiness direct towards

141

God our every purpose and effort—when we learn this, our doubt gives place to confident expectation and adoring gratitude. For we are sure that the Spirit is able to accomplish, even in us, God's purpose of holiness."[327] (See comments on 8:1-11.)

"Death to Sin" is clearly portrayed in 6:1-14. (1) Death to sin symbolized, 3-4; (2) Death to sin dramatized, 6; (3) Death to sin realized, 11-14.

(2) *Sanctification as a new obedience* (6:15-23) This section emphasizes that those who are, according to v. 14, no longer **under the law, but under grace** have been brought into a relationship of service which means heart obedience (v. 17). Paul says in 19 that this is a human way of regarding it, adopted **because of the infirmity of your flesh.** That is, he has introduced this discussion to make himself completely understood, just in case that what he has said in vv. 1-14 is not sufficiently understandable. At the same time, Paul makes it clear that the words which follow must not be understood in any legalistic sense, but that they should be heard and understood in the light of, and as an application of, what he has just said about our dying with Christ to sin.

He begins by restating the question of v. 1. **What then? shall we sin** (*hamartesomen*, "are we to sin?"), **because we are not under the law, but under grace? God forbid** (15). But this is not merely a repetition of the previous question. The first question was, "Are we to continue *in* sin?" This one is, "Are we to continue *to* sin?" The former deals with the permanent state of sin, the latter with the act of disobedience. In vv. 1-14 the apostle has demonstrated the fundamental incompatibility between grace and sin (*he hamartia,* "the sin"). A man who has died to sin cannot live any longer therein. He has passed out of the old order of death in Adam into the new order of life in Christ—and this life is a holy existence. This man who has come into the new order of grace and life through Christ is therefore a man who has *ceased to sin.* Thus, here in vv. 15-23, Paul demonstrates the fundamental incompatibility between grace and *sinning.* This is made clear by the verb *hamartesomen,* which is aorist subjunctive, and may be literally translated, "Are we to make provision for *a single act* of sin?" Paul answers: *Me genoito,* "May it never be!" (NASB; cf. 13:14.)

[327]Beet, *op. cit.,* p. 226.

Paul exults, **Know ye not that to whom ye yield yourselves servants** (*doulous,* "slaves"; so throughout this section)[328] **to obey, his servants ye are to whom ye obey; whether of sin unto death, or of obedience unto righteousness?** (16) "Man has a lord, one way or the other. He is either a servant of sin, or a servant of obedience. Sin and obedience are therefore not in the first place our actions, but powers which have dominion over us."[329] In putting these two masters in juxtaposition Paul makes it clear that sin is disobedience (cf. 4:15; 5:13-14), no mere unintentional "missing of the mark." *Hamartia* is essentially "lawlessness" (I John 3:4; cf. 8:7). The man who sins is not just a poor marksman; he *aims* at the wrong mark and so misses the right one. Sin is "wilful error."[330] Because sin is such a serious affair, the justified believer who willfully disobeys God finds himself enslaved once again by sin. As our Lord himself warned, "Truly, truly, I say to you, every one who commits sin is the slave of sin" (John 8:34, NASB). And—**the wages of sin is death** (v. 23; cf. 8:13). Paul is echoing God's warning given Adam in the time of his innocence (Gen. 3:3), as well as the word of the prophet, "The soul that sinneth, it shall die" (Ezek. 18:4). *To disobey God is to come again under "the law of sin and death."* On the other hand, slavery to obedience ends in **righteousness.** The next verse shows the significance of this new Christian righteousness.

"But thanks be to God, that though ye were slaves to sin, you became obedient from the heart to that form of teaching to which you were committed, and having been freed from sin, you became slaves of righteousness" (17-18, NASB).[331] The grace of God, which can never be praised enough, means that, though we were servants of sin, we are so no longer; "for when we were told and when we heard the Gospel, we have become obedient to it with all our heart and therefore with our whole existence."[332]

---

[328]Adam Clarke comments: "The word *doulos,* which we translate *servant,* properly signifies *slave;* and a slave among the Greeks and Romans was considered as being his master's property" (*op. cit.,* II, 79).

[329]Barth, *A Shorter Commentary on Romans,* p. 72.

[330]Cf. C. Ryder Smith, *The Bible Doctrine of Sin* (London: The Epworth Press, 1953), pp. 142-43.

[331]The KJV represents the exact Greek wording. But Adam Clarke shows clearly that "although" must be inserted between *that* and *ye* (*op. cit.,* II, 79).

[332]Barth, *loc. cit.*

We have therefore become subjects of that second realm, **servants of righteousness.** Thus "righteousness remains important to the Christian; the only righteousness he has given up is his own, and that in order that he may be in subjection to God's righteousness —which is not less but greater than human righteousness (cf. Matt. v. 20)."[333] What does it mean to be **servants of righteousness?** In this new relationship of grace we are, properly speaking, not dealing with slavery but with freedom. Having been liberated from the servitude of sin, we have become "servants of liberty."[334] The service of God is perfect freedom. This is the paradox of God's righteousness.

At this point Paul inserts his apologetic parenthesis which is applied to what follows: **I speak after the manner of men because of the infirmity of your flesh** (19; cf. 3:5; I Cor. 9:8; Gal. 3:15). He then proceeds: **For as ye have yielded your members servants to uncleanness and to iniquity unto iniquity; even so now yield** (*parestesate,* aorist subjunctive as in v. 13b; present in one decisive act of dedication) **your members servants to righteousness unto holiness** (*hagiasmon,* "sanctification," NASB, RSV). Once again we see the relationship between consecration and sanctification. (See comments on 13.)

Compromise between sin and righteousness is unthinkable. A man cannot serve two masters. These are mutually exclusive attitudes. **For when ye were the servants of sin, ye were free from righteousness. What fruit had ye then in those things whereof ye are now ashamed? for the end of those things is death. But now being made free from sin, and become servants to God, ye have your fruit unto holiness** (*hagiasmon,* "sanctification," NASB, RSV), **and the end everlasting life** (20-22). "As you had a lord then and have a Lord now," Barth paraphrases, "so you were then also free, i.e. from righteousness— a terrible freedom, the inevitable shameful result and fruit of which is death. And in the same way you are free again, i.e., from sin, because you have become servants of God, with the result that by his decision and by the ensuing order, you are sanctified men who, as such, are on the way to eternal life."[335] We have now returned to the high view of sanctification which opened in vv. 11-13. By availing themselves of the full possibilities of God's

---

[333]Barrett, *The Epistle to the Romans,* p. 132.

[334]Barth, *A Shorter Commentary on Romans,* p. 72.

[335]*Ibid.,* pp. 72-73.

grace the Roman Christians may become fully sanctified men with the hope of **everlasting life.**

For the wages of sin is death, but the gift of God is eternal life through Jesus Christ our Lord (23). In this final sentence the contrast between sin and God is hardly more important than the corresponding antithesis between **wages** and **gift.** The old servitude to sin was under the reign of law, and sin accordingly paid a wage, as a matter of debt or obligation; the new servitude to God is under the reign of grace, and God accordingly gives a "gift of grace" (*charisma*), namely, **eternal life.** Within this "gift of grace," says Godet, "is the *fullness of salvation.* Everything in this work, from the initial justification to the final absolution, including sanctification and preparing for glory, is a free gift, an unmerited favor, like the Christ Himself who has been made for us righteousness, holiness, and redemption."[336]

In 6:1-23 we see "The Incompatibility of Grace and Sin." (1) The grace of God is incompatible with continuing in the state of sin, 1-14; (2) The grace of God is incompatible with committing an act of sin, 15-23.

b. Sanctification through death to the law (7:1-25). The present discussion is related to what Paul said in 6:14, that the Christian is "not under law, but under grace." What followed in 6:15-23 dealt with an objection, Are we therefore to sin, since we are not under law, but under grace? Paul's answer to this specious question employed the analogy of slavery. It is unthinkable, said he, that the Christian should sin, for his life is now to be lived under the new order of obedience. The Christian is a slave of "obedience unto righteousness," just as formerly he was a slave "of sin unto death." Indeed, only the man who has been set free from sin *can* serve God in obedience. Since he is in sub-

---

[336]*Op. cit.,* p. 262. But while our salvation is wholly "a gift of grace," it is no "cheap grace." *To the man under grace* Paul here says that **the wages of sin is death** (cf. 8:13). Throughout this entire passage "it is certain that he conceives the possibility of a return to the service of sin—a return which would lead them to eternal death as certainly as other sinners. . . . A single affirmative answer to the question: 'Shall I commit an act of sin, since I am under grace?' might have the effect of placing the believer again on the inclined plane which leads to the abyss" (Godet, *ibid.*). Life **under grace** therefore means a life of serious and concentrated endeavor to live under the rule of God's righteousness. At every juncture of our human existence we face the awesome alternatives of sin and grace, and hence of **death** and **eternal life** (cf. 8:13).

jection to the righteousness of God (not his own), he can serve
God fruitfully, and see sanctification and eternal life result from
his service. Now in this section Paul introduces a fresh analogy,
that of marriage, to make substantially the same point.[337]

(1) *Freedom from the law* (7:1-6). **Know ye not, brethren,
(for I speak to them that know the law,) how that the law hath
dominion over a man as long as he liveth?** (1) The first clause,
Know ye not (*e agnoeite*) means, "Surely you know this—that
the reign of law has been superseded by that of grace. Or do you
need to be told that death brings an end to the claims of law, and
therefore that the dispensation of the law ceased with the death
of Christ?" The parenthetical sentence is, *Ginoskousi gar nomon
lalo.* Translated literally, it reads, "I am talking to those who
are acquainted with law." The absence of the article seems to
show that what is meant here is neither the Mosaic nor the
Roman law, but a general principle of all law—that death clears
all scores, and that a dead man is no longer subject to prosecu-
tion.[338] The **brethren** are therefore Christian brothers rather than
fellow Jews related under the law of Moses.

The analogy of marriage follows in 2-3. **For the woman
which hath an husband is bound by the law to her husband so
long as he liveth; but if the husband be dead, she is loosed from
the law of her husband. So then if, while her husband liveth,
she is married to another man, she shall be called an adulteress:
but if her husband be dead, she is free from that law; so that she
is no adulteress, though she be married to another man.** Typical
of many interpreters, Knox calls this figure "awkward" and "confused."[339] The clue to consistency, however, is found in 6:6, in
the concept of the "old man" who dies with Christ to sin; at the
same time his death is to the law (cf. Gal. 2:19-21). In both instances the death of the *old* man is followed by the resurrection
of the *new* man. "The 'self' of the man is double; there is an 'old
self' and a 'new self'; or rather the 'self' remains the same
throughout, but it passes through different states, or phases."[340]
Bearing this in mind, we find Paul is using a consistent metaphor:
(*a*) **The woman** is the true self, the ego, which is permanent
through the transition; (*b*) **the** (first) **husband** is our old status
in Adam; (*c*) **the law of her husband** is the OT law which con-

[337]Barrett, *The Epistle to the Romans,* p. 135.
[338]ICC, "Romans," p. 172.   [339]IB (Exegesis), IX, 487.
[340]ICC, "Romans," p. 172.

demned that old state; (d) the new marriage is the new union with Christ which the Christian enjoys.

"The living man to whom Paul is referring [in 2a], who is therefore subject to the law, is man 'in the flesh' (7.5), who therefore lives as 'the old man' (6.6). The law no doubt applies to him and binds him: the 'law of sin and death' (8:2), the only law with which, according to the question he has to answer, Paul is concerned."[341] It is the law which, according to 7:5, **did work in our members** [as unbelievers] **to bring forth fruit unto death.** So long as the old man of sin lives, and under every circumstance, his life is under this law. "In other words so long as we (the husband) live in the flesh as that old man, we (the wife) are governed by the law, that binds him and therefore ourselves."[342]

The death of the **husband** in 2 is the death of "our old **man**" in and with Christ. When we died with Christ to sin (as described in 6:2-6), we were **loosed from the law of the husband,** i.e., from "the law of sin and death" (cf. 8:2). **So then if, while her husband liveth, she be married to another man, she shall be called an adulteress.** "In other words, without the death of the old man any attempt to withdraw from the law of sin and death, any attempt to escape sin and death could only result in our being, more than ever, convicted of sin and condemned to death by that same law."[343] Whatever we achieve in this direction is nothing but what the OT calls adultery against God—"every kind of idolatry and every kind of confidence in our own works, sin, which does not expel sin but brings it to perfection and which can only make our sentence of death irrevocable.[344] But with the death of her husband—i.e., the death of Christ and our death with Him—**she is free from that law; so that she is no adulteress, though she be married to another man** (the living Christ). Under the law we were united with sin; when we died in and with Christ at Calvary, we were liberated from the law, "the law of sin and death"; in rising with Christ to newness of life we were united with Him in a new bond of faith and love. This is precisely what Paul says in the next verse.

Wherefore, my brethren, ye also are become dead to the law by the body of Christ; that ye should be married[345] **to an-**

---

[341]Barth, *A Shorter Commentary on Romans,* p. 77.
[342]*Ibid.*   [343]*Ibid.,* p. 78.
[344]*Ibid.*   [345]*Genesthai,* lit., "become" to another.

147

other, even to him who is raised from the dead, that we should
bring forth fruit unto God (4). The body of Christ here is the
body of Jesus which was put to death on the Cross; in and with
that body I died, *potentially* when He died and *actually* when I
identified with His death in faith. But my death was simply a
prelude to my being raised from the dead, in order that I might
become a part of the Church, the new bride of Christ. And, as the
old marriage was fruitful unto death (v. 5: cf. Gal. 5:19-21), so
the new union is fruitful unto God (v. 4; cf. Gal. 5:22-23). "But
now we have been released from the Law, having died to that by
which we were bound, so that we serve in newness of the Spirit
and not in oldness of the letter" (6, NASB). "Being bound to the
Law is captivity, being bound to the living Christ is freedom.
There it is enslavement in the letter, here freedom in the Holy
Spirit."[346] This is the newness of the Spirit, being bound to Him
"whose service is perfect freedom."

Paul's "awkward" and "confused" metaphor turns out to be
a convincing summation of the whole problem of law and sin,
Christ and holiness. But it raises acutely a new question which
demands an answer. With this new question the next section
opens.

(2) *The function of the law* (7:7-13). What shall we say
then (7), in view of the foregoing position—in view of the mysterious link between sin, law, and death? Paul has just demonstrated that to be set free from one is also simultaneously a
deliverance from the others and that, equally, liberation from one
can occur only if there is also deliverance from the other two.
This raises a serious question, Is the law sin? Since under the
law "the motions of sins" (5) are stirred, and the "fruit" of this
is death, is the law itself a power opposed to God? God forbid
(*me genoito*, "May it not be so!"). Paul explains, Nay, I had
not known sin, but by the law: for I had not known lust (*epithy-
mian*, every kind of illicit desire[347]), except the law had said,
Thou shalt not covet (*ouk epithymeseis*, 7).[348] Compare 3:20;
4:15; 5:13. The inward rebellion against the Creator by which

---

[346]Brunner, *op. cit.*, p. 58.   [347]ICC, "Romans," p. 179.

[348]Dodd points out that it is highly significant that Paul chose the one
commandment of the second table which deals with the inner life, rather
than overt action. If the motive is strong enough, one may discipline himself into conformity to any of the others. "But can he by a similar process
control the desire to do these forbidden things?" (*Op. cit.*, p. 110.)

the self usurps the place of God as the end of life exists everywhere; and everywhere there exists enough light to make such rebellion responsible and blameworthy (cf. 1:19-20; 2:14-15). But only where **the law**—the explicit command of the living God— exists can sin emerge in perceptible and measurable form. **The law** turns sin into transgression. This, however, does not exhaust Paul's meaning here. " 'Knowing sin' does not mean merely perceiving its existence, but experiencing it. The law is not simply a reagent by which the presence of sin may be detected; it is a catalyst which aids and even initiates the action of sin upon man."[349] The law stirs up illicit desire. This desire is "precisely that exaltation of the ego which we have seen to be the essence of sin" (see comments on 1:19-23). But God's law says, **Thou shalt not covet.** Thou shalt not live by the law of illicit desire, but "thou shalt love the Lord thy God with all thine heart, and with all thy soul, and with all thy might" (Deut. 6:5). *The law commands our total devotion to God.*

But sin, taking occasion by the commandment, wrought in me all manner of concupiscence (8). Here sin slips in, in the guise of the serpent in the Garden. "But the serpent said to the woman, 'You will not die . . . you will be like God' " (Gen. 3: 4-5, RSV). Thus evil desire was conceived in the heart of man— pride, self-exaltation, the perverse desire to imitate God in His power. **Concupiscence** here translates *epithymia* (cf. v. 7). It is the overweening desire for the heights of self-exaltation (cf. Isa. 14:12-14). Sin would dethrone God and exalt the creature. **Taking occasion** (*aphormen labousa*, "getting a start," or "finding something to take hold of") **by the commandment** means that sin "found a base of operations in God's prohibition."[350] Law gives sin the opportunity it wants. As the little girl said, "The Ten Commandments put ideas in our heads!"

In vv. 8-9, Paul seems to be describing a happy childhood: **For without the law sin was dead**—inert, lifeless. **For I was alive without the law once.** Dodd makes an interesting observation on this. " 'I lived my own life, without law' [we say as we look back on our childhood]: nothing could more aptly set before us the lusty little boy, discovering every day new powers in himself, new opportunities for fun and mischief. We speak of the 'age of innocence,' but the little innocent is in actual fact greedy, inter-

---

[349]Barrett, *The Epistle to the Romans*, p. 141.
[350]ICC, "Romans," p. 179.

fering, quarrelsome, completely regardless of the rights and conveniences of other people. But sin is never counted in the absence of law."[351] This is to say that during the period of our childhood innocence sin is present even though it is not active in its God-dimension. We are born "curved in ourselves" (Luther). Self-centeredness is a compulsion of our nature. So Paul continues, **When the commandment came, sin revived** (*anezesen,* "sprang to life," Moffatt), **and I died**—just as God had warned (Gen. 2:17). This death is not physical; it is *spiritual death:* the proud separation of the self from God's lordship, with the resultant judgment of God and the sense of estrangement, guilt, and loneliness (see Gen. 3:7-10).

We must now ask a question: Is 7:7-25, where Paul uses the first person singular throughout, his own spiritual autobiography, or does he use this as simply a literary device? Scholarly opinion is divided on this question, but it is practically impossible to escape the conviction that Paul is drawing from his own experience,[352] although he is certainly using it as a basis for generalizing on the whole problem of sin, law, and grace. For example, in 8:1-4 he shifts from "I" to "we," and in 8:5-8 he uses "they," only to change to "you" in 8:9. Later in c. 8 he intermingles all four persons (beginning at v. 16). When the apostle says, **When the commandment came, sin revived, and I died,** he was probably referring to his *Bar Mitzvah.* At the age of 13, he, as

---

[351]*Op. cit.,* p. 111. This recalls Augustine's famous account of the pear-stealing incident, recorded in the second book of his *Confessions.* "There was a pear-tree near our vineyard," Augustine writes, "laden with fruit. One stormy night we rascally youths set out to rob it and carry our spoils away. We took off a huge load of pears—not to feast upon them ourselves, but to throw them to the pigs—though we ate just enough to have the pleasure of forbidden fruit. They were nice pears, but it was not the pears that my wretched soul coveted, for I had plenty better at home. I picked them simply in order to be a thief. The only feast I got was a feast of iniquity, and that I enjoyed to the full. What was it I loved in that theft? *Was it the pleasure of acting against the law, in order that I, a prisoner under rules, might have a maimed counterfeit of freedom, by doing with impunity what was forbidden, with a dim similitude of omnipotence?"* (abridged by Dodd from *Conf.* II. 4-6; *ibid.,* p. 109).

[352]"Although the contrary view has been argued, it seems all but indubitable that this whole section of the letter (vss. 7-25) is autobiographical. In using the first personal pronoun Paul is not trying merely to give vivid expression to what is imaginary or hypothetical. The passage rings too true and, especially as vs. 24 is reached, strikes too terribly poignant a note to be explained in any such way" (Knox, IB, IX, 499).

other Jewish boys, became a "Son of the Commandment" and assumed responsibility before the law of God. At that moment in Paul's experience he heard within the depth of his consciousness God's "Thou shalt not"; whereupon something within him rejoined, "I will!" "Sin became alive, and I died" (NASB). When we turn back to the account in Genesis 3, all we need to add is reference to the precise warning, "In the day that thou eatest thereof thou shalt surely die" (Gen. 2:17). But this is more than Paul's confession; it is Mr. Everyman's autobiography. "For all have sinned and fall short of the glory of God" (3:23, RSV). This is every person's experience as he passes the threshold of moral accountability.[353] The solitary exception to this rule was Jesus Christ, the Second Adam.

The process may be summarized: **And the commandment, which was ordained to life, I found to be unto death** (10). Sin perverts the law of God into "the law of sin and death" (cf. 8:2). **For sin, taking occasion by the commandment, deceived me, and by it slew me** (11). The account of the Fall is still in the background of Paul's thinking. Sin *deceives* by making promise of power, pleasure, and wisdom (cf. Gen. 3:5-6). All it can really offer, however, is *death*.

Even having said this, Paul goes on to absolve the law from the charge of guilt. **Wherefore the law is holy, and the commandment holy, and just, and good** (12). It is holy because "it springs from, and partakes of, the holy nature of God."[354] Wesley writes elsewhere, "God forbid that we should suppose it is the cause of sin, because it is the discoverer of it; because it detects the hidden things of darkness, and drags them out into open day." Furthermore, the law is **just.** "It renders to all their due. It prescribes exactly what is right, precisely what ought to be done, said, or thought, both with regard to the Author of our

---

[353]"Sin thus exists in two forms, in *principle* and in *act*. Before we come to the age of responsibility, God does not take sin into account, for "sin is not imputed when there is no law" (5:13). As we have seen, childhood is no mere time of innocence, yet we are not held accountable for our inbred sin. When the commandment, however, provokes us to "transgression" (cf. 4:15), we suffer spiritual death; our sin-problem is then twofold, we are both guilty and corrupt. Salvation accordingly must be twofold.

[354]Wesley's *Explanatory Notes upon the New Testament*, p. 544. The next four quotations are from Wesley's sermon on "The Original Nature, Property, and Use of the Law," *Sermons*, I, *The Works of John Wesley*, V, 439-42.

being, with regard to ourselves, and with regard to every creature which He has made. It is adapted, in all respects, to the
nature of things, of the whole universe, and every individual."
That is to say, the law describes right relationships. Since the
law comes from God, who created us, it sets forth the only conditions under which life can be truly fulfilled. It is thus an index
to the very structure of reality. Finally, the law is **good.** Not only
does it flow from the goodness of God, but it is good in the sense
that it is perfectly adapted to human need. "The law itself is
righteousness, filling the soul with a peace which passeth understanding, and causing us to rejoice evermore, in the testimony
of a good conscience toward God." In the life of a fully sanctified
man God's law is seen in this light, so that he can say with the
Psalmist, "The statutes of the Lord are right, rejoicing the heart"
(cf. Ps. 19:8-11).

Furthermore, rather than setting aside this law, the gospel
proclaims it. Barth affirms that "the Law is (3:21) the confirmation of the Gospel, the form, the shell in which the Gospel comes
to us men. How could the Gospel come to us but in the form
of exhortation, warning, instruction, decree, commandment and
prohibition? . . . As a form of the Gospel, far from being sin, the
Law is the form in which God's grace is revealed. And as such it
is holy, and what it commands—each one of its commandments—
is holy and just and good."[355]

In v. 13, Paul asks, **Was then that which is good made death
unto me?** He answers, **God forbid. But sin, that it might appear
sin, working death in me by that which is good; that sin by the
commandment might become exceeding sinful.** The catch is
that the law (and the gospel in the form of law) "is proclaimed
in the realm of sin. It is given to sinful man. Because of the
dominion of sin in his eyes, ears and hands, it becomes that other
law from which he has to be liberated and from which he is in
fact liberated" through faith in Christ (cf. vv. 1-4).[356] The law,
commanding my total devotement to God (Deut. 6:4-5; Matt. 22:
35-40; cf. Matt. 5:17), simply intensifies my sinful predicament.
It commands what I as a sinful man can never fulfill. Even if I
succeed in disciplining myself to the point where I am morally
upright and just, I only refine my sin into self-righteousness and
spiritual pride, which is sin in its quintessence. Thus God's holy

---

[355]*A Shorter Commentary on Romans,* pp. 80-81.   [356]*Ibid.,* p. 81.

commandment makes my **sin . . . exceeding sinful.** It leaves me stranded on my Tower of Babel.[357]

(3) *The futility of the law* (7:14-25). Paul puts the two complementary facts side by side in v. 14. **For we know that the law is spiritual: but I am carnal, sold under sin.** The law is spiritual (*pneumatikos,* "as the Manna and the Water from the Rock were 'spiritual' (I Cor. x. 3, 4) in the sense of being 'Spirit-caused" or 'Spirit-given,' " with the further connotation that the character of the law corresponds with its origin.[358] **But I am carnal** (*sarkinos,* "made of flesh and blood," I Cor. 3:1) and as such morally impotent in the face of temptation (see comments on 5:12).[359] **Sold under sin** expresses the idea of slavery. Barrett translates, "I am a man of flesh, sold as a slave so as to be under the power of sin."[360] **For that which I do I allow not** (*ou ginosko,* "I do not understand," NASB; 15). The RSV renders it, "I do not understand my own actions." Paul then explains: **For what I would, that do I not; but what I hate, that do I.** "My own behaviour baffles me. For I find myself not doing what I really want to do but doing what I really loathe" (Phillips). Every morally sensitive person understands Paul here. Ovid is often quoted in this connection:

> *My reason this, my passion that, persuades.*
> *I see the right, and approve it too;*
> *I hate the wrong, and yet the wrong pursue.*[361]

---

[357]*Ibid.* "While the Law wanted to be my good and to procure life for me, sin enticed me to the wrong belief that I was something different from, something better than a sinner. It made me regard myself as fundamentally good and therefore able to help myself. It enticed me to do the very thing which the Law does not allow in apparent obedience to the Law: to try to make myself guiltless by my own goodness. In this abuse of the commandment given to me sin has become 'exceedingly sinful' and wounded me mortally" (*Ibid.,* pp. 83-84).

[358]ICC, "Romans," p. 181.

[359]Paul is not advancing any Hellenistic doctrine of dualism. Rather he is employing the OT doctrine of flesh. "The idea that the flesh might be the principle of sin is foreign to the Old Testament. . . . but the weakness of the flesh is a very favorable ground for sin, as is shown in the early pages of Genesis. In the Old Testament, flesh is always that which distinguishes man qualitatively from God, not in the sense of a matter-spirit dualism, but of a contrast between strength and weakness (Gen. 6.3; Is. 31.3; 40.6; 49.26; Jer. 12.12; 17.5; 25.31; 32.27; 45.5; Ez. 21.4; Ps. 56.5; 65.3; 78.39; 145.21; 2 Chr. 32.8" (Jacob, *Theology of the Old Testament,* p. 158).

[360]*The Epistle to the Romans,* p. 146.   [361]*Metamorphoses* VII. 19-20.

Epictetus' words are even nearer Paul's: "What he wants he does not do, and what he does not want he does."[362] And a modern poet confesses:

> *I like, dislike, lament for what I could not;*
> *I do, undo; yet still do what I should not,*
> *And, at the selfsame instant, will the thing*
> *I would not.*
>
> —Francis Quarles[363]

A further point now emerges as Paul writes, **If then I do that which I would not, I consent unto the law that it is good** (16). "We find man in a state of rebellion against God, and under sentence of death. For this unhappy situation the law is not to blame. But neither, it now appears, am 'I,' for I agree with the law, and disapprove of the sins which I myself commit."[364] What in fact is happening is that **it is no more I that do it, but sin that dwelleth in me** (17). Paul proceeds to develop this fresh point in vv. 18-20. **For I know that in me (that is, in my flesh,) dwelleth no good thing: for to will is present with me; but how to perform that which is good I find not. For the good that I would I do not: but the evil which I would not, that I do. Now if I do that I would not, it is no more I that do it, but sin that dwelleth in me.**

It is important to distinguish here between **I** and **me** (or **my flesh**). Paul is conscious of two selves at war within himself. The one **I**, or self, consents **unto the law that it is good**, and wills and chooses what the other does not practice (v. 16). This ego, he expressly tells us in v. 22, is the **inward man**, and in v. 23 he identifies it as the **mind** (*nous*) or reason. The other **I**, called **my flesh** in 18, does things which baffle the **mind** or **inward man**. This lower, "outward" self (cf. II Cor. 4:16) is further identified as **my members** (v. 23) and as **the body of this death** (or "this body dominated by death," v. 24). In 6:6 he had also spoken of "the body of sin," meaning "sin's body" or "the body dominated by sin." Here the same idea is expressed, but he is thinking especially of sin's awful consequences.

---

[362]*Discourses* II. 26:4.

[363]"O How My Will Is Hurried To and Fro," in *Emblems Divine and Moral* (New York: Robert Carter & Bros., 1857), p. 202.

[364]Barrett, *The Epistle to the Romans*, p. 147.

The key to understanding this divided or warring personality is **sin that dwelleth in me** (20). This indwelling sin corresponds to the indwelling Spirit of the next chapter (8:9). Indwelt by sin, my lower, or fleshly, nature dominates my true self which delights **in the law of God** (22); but indwelt by the Spirit of God, my **flesh** is dead and deposed (8:3, 9). Indwelt by sin, I am subject to disintegration and death; indwelt by the Spirit, I experience integration and life. In this passage, therefore, Paul is not describing man in the image of God; he is depicting fallen man, man in rebellion against his Creator and therefore corrupt and depraved (cf. 1:21-25). **Flesh** is thus unrenewed man, man cut off from God and subjected to sin. In my fallen humanity sin reigns. **For to will is present with me; but how to perform that which is good I find not** (18). As a creature of **flesh**, my will is bound by sin. For sinful man to boast of free will is therefore vain; he is free only to sin. Like a man sinking in the quicksand, the more he struggles to free himself, the deeper he mires; his only hope is from outside himself. While he is not free to extricate himself from the power of sin, he can call on Jesus Christ and reach out a hand of faith (v. 25).

What does this amount to? That there is a **law** (*nomos*), **that, when I would do good, evil is present with me** (21). This verse describes in fresh terms the state described in vv. 15-16, 18b-19. It is complicated, however, by the use of the word **law**. There are three major interpretations.[365]

(i) Throughout the chapter **law** means the Mosaic law. Thus v. 21 means, "This is what I find the law—a life under the law—to come to in my experience: when I wish to do good, evil is present with me" (Denney). This view is supported by vv. 8, 11.

(ii) **Law** means "rule" or "principle." This view is attractive, but it requires that Paul use the word *nomos* in a radically different sense from its generally understood meaning.

(iii) **Law** here suggests a lawlike rule, which is an evil parallel to the law of Moses. Thus there are two laws: the true law of Moses and the counterfeit of this, which is the result of sin (note the two "laws" in v. 23).

Of these views, (i) and (iii) are not far apart. By struggling

---

[365]Cited by Barrett, *The Epistle to the Romans*, p. 149. These three interpretations are given by Barrett.

to perform God's law in the weakness and corruption of my flesh I transform that very law into **the law of sin** (*to nomo tes hamartias*, "sin's law," or "the law which has become the instrument of sin," 23; cf. vv. 8, 11). **For I delight in the law of God after the inward man** (*kata ton eso anthropon*, "in my inmost self," 22, RSV). "The RSV translation is excellent," says Knox, "not only because 'man' here clearly means 'self', but also because the phrase seems to suggest Paul's conception that the part of him which assents to, even delights in, the law of God is his true, his real, self."[366] We must sharply disagree with Barrett's idea, however, that this "inner self" is "the 'new man' implied by vi. 6."[367] Paul is describing man in the flesh, **sold under sin** (v. 14). Even this man "delights" in the law of God "in [his] inmost self" or **mind** (v. 23). **But I see another law in my members, warring against the law of my mind, and bringing me into captivity to the law of sin which is in my members** (23). Earlier in this passage (in vv. 14, 18) the sin leading man to death is attributed to the **flesh** (*sarx*), but now **the law of sin** is spoken of as ruling **in my members**, i.e., in my body (*soma*). "The queer saint who is led astray by sin and endeavours to put his hands on God's grace is in fact a man rent in two. . . . Which of the two is he? One thing is certain. Whichever of the two he may be, he is not the man who achieves that which, all too boldly, he has undertaken! And it is certain that in the split of this double existence between desire and achievement he is a man who is doomed to death."[368]

O wretched man that I am! Paul cries; **who shall deliver me from this body of death?** (24, marg.) Here **body** (*soma*) means "the sin-ruled self, the self under the sway of sin [as in 6:6*b*]—and that cry applies not to release from the *soma* absolutely, but release from this *soma* as it is ruled through and through by 'flesh,' and that really means release from 'flesh' itself. According to Rom. 8:9, 'flesh' is deposed, and when the next verse says 'if Christ is in you, although your *soma* is dead because of sin,' that means the *flesh-ruled soma* (again equivalent to *flesh* itself) is eliminated (and it is eliminated . . . because sin has been condemned; cf. v. 3)."[369] Since **the wages of sin is death**

---

[366]IB (Exposition), IX, 502.   [367]*The Epistle to the Romans*, p. 150.

[368]Barth, *A Shorter Commentary on Romans*, p. 86.

[369]Rudolph Bultmann, *Theology of the New Testament* (New York: Charles Scribner's Sons, 1951), I, 200.

(6:23), the sin-ruled body is "the body which is given over to death,"[370] or "the death-ridden body."

The glorious statement, **I thank God through Jesus Christ our Lord** (25), is itself grammatically an incomplete answer to the question which he has just raised. "It seems better to understand that Paul, having given a long description of his former unhappy state, can no longer contain himself, and almost before he is ready comes out with the answer to his great problem. Then more calmly he writes a general statement which is a summary of what he has been saying in the past eleven verses."[371] It is a preview of what he is going to enlarge upon in c. 8.

The balance of this verse summarizes the dreary state of man in the flesh, as set forth in the preceding section: **So then with the mind I myself serve the law of God; but with the flesh the law of sin.** In his translation of Romans, Moffatt has taken this last sentence, removed it from its place at the very end of the chapter, and inserted it just before v. 24. This makes a logical, neat arrangement of Paul's thought, and Dodd attempts to justify the rearrangement, even though there is no manuscript support for it whatever.[372] The fact that Paul often writes without slavish regard to logical order militates against making this rearrangement.

Who then is this **wretched man?** He is the man of **flesh, sold** as a slave **under sin** (14). That is to say, he is the "old man" of sin, we ourselves who "were in the flesh," in whom "the motions of sins, which were by the law, did work in our members to bring forth fruit unto death" (5). This "old man" died in and with "the body of Christ," in order that we might be united with Christ and "bring forth fruit unto God" (4). Thus the **wretched man** of vv. 7-25 is *fallen, sinful man confronted by the law.* "The character here assumed is that of a man, first ignorant of the law, then under it, and sincerely, but ineffectually, striving to serve God. To have spoken this of himself, or any true believer, would have been foreign to the whole scope of the discourse; nay, utterly contrary thereto, as well as to what is expressly asserted (viii.2)."[373]

[370]ICC, "Romans," p. 158.

[371]Donald M. Davies, "Free from the Law," *Interpretation*, VII (April, 1953), 162.

[372]*Op. cit.*, pp. 114-15.

[373]Wesley, *Explanatory Notes upon the New Testament*, pp. 543-44.

Paul here confesses in the first person "that the encounter of the Adamite man with the Law is essentially his own origin and that of all believers. . . . Here from the vantage point of his faith in the crucified One, he is describing the essence of his pre-Christian existence. This is *Adamite man under the law, seen with the eye of faith.*"[374] Goppelt sees the model for vv. 14-25 to be what the Pharisees did to Jesus: they wanted to do good and keep God's law but in guilty ignorance did just the opposite. "The 'I' in Rom. 7 has become aware of the existence and at the same time the inescapability of this rebellion."[375] He is caught in the schism between consenting and not performing, between longing for righteousness and actually striving for self-righteousness; he is "fallen" in this dilemma and cannot escape it. He is **flesh:** he wants to do good, but he cannot. It is not until this self-awareness occurs that salvation by the law becomes impossible and the "pre-Christian situation" hopeless.

To begin with, this is undoubtedly Paul's own encounter with the law, as a "Pharisee of the Pharisees" (but viewed from the perspective of his new relationship to Christ). "The whole description is so vivid and so sincere, so evidently wrung from the anguish of direct personal experience, that it is difficult to think of it as purely imaginative."[376] Nygren thinks that Paul's cry in v. 25 is theatrical if it refers to something that is past.[377] But in fact, the memory of those terrible days when he was longing for the fellowship with God which always eluded him brings words of this nature quite naturally to his lips. The whole experience is etched so vividly in Paul's memory that, when he recounts it, he slips naturally into the dramatic present. It is simply a reminder of the intensity of the experience.[378] But now the old "I" is crucified with Christ (6:1-11) and God's law is reestablished through the gift of the Spirit (8:1-11). Paul's testimony at the time of writing the Epistle was not 7:7-25, but 8:1-4. His witness is summed up in one shining sentence: "For the law of the Spirit of life in Christ Jesus hath made me free from the law of sin and death" (8:2). "It would stultify his whole argument if he now confessed that, at the moment of writing, he was a *miserable wretch, a prisoner to sin's law* (verses 24, 23)."[379]

The freedom with which Paul moves from "I" to "we,"

---

[374]Goppelt, *Jesus, Paul and Judaism*, pp. 139-40.   [375]*Ibid.*, p. 140.

[376]ICC, "Romans," p. 186.   [377]*Op. cit.*, pp. 288-90.

[378]Davies, *op. cit.*, pp. 161-62.   [379]Dodd, *op. cit.*, p. 108.

"they," and "you," however, in this whole discussion (cf. 8:1-11), proves that he is generalizing upon the basis of his own struggle and deliverance. Fallen man inevitably changes the law of God into the law of sin (25). Because he is flesh, he is morally weak and corrupt. Sin tyrannizes him, drags him about as a helpless slave. The more desperately he struggles against his captivity, the more grave his situation, for in the process of seeking to lay hold upon the righteousness of the law he becomes a man rent in two, a man doomed to death! Man *cannot* deliver himself from his existence under the law of sin. But in v. 25 there comes a sigh of relief, which marks a dividing line between the period of conflict and defeat and a period where the conflict is practically ended. There are three steps which may be clearly discerned: (1) the life of unconscious morality, marked by happy ignorance (and premoral manifestations of sin; see comments on 9a); (2) then the sharp encounter between the law and sin (9b-24); (3) the end which is at last put to this divided condition by the intervention of Christ and the appropriation of the sanctifying Spirit (vv. 25a; 8:1-11). "Law and the soul are brought face to face with each other, and there is nothing between them. Not until we come to ver. 25 is there a single expression used which belongs to Christianity. And the use of it marks that the conflict is ended."[380] Clearly, the **wretched man** is the awakened sinner, struggling in vain for deliverance from indwelling sin. To apply these verses to the Christian believer would be to admit practically that the grace of Christ is as powerless against sin as is the law. The thrust of the whole argument is to demonstrate that the grace of God in Christ can do "what the law could not do" (8:3), to show that under grace a man has been freed from sin.[381]

[380]ICC, "Romans," p. 186.

[381]The position here advocated was essentially that of Origen and most of the Greek fathers. Augustine and many of the Latin fathers believed that Paul in this passage is speaking primarily of the Christian. The Reformers took this latter view, but Arminius returned to the early Greek view and defended it masterfully. See *The Writings of James Arminius* (Grand Rapids: Baker Book House, 1965), II, 195-453, for a point-by-point attack upon the position that these verses describe present Christian experience. Wesley followed Origen and Arminius, as did Adam Clarke (*op. cit.,* pp. 86-93). Beet defends this same position, affirming, "If these words refer to a justified person, they stand absolutely alone in the entire New Testament" (see *op. cit.,* pp. 217-22). Among more recent defenders of this interpretation are Godet (*op. cit.,* pp. 280-94), Sanday and Headlam (ICC, "Romans," pp. 104-16), and Dodd (*op. cit.,* pp. 104-16).

A qualification must now be added. Paul's intent throughout c. 7 has been clear: *the law cannot sanctify*. From this perspective, the question as to whether vv. 14-25 apply to the unregenerate or the regenerate man is not really Paul's concern. As 3:19-20 shows the powerlessness of the law to *justify* ("by the law is the knowledge of sin"), vv. 14-25 reveal the impotence of the law to *sanctify* ("by the commandment" sin becomes "exceeding sinful," 13). In the beginning of the Christian life it appears that the believer has permanently moved out of vv. 14-25 into 8:1-11, but it is the universal experience of believers and the presupposition of this entire discussion of sanctification in Romans that a justified man does *not* move immediately from the state of sin to the condition of entire sanctification. "In spite of the present tense," Goppelt truly observes, "the 'I' of Rom. 7.14-25 is like the 'I' of Rom. 7.7-13, in both cases basically the past tense for the 'I' of faith, but *a past tense which always lies under the 'I'*. . . . It is a past tense which time and time again becomes partially present experience for every Christian when faith and the Spirit decline."[382] To the extent, therefore, that a believer has not met the conditions of 6:11-13, to that extent sin still remains to trouble his newfound peace. To the extent that he is depending upon his own self-effort for sanctification, to that extent he is yet under the law. Having begun in the Spirit, he is seeking to be made perfect by the flesh (cf. Gal. 3:3). Not until he ceases from his own works does he enter the rest of faith (cf. Heb. 4:9-10). Something of this divided condition and occasional defeat is therefore present experience for the believer until he is cleansed from remaining sin by the sanctifying power of the Spirit (cf. Acts 15:8-9). Thus, while vv. 14-25 most assuredly have a *primary* application to the unrenewed man in his encounter with God's law, they have a *secondary* meaning for the man who is "yet carnal," not in the sense of being dominated by the flesh, but of being a "babe in Christ" and therefore troubled by a remaining self-bias (see I Cor. 3:1-4).[383]

We are now ready to hear Paul's doctrine of sanctification

---

[382]*Op. cit.*, p. 141.

[383]In this connection it is instructive to contrast Gal. 5:19-21 with I Cor. 3:1-4. Both describe the flesh, but from different perspectives. Gal. 5:19-21 delineates the flesh in its full control of human existence—flesh in the unregenerate; whereas I Cor. 3:1-4 describes the flesh in those who have been justified and born of God, but who are not "spiritual" (I Cor. 2:15) or "perfect" (I Cor. 2:6; cf. Heb. 5:12—6:3).

through the Holy Spirit. We are as incapable of sanctifying ourselves as we are of justifying ourselves; but thanks be to God, just as we can be "justified freely" through the propitiation of Christ (3:21-28), we may be "sanctified wholly" through the power of the Holy Spirit (8:1-11; cf. I Thess. 5:23-24). To disclose this second glorious truth is the apostle's purpose in c. 8, and to learn it is to know vital Christianity.

c. Sanctification through the Spirit (8:1-27). Only twice thus far in his discussion of the new life in Christ has the apostle made explicit reference to the Holy Spirit (5:5; 7:6). Both of these references, however, were definitive and relate to what he is about to say in this section. Paul declares that God's love has been poured into our hearts by the Holy Spirit (5:5). This harks back to the prophecy of Isaiah: "For I will pour water upon him that is thirsty, and floods upon the dry ground: I will pour my spirit upon thy seed, and my blessing upon thine offspring" (Isa. 44:3). The same word occurs again in Acts 2 to describe the outpouring on the Day of Pentecost. Peter quotes the prophecy of Joel, "And it shall come to pass in the last days, saith God, I will pour out of my Spirit upon all flesh" (Acts 2:17; cf. Joel 2:28). This has led A. Skevington Wood to call this section "the Pentecost of Romans."[384]

In 8:1-27 the word Spirit occurs 20 times. John Knox observes, "The Spirit is the theme of this culminating section of the argument which began at 6:1 with the question, 'Are we to continue in sin that grace may abound?' "[385] The ultimate answer to the problem of man's sinfulness is the *sanctifying* Spirit, who comes as the culminating Gift of God to apply to our souls the benefits of Christ's redemptive sacrifice. As this passage unfolds, we shall see how the Spirit not only sanctifies our human existence (1:17), but is also the Pledge of our final redemption (18-25). While we may be delivered from the *flesh* by His sanctifying presence and activity (something the law could never do, 7:7-25), our *bodies* still bear the marks of racial sin. But when the new age is consummated by the resurrection, our bodies shall also be redeemed. Meanwhile the Spirit helps us in our frailty and struggle (8:26-27). Such is the theme of this section.

[384]*Life by the Spirit* (Grand Rapids: Zondervan Publishing House, 1963), p. 11.

[385]IB, IX, 504.

(1) God's act in Christ (8:1-4). In these four verses, W. H. Griffith Thomas found "The Saving Activity of God." (1) The glorious fact, 1; (2) The perfect explanation, 2; (3) The divine cause, 3; (4) The practical purpose, 4.

Paul fairly shouts, **There is therefore now no condemnation to them which are in Christ Jesus** (1). **Therefore** has the force of, "In view of what has been previously said, we can declare." We must go back beyond 7:7-25 to find the real point of contact with Paul's argument. On the one hand, we have a normal progression of thought if we connect 8:2 with the cry of thanksgiving in 7:25a. **What the law could not do in that it was weak through the flesh** (3) God has accomplished through sending His Son as a Sacrifice for sin. Therefore since **God** has **condemned sin,** we who are in Christ are not condemned anymore. On the other hand, if we interpret 7:7-25 to describe our existence "under the law" and "in the flesh"—i.e., as our past life as fallen men in the succession of Adam—Paul's conclusion here in 8:1 is directly related to 7:6 (just as 7:7-25 is related to 7:5).

The movement of thought in cc. 7—8 is therefore thus: First, "When we were in the flesh, the motions of sins, which were by the law, did work in our members to bring forth fruit unto death" (7:5). This condition is explicitly described in 7:7-25. Secondly, "But now we are delivered from the law, that being dead wherein we were held; that we should serve in newness of spirit ['the Spirit,' NASB], and not in the oldness of the letter" (7:6). This new life in the Spirit is described in 8:1-27. **Now** is the tie that binds 8:1 to 7:6. "But now we have been released from the law" (7:6, NASB). "There is therefore now no condemnation for those who are in Christ Jesus" (8:1, NASB).

The **condemnation** (katakrima) from which we have been delivered is more than judicial acquittal. Those who are **in Christ Jesus** are not only "not under law" (6:14); they are no longer "in the flesh" (v. 9). The condition and situation described in 7:7-25 is past, at least so far as their being determined by the flesh is concerned (see comments on 5-13). "They do not have the disposition, the structure and the inclination of the flesh but of the Spirit."[386] They have turned their backs on the flesh as their existence dominated by sin and have turned their faces to the Spirit as the Power of the law of grace. Though they may be

[386]Barth, A Shorter Commentary on Romans, p. 91.

tormented by remaining sin, they are enabled by the Spirit of God to conquer the flesh and therefore to **walk not after the flesh, but after the Spirit.**[387] **There is therefore now no condemnation** "for inward sin, even though it does now remain."[388]

In v. 2, Paul reverts to the autobiographical strain of the previous chapter: **For the law of the Spirit of life in Christ Jesus hath made me free from the law of sin and death.** In v. 1 we have **them**; here it is **me.** In 4 it is **us.** What we have here in 2 is obviously personal experience. Phillips Brooks declared, "This is Paul's cry of triumph over the greatest emancipation of his life."[389]

Immediately, however, we are confronted with a paradox. Paul has just been saying that we are delivered from the law, but now he declares that his deliverance is by the application of another law. The paradox is compounded by the fact that he uses the same word (*nomos*) in both cases. **The law (***nomos***) of the Spirit of life in Christ Jesus hath made me free from the law (***nomou***) of sin and death.** "That is a remarkable and perhaps puzzling feature of Paul's experience. He found that only law can liberate from law. He did not cast off restraint when he came to Christ. He submitted to a new law."[390] Barth insists that this **law of the Spirit of life in Christ Jesus** is God's law reestablished by grace. Admittedly, it is smoother to translate *nomos* as "a regulative principle" or paraphrase it to mean something like "religion." But Barth is convinced that Paul means here that "the Law *itself* breaks 'through' that perverted form of a law of sin and death, and shows itself in its true form as the Spirit which moves this man to seek God's grace. In so doing it also liberates this *man* from this perverted form of the law and from the distress

---

[387]Although this last clause is not found in the best Greek MSS, it fits well in v. 1 as a qualification of what it means to be in Christ Jesus. Actually it is borrowed from v. 4 and is omitted here in all modern versions.

[388]Wesley, *Sermons*, I, 91. "That the corruption of nature does still remain, even in those who are the children of God by faith; that they have in them the seeds of pride and vanity, of anger, lust, and evil desire, yea, sin of every kind; is too plain to be denied, being matters of daily experience. And on this account it is, that St. Paul, speaking to those whom he had just before witnessed to be 'in Christ Jesus' (I Cor. 1.2,9,) . . . yet declares, 'Brethren, I could not speak unto you as unto spiritual, but as unto carnal, even as unto babes in Christ' (I Cor. iii.1:) 'Babes in Christ'; so we see they were 'in Christ'; they were believers in low degree. And yet how much of sin remained in them!" (*Ibid.*)

[389]Quoted by Wood, *op. cit.*, p. 21.   [390]*Ibid.*, p. 22.

which in that form it must cause him, and so too it makes this man break through to the path of life, hope and innocence."[391]

In order to put Paul's words in their broadest perspective we do well to recall again the OT promise of the Spirit, which the apostles declare everywhere is now fulfilled. We have already made reference to Isa. 44:3 and Joel 2:28. But there are two other even more significant predictions. Ezekiel (36:26-27) had foretold: "I will put my spirit within you, and cause you to walk in my statutes." And Jeremiah had prophesied, "I will put my law in their inward parts, and write it in their hearts" (Jer. 31: 31-34; cf. Heb. 10:14-17). Beet therefore comments in this connection: "That the Holy Spirit, given to those who believe the words of Christ, prompts and enables them to obey the words of Moses and the prophets is another harmony of the Old and New, and therefore confirms the divine origin of both. And, that Christ came in order that the Law might be fulfilled, proves the importance and the eternal validity of the Law."[392]

The Spirit is the Mediator of this great miracle of grace. Through union with **Christ** we receive "the liberator Spirit."[393] By the gift of the Spirit we are emancipated from the law of sin and death. The Spirit restores God's law once again as a law that is "holy, and just, and good" (7:12; see comments). The law once again becomes "spiritual" (7:14), for "where the Spirit of the Lord is, there is liberty" (II Cor. 3:17). In the power of the sanctifying Spirit we are brought into a new relationship with God, "whose service is perfect freedom."

Paul also speaks of Him as **the Spirit of life** (2). As the Nicene Creed invites us to confess, He is "the Lord and Giver of life." He was the Life-Giver in creation (Gen. 1:2). He is the Life-Giver in the new birth (John 3:5). Here He is the Life-Giver in sanctification, bringing to an end the tyranny of the flesh and delivering us into that perfect love which is the fulfillment of God's law (4). He is also the Life-Giver in resurrection, as we shall see (11). Here in v. 2 the Holy Spirit liberates the believer from sin. "He writes the law of God with living fire in

---

[391]*A Shorter Commentary on Romans*, pp. 89-90.

[392]*Op. cit.*, p. 226. As we shall observe in the comments on v. 4, Paul is certainly implying here a distinction between the moral law and the ritual or ceremonial law of the OT.

[393]Wood, *op. cit.*, p. 23.

our hearts," said Luther, "and consequently the law is not doctrine but life, not word but reality, not a sign but very fulness."[394]
But this is all in Christ Jesus. "The Spirit is the vehicle, but
it is 'Christ who is our life' (Col. 3:4), just as the Spirit is the
Sanctifier but Christ is the sanctification (I Cor. 1:30). 'The
Spirit is never regarded as the *content* of the quickened life,'
Fr. Lionel Thorton concludes after carefully examining the New
Testament evidence. 'The Spirit is the quickening cause; and the
indwelling Christ is the effect of the quickening.' "[395] As Jesus
himself said of the Comforter, "He shall not speak of himself; but
. . . He shall glorify me: for he shall receive of mine, and shall
shew it unto you" (John 16:13-14).

In v. 3 we read, **For what the law could not do, in that it
was weak through the flesh, God sending his own Son in the
likeness of sinful flesh, and for sin, condemned sin in the flesh.**
What was it **the law could not do?** *It could not sanctify.* It could
arouse sin to activity (7:9-13), but it could not cast sin out. This
was because it was **weak through the flesh.** Its appeal was to
man in his fallen and helpless condition. Natural man is *psychikos,* "unspiritual" (I Cor. 2:14, RSV). He is cut off from God
and is subject to sin; therefore he cannot render true devotion
to God (cf. 7:14-25). The law "could not make men free. That
is to say, [it] could not set human feet upon the rock of Eternity
and rid them of the sentence of death which had been pronounced
upon them."[396]

But **what the law could not do . . . God sending his own Son
in the likeness of sinful flesh, and for sin, condemned sin in the
flesh.** What could not be accomplished by the law God performed
through the Incarnation. He sent **his own Son**—"The expression
is intended to emphasize the unique bond of love uniting the
Father to the Son"[397]—"in the likeness of sin's flesh" (*en homoiomati sarkos hamartias,* "in the likeness of *sin-controlled flesh*").[398]
The unique **Son** appeared in human **flesh** "in His impenetrable
incognito."[399] In the eyes of His contemporaries He was a man

---

[394]Quoted by Wood, *ibid.*   [395]Wood, *ibid.,* p. 24.
[396]Barth, *The Epistle to the Romans,* p. 276.

[397]Leenhardt, *op. cit.,* p. 203. This verse assumes the preexistence of the
Son (cf. 1:4; 8:29, 32; I Cor. 1:9; 15:28; II Cor. 1:19; Gal. 2:20; 4:4, 6; Col.
1:13; I Thess. 1:10).

[398]Barth, *The Epistle to the Romans,* p. 278.
[399]*Ibid.,* p. 279.

like all other men (cf. Phil. 2:7). " 'In the likeness of flesh of sin' is one of those exact Scripture phrases which admit of no change," Lenski comments here. " 'The likeness of flesh' would be Docetism, Christ would then be without real flesh; 'the flesh of sin' would be Ebionitism, Christ would then have had sinful flesh; but 'likeness of flesh of sin' is gospel doctrine, Christ assumed our flesh but not its sinfulness."[400]

But *Cur Deus Homo?* "Why did God become man?" It was **for sin** (*peri hamartias*). This phrase may mean "for a sin offering," as in II Cor. 5:21 (so NASB, NEB). But the Greek may mean simply "on account of sin" (Berk.). "The Son of God," says Barrett, "was sent 'to deal with sin.' "[401] He came to meet the tyrant on his own ground and in his own realm—**in the flesh.** As a Denizen of the **flesh,** He **condemned sin in the flesh.** The verb **condemned** means more than to register disapproval; the law does that. He " 'pronounced the doom of Sin.' Sin was thenceforth deposed from its autocratic power."[402] In the flesh-and-blood body of a Man, on the very territory of sin, so to speak, God doomed sin. "By His life of perfect obedience, and His victorious death and resurrection, the reign of sin over human nature has been broken."[403] He is *Christus Victor.* Because He died and rose again, sin is a defeated power, a dethroned tyrant. "The sting of death is sin, and the strength of sin is the law. But thanks be to God, which giveth us the victory through our Lord Jesus Christ" (I Cor. 15:56-57).

The reason for v. 3 is given in 4: **That the righteousness of the law** (*to dikaioma tou nomou,* "the just requirement of the law," RSV) **might be fulfilled in us, who walk not after the flesh, but after the Spirit.** "Righteousness *by* the law is an impossibility," writes Skevington Wood. "Righteousness *of* the law, that is the righteousness which the law demands but can never provide, is gloriously possible when the Spirit applies to our hearts the full benefits of Christ's atoning death."[404] What is "the just requirement of the law"? Let the apostle furnish his own answer. "Owe no man any thing, but to love one another: for he that loveth another hath fulfilled the law. Love worketh no ill to his neighbour: therefore love is the fulfilling of the law" (13:8, 10). And whence this love? The love of God is poured

---

[400]Quoted by Wood, *op. cit.,* p. 27.   [401]*The Epistle to the Romans,* p. 156.
[402]C. Anderson Scott, *op. cit.,* p. 1153. [403]Dodd, *op. cit.,* p. 93.
[404]*Op. cit.,* p. 29.

into our hearts by the Holy Ghost (cf. 5:5). The emphasis is on **in us.** "Not in heavenly angels: in **us.** Not in haloed saints: in **us.** not in spiritual specialists: in **us.**"[405] The last clause is, **In us, who walk not after the flesh, but after the Spirit.** The meaning will become clearer as we consider the next paragraphs.

The preceding sections (7:1—8:4) set forth "The Christian and the Law." (1) Freedom from the law, 7:1-6; (2) Function of the law, 7:7-13; (3) Futility of the law, 7:14-25; (4) Fulfillment of the law, 8:1-4.

(2) *Life in the Spirit* (8:5-11). "Those of whom the apostle had said that they are no longer 'in the flesh' (7:5) cannot evidently live 'according to the flesh.' "[406] **For they that are after the flesh** (*kata sarka,* according to the flesh) **do mind the things of the flesh; but they that are after the Spirit** (*kata pneuma,* according to the Spirit) do mind **the things of the Spirit (5).** It is evident that Paul has precisely the same situation in mind as he treats in Galatians. "For the flesh lusteth against the Spirit, and the Spirit against the flesh: and these are contrary the one to the other: so that ye cannot do the things that ye would" (Gal. 5:17). **The flesh** and **the Spirit** are two conflicting ways of life. To be **after the flesh** is to be incapable of doing **the things of the Spirit;** to be **after the Spirit** is to be incapable of doing **the things of the flesh.** To either type of person Paul says, "You cannot do the things that you would." The man "according to the flesh" cannot live "according to the Spirit." This was Paul's theme in 7:14-25. The man "according to the Spirit" cannot live "according to the flesh." This is his theme in c. 8. There is one important distinction, however, to be noted. The life of the flesh (*kata sarka*) is one of bondage; the life of the Spirit (*kata pneuma*) is one of freedom. Thus while the man *kata sarka* **cannot please God** (v. 8), the man *kata pneuma* still possesses the freedom to sin (Gal. 5:1, 13); the warning in 8:13 makes this clear. Life in the Spirit does not rule out the possibility of sin, but it does impart the power *not to sin.* A man living "according to the Spirit" cannot sin, however, and still be *kata pneuma.* In this sense it may be said to him, "You cannot do the things that you would."

Those who belong to Christ have put the flesh to the Cross (cf. Gal. 5:24). The mortal combat between these two principles is thus settled, and the believer "enjoys the peaceful fruits of victory." Not that he is immune from temptations, but sin no longer gets the upper hand. This is what John Wesley discovered after his conversion at Aldersgate Street. Immediately following the account of his heartwarming experience, he added in his *Journal:* "After my return home, I was much buffetted with temptations; but cried out, and they fled away. They returned again and again. I as often lifted up my eyes and He 'sent me help from His holy place.' And herein I found the difference between this and my former state chiefly consisted. I was striving, yea, fighting with all my might under the law, as well as under grace. But then I was sometimes, if not often, conquered; now I was always conqueror."[407] This is the experience of everyone who is born of God. "What would be the use of the new birth, of redemption at all," Johannes Weiss asks, "if it could not end that miserable stress and slavery?"

In v. 4 the apostle speaks of those "who walk not after the flesh, but after the Spirit." In 5 he goes deeper by passing from the believer's *walk* to his *essential being.* "This is literally an ontological statement," says Wood, "for the Greek participle *ontes* from which that philosophical term is derived appears here in the text."[408] Paul says, **They that are** (*ontes*) **after the flesh . . . they that are after the Spirit** (although the participle is not actually repeated in the second part of the clause).

Verse 6 presents a stark contrast: **For to be carnally minded is death; but to be spiritually minded is life and peace.** NASB translates this: "For the mind set on the flesh is death, but the mind set on the Spirit is life and peace." The Greek phrase is *to phronema tes sarkos;* literally, "the mind of the flesh." Wesley sees the mind set on the flesh as having its "affections fixed on such things as gratify corrupt nature: namely, on things visible and temporal; on things on the earth, on pleasure (of sense or imagination), praise or riches."[409] Undoubtedly this is an *ethical* experience, but it really goes beyond this. Wood holds we are justified in thinking of such a condition as "an *existential* experience—that is to say, having to do with the essential meaning of life."[410] **The flesh** is more than the sensual; it is more than

---

[407]*The Works of John Wesley* (Kansas City: Nazarene Publishing House, n.d.), I, 103-4.

[408]*Op. cit.,* p. 35.   [409]*Explanatory Notes upon the New Testament,* p. 547.
[410]*Op. cit.,* p. 36.

sexual lust. **Flesh** is man living on the earthly, material level, divorced from any contact with the spiritual. This is implied in Jesus' statement to Nicodemus: "That which is born of the flesh is flesh . . . Marvel not that I said unto thee, Ye must be born again" (John 3:6-7; cf. I Cor. 2:14). Such an existence is **death.** Verse 5a reads literally, "The mind of the flesh—death." It is death *now:* "death that comprises all the miseries arising from sin, both here and hereafter" (Amp. NT).

In contrast to this is "the mind of the Spirit" (*to phronema tou pneumatos*). In order to get the full impact of this contrast we should read I Cor. 2:9-16. Those things which are hidden to the eye of the natural (*psychikos*, unspiritual; 14, RSV) man "God hath revealed . . . unto us by his Spirit." For "we have received . . . the spirit which is of God; that we might know the things that are freely given to us of God." If "the mind of the flesh" is earthbound, "the mind of the Spirit" is set on "those things which are above, where Christ sitteth on the right hand of God" (Col. 3:1). The true life of such a man is "in the heavenly places in Christ" (Eph. 1:3; 2:6). Later in this chapter Paul speaks of "the firstfruits of the Spirit" (23); this means that the Spirit is a foretaste, or advance installment, of the glory which shall be revealed to us at Christ's coming (cf. II Cor. 1:22).

If "the mind of the flesh" is **death,** "the mind of the Spirit" is **life** (*zoe*) **and peace** (*eirene*). Two different words are translated "life" in the NT. One is *bios*, which means biological life. The other is the word here (*zoe*). "Now the strange thing is that in classical Greek *zoe* is used as inferior to *bios*. *Bios* is life as lived in extent—the duration of days: whereas *zoe* is the life by which we live, the principle of life. The Bible reverses the order and lifts *zoe* to the pinnacle of supremacy."[411] This is not hard to understand. For the man in Christ, the principle of life is something more than breath; it is **the Spirit** himself. He is the Breath of our new life in Christ, and so *zoe* is lifted to a still higher plane and signifies "the life of God in the soul of man" (Henry Scougal). It is the very life of God communicated by the Holy Spirit. *Zoe* is essentially the life of holiness; for it is "the law of the Spirit of life [*zoes*] in Christ Jesus" which sets us "free from the law of sin and death" (2). So Archbishop Trench has said, "Of that whereof I predicate absolute *zoe*, I predicate absolute holiness of the same. Christ affirming of Himself, *ego eimi he zoe*

[411]*Ibid.*, pp. 38-39.

(I am the life, John 14:6; cf. I John 1:2), implicitly affirmed of Himself that He was absolutely holy; and in the creature, in like manner, that only *lives*, or triumphs over death, death at once physical and spiritual, which has first triumphed over sin. No wonder, then, that Scripture should know no higher word than *zoe* to set forth the blessedness of God, and the blessedness of the creature in communion with God."[412]

Verse 7 sets forth the essential nature of the fleshly spirit: **The carnal mind** (*to phronema tes sarkos*, the mind of the flesh) **is enmity against God** (*echthra eis theon*, "hostile toward God," NASB): **for it is not subject to the law of God, neither indeed can be.** The mind of the flesh is essentially *sin:* "Sin is lawlessness" (*He hamartia estin he anomia*, I John 3:4). The carnal mind is therefore a lawless mind, a sinful mind; as such it **is not,** cannot be, **subject to God's law. So then they that are in the flesh** (*oi de en sarki ontes*) **cannot please God** (8). Here **in** (*en*) is not locative but instrumental; to be **in the flesh** is to be under the domination of the flesh—it indicates a way of life and not a sphere. *En sarki* is practically synonymous with *kata sarka.* We are **in the flesh** when we are living **after the flesh** or "according to the flesh" (5). Such a state is hostile to the Spirit and therefore cannot possibly be pleasing to God; hence it is a state of death (6).

Verse 9 is not addressed to the saints in heaven but to the saints in Rome: **But ye are not in the flesh, but in the Spirit** (*en pneumati*), **if so be that the Spirit of God dwell** (*oikei*, makes His home) **in you.** These men were still in the body (*soma*) but were *not* in the flesh (*sarx*).[413] This proves conclusively that here *sarx* cannot possibly mean "the sphere of the material." As *en sarki* means life "according to the flesh," *en pneumati* means life *kata pneuma*, "according to the Spirit." The believer's inner man is under the motivating, empowering force of the Holy Spirit. "For the Christian, the flesh is dead and deposed (Rom. 8:2 ff.); it is excluded from participation in the Reign of God (I Cor. 15:50), while the *soma*—transformed, i.e. released from the dominion of the flesh—is the vehicle of the

[412]Quoted by Wood, *ibid.*, p. 39.

[413]In Gal. 2:20, Paul uses the phrase *en sarki* in the locative sense, meaning "in the present, earthly body—with all its limitations, weaknesses, and temptations" (R. E. Howard, "Galatians," *Beacon Bible Commentary* (Kansas City: Beacon Hill Press, 1965), IX, 52.

resurrection life. The *soma* is man himself, while *sarx* is a power that lays claim to him and determines him. That is why Paul can speak of a life *kata sarka* (according to the flesh) but never of a life *kata soma* (according to the body)."[414] To the man in whom the Spirit makes His home, God says, "Your body is the temple of the Holy Ghost which is in you . . . therefore glorify God in your body [*soma*]" (I Cor. 6:19-20).

Verse 9 should be placed in juxtaposition with 7:20, in order to understand its full significance. In 7:20, indwelling sin (*he oikousa en emoi hamartia*) determines the existence of the man under law: his life is "in the flesh" and "according to the flesh" because "the sin" (*he hamartia*) dwells, or makes its home, in him. In v. 9 the indwelling Spirit (*pneuma theou oikei en humin*) motivates and empowers the man who is "not under law, but under grace" (6:14): his life is "in the Spirit" and "according to the Spirit." "Thus it is understandable," Leenhardt points out, "as it would not be if these phrases had a locative significance, that the apostle can say without difference of meaning: 'you are in the Spirit' and 'the Spirit is in you.' Both expressions have a common meaning, namely, *the Spirit governs your existence.*"[415]

Now if any man have not the Spirit of Christ, he is none of his. And if Christ be in you, the body is dead because of sin; but the Spirit is life because of righteousness (9b-10). Here **Christ . . . in you** is parallel to the earlier part of v. 9: **Ye . . . are in the Spirit** and **the Spirit of God dwell**(s) **in you.** Not only is **the Spirit** the **Spirit of God** and **of Christ,** but also **Christ** is substituted for **the Spirit.** None of these expressions by itself conveys completely all that has been suggested concerning the action of the Spirit. Paul uses them to complement each other, since "he visualizes in turn the restored communion with God from the point of view of its origin and efficient cause, from the point of view of its realization or instrumental cause, and from the point of view of its completion or final cause. The *Spirit* is at one and the same time the author of this communion, the essence of this communion, and the consummation of this communion. Similarly with regard to *Christ,* whose presence is the very foundation of this communion which in turn consists in and is secured by this presence."[416]

[414]Bultmann, *op. cit.,* p. 201.   [415]*Op. cit.,* p. 207.

[416]*Ibid.* (italics mine).

In the expression, **Now if any man have not the Spirit of Christ,** Wesley understands Paul to be saying, "He is not a member of Christ; not a Christian; not in a state of salvation. This is a plain, express declaration, which admits of no exception."[417] To **have . . . the Spirit of Christ** is obviously both a spiritual and an ethical experience. By and through the Spirit, Christ (i) dwells in the believer and (ii) brings him into conformity "to the image of" the "Son" (29). As the Guest within, Christ "becomes the true 'I' (Gal. 2:20), and exercises His authority at the very centre of the human person through the agency of the Holy Spirit."[418] This is something more than mystical experience; it means that Christ re-presents himself through my redeemed personality. This, Paul says, is the unfailing mark of the Christian. While it is true, however, that every believer *has* the Spirit of Christ, not every Christian is *filled* with the Spirit (cf. I Cor. 2:6, 15-16; 3:1-4; Eph. 3:14-19; 5:18).

Now, Paul goes on to say, **if Christ be in you, the body is dead because of sin** (*to soma nekron dia hamartian*); **but the Spirit is life because of righteousness** (*to pneuma zoe dia dikaiosynen*). Does this mean that **the body is dead** in the sense of 6:6 and of the argument which has preceded this claim, or does v. 10 point forward to v. 11 and mean simply that the body is **mortal** because of Adam's sin? Authorities are almost evenly divided. Bultmann stands foremost among those who insist on the former interpretation. He argues Paul means "that the *flesh-ruled soma* (again equivalent to *flesh* itself) is eliminated (and it is eliminated 'because of sin'—i.e. because sin has been condemned; cf. v. 3)."[419]

Barrett also advocates this position. "If Christ is you, two consequences follow. On the one hand your body is dead. 'Your body' is 'you', and you are dead; for this see vi. 2-11; vii. 1-6. Of course it remains true that this baptismal death must be constantly realized (vi. 11). . . . On the other hand, while the body is dead, the Spirit (of God) is life-giving. Paul does not mean that the (human) spirit is alive, and imply thereby a strict dichotomy of body and spirit. If he had meant this he would have said, 'The spirit is alive', not 'the spirit is life'. The human self is dead—to

[417]*Explanatory Notes upon the New Testament, loc. cit.*

[418]Leenhardt, *op. cit.*, p. 209, fn.

[419]*Op. cit.*, p. 200.

sin; the Spirit is able to give life—because . . . man is now rightly related to God in whose gift the Spirit lies."[420]

Other authorities think Paul's thought at this point has turned forward to the resurrection, for he says next: **But if the Spirit of him that raised up Jesus from the dead dwell in you, he that raised up Christ from the dead shall also quicken your mortal bodies** (to *thneta somata*) **by his Spirit that dwelleth in you (11).**[421] Here both a future gift and a present grace merge with each other. The reference is undoubtedly to the resurrection of the body which will occur when Christ returns; on that day our **mortal bodies** will be made alive.[422] But as believers we now have "the firstfruits of the Spirit" (23). The resurrection of Christ was the beginning of every blessing that we have through Him. Through the risen Lord we have received even now the quickening power of the Holy Spirit. Thus Paul is thinking here of all those revivifying forces which broke into history with Christ's victory over death and which are mediated to us through the Spirit. Salvation is therefore more than a matter of the soul; salvation touches the whole man, body and soul, both here and hereafter. In this passage particularly the Spirit is seen as the life-giving Breath of God, His mighty power by which creation is renewed.

In 8:1-11 we see "Freedom from Sin and Death." (1) The source of freedom, 2, 9; (2) The scope of freedom, 5-8; (3) The sequel to freedom, 2-4, 11 (W. T. Purkiser).

3. *Obligations and privileges in the Spirit* (8:12-17). Thus, then, the indwelling Spirit offers the believer new possibilities of existence. It is for the believer to recognize this opportunity, and act upon it. New obligations are now imposed upon the man who has died and risen with Christ; we owe something to the One who has set us free. Verses 12-14 should be read together, for they form one complete thought: **Therefore, brethren, we are debtors, not to the flesh, to live after the flesh** (kata sarka). **For if ye live after the flesh, ye shall die: but if ye through the**

---

[420]Barrett, *The Epistle to the Romans*, p. 159.

[421]If we adopt this view, we must still recognize the essential correctness of the other. Either position seems to be grammatically possible and theologically correct, and it is difficult to determine the orientation of Paul's thought at this transition.

[422]Notice that Paul does not say *flesh*, for "flesh and blood cannot inherit the kingdom of God" (I Cor. 15:50). In the resurrection man will have *soma* (for he is *soma*), but not *sarx*.

Spirit do mortify the deeds of the body (*ei de pneumati tas praxeis tou somatos thanatoute*, "if by the Spirit you are putting to death the deeds of the body," NASB), **ye shall live. For as many as are led by the Spirit of God, they are the sons of God.**

The debt we owe the Spirit is a debt of loving gratitude to the One who has made us "free from the law of sin and death" (2). The alternative presented is a familiar one in Romans: life according to the flesh or life according to the Spirit. Equally known is the end to which each way leads: death or life. "However, Paul now clarifies the nature of this life according to the Spirit, by saying that it consists in putting to death the deeds of the body through the power of the Spirit."[423] It is important that we try to grasp just what Paul means here. He is most certainly not advocating ascetic mortification, which is based on the idea that the body is a weight upon the soul. Paul is not positing any Hellenistic body-soul dualism. As we have seen, for him the body (*soma*) is the self expressed concretely. What the believer is obligated to do is, if we may borrow Oswald Chambers' happy expression, to *sacrifice the natural for the sake of the spiritual.* By the Spirit we are to reckon that the members of our body are dead to sin and that we are "alive unto God" (cf. 6:11-13). "The members of the body undergo death as it were in order to become more alive than ever through the flowering of their . . . [possibilities] which sin had suppressed. They now become instruments available to the Spirit."[424] The Christian who does not thus sacrifice his body faces the threat of death. So long as he lives he faces the option of dying *to* sin or dying *in* sin. However, the Christian life is no seesaw affair for one who has really died to sin. As Paul has just told us, he is no longer "in the flesh," for the Spirit has come to make His home within. Through the indwelling Spirit, Christ exercises His authority within the very center of his heart. To **mortify the deeds of the body** is thus no matter of self-castigation but of maintaining an attitude of obedience as we continue in the hallowed *communion* of the Spirit (cf. II Cor. 13:14).[425]

---

[423]Leenhardt, *op. cit.*, p. 211.   [424]*Ibid.*

[425]"Perhaps it would be fitting to replace the term union by that of communion, which is more respectful of that dimension of personal reality in which the relations of the sinner restored to fellowship with God through Jesus Christ are situated. Thus we shall characterize the Pauline mysticism as *a relation of communion,* dynamic and based on divine initiative" (*ibid.*, p. 209, fn.).

Paul wants his readers to understand that this mortification of our bodily impulses by the Spirit should not lead to a relapse into legalism. **For as many as are led by the Spirit of God, they are the sons of God.** Mortification is not the basis but the result of our relationship with God. The presence of the Spirit in our hearts is the result of a change in our relations with God, a change in which God has taken the initiative. He sent His Son so that His rebellious children might become His sons by the procedure of adoption. Mortification thus shows that God has reestablished filial relations. It flows from the renewed presence of the Holy Spirit within our hearts. Hence all anxious fear is out of place. **For ye have not received the spirit of bondage again to fear; but ye have received the Spirit of adoption, whereby we cry, Abba, Father** (15). The apostle goes into this thought even more fully in Gal. 4:1-7. Under the law, the highest relationship with God one may know is that of servitude—i.e., scrupulous endeavor to please God, which is inevitably accompanied by **the spirit of bondage . . . to fear.** But under grace, our relationship is that of *sonship*—i.e., a filial relationship of love characterized by joyous and grateful obedience. "But when the fulness of time was come, God sent forth his Son, made of a woman, made under the law, to redeem them that were under the law, that we might receive the adoption of sons. And because ye are sons, God hath sent forth the Spirit of his Son into your hearts, crying, Abba, Father. Wherefore thou art no more a servant, but a son" (Gal. 4:4-7).

The Aramaic **Abba** is a clue to Paul's thought. It was the intimate family term for *Father*. Every language has such a word; in medieval Latin that word was *papa,* and in French it is *dada* (from which we get the English "daddy"). Although the Jews addressed God with the reverential *Abbi,* no Jew would think of saying **Abba.** This was the word Jesus used when He prayed (cf. Mark 14:36). As His disciples heard Him speak so intimately with the Father, they requested, "Lord, teach us to pray" (Luke 11:1). They learned to know the same intimacy with God which Jesus enjoyed. **The Spirit of adoption** which we receive when we are justified by faith is the answer to the disciples' petition. The Spirit puts into our hearts the spirit of sonship and on our lips **Abba, Father.** "He became what we are, that we might become what He is."[426] One qualification must be added, however, to safeguard the uniqueness of Jesus. He is the Son

[426]Irenaeus.

of God by nature (cf. John 1:18), we by adoption. Yet through the incarnation of the Son (cf. 8:3; Gal. 4:4) we are introduced into the circle of divine fellowship (cf. John 17:17-26).

Therefore we read: **The Spirit itself** ("himself," NASB, RSV) **beareth witness with** (*symmartyrei,* witnesses along with) **our spirit, that we are the children of God** (16). Paul is declaring that there is a "joint-witness"[427] between the Spirit of God and the human spirit (or conscience). First and foremost is the witness of God's Spirit, which in Wesley's classic phraseology "is an inward impression on the soul, whereby the Spirit of God directly witnesses to my spirit, that I am a child of God; that Jesus Christ hath loved me, and given himself for me; and that all my sins are blotted out, and I, even I, am reconciled to God."[428] The witness of the human spirit, which necessarily *follows* [429] and *corroborates* the witness of the divine Spirit, "is nearly, if not exactly, the same with the testimony of a good conscience towards God; and is the result of reason, or reflection on what we feel in our souls. Strictly speaking, it is a conclusion drawn partly from the word of God, and partly from our own experience. The word of God says, every one who has the fruit of the Spirit is a child of God; experience, or inward consciousness, tells me, that I have the fruit of the Spirit; and hence I rationally conclude, 'Therefore I am a child of God.' "[430] Wesley seems here to have penetrated to the heart of Paul's meaning.

[427]ICC, "Romans," p. 203.

[428]Sermons, I, *op. cit.,* pp. 115 and 124-25.

[429]"That this testimony of the Spirit of God must needs, in the very nature of things, be antecedent to the testimony of our own spirit, may appear from this single consideration: We must be holy of heart, and holy in life, before we can be conscious that we are so; before we can have the testimony of our spirit, that we are inwardly and outwardly holy. But we must love God, before we can be holy at all; this being the root of all holiness. Now we cannot love God, till we know that he loves us. 'We love him, because he first loved us.' And we cannot know his pardoning love to us, till his Spirit witnesses it to our spirit. Since, therefore, this testimony of his Spirit must precede the love of God and all holiness, of consequence it must precede our inward consciousness thereof, of the testimony of our spirit concerning them" (Sermons, I, *op. cit.,* pp. 115-16).

[430]Sermons, I, *op. cit.,* p. 125. Barth writes in the same vein: "Ecstasies and illuminations, inspirations and intuitions, are not necessary. Happy are they who are worthy to receive them! But woe to us, if we wait anxiously for them! Woe be to us, if we fail to recognize that they are patchwork by-products! All that occurs to us and in us can be no more than an answer to what the Spirit Himself says" (*The Epistle to the Romans,* p. 298).

The first privilege of an adopted son, therefore, is to call God **Father.** Through the presence of Christ within and the working of His Spirit our sonship becomes a blessed experience of communion with God. The second privilege of the adopted son is that he becomes an heir of his adoptive Father's wealth. **And if children, then heirs; heirs of God, and joint-heirs with Christ; if so be that we suffer with him, that we may be also glorified together (17).** We might say that the aim of adoption is to make someone a beneficiary of goods of which he would otherwise have been deprived. The metaphor borrowed from the Roman law court therefore suits the dispensation of grace.[431] The idea of inheritance emphasizes the gratuity of the wealth received. Paul sees in the fact of adoption a privilege which was passed on to sinners by the Son, the Heir *par excellence,* He in whom the promise of inheritance, made to Abraham (4:13; cf. Gal. 3:29), had found its supreme fulfillment.

We are **joint-heirs with Christ; if so be that we suffer with him, that we may be also glorified together.** There is no sharing in Christ's glory unless there is sharing in His sufferings. Sufferings and then glory were the appointed order for Christ (cf. I Pet. 1:11); the same applies to those who are His **joint-heirs.** It is important to note that they suffer **with** Him, and this joint participation is stressed in the case of both the suffering and the glorification. The sufferings of the children of God are regarded by Paul as the sufferings of Christ (II Cor. 1:5; Phil. 3:10; Col. 1:24; II Tim. 2:11; cf. I Pet. 4:13 and Mark 10:39). Dietrich Bonhoeffer, who was put to death as a Christian martyr by the Gestapo on April 9, 1945, wrote from the crucible of his own sufferings: "In the fellowship of the crucified and glorified body of Christ we participate in his suffering and glory. His cross is the burden which is laid on his Body, the Church. All its sufferings borne beneath this cross are the sufferings of Christ himself. This suffering first takes the form of the baptismal death [of 6:3-4]. . . . But there is a far greater form of suffering than this, one which bears an ineffable promise. For while it is true that only the suffering of Christ himself can atone for sin, and that his suffering and triumph took place 'for us,' yet to some, who

---

[431]The term **adoption** (*huiothesia*) was unknown to the Jews and is not found in the LXX; the word was borrowed from the *koine* Greek and adapted by Paul to the gospel.

are not ashamed of their fellowship in his body, he vouchsafes the immeasurable grace and privilege of suffering 'for him,' as he did for them."[432] Such suffering with Christ cannot but end in glory with Him.

In 8:12-17, Paul shows us "The Christian Life." (1) Its discipline, 12-13; (2) Its direction, 14; (3) Its devotion, 15; (4) Its discernment, 16; (5) Its dominion, 17 (W. T. Purkiser).

(4) *The firstfruits of the Spirit* (8:18-27). Our Christian existence has three temporal dimensions: past, present, and future. It is based on the Foundation which has been laid, Christ (I Cor. 3:11); it lives in the present by the power of the Spirit; it reaches out toward the full redemption in the future. After having thoroughly dealt with the first two, Paul now turns to the third, the hope we have in Christ. But even so, the Spirit is still central as the foretaste of this future glory. This is the meaning of the key phrase in the section, **the firstfruits of the Spirit** (23). God bestows the Spirit upon the believer as the anticipation of **the glory which shall be revealed** (18) when Christ comes to consummate his salvation.

The immediate link in the preceding section is v. 15, where Paul speaks of "the Spirit of adoption." He realizes that this adoption is incomplete. "It is assured to the believer, but it is not yet apparent to the world. It is a concealed sonship. It is obscured by the body of our humiliation. But at the end of the age, when the Lord returns for His own and then with His own, that sonship will be revealed. All will see that adoption is a fact. The Spirit is the first fruits of that coming disclosure. 'Beloved, we are God's children now; it does not yet appear what we shall be, but we know that when he appears we shall be like him, for we shall see him as he is' (I John 3:2)."[433]

Paul now begins to describe the interim period, showing how Christians should take courage both from the prospect of glory and from the assistance already given them by the Holy Spirit.[434] **For I reckon that the sufferings of this present time are not worthy to be compared with the glory which shall be revealed in us** (18). When he says, **I reckon** (*logizomai*), he means, "I

---

[432]Op. cit., pp. 272-73.   [433]Wood, *op. cit.,* p. 105.

[434]See Barrett, *The Epistle to the Romans,* p. 165.

judge after careful deliberation." **This present time** is the period in which the Christians' **sufferings** occur. It is "this age" or "this present age" in contrast to "the age to come" (cf. 12:2; Gal. 1:4; Eph. 1:21, where "world" translates *aion,* which is properly rendered "age"). The age to come is the age of resurrection and glory to be revealed at Christ's return. Godet notes the significance of this fact for Christian experience: "As to the spirit we are in the *age to come;* as to the body, in the *present age.*"[435] For the doctrine of holiness this means that, while the body of the fully sanctified believer is no longer the instrument of sin (see comments on 6:6 and 8:9-10), it is still unredeemed (cf. v. 23, and comments there).

Sufferings then belong to this present age, between the advents of our Lord. **Glory** belongs to the age to come. And the one bears no kind of comparison with the other. As Moffatt puts it, **sufferings** are "a mere nothing" when set against **the glory which shall be revealed in us.** The phrase **in us** (*eis hemas*) may mean "to us" (NASB, RSV), although the KJV may be nearer Paul's thought. The glory which is promised will not only be revealed to us but will transform us (Phil. 3:21).

So great is this glory that **the earnest expectation of the creature** (*tes ktiseos,* the creation, cf. 1:20; v. 22) **waiteth for the manifestation** (*apokalypsin,* "revealing," NASB, RSV) **of the sons of God** (19). How much of created reality is awaiting the revelation of the sons of God? We may exclude angels, for they are not subjected to vanity and the bondage of corruption. Satan and demons must be excluded, for they cannot be regarded as awaiting **the manifestation of the sons of God.** The children of God are not included, for they are expressly distinguished in this very verse. The unregenerate are not included, for they entertain no such expectation. "The creation" thus means the natural order, cursed as it is in consequence of Adam's sin (Gen. 3:17). We are here told of "the one far-off divine event to which the whole creation moves." Phillips phrases it: "The whole creation is on tiptoe to see the wonderful sight of the sons of God coming into their own." This is what the late Professor G. T. Thomas of Edinburgh calls "a scientific fact viewed theologically."[436]

Paul has introduced this point because his main object in mentioning the creation is to emphasize the certainty of future

---

[435]*Op. cit.,* p. 313.   [436]Cited by Wood, *op. cit.,* p. 108.

salvation for Christians. His concern is not with creation for its own sake, but having brought the subject up he feels the matter requires further explanation. "For the creation was subjected to futility [**vanity**], not of its own will, but because of Him who subjected it, in hope that the creation itself also will be set free from its slavery to corruption into the freedom of the glory of the children of God" (20-21, NASB). Paul says three things here: (1) the created order "was made the victim of frustration" (NEB); (2) this was not of its own will; (3) it was subjected in hope. This can mean only that creation was not corrupted through any fault of its own; it was involved in the fatal defection of Adam. But this curse upon nature, though arising out of man's sin, was imposed upon it by the Creator. Since creation is under the control of God, it has never been without hope. The world as we know it is *not* "the best possible of all worlds." It shares in the misery and purposelessness of man's sinful existence. But since it was not enslaved by its own will, God reserves a hope in its behalf.

The **hope** of creation is that it shall share in the redemption of mankind. In the mystery of God's eternal purpose, the two go hand in hand and are inseparably united. "Just as God, on the day of resurrection, will give man a body which corresponds to the new aeon of glory, a 'spiritual body,' so He will create a corresponding new cosmos, 'new heavens and a new earth.' "[437] The prophecy of Isaiah which predicts the new heaven and earth is preceded by the analogy of labor pains (Isa. 66: 7-9, 22). These are anticipated in **this present time** by the natural order, struggling even now to be delivered from its bondage. This is the thought of vv. 22-23.

For we know that the whole creation groaneth and travaileth in pain together until now. And not only they, but ourselves also, which have the firstfruits of the Spirit, even we ourselves groan within ourselves, waiting for the adoption, to wit, the redemption of our body. The subject, **We,** is explained by v. 23: we ourselves, who have the firstfruits of the Spirit. "This, then, is not a matter of general knowledge, as if everyone was aware of nature's pangs. That is plainly not so. Even the scientists whose task it is to examine the phenomena of the material universe, are unable to trace the evidence, unless aided by revelation. This is

---

[437]Nygren, *op. cit.,* p. 332.

something we know as Christians, because God the Creator has told us in His Word."[438] **The whole creation** groans and travails in the labor of childbirth **until now.** This latter phrase "indicates that the birth of the new order has not yet taken place, but it also is a token that the birth pangs have not ceased and that hope has not been quenched."[439]

"And not only this, but also we ourselves, having the first-fruits of the Spirit, even we ourselves groan within ourselves, waiting eagerly for our adoption as sons, the redemption of our body" (NASB). "And not only this" indicates that the argument is being carried one step further. While the creation is **subjected . . . in hope** (20), we possess **the firstfruits** (*aparche*, the "first installment" or "down payment") **of the Spirit.** The indwelling Spirit is the foretaste of our heavenly glory, the anticipation of our future redemption. In two other Epistles, Paul conveys this same teaching about the Spirit by the use of *arrabon*, which means "pledge" or "earnest" (II Cor. 1:22; 5:5; Eph. 1:14). In modern Greek *arrabon* is employed for an engagement ring, as the pledge or earnest of the coming marriage. The indwelling Spirit is the believer's assurance of God's better day. *Aparche*, however, is an even stronger metaphor than *arrabon*. The **first-fruits** are a specimen crop of the glory which shall be ours when Christ returns. As the grapes of Eshcol, brought back by Caleb and Joshua from the land of Canaan, were meant to whet the appetite of the Hebrews for the Promised Land, so the Holy Spirit introduces us to the taste of heaven.

> *Once heaven seemed a far-off place,*
> *Till Jesus showed His smiling face.*
> *Now it's begun within my soul;*
> *'Twill last while endless ages roll.*

The **adoption** for which we are **waiting** is the full **manifestation** of our status as **the sons of God.** By the witness of the Spirit we know that we have been adopted into God's family: by "the Spirit of adoption . . . we cry, Abba, Father" (15-16). But when Christ returns, there shall be a public proclamation of this glorious fact to the whole world (cf. 19). Writing of this same wondrous event, Paul says in another Epistle: "We shall not all

---

[438]Wood, *op. cit.,* p. 111.

[439]Murray, *op. cit.,* p. 305.

sleep, but we shall all be changed, in a moment, in the twinkling of an eye, at the last trump: for the trumpet shall sound, and the dead shall be raised incorruptible, and we shall be changed" (I Cor. 15:51-52). This change will be **the redemption of our body**, which still exists in this present age as "the body of our humiliation" (Phil. 3:21, ASV). (Cf. v. 11 and comments on v. 18.) While the body is dead to sin (6:6-7; 8:3, 9-10) if we are fully consecrated to God (6:13) and sanctified (6:19), it still must be constantly sacrificed to God through the power of the Spirit (8:13) and kept subject to our consecrated purpose as Christians (I Cor. 9:27).

As we have already seen, the *body* is not sinful, but the *flesh* is (8-9). When the body is presented to God as a "living sacrifice" (12:1), it becomes in very truth "the temple of the Holy Ghost" (I Cor. 6:19), through which we may "glorify God" (I Cor. 6:20). Nevertheless it is still unredeemed. The sense in which this is true is suggested in v. 26. Even though we are indwelt by the Holy Spirit, we are beset by **infirmities**. These include the bodily sufferings which eventuate in physical death, with all the anguish of spirit implied by what we call human suffering. Why the righteous suffer is the enigma of **this present time** (18). Paul makes no effort to solve this riddle here; he is content at the moment to remind us by the word of God that suffering shall in God's time be swallowed up in **glory**. The **redemption of the body** will mean the end of human suffering.

But Paul surely means more than this. Because of **our infirmities** the **Spirit maketh intercession for us with groanings which cannot be uttered** (26). The **groanings of the Spirit** are the birth pangs of our bodily redemption, just as the groanings of the **whole creation** are the travail of nature's redemption (22). As the creation is frustrated, or **subject to vanity** (20), so **our infirmities** frustrate the Holy Spirit and cause Him to groan within us. **Our infirmities** must surely encompass the whole array of human frailties: the racial effects of sin in our bodies and minds, the scars from our past sinful living, our prejudices which hinder God's purposes, our neuroses which bring emotional depressions and cause us at times to "act out of character," our temperamental idiosyncrasies, our human weariness and fretfulness, and a thousand faults our mortal flesh is heir to. "For we have this treasure in earthen vessels, that the excellency of the power may be of God, and not of us" (see II Cor. 4:7-11,

16). We may add to this list our "involuntary transgressions" of God's perfect law.[440]

A full-orbed doctrine of Christian perfection must place the truth of entire sanctification within the framework of **this present time** (v. 18), which is characterized by **infirmities**. The *tyranny* of the flesh is ended by the sanctifying presence of the Holy Spirit, but not the *weakness* of the flesh. Using the term, therefore, in its OT sense, we must confess with Paul, "The life which I now live in the flesh [of weakness and infirmity] I live by the faith of the Son of God" (Gal. 2:20). Furthermore, the man who is indwelt by the Spirit must confess, "I know that in me (that is, in my flesh,) dwelleth no good thing" (7:18)—that is, *apart from the presence of Christ in my life I am flesh*. In Wesley's words, we have no "stock of holiness" in us; whatever holiness we enjoy at any moment is in us by His indwelling presence, "for without me ye can do nothing" (cf. John 15:1-6).[441] To see this is to understand that our sanctification is wholly His work. With Harriet Auber, we gladly confess,

> *And every virtue we possess,*
> *And every victory won,*
> *And every thought of holiness*
> *Are His alone.*

In the Philippian letter Paul puts this truth in its fullest perspective. First, "it is God which worketh in . . . [me] both to will and to do of his good pleasure" (2:13). But in view of the hope of "the resurrection from the dead" (3:11, NASB), I must confess that, even though I may be classed with those who are

---

[440]In his *Plain Account of Christian Perfection*, Wesley is quite explicit at this point. "It follows, that the most perfect have continual need of the merits of Christ, even for their actual transgressions, and may say, 'Forgive us our transgressions.' . . . I believe there is no perfection in this life as excludes these involuntary transgressions which I apprehend to be naturally consequent on the ignorance and mistakes inseparable from mortality. Therefore *sinless perfection* is a term I never use, lest I should seem to contradict myself" (*Works of John Wesley*, XI, 395-96). Christian perfection is not in the legal but in the evangelical order in which "love is the fulfilling of the law," "love filling the heart, expelling pride, anger, desire, self-will" (*ibid.*, pp. 414-17).

[441]*Ibid.*, p. 417. "The best of men may say, 'Thou art my light, my holiness, my heaven. Through my union with thee, I am full of light, of holiness, and happiness. But if I were left to myself, I should be nothing but sin, darkness, hell.'"

"perfect" (3:15; cf. I Cor. 2:6, 15-16), I am not "perfected" (*teteleiomai*, 3:12)—in the sense of **the redemption of our body** (23). Nevertheless, "I am confident of this very thing, that He who began a good work in me will perfect it [*epitelesei*] until the day of Christ Jesus" (1:6, NASB).

But we are saved by hope (24)—the hope of the resurrection. **Are saved** (*esothemen*) is better rendered "were saved" (RSV). When we were saved, Paul is saying, it was in the hope of our final redemption. "If Christianity be not altogether restless eschatology," Barth says in his characteristic incisiveness, "there remains in it no relationship whatever to Christ."[442] "We have been saved from the sinking ship into the lifeboat," Beet writes, "but not yet into the haven."[443] We shall be safe home in the port only when in the glorified body we are forever with the Lord.[444]

But hope that is seen is not hope: for what a man seeth, why doth he yet hope for? These clauses scarcely need comment; they express the obvious truth that hope is no longer hope when the thing hoped for is realized. "They provide, however, a patent example of the two uses of the term hope. In the first clause, 'hope' refers to the thing hoped for, the object of hope; in the second, hope denotes the state of mind entertained in reference to the thing hoped for."[445] Verse 24 thus prepares for the next statement: **But if we hope for that we see not, then do we with patience wait for it** (25). "Hope then ever draws patience with it," says Calvin. "Thus it is a most apt conclusion—that whatever the gospel promises respecting the glory of the resurrection, vanishes away, except we spend our present life in patiently bearing the cross and tribulations."[446]

It is at this point that Paul reminds his readers of the gracious assistance of the Holy Spirit in their **infirmities** (26). In the preceding verses the accent falls upon the **sufferings** and the **hope** afforded in these; in vv. 26-27 the emphasis is upon **our infirmities** and the help given for their relief. "As hope sustains us in suffering, so the Holy Spirit helps our infirmity."[447] **For we know not what we should pray for as we ought** shows how helpless we are in **our infirmities** and lays the basis for the special

---

[442]*The Epistle to the Romans,* p. 314.   [443]*Op. cit.,* p. 250.
[444]Wood, *op. cit.,* p. 114.   [445]Murray, *op. cit.,* p. 309.
[446]*Op. cit.,* p. 176.   [447]Murray, *op. cit.,* p. 311.

kind of help afforded by the Holy Spirit. "Prayer covers every aspect of our need, and our weakness is exemplified and laid bare by the fact that we know not what to pray for as is meet and proper," understanding *katho dei* in the sense of "as is meet." "We do not know how to pray as the exigencies of our situations demand" (cf. II Cor. 12: 7-10).[448] It is at this point of "weakness" (cf. II Cor. 12:9) that **the Spirit** comes to our help. This is grace in the subjective sense—the gracious assistance of the Holy Spirit who **maketh intercession for us with groanings which cannot be uttered.**

As the children of God we have two divine Intercessors. Christ is our Intercessor in heaven, "at the right hand of God" (34; cf. Heb. 7:25; I John 2:1). The Holy Spirit is our Intercessor within (cf. John 14:16-17, where *allon parakleton* may be rendered "another Intercessor," NASB, marg.). He intercedes **with groanings which cannot be uttered.** Whatever view we may adopt with regard to these groanings, we must not overlook the fact that they are groanings of which the Holy Spirit is the Author. More deeply, they are the groanings of the Spirit himself. In laboring to give birth to our resurrected bodies He groans within us. At the same time these are our groanings also. "We cannot reasonably think of the Holy Spirit himself, apart from the agency and instrumentality of those on whose behalf he intercedes, as presenting his intercessions to the Father in the form of his own groanings."[449] This is clearly implied in the next statement.

And he that searcheth the hearts knoweth what is the mind of the Spirit, because he maketh intercession for the saints according to the will of God (27). Only as we appreciate the main thought of v. 26, that the groanings of the saints register the intercession of the Holy Spirit, can we understand this verse. **He that searcheth the hearts** is God the Father (cf. Ps. 139:1, 23; Jer. 17:10; Acts 15:8-9; I Cor. 4:5; Heb. 4:13). **The mind of the Spirit** in this instance is not the mind of Christ created in us (cf. I Cor. 2:15-16) but the mind of the Holy Spirit himself; this is shown by what follows—**because he maketh intercession for the saints according to the will of God.** It is the Holy Spirit who makes intercession. Since His intercession is in accord with the mind and will of God, this is the guarantee that the Searcher

---

[448]*Ibid.*   [449]*Ibid.*, p. 312.

of our hearts knows the content and intent of the intercession. Therefore we have the confidence expressed elsewhere in one of the apostle's great prayers, that God does "exceeding abundantly above all that we ask or think, *according to the power that worketh in us*" (Eph. 3:20)—i.e., through the intercession of the Holy Spirit.

d. *Our security in Christ* (8:28-39). We now come to the climax of the section. Throughout the chapter Paul's perspective has been widening step by step, until at last we have come to a survey of God's eternal purpose. The present age ("this present time," 18) is not the first, as its comparison with God's new age might suggest. Just as the present age is to be followed by eternity, it has already been preceded by an eternity. Only when we view our present existence set in God's purpose, which extends from eternity to eternity, do we get the right and fullest perspective. Then we are in a position to see that **all things** which come to the Christian in this life—and thus the sufferings of the present age—must **work together for good** to him.

(1) *God's eternal purpose consummated* (8:28-30). All that is negative in this life is seen to have a positive purpose in the execution of God's eternal plan. Superficially, "the sufferings of this present time" seem to hinder God's purpose for us; but in actual fact everything which seems to frustrate God's purpose comes to serve its accomplishments. "The result is that nothing can harm the Christian. Even the onslaught of the powers of destruction[450] belongs to that which must work together for good."[451] **And we know that all things work together for good to them that love God, to them who are the called according to his purpose** (28).

The **we know** here in 28 seems to be in contrast to "we know not" in v. 26. *We* may not know, but "he that searcheth the hearts knoweth" (27); *He* knows, and we may know in Him. Verse 28 is therefore a connecting link between what Paul has just written and what he is about to tell us. "The Spirit brings assurance not only of sonship, as in v. 16, but of security."[452] We know only because the Spirit knows, and communicates His knowledge to us.

---

[450]See vv. 35-39, where these powers are enumerated.

[451]Nygren, *op. cit.*, p. 338.   [452]Wood, *op. cit.*, p. 124.

A small but significant group of authorities add "God" (*ho theos*) as the subject of the sentence. Sanday and Headlam accept the insertion as a correction of the text. The NASB thus translates, "And we know that God causes all things to work together for good to those who love God, to those who are called according to His purpose." The RSV feels the awkwardness of repeating the word God and renders it, "We know that in everything God works for good with those who love him, who are called according to his purpose." If we omit *ho theos* as the subject, we must still take the verb *synergei* as a transitive, "causes all things." The NEB reverts to an ancient interpretation, which makes the Spirit in v. 27 the subject: "And God who searches our inmost being knows what the Spirit means, because he pleads for God's own people in God's own way; and in everything, as we know, he co-operates for good with those who love God and are called according to his purpose." But it is not the idea of "voluntary co-operation" which is here expressed, "but the authoritative over-riding of divergent and even antagonistic factors so that despite themselves they collaborate for the ultimate good of those who love God."[453] Only thus can we understand the force of *synergei,* which as we have seen must mean "to cause, or make to work together."

If we omit *ho theos,* therefore, we must still presuppose that God, not **the Spirit,** is the implied subject. In this case *ton theon* should be rendered as pronoun for the sake of grammatical smoothness. **All things** (*panta*) is properly "everything," not simply the **all things** (*ta panta,* 32) of the spiritual order. Paul is including literally "everything." Things which independently or of themselves would prove to be our undoing God causes to work for our ultimate good. This **we know,** if we have the Spirit.

This knowledge is the property, first, of **them that love God** (*tois agaposin ton theon*). Paul rarely describes Christians as those who **love God** (only here and I Cor. 2:9; 8:3; cf. Eph. 6:24). He usually prefers the term believe (or the noun faith). There is not a single instance where the noun *agape* clearly means our love to God. *Agape,* for Paul as for John (I John 4:10, 16), is primarily the love God has showed to us in sending His Son (5:5-8; cf. John 3:16). "The love of God, which is in Christ Jesus our

---

[453]*Ibid.,* pp. 126-27. Wood's authority here is Moulton and Milligan's *Vocabulary of the Greek Testament.* Thayer quotes Fritzsche: "For them that love God, God coworking provides all things for good" (*op. cit.,* p. 603).

Lord" (39), is also God's own love toward us in Christ. Verse 28 then is one of the few places where Paul speaks of the Christian's love for God; but the Christian does love God (see Matt. 22: 37-38) and "our Lord Jesus Christ in sincerity" (Eph. 6:24). "Those who love God" (NASB) is thus a sufficient name for Christians. But as Jesus' quotation of Deut. 6:4-5 indicates, love for God is more than an emotional response—it is the devotion of one's total personality to God. It is the devotement of Job, whose love was not for selfish reasons (Job 1:9-12; 2:4-10). It is the devotion which says, "Though he slay me, yet will I trust in him" (Job 13:15). Adam Clarke notes that those who love God are those "who live in the *spirit of obedience.*"[454]

The conviction that God makes **all things work together for good** is the privilege, secondly, of those **who are the called according to his purpose** (*tois kata prothesin kletois ousin*). See comments on 1:6. As Christians we **love God,** but this says nothing as to why all things are made to **work together** for our good. "The reason for that is not found in . . . [us], but in God's objective, eternal purpose. Those who love God have not brought that about themselves; it has been given to them through the calling that has come to them from God, which has its basis in His eternal purpose."[455] "Calling" is the realization in history of God's eternal **purpose,** and it is in this **purpose** that the ultimate assurance of salvation rests. Verse 29 deals with what may be called the pre-temporal aspects of that purpose; v. 30, with the temporal, which also looks beyond history to the final glory.

In designating Christians as those who **love God,** Paul is viewing the Christian life subjectively; but in going on to refer to them as **the called according to his purpose,** he raises the whole discussion to the objective plane of the divine purpose. He then proceeds with a series of sentences which have been called the most objective to be found in the NT. **For whom he did foreknow, he also did predestinate to be conformed to the image of his Son, that he might be the firstborn among many brethren. Moreover whom he did predestinate, them he also called: and whom he called, them he also justified: and whom he justified, them he also glorified** (29-30).

"These are mighty affirmations which are closely knit together and stretch *from eternity—through time—to eternity.*"[456]

[454]*Op. cit.,* p. 101.   [455]Nygren, *op. cit.,* p. 339.
[456]*Ibid.,* p. 340.

"Before the foundation of the world" God purposed to create a holy people in Christ (Eph. 1:4). It is that eternal purpose which is fulfilled in time when God calls and justifies men and which is consummated in eternity when He finally glorifies them. Thus the whole scheme of redemption—from election to final glorification—is utterly in God's hand. There is no place for either chance or arbitrariness, for it is all the purposeful activity of the God who reveals himself as holy love.

The next chapter will deal in detail with divine election, but the doctrine is introduced here. Election means that "all things are of God, who hath reconciled us to himself by Jesus Christ" (II Cor. 5:18). God's will has absolute priority in both creation and redemption. That God has "chosen" to create the cosmos is the reason created things exist; that God has "chosen" to make us men as His creaturely image is the ground for our existence as men; that God has loved us "from the foundation of the world" and "chosen" us in Christ is the explanation of our salvation.[457] This is surely the meaning of **foreknow:** He "foreloved"[458] and "forechose" us *in Christ*.[459] Christ is God's beloved Son; in Him we also are beloved of God (Eph. 1:4-5). We must remember that "we are not dealing here with a rigidly thought out and expressed determinist philosophy, but with a profound religious conviction,"[460] so that, as Dodd aptly observes, the best commentators upon this passage are not the great theologians but the great hymn writers of the Church.[461]

Those who **love God** are thus those whom from eternity God has chosen to enjoy His salvation. They are those whom God has redeemed by His amazing grace. In colorful imagery Barth

---

[457]Brunner, *op. cit.*, p. 77.

[458]The meaning of **foreknow** must be determined by the biblical use of the word "know," which is very marked and clear. It describes the "knowledge" of marriage (Gen. 4:1, 25). It is used to set forth God's election of Israel: "You only have I known of all the families of the earth" (Amos 3:2); "I did know thee in the wilderness" (Hos. 13:5). To the reprobates on the day of judgment Christ will say, "I never knew you" (Matt. 7:23). God's foreknowledge is thus His electing love, His purpose to create a people for His possession and fellowship.

[459]Our election is *in Christ*, who is **the firstborn among many brethren.** Christ is the Elect; we are the elect in Him (Eph. 1:4). God's eternal "decree" is that we shall be saved through faith in Christ (John 3:16). This will become increasingly explicit in c. 9. See comments there for an enlargement of this idea.

[460]Barrett, *The Epistle to the Romans*, p. 170.   [461]*Op. cit.*, p. 141.

writes, "He knew about them and by knowing and thinking about
them he gave them their purpose—both in advance, i.e. by himself, in the power of his almighty mercy which existed before the
world was (Eph. 1:4). While they were yet deaf he called them
by his word, while they were yet ungodly he told them, in the
hearing of the whole celestial creation, that they were righteous,
while they were yet subject to temptation he clothed them with
his own glory."[462] This is because He is "God, who quickeneth
the dead, and calleth those things which be not, as though they
were" (4:17). Our redemption is therefore not the working out
of our fickle human purposes or of our self-initiated choices;
rather it represents the outworking of God's eternal plan. Only
by resting in this faith can we know peace and security.

Foreknowledge and election issue in predestination, and predestination means that our God-fashioned destiny is that we be
conformed to the image of his Son.[463] Christ is at once "the image
of God" (II Cor. 4:4; Col. 1:15) and the image of true man. "In
the God-Man, Jesus Christ, has not only been manifest to us who
God is, but also what man is and ought to become according to
his true nature."[464] The process of metamorphosis by which we
are gradually changed into the *Imago Dei* disclosed in Christ is the
work of sanctification through the Holy Spirit (cf. 12:2). "But we
all, with unveiled face beholding as in a mirror the glory of the
Lord, are being transformed into the same image from glory to
glory, just as from the Lord, the Spirit" (II Cor. 3:18, NASB).
When this purpose is finally realized—i.e., when we have received
"the redemption of our body" (v. 23)—"we shall be like him, for
we shall see him as he is" (I John 3:2). At present we are "conformed [*symmorphizomenos*] to his death" (Phil. 3:10); we shall
be conformed (*symmorphos*, used here by Paul) to the body of
Christ's glory (Phil. 3:21).

[462]*A Shorter Commentary on Romans*, pp. 104-5.

[463]In addition to Eph. 1:4, cf. II Thess. 2:13; I Pet. 1:2. Predestinated
(*proorisen*) means literally "marked out beforehand" (only here and Eph.
1:5, 11; Acts 4:28; I Cor. 2:7). "A parent who, before his child is old enough
for a trade, chooses a trade for him, predestines the boy. He *marks out
beforehand* a path in which he designs him to go. The purpose, whether
carried out or not, is predestination. . . . Before they were born, and
therefore from eternity, God resolved that believers should be made like
His only begotten Son. . . . Predestination is simply a purpose; and by no
means implies the inevitable accomplishment of that purpose" (Beet, *op. cit.*,
pp. 256-57).

[464]Brunner, *loc. cit.*

In v. 29 we have returned to the thought of the new humanity in Christ (see 5:12-21). Only here the picture is of Christ as the eldest in God's redeemed family, **the firstborn among many brethren.** He, the Son of God by nature (vv. 3, 32), is the Heir of God; we, God's adopted sons (vv. 14-15), are "joint-heirs with him" (17) of the predestined glory.

Predestination is accomplished in time: **Moreover whom he did predestinate, them he also called**—i.e., in conversion (cf. I Cor. 7:18; Gal. 1:6; Col. 3:15). "The *klesis* is not *au salut* [to salvation], at least in the sense of final salvation, but simply to become Christians."[465] **Called** implies a summons or invitation which has been obeyed (cf. Acts 26:19). This call is by the word of God (10:13-17) and the Spirit (John 6:44). **And whom he called, them he also justified,** "because they responded in faith to his call."[466] With justification Paul has reached the present; but so sure is he of the purpose of God that he can go on and describe the future in the past tense: **And whom he justified, them he also glorified** (cf. 17, "if so be that . . . [they] suffer with him"; also 11:22 and Col. 1:21-23). "St. Paul does not affirm, either here or in any other part of his writings, that precisely the same number of men are called, justified, and glorified. He does not deny that a believer may fall away and be cut off between his special calling and his glorification (xi. 22). Neither does he deny that many are called who never are justified [cf. 10:21]. He only affirms that this is the method whereby God leads us step by step toward heaven."[467]

---

[465]ICC, "Romans," p. 217.

[466]Barrett, *The Epistle to the Romans, loc. cit.*

[467]Wesley, *Explanatory Notes upon the New Testament*, p. 551. This is "not a quantitative limitation of God's action, but its qualitative definition" (Barth, *The Epistle to the Romans*, p. 346), "the final statement of the truth that justification, and, in the end, salvation also, are by grace alone, and through faith alone" (Barrett, *The Epistle to the Romans*, p. 171). Erdman explains: "In all this majestic movement whereby these successive stages of the divine purpose are carried into effect, nothing is stated as to the agency or activity or responsibility of believers. Here the thought is of God. That Paul also believed and taught . . . the responsibility of man . . . must not be forgotten. Nor does he ever try to reconcile these two spheres of truth. However, in seeking to encourage us to patience in suffering and to confident expectation of future glory, he wisely fixes the attention wholly upon that which must be ultimate in all our thinking and our thanksgiving, namely, upon the mysterious, loving, eternal purpose of God" (*op. cit.,* pp. 94-95).

"Saved by Hope" is the theme of 8:18-30. (1) Our hope, 18-25; (2) Our help, 26-27; (3) Our high calling, 28-30 (W. T. Purkiser).

(2) *Certainty in Christ* (8:31-39). There is in the election and calling of God an immense assurance for the Christian in a world where so much is against him. **What shall we then say to these things? If God be for us, who can be against us?** (31) That, says Brunner, is the salvation against which everything in opposition to us cannot prevail.[468] Of God's goodwill toward us there can be no possible doubt: "But God commendeth his love toward us, in that while we were yet sinners, Christ died for us" (5:8). That carries with it everything else. **He that spared not his own Son, but delivered him up for us all, how shall he not with him also freely give us all things?** (32) He who bestowed upon us "his unspeakable gift" certainly will not deny us the smaller tokens of His love.

"God is for us" (31, NASB). If this is to be an inward certainty to us, the accusation which is **against us** must be removed and we must be changed in the very core of our beings. Thank God, that accusation has been swallowed up in the reconciling death of His own Son. Through the blood of the Crucified One I am justified. **Who shall lay any thing to the charge of God's elect? It is God that justifieth** (33). Or, as Moffatt puts it, "When God acquits, who shall condemn?" Though we have all sinned and fallen short of the glory of God (3:23), we have been "justified freely by his grace through the redemption that is in Christ Jesus" (3:24). And "God's love has been poured into our hearts through the Holy Spirit" (5:5, RSV). "God for us" means "God is love." "The love of Jesus is the love of God, the love of God is the love which Jesus Christ has brought to us who are afraid of God because of sin and grants to everyone who believes in him."[469]

But, after all, may not Christ himself condemn us, His unprofitable servants? "For we must all appear before the judgment seat of Christ" (II Cor. 5:10). Will His sentence be one of condemnation? This is unthinkable, for "there is therefore now no condemnation to them which are in Christ Jesus" (8:1). **Who is he that condemneth? It is Christ that died** for us (34) "when we were enemies" (5:10), **yea rather, that is risen again. Far**

---

from condemning us, even **at the right hand of God** He **maketh intercession for us.** The Judge is the Advocate for our defense![470]

Dodd is probably correct in assuming that Paul is here quoting from a primitive version of the Apostles' Creed, which many scholars believe originated in Rome: "He was crucified, dead, and buried; the third day he rose again from the dead, and sitteth on the right hand of God; from thence he shall come to judge the quick and the dead." Dodd writes: "But lest the thought of Christ as Judge should lead Christians to fear for their salvation, he reminds them of another idea which also was deeply fixed in Christian belief, though it did not get into the Creed. 'He ever liveth to make intercession for them,' says the Epistle to the Hebrews (vii.25) . . . 'If any man sin,' says I John (ii.1), 'we have an advocate with the Father, Jesus Christ the righteous.' "[471]

But can we believe in the love of God in the face of everything we must go through again and again? For things do not happen the way some people interpret 8:28—that Christians will fare better than others. Paul knew better than this. For him, and for many thousands of faithful witnesses to Christ, the Christian life meant **tribulation . . . distress . . . persecution . . . famine . . . nakedness . . . peril . . . or sword.** As it is written, **For thy sake we are killed all the day long; we are accounted as sheep for the slaughter** (35-36). The disciple is not above his Master. If they crucified Him, if His life was suffering, should it be better for His disciples? If God was able through His sufferings to give proof of divine love, then the sufferings of Christians should not obscure that love.

Paul writes: **In all these things we are more than conquerors through him that loved us** (37). There is one thing of which we cannot be deprived, our union with Him and a daily new experience of His love in the midst of trouble and distress.

The Gospel is a message of triumph. . . . The life in the Holy Spirit is no longer that lamentable swaying to and fro between victory and defeat which characterizes the condition of the man under the Law; it is victorious life. Paul uses here a strong and untranslatable expression. We are "excessively victorious." The joy of victory is the sign of the life in the Spirit in the same way as the wretched sinfulness is the mark of legalism. It is true that whoever truly belongs to Christ never leaves the groaning behind as long as he lives on earth, but he does leave the moaning and anxiety. The

---

[470]Dodd, *op. cit.*, pp. 143-44.   [471]*Ibid.*, p. 144.

note of victory is the visible mark of those who are united with the Victor.[472]

Everything else depends upon the inward assurance—**I am persuaded** (38). The inner witness of the Spirit (15-16) corroborated by the power of new life in Christ (cf. II Cor. 5:17) is the assurance which produces deep certainty. Then, but only then, can I affirm with the apostle, **I am persuaded, that neither death, nor life, nor angels, nor principalities, nor powers, nor things present, nor things to come, nor height, nor depth, nor any other creature, shall be able to separate us from the love of God, which is in Christ Jesus our Lord** (38-39).

This assurance is not automatic; it must fight its way through both natural and supernatural opposing forces. Demonic powers continually cast doubts on this persuasion as though it were untenable superstition. "But whatever adversaries assail us and our faith, one thing they cannot do: separate us from Christ, make obscure or incredible the love of God which we have known in Christ. What Paul has taught us in these eight chapters is not a beautiful theory but experience tried in the fiery trial of suffering and struggle."[473]

Jesus Christ is Lord. He is Lord over **life** and **death,** for He was crucified and raised from the dead. He is Lord over all **principalities** and **powers,** for He triumphed over them in the Cross (Col. 2:15). He is Lord of **things present** and **things to come,** for it is in Him that God elected us in love and it is in Him that we shall enter God's final glory. **In Christ Jesus our Lord** "God is for us"; in Him "we overwhelmingly conquer" (37, NASB) in the triumph of assurance and faith. Our final glorification is conditional upon our suffering with Him (17) and our continuing in the goodness of God (11:22); nevertheless Paul's accent is upon the sufficiency of God's grace. We are "confident of this very thing, that he which hath begun a good work in . . . [us] will perform it until the day of Jesus Christ" (Phil. 1:6).

From vv. 29-39, Paul Rees expounds the theme, "If God Be for Us." (1) Electively in the purposes of His grace, 29-30; (2) Efficaciously in the cross of Christ, 32; (3) Encouragingly in His providences 35-37; (4) Eternally in the fellowship of His love, 38-39.

---

[472]Brunner, *op. cit.*, pp. 80-81.   [473]*Ibid.*, p. 82.

W. T. Purkiser finds "Victory in Christ" hymned in 8:31-39. (1) Its source, 31-34; (2) Its scope, 35, 38-39; (3) Its secret, 37, 39.

C. GOD'S RIGHTEOUSNESS IN HISTORY, 9:1—11:36

This section in Romans has been variously understood. It has been called a *theodicy*, a justification of the ways of God with men. There is truth in this view, for Paul is wrestling here with the problem of why God has apparently set aside His people Israel. Have God's calling and promise failed? Has He thereby proved to be unrighteous? But to call this a theodicy is to presume that we can justify God, when in reality God is not accountable to man; it is the other way around. The purposes and ways of God transcend human reason (Isa. 55:9); otherwise God is not God. "A God comprehended is no God" (Tersteegen).[474] As he concludes this section Paul quite appropriately rises to the heights of adoration in the face of the divine mystery (11:33-36).

Others have called this section *Paul's philosophy of history*. We have here, however, no inclusive historical view of how God controls the world and leads it to its final goal, but "a prayerful wrestling with God himself." Rather than giving us a step-by-step account of God's unfolding purpose in history these chapters trace "a step-by-step self-disclosure of God for faith."[475]

A third school understands this section as *Paul's doctrine of predestination*. But, as Nygren points out, the classical treatment of predestination is found in 8:28-30. "If one uses chapters 9—11 as his point of departure in studying Paul's view of predestination, he ends with a false picture of it."[476] Thus Brunner: "Of a double decree (predestination), one leading to eternal life and the other to eternal damnation, this passage teaches just as little as any other part of Holy Scripture."[477] The clue to understanding Paul's statements of divine sovereignty and election is (1) to set them within the framework of 8:28-30 (see comments), and (2) to grasp clearly that in these chapters "he is discussing na-

---

[474]Cited by Rudolph Otto, *The Idea of the Holy* (trans. by J. W. Harvey) (London: Oxford University Press, 1957), p. 25.

[475]Goppelt, *op. cit.*, p. 133.

[476]*Op. cit.*, p. 354.

[477]*Op. cit.*, p. 86; cf. p. 99 also.

tional conversion and not individual salvation."[478] The question
is, Why has God apparently set aside ancient Israel and chosen
the Church to be the new people of God?

Moreover, it is a mistake to view these chapters as independent, or unrelated to the rest of the Epistle. Dodd thinks they
constitute a sermon the apostle had preached and which he incorporated here "to save a busy man's time and trouble in writing
on the subject afresh."[479] It is even more difficult to understand
Barth's contention that cc. 9—11 "cannot be simply a continuation
of the argument in 1.18—8.39."[480] Rather, they appear to be
precisely this. The theme is still "the righteousness of God" (in
the sense Paul has earlier developed it; cf. esp. 9:30—10:4), which
becomes even brighter and more certain as his argument unfolds.
The final vision of God's righteousness in c. 11 is so glorious that
Paul breaks out in ecstatic adoration and praise of the unsearchable "depths of the riches both of the wisdom and knowledge of
God" (11:33).[481]

While these chapters are integral to Paul's doctrine of God's
righteousness, they nevertheless constitute a unit. "The three
chapters form a trilogy: the first deals with divine sovereignty,
the second with human responsibility, the third with universal
blessing; the first with 'election,' the second with 'rejection,' the
third with 'restoration'; the first with the past, the second with
the present, the third with the future."[482]

Furthermore, these chapters are just as much God's word
to us as the previous chapters. Israel is representative of those
who in all times have sought salvation by the law, i.e., by their
own merit and righteousness. The proclamation that men are
"justified by faith apart from works of the Law" (3:28, NASB)

---

[478]Erdman, *op. cit.*, p. 99. "That Paul had not here the least thought of
personal election or reprobation is manifest, (1) because it lay quite wide
of his design, which was this, to show that God's rejecting the Jews and
receiving the Gentiles was consistent with His word; (2) because such a
doctrine would not only have had no tendency to convince, but would have
evidently tended to harden, the Jews; (3) because when he sums up his
argument in the close of the chapter, he has not one word, or the least intimation, about it" (Wesley, *Explanatory Notes upon the New Testament*,
p. 554).

[479]*Op. cit.*, pp. 148-50.

[480]*A Shorter Commentary on Romans*, p. 110.

[481]Goppelt, *op. cit.*, pp. 151-53; Nygren, *op. cit.*, p. 357.

[482]Erdman, *op. cit.*, p. 100.

accordingly here reaches its final climax. The peril and plight of Israel is that of every man who refuses the salvation freely offered through Christ. Nevertheless, the amazing mercy of God is extended to every son of Adam's race, for He has "concluded them all in unbelief, that he might have mercy upon all" (11:32).

1. *The Problem of Faith* (9:1-5)

The apostle is about to broach a subject he shrinks back from directly announcing. The strong asseveration we find in 1-2 indicates both the gravity of his own feeling and conviction and the awareness that his fellow countrymen may doubt his sincerity. With great tact and delicacy he moves into his subject. **I say the truth in Christ** (*en Christo*, "as one united with Christ"; cf. II Cor. 2:17; 12:19), **I lie not, my conscience also bearing me witness in the Holy Ghost, that I have great heaviness and continual sorrow in my heart** (1-2).

Paul's shout of joy has become a sob of compassion. **For I could wish that myself were accursed from Christ for my brethren, my kinsmen according to the flesh** (3). It is a paradox of Christian experience that "a high degree of spiritual sorrow and of spiritual joy may consist together."[483] By declaring his sorrow for his unbelieving **kinsmen** Paul would disabuse their minds that he is speaking from any prejudice. He is groaning in the Spirit (cf. 8:26-27) for their salvation (cf. Matt. 9:36). Paul employs the emphatic **I . . . myself** (*autos ego*) to emphasize his willingness for personal sacrifice. These words have even more force when we recall that he has just asserted that nothing in heaven or earth can "separate us from the love of God which is in Christ" (8:39).

He says, **For I could wish . . . myself accursed** (*anathema*, "devoted to destruction"; cf. I Cor. 16:22; Gal. 1:8-9) **from Christ** ("separated from Christ," NASB) **for my brethren . . . according to the flesh** (*kata sarka*). This prayer is similar to that of Moses, "Yet now, if thou wilt forgive their sin—; and if not, blot me, I pray thee, out of thy book" (Exod. 32:32). This is the language of *agape* (cf. 5:8), but it is a prayer impossible of fulfillment for finite man. Only the Infinite and Holy One could really become a curse for us and thereby effect our salvation (Gal. 3:13-14). But *agape* in the heart of the Christian prompts

[483]Wesley, *Explanatory Notes upon the New Testament*, p. 554.

him to "fill up" the afflictions of Christ (cf. II Cor. 5:18-21; Col. 1:24).

Paul states two reasons for his deep compassion. First, these are his **kinsmen according to the flesh.** The apostle never lost his feeling of identity with his brother Israelites. He suffered within himself "the conflict between the present spiritual condition of Israel and its divine history."[484]

The second reason for Paul's compassion consists in the divinely bestowed privileges which have been given to the chosen people (cf. 3:1-3). They are **Israelites** (4), partakers of the promises made to Jacob, to whom the name "Israel" was given. In cc. 1—8, Paul speaks of "Jews"; but in cc. 9—11, of "Israel." **Israelites** are God's people "standing within God's covenant and called to God's salvation."[485] "For Israel is a nation holy unto God, and a nation of inheritance for its God, and a nation of priesthood and royalty and a possession" (Jubilees 33:18; cf. Deut. 7:6-9; I Kings 8:51, 53).

Theirs is **the adoption** (*huiothesia*, "status of an adopted son"; cf. 8:15 with comments). Here the word implies the relationship with God described in Exod. 4:22; Deut. 32:6; Jer. 31:9; Hos. 11:1.

Theirs is **the glory** (*he doxa*), "the visible presence of God among His people," the Shekinah. "No other nation was ever thus favoured."[486]

Theirs are **the covenants** (*hai diathekai*). The plural does not refer to the old and new covenants, but probably to the covenants with the patriarchs and with Moses (Gen. 6:18; 9:9; 15:18; 17:2, 7, 9; Exod. 2:24; 19:5; etc.), repeated often and binding them as the people of God. Some MSS have the singular, "covenant," in

---

[484]Brunner, *op. cit.*, p. 83.

[485]Goppelt, *op. cit.*, p. 135. " 'Jew' is the man of Jewish blood bound to the Law. Since this is the essential hallmark of the Jew, Paul can no longer refer to himself as a Jew after his conversion without qualification; he is only a 'Jew by birth' (Gal. 2:15). He can become 'as a Jew' to the Jews, namely, 'to those under the law as one under the law—though not myself under the law' (1 Cor. 9:20). However, even as a Christian he can still continue to call himself a 'Hebrew' (Phil. 3:5; 2 Cor. 11:22) as a child of a Jewish-Palestinian family, and an 'Israelite' (2 Cor. 11:22; Rom. 11:1; cf. Phil. 3:5) as a member of the nation standing within God's covenant and called to God's salvation" (*ibid.*).

[486]Clarke, *op. cit.*, p. 109.

which case the reference would be to the covenant made at Mount Sinai.

Theirs is **the giving of the law** (*he nomothesia*), which signified "the dignity and glory of having a law communicated by express revelation, and amidst circumstances so full of awe and splendour."[487]

Theirs are **the service of God** (*he latreia,* "the temple service," NASB) and **the promises** (*hai epangeliai,* the promises of the Messiah in the OT).

Theirs are **the fathers** (5; *hoi pateres,* "the patriarchs"; cf. Acts 3:13; 32), who as saintly ancestors left a holy heritage to Israel.

Finally, their supreme privilege was that through their fathers **as concerning the flesh Christ came, who is over all, God blessed for ever. Amen.** The Greek reads: *Kai ex hon ho Christos to kata sarka* ("from whom [is] the Christ according to the flesh"), *ho on epi panton* ("the One who is over all"), *theos eulogetos eis tous aionas, amen* ("God blessed unto the ages. Amen."). Sanday and Headlam give a lengthy summary of the interpretation of 5, a verse which has "probably been discussed at greater length than any other in the NT." They see four possible interpretations:[488]

(*a*) Placing a comma after *sarka* and referring the whole passage to Christ (ERV, Phillips, RSV, marg.).

(*b*) Placing a full stop after *sarka* and translating, "He who is God over all be blessed for ever," or, "is blessed forever" (ASV, marg., RSV, NEB, Moffatt).

(*c*) With the same punctuation translating, "He who is over all is God blessed forever" (ASV, marg.).

(*d*) Placing a comma after *sarka* and a full stop at *panton,* "who is over all. God be (or is) blessed for ever" (ASV, marg.).

It is difficult to decide between these possibilities. The original MSS were devoid of any sort of punctuation. It may be significant that "an immense preponderance of the Christian writers

---

[487]Vaughn; cited by ICC, "Romans," p. 231.

[488]ICC, "Romans," p. 233. Like the KJV, the NASB leaves the question of interpretation undecided.

of the first eight centuries refer the word to Christ,"[489] although there is no evidence they arrived at this conclusion on dogmatic grounds; the verse is rarely cited in controversy. Apparently the language of the passage indicated this meaning.

The grammatical evidence seems to favor (a), [490] unless the words *ho on epi panton theos* contain in themselves too marked a contrast to the preceding clause. If we adopt this interpretation, the phrase *to kata sarka* contrasted with *theos* parallels the contrast in 1:3-4 between *kata sarka* and *kata pneuma hagiasunes* (see comments). The course of Paul's argument here has led him to lay stress on the human birth of Christ as an Israelite; this one-sided emphasis must be corrected. *To kata sarka* leads us to expect an antithesis, and we find just what we should have expected in *ho on epi panton theos*. However, although Paul regards Christ as being **over all** creation (I Cor. 11:3; 15:25; Phil. 2:5-11; Col. 1:13-20), he regularly refers to Him as "Lord" rather than **God** (I Cor. 8:6; Eph. 4:5-6; I Tim. 1:1-2; 5:21; Titus 1:4; but cf. Titus 2:13, NASB, RSV). Nevertheless, Paul may here have chosen *theos* because he "wishes to say that Christ was in human terms a Jew, but in fact God."[491] Paul would thus be saying, " 'According to the flesh,' *kata sarka*, Christ belongs to Israel; but 'according to the Spirit,' *kata pneuma*, He is 'God who is over all, blessed forever."[492]

2. The First Answer: God's Promise Only to Believers (9:6-29)

In this section the apostle gives his first clear answer to the question implied in v. 6: Has the word of God failed? "No," says Paul. "God's word of promise from the very beginning meant only those elected by God's free grace."[493]

a. The children of promise are the children of God (9:6-13). In v. 6, Paul asserts that it is **not as though** (*ouch hoion de hoti,* "the case is not as though")[494] **the word of God** (in the sense of

---

[489]*Ibid.,* p. 234. Among the proponents of the above interpretation were Irenaeus, Hippolytus, Novatian, Athanasius, Epiphanius, Basil, Gregory of Nyssa, Chrysostom, Theodoret, Augustine, Hilarius, Ambrosius, Hieronymus, Cyril of Alexandria, and Origen.

[490]See Barrett, *The Epistle to the Romans,* pp. 178-79, in addition to ICC, "Romans," p. 233-38.

[491]Barrett, *ibid.*

[492]Nygren, *op. cit.,* p. 356.

[493]Goppelt, *op. cit.,* p. 153.

[494]ICC, "Romans," p. 240.

the declared purpose of God) **hath** failed (*ekpeptoken,* "fallen to the ground," Wesley). **If Israel** is understood· in a physical or mechanical sense, it cannot be denied that the majority of Israel have set aside the word of God, which accordingly has "fallen to the ground." But Israel is not a term like Greece or Rome; Israel is not created by blood and soil, but by the promise of God. God is free to declare who **Israel** is, and **they are not all Israel, which are of Israel.** "The sum is, God accepts all believers, and them only; and this is in no way contrary to His word. Nay, He hath declared in His word, both by type and by express testimonies, that believers are accepted as the 'children of promise,' while unbelievers are rejected, though they are 'children after the flesh.' "[495]

In v. 7, Paul is denying a universally accepted viewpoint, that all who appear or claim to be Israel are really **the seed of Abraham** (cf. John 8:39). **Neither, because they are the seed of Abraham, are they all children.** It is essential that we grasp Paul's idea of "Abraham's seed" (cf. 4:13, 16, 18; Gal. 3:16, 19, 29). The Galatian passages are particularly important, for they show that "seed" is a collective term which focuses upon one Descendant of Abraham, Christ. This passage is therefore Christological. Christ is the "seed" of promise (Gal. 3:16), but this includes those who by faith are "in Christ" (Rom. 4:13, 16, 18; Gal. 3:29). "It is *in Christ* that the promises of God are fulfilled. Thus the thought of v. 4 receives a severe qualification: the promises do belong to Israel, but—what Israel?"[496]

The apostle cites Gen. 21:12 to illustrate his point: **In Isaac shall thy seed be called.** This obviously means: **They which are the children of the flesh, these are not the children of God: but the children of promise are counted for the seed** (8). Although Abraham had several children besides Isaac (Gen. 25:1-4), here the reference is to Ishmael (cf. Gal. 4:21-31). The word **counted** (*logizetai*) is one of the important words in the Epistle; the most fruitful comparison here is with 4:3, "Abraham believed God, and it was counted [*elogisthe*] unto him for righteousness" (quoted from Gen. 15:6). "It points to the creative freedom of God, who creates 'righteousness' by 'counting' it, and annuls sin by not 'counting' it (iv.6, 8). He can raise up sons of Abraham

[495]Wesley, *Explanatory Notes upon the New Testament*, pp. 555-56.
[496]Barrett, *The Epistle to the Romans*, p. 181.

out of stones (Matt. iii.9; Luke iii.8), and freely determines what
is 'seed' and what is not."[497] It is evident that **seed** is bound up
with **promise**. Ishmael was a true son of Abraham, but his birth
was by natural generation. Isaac, on the other hand, was born
as a result of the creative word of God's promise (cf. 4:19). **For
this is the word of promise, At this time will I come, and Sarah
shall have a son** (9).

And not only this (*ou monon de;* cf. 5:3 for an even stronger
use of this phrase) has the meaning: "You may find some flaw
in the previous illustration. After all, Ishmael's mother was the
slave Hagar, while Isaac's mother was the princess Sarah (Gal.
4:21-31). You might even argue that, as Isaac's descendants, all
Israelites are children of promise. The instance I am about to
quote will safeguard my argument against such false conclusions."
**When Rebecca also had conceived by one, even our father Isaac;
(for the children being not yet born, neither having done any
good or evil, that the purpose of God according to election might
stand, not of works, but of him that calleth;) it was said unto
her, The elder shall serve the younger. As it is written, Jacob
have I loved, but Esau have I hated** (10-13). The last sentence
is a Hebrew idiom meaning, "I have preferred Jacob to Esau."

By one (*ex henos*) is emphatic. **Jacob** and **Esau** not only have
the same father; they also have the same mother, and their origin
goes back to one moment of conception. Thus the defective conditions which might be found in the previous illustration are overcome. The difference between **Jacob** and **Esau** is a matter of
divine election and not of human ancestry or merit. God is absolutely free; whatever happens is by His sovereign purpose, which
works itself out in the process of election: **that the purpose of God
according to election might stand, not of works, but of him that
calleth.** "Calling" and "faith" are corresponding terms; faith is a
positive response to God's call, as the example of Abraham makes
clear (cf. Gen. 12:1-4; Heb. 11:8). **Works** and "calling" are related here as works and faith were earlier related (cf. 4:4-5 with
comments). "Not works but faith leads to justification; not works
but God's call admits to the promise. These are different ways of
expressing the same truth."[498] Obviously, Paul is still developing
his doctrine of justification by God's free grace.

When he declares, **The elder shall serve the younger** (12), his

[497]*Ibid.*   [498]*Ibid.*, pp. 181-82.

reference is not to the two brothers but to their posterity. **Esau was never subject to Jacob,** but the Edomites (his descendants) were often subjected to Israel. With this word from Gen. 25:23 the prophet Malachi (Mal. 1:2-5) is in agreement: **Jacob** (Israel) **have I loved, but Esau** (Edom) **have I** (comparatively) **hated.** The context in Malachi makes clear that it is the nations of Israel and Edom that are in view. This is an example of the common oscillation in biblical (and especially OT) thought between individual and corporate personality (cf. 5:12-21). "Israel was the elect nation, and Edom had incurred the wrath of God because of their unbrotherly conduct towards Israel in the day of Israel's calamity."[499] "Observe," says Wesley, "(1) this does not relate to the person of Jacob or Esau; (2) nor does it relate to the eternal state either of them or their posterity. Thus far the apostle has been proving his proposition; namely, that the exclusion of a great part of the seed of Abraham, yea, and of Isaac, from the special promises of God, was so far from being impossible, that, according to the Scriptures themselves, it had actually happened."[500]

The substance of Paul's argument is that God operates on the basis of His elective purpose. In developing his argument he uses **seed** in two ways, (*a*) to define the natural descendants of Abraham (*7a*) and (*b*) the children of promise (*7b*). As we have seen, in the spiritual sense **the seed of Abraham** contracted until it became Christ (Gal. 3:16) and was subsequently expanded to include those who are in Christ (Gal. 3:29). "This means that election does not take place (as might at first appear from Paul's examples) arbitrarily or fortuitously; it takes place always and only *in Christ.* They are elect who are in him; they who are elect are in him."[501] It has been the failure to grasp this cardinal point which has caused confusion over Paul's doctrine of predestination and election. The next section will throw further light on this idea.

b. God is sovereign in mercy and wrath (9:14-29). Paul has just shown that everything depends on God's purpose and

[499]Bruce, *The Epistle of Paul to the Romans,* p. 193.

[500]*Explanatory Notes upon the New Testament,* p. 557.

[501]Barrett, *loc. cit.* See comments on 8:28-30. Thus the "elect" are those who respond in repentance and faith to the call of God and who *endure unto the end* (Matt. 24:13; I Cor. 9:27; II Pet. 1:10).

election, and nothing on our works (11). That God chose Abraham, Isaac, and Jacob did not depend upon anything in them; Jacob was not even born when God chose him and established His promise for him. The choice depended solely on God's gracious will. But this is the nature of grace and promise. If it depended on anything else, grace would not be grace and the promise would not be promise.[502]

If everything lies within the purpose of God in election, it seems to follow that God is unjust. **What shall we say then,** in view of the foregoing argument? **Is there unrighteousness with God?** (14) Paul is as anxious as we to deny this suggestion. **God forbid.** But how can the objections be met?[503]

Paul begins with an OT quotation. **For he saith to Moses, I will have mercy on whom I will have mercy, and I will have compassion on whom I will have compassion** (15; Exod. 33:19). He simply disallows the objection. God is sovereign in dispensing mercy.[504] Mercy cannot be earned; it can only be received in faith and gratitude. If man could deserve this grace, it really would not be mercy (cf. 4:2-4). **So then it is not of him that willeth, nor of him that runneth, but of God that sheweth mercy** (16). God, not man, defines the terms upon which He will receive us into His favor. "Let the wicked forsake his way, and the unrighteous man his thoughts: and let him return unto the Lord, and he will have mercy upon him; and to our God, for he will abundantly pardon." Immediately the Lord adds, "For my thoughts are not your thoughts, neither are your ways my ways, saith the Lord" (Isa. 55:7-8). In the fullness of time those terms have become *faith in Christ* as the means of God's righteousness (3:21-28; cf. 9:30—10:4). What right has he that **willeth** (cf. 7:

---

[502]Nygren, *op. cit.*, p. 364.

[503]In 3:5-8, Paul has declared the justice of God. There is no place for **unrighteousness** (*adikia*) with God; the whole gospel is rather a display of His righteousness (*dikaiosyne theou*, 1:17). "But in Paul's 'By no means!' there is a more fundamental fact. Paul does not merely answer the question with a negative. He denies the propriety of the framing of the question" (*ibid.*, p. 365).

[504]"The point to note is that these verses emphasize not only the freedom of God, but his mercy. . . . Mercy (*eleos;* verb, *eleein*) is the keynote of chs. ix-xi, as will appear at point after point. . . . Here where the word first occurs, it may suffice to point onwards to the last occurrence: God has shut up all men to disobedience, in order that he may deal with all men in mercy (xi.32)" (Barrett, *The Epistle to the Romans*, p. 185).

14-25) to think that he can bring God to his terms (cf. vv. 31-32)? We come on God's terms, or we do not find mercy. But this is no piece of divine arbitrariness; our redemption in Christ is the outworking of **mercy.** It is because God is merciful that we may be justified by faith; and God is determined to treat us on the basis of mercy. Indeed, if He should treat us otherwise, who should survive? (Cf. Ps. 130:3-4).[505]

But God is also sovereign in wrath. **For the scripture saith unto Pharaoh, Even for this same purpose have I raised thee up, that I might shew my power in thee, and that my name might be declared throughout all the earth. Therefore hath he mercy on whom he will have mercy, and whom he will he hardeneth (17-18).** Paul's quotation here is a free rendering of Exod. 9:16. This quotation makes possible two new points. Pharaoh had been raised up: (1) as an occasion for the display of God's **power,** and (2) in order that God's **name might be declared throughout all the earth.** If there had been no "Pharaoh of the oppression" there would have been no Exodus, with the display of God's almighty power.[506]

[505]Here, then, is the *second* safeguard against the idea of divine arbitrariness in election: the process is the outworking of God's character as *agape* love (cf. Eph. 1:4-5, RSV). For the first safeguard see 8:28-30 and v. 7 with comments.

[506]Wesley notes that God gave Pharaoh ample opportunity and encouragement to repent before making him the object of His wrath and power. "For this cause have I raised thee up—That is, Unless thou repent, this will surely be the consequence of My raising thee up. . . . Perhaps this may have a still further meaning. It seems that God was resolved to show His power over the river, the insects, other animals (with the natural causes of their health, diseases, life, and death), over the meteors, the air, the sun (all of which were worshipped by the Egyptians, from whom other nations learned their idolatry), and at once over all their gods, by that terrible stroke of slaying all their priests, and their choicest victims, the firstborn of man and beast; and all this with a design, not only to deliver His people Israel (for which a single act of omnipotence would have sufficed), but to convince the Egyptians, that the objects of their worship were but the creatures of Jehovah, and entirely in His power, and to draw them and the neighbouring nations, who should hear of all these wonders, from their idolatry, to worship the one God. For the execution of this design . . . God was pleased to raise up to the throne of an absolute monarchy, a man, not whom He had made wicked on purpose, but whom He found so, the proudest, the most daring and obstinate of all the Egyptian princes; and who, being incorrigible, well deserved to be set up in that situation, where the divine judgments fell the heaviest" (*Explanatory Notes upon the New Testament,* pp. 557-58).

Barrett makes the very fine point that "in the present time, Israel (like Pharaoh in his) exists for a double purpose, (i) to provide the occasion or context for a divine act of deliverance— that in which men are freed from the law, and thereby from sin and death; (ii) to act so as to cause the publication of God's act of deliverance through all the world—which took place precisely because Israel rejected the Gospel (xi.11, 15, 19, 25)."[507] In this manner God overrules the self-will of humankind and makes the wrath of men to praise Him.

There are two sides to the matter of divine sovereignty. "He has mercy on whom He desires" (NASB); that is one side of the matter. The other side is, "He hardens whom He desires." While we must not soften this truth, "hardening" does not imply final rejection. We have already encountered this thought in 1:24, 26, 28, where it is said that God gives men up to sin. "When man turns to sin, he does so of his own volition; but at the same time the wrath of God commits him to it."[508] There is a parallel passage in another Epistle. To those who believe and are being saved the gospel is "the savour of life unto life"; but to those who are perishing in unbelief, "the savour of death unto death" (cf. II Cor. 2: 15-16). From first to last God's purposes are governed by mercy. Nonetheless, "hardening" is an offensive word, and Paul imagines his interlocutor raising another objection, which follows.

Thou wilt say then unto me, Why doth he yet find fault? For who hath resisted his will? (19) If God treats men as Paul has explained, they have no moral responsibility. God has no right to condemn a sinner whom He himself has hardened. But Paul raises this question, not to answer it, but to remove it. We look in vain for Paul to answer the problem of the relation of divine sovereignty to human freedom. He affirms both truths at one and the same time, without any attempt at theologizing. The basis of Israel's rejection lies within God's purpose, but in the next answer he charges Israel with responsibility for refusing God's call. The only answer he gives is that God is God and that man has no right to call Him to account.[509] **Nay but, O man, who**

[507]*The Epistle to the Romans*, p. 187.   [508]Nygren, *op. cit.*, p. 367.

[509]For Paul divine sovereignty and human freedom find their reconciliation in Christian experience. We know that if we are saved, it is by God's grace, and that if we are lost, it is by our own perversity. The apostle is determined to preserve both of these convictions, to safeguard both the divine priority and the human responsibility in salvation.

art thou that repliest against God? Shall the thing formed say to him that formed it, Why hast thou made me thus? Hath not the potter power over the clay; of the same lump to make one vessel unto honour, and another unto dishonour? (20-21)

God is not answerable to man. For the creature to pass judgment upon the Creator is sinful pride, an attempt to bridge the eternal chasm which separates God from all created existence. "Yet God can be relied upon to act in consistency with His character, which has been disclosed supremely in Christ. With such a God to trust, why should any of His people question His ways?"[510] Paul insists that, just as a human potter may fashion of his clay any vessel he chooses, so God has perfect liberty to make what He wills of the humanity He has created for His glory, and man has no more right to answer back than the potter's clay.[511] "But the trouble is that man is not a pot; he *will* ask, 'Why did you make me like this?' and he will not be bludgeoned into silence."[512] "Of course man is not a pot," Barrett rejoins, "and obstinate questions arise in his mind. It is because the mind asks questions about the divine government of the universe that works like Romans are written. To stress this point, however, is to emphasize a detail in the analogy instead of the major comparison, which is between the final responsibility of the potter for what he produces, and the final responsibility of God for what he does in history. 'Everything depends, not on man who exercises his will ... but on the merciful God' (v. 16)."[513]

What Paul has just said about Pharaoh is now transferred to Israel. **What if God, willing to shew his wrath, and to make his power known, endured with much longsuffering the vessels of wrath fitted to destruction: and that he might make known the riches of his glory on the vessels of mercy, which he had afore prepared unto glory, even us, whom he hath called, not of the Jews only, but also of the Gentiles? (22-24)** As God . . . endured with much longsuffering the perversity of Pharaoh, He has also endured the unbelief of Israel. As Pharaoh's hardening and unbelief furnished the occasion for a demonstration of God's power and the spread of His name throughout the earth, so Israel's hardening and disobedience have provided the occasion

[510]Bruce, *The Epistle of Paul to the Romans*, p. 195.

[511]See Isa. 29:16; 45:9-10; Jer. 18:1-6.

[512]Dodd, *op. cit.*, p. 159.

[513]*The Epistle to the Romans*, p. 188.

for a display of **the riches of his glory** in saving those who believe in Christ and for the worldwide publication of the gospel.

In the framework of vv. 22-24 we have the following sequence: (*a*) **God ... endured** (*b*) **because He was willing** (*c*) **in order that.** Clause (*c*) is easy to understand. What God has done, He has done in order to **make known the riches of his glory on the vessels of mercy,** i.e., those **whom he hath called, not of the Jews only, but also of the Gentiles.** Clause (*a*) is not too difficult. God's endurance and long-suffering refer to the fact that He has not yet brought in His day of wrath (2:5); He seeks to lead men to repentance (2:4). Between these two, clause (*b*) seems to mean that God wished to reveal both His wrath against sin and His saving power (cf. 3:26). "What then if this is the purpose that lies behind God's election? In glory and in wrath he is manifesting his righteousness, and all his actions are rooted in the mercy with which alone he will deal with men."[514]

A series of OT quotations follows in vv. 25-29, to show that, in calling His Church from Jews and Gentiles, God has fulfilled His word of promise in the way it was intended from the beginning. **As he saith also in Osee** (Gk. for Hosea), **I will call them my people which were not my people; and her beloved, which was not beloved** (25; Hos. 2:23; cf. I Pet. 2:10). Paul then quotes from an earlier verse in the same prophecy: **And it shall come to pass, that in the place where it was said unto them, Ye are not my people; there shall they be called the children of the living God** (26; Hos. 1:10). Although Paul is undoubtedly thinking of the call of the Gentiles, it is possible he was also thinking (as did Hosea) of the temporary lapse of Israel and their subsequent salvation (cf. 11:25-26).

Two passages from Isaiah follow. **Esaias** (Gk. for Isaiah) **also crieth concerning Israel, Though the number of the children of Israel be as the sand of the sea, a remnant shall be saved: for he will finish the work, and cut it short in righteousness: because a short work will the Lord make upon the earth** (27-28; Isa. 10: 22-23). The **remnant** (*to hypoleimma*) means Paul and his kinsmen (3) who have come to believe in Christ. That this **remnant** should exist at all witnesses to the mercy of God, for, **except the Lord of Sabaoth** (Lord of Hosts) **had left us a seed, we had been as Sodoma** (Sodom), **and been made like unto Gomorrha** (29;

---

[514]*Ibid.*, pp. 190-91.

Isa. 1:9). Once again we encounter the word **seed,** which is here identified with the **remnant** of grace, i.e., those who believe in Christ.

The above quotations testify to the fact that God has completely fulfilled His promise. They provide OT support for Paul's gospel of free grace. The Church of Jesus Christ, made up of both Jews and Gentiles who believe, has been elected by God's free grace and constitutes the promised **remnant.**[515]

3. The Second Answer: Israel Rejected Because of Unbelief (9:30—10:21)

Having considered the problem of Israel's rejection from the standpoint of divine election, Paul now considers it from the standpoint of human responsibility. His aim in this section is to point out the guilt of Israel. God has rejected Israel because Israel has rejected the Messiah (9:30-33). In their zeal for law-righteousness they have rejected the righteousness of God (10:1-13). Their guilt is seen to be inexcusable. God has called Israel to salvation by the word of His promise, but Israel has refused to its own guilt (10:14-21).

a. Why Israel stumbled (9:30-33). **What shall we say then?** means, What is to be concluded from all that has been said? The answer is, **That the Gentiles** (*ethne;* not all Gentiles, or Gentiles as a whole, as in 11:25, but some among the Gentiles), **which followed not after righteousness, have attained to righteousness, even the righteousness which is of faith. But Israel, which followed after the law of righteousness, hath not attained to the law of righteousness. Wherefore? Because they sought it not by faith, but as it were by the works of the law** (30-32).

Just as tax collectors and harlots had entered the kingdom of God in the days of Jesus' earthly ministry, so believing Gentiles, who had never shown an interest in being righteous before God, were now being pardoned and received into the favor of God. But Israel, which constantly strove to be righteous, was being judged unrighteous. Why? Because Israel thought righteousness could be obtained by pursuing it "by works" (*ex*

---

[515]"It is in this connection, and not before this, that we have the first instance of primitive Christian theology appropriating the Old Testament idea of the 'remnant' " (Goppelt, *op. cit.,* p. 155).

ergon).[516] However much Israel strives after righteousness, she cannot attain it because the righteousness God requires and bestows is **by faith** (*ek pisteos*). The "just requirement of the law" cannot be met by those who follow the way of legal righteousness but only by those "who walk not after the flesh, but after the Spirit" (8:3, RSV; cf. 2:25-29 with comments).

Paul has said in the first answer that "it is not of him that willeth, nor of him that runneth,[517] but of God that sheweth mercy" (v. 16). That is confirmed here. "Had it depended on the will or exertion of man, the result would have been the opposite. Then the Jews, who sought after righteousness, would have found it; and the Gentiles, who did not seek it, would have been rejected. But God has proceeded in quite the opposite way."[518] Thus we see how closely the two answers belong together. Israel, striving after righteousness, failed to achieve it; Gentiles, hearing the preaching of the gospel, discovered faith and thereby stumbled unexpectedly upon the divine righteousness, like the farmer in Jesus' parable of the hidden treasure (Matt. 13:44).

If Gentile believers stumbled unexpectedly upon the treasure of God's righteousness, Israel "stumbled over THE STUMBLING-STONE" (NASB; Isa. 8:14, LXX). **Stumbled** (*prosekopsan*) does not mean "to stumble over by inadvertence," but "to be annoyed with," "show irritation at."[519] To the Jews the cross of the Messiah was an **offence** (*skandalon*, 33), which irritated and annoyed them into indignation. "Since we are angry with an obstacle in our path which we have struck and hurt our foot

---

[516]Paul's phrase in 32 is *all hos ex ergon*, "but as though it were by works" (NASB). The *hos* introduces a subjective idea. "St. Paul wishes to guard himself from asserting definitely that *ex ergon* was a method by which *nomon dikaiosunes* might be pursued. He therefore represents it as an idea of the Jews, as a way by which they thought they could gain it" (ICC, "Romans," p. 280). He does not say Israel made *righteousness* its aim but "a law of righteousness" (*nomon dikaiosunes*). It misused the law as a means of attaining righteousness. It is proper to seek righteousness— i.e., a right relationship with God—but to seek it "by works" produces at most a human righteousness (cf. 10:3).

[517]In v. 30, Paul employs *diokonta* and *katelabe*, which are correlative terms for pursuing and overtaking. The metaphor, as in *trekontos* (the verb used in v. 16), is taken from the racecourse, and the words were used without losing sight of the original meaning. *Diokein* is a characteristic Pauline word occurring in letters of all periods.

[518]Nygren, *op. cit.*, p. 376.   [519]ICC, "Romans," *loc. cit.*

against. . . . thus the Jews are said *proskopsai to litho tou pros-
kommatos*, i.e. to have recoiled from Jesus as one who failed to
meet their ideas of the Messiah."[520]

This God foresaw: **As it is written, Behold, I lay in Sion a
stumblingstone and rock of offence: and whosoever believeth on
him shall not be** ashamed (33). This is a fusion of Isa. 28:16 with
words from Isa. 8:14, both from LXX.[521] Paul inserts *ep auto*, to
make the prophecy apply personally to the Messiah: "He who
believes *in Him* shall not be put to shame." In 10:11 he inserts
the same phrase again in order to emphasize the personal reference of faith. **Shall not be ashamed** (*kataischynthesetai*) is probably based on a different Hebrew reading of Isa. 28:16.[522] The
accepted Hebrew text reads, "He that believeth shall· not make
haste"; i.e., "The man who stands on God's foundation will 'keep
his head when all about him are losing theirs and blaming it on
him'; he will not fuss and rush around but trust in God, confident
that His purpose will be accomplished in His own time."[523]

Barrett distinguishes three points here:

> (i) It is the man who has faith who is not put to shame. This
> *sola fide* was, historically speaking, the primary source of scandal
> to the Jews (cf. I Cor. i. 22 f.). They preferred the way of law, by
> means of which they hoped to establish their own righteousness,
> and to avoid submitting to God's (x. 3). Here we are driven back
> to the theme of God's mercy, for only faith is the proper response to
> mercy.

> (ii) The stone is Jesus Christ himself, who has the double effect
> of creating both offence and faith (see 1 Cor. i. 18; 2 Cor. ii. 15). He

---

[520]Thayer, p. 548.

[521]The passage is quoted to the same effect in I Pet. 2:8. In Isaiah, God
himself is "a sanctuary" against the Assyrian invasion which will sweep over
Israel like a flood, a Rock on which those who put their trust may stand
secure. But from the very beginning *rock* (*lithos*) was applied to Christ,
primarily with reference to Ps. 118:22, "the stone which the builders refused" (cf. Matt. 21:42; Mark 12:10; Luke 20:17; Acts 4:11). The other
passages where the word *lithos* was used in LXX came to be applied as here
(cf. Eph. 2:20, where *akrogoniaiou* is almost a proper name). By the time
of Justin Martyr *lithos* is practically a name of the Christ. Paul was simply
using a designation which was familiar to his readers.

[522]The LXX translators probably read the Hebrew text before them
as *lo' yebosh* ("will not be ashamed") instead of *lo' yahish* ("will not
haste").

[523]Bruce, *The Epistle of Paul to the Romans*, p. 200.

himself is the "seed of Abraham"; election and rejection are both in him, and it is impossible for men to glimpse God's eternal purposes apart from him.

(iii) All these truths, as the quotation itself shows, have the authority of Scripture. The Jews' own Bible proclaims the offensive Christ, whose obscurity and suffering scandalized his own people (v. 5), just as it commends, even through the law, the way of faith.[524]

b. Men's righteousness versus God's righteousness (10:1-13). There is no break in the argument between 9:30-33 and 10:1-13, but before expanding his argument Paul pauses a moment to express his sorrow and affection for his unsaved **brethren** (*adelphoi*, 1). The position of the word here is emphatic. **Brethren** is the form of address the apostle always uses when he wishes to give special emphasis to a thought. **My heart's desire and prayer to God for Israel is, that they might be saved.** "My brothers, from the bottom of my heart I long and pray to God that Israel may be saved" (Phillips). **For Israel** (*tou Israel*) is not in the best attested MSS; it may be merely an explanatory gloss, or may have arisen through the verse being used as the beginning of a lesson in church services.[525]

For I bear them record (2, *martyro*) seems to be an allusion to Paul's former conduct, and to say, "I know something of it, of that zeal."[526] **They have a zeal of God** (*zelon theou*, "zeal for God," NASB; obj. genitive). Paul uses the very word the Jew himself would have selected to express that zeal on which more than anything else he prided himself. But that zeal was **not according to knowledge** (*kat epignosin*, a word used almost technically for the knowledge of God; cf. Col. 1:9). *Epignosis* was the highest and most perfect form of *gnosis*. "They had a zeal without knowledge," Wesley reminds us; "we have a knowledge without zeal."[527]

Being ignorant (3, *agnoountes*) means "not knowing," "being ignorant of," rather than "misunderstanding." Here the fact of Israel's ignorance is noted, without considering how far it is culpable. The point of their culpability he makes in vv. 14-21.

---

[524]*The Epistle to the Romans*, p. 194.

[525]ICC, "Romans," p. 282.

[526]Godet, *op. cit.*, p. 375. Cf. Gal. 1:13-14; Phil. 3:6.

[527]*Explanatory Notes upon the New Testament*, p. 561.

Being ignorant of God's righteousness, and going about (*zetoun-tes*, "seeking," RSV) **to establish their own righteousness, (they) have not submitted themselves unto the righteousness of God.** The phrase, **to establish** (*stesai*), indicates their pride in their endeavor. "They would erect a righteousness of their own as a monument to their own glory and not to God's."[528] Israel's striving was wrong, not only because it could not fulfill the law in its entire breadth and depth (cf. 2:14-29, with comments), but also because its striving itself was already wrong. "Israel's striving for righteousness by the Law was, as Rom. 7 shows, inevitably a striving for 'their own righteousness.' They were really seeking what the brother of the prodigal was seeking, not unification with the Law but rather their own worthiness. One's 'own righteousness' is the recognition to which man lays claim by virtue of his fulfilling the law."[529]

The righteousness of God (*ten tou theou dikaiosynen*) **and their own** (*ten idian*) thus contrasts two methods of righteousness. The first is the righteousness which comes from God through faith. The other is a righteousness they hoped to win by their own methods and merits, but this turned their striving into sin. "In their eagerness to pursue after the latter, they had remained ignorant of and had not submitted to the method (as will be shown, a much easier one) which God Himself had revealed."[530] See Phil. 3:9, where the same contrast is drawn; also see comments on 1:17 and 3:21-31.

The apostle has just contrasted the two methods of obtaining righteousness. One, that ordained by God, is a method "by faith" (*ek pisteos*, 9:32); the other, that pursued by the Jews, is by the law (*dia nomou*). The latter has ceased with the coming of Christ. **For Christ is the end** (*telos*, termination) **of the law for righteousness to every one that believeth** (4). God gave the law in order to show up sin as the exceeding sinful thing it is; it turns our very striving for righteousness into a claim for personal virtue in the eyes of God. "In order to condemn this inevitable and ultimate slavery to sin and to free them from it, *God replaced the mediatorial role of the law with that of Christ,* not in chronological

---

[528]Vincent, *op. cit.*, p. 112.

[529]Goppelt, *op. cit.*, pp. 155-56.

[530]ICC, "Romans," p. 283.

sequence, but 'for every one who has faith.' "[531] **The law** (*nomou*) is not the Mosaic law but law as a principle. Although the absence of the article may be explained on grammatical grounds, the whole drift of the apostle's argument supports the idea that the term is general. This verse condemns *all human striving* after the favor of God; only through Christ can we be forgiven and accepted. **Christ is the end of the law** (*telos nomou Christos*) here is an exact parallel to *choris nomou* ("apart from law") in 3:21. In c. 3, God's righteousness is *eis pantas tous pisteuontas* ("for all who believe," NASB); here it is *panti to pisteuonti*, **to every one that believeth.** Paul is back again with his old theme, the contrast between righteousness by law and righteousness through faith.

In v. 5 the apostle writes: **For Moses describeth the righteousness which is of the law** (*ex nomou*), **That the man which doeth** (*ho poiesas*, "the one practicing") **those things shall live** (*zesetai*, "shall obtain life in its deepest sense both here and hereafter;" see comments on 8:6) **by them.** In Lev. 18:5 we have the principle of righteousness by the law expressed: the man who practices the precepts of the law will thereby attain to life. "But what is wrong with this?" it might be asked. Simply that no one has ever succeeded in obeying the law (cf. 2:1-24). On this basis the whole world stands guilty before God (3:19-20). Even though Paul could describe his earlier career as "touching the righteousness which is in the law, blameless" (Phil. 3:6), he knew it was blameless only in the sight of men; before God his striving was sin in its highest form of self-righteousness (7:14-25).

To illustrate the righteousness which comes through faith Paul goes to another place in the Pentateuch (Deut. 30:11-14). These words he finds suited to the language of **the righteousness which is of faith** (6), and he gives a brief running commentary on them in this sense.[532] **The righteousness which is of faith**

---

[531]Goppelt, *loc. cit.* Cf. Eph. 2:15 and Col. 2:14, where the theological idea of this verse is expanded and the death of Christ is specifically declared to be the termination of the law. The interpretation of this verse has been confused by incorrect translations of *telos*, to mean "aim" or "fulfillment." Sanday and Headlam insist that *telos* never means *teleiosis*. It is true that the law is the *paidagogos* ("schoolmaster," Gal. 3:24; "custodian," RSV) to lead us to Christ, and that Christ can be described as the "goal" or "aim" of the law (Matt. 5:17); but if this were Paul's meaning here, *Christos* would become the predicate and *telos* would require the article, and *nomos* would have to be restricted to the Mosaic law (ICC, "Romans," pp. 284-85).

[532]Bruce, *The Epistle of Paul to the Romans*, p. 201.

speaketh on this wise, Say not in thine heart, Who shall ascend
into heaven? (that is, to bring Christ down from above:) as
though He had never become incarnate on earth. Or, Who shall
descend into the deep? (that is, to bring up Christ again from
the dead.) as though He had not already been resurrected. But
what saith it? The word is nigh thee, even in thy mouth, and in
thy heart: that is, the word of faith, which we preach; that if thou
shalt confess with thy mouth the Lord Jesus, and shalt believe in
thine heart that God hath raised him from the dead, thou shalt
be saved. For with the heart man believeth unto righteousness;
and with the mouth confession is made unto salvation (6-10).
Bruce points out that Paul's exposition of this passage is in line
with the *pesher* style made familiar to us from the Qumran texts,
where righteousness is understood as a gift of God to be received
by faith.[533]

This passage means that, through the Incarnation and Resurrection, Christ is near us and immediately with us. In its literal
meaning this passage refers to God's law, but in the deeper sense,
intended by God beforehand, it refers to **the word of faith** (8).
"Christ has come from heaven, He has arisen from the dead, salvation is at hand, and the word about this salvation is immediately
near us."[534] To show how near this word is to us the OT passages
use two different expressions: (1) the word is **in thy mouth** (*en
to stomati sou*) and (2) **in thy heart** (*en te kardia sou*). Notice
how Paul lays hold of these expressions in vv. 9-10. **With the
heart** (*kardia*) **man believeth unto righteousness** (*eis dikaiosynen*), **and with the mouth** (*stomati*) **confession is made unto
salvation** (*eis soterian*). **Righteousness** and **salvation** are not
two different things (see 1:16-17 for commentary on these two
terms). Paul is employing Hebrew parallelism of the sort common in the OT, where the same idea is repeated in different
phraseology.

The NEB translates v. 9 in such a way as to preserve the
primitive Christian confession enshrined therein: "If on your
lips is the confession, 'Jesus is Lord.' " This is the confession which
no one can make "except by the Holy Spirit" (I Cor. 12:3, NASB,
RSV). Just as Simon confessed Jesus as "the Christ, the Son of
the living God," through the revelation of the Father (Matt. 16:
16-17), the Christian confesses "Jesus is Lord" (*Kyrios Iesous*),

---

[533]*Ibid.*, p. 204.   [534]Nygren, *op. cit.*, p. 382.

through the instrumentality of the Holy Spirit. This is the evidence of salvation (cf. I John 4: 2-3, 15).[535]

In v. 11, Paul continues, **For the scripture saith, Whosoever believeth on him shall not be ashamed** (cf. Isa. 28: 16; see 10: 33 with comments). Here Paul adds **whosoever** (*pas*) to bring out the point on which emphasis is to be laid. He introduces a proof from the OT for the statement that faith is the condition of salvation, and at the same time he makes the quotation an occasion for introducing a second point in the argument, viz., the universal character of the new method of obtaining righteousness.[536] **For there is no difference between the Jew and the Greek: for the same Lord over all is rich unto all that call upon him** (12). In 3: 22-23, Paul spoke of the absence of **difference** between Jew and Greek in a negative—"all" without distinction "have sinned" and fall short of the divine "glory." Here he makes the corresponding positive statement—all without distinction have **the same Lord** and enjoy the rich resources of His goodness and glory.[537] "Calling upon God" implies, and is the outward expression of, faith (cf. 14). Paul draws the word from the quotation used in the next verse, already in his mind: **For whosoever shall call upon the name of the Lord shall be saved** (13; Joel 2: 32). The reference to "the day of the Lord" in the context of Joel indicates the Messianic nature of the promise. This is how Peter interprets Joel in his Pentecostal sermon (cf. Acts 2: 16-21).

The term **Lord** (*Kyrios*) is applied to Christ by Paul in quotations from the OT in I Cor. 2: 16; 10: 21, 26; II Cor. 3: 16; II Thess. 1: 9. In LXX, *Kyrios* translates the ineffable name Yahweh. To confess Jesus as *Kyrios* is to confess our faith in His essential deity.

c. *Israel's unbelief inexcusable* (10: 14-21). God's sure word of promise is, "Whosoever shall call upon the name of the Lord shall be saved" (13). The trouble was, Israel had not called upon that name. Where was the fault? In vv. 14-15, Paul answers this question by constructing a chain of connecting links and enquiring which link has failed.[538] **How then shall they call on him in whom they have not believed? and how shall they believe in him**

---

[535]The reference here is to the initial confession made in Christian baptism, "the answer of a good conscience" (I Pet. 3: 21).

[536]ICC, "Romans," p. 290.

[537]Barrett, *The Epistle to the Romans*, p. 202.

[538]*Ibid.*, p. 203.

of whom they have not heard? and how shall they hear without a preacher? and how shall they preach, except they be sent? The links in the chain are self-evident. Men are urged to call upon the name of the Lord and be saved; but they will not call upon that name unless they have been moved to believe in Him; they cannot believe in Him unless they have heard of Him; they cannot hear about Him unless someone proclaims the gospel to them; and no one can proclaim the saving word unless he has been sent. The preacher is an "apostle" in the primary sense of the word.[539]

The chain of the argument is complete. Paul now shows that God has not failed to send preachers (15) and adds, a few verses further, that Israel did not fail to hear (18-19). He anticipates this conclusion in v. 16. The chain breaks at the point of faith.

In His goodness and mercy God has **sent** His messengers. Of those who bring the joyful news of salvation the prophet spoke centuries before: **How beautiful are the feet of them that preach the gospel of peace, and bring glad tidings of good things!** (15; Isa. 52: 7) Paul quickly moves to the next fact: **But they have not all obeyed the gospel. For Esaias (Isaiah) saith, Lord, who hath believed our report?** (16; Isa. 53:1)

Verse 17 is a logical conclusion of the argument in 13-15a: **So then faith cometh by hearing, and hearing by the word of God.** *Christou* (Christ) is better attested than **God** (*theou*). "So faith comes from hearing, and hearing by the word of Christ" (NASB). "Hearing by the word of Christ" (*dia hrematos Christou*) means "a message concerning Christ." "That which when heard is *akoe* is when spoken *hrema*, and it is the condition of faith. The construction in *hrema Christou* is the same as in *to hrema tes pisteos* in ver. 8. The words could not signify Christ's command."[540] The condition of Christian faith is "the preaching of Christ" (RSV; cf. vv. 6-9). In this sense faith is a gift from God: its basis is "the word of Christ." But God does not believe for us, otherwise Israel would not be guilty. This latter idea is precisely the apostle's point in the next verse.

But I say, Have they not heard? Yes verily, their sound went into all the earth, and their words unto the ends of the world (18). The process of convicting Israel is now under way.

[539]See comments on 1:1.

[540]James Denney, "St. Paul's Epistle to the Romans," *The Expositor's Greek Testament* (Grand Rapids: Wm. B. Eerdmans Pub. Co., n.d.), II, 674.

But I say (*alla lego*) introduces a plea in their behalf. Since it is Paul who is speaking, his question, **Have they not all heard?** suggests his opinion as to the answer. "To hear is necessary to believe; do you mean to say that they have not heard?" The contrary is so clearly the case that there is a touch of derision in the proof that Paul offers. **The words of the gospel have gone into all the earth.** The words of Ps. 19:4 (LXX) are quoted as an expression and proof of this. Here is another adaptation of scripture (cf. 5-8). As Denney comments, this is legitimate enough if we remember that Paul knew the extent to which the gospel had been proclaimed (cf. Col. 1:6, 23). "It was as widely diffused as the Diaspora, and the poetic inspired expression for this had a charm of its own."[541]

But I say (19; *alla lego*) is a second attempt to introduce a plea in Israel's behalf. **Did not Israel know?** "You cannot say they did not *hear;* you certainly do not mean to say then, do you, that Israel did not *understand?*" The introduction of the word **Israel** here is significant. From this point on the contrast between Israel and the Gentiles is the key to Paul's argument. Above all peoples, Israel should have understood God's message. **First Moses saith** (*protos Mouses legei*) means virtually, "Even Moses, at the beginning of Israel's history, says."

The point of citing Deut. 22:21 here is not very clear: **I will provoke you to jealousy by them that are no people, and by a foolish nation I will anger you.** Like the passages quoted in 9: 25-26, this verse might have been adduced by Paul to prove that Gentiles were to be called of God in order to rouse Israel to jealousy; but "to be in place here, there must be also the latent idea that if peoples beyond the covenant (who were not peoples at all), and unintelligent peoples (i.e., idol worshippers) could understand the Gospel, a privileged and religiously gifted people like the Jews was surely inexcusable if it failed to understand it."[542]

The next quotation from Isaiah enforces the same idea. **But Esaias is very bold** (*Hesaias de apotolma*, "Isaiah breaks out boldly"), **and saith, I was found of them that sought me not; I was made manifest unto them that asked not after me** (20; Isa. 65:1, LXX, with clauses in reverse order). Isaiah has in mind God's spontaneous, unmerited love, which takes the initiative in

[541]*Ibid.*   [542]*Ibid.*

offering, unsolicited, mercy to faithless Israelites who made no appeal to Him and never sought Him. Paul applies this, like the similar passages quoted in 9:25-26, to the reception of the gospel by the Gentiles. The part of the verse not quoted here, "I said, Behold me, behold me, unto a nation that was not called by my name," refers to the Gentiles, and this tradition of its application Paul may have learned from Gamaliel. If God has been recognized and **found** under conditions so unfavorable, surely Israel is inexcusable in missing the meaning of the gospel. "The very calling of the Gentiles, predicted and interpreted as it is in the passages quoted, should itself have been a message to . . . [Israel], which they could not misunderstand; it should have opened their eyes as with a lightning flash to the position in which they stood— that of people who had forfeited their place among the people of God—and provoked them, out of jealousy, to vie with these outsiders in welcoming the righteousness of faith."[543]

In v. 21 the outstretched hands of God symbolize His incessant, pleading love which Israel had consistently despised: **But to Israel he saith, All day long I have stretched forth my hands unto a disobedient and gainsaying people** (cf. Isa. 65:2, LXX). In v. 3 the apostle spoke of Israel's ignorance of God's righteousness, without enquiring how far such misunderstanding is culpable; but here we see that such ignorance has its root in the will, "in the pride of a heart which is determined to have a righteousness of its own without coming under any obligation to God for it, and which therefore cannot assume the attitude to which the Gospel becomes credibly Divine."[544] Israel stands inexcusable because she has stubbornly refused God's proffered grace (cf. Acts 7:51-53).

Romans 9 takes Israel's unbelief as God's judgment which hardens hearts; c. 10 acknowledges it as the standing guilt of Israel's disobedience, rooted in the profound wickedness of the human heart. This double realization is almost as far as the rest of the NT goes in the face of Israel's unbelief (cf. Matt. 23:37; Mark 4:11-12; John 12:37-40; Acts 28:25-28). But Paul is led even deeper into God's redemptive purpose, as we shall see in c. 11.[545]

4. The Third Answer: Israel's Rejection Not Final (11:1-32).

Paul now returns to his initial problem: **Hath God cast away his people?** (1) In the preceding chapters, the apostle has dealt

---

[543]*Ibid.*, pp. 674-75.   [544]*Ibid.*, p. 675.   [545]Goppelt, *op. cit.*, pp. 156-57.

with the problem of Israel's rejection from two points of view. In his first answer he has spoken of the sovereignty of God: God chooses whom He will, and whom He will He rejects, and man can present himself with no claims to God. God's people are freely chosen by grace through faith (9:6-29). In his second answer he has shown that Israel's rejection is her own fault. God's promises depend upon faith, but Israel seeks her own righteousness by the law. Israel's rejection is the consequence of her unbelief (9:30—10:21).

What would be the situation if Paul said no more? It would mean that Israel's rejection is final; that God intended it to be so, and Israel deserved it. But this is not the last word on the problem. "Of what use was all God's procedure with His peculiar people, if, when the fullness of times has come, they are simply to be rejected? That is a question which absolutely demands an answer."[546] Has God rejected that people which as a whole had received the special benefits enumerated in 9:4-6? The answer is a resounding **God forbid.** The rejection of Israel is not final: for (1) even now there is a remnant of Israel in the Church (1-10); (2) the fall of Israel became the salvation of the Gentiles, and therein we see an intimation of her final acceptance (11-24); and (3), in the last place, Israel as a whole is destined to receive the Messianic salvation (25-32).

a. A remnant now in the Church (11:1-10). In denying the rejection of Israel, Paul in essence here repeats his first answer given in 9:6-13: God has not rejected His people, for they are present in the elect remnant. Yet there is a difference in tone here. "There the word was: only a remnant. Here it is: *already a remnant!*"[547] There the remnant was only those elected by God's free grace; here it is the firstfruits (cf. 16) of Israel's restoration.

I say then (1, *lego oun*) is an emphatic phrase, marking a new stage in Paul's argument. **Hath God cast away his people?** The form of the Greek question (beginning with *me*) implies a negative answer. This is reinforced by the juxtaposition of **God** (*ho theos*) and **his people** (*ton laon autou*). Israel is **his people**; therefore He cannot reject them. Furthermore, more than once we find in the OT (I Sam. 12:22; Ps. 94:14) the promise, "The Lord will not forsake his people" (*ouk aposetai Kyrios ton laon*, LXX).

---

[546]Nygren, *op. cit.*, p. 390.   [547]Goppelt, *op. cit.*, p. 158.

By using words which were so well-known Paul reminds his readers of the promise, and thus again implies a negative answer.[548]

God forbid is a repudiation with horror of the thought of Israel's rejection. "All his feelings as an Israelite make it disloyal in him to hold it."[549] **For I also am an Israelite, of the seed of Abraham, of the tribe of Benjamin** (cf. Phil. 3:5). Seed is used here without the special sense it has in 9:7. We may paraphrase, "How can anyone think that God has rejected His people? No Israelite could believe such a thing, and I am an Israelite." From the reference to Elijah which follows, however, Paul may be saying, "More than most of my fellow Israelites, I was victim of that zeal for the law which was blind to Christ. The grace that saved me can save anyone. Together with me a remnant has already been saved."

The existence of Jewish Christians, such as Paul, would thus be proof that **God hath not cast away his people which he foreknew** (*hon proegno*, 2). For **foreknew** see comments on 8:29. Paul's reference is to the many passages which speak of God's election of Israel to be His special people (see on 9:4). God will not go back on His ancient choice (cf. 29).

Since Jewish Christians are such a small minority of the nation as a whole, their existence is not a full answer to the problem. This fact, however, suggests an approach which Paul follows. **Wot ye not** (*he ouk oidate*, "Do you not know?" RSV) **what the scripture saith of Elias** (*en Eleia*, "in the section of Scripture which narrates the story of Elijah") **?**[550] **how he maketh intercession to God against Israel** (*entygchanei to theo kata tou Israel*, "accuses Israel before God"),[551] **saying, Lord, they have killed thy prophets, and digged down thine altars; and I am left alone, and they seek my life** (2-3). With this lamentation about Israel (cf. 9:1-5; 10:1) Paul seems to stand before God as lonesome as Elijah on Horeb (cf. I Kings 19:9-10). This is the posture in

---

[548]ICC, "Romans," p. 309.

[549]*Ibid.*

[550]*En Elia* reflects a usage in Rabbinic Hebrew. The OT was divided into paragraphs to which titles were given according to their subject matter, and these came to be commonly used in quotations as references. Many instances may be quoted from Hebrew commentators as well as from the Talmud.

[551]ICC, "Romans," p. 311.

which he stands, and this is the posture in which he receives God's illuminating and comforting counsel in vv. 4-5.[552]

But what saith the answer of God unto him? I have reserved to myself seven thousand men, who have not bowed the knee to the image of Baal. Even so then at this present time also there is a remnant (*leimma,* "remainder"; cf. Isa. 6:13; 10:20-22) **according to the election of grace.** Together with Paul a remnant has already been saved. "Israel in that day stands in God's grace no less than in the days of Elijah."[553] "There is an analogy, St. Paul argues, between this situation and that of his own day. The spiritual condition is the same. The nation as a whole has rejected God's message, now as then; but now as then also there is a faithful remnant left, and if that be so God cannot be said to have cast away his people."[554]

At v. 6, Paul introduces a brief parenthesis: **And if by grace, then is it no more of works: otherwise grace is no more grace.** This **election** (5) is according to God's **grace**—that is, it is the choice of those who believe (cf. 9:6-13) and not an election of those who have earned it by their works. Unless election is on this wise, **grace is no more grace.** The rest of the sentence in the KJV, **otherwise work is no more work,** is generally regarded as a scribal gloss (cf. NASB, RSV). The observation was probably written as a marginal note by some scribe who thought he could state the converse to the principle stated in the first half of the verse, and was later incorporated by error into the text.[555]

What then (*ti oun,* 7) is the result? In what way can we soften the harsh assumption made in v. 1? It is indeed true that **Israel hath not obtained that which he seeketh for,** namely, righteousness (cf. 9:31; 10:3); **but** at the same time **the election** (*he de ekloge*) **hath obtained it.** The abstract form *he de ekloge* for the concrete "the elect" (*hoi eklektoi*) lays the stress on the idea of election rather than the elect individuals. "Paul has already said that Israel as a whole has, through seeking [righteousness] by means of works, failed to achieve this goal, though the Gentiles, who, in the nature of the case, could reach it by faith alone, had achieved it. He now adds to the Gentiles, and subtracts from the people as a whole, the elect remnant, who also, like the Gentiles,

---

[552]Goppelt, *loc. cit.*   [553]*Ibid.*
[554]ICC, "Romans," *loc. cit.*
[555]Bruce, *The Epistle of Paul to the Romans,* p. 214.

attained it just because they did not (*ex hypothesi*) attempt to attain it, but received it as part of the act of grace by which they were constituted."[556]

And the rest were blinded (*eporothesan*, "hardened," NASB, RSV). Israel, less the remnant, stood outside the relation of grace and consequently were "hardened." "Their religious enthusiasm was turned to sin."[557] This was in accordance with what is written, **God hath given them a spirit of slumber** (*pneuma katanyxeos*, a spirit of torpor or dull insensibility to everything spiritual, such as would be produced by drunkenness or stupor; Isa. 29:10), **eyes that they should not see, and ears that they should not hear** (8; Deut. 29:4).

In vv. 9-10, Paul quotes from the LXX of Ps. 68 [69 in RSV]: 23-24, ascribed in the title to David. **And David saith, Let their table be made a snare, and a trap, and a stumblingblock, and a recompence unto them: let their eyes be darkened, that they may not see, and bow down their back alway.** "Their table is their table-fellowship: the unity, and interrelatedness created by the law and so highly valued in Judaism were no more than a delusion since they were a union in sin (iii. 20), not righteousness. The bent back is a symbol of bondage; compare Gal. iv. 25."[558]

b. Israel's fall the Gentiles' salvation (11:11-24). Paul now asks the ultimate question: **Have they stumbled so that they should fall** (forever)? (11) The meaning of the passage is given by noting the contrast between **stumbled** (*ptaiein*) and **fall** (*pesein*). A man who stumbles may recover himself, or he may fall completely. Hence *pesosin* is here used of a complete and irrevocable fall (Isa. 24:20; Heb. 4:11).[559]

God forbid. The apostle indignantly rejects the thought that the final fall of Israel was the contemplated result of their transgression. The result of it has already been the calling of the Gentiles, and the final purpose is the restoration of Israel also. **Through their fall** (*to auton paraptomati*, "by their false step," continuing the metaphor of *eptaisan*) **salvation is come unto the**

---

[556]Barrett, *The Epistle to the Romans*, p. 210.
[557]*Ibid.*   [558]*Ibid.*, p. 211.

[559]ICC, "Romans," pp. 320-21. It is no argument against this position that the same word is used in vv. 22-23 of a fall which is not irrevocable; the meaning in each case is determined by the context, and here the contrast with *eptaisan* suggests a fall that is irrevocable.

Gentiles (cf. Acts 13:45-48; cf. 8:4; 11:19; 28:25-28), **to provoke them to jealousy.** The phrase **to provoke them to jealousy** is Paul's interpretation of Deut. 32:21 (already quoted in 10:19). "It is by the blessing He bestows on those who were formerly a 'no-people' in relation to Him, by the salvation which 'a foolish nation' has received through readily embracing the gospel, that God will provoke Israel to jealousy."[560]

In v. 12, Paul reasons: If an event which has been so disastrous to the nation has had such a beneficial result, how much more beneficial will be the result of the "full inclusion" (RSV) of Israel in the Messianic kingdom? **Now if the fall of them be the riches of the world** (*ploutos kosmou*, the enriching of the world by the throwing open to it the kingdom of the Messiah; cf. 10:12),[561] **and the diminishing of them** (*to hettema auton*, "their failure," NASB) **the riches of the Gentiles; how much more their fulness** (*to pleroma*, "their full and completed number"; "their fulfillment," NASB)?

For I speak to you Gentiles (13). Paul remembers that the majority of his readers are Gentiles, and he has now come to the point where what he has to say touches them directly. He reminds them, **I am the apostle of the Gentiles** (*ethnon apostolos*, "an apostle of Gentiles," NASB). **I magnify** (*doxazo*, glorify) **mine office: if by any means I may provoke to emulation them which are my flesh, and might save some of them** (14). "Do not think," we may paraphrase, "that what I am saying has nothing to do with you Gentiles. It makes me even more zealous in my work for you. I glorify my ministry to you Gentiles (by my faithful discharge of it) if by any means I may save some of my kinsmen" (cf. I Cor. 9:21; for this interpretation of *doxazo* see John 17:4; II Thess. 3:1).

After the personal explanation of vv. 13-14, which interrupts his argument, Paul returns to the ideas of v. 12. **For if the casting away of them** (*apobole*, their rejection by God because of their unbelief) **be the reconciling of the world** (*katallage kosmou*, a world's reconciliation; cf. 5:11; II Cor. 5:19), **what shall the receiving of them** (*he proslempsis*, the reception of Israel into God's favor and into the Messianic kingdom) **be, but life from the dead** (*zoe ek nekron*)? (15) Because of Israel's rejection of

[560]Bruce, *The Epistle of Paul to the Romans*, p. 216.
[561]ICC, "Romans," p. 322.

the Messiah and the righteousness of God, reconciliation was accomplished through the Cross; and this act of rejection diverted the gospel to the Gentiles (cf. Matt. 22:1-10; Mark 12:1-11). If the world has benefitted so wondrously through the Jewish *rejection* of Christ and God's righteousness, what shall their *reception* of the Saviour be but **life from the dead?** This phrase is taken by many authorities in a technical sense. Bearing in mind that both "reconciliation" and "life from the dead" are probably eschatological terms, we may understand the verse to mean: "The final return of Israel (v. 26) will be the signal for the resurrection, the last stage of the eschatological process initiated by the death and resurrection of Jesus. The full conversion of Israel therefore stands on the boundary of history."[562] Other scholars, however, regard the phrase figuratively "as a description of an unimaginable blessing."[563]

Verse 16 marks the beginning of Paul's argument that the salvation of Israel is possible (16-24). **For if the firstfruit be holy, the lump is also holy: and if the root be holy, so are the branches.** "The Gentile Christians . . . have no reason to scorn fallen Israel in Pharisaic self-satisfaction instead of longing for its conversion. Even though only the elect are the seed of promise and by now a part of the redeemed community (Rom. 9.9 ff.), yet all the natural children of Abraham (at least in keeping with I Cor. 7.14) are sanctified (Rom. 11.16), ordained to be God's possession."[564]

The metaphor for the first part of this verse is taken from Num. 15:19-20, "Then it shall be, that, when ye eat of the bread of the land, ye shall offer up an heave offering unto the Lord. Ye shall offer up a cake of the first of your dough for an heave offering: as ye do the heave offering of the threshingfloor, so shall ye heave it." By the offering of the firstfruits the whole mass was consecrated; thus the holiness of the patriarchs of Israel consecrated the whole people from whom they came.

The same thought is expressed in the second image of **the root**

---

[562]Barrett, *The Epistle to the Romans*, p. 215. Cf. Goppelt, *op. cit.*, pp. 161-67, for a scholarly defense of this position.

[563]Denney, *op. cit.*, p. 679. Sanday and Headlam present both views, without committing themselves to either. Denney's objection is based in part upon the argument that Paul would have used *anastasis* rather than *zoe ek nekron* if he were speaking technically of the end.

[564]Goppelt, *op. cit.*, p. 159.

(*hriza*) and the branches (*kladoi*), which is considerably expanded in vv. 17-24. The nation of Israel is a tree: its roots are the patriarchs, and individual Israelites are its branches. As the patriarchs were holy (i.e., belonged to God in a special manner, as the root of His saving community among mankind), so are all Israelites who belong to the stock of the tree and are nourished by the sap which flows up to them from that root.

Paul proceeds in 17-18 to expand the metaphor. **And if some of the branches be broken off** (the unbelieving Israelites), **and thou** (the Gentile believer), **being a wild olive tree, wert graffed in among them** (*en autois*, "in their place," RSV), **and with them partakest of the root and fatness of the olive tree** (*synkoinonos tes hrizes tes piotetos tes elaias egenou*, "the rich root of the olive tree," NASB; cf. 10:12); **boast not against the branches. But if thou boast, thou bearest not the root, but the root thee.** "At the best the Gentile [believer] only shares with Jews in the virtues of a root which is not Gentile, but Jewish; he has his part in the consecration of the patriarchs, the one historical root of the people of God, and in the blessings God attached to it."[565] This illustration is drawn from Jer. 11:16 and Hos. 14:6. It seeks to express the continuity of God's redemptive activity in history; God ties himself to men. "Consequently salvation is to be found only in historical continuity by inheriting promises given to the fathers: The Gentile Christians are what they are only because they have become 'Abraham's seed.' Consequently there is still hope for unbelieving Israel."[566]

The purpose of the illustration is to prevent any false sense of security on the part of Gentile Christians. **Thou wilt say then, The branches were broken off, that I might be graffed in. Well; because of unbelief they were broken off, and thou standest by faith. Be not highminded, but fear: for if God spared not the natural branches, take heed lest he also spare not thee (19-21).** The continuity between Israel and Gentile believers is not intrinsic; it rests solely on God's faithfulness and their continuing faith. God did not spare Israel when she fell into **unbelief (20)**; neither will He preserve Gentile Christians unless they stand fast **by faith** and **continue in his goodness (22;** cf. 8:17; Col. 1:21-23).

In 23-24, Paul draws a second lesson which is even more significant. **And they also, if they abide not still in unbelief, shall be graffed in: for God is able to graff them in again. For**

[565]Denney, *op. cit.*, p. 680.   [566]Goppelt, *op. cit.*, p. 160.

if thou wert cut out of the olive tree which is wild by nature, and wert graffed contrary to nature into a good olive tree: how much more shall these, which be the natural branches, be graffed into their own olive tree? Goppelt points out that the attitude of Gentile Christians toward unbelieving Israelites is a touchstone of their relationship with God. "They do not stand in faith unless they confess that the grace which saved them can also save those most hopelessly lost, therefore, above all, the severed branches of the people of the old covenant. They are in faith only if it is their 'heart's desire that they may be saved' (Rom. 10.1), and if they are certain that this petition in spite of everything is not hopeless, but that 'God is able to graft them in again' by bringing them to faith."[567]

The strength of Paul's argument lies in the fact that the process he describes is **contrary to nature** (*para physin*). It is a process never performed in horticulture. The cultivated branch is always engrafted upon the wild stock, and never the other way around. Paul disarms his critics by acknowledging that he is aware of the unnaturalness of the particular kind of grafting he describes. But if, **contrary to nature**, God has grafted wild olive branches into His cultivated tree, certainly He is able to graft the natural branches in again. The restoration of Israel is a divine possibility. **God is able** (23).

c. *"All Israel shall be saved"* (11:25-32). Paul has affirmed the possibility of Israel's conversion to Christ, but *will this possibility be realized?* In order to answer this question Paul reveals to us a **mystery**, "a portion of God's plan of salvation announced to him by revelation, which will come true in the last days."[568] Paul writes **that blindness in part** (*porosis apo merous,* "a partial hardening," NASB; "partial blindness," NEB; "a hardening has come upon a part," RSV) **is happened to Israel, until the fulness of the Gentiles** (*to pleroma ton ethnon,* "the Gentile world as a whole, just as in ver. 12 *to pleroma* is the Jewish nation as a whole")[569] **be come in** (25). "The 'full number of the

---

[567]*Loc. cit.*

[568]*Ibid.* Cf. I Cor. 2:7; Eph. 3:3-4; 16:25. Mystery (*to mysterion*) is a "revealed secret" (I Cor. 2:7-10). This mystery, which has been revealed in Christianity, is the eternal purpose to save mankind in Christ, and all that is implied in that (Rom. 16:25; I Cor. 2:1, 7; Eph. 1:9; 3:3-4; Col. 1:26-27; I Tim. 3:16).

[569]ICC, "Romans," p. 335.

Gentiles' does not mean 'all Gentiles, without exception,' nor the Gentiles predestined to be saved, but rather that multitude of Gentiles comparable to the richness of the grace of God."[570] **And so**—i.e., after this hardening of part of Israel and the salvation of the Gentiles made possible by it—**all Israel shall be saved** (26). " 'All Israel,' analogous to the full number of the Gentiles, does not mean the sum of all the members of the Jewish people, nor the host of the predestined in Israel, but Israel as a whole people."[571] After **all Israel** is **saved**, there will still be unbelieving Jews, just as after "the full complement of Gentiles" are saved, there will be unbelieving Gentiles.

As in all "genuine prophecy,"[572] Paul does not spell out the details of how this prediction will be fulfilled. It appears to be "a miraculous event coming just before the impending Parousia of Christ (Rom 13.11 f.) and following the conversion of the nations, perhaps even caused by this conversion; for according to Rom. 11.15 Israel's conversion means the days of the final fulfillment."[573]

[570]Goppelt, *loc. cit.*

[571]*Ibid.*, pp. 160-61. Cf. I Kings 12:1; II Chron. 12:1; Dan. 9:11. Karl Barth takes an opposing view as to the meaning of **all Israel**. In his comments on 11:26 he writes: "The 'mystery' does not in any sense consist in a change which we can one day expect in relation to Israel; in the reingrafting, according to the nature of Israel and in establishment of its election, of branches which are now severed. . . . The latter will indeed be the natural event already announced and prepared by the calling and conversion of the Gentiles, and in a twofold sense definitely to be expected along with it. The mystery, on the other hand, consists in the hiddenness of the meaning of the fact that this event has not yet taken place. Thus 'all Israel' (the community of those elected by God in and with Jesus Christ from Jews and also from Gentiles) will be saved in the way which is now disclosed in the relationship of the Church and the Synagogue, that is, in such a way that the first will be last and the last first" (*Church Dogmatics*, II/2, pp. 299-300). Cf. *The Epistle to the Romans*, pp. 415-16. Barth's interpretation, however, conflicts not only with **and so** and **Israel**, but also with the central intention of cc. 9—11. If Paul's prediction, **And so all Israel shall be saved**, means *only* that the Church in which Jew and Gentile are one (Eph. 2:11-22) shall all be saved in the same manner, i.e., through faith in Christ, the question with which c. 11 opened is left unanswered. Cf. Bruce, *The Epistle of Paul to the Romans*, pp. 221-22.

[572]Goppelt, *loc. cit.*

[573]*Ibid.* "Only the church that views unbelieving Israel in the light of Rom. 9-11 will be divorced from all false security in its own salvation and all contempt toward those who have fallen; only such a church . . . will also be performing the service it owes to Israel, namely, unabridged witness to Christ" (*ibid.*, p. 167).

The last part of 26 and all of 27 is a quotation from Isa. 49:20, as found in the LXX, with the concluding words added from Isa. 27:9. **As it is written, There shall come out of Sion the Deliverer, and shall turn away ungodliness from Jacob: for this is my covenant unto them, when I shall take away their sins** (26-27). "The reference is to a manifestation to Israel of her divine Redeemer— a manifestation which Paul may well identify in his mind with the parousia of Christ."[574]

As concerning the gospel (28; *kata men to euangelion,* "as regards the Gospel order, the principles by which God sends the Gospel into the world"),[575] **they** (the Jews) **are enemies** (*echthroi,* alienated from God through unbelief) **for your sakes** (*di humas,* "for your sake, in order that you by their exclusion may be brought into the Messianic kingdom").[576] **But as touching the election** (*kata de ten eklogen,* "as regards the principle of election"; "because they are of the chosen race"),[577] **they are beloved for the fathers' sakes** (*dia tous pateras;* cf. 9:4; 11:16-17; for the sake of the patriarchs from whom they have sprung). Paul means that the promises of God made to the fathers of Israel are secured to their descendants, not on the ground of merit, but on the ground of God's fidelity to His word. **For the gifts and calling of God are without repentance** (29). God does not repent of the choice He has made of Israel (cf. v. 2).

God's plan is to make disobedience an opportunity for showing mercy—first to Gentile believers, then finally to Israel. **For as ye** (Gentiles) **in times past have not believed God, yet have now obtained mercy through their** (the Jews') **unbelief: even so have these also now not believed, that through your mercy they also may obtain mercy** (30-31). Denney speaks of "a Divine purpose mastering all the random activity of human wills; a purpose which is read out by the Apostle in verse 32: God shut them all up [*synekleisen,* 'has consigned,' RSV] into disobedience that He might have mercy upon them all." [578] Since salvation is by free grace, Jews and Gentiles alike have been made to feel the need of that grace by being shut up under disobedience (cf. 5:18).

---

[574]Bruce, *The Epistle of Paul to the Romans,* p. 222.

[575]ICC, "Romans," p. 337.

[576]*Ibid.* The strong implication of this passage is that the Roman church was predominantly Gentile.

[577]*Ibid.*   [578]*Op. cit.,* pp. 684-85.

"Here at length the full meaning of Paul's 'double predestination' is revealed. God has predestinated *all men* to wrath and he has predestinated *all men* to mercy. If they were not predestinated to the former they could not be predestinated to the latter. . . . Paul does not intend to make a definite pronouncement about the ultimate destiny of each individual man. But the hope of mankind is more, not less, secure because it is rooted in the truth about God, rather than in a truth about man himself."[579] Paul says almost the same thing in Gal. 3:22. God has shut all men up in sin and judgment (cf. 3:19-20) only that He may have an opportunity of dispensing His saving mercy to all.

Paul's commission as the apostle to the Gentiles was to declare that Gentiles in Christ should be fellow heirs of the promise through the gospel (Eph. 3:6). God in Christ has "broken down the middle wall of partition" which separates Jews from Gentiles and both from God, and He has reconciled both to himself as a new creation "in one body," the Church of Jesus Christ (Eph. 2:14-16). The prospect in this sublime prophecy "of Israel's homecoming after the Gentiles have come in, crowns Paul's stunning vision of God's redemptive economy which the Spirit of the crucified Lord had disclosed to him."[580]

---

[579]Barrett, *The Epistle to the Romans*, p. 227. Paul's doctrine of "double predestination" is not therefore to be identified with the doctrine that God, before He had created the universe, decreed that a certain number of men should be saved and that the rest should be passed by to perish as the just consequence of their sins. The Calvinistic doctrine of unconditional predestination is generally known as "double predestination." "No mere *permissive* act of God must here be understood by the clause [**that he might have mercy upon all**]. The Apostle is speaking of the divine arrangement, by which the guilt of sin and the mercy of God were to be made manifest . . . taking no account, for the time, of human agency; which, however, when treating of us and our responsibilities, he brings out into as prominent a position [for example, 9:30—10:21]. . . . But there remains some question, *who are the* all men *of both clauses? Are they the same? And if so, is any support given to the notion of a general restoration of all men?* Certainly they are identical: and signify *all men*, without limitation. But the ultimate difference between the all men who are shut up under disobedience, and the all men upon whom mercy is shewn is, that by all men *this mercy is not accepted*, and so men become *self-excluded* from the salvation of God. GOD'S ACT remains the same, equally gracious, equally universal, whether men accept His mercy or not. This contingency is *here not in view;* but simply *God's act* itself" (Henry Alford, *The New Testament for English Readers* [Chicago: Moody Press, n.d.], pp. 947-48).

[580]Goppelt, *op. cit.*, p. 167.

5. Doxology (11:33-36)

God has granted Paul a glimpse of His eternal purpose, and the apostle stands amazed with wonder, **O the depth of the riches both of the wisdom** (*sophia*) **and knowledge** (*gnosis*) **of God! how unsearchable are his judgments, and his ways past finding out!** (33) God's thoughts are not our thoughts, neither are His ways our ways (cf. Isa. 55:8-9).

> What Paul adores is the unsearchable wealth of love that enables God to meet and far more than meet the appalling necessities of the world; love less deep would soon be bankrupt at the task. In *sophia* and *gnosis* the intellectual resources are brought into view with which God has ordered, disposed and controlled all the forces of the world and of man's history so as to make them subservient to His love. The world, with its conflict of races, religions, passions and even vices, may seem to be a realm of chaos; but when we see it in the light of God as Paul did, we see the signs of wisdom and knowledge, of a conscious purpose transcending human thought, and calling forth adoring praise.[581]

In vv. 34-36 two OT quotations follow: **For who hath known the mind of the Lord? or who hath been his counsellor?** (Isa. 60:13, LXX) God's counsels are profound and inscrutable. As Tersteegen said, "A God comprehended is no God at all." The second quotation takes a different approach: God acts in grace, and it is therefore impossible to build up a store of merit with Him in order to claim a reward; whatever He gives He gives freely. "With God, man never earns a recompense; he can only be loved and treated with mercy."[582] **Or who hath first given to him, and it shall be recompensed unto him again?** (35; cf. Job 35:7) God is the Source of all wisdom and of all love: **For of him, and through him, and to him, are all things: to whom be glory for ever. Amen** (36). "The universe of grace, with all that goes on in it for the common salvation of Jew and Gentile, is of God and through God and to God. To Him be the glory which such a display of wisdom and love demands."[583] "The *sola gratia* and *sola fide* of these eleven chapters can issue only in this *soli Deo gloria*."[584]

[581]Denney, *op. cit.*, p. 686.
[582]Barrett, *The Epistle to the Romans*, p. 229.
[583]Denney, *loc. cit.*
[584]Barrett, *loc. cit.*

"The Good and Perfect Will of God" is outlined in 11:33—12:2. (1) In creation, 11:36; (2) In conversion, 12:1, **mercies;** (3) In consecration, 12:1, **present your bodies;** (4) In cleansing, 12:2, **transformed, renewing;** (5) In commitment, 12:2, **prove** (W. T. Purkiser).

Section III   The Fruits of God's Righteousness

Romans 12:1—15:13

In the doctrinal section just concluded Paul has announced *The Gospel of God's Righteousness*, or the *way* of salvation. This is the way of justification through Christ, whereby the sinner is reconciled to God by faith (cc. 1—5), then sanctified in Christ by the communication of the Spirit (cc. 6—8). As it was Israel's refusal of God's proffered righteousness which occasioned their rejection from the Messianic kingdom and the inclusion of the Gentiles therein, so it will be Israel's future acceptance of this righteousness which will mean their ultimate salvation (cc. 9—11). But what are *The Fruits of God's Righteousness?* What is the *life* of salvation? Paul sketches his answer in this practical section. In cc. 12—13 he makes a general application of *agape* love as the characteristic principle of the Christian life, pointing out how this principle manifests itself both within and outside the Christian fellowship. Paul's language in these chapters shows an indebtedness to the teachings of Jesus as recorded in the Gospels, and an impressive list of parallels can be drawn up between cc. 12—13 and the Sermon on the Mount. He then applies the *agape* principle to the problem of differences of religious opinion within the Christian fellowship (14:1—15:13).

These two major divisions of the Epistle correspond to the distinction between *kerygma* (the proclamation of God's salvation in Christ) and *didache* (instruction given to believers, particularly in the area of ethics) found throughout the NT. Repeatedly in Paul's letters doctrinal exposition is followed by ethical instruction.[1] But here, as in Ephesians (cf. Eph. 4:1), the transition from doctrine to exhortation is definite and, one might almost say, abrupt.[2]

It is imperative, however, that we grasp the vital relationship which exists between the two divisions of Romans. The Christian ethic is grounded in the grace of God. Nowhere does Paul attempt to define a Christian *summum bonum,* and to deduce from this a hierarchy of virtues. Just as foreign would be the Pharisaic

---

[1] Exceptions are I and II Corinthians and Philippians.

[2] Cf. Galatians (5:1) and Colossians (3:5), and, less markedly, I and II Thessalonians.

Halakha, or Rule of Conduct, derived from a fixed code of commandments regarded as divine and unalterable. "He does not think of right conduct either as conformity with a code or as adding of virtue to virtue in a discipline of self-culture. It is the *harvest of the Spirit*—a spontaneous reaction of the inward spirit of a man, controlled by the Spirit of God, to the successive situations in which he finds himself as he lives with other men in society."[3] All the apostle does in this section, therefore, is to indicate in a general way how the Spirit of Christ will prompt a believer to behave both within the Church and in society in general. It is for this reason that the division is captioned "The Fruits of God's Righteousness" (cf. Gal. 5:22-23). Any attempt to outline this section too neatly and logically is futile. We concur with John Knox's observation: "Many proposals have been made, and the one adopted here is probably no better than several others."[4]

A. The Basis of Christian Ethics, 12:1-2

1. *Consecration* (12:1)

I beseech you therefore, brethren, by the mercies of God, that ye present your bodies a living sacrifice, holy, acceptable unto God, which is your reasonable service. In one of the finest passages in his definitive commentary on Romans, Godet shows how **therefore** (*oun*) is the connecting link between the two parts of the Epistle. Ancient religion, he reminds us, was **service** (*latreia*), or *cultus,* which centered in **sacrifice** (*thysia*). In Leviticus four kinds of sacrifice are enumerated; but they may be reduced to two: the first, comprising those sacrifices offered before reconciliation and to obtain it (the sin offering and the trespass offering); the second, the sacrifices offered after reconciliation and serving to celebrate it (the whole burnt offering and the peace offering). He sees the grand divisions of Romans as explained by this contrast.

> The fundamental idea of the first part, chaps. i.-ix., was that of the sacrifice offered by God for the sin and transgression of mankind; witness the central passage, iii.25 and 26. These are *the mer-*

---

[3]Dodd, *op. cit.,* p. 189. Brunner cautions against our saying "after the 'dogmatics', the 'ethics'. . . . But as the fruit grows from the sap of the tree, so this instruction for the true Christian life grows out of what has been previously told us about God's merciful dealings with us" (*op. cit.,* pp. 101-2).

[4]IB, IX, 579.

cies of God to which Paul appeals here, and the development of which has filled the first eleven chapters. The practical part which we are beginning corresponds to the second kind of sacrifice, which was the symbol of consecration after pardon had been received (the holocaust, in which the victim was entirely burned), and of the communion re-established between Jehovah and the believer (the peace-offering, followed by a feast in the court of the temple). *The sacrifice of expiation offered by God in the person of His Son should now find its response in the believer in the sacrifice of a complete consecration and intimate communion.*[5]

I beseech (*parakalo*) may be rendered "I exhort" (Wesley), "I appeal" (RSV), "I urge" (NASB), "I beg" (Phillips), "I implore" (NEB). It differs from a legal commandment in that it appeals to a sentiment already existing in the heart, **the mercies of God** (*ton oiktirmon tou theou*, "the compassions of God"; cf. 9:15b).[6] The word may also mean "comfort."[7] "To exhort is to speak words calculated to move to action or endurance."[8] "In grateful recognition of what God in His infinite compassions has done for you in pardoning you your sins and receiving you back into His favor through Christ, I exhort you to make to Him a complete consecration of **your bodies** as a **living sacrifice.**" This is Paul's appeal to the Roman **brethren** (*adelphoi;* cf. 1:13).

Present (*parastesai*) is not *per se* a sacrificial term. In 6:13, 16, 19, it is translated **yield** as well as **present,** and is used to express the idea of putting the body at the disposal of God or of sin (cf. also II Cor. 4:14; 11:2; Eph. 5:27; Col. 1:22, 28). *Parastesai* is aorist and therefore implies that consecration is an *act* (cf. comments on 6:13). The Christian is urged to present his body once for all for the service of God. By the same token consecration is also an *activity*, "a crisis and a process . . . a gift and a life."[9]

The Roman Christians are exhorted to put their **bodies** (*ta somata*) at God's disposal. Sanday and Headlam insist that *ta somata* is to be taken literally, like "your members" in 6:13. "Our

[5]*Op. cit.,* pp. 424-25 (italics mine).

[6]In 9:15, **I will have compassion** (*oiktireso*) is parallel to **I will have mercy** (*eleeso*); cf. 11:32 also.

[7]"By *exhorting* them, i.e. by strengthening them in faith, Paul *comforts* the Christians in their lives in time and in the world. And by *comforting* them he *exhorts* them" (Barth, *A Shorter Commentary on Romans,* p. 149). *Parakalo* is the root of *parakletos* (cf. John 14:16, 26; 15:26; 16:7).

[8]Beet, *op. cit.,* p. 332. Cf. v. 8; 15:30; 16:17.

[9]Erdman, *op. cit.,* p. 131.

members are to be *hopla dikaiosunes to theo* (vi. 13); our bodies
(*ta somata*) are to be *mele Christou* (I Cor. vi. 15); they are the
temple of the Holy Spirit (*ib.* ver. 19); we are to be pure both
in body and in spirit (*ib.* vii. 34)."[10] But surely Sanday and
Headlam are wrong in contrasting *ta somata* with *tou noos* in v. 2.
Denney observes that **your bodies** in 12:1 is not exactly the same
as "yourselves" in 6:13, "yet no stress is to be laid on the words
as though Paul were requiring the sanctification of the body as
opposed to the spirit: the body is in view here as the instrument
by which *all* human service is rendered to God, and the service
which it does render, in the manner supposed, is not a bodily but
a spiritual service."[11] In biblical psychology body and spirit are
a *unit* (cf. comments on 6:6). The Christian's body is "his individual personality as an acting concrete whole."[12]

This *whole person* is to become a **living sacrifice** for God.
Chrysostom strikingly asks:

> How can the body become a **sacrifice?** let the eye look upon
> nothing evil, and it has become a sacrifice; let the tongue speak noth-
> ing shameful, and it has become an offering; let the hand do
> nothing unlawful, and it has become a burnt-offering. Nay, this is
> not sufficient, but we need the active practice of good,—the hand
> must do alms, the mouth must bless them that curse, the ear must
> give attention without ceasing to divine lessons. For a sacrifice
> hath nothing impure, a sacrifice is the firstfruit of other things.
> And let us therefore with our hands, and our feet, and our mouth,
> and all our other members, render firstfruits unto God.[13]

This **sacrifice** is **living** (*zosan*) in opposition to the OT sacrifices,
which were slain animals. We die to nothing but sin, that we
may live wholly unto Him who died for us and rose again (cf.

---

[10]ICC, "Romans," p. 352. "The victim to be offered is *the body* of the
victim" (Godet, *op. cit.,* p. 425).

[11]*Op. cit.,* p. 687.

[12]Dodd, *op. cit.,* p. 190. To present the body, says Beet, "is practically
the same as presenting ourselves to God: for only through our body does
the world act upon us and we upon the world" (*loc. cit.*). "By 'body' Paul
means the whole human person" (Barrett, *The Epistle to the Romans,*
p. 231). "To present their bodies—the whole person" (Barth, *A Shorter
Commentary on Romans,* pp. 149-50). "The organ of action, the body, must
now become an organ and instrument of God" (Brunner, *op. cit.,* p. 102).
"Your bodies—that is, yourselves; a part is put for the whole; the rather, as
in the ancient sacrifices of beasts, the body was the whole" (Wesley
Explanatory Notes upon the New Testament, p. 568).

[13]Quoted by Alford, *op. cit.,* p. 949.

6:11; II Cor. 5:14-15, NASB, RSV). Audrey J. Williamson comments on **present your bodies a living sacrifice**: "This is the master word for the outward life of a Christian. It is more than surrender. We are to be *consumed* . . . upon *God's holy altar of service.*"[14] Just as the soldier sacrifices himself for his country in time of war, or the scientist sacrifices himself to advance medical knowledge to be used for the healing of mankind, so the Christian offers himself for the Kingdom. This implies a constant sacrifice of the physical for the sake of the spiritual in the sense that Paul spoke of it in I Cor. 9:24-27.

The **sacrifice** we offer God must also be **holy** (*hagian*). The Christian's life is to be the antithesis of 1:24. He is to recognize that his body belongs to God and that it is to be set apart for His use. He is to be without sin, to become in very truth "the temple of the Holy Spirit" (I Cor. 6:19-20; cf. I Pet. 1:14-16). "Observe that the way has been prepared for this injunction in vi. 13, 19, 22. It means that morality is lifted out of the sphere of convention or calculated expediency, and associated with all that is loftiest and deepest in the universe of our experience."[15]

Such a sacrifice will be **acceptable unto God** (*to theo euareston*, well pleasing to God; cf. 14:28; II Cor. 5:9; Eph. 5:10; Phil. 4:18). "This body, full of life and constantly employed for good, will present a *well-pleasing* spectacle to the eye of God; it will be an 'offering of sweet-smelling savour' in the N.T. sense."[16]

Moreover, says the apostle, this offering is **your reasonable service** (*ten logiken latreian hymon*). It is difficult to find a satisfactory rendering for this phrase. Etymologically, *logike* means "pertaining to the *logos*, or reason," and therefore implies a service which befits a rational creature. Epictetus declared, "If I were a nightingale I would do what is proper to a nightingale . . . but in fact I am a rational (*logikos*) creature, so I must praise God."[17] The RSV renders the phrase, "your spiritual worship"; NASB, "your spiritual service of worship"; NEB, "the worship offered by mind and heart" (marg., "the worship which you, as rational creatures, should offer"). **Service** (*latreia*) was used in 9:4 of "the service of God" or the "worship" (RSV; cf. NEB,

---

[14]*Overcome Evil with Good* (Kansas City: Beacon Hill Press of Kansas City, 1967), p. 17.

[15]Dodd, *op. cit.*, pp. 190-91.   [16]Godet, *op. cit.*, p. 426.

[17]*Discourses*, I, xvi. 20 f.; quoted by Barrett, *The Epistle to the Romans*, p. 231.

"the temple worship") ordained for the Israelites. *Logike latreia* would thus appear to mean "the service of obedience as the only reasonable or logical response to the grace of God."[18] Barth thinks it should be rendered "your logical worship." "It is logical, it simply stands to reason that the life of the man on whom God's mercy has been bestowed is . . . such a life . . . as is intended to be presented to God."[19]

2. *Entire Sanctification* (12:2)

In v. 2, we have a continuation of the thought in v. 1: **And be not conformed to this world: but be ye transformed by the renewing of your mind, that ye may prove what is that good, and acceptable, and perfect, will of God.** The word **and** (*kai*) signifies here: *and this means.* To be sacrificed in body and consecrated to the service of God implies that we (1) **be not conformed** to *this age* (*aioni*) but (2) **be . . . transformed** as befitting members of *the coming age.* "The contrast between this age and the age to come is obviously in Paul's mind when he uses these contrasting verbs."[20]

This age, as opposed to the age to come (cf. Eph. 1:21), is "evil" (Gal. 1:4); Satan is its "god" (II Cor. 4:4). All of us in our unregenerate condition "formerly walked according to the course of this age . . . in the lusts of our flesh" (Eph. 2:2-3, NASB, marg.). But as men of faith we have been resurrected with Christ and transferred to His heavenly realm (Eph. 2:4-10; cf. Col. 1:13). When Christ arose from the dead "the powers of the age to come" (Heb. 6:5, NASB) became operative in history. Those who have died with Christ and been raised with Him to **newness of life** (6:4) have become members of the coming age. "*In Christ* they have entered the new age; already they have

[18]Bruce, *The Epistle of Paul to the Romans,* p. 226.

[19]*A Shorter Commentary on Romans,* p. 150. Knox thinks the word "spiritual" is better than "rational." He suggests it means, " 'This worship is appropriate to your new spiritual life'; or it may be, 'This worship is really God's Spirit offering your worship for you' (cf. 8:26-27)" (IB, IX, 581). But in I Pet. 2:5, where we read of "spiritual sacrifices," the adjective is *pneumatikas.*

[20]Knox, IB, IX, 528. The age to come is not mentioned by name, but it is glimpsed in the expression **the renewing** (*anakainosis*) **of your mind;** for the new man has a new mind, the mind of Christ (I Cor. 2:16), which corresponds to the new age (Nygren, *op. cit.,* p. 419).

received the first-fruits of the Spirit (viii.23), and are under obligation not to the flesh but to the Spirit (viii.12)."[21]

Here the obligations of this new life in Christ are expressed in a fresh way. Christians must not be **conformed** (*syschematizesthe*) to this age but **transformed** (*metamorphousthe*, lit. "be metamorphosed") by the constant **renewing** (*anakainosei*) of the **mind** (*tou noos*). They have a present model to be rejected, then a new type to be discerned and realized. The model to be rejected is that presented to them by this present age, or, as we should say, the reigning *fashion* of the world. The term *schema* denotes the manner of holding oneself—attitude, pose; and the verb *schematizesthai*, used here and derived from it, means the adoption or imitation of this attitude or posture. The consecrated believer must not only reject the fashion of the world; he is to be *metamorphosed*. The term *morphe*, "form," denotes, not an external pose suitable for imitation, like *schema*, but an organic form, the natural product of a principle of life which manifests itself thus. Sanday and Headlam paraphrase, "Do not adopt the external and fleeting fashion of this world, but be ye transformed in your inmost nature."[22] Phillips translates, "Don't let the world around you squeeze you into its mold, but let God remold your minds from within." The Greek verb is rendered "transfigure" in the transfiguration accounts at Matt. 17:2 and Mark 9:2. Transformation, or transfiguration, is *from within* by the working of God.

Godet points out that this double exhortation refers to "two continuous incessant acts which take place on the basis of our consecration performed once for all."[23] **Be ye transformed** has the force of "go on being transformed." "Instead of yielding to the influences which tend to shape us into the likeness of things around, we must day by day undergo a change in the opposite direction."[24] The only other place this verb appears in the NT is

---

[21]Barrett, *The Epistle to the Romans*, p. 232.

[22]ICC, "Romans," p. 353. On the distinction between *schema* and *morphe* see Lightfoot, *St. Paul's Epistle to the Philippians* (London: Macmillan & Company, 1913), p. 110. Chrysostom comments, "He says not change of fashion, because virtue's not a fashion, but a kind of real *form*, with a natural beauty of its own, not needing the trickeries and fashions of outward things, which no sooner appear than they go to naught. For all these things, even before they come to light, are dissolving. If then thou throwest the fashion aside, thou wilt speedily come to the form" (ICC, *loc. cit.*).

[23]*Loc. cit.*   [24]Beet, *loc. cit.*

in II Cor. 3:18, where Paul declares that believers "are being transformed" into the likeness of Christ "from one degree of glory to another" by the operation of the Spirit (NASB, RSV). As Denney reminds us, this process is properly described as *sanctification*.[25] See comments on 6:13, 19, 22 (cf. also 15:16).

Here the apostle explains that this transformation is **by the renewing** (*te anakainosei*) **of your mind** (*tou noos*). **Renewing** comes from the adjective *kainos*, which "denotes the new primarily in reference to quality, the fresh, unworn."[26] God gives up to "blindness" the minds of those who reject Him (1:21), so that moral values no longer appear in their true light. Depravity of the whole man is the result (1:28). But to those who believe, God gives back the power of correct moral vision. To reject the conventional judgments of society and experience the grace of entire sanctification is to be given a fresh and independent insight into moral realities.[27] "And, since a man's character is formed by his estimate of what is good or bad, the restoration of the moral vision gradually changes the whole man."[28]

There seems to be the further suggestion of moral strength. The *nous* of the awakened sinner perceives to some extent the law of God, but it is too weak to throw off the bondage of sin (7:14-25). The thought of renewal here therefore suggests renewed moral power by the action of the Holy Spirit, so that the mind which discerns God's will with increasing clarity is regnant and victorious.[29] "Our bodies are to be pure and free from all the stains of passion; our 'mind' and 'intellect' are to be no longer enslaved by our fleshly nature, but renewed and purified by the gift of the Holy Spirit."[30]

In another Epistle, Paul says, "We have the mind [*nous*] of Christ" (I Cor. 2:16). This is the ability to **prove** (*dokimazein*, "appreciate" or "discern") **what is the will of God**, (viz., that which is) **good** (*agathon*), **and acceptable** to God (*euareston*, "well-pleasing" to God),[31] **and perfect** (*teleion*, enabling us to realize the true *end* of our human existence and thereby

[25]*Op. cit.*, p. 688.

[26]J. H. Thayer, *Greek-English Lexicon of the New Testament* (New York: American Book Co., n.d.), p. 318.

[27]Dodd, *op. cit.*, p. 192.   [28]Beet, *loc. cit.*

[29]Cf. Knox, *loc. cit.*   [30]ICC, "Romans," p. 354.

[31]The same adjective used in v. 1; in all nine cases of the adjective and three of the verb *eurastein* which are found in the NT the thought is that of being "well-pleasing" to God.

completeness). Dodd comments, "We may recall that our psychologists regard the impulse toward completeness as 'the most compelling motive of life,' and often find in it the basis of 'natural' ethics. Thus the will of God for man is not some mysterious and irrational form of holiness (such as leads to superstitious distinctions of days and food and the like; see chap. xiv.). It consists in that kind of life which the *renewed mind* of the Christian man can prove to be good in itself, satisfying, and complete."[32]

In 12:1-2 we see that "The Christian's Calling" is to: (1) Consecration—**Present your bodies;** (2) Separation—**Be not conformed;** (3) Transformation—**Be ye transformed** (Ralph Earle).

B. CHRISTIAN LOVE WITHIN THE CHURCH, 12:3-13

1. *The Humility of Love* (12:3-8)

Paul begins, **For I say** (3). The preposition **for** (*gar*) suggests that "humility is the immediate effect of self-surrender to God."[33] He illustrates this by his own position. He speaks **through the grace** (*charitos*) **given** to him as an apostle (1:5; 15:15), and therefore without pride. But he does speak with the God-given authority commensurate with this **grace,** and thus puts his Christian understanding and love at the service of the Church. He speaks to **every man** (*panti*) in the Roman congregation, for **every man** (*ekasto*) has been **dealt** some spiritual gift (cf. v. 6).

The apostolic exhortation is **not to think** of oneself **more highly than** one **ought to think; but to think soberly.** In the Greek there is a play on words—*phronein eis to sophronein:* "Turn the *phronein,* the energy of the mind, into a *sophronein,* a recognition of, and respect for, its limits." Sober-mindedness is one of the Greek virtues, ranked by Aristotle in his *Nichomachaean Ethics* next to courage. For him it means soundness of mind, discretion, moderation, especially in the things of sense. But for Paul sober-mindedness is determined by a different frame of reference; his thought is God-centered. We are **to think soberly, according as God hath dealt to every man the measure of faith** (*metron pisteos*). Every believer has received from God a *charisma* (cf. v. 6), a gift of faith "which God has assigned him" (RSV). Faith here means "achieving faith," the power from God to accomplish things (cf. I Cor. 13:2). "Men's opinions of them-

---

[32]*Op. cit.,* p. 193.   [33]Gifford; quoted by Denney, *loc. cit.*

selves should be in proportion not to natural capacities but to God's gifts; if this is so they will never (even though God calls them to be apostles) be boastful, for they will remember that they have nothing they have not received (I Cor. iv.7)."[34] This acknowledgment cuts the taproot of pride. It enables one to "take a sane view of oneself" (Moffatt). Paul's thought here is thus in line with that of Aristotle and the Greek ethicists, but the religious background of the apostle's teaching gives a deeper meaning to the precept, "Know thyself," while it also points the way to put it in practice.[35]

Christian humility has yet another basis. To be "in Christ" is to be incorporated into a social whole in which individualism may be overcome in a loving concern to serve others. **For as we have many members in one body, and all members have not the same office; so we, being many, are one body in Christ, and every one members one of another (4-5).** For Paul, the Church is the body of Christ. The **as . . . so** indicates that we have here only a simile or analogy, but the implication is clear: "In Christ" we are a corporate fellowship. Believers have varied functions which nevertheless are essential to the proper working of the body of which they are parts; there is therefore no place for any to think too highly of himself. The full import of Paul's thought becomes clear if we read I Corinthians 12 as a commentary on it. Whatever gift one has received marks out that individual for a particular line of service, to which he must devote himself.

The apostle therefore proceeds: **Having then gifts differing according to the grace that is given to us** (cf. v. 3), **whether prophecy, let us prophesy according to the proportion of faith (6).** The term **gifts** (*charismata*) has occurred several times with different meanings (1:11; 5:15; 6:23; 11:29); "here it means an actualization, a practical expression, of the grace (*charis*) of God under which the Church stands. In this sense the whole life of the Church, not its ministry only, is 'charismatic'."[36] **Prophecy** was the gift of inspired speech; it sometimes, but not always, included the power of prediction (Acts 11:27-28; 21:10-11). The meaning of **faith** (*tes pisteos*) here is the same as in v. 3 (see comment there). **Proportion** (*analogian*) probably means much the same as **measure** in v. 3. The Greek *tes pisteos*

[34]Barrett, *The Epistle to the Romans*, p. 235.

[35]Dodd, *op. cit.*, p. 194.   [36]Barrett, *The Epistle to the Romans*, p. 237.

may be translated "the faith" in the sense of "the Christian faith," but this does not appear to be Paul's meaning.[37] Like other Christians, the prophet must be sober-minded about his activity and importance.

Paul continues, **Or ministry** (*diakonian*), **let us wait on our ministering** (7). *Diakonia* simply means "service" (NASB, RSV). It was used generally of all Christian service (11:13; I Cor. 12:5; Eph. 4:12) or specifically of ministering to the temporal needs and bodily wants (I Cor. 16:15; II Cor. 8:4; cf. **he that giveth, he that sheweth mercy,** v. 8). It was already on the way to becoming a technical term (cf. *deacon* in 16:1; Phil. 1:1; I Tim. 3:8; cf. Acts 6:1-4).

Verses 7-8 add: **Or he that teacheth, on teaching; or he that exhorteth, on exhortation.** Placed beside **teaching,** the word **exhortation** suggests preaching. For the meaning of **exhortation** (*parakalon*) see comments on v. 1. However, Barrett reminds us that we must avoid making too sharp a distinction between **teaching** and **exhortation.** "Each means a communication, effected in different ways, of the truth of the Gospel to the hearer; in the one it is explained, in the other applied. Yet it could never be explained without application or applied without explanation."[38]

He that giveth, let him do it with simplicity (8; *en aploteti,* "with liberality," NASB, RSV; "with all your heart," NEB). It is openhanded and openhearted generosity, giving out of compassion and singleness of purpose (cf. Matt. 6:1-4). **He that ruleth** (*ho proistamenos,* "he who presides"), **with diligence** (*en spoude,* "with zeal," RSV). This may be an exhortation to Christian fathers to preside diligently over their households (I Tim. 3:4). Or it may be addressed to those who preside over churches (I Thess. 5:12; I Tim. 5:17). There is no indication in the NT whether the "president" presided at a Christian service of preaching and teaching (like the president of a Jewish synagogue), at the Lord's Supper, or in a church meeting convened for deliberative or disciplinary purposes. Nor is it clear whether this was a

---

[37]Wesley, however, translates *analogian tes pisteos* "the analogy of faith." " 'According to the analogy of faith' means 'according to "the oracles of God" ': according to the general tenor of them; according to that grand scheme of doctrine which is delivered therein, touching original sin, justification by faith, and present, inward salvation" (*Explanatory Notes upon the New Testament,* pp. 569-70).

[38]*The Epistle to the Romans,* p. 238.

distinct office or a function exercised jointly with others or in turn.[39] It was, however, a *charisma* of the Spirit just as much as prophecy or teaching.

He that sheweth mercy, with cheerfulness suggests that when a man practices charity he should do so with a joyful heart. "To a Christian, kindness is a delight, not a duty."[40]

From 12:6-8, Maclaren discusses "Grace and Graces." (1) The grace that gives the gifts, 6a; (2) The graces that flow from the grace, 6b-8; (3) The exercise of the graces, 6b-8.

2. The Sincerity of Love (12:9-13)

This section starts out: **Let love** (*agape*) **be without dissimulation** (*anypokritos*, "without hypocrisy," NASB; "genuine," RSV; "in all sincerity," NEB). In I Corinthians 12 the enumeration of the gifts of the Spirit leads up to the conclusion (in c. 13) that *agape* love is greater than all gifts. Here the train of thought is the same, though the link is not expressed.

For Paul, as for John (I John 4:7-10), *agape* is the essential nature of God, His redemptive goodness expressed concretely in the Cross (5:8). It is poured into our hearts by the Holy Spirit (5:5) and as such is the supreme and all-inclusive gift of the Spirit (I Cor. 12:31—13:13). It is not by chance that *agape* is here, as elsewhere in Paul's writings, mentioned as first among the virtues of the Christian life. For example, when he enumerates "the fruit of the Spirit" it is *agape* he names first (Gal. 5:22). This is not because **love** is simply the first in a series of comparable virtues, but because it is the comprehensive manifestation of the Spirit (see Gal. 5:6; I Tim. 1:5). If love is sincere, all that to which Paul exhorts the church will follow.

Agape, however, is not vapid sentimentality; it is a vigorous moral quality. When it is genuine, it will **abhor that which is evil, cleave to that which is good.** Of Christ, who was the Incarnation of God's love, it is written, "Thou hast loved righteousness, and hated iniquity" (Heb. 1:9). There is always something inexorable about divine love; it never condones evil. *Agape*'s holy love.

While *agape* is universal (cf. Matt. 5:43-48), it has a special manifestation within the Christian fellowship. Paul exhorts: **Be kindly affectioned** (*philostorgoi*—"a proper term for family

---

[39]*Ibid.*, p. 239.   [40]*Ibid.*

affection")[41] **one to another with brotherly love** (*te philadelphia;* 10). The term *philadelphia* is literally "brotherly love," i.e., the love which binds God's children together as a family (cf. II Pet. 1:7). "The moral purity required in ver. 9 is not the only mark of Christian love; since they are members of one family, their love is to have the character of strong natural affection (*storge*); it is to be warm, spontaneous, and constant."[42] Moreover, sincere love is other-regarding: **in honour preferring one another** (cf. I Cor. 13:5; Phil. 2:3). NASB translates, "Give preference to one another in honor."

Zeal in all our Christian duties is the natural consequence of *agape* filling our hearts. **Not slothful in business** (11; *te spoude me okneroi*) is literally "in zeal not flagging." The following clauses show that the words are being used in a spiritual sense. Of Jesus it was said, "The zeal of thine house hath eaten me up" (John 2:17; cf. Ps. 69:9). When the love which moved Him dwells in us, we will be **fervent in spirit** (*to pneumati zeontes*). "The parallel with 'the Lord' shows that here 'Spirit' means not the human spirit but the Holy Spirit."[43] The RSV translates v. 11, "Never flag in zeal, be aglow with the Spirit, serve the Lord."

The exhortation continues: **Rejoicing in hope; patient in tribulation; continuing instant in prayer** (12). For **hope** see comments on 5:2; for **tribulation**, 5:3; for patience, 2:7; for **continuing instant in prayer**, cf. I Thess. 5:17. The Christian life, for all its fervent zeal, can never be so busy "doing" that it fails to look beyond all human activity—in **hope** that endures tribulation and in **prayer** which brings a constant renewal of the Holy Spirit.

The apostle makes two final applications of *agape* in the Christian community: **Distributing to the necessity of saints; given to hospitality** (13). For **saints** see comments on 1:7. From the very beginning hospitality was recognized as a foremost Christian virtue. The early Christians looked upon themselves as the new people of God scattered among the nations and therefore bound together as members of a body and as brothers in one family. The practical expression of this conviction would demand that whenever they went from one place to another they would find a home among the Christians where they visited. See Heb. 13:2; I Tim. 3:2; Titus 1:8; I Pet. 4:9.

[41]ICC, "Romans," p. 361.   [42]Denney, *op. cit.,* p. 691.
[43]Barrett, *The Epistle to the Romans,* p. 240.

C. CHRISTIAN LOVE OUTSIDE THE CHURCH (12:14—13:14)

1. *Loving Our Enemies* (12:14-21)

The apostle now composes a passage which strikingly echoes our Lord's teachings in the Sermon on the Mount: **Bless them that persecute you; bless, and curse not** (14; cf. Matt. 5:44; Luke 6:28). It is this heavenly ability of *agape* to **bless them that persecute you** which lifts it above all human love. "If you love those who love you," our Lord asks, "what do you do more than others?" (Matt. 5:46-47, NASB) Human love is conditioned by the goodness or lovableness of its object; *agape* is unconditioned in this sense—it spontaneously gives itself for its enemies (5:8-10). In Christian experience this love is essentially God's own *agape* poured into our hearts by the Holy Spirit (5:5; cf. I John 4:10, 19). It was this love demonstrated by the martyr Stephen which registered in Paul's conscience and helped to prepare the way for his conversion (cf. Acts 7:54-60).

Love reigning in our hearts prompts us to fulfill the apostle's next command: **Rejoice with them that do rejoice, and weep with them that weep** (15). Chrysostom observed that it requires more Christian grace to rejoice with the joyful than to weep with the sorrowful. "Nature" enables us to weep with a fellow human being who has suffered calamity, but to rejoice with another in his good fortune requires divine love "so as not only to keep from envying, but even to feel pleasure with the person who is in esteem." He suggests that this is why Paul places that exhortation first.[44]

The next plea seems to be directly applicable to the Christian fellowship: **Be of the same mind one toward another** (16). Gifford paraphrases: "Let each so enter into the feelings and desires of the other as to be of one mind with him."[45] There is a parallel passage in Phil. 2:2-4, where the injunction to be "like-minded" is followed by a statement of the only way in which this is possible in a Christian sense: "Have this mind among yourselves, which you have in Christ Jesus" (Phil. 2:5, RSV).

The negative injunctions which follow help to reinforce Paul's thought in that they forbid what would destroy the unanimity of love. **Mind not high things** (*ta hypsela;* cf. comments on 3), **but condescend to men of low estate** (*tois tapeinois synapagomenoi*). Although the contrast with *ta hypsela* has caused some to con-

---

[44]Quoted in ICC, "Romans," p. 363.   [45]Quoted by Denney, *op. cit.,* p. 693.

sider *tois tapeinois* also to be neuter, most translators follow the
KJV in taking the latter to be masculine. "Do not be haughty in
mind, but associate with the lowly" (NASB; cf. RSV and NEB).
Phillips translates, "Don't become snobbish, but take a real interest in ordinary people." **Be not wise in your own conceits** is
a quotation from Prov. 3:7.

Paul's next exhortation again broadens the Christian's obligations: **Recompense to no man evil for evil** (17; cf. I Thess. 5:15;
I Pet. 3:9). **No man** (*medeni*) means "no one, Christian or non-
Christian." Nothing can ever justify revenge in a Christian heart
(cf. Matt. 5:38-48). The Christian must exemplify nobility of
spirit. **Provide things honest in the sight of all men** should
probably be rendered, "Take thought for what is noble in the
sight of all" (RSV). A Christian cannot stoop to meanness of
spirit; even the pagan conscience condemns ignoble conduct.[46]

The Christian must be a man of peace, striving always for
peaceful relations with his neighbors in the world. This is one
of the primary social obligations of *agape*. So Paul continues, **If
it be possible, as much as lieth in you, live peaceably with all
men** (18). Christ's man will go to all lengths to maintain a harmonious relation with **all men**. If collisions occur, as they almost
inevitably will, the provocation must not come from the Christian's side. When conflict comes, he must maintain a spirit of
forgiveness, leaving the matter of his vindication with God. Accordingly we read, **Dearly beloved, avenge not yourselves, but
rather give place unto wrath** (19; *dote topon te orge*, "give room
or place to the wrath [of God]," cf. 2:5-6). The meaning is, "Do
not take justice into your own hands; let God's wrath punish"
(cf. Eph. 4:27).[47] **For it is written, Vengeance is mine, I will
repay, saith the Lord** (from Deut. 32:35; the LXX reads, "In the
day of vengeance I will repay").

Paul now quotes Prov. 25:21-22 exactly as in the LXX.
Therefore (*alla*, "but") **if thine enemy hunger, feed him; if he
thirst, give him drink: for in so doing thou shalt heap coals of
fire on his head** (20). The apostle does not mean that we are to
be consoled for our kindness by the knowledge that our enemy
will be punished. This would be to have a malicious motive. Such

---

[46]This implies that there is a certain moral standard common to all men
and recognized as universally praiseworthy. See comments on 2:14-15 for a
discussion of natural ethics.

[47]For *te orge* as used absolutely of God's wrath, cf. 5:9 and I Thess. 2:16.

an attitude would be utterly contrary to the meaning of *agape*
and would violate the context of both Proverbs and our passage.
Paul's intent is brought out by the next exhortation, **Be not
overcome of evil, but overcome evil with good** (21). His thought
is that of his Master in Matt. 5:38-42. What we do must be for
our enemy's good; by the power of *agape* we must strive to make
of him a friend and a child of God. "Coals of fire must mean,
as most commentators since Augustine have said, 'the burning
pangs of shame' which a man will feel when good is returned for
evil, and which may produce remorse and penitence and contri-
tion."[48]

Dodd considers the last sentence of this chapter "an admi-
rable summary of the teaching of the Sermon on the Mount,
about what is called 'non-resistance' " and it expresses, he thinks,
"the most creative element in Christian ethics."[49]

2. *Living as a Citizen* (13:1-7)

This section on the Christian's obligation to the state is
unique in Paul's letters. One wonders why it occurs in this particular Epistle. Is it because he is writing to the church in Rome,
the seat of the empire, where political concerns would naturally
be strong? Or were there reasons, unknown to us, why he addressed the Romans in this manner? Perhaps the Jewish disturbances which led to Claudius' edict were in the background.[50]

There may have been a theological reason for including this
explanation of the role of the state. In the previous chapter the
apostle has cautioned Christians against conformity to this present
world (12:2). Should they disavow loyalty to its institutions and
authorities? Should they be in subjection to "the princes of this
world" (I Cor. 2:6)? Since Jesus only is Lord (I Cor. 8:6; Phil.
2:9-11), is there place for any other dominion? Since the Christian's citizenship is in heaven (Phil. 3:20), is he not free from
the obligations of earthly citizenship? From time to time these
inferences have been drawn, and it may have been the knowledge
of some such pattern of thought in the church at Rome which
caused Paul to write as he did. There is no positive indication,
however, that he is replying to such a specific situation.

[48]ICC, "Romans," p. 365.   [49]*Op. cit.*, p. 201.

[50]See Introduction, p. 23. There seems to be evidence that the Jews in
Rome were "notoriously bad subjects," and it may be that this spirit of
anarchy carried over into the Roman church. See Denney, *op. cit.*, p. 695.

The connection between the discussion of state authority and the preceding section is actually quite close. In fact the break between cc. 12 and 13 is more apparent than real; Paul has been led to introduce his new topic by the very movement of his ideas. In 12:14-21 he has insisted that the Christian is essentially a man of peace who refuses to resist evil. Does this policy of nonresistance mean the overturn of justice in human affairs? This counsel is hardly to be put forward as a way of life to be followed by all men. Furthermore, should it be generalized as applicable to every situation in which the Christian may find himself? Thus for many reasons there arises the question as to what the Christian attitude should be toward civil authorities whose responsibility it is to curb lawless actions. Is civil government contrary to the will of God?[51]

In answering this question Paul interrupts his discussion of *agape,* which he resumes in 13:8-10. The fact that he places this section in the midst of a passage in which he is explaining the nature of Christian love implies strongly that the conflict between *agape* and civil justice is not to be understood in terms of antithesis but in terms of things that are complementary. The Christian is a citizen of two orders, and Paul seems to be saying with the Master, "Render therefore unto Caesar the things which are Caesar's; and unto God the things that are God's" (Matt. 22:21).

Finally, it is important to see that Paul's treatment of the role of the state is positive. It serves the "good" of man (v. 5). While the state must not be confused with the Church and is a stranger to God's love in Christ, it nevertheless operates within the providential will of God. It is this view which forms the basis for the Christian's attitude of obedience to the civil authorities.

The section begins with the word of counsel, **Let every soul be subject unto the higher powers** (1; *exousiais hyperechousais,* "the governing authorities," NASB, RSV). **Every soul** (*pasa psyche*) is a Hebraism suggesting the idea of individual duty. This view of submission to established authority was widely held in Judaism. It finds its first expression in Daniel (2:21, 37-38; 4:14, 26). In the apocryphal book of *Wisdom* we read, "Hear therefore, O ye kings, and understand; learn, ye that be judges of the ends of the earth. . . . For power is given you of the Lord, and sovereignty from the Highest, who shall try your works, and

[51]Leenhardt, *op. cit.*, p. 322.

search out your counsels. Because, being ministers of his kingdom, ye have not judged aright, nor kept the law, nor walked
after the counsel of God" (6:1-4). The idea here is the same as
Paul's: **There is no power but of God: the powers that be are
ordained of God.** *Wisdom,* however, addresses its warning to
rulers rather than subjects. The conception that civil authorities
rule by divine ordination is the common idea and actually has
both implications (viz., that rulers should discharge their responsibilities worthily, and subjects should respect and obey
them).[52]

The state is not simply a civil compact; it exists by divine
order. With *Wisdom,* Paul would certainly agree that not all that
the authorities do is necessarily in agreement with God's will.
"There are good and bad authorities, God-fearing and godless
governments. There are some authorities that use their powers
in harmony with God's will, and others that misuse their powers
and tramp the will of God under their feet. But Paul is not now
talking about such distinctions. He is speaking of that which all
authorities have in common, namely, that they are instituted by
God. That there are governments in the world is not an arbitrary
invention of man's; it is a fact ordained by God."[53]

On the basis of this fundamental issue Paul makes his first
practical point: **Whosoever therefore resisteth the power, resisteth the ordinance of God: and they that resist shall receive
to themselves damnation** (2; *krima;* "condemnation," Wesley,
NASB; "judgment," RSV). To oppose authority is to oppose God,
and such opposition is bound to be punished. Since *krima* is
punishment which comes through the human instrumentality of
the state, it is temporal rather than eternal. Nevertheless, it is
the judgment and "wrath" of God (cf. v. 5) which is being
executed in the process.

The role of government is here portrayed in negative terms:
it punishes those who resist its orders. If anarchy is to be prevented, governing authorities must be invested with powers of
repression and punishment. On the other hand, **Rulers are not a
terror to good works** (3). The positive side of government is not
always apparent, for its primary purpose is to restrain the irre-
sponsible exercise of freedom. By its very nature it comes into
collision with lawless persons. But the person who exercises
self-discipline finds no conflict with the state. He has no reason

[52]Knox, IB, IX, 602.   [53]Nygren, *op. cit.,* p. 428.

to **be afraid of the power.** "The citizen whose intention it is to live in his sphere and to play his part, without trespassing on the rights of his neighbour, is acting in the same sense as state authority and has nothing to fear from the latter; he is performing a good work for which he will be praised by the authority of the state."[54]

Since the state is by divine ordination Paul can take another step and declare that the civil authority is **the minister of God to thee for good** (4; cf. *Wisdom* 6:4, where rulers are spoken of as "ministers of his kingdom"). The magistrate is God's minister (*diakonos*, servant) to preserve peace and tranquility in society. **But if thou do that which is evil, be afraid; for he beareth not the sword in vain: for he is the minister of God, a revenger to execute wrath upon him that doeth evil.** "The sword was carried, if not by, then before the higher magistrates, and symbolized the power of life and death which they had in their hands."[55] That is to say, the magistrate's sword is here "the instrument of capital punishment, which God authorizes him to inflict."[56] This, however, does not sanction the practice of capital punishment as it may happen to prevail in a given society. The Christian conscience has a right to question and change the laws of a state in order to bring them to accord with God's will as he understands it.

Quimby has put the matter well: "Today under our different form of government, in case of injustice, this teaching of Paul cannot be made to mean: Never object to any law, never agitate for repeal or change, never seek reforms. But it meant then, and it still means most properly: Never flout decent public order! Along that path lies anarchy and chaos. It is anti-God, for God is the God of order."[57]

Rulers are to be obeyed not only because they have the power of life and death over their subjects but also because it is right. **Ye must needs be subject, not only for wrath, but also for conscience sake** (5). Conscience recognizes the right of the state as an order of God, to command our obedience.[58] The state re-

---

[54]Leenhardt, *op. cit.*, p. 330.   [55]Denney, *op. cit.*, p. 697.
[56]Wesley, *Explanatory Notes upon the New Testament*, p. 572.
[57]*Op. cit.*, p. 183.
[58]The apostle would certainly agree that the Christian conscience might move him to say with Peter and John, "We ought to obey God rather than men" (Acts 5:29; cf. Acts 4:18-21). Even so, the conscientious objector must be prepared to suffer the punishment which the state dictates, for as a Christian he believes that even an evil state is better than anarchy.

quires not only the goodwill but also the active support of its citizens. Paul writes, **For this cause pay ye tribute also** (6). The term **tribute** (*phorous*) is often used of payments made by a subject nation but here it probably means any imposts made for the support of the government. Most modern versions translate the word as "taxes." Moreover, the authorities are **God's ministers, attending continually upon this very thing** (not collecting taxes, but promoting good and restraining evil). The word translated **ministers** (*leitourgoi*) was a common term for public officials, and especially for those who carried out public works in the service of the state. "The word in itself (although Paul uses it to describe his own office—xv. 16) is not a theological term, but derives theological significance from the genitive, 'of God'. The Roman magistrates, little though they knew it, were public servants not of Rome but of God; it was his work they did. In this lay their true authority, and their right to receive 'dues'."[59]

Paul's conclusion is, **Render therefore to all their dues: tribute** (*phoron*) **to whom tribute is due; custom** (*telon*) **to whom custom; fear to whom fear; honour to whom honour** (7). Various distinctions have been made between *phoros* and *telos*. Lietzmann defines the distinction as being between direct and indirect taxes respectively.[60] Sanday and Headlam think *phoros* designates the tribute exacted by a foreign master-nation, and *telos*, ordinary taxation.[61] Knox is probably right when he suggests, "Perhaps Paul has no particular distinction in mind; certainly he does not think of **respect** and **honor** as separately due to two distinct classes of men. . . . The point is that whatever one truly owes another (i.e., **their dues**), whether it is money or respect, one must fully pay."[62]

In 13:1-7, Paul indicates "The Christian's Twofold Attitude Toward His Government." (1) Submission, 1-5; (2) Support, 6 (Ralph Earle).

3. Discharging Our Obligation (13:8-10)

Paul has now concluded his theological treatment of civil law. What is the relation of that law to the law of Moses? This passage shows that there is no conflict or contradiction, because the love which fulfills the law of God means loving one's neighbor as oneself.

---

[59]Barrett, *The Epistle to the Romans*, p. 247. [60]Knox, IB, IX, 604.
[61]ICC, "Romans," p. 368.   [62]IB, IX, 605.

The transition is from the precept, "Render therefore to all their dues," to its negative corollary: **Owe no man any thing** (8). This means, Do not *continue* in a state of owing any of the obligations referred to in v. 7, but fulfill and discharge them. "Get rid of all debts, not by denying, ignoring, or evading them, but by paying them: there is only one debt of which one can never get rid—the debt of love."[63] "Owe nothing to anyone except (*ei me*) to love one another" (NASB). Barrett paraphrases, "Let your only indebtedness be the mutual love you are bound to owe as Christians."[64]

The debt we owe is not constituted by any natural relationship but is created by God's command: **For he that loveth another** (*ton heteron*, "the other") **hath fulfilled the law** (God's law). It is significant that Paul does not say "neighbour" here as in vv. 9 and 10. He is stating a moral principle. "Just as Christian faith means that a man is prepared to worship and obey God rather than himself, so Christian love means that his attention is directed away from himself and towards those who are essentially other than himself (cf. Phil. ii.4)."[65] Love for "neighbour" can quite easily be made to mean love for the one who is like-minded and congenial; but love is not Christian unless it includes the man who differs from me in every way.[66]

Paul proceeds to show the manner in which love fulfills the law. **For this, Thou shalt not commit adultery** (Exod. 20:14; Deut. 5:18), **Thou shalt not kill** (Exod. 20:13; Deut. 5:17), **Thou shalt not steal** (Exod. 20:15; Deut. 5:19), **Thou shalt not covet** (Exod. 20:17; Deut. 5:21), **and if there be any other commandment, it is briefly comprehended in this saying, namely, Thou shalt love thy neighbour as thyself** (9; Lev. 19:18). The apostle here echoes Jesus' summation of God's law in two "great commandments" (cf. Matt. 22:34-40; Mark 12:29-31). The meaning is clear: If you love your neighbor (assuming that we put into this word the meaning of "the other" in v. 8), you will not offend against him in any way. As Paul goes on to say, **Love worketh no ill to his neighbour: therefore love is the fulfilling of the law** (10).

Love filling the heart and banishing ill will—this constitutes the fulfillment of the law's requirement. The law does not de-

[63]*Ibid.*
[65]*Ibid.*

[64]*The Epistle to the Romans,* p. 250.
[66]*Ibid.;* see Matt. 5:46-47.

mand of the Christian absolute perfection in every detail of conduct; it requires a motive of love. The Christian life is not to be a scrupulous straining after an impossible ideal of perfection but rather a joyous surrender of the self to God's love in Christ. Christian love has its source in God (I John 4:10); it is poured into our hearts by the Holy Spirit, who is given to us (5:5). By this gift of the Spirit the believer is enabled to fulfill "the just requirement of the law" (8:4, RSV). This John Wesley termed Christian perfection: "the loving God with all our heart, mind, soul, and strength. This implies that no wrong temper, none contrary to love, remains in the soul; and that all the thoughts, words, and actions, are governed by pure love."[67]

4. *Awaiting the Consummation* (13:11-14)

The apostle now concludes this section by reminding us that Christians are to live a life in keeping with the new age which is about to burst upon us in its glory with the coming of Christ. We must not be conformed to the scheme of this present age; our minds must be transformed into harmony with God's new age (12:2). Thus in coming to the end of these exhortations Paul returns to his starting point.

We know **the time** (11; *ton kairon*) in which we live. The Greek word signifies "divine timing" in distinction from *chronos,* which is calendar time. *Kairos* is a divinely determined moment in the time process, and is used technically in the NT with reference to the time before Christ's Parousia (I Cor. 7:29). **Knowing the time,** we do not behave as those who are unaware that the end is near. We realize **that now it is high time to awake out of sleep: for now is our salvation nearer than when we believed.**

We live in expectation of the day of **salvation** which is dawning. In one sense our salvation is a present reality, but in another sense it is incomplete until Christ returns to give us His glory (see 8:17-23). It is this future salvation that Paul speaks of when he says that **now our salvation is nearer than when we believed.** Every day we live brings us nearer "the day of the Lord," closer to the day of the revelation of His glory.

[67]"A Plain Account of Christian Perfection," *The Works of John Wesley,* XI, 394.

Earlier in this letter Paul spoke of the old age as the age of sin and death which stands under the wrath of God. Now he compares it with the night. **The night is far spent, the day is at hand** (12). As long as the old age lasts, **the night** continues. But the turning point has come, with Christ. "The dayspring from on high hath visited us" (Luke 1:78). The night continues of course, but it moves swiftly toward the daybreak. Those who are Christ's belong no longer to the night; they are men of the morning, for they have seen the breaking of God's new **day.**

The apostle now insists that our ethical life must conform to the fact that we are those of the day: **Let us therefore cast off the works of darkness, and let us put on the armour of light.** Elsewhere, **the works of darkness** are called "the works of the flesh" (Gal. 5:19-21). Here an abbreviated list is given: **rioting** (*komois*, "carousing," NASB; "reveling," RSV) **and drunkenness, chambering** (*koitais*, "sexual promiscuity," NASB; "debauchery," RSV) **and wantonness** (*aselgeiais*, "sensuality," NASB; "licentiousness," RSV), **strife and envy** (13). All these belong to **the night.** In place of these we must put on **the armour of light.**

The entire exhortation is summarized in one shining sentence: **But put ye on the Lord Jesus Christ, and make not provision for the flesh, to fulfil the lusts thereof** (14). "Herein is contained the whole of our salvation," Wesley comments. "It is a strong and beautiful expression for the most intimate union with Him, and being clothed with all the graces which were in Him. The apostle does not say, Put on purity and sobriety, peacefulness and benevolence; but he says all this and a thousand times more at once, in saying, Put on Christ."[68] But, to **put on** ... **Christ** means to put off **the flesh** (cf. 8:8-9).

In Paul's terminology the entire Christian life may be described as a putting off and a putting on. The process begins in justification and baptism. "For as many of you as have been baptized into Christ have put on Christ" (Gal. 3:27; cf. 6:3-4). But that which happened implicitly in conversion must be made experientially real (6:11-13). All that belongs to the old age must be put off; all that belongs to the new must be put on. "But now ye also put off all these; anger, wrath, malice, blasphemy, filthy communication out of your mouth. Lie not one to

---

[68]*Explanatory Notes upon the New Testament*, p. 573.

another, seeing that ye have put off the old man with his deeds; and have put on the new man, which is renewed in knowledge after the image of him that created him. Put on therefore, as the elect of God, holy and beloved, bowels of mercy, kindness, humbleness of mind, meekness, longsuffering. And above all these things put on charity [*agape*], which is the bond of perfectness" (Col. 3:8-10, 12, 14; cf. Eph. 4:22-24). **Put ye on the Lord Jesus Christ, and make not provision for the flesh, to fulfil the lusts thereof**—that in one pithy sentence is what it means to be a Christian.

D. CHRISTIAN LOVE AND DIFFERENCES OF OPINION, 14:1—15:13

The final paragraph of the preceding section seems to conclude the ethical section of the Epistle. Knox observes that although different in form and content that passage is identical in function with the concluding exhortation of the Sermon on the Mount in both Matt. 7:24-29 and Luke 6:46-49. We have, therefore, in 14:1—15:13 something of a postscript to Paul's ethics.[69]

It has been customary to regard this plea for unity amidst diversity of religious opinion as directed to a specific situation which existed in the Roman church, but efforts to identify the sect or party which created the issue have not succeeded.

At first the man who is **weak in the faith** (1) seems to be a converted Jew who has not yet freed himself from the scruples of the Mosaic law. But the fact that he is a vegetarian (2), a man who will neither **eat flesh** nor **drink wine** (21), points to the Essenes, who are known to have been vegetarians and abstainers. Yet it is possible that the weak brother is a Gentile recently converted from idolatry who refuses to eat meat because that which he must buy at the markets has been previously consecrated to pagan divinities. Paul devotes three chapters of I Corinthians to this problem (I Corinthians 8—10).

These exhortations may not therefore be prompted by anything Paul knew about a specific situation in the Roman church. Rather, like the rest of the ethical section, they may be general instruction arising from issues with which Paul has had to deal elsewhere. Knox points out that in Corinth, where the apostle was at the time he wrote Romans,[70] he had seen the unity and

[69]IB, IX, 612-13.   [70]See Introduction, "Place and Date of Writing."

harmony of the church threatened by two forces: diversities of gifts and differences of religious opinion. He reminds us that Romans 12:3-8 corresponds with I Corinthians 12 and 14, where Paul dealt with the first of these issues, while Rom. 12:9-21 may be compared with I Corinthians 13. Moreover, this present section bears a striking resemblance to I Corinthians 8—10. "Thus we find that two of the major sources of the disorder at Corinth are taken up for discussion in Romans, and taken up in connection with a discussion of love which bears many resemblances to the treatment of that *same theme* in that *same connection* in the Corinthian letter."[71] He thinks the inference we must draw is that Paul deals with these themes in Romans because of difficulties he has had in Corinth rather than because of any specific knowledge he may have had of Rome.

This inference finds further support in the fact that the treatment of these matters is more general in Romans than in Corinthians. In I Corinthians it is clear that the issue with relation to spiritual gifts is the specific matter of speaking in tongues, whereas Rom. 12:3-8 is a more generalized discussion of gifts. And with regard to the weak, whereas in I Corinthians Paul's concern is primarily with those who scruple about meat offered to idols, the reference in Romans, as we have seen, is more vague and diffused.[72]

1. The Strong and the Weak (14:1-12)

Paul begins with an abrupt injunction: **Him that is weak in the faith** (*ton de asthenounta te piste*) **receive ye** (1). "One is weak in respect of faith who does not understand that salvation is of faith from first to last, and that faith is secured by its own entireness and intensity, not by timorous scrupulosity of conscience."[73] Nevertheless, the Romans are commanded to **receive** (*proslambanesthe*) this fearful believer into full Christian fellowship. The verb is often used of God's gracious acceptance of men: if God receives this wavering man, so must we. Godet points out that Paul's employment of the participle *asthenounta* instead of the adjective meaning weak (*asthene*) denotes one who is for the time feeble, but who may become

---

[71]IB, IX, 614-15.
[72]*Ibid.*, p. 615. See ICC, "Romans," pp. 399-403 for a full discussion of this issue.
[73]Denney, *op. cit.*, p. 701.

strong.[74] Within the church he may come to a more adequate understanding of the gospel and thus to "the full assurance of faith" (cf. Heb. 10:19-23).

The **weak** brother must be received, **but not to doubtful disputations** (*me eis diakriseis dialogismon*). The Greek phrase means "but not to pass judgments on his thoughts."[75] He cannot be argued out of his views; arguments would only confirm him in them. He must grow out of his limited ideas, and meanwhile he is not to be criticized and censured, but loved (cf. I Thess. 5:14).

The apostle proceeds to describe the two classes to which he is referring. **One believeth** (*pisteuei*, has faith) **that he may eat all things: another, who is weak, eateth herbs** (2; *lachana esthiei*, "eats only vegetables," RSV). Sanday and Headlam understand Paul to be writing generally. "He takes, on the one side, the man of thoroughly strong faith, who has grasped the full meaning of Christianity; and on the other side, one who is, as would be generally admitted, overscrupulous, and therefore is suitable as the type of any variety of scrupulousness in food which might occur."[76]

Paul then gives a suitable word to each group. **Let not him that eateth despise him that eateth not; and let not him which eateth not judge him that eateth: for God hath received him** (3). The man of knowledge is prone to **despise** his scrupulous brother, while the temptation of the hyper-conscientious man is to **judge** the man who does not adhere to his scruples. Paul reminds this latter man that **God hath received** his brother. Through Christ He has admitted him into His gracious favor without imposing upon him minute and exacting rules. The brother must not therefore be criticized or censured for neglecting practices which God has not required.

The sharpness of the rebuke which follows shows that Paul, with all his love and consideration for the weak, was alert to the ever present tendency of the very conscientious person to lapse from scrupulosity about his own conduct into loveless Pharisaism toward that of others. **Who art thou that judgest another man's servant? to his own master he standeth or falleth** (4). "Who are you to set yourself up as a brother's judge or master? Do you not know that he is answerable to God, not to you?" (Cf.

[74]*Op. cit.*, p. 454.   [75]ICC, "Romans," p. 384.   [76]*Ibid.*, p. 385.

258

I Cor. 4:3-5.) **Yea, he shall be holden up: for God is able to make him stand** (cf. Phil. 1:6). "Do not take too gloomy a view of your brother's chances of salvation. The grace of God is sufficient to uphold him." Paul is aware of the dangers of spiritual sophistication (see I Cor. 8:1-3; 10:12), yet "he is confident that Christian liberty, through the grace and power of Christ, will prove a triumphant moral success."[77]

The apostle now passes on to another question of essentially the same nature—the religious observance of days. **One man esteemeth one day above another** (5). Here is a man who insists on observing the Jewish Sabbath, or perhaps the feast and fast days of Judaism. In Galatians, Paul expressed concern for his converts who had lapsed into such legalism: "Ye observe days, and months, and seasons, and years. I am afraid of you, lest by any means I have bestowed labour upon you in vain" (4:10-11). Since the Galatians had begun in the freedom of full Christian faith (1:6; 3:1-3), Paul considered their lapse a falling from grace (5:4). In this Roman letter he simply considers the principles which underlie such practices.

Here, however, is **another** man who **esteemeth every day alike.** This does not mean that **another** treats every day as secular; it may mean he regards every day as sacred, as dedicated to the service of God. In Hebrews we read, "There remaineth therefore a rest [*sabbatismos,* a keeping of the sabbath] to the people of God. For he that is entered into his rest, he also hath ceased from his own works, as God did from his. Let us labour therefore to enter into that rest" (4:8-10). For the Christian who has entered "into that rest" *every day* is a sabbath unto God. This was certainly Paul's attitude.

What solution does the apostle propose? Simply this, **Let every man be fully persuaded in his own mind.** That is, let him decide on the basis of his personal relationship to the Lord. **He that regardeth the day, regardeth it unto the Lord; and he that regardeth not the day, to the Lord he doth not regard it** (6).[78] The scrupulous man who observes the Jewish Sabbath (and/or any other fast and feast days on the Jewish calendar) does so because he believes this is what **the Lord** requires; he

---

[77]Denney, *op. cit.,* p. 702.

[78]Although the negative side of the statement is not found in the best MSS, the thought is certainly implied, as the second half of the verse suggests.

who does not observe these days disregards them because he is
convinced that Christ's death on the Cross cancelled "the law of
commandments contained in ordinances," including the observance of the Mosaic Sabbath (Eph. 2:11-22; Col. 2:13-17).[79] But
still such matters are scruples of the private conscience, and
every Christian must decide for himself what God's will is for
him in these questions. By the same token, **He that eateth, eateth
to the Lord, for he giveth God thanks; and he that eateth not,
to the Lord he eateth not, and giveth God thanks.**

Paul now proceeds to elaborate upon this truth of the believer's responsibility to the Lord. **For whether we live, we live
unto the Lord; and whether we die, we die unto the Lord:
whether we live therefore, or die, we are the Lord's. For to
this end Christ both died, and rose, and revived, that he might
be Lord both of the dead and living** (7-9). From the context
it is evident when the apostle says that **none of us liveth to himself** he does not mean (as is often supposed) that our actions
affect our fellowmen. He means that we live in relation to Christ.
Both our life and our death are **unto the Lord**—nothing in life
or death can separate us from Him (cf. 8:35-39), for by His
death and resurrection He became **Lord both of the dead and
living.**

Paul now applies the argument pointedly to the questions
he is discussing. **But why dost thou judge thy brother? or why
dost thou set at nought thy brother? for we shall all stand before the judgment seat of Christ** (10; cf. II Cor. 5:10). We are
responsible to Christ: we shall appear before Him; there is therefore no place for uncharitable judgments or self-righteous exclusiveness between Christian men. The apostle supports his
warning of the universal character of God's judgment by quoting
from Isa. 45:23. **For it is written, As I live, saith the Lord, every
knee shall bow to me, and every tongue shall confess to God**
(11). We conclude therefore that it is to **God** and not to man
that each of us has to give account. **So then every one of us
shall give account of himself to God** (12). Notice how easily
Paul passes from **Lord** to **God.** The Father and the Son were so

[79]The Church has from the beginning observed the first day of the week
as "the Lord's day" in commemoration of Christ's resurrection (John 20:1,
19; Acts 20:7; I Cor. 16:2; Rev. 1:10). Both the existence of the Church as
the body of Christ and the Lord's day as the Church's day of worship are
living memorials of the Resurrection.

united in his mind that they are often interchanged. "God, or Christ, or God through Christ, will judge the world. Our life is in God, or in Christ, or with Christ in God. The union of man with God depends upon the intimate union of the Father and the Son."[80]

2. Walking in Love (14:13-23)

The thought of the previous paragraph is assumed and summarized: **Let us not therefore judge one another any more** (13). Neither strong nor weak is in a position to adopt the superior attitude of the judge. All critical and censorious feelings must cease. Paul then presses on to a further point, using the word **judge** in a play on words: **But judge this rather, that no man put a stumblingblock or an occasion to fall** (*skandalon*) **in his brother's way.** Sanday and Headlam think Paul derived the word *skandalon* and the whole thought of this sentence from our Lord's words reported in Matt. 18:6-7 (cf. I Cor. 8:9-13).

It is evident that the apostle is now addressing the strong. Speaking as a man of knowledge, he says: **I know, and am persuaded by the Lord Jesus, that there is nothing unclean of itself: but to him that esteemeth any thing to be unclean, to him it is unclean** (14). This may mean that Paul knew Jesus' teaching on this matter (see Mark 7:14-23). A careful comparison of the ethical teachings in his Epistles reveals that the apostle was intimately acquainted with our Lord's precepts. The phrase **by the Lord Jesus** (*en kyrio Iesou*), however, may mean "in the Lord Jesus" (NASB, RSV) in the sense of "as a Christian" (NEB). The claim that **there is nothing unclean of itself** must not be wrested out of its context here; Paul is speaking of meats (cf. Acts 10:13-15). But many a person can still be found who regards a certain food as **unclean**; if he were to eat it, he would be defiled, not because the food is in itself unclean, or offensive to God, but because his action is an offense against his conscience (cf. v. 23). To this person, **it is unclean**; for as a doubtful eater he cannot give God thanks (v. 6).

Bearing in mind this last point, we understand Paul's next statement. **But** (*gar*, for) **if thy brother be grieved with thy meat, now walkest thou not charitably** (15). How may this

---

[80]ICC, "Romans," p. 389. In the best MSS, v. 10 reads: "We must all appear before the judgmeat seat *of God* [*theou*]." In vv. 7-9, however, it is **the Lord** to whom we are answerable.

brother be grieved? For one thing, it will pain his overly sensitive conscience to see you do what he (however wrongly) regards as sinful. But the real damage occurs when he is emboldened by your example to do what he believes God forbids him to do. He who eats with a bad conscience is a waverer who is condemned by his doubts. Hence Paul warns, **Destroy not him with thy meat, for whom Christ died.** "And through thy knowledge shall the weak brother perish, for whom Christ died? But when ye sin so against the brethren, and wound their conscience, ye sin against Christ" (I Cor. 8:11-12). To grieve or offend a brother is therefore to cause him to fall into sin and perhaps to perish out of Christ.

Verses 1-15 show "The Christian's Attitude Toward His Brother." (1) Accepting differences of opinion, 1-6; (2) Avoiding censure, 7-11; (3) Avoiding giving offense, 12-15 (Ralph Earle).

The truth of 15 is expressed more generally in the next verse: **Let not then your good be evil spoken of** (16). The expression **your good** (*hymon ton agathon*) is somewhat indefinite, but in view of the context it can only mean "your Christian freedom," "the freedom of conscience which has been won by Christ, but which will inevitably get a bad name if it is exercised in an inconsiderate loveless fashion."[81]

To insist upon our freedom without regard to the conscientious scruples of others is not only to fail in Christian love but to misunderstand the nature of Christian experience. **For the kingdom of God is not meat and drink** (*brosis kai posis*, "eating and drinking," NASB); **but righteousness, and peace, and joy in the Holy Ghost** (17). "Faith is not 'faith to eat all things' (v. 2); Christian privilege is not the privilege of being able to eat and drink what one likes."[82] Rather, faith is that relation to God which brings "the fruit of the Spirit" (cf. Gal. 5:22-23). Generally, in Paul's letters righteousness and peace describe an objective relation to God; but here **joy** is certainly subjective and probably determines the sense of the other two words. **Righteousness** is therefore righteous action and **peace** a peaceful state of mind springing from a relation of peace with God.

In the Holy Ghost believers anticipate the blessings of the coming **kingdom of God** (cf. 8:11, 23). For Paul, **the kingdom**

---

[81]Denney, *op. cit.*, p. 705.   [82]Barrett, *The Epistle to the Romans*, p. 264.

of God (as distinct from the present kingdom of Christ) is the future inheritance of the people of God (cf. I Cor. 6:9-10; 15:50; Gal. 5:21; Eph. 5:5; I Thess. 2:12; II Thess. 1:5); but in the Holy Ghost its blessings can be enjoyed here and now.[83] It is this joy in the Holy Ghost that we should seek, rather than the pleasures of eating and drinking.

Verse 17 gives us "The Meaning of True Religion." It is not a matter of externals—not meat and drink. Rather it is: (1) Righteousness, inward and outward; (2) Peace, "with God" and "of God"; (3) Joy, "the echo of God's life within" (Ralph Earle).

The next sentence follows immediately. For he that in these things (*en touto,* in this; "on the principle implied by these virtues")[84] serveth Christ is acceptable to God, and approved of men (18). That is, the man is well-pleasing to God who serves Christ by being righteous and conciliatory and charitable toward others, not by selfishly insisting on his Christian liberty (cf. I Cor. 9:1-23). This man says with Paul, "For though I am free from all men, yet have I made myself servant unto all" (I Cor. 9:19).

Let us therefore follow after the things which make for peace, and things wherewith one may edify another (19). "The practical rule implied here is that, when anything is morally indifferent to me, before I act on that conviction, I must ask how such action will affect the peace of the Church and the Christian growth of others."[85] This determines the sense of the next sentence. For meat destroy not the work of God (20), i.e., not now the individual Christian (as in v. 15), but the Church as the temple of God (cf. I Cor. 3:15-16).

Paul now returns to a point further back in his argument: All things indeed are pure; but it is evil for that man who eateth with offence (cf. v. 14). Both statements are true, but the apostle turns at once to give specific advice to the strong: It is good neither to eat flesh, nor to drink wine, nor any thing whereby thy brother stumbleth (21).[86] The meaning is: "I

[83]Bruce, *The Epistle of Paul to the Romans,* p. 252.

[84]ICC, "Romans," p. 392.

[85]Denney, *op. cit.,* p. 706.

[86]The balance of the sentence is not in the best MSS. Though it should be regarded as a scribal gloss, the meaning is in harmony with the preceding authentic phrase.

would live like an Essene rather than do anything to offend my brother."[87] This is disciplining my life through Christian *agape*.

Hast thou faith? (in the sense of vv. 1-6) **have it to thyself before God** (22). "True faith is an invisible relation between man and God, a confidence in God so complete that the man who has it knows that no religious scrupulosity can add to the security of his relation with God."[88] But the moment such faith begins to parade itself as a selfish demonstration of freedom, it ceases to be faith. The apostle clearly sanctions the position of the stronger brother, as he has tacitly done throughout the chapter. "But it is the man who is sure of his freedom of these things in Christ, just as it is the man who has real wealth or real learning, who makes no offensive display."[89] This leads to the next assertion, **Happy is he that condemneth not himself in that thing which he alloweth.** Yet a man may "allow" himself an indulgence for which his own conscience may later condemn him. For this reason the "strong" believer must "take heed lest he fall" (I Cor. 10:12; cf. Gal. 6:1).

But (*de*) **he that doubteth is damned** (*katakekritai,* "condemned," NASB) **if he eat: for whatsoever is not of faith is sin** (23). The condemnation the Christian incurs who acts against his scruples is not simply subjective: "It is not only that his own conscience pronounces clearly against him after the act, but that such action incurs the condemnation of God. . . . Everything a Christian man does that cannot justify itself to him on the ground of the relation to Christ is sin. . . . All a man cannot do remembering that he is Christ's—all he cannot do with the judgment-seat (ver. 10) and the cross (ver. 15) and all their restraints and inspirations present to his mind—is sin."[90]

In the light of Paul's total position (which identifies him with the stronger brother; see 15:1) we should not conclude that a Christian must forever be in bondage to such scruples as we have been considering. The Christian conscience must be "trued" by the mind of Christ. To study the Gospels is to be struck by the fact that for Jesus the great issues of faith and life are at the opposite pole from such matters as dietary taboos (Mark 7:18-23) or even the punctilious observance of the Sab-

---

[87]ICC, "Romans," p. 393.   [88]Barrett, *The Epistle to the Romans,* p. 266.
[89]James K. Stifler, *The Epistle to the Romans* (Chicago: Moody Press, 1960), p. 230.
[90]Denney, *op. cit.,* p. 707.

bath (Matt. 12:1-13). For our Lord "the weightier matters of the law" have to do with God's requirement for "justice, mercy, and faith" (Matt. 23:23). The believer who is "weak in the faith" must understand that his salvation is wholly by grace through faith (as Paul has argued throughout this Epistle). It is therefore not dependent upon a scrupulous keeping of every jot and tittle of the law. "The just requirement of the law" is that a man shall express in all his personal and social relationships the spirit of Christian *agape* (cf. 13:8-11). The word which this man must hear is that of the prophet Micah, "He hath shewed thee, O man, what is good; and what doth the Lord require of thee, but to do justly, and to love mercy, and to walk humbly with thy God?" (Mic. 6:8) But until this word is clearly understood, he must be true to the limited light he has received.

3. *Following Christ's Example* (15:1-13)

The fourteenth chapter has a certain completeness in itself, and we can understand that if copies of the Epistle were sent as a circular letter to different churches, some might have ended with 14:23, to which the Doxology (16:25-27) might have been appended, as in many MSS.[91] But it is unquestionably the same subject which is continued in this section. It is still the relations of the strong to the weak with which Paul is concerned, but he now makes a new appeal for unity based upon the example of Christ. The strong must act in the spirit of Christ (vv. 1-6), and in His spirit the strong and weak must receive one another (vv. 7-12). He then pronounces the first of several benedictions (v. 13).

a. Christ's example to the strong (15:1-6). Paul now identifies himself with the strong: **We then that are strong ought to bear the infirmities** (*ta asthenemata,* the weaknesses) **of the weak, and not to please ourselves** (1). The scrupulosity of the weak is a burden to be borne by the **strong.** This word of admonition is needed, for it is an easy matter for self-pleasing to shelter itself under the guise of Christian principle. If the **weak** are deficient in knowledge, the **strong** tend to fall short on love. Paul felt it necessary to warn the knowledgeable of Corinth, " 'Knowledge' puffs up, but love builds up" (I Cor. 8:1, RSV). It is for this love which edifies that Paul pleads (cf. Gal. 6:2).

---

[91]See Introduction.

Let every one of us please his neighbour (2). Eating and drinking may please the palate, but the Christian must seek to **please his neighbour**. But the **neighbour** may be pleased to his hurt, so Paul adds that he must be pleased **for his good to edification.** To afford him pleasure which does not build him up is not for his good (cf. 14:16, 19).

"If it should seem burdensome and grievous to some strong Roman to live narrowly for the sake of the weak, the consolation and dignity of such a life are that Christ lived it"[92]—**For even Christ pleased not himself** (3). Paul's verb sums up the life and character of Christ: His very existence was one of self-giving for others (cf. Phil. 2:5-8). Yet instead of appealing to the life of Christ to support his statement, the apostle cites a prophecy: **But, as it is written, The reproaches of them that reproached thee fell on me** (Ps. 69:9). This psalm is quoted throughout the NT as having some reference to Christ.[93] It describes Him as being so identified with the cause of God that He endures in His own person the assaults of the enemies of God. **Reproaches** fell upon Christ because He **pleased not himself,** but lived to please God in the work of redemption. If self-pleasing had been the guide of His life, He would have escaped the shame and reproach which were heaped upon Him; but living as He did to please God, to serve His will for the salvation of men, these reproaches came, and thus were God's.

Paul justifies this use of the Scriptures on the principle, **For whatsoever things were written aforetime were written for our learning, that we through patience and comfort of the scriptures might have hope** (4). This one verse, culled from the OT, moves Paul to say that every part of the same Scriptures was written for the same purpose—**for our learning** (cf. II Tim. 3:16). The OT abounds in instances of a self-denying life bringing glory to God; thus it stimulates our **patience** and gives us **comfort** or encouragement. The record of these instances becomes a proof that, as God dealt with His servants then, so will He deal with us now. It is by means of this **patience and comfort** derived from the OT that **hope** arises (cf. 5:3-4).[94]

After the digression of the previous verse, Paul returns to

[92]Stifler, *op. cit.,* p. 233.

[93]John 2:17 (Ps. 69:9); John 15:25 (Ps. 69:4); Matt. 27:34 (Ps. 69:21); Acts 1:20 (Ps. 69:25).

[94]Stifler, *op. cit.,* 234.

his subject and sums up his plea by a prayer for the unity of the Roman church: **Now the God of patience and consolation grant you to be like-minded one toward another according to Christ Jesus: that ye may with one mind and one mouth glorify God, even the Father of our Lord Jesus Christ** (5-6). It is **God** who is the Source of the **patience and consolation** offered us in Scripture. These graces are the gift of God, but they are imparted by Him through the written Word. It is by these two Christian qualities, also, that God will make them **like-minded one toward another.** Once again Paul's admonition to the Philippians comes to mind, "Have this mind among yourselves, which you have in Christ Jesus" (Phil. 2:5, RSV). This does not mean that they will come to a common understanding on the questions of vegetarianism, Sabbath keeping, and such matters. They will, however, come to unanimity of spirit, so that **with one mind and one mouth** they may **glorify God.** This is true Christian unity, "the unity of the Spirit in the bond of peace" (Eph. 4:3; cf. John 17:21-23, 26).

b. Christ's example to all (15:7-13). Paul now makes an appeal to the entire church: **Wherefore receive ye one another, as Christ also received us to the glory of God** (7). The verb **receive** brings us back to the topic sentence of this section in 14:1. Knox paraphrases the general intention of vv. 7-12 thus: "Just as Christ came under the law in order that He might bring about the fulfillment of God's purpose of salvation for both Jew and Gentile [which has been set forth in chs. 9—11], you Gentiles should be willing to bear with the scruples of some of your less mature and less fully emancipated brethren."[95] Since Christ has **received** both groups, they are bound to **receive . . . one another.**

Verses 1-7 show us "The Christian's Attitude Toward His Weaker Brother." (1) Unselfish upholding, 1-4; (2) Unselfish understanding, 5-6; (3) Unselfish unity, 7 (Ralph Earle).

The gracious acceptance that Christ has given to men has led to two different results: **Now I say that Jesus Christ was a minister of the circumcision for the truth of God, to confirm the promises made unto the fathers, and that the Gentiles might glorify God for his mercy** (8-9). God's reception of the Jews led to His being glorified for His **truth,** that is, faithfulness to His

[95]IB, IX, 637-38.

promises made unto the fathers. His reception of the Gentiles led to God's being glorified for His **mercy;** for without having promised anything to them directly, He has given everything to them as well as to the Jews. "And hence it is, that with the voice which rises from the people of Israel to celebrate God's faithfulness, there should henceforth be joined that of the Gentile world magnifying His grace."[96] Godet goes on to make the observation that the Gospel of Matthew illustrates that which strikes the Jew with reference to Christ's coming, viz., the fulfillment of OT prophecy. On the other hand, the Gospel of Luke reveals that the heart of the Gentile is moved by the view of God's mercy in Christ.

In carrying out this double purpose Paul declares that Christ was made **a minister of the circumcision.** This can mean only what he says in his Galatian letter: "God sent forth his Son, made of a woman, made under the law, to redeem them that were under the law, that we might receive the adoption of sons" (4:4-5). The Son of God submitted to the irksome limitations of the Mosaic law in order to carry out the scheme of salvation. He thus provides an example for all strong Christians (cf. v. 3). If Jesus Christ submitted himself to the burdensome restrictions imposed upon Him by the Pharisaical interpretation of the OT, in order to bring about God's plan of salvation for both Jew and Gentile, the Gentiles should be willing to bear with the scrupulosity of their less enlightened brethren.[97]

The inclusion of **the Gentiles** is not to be regarded as accidental; it was predicted in Scripture. **As it is written, For this cause I will confess to thee among the Gentiles, and sing unto thy name** (Ps. 18:49). The point of this quotation, as in those that follow in 10-12, lies in the reference to **the Gentiles,** and, secondarily, in the offering of praise for God's faithfulness and mercy. **And again he saith, Rejoice, ye Gentiles, with his people** (Deut. 32:43). **And again, Praise the Lord, all ye Gentiles; and laud him, all ye people** (Ps. 117:1). **And again,**

---

[96]Godet, *op. cit.,* p. 471.

[97]This interpretation seems to argue that the division existing at Rome was simply between Jew and Gentile; but we have seen how this oversimplifies the problem. Paul is rather arguing from the greater to the lesser—if God can unite these two, He can unite anyone. Or possibly v. 6 concludes his argument and vv. 7-13 are added as a summary which looks back to cc. 9—11 as well as to c. 14 (Barrett, *The Epistle to the Romans,* pp. 272-73).

Esaias saith, **There shall be a root of Jesse, and he shall rise to reign over the Gentiles; in him shall the Gentiles trust** (*elpiousin,* hope; Isa. 11:10).

The discussion of the relations between strong and weak in the Roman church concludes with a brief benediction upon the readers. **Now the God of hope fill you with all joy and peace in believing, that ye may abound in hope, through the power of the Holy Ghost** (13). God is described as **the God of hope,** evidently because of the last words of the preceding quotation: "In him shall the Gentiles hope" (RSV). The richer the possession of present blessings **(joy and peace)** which the believer derives from **believing,** the more does his soul rise to an apprehension of future blessing, and according to Paul's expression here, "overflow with hope" (NEB). The last words, **the power of the Holy Ghost,** point the readers back once more (as in 14:17) to the true power they ought to seek, in contrast to the false expression of power by which one selfishly displays his freedom. When our freedom is under **the power of the Holy Ghost,** we say with the apostle what he said of himself: "For though I be free from all men, yet have I made myself servant unto all, that I might gain the more. To the weak became I as the weak, that I might gain the weak: I am made all things to all men, that I might by all means save some. And this I do for the gospel's sake" (I Cor. 9:19, 22-23).

Section **IV** *Personal Conclusion*

Romans 15:14—16:27

The substance of the Epistle is now finished, and there remain only the concluding sections of personal explanation, greeting, and encouragement.

Godet shows how the conclusion correlates with Paul's preface (1:1-15).[1] First, the apostle apologizes for the boldness with which he has written the Roman Christians, by reminding them of his mission to the Gentiles (15:14-21). This corresponds to 1:14-15, where he declares himself a "debtor" to all Gentiles, the Romans included. He then explains what has thus far kept him in the east (15:22-33). This completes what he has said in 1:11-13 of the impossibility of making his way earlier to Rome. The personal salutations of 16:1-23 correspond to the address of 1:7, "To all that are at Rome, beloved of God." Finally, the doxology (16:25-27) brings us back to the opening assertion of the letter, that of the fulfillment of the divine plan by the gospel which had been "promised afore by his prophets in the holy scriptures" (1:1-2).

A. PAUL'S APOLOGY FOR HIS ADMONITIONS, 15:14-21

As in 1:8, Paul begins with a reference to the good report of the Roman church. He courteously apologizes for the warmth of feeling with which he has written, especially in the preceding section. His opening statement is tactful. **And I myself also am persuaded of you, my brethren, that ye also are full of goodness, filled with all knowledge, able also to admonish one another (14).** "Though I have spoken so strongly at times, this does not mean that I am not aware of the spiritual earnestness of your church."[2] He acknowledges both their **goodness** of heart and the fullness of their Christian **knowledge.**

The apostle continues, **Nevertheless, brethren, I have written the more boldly unto you in some sort** (*apo merous,* "on some points," NASB, RSV), as **putting you in mind (15).** The NEB translates this, "I have written to refresh your memory, and written somewhat boldly at times" (in view of the fact that the Roman church was not of his planting).[3] "Paul has written only *on some points*—as though to say, 'I know there is much which you could teach me about the Christian life' [cf. 1:11-12] —points on which the special grace given him as the Apostle of

[1]*Op. cit.,* p. 475.   [2]ICC, "Romans," p. 403.
[3]Bruce, *The Epistle of Paul to the Romans,* p. 260.

the Gentiles both requires and qualifies him to write" (cf. 1:5; 12:3).[4]

He now calls his service of the gospel a priestly service, in which he is the mediator of God's love in Christ to the Gentiles and the one through whom the Gentiles offer themselves as a sacrifice to God (cf. 12:1). He speaks of himself as **a minister of Jesus Christ to the Gentiles, ministering the gospel of God, that the offering up of the Gentiles might be acceptable, being sanctified by the Holy Ghost** (16). Three Greek words are employed as sacrificial terms. In the LXX **minister** (*leitourgon*) is used definitely and technically of a priest; in the Hebrew Epistle, Christ is described as "a minister [*leitourgos*] of the sanctuary, and of the true tabernacle" (Heb. 8:2). **Ministering** (*hierourgounta*) has the sense of "being the sacrificing priest" **of the gospel of God.** Paul is a priest, his proclamation of the gospel a priestly service; his Gentile converts are **the offering** (*he prosphora*) he presents to God.

We noted earlier[5] that the OT priest offered two general kinds of sacrifices: (1) those offered to effect the reconciliation of sinners to God (the sin offering and the trespass offering) and (2) those offered after reconciliation to celebrate the fact of atonement (the whole burnt offering and the peace offering). As a priest under God's new covenant Paul ministered the gospel as (1) the medium of God's redeeming love in Christ by which He reconciles sinful men to himself (3:21-26; cf. II Cor. 5:18-21), and (2) as a call for redeemed men to present themselves to God as "a living sacrifice, holy and acceptable to God, which is . . . [their] spiritual worship" (12:1, RSV; cf. 6:13). As Godet notes, these correspond to the two major divisions of Romans.[6]

Being sanctified by the Holy Ghost is a key phrase. "There were some, no doubt, who maintained that Paul's Gentile converts were 'unclean', because they were not circumcised. To such cavillers Paul's reply is that his converts were 'clean', because they were sanctified by the Holy Spirit who had come to

---

[4]Knox, IB, IX, 644.   [5]See comments on 12:1.

[6]*Op. cit.*, pp. 424-25. "In the new economy which God has established in Jesus Christ, the gospel proclaimed by the apostle is the new way by which the sinner is reconciled to God: it brings the sinner to the obedience flowing from faith in Christ, the sacrificial victim who replaces every other. But the sacrifice of Christ includes and implies the sacrifice of every believer who is united to the Crucified by faith and baptism (cf. 6:2-3). Through this union the sinner becomes with Christ an offering that is living, holy, and well-pleasing to God" (Leenhardt, *op. cit.*, p. 368).

dwell within them. . . . Similarly, Peter at the Council of Jerusalem reminds his fellow-Jewish believers how, when the Gentiles heard the gospel, God gave them the Holy Spirit 'even as he did unto us; and put no difference between us and them, purifying their hearts by faith' (Acts xv. 8 ff.)."[7]

The realization of this great truth gives Paul a proper pride and confidence in his ministry. **I have therefore whereof I may glory through Jesus Christ in those things which pertain to God (17).** The words **through Jesus Christ** soften Paul's glorying (cf. Gal. 6:14). His **glory** was not in himself but in Christ. **For I will not dare to speak of any of those things which Christ hath not wrought by me (18)** is better translated, "For I will not venture to speak of anything except what Christ has wrought through me" (RSV). And what was this? **To make the Gentiles obedient** (cf. 1:5; 16:26), **by word and deed, through mighty signs and wonders, by the power of the Spirit (18-19)**.[8]

Paul's apostolic ministry is here attested by miracles wrought in the power of the Holy Spirit. **Signs and wonders** (*semeia kai terata*) are throughout the NT employed to express what we call miracles. *Teras* implies anything marvelous or extraordinary in itself; *semeion* represents the same event, but viewed as a sign or token of the agency by which it is accomplished or the purpose it is intended to fulfill. In John's Gospel, Jesus' miracles are viewed as signs (*semeia*) of His heavenly glory. Often a third word, *dynameis,* is added, to indicate that these works are the exhibition of more than natural power. Here Paul varies the expression by saying the deeds accomplished in his ministry were wrought "in the power of signs and wonders" (*en dynamei semeion kai teraton*). This **power** is further qualified as **the power of the Spirit** (*en dynamei pneumatos*). "There can be no doubt," say Sanday and Headlam, "that St. Paul in this passage assumes that he possesses the apostolic power of working what are ordinarily called miracles."[9] The historical narrative of Acts supports this claim (cf. Heb. 2:3-4).

[7]Bruce, *loc. cit.* Cf. Leenhardt, *op. cit.,* pp. 368-69.

[8]**Of God** should be omitted here, since *theou* is not in the best MSS.

[9]ICC, "Romans," p. 406. "The evidence for the existence of miracles in the Apostolic Church is twofold: on the one hand the apparently natural and unobtrusive claim made by the Apostles on behalf of themselves or others to the power of working miracles, on the other the definite historical narrative of the Acts of the Apostles. The two witnesses corroborate each other" (*ibid.*).

We must bear in mind that Paul's purpose throughout this section is to defend his claim to a divine commission as apostle to the Gentiles. That his mission has been powerful and effective is a fact no one can deny, and he offers his record to the Roman church as part of his credentials. He has taken the eastern provinces of the Roman Empire as his territory, exclusive of those places where other Christian missionaries have labored. His work in this territory is now finished, since **from Jerusalem, and round about unto Illyricum** (see map 1) he has **fully preached the gospel** (*peplerokenai to euangelion,* "completed the preaching of the gospel," NEB) **of Christ.** Paul's work in the east is complete.

The mention of **Jerusalem** as the starting point of his ministry can be explained by the fact that he considered the mother church as the base of the entire Christian movement (cf. Luke 24:47; Acts 1:4, 8; 8:14; 9:22; 15:2). **Illyricum** represents the westernmost point of his ministry. There is no mention of this province (which borders the eastern shore of the Adriatic Sea) in Acts or any of Paul's letters up to this time. There is reason to believe, however, that he may have evangelized Illyricum during his extended stay in Ephesus on his last journey. There is indication that he crossed into Macedonia in the summer or autumn of A.D. 55 (cf. II Cor. 2:12-13) and spent the next 15 or 18 months in Macedonia and Achaia (see map 1). It must have been within this period that he traveled along the Egnatian Way westward to the frontier of Illyricum, probably crossing into Illyricum and preaching the gospel there. There seems to be no other point where a journey to Illyricum can be fitted into his itinerary.[10]

Within the area, however, between **Jerusalem** and **Illyricum** there were places where he had not preached. He believed his

---

[10]Bruce, *The Epistle of Paul to the Romans,* p. 261. Sanday and Headlam have a different explanation, however, fitting Illyricum into Paul's second journey. "Strabo, describing the Egnatian way from the Adriatic seacoast, states that it passes through a portion of Illyria before it reaches Macedonia, and that the traveller along it has the Illyrian mountains on his left hand. St. Paul would have followed this road as far as Thessalonica, and if pointing Westward he had asked the names of the mountain region and of the peoples inhabiting it, he would have been told that it was 'Illyria.' The term therefore is one which would naturally occur to him as fitted to express the limits of his journeys to the West" (ICC, "Romans," pp. 407-8).

commission was to preach the gospel where Christ was not known, in order not to compete with other missionaries. **Yea, he continues therefore, so have I strived to preach the gospel, not where Christ was named, lest I should build upon another man's foundation** (20). Paul describes his work elsewhere as laying a "foundation stone" (I Cor. 3:10).

He then describes in v. 21 the aim of his mission in the words of an OT quotation: **But as it is written, To whom he was not spoken of, they shall see: and they that have not heard shall understand** (Isa. 52:15, LXX). Paul correctly takes these words to apply to the extension of the knowledge of the Suffering Servant to places where His name has not been mentioned. Isaiah is speaking of the surprise of nations and their kings when they see the exaltation of the Suffering Servant whom formerly they had despised.

B. PAUL'S PROPOSED PLANS, 15:22-33

Since he has completed his ministry in the east, Paul is now ready to come to Rome. The reader can sense that he is aware the Roman church may feel his visit is long overdue, and it is for this reason he takes such pains to show them why he has not come to them earlier. **For which cause** (*dio kai*, "For this reason," NASB) **also I have been much hindered from coming to you** (22; cf. 1:13). The reason he has been so far prevented from coming to Rome is not so much the fear that he might build on another man's foundation as the necessity of "completing the preaching of the gospel" (v. 19) in his previously assigned territory.

But now having no more place in these parts, and having a great desire these many years to come unto you (cf. 1:9-11), **whensoever I take my journey into Spain, I will come to you** (23-24). A. T. Robertson comments on Paul's surprising frankness. "Paul is now free to come to Rome because there is no demand for him where he is."[11] But his trip will simply be a stopover on his way to **Spain.** There was no need to stay long in Rome, since the church there was strong and flourishing; it was Spain which was beckoning him. Spain was a Roman province with many Jews in it, and Paul would not be satisfied until

[11]*Word Pictures in the New Testament* (Nashville: Broadman Press, 1931), IV, 422.

he proclaimed Christ on the western rim of the empire. To use Wesley's words, the world was his parish.

I trust to see you on my journey, he continues, **and to be brought on my way thitherward** (*propempthenai ekei,* "helped on my way there," NASB) **by you, if first I be somewhat filled with your company.** The latter clause is translated in the RSV, "once I have enjoyed your company for a little."

He now mentions a further reason which will cause some delay in his visit to Rome, and his missionary journey to Spain. **But now I go unto Jerusalem to minister unto the saints (25).** The phrase, **to minister unto the saints** (*diakonon tois hagiois*) is almost a technical expression in Paul for the contributions made by the Gentile Christians to the church at Jerusalem.[12] The members of the church at Jerusalem are **the saints** *par excellence* (cf. I Cor. 16:1; II Cor. 9:12). But Paul's converts and other Gentile Christians have become "fellowcitizens with the saints" (Eph. 2:19), the holy people of God. (Cf. 1:7, with comments. Further details about the collection are found in I Cor. 16:1-4 and II Corinthians 8—9. It was an undertaking to which Paul attached great importance.)

For it hath pleased them of Macedonia and Achaia[13] (see map 1) **to make a certain contribution for the poor saints which are at Jerusalem (26).** The verb **hath pleased** (*eudokesan*) implies that their contribution was voluntary, and made with heartiness and goodwill (cf. 10:1; I Cor. 1:21; Gal. 1:15). From the very beginning there appears to have been a sizable group of poor saints in the Jerusalem church (cf. Acts 2:44-45; 4:34-35; 6:1-3; 11:27-30). It seems that the Jerusalem Christians referred to themselves as "the poor" (cf. Gal. 2:10), and in later years Jewish Christians were known as Ebionites (from the Heb. form *ebyonim,* "poor").

Paul emphasizes the goodwill with which the contribution was made, by repeating the verb **pleased** (*eudckesan*), but he

---

[12]ICC, "Romans," p. 412. Cf. II Cor. 8:4; 9:1.

[13]"Paul mentions the Christians in these two provinces here probably because he had been for several months past in close touch with them. But we have his own testimony in I Cor. xvi. 1 that he had organized a similar collection in the churches of Galatia, and the presence of Tychicus and Trophimus with him at this time (Acts xx.4; cf. xxi.29) indicates that the churches of Ephesus and other cities in the province of Asia also had a share in this ministry" (Bruce, *The Epistle of Paul to the Romans,* p. 264).

275

goes on to point out that in another sense they were simply repaying a just debt. **It hath pleased them verily; and their debtors they are. For if the Gentiles have been made partakers of their spiritual things, their duty is also to minister unto them in carnal things (27).** Spiritual (*pneumatikos*) and **carnal** (*sarkikois*) are characteristic Pauline words (cf. I Cor. 9:11; II Cor. 10:4). The NASB renders this, "For if the Gentiles have shared in their spiritual things, they are indebted to minister to them also in material things." The verb **to minister** (*leitourgesai*) possibly suggests that Paul thought of this offering as a further extension of his priestly service (cf. v. 16). In II Cor. 9:12 he calls the collection a "service" (*leitourgia*), from which we derive the word "liturgy."

He now resumes his argument and restates his plans to visit Rome. **When therefore I have performed this, and have sealed** (*sphragisamenos*) **to them this fruit, I will come by you into Spain (28).** Instead of **sealed to them this fruit,** the NEB reads, "and delivered the proceeds under my own seal." Paul implies that by taking the contribution to Jerusalem and presenting it to the church there, he puts his "seal" upon it (as a steward would put his seal upon fruit gathered under his direction). He would thus show that it is the fruit of his ministry among the Gentiles. Bruce, however, thinks perhaps "it is not Paul's own seal that we should think about, but the seal of the Spirit; here is conclusive confirmation of His work among the Gentiles."[14]

Paul now gives his personal testimony. **And I am sure that, when I come unto you, I shall come in the fulness of** (*pleromata*) **the blessing of the gospel of Christ (29).** The words **of the gospel** (*euangeliou tou*) are wanting in all the best MSS. Paul is coming to Rome **in the fulness of the blessing . . . of Christ.** He was conscious of the fullness of the Spirit (cf. Eph. 5:18); he would thus be able to bestow upon the Romans a spiritual *charisma* (cf. 1:11, with comments).

The reference to his visit to Jerusalem reminds the apostle of the dangers and anxieties which that trip implies. This leads him to conclude the section with an earnest entreaty to the Roman Christians to join in prayers in his behalf. **Now I beseech you, brethren, for the Lord Jesus Christ's sake, and for the love of the Spirit, that ye strive together with me in your prayers to God for me; that I may be delivered from them that**

[14]*Ibid.*, p. 265.

do not believe in Judaea; and that my service may be accepted of the saints; that I may come unto you with joy by the will of God, and may with you be refreshed (30-32). His appeal is based on the common devotion to the Lord Jesus Christ and love of the Spirit which the Romans share with Paul. The term he employs, strive together, describes the prayer that is needed. It is "an intense energy of prayer, wrestling as it were,"[15] indicative of how much risk Paul thinks of himself as running when he goes to Jerusalem.

Paul was not only concerned about the treatment he would receive from the unbelieving Jews, but he also had misgivings about how this offering would be accepted by the church in Jerusalem. As it turned out, the church apparently received his contribution with gratitude (Acts 21:17-20). However, his fears of what the unbelieving Jews would do proved to be well-grounded. At the order of James, Paul went to the Temple and performed certain traditional Jewish rites in an effort to disarm the prejudice of his fellow Jews. His presence, however, caused a riot. He was almost lynched, but was rescued by the Roman guard (Acts 21:20-34). Ultimately he was sent to Rome as a prisoner.

"The course of history, therefore, has given a deep colour of tragic irony to this section of the letter. The man who writes to Rome, full of far-reaching schemes, who is planning to visit the capital on his way to remoter fields of enterprise, was brought to Rome worn by years of imprisonment, in chains, his hope disappointed, his active career at an end."[16] Thus in the mystery of providence did the apostle come by the will of God to Rome.

This section concludes with a brief but characteristic Pauline benediction: Now the God of peace be with you all. Amen (33).

C. INTRODUCTION OF PHOEBE, GREETINGS AND WARNINGS, 16:1-24

1. *Introduction of Phoebe* (16:1-2)

An ancient letter, like a modern one, usually ended with good wishes for the recipient and greetings to friends. But be-

---

[15]Thomas, *op. cit.*, p. 408. Sanday and Headlam observe: "It has been pointed out how strongly these words make for the authenticity and early date of this chapter. No one could possibly write in this manner at a later date, knowing the circumstances under which St. Paul actually did visit Rome" (ICC, "Romans," p. 414).

[16]Dodd, *op. cit.*, p. 233.

fore sending greetings to the Romans, Paul adds a few sentences by way of a postscript to introduce to the church of Rome a deaconess (*diakonon*) **of the church . . . at Cenchrea** named **Phebe** (1). Cenchrea was the eastern seaport of Corinth (see map 1), and Phoebe was probably planning a trip to the capital city. A letter of introduction would give her an entree to the church there.

Such letters of recommendation were widely used in the Early Church. Paul elsewhere asks of the church at Corinth, "Do we need, as some do, letters of recommendation to you?" (II Cor. 3:1, RSV) There was a necessity for such letters in the case of less known persons. A church must know that a stranger arriving and seeking hospitality (cf. 12:13) is not an impostor.

Paul urges the Romans **to receive** Phoebe **in the Lord, as becometh saints** (2; *axios ton hagion,* "in a manner worthy of the saints").[17] They were to admit her to the privileges of the Christian fellowship in Rome and **assist her in whatever business she** might have **need** of them. He informs the Romans that **she hath been a succourer** (*prostatis,* "helper," NASB) **of many.** *Prostatis* is sometimes equivalent to the Latin *patrona,* a legal representative or wealthy patron. Sanday and Headlam think the expression here suggests that Phoebe was a person of some wealth and position, who was thus able to act as patroness of the church at Cenchrea.[18] But other authorities understand the term as referring to her work as a *diakonos* (v. 1). The duties of a *diakonos* could be performed by either men or women. This is suggested by I Tim. 3:11, where "their wives" is more probably to be rendered "women" (NASB), i.e., "women-deacons" ("deaconesses," NEB, marg.).

In any event we are to assume that Phoebe was to deliver the letter to the Roman congregation. Private individuals such as the apostle had to make their own arrangements for the conveyance of letters; only public officials and their friends could make use of the imperial postal service.[19]

2. Personal Greetings (16:3-16)

The apostle now sends personal greetings to some two dozen members of the Roman church. These are Christians he has

---

[17]ICC, "Romans," p. 417.   [18]*Ibid.,* p. 418.
[19]Dodd, *op. cit.,* p. 235.

known elsewhere in his travels who have found their way to the Roman metropolis.[20]

In an effort to identify some of the "saints . . . of Caesar's household" mentioned in Phil. 4:22, Bishop Lightfoot has collected impressive evidence which bears on the possible identification of some of the persons here mentioned. Most of the evidence comes from inscriptions found in the imperial burial grounds. He found all the *names* which appear in these verses; in two or three instances he seems to have established a probable connection between Paul's list and known members of "Caesar's household."[21] Since Lightfoot's time other scholars have examined both the Roman and Ephesian inscriptions in the effort to identify these individuals. The very least that can be said from the collected evidence is that the names in these verses are better attested at Rome than at Ephesus.[22]

Heading the list are **Priscilla and Aquila** (*Priscan kai Akylan*, "Prisca and Aquila," NASB, RSV), **my helpers in Christ Jesus (3)**. **Priscilla** is the diminutive for Prisca. Luke calls her by this more familiar name (cf. Acts 18:2, 18, 26), but Paul prefers Prisca (cf. I Cor. 16:19, NASB, RSV; II Tim. 4:19). Both Luke and Paul generally name her before Aquila, her husband. This may be because she was the stronger personality of the two, but there is evidence that she was of superior social rank. Prisca may have belonged by birth or manumission to the *gens Prisca*, a noble Roman family, while Aquila was a Jew from Pontus in Asia Minor (Acts 18:2).[23]

Prisca and Aquila were expelled from Rome in A.D. 49 by Claudius' edict,[24] whence they removed to Corinth, where Paul met them (Acts 18:1-3). Later they removed to Ephesus, where they may have been involved in the troubles described in Acts 19:23-40; in these they may have **laid down their own necks**

---

[20]See Introduction, "The Problem of Chapter 16."

[21]*St. Paul's Epistle to the Philippians* (London: The Macmillan Co., 1913), pp. 171-78.

[22]Bruce, *The Epistle of Paul to the Romans*, p. 269. Cf. also Dodd, *op. cit.*, pp. xx-xxiv, 236-40; ICC, "Romans," pp. 422-28.

[23]ICC, "Romans," pp. 418-20.

[24]See Introduction, "The Church at Rome."

for Paul's **life** (4). When the edict of banishment was no longer in force, they returned to Rome.[25]

The gratitude which both Paul and **all the churches of the Gentiles** felt toward this Christian couple is understandable. They had not only been devoted to Paul but had rendered important services in connection with the founding of the church in both Corinth (Acts 18:2-3) and Ephesus (Acts 18:18-28).

The apostle also sends greetings **to the church . . . in their house** (5; cf. I Cor. 16:19). Such household churches are mentioned elsewhere in the NT (Col. 4:15; Philem. 2). We also read of entire households becoming Christians together (Acts 10:44-48; 16:5, 30-34; 18:8; I Cor. 1:16). The household included, in addition to members of the immediate family, slaves and dependents, who were members of the *familia* (in the Roman sense). If it was a large and influential household, with commodious accommodations, Christian neighbors would attach themselves to it also. Thus, while the household of **Priscilla and Aquila** might consist of their children and other relatives, their slaves, employees, and tenants, it would also include other "brothers in Christ" who met at their table for the Lord's Supper. At death these Christian "brothers" had the right to be buried in the family vault. Several of the catacombs of Rome can be shown to have developed out of such familial burial places.[26] Furthermore, some of the oldest churches in Rome appear to have been built on the sites of such houses used for Christian worship.[27]

There is no reason to suppose that the church which met in the house of Priscilla and Aquila was composed of all the Roman Christians. Similar bodies seem to be implied in 14-15. There is no decisive evidence until the third century of the existence of church buildings as such.

---

[25]Dodd points out that there is no reason to suppose that their Roman establishment was closed down during the years they were away; all they would need to do would be to install a *procurator* who was not a Jew, and he could carry on the business as usual. Again, the establishment at Ephesus need not have been closed when they returned to Rome (cf. II Tim. 4:19). "Thus they could have a 'household' (which in their case would consist mainly of their business and industrial staff) at Ephesus and at Rome at the same time; and each household would contain a body of Christian slaves and dependents" (*op. cit.*, p. xxi).

[26]*Ibid.*, p. 237.   [27]Denney, *op. cit.*, p. 719.

In v. 5 there is a greeting to **my wellbeloved Epaenetus, who is the firstfruits of Achaia unto Christ.** For **Achaia** we should read *Asia,* which is better attested. This was the province of Asia, with Ephesus as the chief city. The name has been found on inscriptions in both Ephesus and Rome.[28]

Mary (6; *Marian*) may be either a Jewish or a Roman name. In favor of the latter it may be observed that apparently in other cases where Paul is referring to Jews he speaks of them as his kinsmen (cf. vv. 7, 11). Mary had **bestowed much labour** on the Roman church.[29] Paul notes this, not for the sake of the church, but as words of praise for Mary herself.

Andronicus and Junia Paul salutes as **my kinsmen, and my fellowprisoners, who are of note among the apostles, who also were in Christ before me** (7). Like Priscilla and Aquila, Andronicus and Junia are probably husband and wife.[30] Since Paul was converted not more than four or five years after the Resurrection, we must connect this couple with the primitive Jerusalem church. As they were Jews with Greek or Graeco-Roman names, they probably belonged to the Hellenistic circle whose leaders were Stephen, Philip, and their associates. Like others in this group (Acts 8:4-5; 11:19-21), they became missionaries, or **apostles** in the wider sense (cf. 1:1, with comments). Among the wider body of apostles Andronicus and Junia were **of note.** We do not know when they had been **fellowprisoners** with Paul, but the expression does not necessarily mean that they had been in the same prison together.

Amplias (8) is an abbreviation of Ampliatus, which is the form in the best attested MSS. Dodd points out that in one of the early Christian tombs the one word *AMPLIATI* is found in fine uncial lettering of the first or early second century. "The position and character of the tomb suggest that it belonged to a person held in especial respect. It is quite possible that he is our 'Ampliatus beloved in the Lord.' In any case, we have early evidence of a Roman Christian family bearing this name."[31]

---

[28]ICC, "Romans," p. 421.

[29]The better attested reading is "you" instead of **us** (NASB, RSV).

[30]**Junia** (*Iounian*), however, may be masculine, although it is less usual as a man's name. Chrysostom does not consider the idea of a female apostle impossible. Of Junia he says, "Oh! how great is the devotion of this woman, that she should be even counted worthy of the appellation of apostle!" (ICC, "Romans," p. 423.)

[31]Dodd, *op. cit.,* pp. xxii-xxiii.

Urbane (9; *Urbanus*) was a very common name, meaning "of the city" (*urbs*). It is found in a number of Roman inscriptions.[32] On the other hand, **Stachys** is quite rare. "Yet at least one person so called held an important office in the household [of Caesar] near the time when St. Paul wrote."[33]

Apelles (10) was a name sufficiently common among the Jews of Rome to be used by Horace as a typical Jewish name— "*credat Iudaeus Apella*" (*Satire* i. 5. 100).[34]

Paul's next salutation is significant. Those **of Aristobulus' household** (*tous ek ton Aristoboulou*) means Christians belonging to the household of Aristobulus. Lightfoot makes Aristobulus the grandson of Herod the Great. "Now it seems not improbable, considering the intimate relations between Claudius and Aristobulus, that at the death of the latter his servants, wholly or in part, should be transferred to the palace. In this case they would be designated *Aristobuliani*, for which I suppose St. Paul's *hoi ek ton Aristoboulou* to be an equivalent. It is at least not an obvious phrase, and demands explanation."[35]

It is noteworthy that after saluting **them which are of Aristobulus' household** Paul immediately singles out one whom he designates as his **kinsman,** i.e., his fellow Jew, whose name **Herodion** (11) we might expect to find among the slaves or freedmen of a distinguished member of the Herodian family. This seems to link vv. 10 and 11.[36] Immediately Paul uses the same form of expression in saluting **the household of Narcissus.** The name was common. But here, as in the case of Aristobulus, the expression seems to point to some famous person of the name. The **Narcissus** meant was probably the notorious freedman of Claudius who was put to death shortly after the accession of Nero, and therefore two or three years before this letter was written. His slaves would probably pass into the emperor's hands, and increase "Caesar's household" as *Narcissiani.*[37]

Tryphena and Tryphosa (12), who are next mentioned, were probably sisters and may have been twins. Both names were found in the imperial household about the time Paul wrote this Epistle. Their names mean "Dainty" and "Disdain" and are characteristically pagan; but now these sisters **labour in the Lord.**

---

[32]Lightfoot, *op. cit.*, p. 174.   [33]*Ibid.*
[34]Bruce, *The Epistle of Paul to the Romans*, p. 272.
[35]*Op. cit.*, p. 175.   [36]*Ibid.*
[37]*Ibid.*

The present tense indicates that they were still at work. In contrast, the "much labour" of **the beloved Persis** belongs to some occasion in the past. The adjective **beloved** suggests that Persis was dear to the whole church.[38]

Rufus (13) is a very common name, and would not have attracted attention except for the fact that it occurs in Mark's Gospel. Mark, who wrote for the Romans, describes Simon of Cyrene as "the father of Alexander and Rufus" (15:21). "A person of this name therefore seems to have held a prominent place among the Roman Christians; and thus there is at least fair ground for identifying the Rufus of St. Paul with the Rufus of St. Mark."[39] Paul speaks of Rufus as **chosen in the Lord** ("an outstanding follower of the Lord," NEB).[40] He also salutes **his mother and mine.** When she "mothered" Paul we do not know.

Of **Asyncritus, Phlegon,** and **Hermas** (14) we know nothing at all. **Patrobas** (from Patrobius) may have been a dependent of a famous freedman of the same name in Nero's time, who was put to death by Galba (Tacitus, *Hist.*, i., 49, ii., 95). "Hermas has often been identified with the author of *The Shepherd*, but though the identification goes back to Origen, it is a mistake."[41] **The brethren which are with them** probably suggests a household church (cf. v. 5).

Philologus and Julia (15) here named together are probably husband and wife. Both are very common slave names. Roman ecclesiastical tradition as far back as the fourth century associates **Nereus,** and a companion named Achilleus, with Flavia Domitilla. Flavia was a Christian lady of the imperial household who was banished to the island of Pandateria by her uncle Domitian in A.D. 95, but was released after his death in the following year; her name is perpetuated in the "Cemetery of Domitilla."[42] **Olympas** is an abbreviation of Olympiodorus. **All the saints which are with them** in all likelihood has the same meaning as the concluding phrase of the previous verse. The Roman church was probably composed of a number of household congregations in different sections of the city.

---

[38]Denney, *op. cit.*, p. 720.   [39]Lightfoot, *op. cit.*, p. 176.

[40]**Chosen** in this instance does not seem to carry the common meaning of gospel election: it rather means "choice," hence "outstanding."

[41]Denney, *op. cit.*, p. 721.

[42]Bruce, *The Epistle of Paul to the Romans*, p. 275.

When the Epistle is read in the church, the Christians are to **salute one another with an holy kiss** (16; *en philemati hagio*). The custom of combining greeting and kiss was oriental; it was especially Jewish, and in this way became Christian. In I Pet. 5:14 the kiss is called *philema agapes*. By **holy** (*hagion*) the kiss is distinguished from the ordinary greeting of natural friendship or affection. "It belongs to God and the new society of His children; it is specifically *Christian*."[43] Eventually it became a regular part of the liturgy.

The churches of Christ salute you concludes Paul's greetings. This should read, "All the churches of Christ greet you" (*hai ekklesiai passai tou Christou*).[44] For "all the churches" cf. v. 4; I Cor. 7:17; 14:33; II Cor. 8:18; 11:28. Hort suggests that this unique phrase is used to express "the way in which the Church of Rome was an object of love and respect to Jewish and Gentile Churches alike."[45]

3. *Warning Against False Teachers* (16:17-20)

This admonition is unlike the rest of Romans in both style and substance.

a. Style. It was Paul's custom, after dictating a letter, to take the pen in his own hand and add a brief note. Thus we read in II Thess. 3:17: "The salutation of Paul with mine own hand, which is the token in every epistle: so I write. The grace of our Lord Jesus Christ be with you all. Amen." In Col. 4:18 he writes: "The salutation by the hand of me Paul. Remember my bonds. Grace be with you. Amen." But in two other letters this autograph conclusion runs quite long (I Cor. 16:21-24; Gal. 6:11-18).

We may therefore regard vv. 17-20 as Paul's usual epistolary conclusion. It closes with the benediction he uses with slight variations in every letter, **The grace of our Lord Jesus Christ be with you. Amen.** "We may suppose that he has taken the pen from the hand of his amanuensis to add the brief admonition and 'grace' in his own handwriting, which, as he tells us in 2 Thessalonians, was the invariable mark of an authentic letter from him."[46]

---

[43]Denney, *loc. cit.*   [44]This is a unique expression in Paul.
[45]Quoted by ICC, "Romans," pp. 428-29.
[46]Dodd, *op. cit.,* p. 242.

b. Substance. The fact that Paul now feels himself to be more in direct contact with the Romans may account for the change in tone and subject matter. Throughout the Epistle he has written officially as an apostle to a church he has never visited. Now he assumes a pastoral attitude more characteristic of letters written to his own churches. **Now I beseech you, brethren, mark them which cause divisions and offences contrary to the doctrine which ye have learned; and avoid them (17).**

Who are these false teachers? Sanday and Headlam think they are "probably of a Jewish character."[47] This is quite unlikely. They seem rather to resemble the antinomians the apostle denounces in Phil. 3:18-19. It seems clear, however, that, whoever they are, they have not yet appeared in Rome, nor begun to work there. The warning would thus be a general one, rather than one aimed at a known situation in Rome. The antinomian nature of these teachers is indicated by the next statement. **For they that are such serve not our Lord Jesus Christ, but their own belly** (cf. Phil. 3:19); **and by good words and fair speeches deceive the hearts of the simple.** These teachers are not servants of **the Lord Jesus Christ;** they are slaves of their appetites. But they are smooth and persuasive talkers who are capable of deceiving well-meaning Christians with their captious teachings.

In order to connect v. 19 with the preceding sentence we should insert a connecting statement. "I give this exhortation, separating you altogether from the false teachers, and from those who are liable to be misled by them." Verse 19 then follows naturally: **For your obedience is come abroad unto all men. I am glad therefore on your behalf** (*eph hymin oun chairo,* "over *you* therefore I rejoice"); **but yet I would have you wise unto that which is good, and simple concerning evil.** "What Paul here wishes for the Romans—moral intelligence, not impaired in the least by any dealings with evil—does suggest that antinomianism was the peril to be guarded against. Integrity of the moral nature is the best security: the seductive teaching is instinctively repelled."[48]

He then gives them a promise which echoes Gen. 3:15: **And the God of peace shall bruise Satan under your feet shortly (20).** This implies that divisions are Satan's work, and the sup-

---

[47]ICC, "Romans," p. 429.   [48]Denney, *op. cit.,* p. 722.

pression of them by the God of peace is a victory over Satan. Then comes the benediction: **The grace of our Lord Jesus Christ be with you. Amen.**

4. *Greetings from Friends at Corinth* (16:21-24)

The letter is complete, but, by way of postscript, Paul adds greetings from some of his companions who are with him in Corinth. **Timotheus** (21) is well-known. He was with Paul in Macedonia (cf. II Cor. 1:1) before he came to Corinth. **Lucius** may be the one mentioned in Acts 13:1. **Jason** was once Paul's host (Acts 17:5-9) in Thessalonica. **Sosipater** may be the longer form of Sopater mentioned in Acts 20:4. They are all Paul's **kinsmen**, or fellow Jews.

Then Paul's amanuensis takes the pen again and writes, **I Tertius, who wrote this epistle, salute you in the Lord** (22). See II Thess. 3:17; I Cor. 16:21; Col. 4:18.

Gaius mine host, and of the whole church, saluteth you (23). "As the Epistle to the Romans was written from Corinth this hospitable Christian is probably the same who is mentioned in I Cor. i. 14."[49] Three other persons of the same name are mentioned elsewhere (Acts 19:29; 20:4; III John 1). **Of the whole church** (*ho xenos holes tes ekklesias*) may mean that the whole Christian community met in his house (cf. vv. 5, 14-15). **Erastus** (II Tim. 4:20) was **the chamberlain** (*ho oikonomos,* treasurer) of the city of Corinth. The Greek word means "house-manager" and may indicate that Erastus was city manager of Corinth. He was probably administrator of the city's property.[50] **Quartus** is the Latin name for *fourth.* (Verse 24 is not found in the best MSS, and should be omitted. Note how it repeats 20*b*.)

5. *Doxology* (16:25-27)

Paul's letters generally conclude with a benediction. Even apart from the questions of textual criticism connected with it, this doxology has given rise to much discussion. The closest analogies are found in Eph. 3:20-21; Heb. 13:20-21; and Jude 24-25. Paul's doxologies are usually much briefer (cf. 1:25; 9:5; 11:36; Phil. 4:20). This one is found at various places in extant MSS of Romans. In some it is placed after 14:23, and in others both there and at this place. In one MS it does not appear at all. Because of what he considers the artificial character of the

[49]*Ibid.,* p. 723.   [50]Robertson, *op. cit.,* p. 430.

materials, a conservative and reverent scholar like Denney is
suspicious that it does not belong to the Epistle any more than
the doxology of Matt. 6:13b belongs to the Lord's Prayer.[51]

Sanday and Headlam, on the other hand, agree with Hort
and Lightfoot that we have here "a genuine and original conclusion to the Epistle exactly harmonizing with its contents."[52]
In their commentary on the doxology they point to the various
parts of the Epistle which are summed up in pregnant sentences
in these final verses.

Now to him that is of power to stablish you (25) seems to
echo 14:4. "We are at once reminded that in i. 11 St. Paul had
stated that one of the purposes of his contemplated visit was to
confer on them some spiritual gift that they might be established."[53] **According to my gospel** (*kata to euangelion mou*) repeats 2:16. A salient feature of the Epistle is Paul's desire to set
forth to the Romans his special understanding of the gospel. He
did not regard this understanding as in any way antagonistic to
the common faith of the church (cf. I Cor. 15:1-4) but as complementary to the general tradition.

The phrase **the preaching of Jesus Christ** (*to kerygma Iesou
Christou*) stresses the gospel as the *proclamation* of Christ (cf.
10:8-12; I Cor. 1:21, 23; 2:4; II Cor. 1:19; 4:5; 11:4; Gal. 2:2;
etc.). **According to the revelation of the mystery, which was
kept secret since the world began, but now is made manifest**
(25-26) is parallel to I Cor. 2:7-10 (cf. Eph. 3:3, 5-6; Titus 1:2-3;
II Tim. 1:9-10). For separate phrases cf. 1:16; 3:21; 11:25. This
is the thought that underlies cc. 9—11, and is indirectly implied
in the first eight chapters. God, who rules over all the aeons
which have passed and which are to come, is working out His
eternal purpose in the world. For ages it was a mystery, but
now in these last days this mystery has been revealed through
the gospel.

All the ideas in the remainder of v. 26 are in accordance
with thoughts which run through the Epistle. The expression **by
the scriptures of the prophets** (*dia te graphon prophetikon*) is
in accordance with 1:1-2 and 3:21. It indicates that the new
method of salvation "apart from law, was witnessed by the law
and the prophets." Throughout Romans, Paul stresses the unity
of the Old and New Testaments, showing that the gospel establishes the law (3:31). The same is true of the idea expressed

[51]*Op. cit.*, pp. 723-24.   [52]ICC, "Romans," p. 433.   [53]*Ibid.*

by the phrase **according to the commandment of the everlasting God** (*kat epitagen tou aioniou theou*). "The mission given to the preachers of the Gospel is brought out generally in Rom. x. 15 ff., the special command to the Apostle is dealt on in the opening vv. 1-5, and the sense of commission is a constant thought of this period."[54] The word **everlasting** (*aioniou*) is suggested by **since the world began** (*chronois aioniois*) in v. 25. The formula **the commandment** (*kat epitagen*) occurs in I Cor. 7:6, and in II Cor. 8:8, but with a different meaning; in the sense Paul uses it here it is found in I Tim. 1:1; Titus 1:3.

We find the phrase **the obedience of faith** (*eis hypakoen pisteos*) in 1:5 (cf. 15:18). This is one of Paul's key thoughts in the Epistle. See comments on 1:5 for its crucial significance in his teaching.

The last phrase, **made known to all nations** (*eis panta ta ethne gnoristhentos*), is a commonplace of the Epistle. "In this passage still carrying on the explanation of the *kerygma,* four main ideas of the Apostolic preaching are touched upon—the continuity of the Gospel, the Apostolic commission, salvation through faith, the preaching to the Gentiles."[55]

The Epistle closes with the grand words, **To the only wise God** (*mono sopho theo*) **be glory through Jesus Christ for ever. Amen** (27). A similar expression, "unto . . . the only wise God" (*to mono sopho theo*), is found in I Tim. 1:17. The grand thought is that of 3:29-30—God is **one**; therefore He is the God of both Jews and Gentiles; the gospel is one. God is infinitely **wise**; even when we cannot trace His ways, we can trust His wisdom.

"The doxology sums up all the great ideas of the Epistle. The power of the Gospel which St. Paul was commissioned to preach; the revelation in it of the eternal purpose of God; its contents, faith; its sphere, all the nations of the earth; its author, the one wise God, whose wisdom is thus vindicated—all these thoughts had been continually dwelt on. And so at the end feeling how unfit a conclusion would be the jarring note of vv. 17-20, and wishing to 'restore the Epistle at its close to its tone of serene loftiness,' the Apostle adds these verses, writing them perhaps with his own hand in those large bold letters which seem to have formed a sort of authentication of his Epistles (Gal. vi.11), and thus gives an eloquent conclusion to his great argument."[56]

[54]*Ibid.,* pp. 434-35.   [55]*Ibid.,* p. 435.   [56]*Ibid.,* p. 436.

Bibliography

I. COMMENTARIES

ALFORD, HENRY. *The New Testament for English Readers*. Chicago: Moody Press, n.d.

BARCLAY, WILLIAM. *The Letter to the Romans*. "The Daily Study Bible." Philadelphia: The Westminster Press, 1957.

BARRETT, CHARLES KINGSLEY. *The Epistle to the Romans*. "Harper's New Testament Commentaries." New York: Harper & Brothers, 1957.

————. *Reading Through Romans*. London: The Epworth Press, 1963.

BARTH, KARL. *The Epistle to the Romans*. Translated from the Sixth Edition by EDWIN C. HOSKYNS. London: Oxford University Press, 1933.

————. *A Shorter Commentary on Romans*. Richmond, Virginia: John Knox Press, 1959.

BEET, JOSEPH AGAR. *St. Paul's Epistle to the Romans*. London: Hodder and Stoughton, 1885.

BRUCE, F. F. *The Epistle of Paul to the Romans*. "The Tyndale Bible Commentaries." Grand Rapids: Wm. B. Eerdmans Publishing Company, 1963.

BRUNNER, EMIL. *The Letter to the Romans*. Translated by H. A. KENNEDY. Philadelphia: The Westminster Press, 1959.

CALVIN, JOHN. *The Epistles of Paul to the Romans and Thessalonians*. Translated by ROSS MACKENZIE. Grand Rapids: Wm. B. Eerdmans Publishing Company, 1960.

CLARKE, ADAM. *The New Testament of Our Lord and Saviour Jesus Christ*, Vol. II. New York: Abingdon-Cokesbury Press, n.d.

CRAGG, GERALD. "The Epistle to the Romans" (Exposition). *The Interpreter's Bible*. Edited by GEORGE A. BUTTRICK, et al., Vol. IX. New York: Abingdon-Cokesbury Press, 1951.

DENNEY, JAMES. "St. Paul's Epistle to the Romans." *The Expositor's Greek Testament*. Edited by W. ROBERTSON NICOLL, Vol. II. Grand Rapids: Wm. B. Eerdmans Publishing Company, n.d.

DODD, C. H. *The Epistle to the Romans*. "The Moffatt New Testament Commentary." New York: Harper and Brothers Publishers, 1932.

ERDMAN, CHARLES R. *The Epistle of Paul to the Romans*. Philadelphia: The Westminster Press, 1925.

GODET, F. *St. Paul's Epistle to the Romans*. Translated by A. CUSIN. New York: Funk and Wagnalls, 1883.

GORE, CHARLES. *St. Paul's Epistle to the Romans*, Vol. I. London: John Murray, 1902.

GREATHOUSE, WILLIAM M. *Romans*. "Search the Scriptures," Vol. VI. Edited by NORMAN R. OKE. Kansas City: Nazarene Publishing House, n.d.

HENRY, MATTHEW. *Commentary on the Whole Bible*, Vols. I and VI. New York: Fleming H. Revell Co., n.d.

HODGE, CHARLES. *Commentary on the Epistle to the Romans*. Grand Rapids: Wm. B. Eerdmans Publishing Company, 1950.

289

HOWARD, RICHARD E. "Galatians." *Beacon Bible Commentary*. Edited by RALPH EARLE, *et al.*, Vol. IX. Kansas City: Beacon Hill Press, 1965.

KNOX, JOHN. "The Epistle to the Romans" (Exegesis). *The Interpreter's Bible*. Edited by GEORGE A. BUTTRICK, *et al.*, Vol. IX. New York: Abingdon-Cokesbury Press, 1951.

LEENHARDT, FRANZ J. *The Epistle to the Romans*. Cleveland and New York: The World Publishing Company, 1957.

LIGHTFOOT, J. B. *St. Paul's Epistle to the Philippians*. London: Macmillan Press, 1913.

LUTHER, MARTIN. *Lectures on Romans*. Translated by WILHELM PAUCK. Philadelphia: The Westminster Press, 1961.

LUTHI, WALTER. *The Letter to the Romans*. Richmond, Virginia: John Knox Press, 1961.

MACLAREN, ALEXANDER. *Expositions of Holy Scripture*, Vol. XIII. Grand Rapids: Wm. B. Eerdmans Publishing Co., 1944.

MURRAY, JOHN. *The Epistle to the Romans*, Vol. I. Grand Rapids: Wm. B. Eerdmans Publishing Co., 1959.

NYGREN, ANDERS. *Commentary on Romans*. Translated by CARL C. RASMUSSEN. Philadelphia: Fortress Press, 1949.

QUIMBY, CHESTER WARREN. *The Great Redemption*. New York: Macmillan Company, 1950.

ROBERTSON, ARCHIBALD THOMAS. *Word Pictures in the New Testament*, Vol. IV. Nashville: Broadman Press, 1931.

SANDAY, W., and HEADLAM, A. C. *The Epistle to the Romans*. "The International Critical Commentary." New York: Charles Scribner's Sons, 1929.

SCOTT, C. ANDERSON. "Romans." *The Abingdon Bible Commentary*. Edited by DAVID C. DOWNEY. New York: Abingdon Press, 1929.

SCOTT, E. F. *Paul's Epistle to the Romans*. London: SCM Press, 1947.

STIFLER, JAMES K. *The Epistle to the Romans*. Chicago: Moody Press, 1960.

THOMAS, W. GRIFFITH. *St. Paul's Epistle to the Romans*. Grand Rapids: Wm. B. Eerdmans Publishing Co., 1947.

THOMSON, G. T., and DAVIDSON, F. "Romans." *The New Bible Commentary*. Edited by F. DAVIDSON, *et al.* Grand Rapids: Wm. B. Eerdmans Publishing Co., 1953.

THROCKMORTON, BURTON H., JR. *Romans for the Layman*. Philadelphia: The Westminster Press, 1961.

VINCENT, MARVIN R. *Word Studies in the New Testament*, Vol. III. New York: Charles Scribner's Sons, 1905.

WESLEY, JOHN. *Explanatory Notes upon the New Testament*. London: Epworth Press, 1950 (reprint).

WILEY, H. ORTON. *The Epistle to the Hebrews*. Kansas City: Beacon Hill Press, 1959.

WOOD, A. SKEVINGTON. *Life by the Spirit*. Grand Rapids: Wm. B. Eerdmans Publishing Co., 1963.

WUEST, KENNETH S. *Romans in the Greek New Testament*. Grand Rapids: Wm. B. Eerdmans Publishing Co., 1945.

II. OTHER BOOKS

ABBOTT-SMITH, G. *A Manual Greek Lexicon of the New Testament.* Second Edition. Edinburgh: T. & T. Clark, 1923.

ARMINIUS, JACOB. *The Writings of Arminius,* Vol. II. Grand Rapids: Baker Book House, 1956.

The Apocrypha, According to the Authorized Version. New York: Harper & Brothers, n.d.

ARNDT, W. F., and GINGRICH, F. W. *A Greek-English Lexicon of the New Testament and Other Early Christian Literature.* Chicago: University of Chicago Press, 1957.

BARCLAY, WILLIAM. *The Mind of St. Paul.* London: Collins, 1958.

————. *More New Testament Words.* London: SCM Press, Ltd., 1958.

BARNETT, ALBERT E. *The New Testament, Its Making and Meaning.* New York: Abingdon-Cokesbury Press, 1946.

BARTH, KARL. "Christ and Adam: Man and Humanity in Romans 5." *Scottish Journal of Theology Occasional Papers.* Edinburgh and London: Oliver and Boyd, 1956.

BONHOEFFER, DIETRICH. *The Cost of Discipleship.* New York: Macmillan Company, 1963.

BRUCE, F. F. *The Letters of Paul: An Expanded Paraphrase.* Grand Rapids: Wm. B. Eerdmans Publishing Co., 1965.

BULTMANN, RUDOLPH. *Theology of the New Testament,* Vol. I. Translated by KENDRICK GROBEL. New York: Charles Scribner's Sons, 1951.

DAVIES, D. R. *Down Peacock's Feathers.* New York: Macmillan Press, 1944.

FLEW, R. NEWTON. *The Idea of Perfection.* London: Oxford University Press, 1934.

GOPPELT, LEONHARD. *Jesus, Paul and Judaism.* Translated by EDWARD SHROEDER. New York: Thomas Nelson & Sons, 1964.

HILLERBRAND, HANS J. *The Reformation.* New York: Harper & Row, 1964.

HILLS, A. M. *The Establishing Grace.* Kansas City: Nazarene Publishing House, n.d.

HUNTER, A. M. *Interpreting Paul's Gospel.* Philadelphia: Westminster Press, 1954.

JACOB, EDMOND. *Theology of the Old Testament.* New York: Harper & Brothers, 1958.

LILLIE, WILLIAM. *Studies in New Testament Ethics.* Philadelphia: Westminster Press, 1963.

MORRIS, LEON. *The Apostolic Preaching of the Cross.* Grand Rapids: Wm. B. Eerdmans Publishing Co., 1956.

OTTO, RUDOLPH. *The Idea of the Holy.* Translated by J. W. HARVEY. Second Edition. London: Oxford University Press, 1950.

PURKISER, W. T., ed. *Exploring Our Christian Faith.* Kansas City: Beacon Hill Press, 1960.

RICHARDSON, ALAN. *An Introduction to the Theology of the New Testament.* New York: Harper & Brothers, 1958.

SMITH, RYDER. *The Bible Doctrine of Sin.* London: Epworth Press, 1953.

STAUFFER, ETHELBERT. *New Testament Theology.* Translated by JOHN MARSH. New York: Macmillan Company, 1955.

WESLEY, JOHN. *Works,* Vols. V, VI, XI. Kansas City: Nazarene Publishing House, n.d.

WILLIAMS, COLIN W. *John Wesley's Theology Today.* New York: Abingdon-Cokesbury Press, 1960.

WILLIAMSON, AUDREY. *Overcome Evil with Good.* Kansas City: Beacon Hill Press of Kansas City, 1967.

III. ARTICLES

DAVIES, DONALD M. "Free from the Law." *Interpretation,* VII (April, 1953), 157-62

MINEAR, PAUL S. "The Truth About Sin and Death." *Interpretation,* VII (April, 1953), 142-55.

REUMANN, JOHN. "The Gospel of the Righteousness of God." *Interpretation,* XX (October, 1966), 432-52.

The First Epistle of Paul

to the

CORINTHIANS

Donald S. Metz

Introduction

A. AUTHORSHIP

Practically all New Testament scholars accept the Pauline authorship of I Corinthians. The nearly unanimous assignment of this letter to Paul is expressed by Robertson and Plummer as follows: "Both the external and the internal evidence for the Pauline authorship are so strong that those who attempt to show that the Apostle was not the writer succeed chiefly in proving their own incompetence as critics."[1] Since there is general agreement, it is necessary to suggest only briefly the nature of the internal and external evidence for the Pauline authorship.

The internal evidence points to Paul as the author. The general form of the letter, with its opening greetings, the treatment of practical and doctrinal problems, and a warm benediction in closing, follows the familiar pattern in Paul's Epistles. The style is also Pauline, combining courteous persuasion, passionate exhortation, direct confrontation, and brotherly affection. The language is also typical of Paul. Such phrases as "Jesus Christ our Lord," "in Christ," "the spiritual man," "justified," and "the body of Christ" are all Pauline expressions. Also the letter associates Paul with the Corinthian church in a way which is not at all flattering to the Corinthians. Thus the letter must have been an accurate description of the situation at Corinth or these people would not have permitted it to stand without refutation.

The external evidence also supports the Pauline authorship. In A.D. 95, Clement of Rome referred to I Corinthians as a letter from the Apostle Paul. This is "the earliest example in literature of a New Testament writer being quoted by name."[2] The Muratorian canon, probably appearing at the end of the second century, lists I Corinthians as one of Paul's letters.[3] Tertullian, the father of Latin theology, in his *Prescriptions Against Heretics,* uses I Corinthians as a Pauline support for the doctrine of the resur-

---

[1]*A Critical and Exegetical Commentary on the First Epistle of St. Paul to the Corinthians* ("The International Critical Commentary"; Edinburgh: T. and T. Clark, 1911), p. xvi.

[2]*Ibid.,* p. xvii.

[3]Henry Bettenson, ed., *Documents of the Christian Church* (London: Oxford University Press, 1963), pp. 40-41.

rection.[4] Origen, in a discussion of temptation, also quotes from I Corinthians, and quite naturally refers to Paul as the author.[5]

Paul's authorship of I Corinthians stands above any serious challenge and may be accepted without reservation. In the words of a noted New Testament scholar and historian: ". . . First Corinthians formed the beginning in the earliest collection of the Pauline epistles."[6]

B. City of Corinth

Paul went to Corinth about A.D. 50[7] to conduct an 18-month home missionary campaign. He found himself in a prosperous commercial center. Both land and sea traffic converged on Corinth. The city was built on a narrow neck of land which joined northern and southern Greece (see map 1). All traffic from north to south was funneled through the narrow strip of land dominated by Corinth. In addition, Corinth had natural seaport facilities and a strategic location that made it a thriving shipping center. Most east-west traffic came to the city either to save time or to avoid a long and dangerous journey around the treacherous waters of southern Greece. Cargo could be unloaded, dragged across the narrow, four-mile neck of land, reloaded, and sent out in a much shorter time than traveling several hundred miles around the southern tip of Greece.

About 200 years before Paul arrived in Corinth, a Roman general named Lucius Mummius had plundered and sacked the city in 146 B.C. Julius Caesar rebuilt it in 46 B.C. as a military outpost and as a commercial center of the empire. The city attracted merchants, vagabonds, fortune-hunters, and pleasure-seekers. One writer describes the population in these words:

> The riff-raff of the world was there . . . Scoundrels who found life uncomfortable in their own towns drifted to Corinth. The busy port was notoriously more immoral than any other in the Roman Empire; and that tendency was encouraged because the temple of

[4]S. L. Greenslade, ed., and trans. *Early Latin Theology* ("The Library of Christian Classics"; Philadelphia: The Westminster Press, 1956), p. 54.

[5]Henry Chadwick and John E. L. Oulton, *Alexandrian Christianity* ("The Library of Christian Classics"; Philadelphia: The Westminster Press, 1954), p. 312.

[6]Johannes Weiss, *Earliest Christianity: A History of the Period A.D. 30-150.* (New York: Harper and Brothers, 1937), II, 681.

[7]Jack Finegan, *Light from the Ancient Past* (Princeton, N.J.: Princeton University Press, 1946), p. 282.

Venus (Aphrodite), the sensual Greek goddess, still held sway over the new Roman City.[8]

Here Paul again encountered the Greek mind, as he had in Athens. In Corinth, however, "the Greek intellect was not devoted to science, eloquence, or literature . . . but was given to gaiety and effeminate luxury."[9]

The outstanding building of Corinth was the temple of Venus, "erected on its acropolis, and towering high above the city, as illustrative of the taste and the character of the Corinthians."[10] In Corinth, Christianity came into contact "with all that art could devise for the amusement of life; with all that was adapted to nourish the habits of voluptuousness, with all, refined or gross, that could minister to the pleasures of sense."[11] Corinth was one of the most "luxurious, effeminate, ostentatious, and dissolute cities of the world."[12] It was a place of exceptional immorality and open licentiousness which was encouraged by the worship of Aphrodite, with a thousand temple prostitutes. Recent excavations have discovered 33 taverns behind a colonnade only 100 feet long.[13] The city contained a theatre with a seating capacity of 18,000 people.[14]

So notorious was the depravity of Corinth that the name of the city "had actually passed into the vocabulary of the Greek tongue; and the very word 'to Corinthianize' meant 'to play the wanton.' "[15] Today, except for seven Doric columns which are still standing, and some scattered ruins of masonry, there is nothing left of this once proud city except rubble.[16] It does have a perpetual memorial in the letters that the Apostle Paul wrote to it.

C. THE CHURCH AT CORINTH

God's grace is sufficient to redeem fully and to sustain continually. Many spiritual churches composed of devout and dedi-

[8]H. F. Mathews, *According to St. Paul* (New York: Collier Books, 1962), pp. 40-41.

[9]Albert Barnes, *The Apostle Paul* (Grand Rapids: Baker Book House, 1950), p. 203.

[10]*Ibid.*, p. 204.   [11]*Ibid.*   [12]*Ibid.*

[13]Ralph Earle (ed.), *Exploring the New Testament* (Kansas City, Mo.: Beacon Hill Press, 1955), p. 271.

[14]G. Ernest Wright, *Biblical Archaeology* (Philadelphia: The Westminster Press, 1957), p. 262.

[15]J. Conybeare and J. S. Howson, *The Life and Epistles of Saint Paul* (Hartford, Conn.: S. S. Scranton Co., 1904), p. 419.

[16]William M. Taylor, *Paul the Missionary* (New York: Harper and Brothers, 1882), p. 279.

cated saints have attained a high degree of spirituality in sinful and unfavorable environments. But, unfortunately, the church at Corinth was not such a church, for "there were many complications in the attempt of the early Christians to separate themselves from sinful society."[17] The church at Corinth was a problem church. Paul, in this letter, was led "to denounce the sins which had polluted the Corinthian Church, and almost annulled its right to the name of Christian."[18]

In writing to the Corinthians, Paul reminded them that they were set apart, "called to be saints" (1:2); he complimented those who were enriched in "utterance, and in all knowledge" (1:5); he commended them for their variety of gifts (1:7). But Paul also expressed some serious concern for them. He begged them to come to an agreement among themselves (1:10); he was distressed by the divisions among them (1:11). He drew a graphic picture of the inability of the natural man to understand spiritual concepts (1:18-26). He presented Christ as the supreme object of Christian loyalty and devotion (1:30-31). Paul made a detailed analysis of their spiritual state. And a sordid picture it was. The catalogue of charges that Paul leveled at the Corinthians ran the range from carnal divisions to a denial of the resurrection of Christ. A lesser soul than Paul would have abandoned the church in despair or condemned it in indignation. Paul did neither—he preached Christ to them.

Paul could boldly challenge the Corinthians because he had been God's instrument in founding the church. His arrival in Corinth near the middle of the first century was not a matter of triumphant anticipation nor of confidence based on past success. He had escaped from Macedonia with his life in peril (Acts 17:13-14). From Thessalonica, in Macedonia, Paul had gone to Athens, where he met with little success among either Jews or Greeks (Acts 17:16-33). Leaving Athens, Paul traveled to Corinth (Acts 18:1), where he stayed for 18 months (Acts 18:11). At Corinth, the cesspool of the ancient world, Paul was able to win a number of outstanding converts. First Aquila and Priscilla were convinced and converted. Timothy and Silas came from Macedonia to assist Paul, and soon Crispus, a ruler of a synagogue, was converted. His change of spiritual life was followed by several more conversions. Among these converts were some people of social stature, such as Titus Justus, whose home

[17]Clarence Tucker Craig, *The Beginning of Christianity* (New York: Abingdon Press, 1943), p. 241.

[18]Conybeare and Howson, *op. cit.*, p. 423.

became a meeting place for the church. Aquila and Priscilla, already mentioned, were people of strong character and immense industry. There was also Gaius, "who was a man of means and great hospitality, entertaining Paul and the whole church."[19] Erastus, the city treasurer, became a convert. There may have been other men of stature, but as D. A. Hayes writes: ". . . the majority of the church was made up of poor and uncultured people, some from the middle class and more from the slave population."[20] After 18 months at Corinth, Paul went to Ephesus (Acts 18:19). He left behind one of the largest congregations of the Early Church.

D. Occasion and Purpose of the Letter

After Paul left Corinth, the work of building and consolidating the thriving new church was given to Apollos (Acts 19:1). He was an Alexandrian Jew, an eloquent and learned man (Acts 18:24). He had served his apprenticeship at Ephesus and had preached with a marked fervency the baptism of John (Acts 18:25). In Ephesus his theological education was enhanced by the teaching of Aquila and Priscilla (Acts 18:26). Leaving Ephesus, Apollos had gone to Corinth. No doubt he returned to Ephesus to report on the conditions of the Corinthian church.

In the three years that had passed since Paul left Corinth, the church members had not developed well spiritually. The apostle had written a letter to the church earlier; in I Cor. 5:9 he writes: "I wrote you a letter not to associate with fornicators" (lit.). Apparently the original letter, called by scholars "The Previous Letter," has been lost. Paul received information that the situation at Corinth was getting worse. He mentioned several sources of information.

1. Chloe's people. In I Cor. 1:11, Paul states: "For it has been reported to me by Chloe's people that there is quarreling among you, my brethren" (RSV). This report was unsolicited and unauthorized, yet it was true. One writer refers to it as follows: "Both because the information is said to come from these persons rather than from the Corinthian Church . . . and because of the unfavourable nature of this news, it is safe to assume that these persons were not sent by the Corinthians to bring this news and that their report, therefore, was quite unof-

[19]*Paul and His Epistles* (New York: The Methodist Book Concern, 1915), p. 197.
[20]*Ibid.*

ficial."[21] Deissmann suggests that Chloe may have been a woman of some financial means.[22]

2. News of the situation at Corinth also came as a result of a visit of Stephanas, Fortunatus, and Achaicus to Ephesus (I Cor. 16:17).

3. The most direct news came from the church itself. The rapidly deteriorating condition alarmed some of the members and they sent a letter to Paul. In I Cor. 7:1 he wrote: "Concerning the questions about which you wrote to me . . ." (lit.). So a combination of factors caused the apostle to write a letter to the church. It was designed to deal with its problems and to point its members to a life of holiness in Christ.

In the letter from the Corinthians to Paul there were questions about marriage and celibacy, about food offered to idols, about public worship, and probably some about spiritual gifts. But Paul was also concerned about other problems which plagued this church, such as divisions, a quarrelsome spirit, sexual impurity, and an unchristian spirit. Paul wrote a letter presenting the truth that Christianity required a complete renovation of character and conduct—a new morality based on the redeeming power of Christ.

As Hurd has pointed out, "It can now be said that there is clear evidence that I Corinthians is the fourth stage in an exchange which took place between Paul and the Corinthian Church."[23] These phases of Paul's relationship to the church are as follows:

PHASE 1: Paul's first visit to Corinth and tne establishment of the church.

PHASE 2: Paul's "Previous Letter" to the church at Corinth.

PHASE 3: This phase consisted of two parts. First was the information reported to Paul about Corinth by Stephanas, Fortunatus, and Achaicus and by Chloe's people. In addition to the verbal reports of visitors from Corinth there was the letter written to Paul by the church

[21]John C. Hurd, Jr., *The Origin of I Corinthians* (New York: Seabury Press, 1965), p. 48.

[22]*Paul: A Study in Social and Religious History;* trans. William E. Wilson (First Harper Torchbook; New York: Harper and Brothers, 1957), p. 243.

[23]*Op. cit.,* p. 57.

itself. This letter requested him to advise them on some problems which had developed.

PHASE 4: The writing of I Corinthians. In this first letter Paul dealt with the questions which the church had directed to him. But he went further, and discussed at length the more serious questions which had been called to his attention by the verbal reports about the situation at Corinth.

E. IMPORTANCE OF THE LETTER

The importance of I Corinthians is sharply in focus in the latter half of the twentieth century. Paul dealt with several problems that make the letter relevant today. The first of these is that he was dealing with a church in a secular, urban culture. Deissmann writes: "The cosmopolitan cities were especially his sphere of work. Paul the city-dweller evangelised in the great cities."[24] Another writer says: ". . . unlike the rural character of contemporary Protestantism, the church of the New Testament was urban."[25]

A second reason for the relevance of I Corinthians is the current emphasis on ecumenism. No man possessed a more tolerant spirit than Paul and no man stressed the unity of the church more than he did. But Paul was also careful to base the unity of the church on the doctrine of Christ and the radical change which resulted from a redemptive relationship "in Christ." A third reason that this letter is significant today is the current stress on a "new morality." But Paul's "new morality" came directly from a revelation that "God was in Christ, reconciling the world unto himself." A final reason for the contemporary meaning of I Corinthians is the rise of interest in the work of the Holy Spirit and the gifts of the Spirit. With these vital themes included in the general and specific teachings of this letter to all churches in all ages, the letter called I Corinthians is as relevant as this morning's sunrise.

F. DATE AND PLACE OF ORIGIN

The place of the writing is clearly indicated by Paul's statement: "I will tarry at Ephesus until Pentecost" (I Cor. 16:8).

[24]Op. cit., p. 227.

[25]William Baird, The Corinthian Church—A Biblical Approach to Urban Culture (New York: Abingdon Press, 1964), p. 23.

The precise time at which Paul wrote to Corinth during his three-year ministry in Ephesus is not apparent. There is no indication that the church at Corinth was in any difficulty when Paul finished his ministry there. And a party of Apollos would not have developed during the time that Apollos was there, for certainly he did not consider himself a rival of Paul and Peter, much less of Christ! Time would be needed for the spirit of division and pride to develop.

Again, there is mention of a "previous letter" (I Cor. 5:9). Evidently this first letter was dispatched when the early signs of spiritual rebellion began to appear at Corinth.

Another important item in the dating of the letter is the fact that Gallio was proconsul of Achaia while Paul was in Corinth (Acts 18:12-16). An inscription mentioning a civil official named Gallio has been discovered at Delphi, on the opposite side of the narrow neck of land from Corinth. The inscription can be dated, and suggests that Gallio came to Corinth as proconsul in either A.D. 51 or 52.[26] When time is allowed for the occurrence of the events described in Acts 17 and 18, between Paul's departure from Corinth and the time spent in Ephesus, it can be stated that the letter was written during the last year of Paul's stay in Ephesus, or "somewhere about the mid-fifties."[27] Thus the letter would be one of the apostle's earlier writings.

[26]Wright, op. cit., p. 261.

[27]Leon Morris, The First Epistle of Paul to the Corinthians ("Tyndale New Testament Commentaries"; Grand Rapids: Wm. B. Eerdmans Publishing Company, 1958), p. 29.

Outline

Section I *Prologue*

I Corinthians 1:1-9

Paul was a genius in the area of religious living. However, his genius was not that of a man with one outstanding talent, which was utilized relentlessly to achieve a goal. It was many-sided. He combined genuine courtesy with passionate convictions; he united intellectual brilliance with deep piety; he merged powerful preaching ability with extraordinary missionary labors; he allied a profound concern for the present with an overwhelming expectation for the future. Many of these traits appear in the introduction to the letter.

A. APOSTOLIC GREETINGS, 1:1-3

The apostolic greetings contain three familiar patterns in Paul's approach to a delicate church situation. There is the declaration of his personal apostleship, the note which reminds the church of its spiritual relationship to Christ, and the courteous expression of spiritual concern.

1. Paul's Apostleship (1:1)

Paul was not a reluctant prophet, nor did he have the "preacher's itch." He did not debate with God about his ability to preach and to lead, as did Moses (Exod. 3:11—4:17). Nor did he shrink from the task of preaching, as did Jeremiah (Jer. 1:6). For Paul, to know God's will was to attempt to do it. His willingness to preach may have reflected a particular personality response in the man, but beyond this there was the sense of divine imperative, the recognition of the lordship of Christ, and a submission to God's will. From the time of his conversion on the Damascus road until his death, Paul had one overwhelming purpose—to preach the message of redemption in Christ. Luke, the historian, states that within a few days after Paul's acceptance of the lordship of Christ "straightway he preached Christ . . . that he is the Son of God" (Acts 9:20). Paul never varied from this divinely appointed mission.

a. The divine imperative. Paul was **called**. The divine call is mysterious in its selection, but real and knowable in its expression. To a spiritually sensitive soul like Paul, to be "divinely

305

selected and appointed"[1] to the ministry of preaching was the greatest of honors as well as the highest of obligations. Paul was always careful to present his apostolic credentials (Rom. 1:1; Gal. 1:1; Eph. 1:1). **An apostle** is one who is directly commissioned and dispatched with a message, as a delegate, envoy, or ambassador.[2] The title is used at times in a general sense to include associates and assistants, such as Barnabas. But Lenski writes that "this is evidently not the case when the word is employed in the introduction to a weighty letter. Only the Twelve and Paul are 'apostles' in the strict sense of the term."[3]

By referring to his apostolic commission Paul indicated that it was the sovereign **will of God** and not human merit that qualified men to preach. In the case of the Corinthian church Paul may have desired also to suggest that his authority was God-ordained, not self-assumed. Self-appointed prophets have no vital concern for the church. But a **called . . . apostle** has a concern and a compassion that become a divine imperative which transforms the course of his life. Paul regarded his apostleship as "an express intervention of the divine will."[4] He was called "to be herald and dispenser"[5] in God's redemptive work.

b. *Christ-centered commission.* Paul made his message relevant to his day by preaching about Christ. Bypassing the rational appeal and the oratorical approach, Paul announced at the outset that the foundation of his message was the crucified and resurrected Saviour. He was well aware of man's involvement in sin. But Paul was also aware that no human self-analysis and no personal human power could transform the nature of man. Thus his message was Christ-centered; Paul was always **an apostle of Jesus Christ.** Further, his commission was by **the will of God,** which placed the whole matter of his apostleship beyond any valid challenge.

[1]Joseph Henry Thayer, *A Greek-English Lexicon of the New Testament* (New York: American Book Company, 1889), p. 350.

[2]William F. Arndt and F. Wilbur Gingrich, *A Greek-English Lexicon of the New Testament* (Chicago: University of Chicago Press, 1957), p. 99.

[3]*The Interpretation of St. Paul's First and Second Epistles to the Corinthians* (Minneapolis: Augsburg Publishing House, 1963), p. 19.

[4]G. G. Findlay, "St. Paul's First Epistle to the Corinthians," *The Expositor's Greek Testament* (Grand Rapids: Wm. B. Eerdmans Publishing Co., 1951 [reprint]), II, 757.

[5]*Ibid.*

c. *Brotherly fellowship.* **Sosthenes** was included in the greeting, because Paul was all-inclusive in his outreach, and always individualized his religious concern. He was more concerned with people than with causes. Sosthenes was a Jew by birth and had been a ruler of the synagogue at Corinth (Acts 18: 12-17). When Paul was arraigned before Gallio, Sosthenes either defended Paul or declared himself a Christian. At any rate, he was mobbed and beaten by his own countrymen in the presence of Gallio (Acts 18:17). He was probably with Paul in Ephesus when the apostle was writing. Sosthenes was a noted convert to Christianity in Corinth and well-known to the Corinthian congregation. Paul referred to him as **our brother** or "our colleague."

2. *Spiritual Recognition* (1:2)

Paul's sense of apostleship was always two-dimensional—it came from God and it was directed to the Church of Jesus Christ. In shifting the emphasis of his greeting from personal apostleship to the wider area, Paul suggests four things about the Church. First, it is universal in scope—it is the Church of God. Second, the Church is a unique fellowship—it is separated. Third, the Church has a particular calling or vocation—it is to be saintly. Finally, Christ is the Object of worship in the Church and is the Lord of all the Church.

a. *The universal nature of the Church* (1:2). In the NT the word **church** (*ecclesia*) means "the community of the redeemed."[6] In its primary meaning the Church is "the entire congregation of all who are called by and to Christ, who are in the fellowship of His salvation—the church."[7] The idea of the universality of the Church is found in Acts 2:47; 9:31; and Rom. 16:23.

Here Paul speaks of the **church of God which is at Corinth.** Every individual church is but a fragment of the universal Church of the redeemed—the Church of God. The Corinthian church had a tendency to act as a law unto itself in matters of conduct and of doctrine. But Paul issued the mandate clearly and precisely; it is **the church of God** which happens to be located in **Corinth.** As such it is a member of the whole body. Churches

[6]Hermann Cremer, *Biblico-Theological Lexicon of New Testament Greek,* trans. William Urwick (Edinburgh: T. & T. Clark, 1962 [reprint]), p. 334.
[7]*Ibid.*

may differ in creed, policy, or conduct and yet belong to the body of Christ. But no group can isolate itself from the community of the redeemed and remain part of the Church of God.

b. *The Church is sanctified—separated* (1:2). When Paul refers to the Corinthians as **them that are sanctified in Christ Jesus,** he indicates a unique state of dedication and separation rather than a state of self-righteous isolation. As it is used in the context of this greeting, "the term 'sanctified' signifies set apart to God, and is a designation applied to all believers."[8] The Corinthians, like all followers of Christ, were God's called-out people. They were called to dedication to God and to separation from sin. As believers they had received the grace of regeneration, or initial sanctification. As in any mixed group of Christian people, some of them no doubt had experienced entire sanctification. As one writer states it: "Here is the gospel for a city with all its corruption and licentiousness, vice and ignorance—a gospel that is completely adequate for every situation when it is intelligently preached and intelligently understood."[9]

c. *The Christian vocation* (1:2). The Christian vocation is holiness. Paul calls the Corinthians **saints.** This is a rather generous use of the word in the light of the low spiritual state of these people. However, **saints** here is a general term meaning "members of this church." Yet it means more than nominal membership in the Christian community. When Paul calls the Christian a saint (*hagios*), he means that this man has a specific calling which makes him different because he belongs to God. Barclay writes: "And that difference is not to be marked by the withdrawal from ordinary life and activity, but by showing in ordinary life a difference of quality and character which will mark him out as the man of God."[10] Adam Clarke interprets the words **called to be saints** as follows: "*Constituted saints,* or *invited* to become such; this was the design of the Gospel, for Jesus Christ came to save men from their sins."[11] These church people were

---

[8]W. E. Vine, *I Corinthians* (Grand Rapids: Zondervan Publishing House, 1961), p. 12.

[9]Alan Redpath, *The Royal Route to Heaven* (Westwood, N.J.: Fleming H. Revell Co., 1966), p. 16.

[10]*The Letters to the Corinthians* (Philadelphia: Westminster Press, 1954), pp. 11-12.

[11]*The New Testament of Our Lord and Saviour Jesus Christ* (Methodist Book Concern, n.d.), II, 190.

dedicated to God, were separated to God, and were to indicate their dedication by a sense of vocation climaxing in holiness. As Vine put it, "The phrase 'called to be saints,' literally, 'called saints' . . . does not simply assign the name to them; it signifies 'saints by calling.' "[12]

d. Christ is Lord of the Church (1:2). The entire idea of being sanctified and called as saints assumes the lordship of Jesus. **For all that in every place call upon the name of Jesus Christ our Lord** bow to His authority and leadership. The significant title "Lord Jesus Christ" is used four times in the first 10 verses of this opening chapter, and the title **Jesus Christ our Lord is** used twice (vv. 2, 9). The frequent reminder of the lordship of Christ was particularly meaningful to a church that was split into factions and which had strong tendencies to disregard the sovereign rule of Christ in their lives.

3. *Courteous Spiritual Concern* (1:3)

Paul's approach to a carnal and fractious church was expressed in courteous spiritual concern. He did not evade issues nor did he bypass personal convictions. But he dealt with basic issues and expressed strong convictions in a spirit of courtesy. Paul's method of saying "hello" was to say: **Grace . . . unto you, and peace.**

a. The meaning of grace. **Grace** is defined as the free, undeserved favor, or mercy of God. In its original usage, it refers to something which is "conferred freely, with no expectation of return, and finding its only motive in the bounty and free-heartedness of the giver."[13] But grace is much more than mere favor or goodwill. Grace comes, as Paul declares, **from God our Father** through **the Lord Jesus Christ.** God is the Spring or Source, while Jesus Christ is the Channel or Medium through which it comes. Grace is thus God's holiness and purity extended to man. It is God's willingness to share himself with an undeserving sinner.

b. The presence of peace. The ancient Hebrew greeting was, *Shalom,* **Peace.** But Paul found personal peace only through **the Lord Jesus Christ.** Peace, in the Pauline sense, does not suggest

[12]*Op. cit.,* p. 12.

[13]Richard C. Trench, *Synonyms of the New Testament* (Grand Rapids: Wm. B. Eerdmans Publishing Co., 1963 [reprint of ninth ed.]), p. 168.

laziness, inactivity, or freedom from adverse conditions. It implies inner security without friction. It also means inner peace and outer poise, a sense of harmony and well-being because guilt is gone and the power of sin is broken. Peace is a sense of meaning and purpose which comes from centering one's life on doing God's will.

B. PERSONAL APPRECIATION, 1:4-5

Paul was big-spirited. Apparently without any personal family ties and with no material possessions, his source of satisfaction was in his converts. Thus he could write: **I thank my God always on your behalf, for the grace of God which is given you by Jesus Christ** (4). Even though the people in the church at Corinth were beset by an amazing catalogue of carnal qualities, yet the comparison of their new life in Christ to their old life in corrupt heathenism was a source of satisfaction to Paul. He knew full well the glory and the power, the truly revolutionary nature of redeeming grace. Yet Paul was also realistic enough in his thinking to realize that there was no such thing as "instant sainthood." While he did not condone the sins and the faults, the lack of spiritual growth in the church, he expressed his appreciation for the degree of spiritual progress they had made. Further, he may have desired to state his gratitude in order to temper the severity of his later discussions of their problems.

Paul also appreciated the spiritual enrichment and the knowledge of the Corinthians. He writes: **That in every thing ye are enriched by him, in all utterance, and in all knowledge** (5). Bishop Lightfoot interprets this enrichment as follows: "Not only were the Corinthians rich in the knowledge of the truths of the Gospel, but they were also gifted with the power of enunciating them effectively."[14] The reference suggests that the Corinthians were once utterly destitute spiritually, but now had come into great spiritual wealth. From the context it is clear that Paul had in mind primarily the gift of grace, which is true wealth.

C. DIVINE CONFIRMATION, 1:6-9

Paul's preaching had promised a revolutionary new way of life. This promise was fulfilled with abundant spiritual gifts and power.

---

[14]*Notes on the Epistles of St. Paul* (Grand Rapids: Zondervan Publishing House, 1957 [reprint]), p. 147.

1. *Spiritual Expectation Fulfilled* (1: 6)

The testimony of Christ was the proclamation that as the Son of God He would grant peace, joy, and pardon. Now this testimony was verified and established by their acceptance of the gospel. The verb confirmed (*bebaioo*) is a technical term meaning "guaranteeing the delivery of something of which the earnest had already been paid."[15] Thus when the Corinthians accepted Paul's gospel of Christ, they received a down payment of spiritual wealth which was delivered as promised. When God guarantees delivery, the goods are already in transit.

2. *Abundant Spiritual Gifts* (1: 7)

In the expression so that ye come behind in no gift, the verb come behind means to be deficient in, fall short, to be lacking. Stated in positive terms, the Corinthians had an abundance of spiritual gifts, all that was necessary to salvation. The word gift (*charisma*) is used only by Paul in the NT (except I Pet. 4:10). Paul used the word in two ways. Generally, the word means "the effect of God's gracious dealings, the positive blessing bestowed upon sinners through grace."[16] In this general sense it includes all spiritual graces and all spiritual endowments. It is used by Paul also in a special way to refer to particular spiritual endowments which would be used in the ministry of the gospel of Jesus Christ. Such gifts are discussed toward the end of this letter, in cc. 12—14.

In this first chapter Paul used the word gift in its more general sense. Regarding the use of the word here Bishop Lightfoot writes: "That it is here used in this wider sense, is clear from the context, which shows that St. Paul is dwelling especially on moral gifts, as for instance on holiness of life."[17] God had enriched their lives so that they lacked nothing necessary to salvation.

3. *Spiritual Expectation* (1: 7)

Paul, with the Corinthians, was waiting for the coming of our Lord Jesus Christ. The apostle combined present spiritual vitality with future spiritual anticipation. He *looked out* at life

---

[15]James Hope Moulton and George Milligan, *The Vocabulary of the Greek Testament* (London: Hodder and Stoughton, 1930), p. 108.

[16]Cremer, *op. cit.*, p. 577.   [17]*Op. cit.*, p. 149.

realistically, knowing the sins of man and proclaiming the redeeming grace of God. He also *looked up* expectantly, knowing that the second coming of Christ was the ultimate answer of grace to a world enmeshed hopelessly in sin. The verb translated **waiting for** carries the idea of strong, earnest expectation, and alert watching. The word **coming** (revelation, *apocalypsis*) means literally an uncovering, an unveiling. "Here it refers to the return of the Lord to receive His saints to Himself at His Parousia. . . . It is used of His coming with His saints and angels to dispense the judgments of God. . . ."[18] Paul made the gospel relevant to the current needs of man. But he, along with other NT writers, always made the expectation of the return of the Lord Jesus Christ a spur to spiritual pursuits and a means of spiritual enrichment and of spiritual power (cf. II Pet. 3:11-12; I John 3:2-3).

4. *Spiritual Strengthening* (1:8)

Personal redemption is a matter of crisis and process. Thus Paul declares that the Christ who initially transformed them would continue to **confirm** (establish and strengthen) them. The purpose of this process of nourishment and strengthening was to present the Christian **blameless in the day** (at the coming) **of our Lord Jesus Christ.** Thus the grace of God produces a life that will be irreproachable, or unimpeachable, when the individual stands before Christ. This blameless life is the life of holiness.

5. *God's Faithfulness* (1:9)

Man tends toward doubt, and needs to be reminded of God's faithfulness. Here Paul declares, **God is faithful, by whom ye were called unto the fellowship of his Son Jesus Christ our Lord.** Such passages as Psalms 89, where God's faithfulness is mentioned seven times, and Isa. 11:5; Heb. 10:23; and I John 1:9 testify to this truth. God has called man into a **fellowship** (*koinonia*). Such fellowship includes partnership, common sharing, and communion of spirit.

The prologue to this letter might be called the gospel in miniature. In it Paul presents the basic aspects of all that is involved in man's redemptive relationship to God through Christ.

---

[18]Vine, *op. cit.*, p. 15.

Section **II** The New Faith and
Some Old Problems

I Corinthians 1:10—4:21

The Corinthians had accepted the gospel as a new and revolutionary way of life. Yet many problems persisted in the church. In the Christian life some problems, such as actual sins and trans—gressions, are solved in the new birth (I John 3:8-9). Other problems, such as carnal affections and attitudes, are solved by the cleansing power of the Holy Spirit in the crisis of entire sanctification (I Cor. 3:3; II Cor. 7:1; Eph. 5:25-26). Other problems not related to sin or to the carnal mind are solved by spiritual maturity, growth in grace, and enlarged understanding. The problems of the church at Corinth were due primarily to the carnal mind, although some, such as the problem of marriage and celibacy, may have been due to lack of understanding.

One of the most glaring problems at Corinth was that of spiritual divisions. During Paul's absence the church had developed into clashing cliques and egotistical factions that threatened to tear their fellowship to pieces. The problem was an old one. Paul attempted to show the unchristian nature of a quarreling, divided, critical group of professed believers. He claimed that the new experience in Jesus Christ could solve this ancient problem. In pleading for Christian unity Paul presented several contrasts, or comparisons, between the Spirit-directed life in Christ and the selfish, carnally motivated lives of the Corinthians.

A. INDIVIDUAL PREFERENCE VERSUS DIVINE UNITY, 1:10-17

One of the problems at Corinth was the insistence on personal liberty, even license, rather than unity in Christ. The apostle calls for unity in the church.

1. *Exhortation to Unity* (1:10)

Paul pleads in strong and persuasive words **that ye all speak the same thing.** This is an expression from classical writing used of political communities which are free from tensions, or of different states which conduct cordial diplomatic and commercial relationships.

The word for **divisions** (*schismata*) means "rift," "cleft," or "division." The term is used by Mark (2:21) and by Matthew (9:16) to describe a tear in an old garment. John uses the word (7:43) to describe the division of opinion among the people in regard to Jesus. Paul uses the same word in reference to the snobbish groups which made the observance of the Lord's Supper a mockery (11:18). In the expression **that ye be perfectly joined together** Paul uses a medical term. Barclay explains it as "a medical word which is used of knitting together bones that have been fractured, or joining together a joint that has been dislocated."[1] Paul desires that they come to a right understanding and a unity of opinion, or judgment.

2. *Report of Dissension* (1:11)

Paul had received a report from the household **of Chloe, that there are contentions among you.** Chloe is not known except by the reference at this point. The fact that Paul refers to her serves three purposes. It indicates that these reports were no idle rumors or inconsequential buzzing on the "ecclesiastical grapevine." It also suggests that Chloe was a woman of character and good standing. Further, the reference suggests that the church had elevated women to a place of dignity and respect.

The word Paul uses for **contentions** means bitter quarreling. The Greek (*eris*) is "a term employed by Homer to mean battle-strife in the *Iliad* and 'contention' or 'rivalry' in the *Odyssey*."[2] An even stronger meaning of this word is given in the expression "when hate takes hold of me."[3] The divisions at Corinth were not slight differences of opinions. They were deep-seated quarrels that threatened the existence of the church.

3. *The Divisions in the Church* (1:12)

The divisions in the church were the result of a carnal attachment to human leaders. There was no disagreement among these leaders themselves. But disagreement arose when certain people insisted on the authority of one leader over another. Different ones were saying: **I am of Paul; and I of Apollos; and I of Cephas; and I of Christ.** Thus there appeared to be a fourfold division.

[1]*Op. cit.*, p. 15.   [2]Baird, *op. cit.*, p. 30.
[3]Moulton and Milligan, *op. cit.*, p. 254.

a. *Party of Paul.* The party of Paul probably was a combination of simple and earnest believers and the "old guard," made up of the founding fathers, or charter members. Their concern may have been basically spiritual. But the fact that they exhibited the factious spirit also indicated that they may have desired to use their seniority to exert priorities on the leadership of the church. Or they may have tended to make the freedom in Christ which Paul preached an excuse for unwarranted license. At any rate, Paul was not flattered by their false loyalty to him.

b. *Party of Apollos.* According to Acts 18:24, Apollos was an eloquent man, well-versed in Scripture. With the extreme emphasis on verbal expression in Corinth, it was natural that some would have preferred the eloquent Apollos to the less impressive Paul (II Cor. 10:10). Apollos was an Alexandrian, and may have had a background of intellectual excitement, which, added to his oratorical ability, would have made him a magnetic preacher.

c. *Party of Cephas.* Those who followed the leadership of Peter were either Jewish converts who insisted that Christians should observe the Jewish law or they were Gentile converts who were legalistic in their approach to Christian living.

d. *Party of Christ.* While some scholars debate the matter, it seems valid to accept a fourth party called the "Christ party." William Baird states three possible descriptions of this division. (1) The Christ party was a Judaizing faction made up of converts of James, the brother of the Lord; (2) The Christ party was a libertine group, consisting of people who wanted complete ethical and religious freedom, with no apostolic authority exerted over them; (3) The Christ party was a faction of Gnostics, who loved to parade their knowledge and demanded liberty in thought and act.[4]

4. One Christ and One Baptism (1:13-17)

Paul regarded the Church as the body of Christ (I Cor. 12:12-27). As such the body was united and should not be torn limb from limb by the carnal quarreling of the church. To drive home his point the apostle asked several purely rhetorical questions that could be answered only in the negative.

[4]*Op. cit.,* pp. 32-33.

a. **Is Christ divided?** (13) Is the work of Christ as Saviour and Lord parceled out "between several individuals, so that one possesses one piece of it, another, another?"[5] To profess the name of Christ in the midst of disagreements, quarrels, and divisions is in reality to tear Christ to pieces. Divisions actually deny the lordship of Christ. As John Calvin states it: "For He reigns in our midst, only when He is the means of binding us together in an inviolable union."[6]

b. The first question exalted Christ. In his second question Paul "implies his own comparative insignificance,"[7] **Was Paul crucified for you?** Since no human personality could achieve man's redemption, it was useless to quarrel about human leadership. Only the death of Christ could accomplish man's personal salvation. In view of Christ's crucifixion, all of man's quarreling ought to cease.

c. A third question climaxed the process, **Or were ye baptized in the name of Paul?** " 'Into the name' implies entrance into fellowship and allegiance, such as exists between the Redeemer and the redeemed."[8] The Corinthians had been baptized as *Christians,* not as followers of any human leader.

d. Paul himself had **baptized** only a few persons, 14-17. He was not reflecting on the act of baptism, nor did he imply that he had avoided baptizing freely because he had foreseen what would happen at Corinth. Nevertheless, he was glad that he had not made it a rule to baptize and thus had avoided the dangers of having his converts identify themselves with him. He was commissioned to preach, and the gospel of faith and grace that he proclaimed was as free from outer ritual and ceremony as it was devoid of legal observances.

With the centrality of the Cross in mind Paul could say: **For Christ sent me not to baptize, but to preach the gospel: not with wisdom of words, lest the cross of Christ should be made of none effect** (17). He preached the gospel without any strange oratorical flourishes and with no pretense to intellectual display.

[5]F. Godet, *Commentary on the First Epistle of St. Paul to the Corinthians* (Grand Rapids: Zondervan Publishing House, 1957), I, 80.

[6]*The First Epistle of Paul the Apostle to the Corinthians*, trans. J. W. Frazer ("Calvin's Commentaries"; Grand Rapids: Wm. B. Eerdmans Publishing Co., 1960), p. 28.

[7]Vine, *op. cit.,* p. 19.   [8]Robertson and Plummer, *op. cit.,* p. 13.

His approach was a straightforward declaration of the cross of
Christ. He knew that any attempt to evangelize by worldly wisdom would empty the gospel of meaning until it would "dwindle
to nothing, vanish under the weight of rhetorical ornament and
dialectic subtlety."[9] For Paul **the cross** (*stauros*) described
the death of Christ in the deepest possible humiliation. The cross
was a stake or crossbeam to which condemned slaves or the most
depraved and despised criminals were nailed. The apostle was
well aware that a gospel based on such extreme humiliation was
the absolute opposite of human wisdom. Yet he knew also that
to preach any other message made the gospel void and inoperative.

B. HUMAN WISDOM VERSUS DIVINE POWER, 1:18-31

In the preceding paragraph (10-17) Paul had condemned the
divisions in the church which had risen due to a false concept of
loyalty to human leaders. He had stressed the cardinal fact that
the cross of Christ made unity the normal result of true Christian
fellowship. Now, by a casual reference to the nature of preaching,
he passes to a different emphasis. He leaves temporarily the problem of divisions in the church and begins a discussion on the unchristian stress on human eloquence and wisdom. The idea of
divisions is picked up again in the third chapter.

1. *Preaching—Foolishness to Unbelievers* (1:18-23)

Without any equivocation Paul declares a basic principle of
the redeeming gospel of Christ: **For the preaching of the cross
is to them that perish foolishness; but unto us which are saved
it is the power of God** (18). At first glance it appears that Paul
is advocating a rigid anti-intellectualism. But he was not placing a premium on ignorance. He did not intend "to ground religious knowledge in absurdity nor to reduce theological learning
to a bare minimum."[10] In reality, Paul was attempting to show
that true wisdom, the wisdom of God, is revealed in and through
the cross of Christ. For "to know nothing but Christ and him
crucified is to know everything significant."[11]

To those who are even now in the process of perishing, **the
preaching of the cross** is **foolishness**. The word **foolishness**
(*moria*) refers to anything which is irrational, stupid, or worth-

[9]Lightfoot, *op. cit.*, p. 157.   [10]Baird, *op. cit.*, p. 45.
[11]*Ibid.*

less. On the other hand, to those who believe and accept it, **the preaching of the cross** becomes **the power** (*dynamis*) **of God.** Because it is **power,** "the word of the cross is, after all, the truest wisdom."[12] To illustrate his claim that God's wisdom is actually a power that operates in human affairs, Paul uses several illustrations from history and from contemporary life.

a. The first illustration of God's power as contrasted to human wisdom is taken from a reference in Isa. 29:14: **I will destroy the wisdom of the wise, and will bring to nothing the understanding of the prudent** (19). The allusion in Isaiah is to a political alliance with Egypt which was considered a masterpiece of human wisdom and diplomacy. But in God's sight it was rebellion. The invasion of Sennacherib reduced Judah to poverty and helplessness. In this fashion God showed that "the deliverance granted by Jehovah to His people would be His work, not that of the able politicians who directed the affairs of the kingdom."[13] Not only in the past, but in the future God will continue to set aside the proud claims of man who seeks to shape his destiny apart from divine power.

b. A second illustration of the contradiction between divine power and human wisdom is taken from Isa. 33:18. Paul asks the penetrating question: **Where is the wise? where is the scribe? where is the disputer of this world?** (20) The general reference is to the Assyrian conquerors who came with military power to overwhelm the Jews and to carry off the rewards of conquest. The **wise** probably refers to the proud, self-styled intellectual—the Greek sophist—who could argue any point with apparent sincerity. The **scribe** would be the stubborn interpreter of Jewish law. The **disputer** is a term which includes both the self-confident philosopher and the self-satisfied Jew who relied upon human wisdom for salvation.

God does not look with indifference upon the proud pretensions of man: **Hath not God made foolish the wisdom of this world?** (20) He makes all of man's vaunted wisdom look foolish. Bishop Lightfoot writes that God renders man's wisdom vain in two ways: "(1) by exhibiting its intrinsic worthlessness and corrupt results, and (2) by the power of the Cross set in opposition to it and triumphing over it."[14]

---

[12]Findlay, *op. cit.,* p. 767.   [13]Godet, *op. cit.,* p. 92.
[14]*Op. cit.,* p. 160.

c. A third illustration of the failure of human wisdom is a sweeping indictment of all mankind: **For after that in the wisdom of God the world by wisdom knew not God, it pleased God by the foolishness of preaching to save them that believe (21).** Earlier forms of revelation had appealed to man through reason and understanding. Concerning the failure of human reason in submitting to God, Godet writes: "Man not having recognized God . . . by the healthy use of his understanding, God manifests Himself to him in another revelation which has the appearance of folly."[15] Man's blighted reason is futile as a means of a personal relationship to God. Thus it pleased God to resolve that problem, by means of the apparent **foolishness of preaching** (Gk. *keryma,* "the message") **to save** those that accept and **believe.**

d. A fourth contrast of divine power and human wisdom used by Paul was the contemporary attitude of the Jews and the Greeks (22-23). **The Jews** demanded practical signs and evidences in ceremonial observances and in legal specifications. **The Greeks** insisted upon rational explanations and sought for speculative systems. In both instances the Jews and the Greeks were in fact demanding that God reveal himself in harmony with their particular ideas.

But instead of reducing God to man's concept, Paul said: **We preach Christ crucified, unto the Jews a stumblingblock, and unto the Greeks foolishness (23).** The essence of the gospel is the heralding of a message from God, not the accommodation of God to man's wisdom. The message is that of the crucified Christ. The verb **crucified** is a present particple. The significance of this form is stated by Morris: "Not only was Christ once crucified, but He continues in the character of the crucified one. The crucifixion is permanent in its efficacy and its effects."[16]

The nationalistic ideas of the Jews, who sought for a political leader, would not accept a crucified Messiah. Thus Christ became a **stumblingblock,** an occasion of insult, and a spiritual deathtrap. The Greeks sought for a universe in which harmony, rationality, and beauty were the ruling forces. So the Cross with its apparent ugliness, folly, and tragedy was unmitigated foolishness.

2. *Preaching—God's Power to Believers* (1:24-25)

To those who know by personal experience the call of God there is one grand, overarching fact about Christ—He is both

---

[15]*Op. cit.,* p. 99.   [16]*Op. cit.,* p. 46.

the wisdom and the power . . . of God. From the order of the wording, **Christ the power of God, and the wisdom of God** (24), it is apparent that one must experience God's redeeming power in salvation from sin before he realizes the wisdom of God. Jesus Christ is God's **power** because He saves from sin. He is God's **wisdom** because in Him God's nature, purposes, and designs are revealed to man. Christ hanging on the Cross may appear to be a scandal, an embarrassment, an utter foolishness. But this climactic act of God's love, grace, and mercy, although it appears to be weak, is more powerful than any wisdom or force that man can produce.

In 1:1-25 there is the picture of "A Dynamic Church in a Secular World." (1) Challenged by a holy calling, 1-2; (2) Unified by a common purpose, 10; (3) Inspired by a saving message, 22-25.

3. Preaching—God's Method of Deliverance (1:26-31)

To reinforce his assertion that human wisdom stands in opposition to divine power, Paul asks that the people make a roll call of their group. If they do this, they will discover that most of them have come from the lower class of society, for **not many wise men after the flesh, not many mighty, not many noble, are called** (26). This does not mean that God does not call all men to repentance and to redemption. All are called, and occasionally a person of high standing will respond.

As Barclay points out, even in NT times people from the highest ranks of society became Christians.[17]

> There was Dionysius at Athens (Acts 17:34); Sergius Paulus, the proconsul of Crete (Acts 13:6-12); the noble ladies at Thessalonica and Berea (Acts 17:4, 12); Erastus, the chamberlain, probably of Corinth (Romans 16:23). In the time of Nero, Pomponia Graecina, the wife of Plautius, the conqueror of Britain, was martyred for her Christianity. . . . Flavius Clemens, the cousin of the Emperor himself, was martyred as a Christian. Towards the end of the second century Pliny, the governor of Bithynia, wrote to Trajan the Roman Emperor, saying that the Christians came from every rank in society.[18]

And in A.D. 312, King Constantine formally accepted Christianity as his religion.

[17]*Op. cit.,* p. 23.   [18]*Ibid.*

But such people as those were the exception. The great mass of Christians was composed of slaves, freedmen, simple and humble folk. Barclay quotes from the writings of Celsus, who, about A.D. 178, described the Christians as follows: "We see them in their own houses, wool dressers, cobblers and fullers, the most uneducated and vulgar [common] persons."[19] Thus not many **wise men**, or lovers of human wisdom and understanding, were believers; nor did the **mighty**, the leading and outstanding people, accept Christ; neither did the **nobles**, or those of royal rank or noble birth, submit to Christ, except in rare instances.

Paul emphasizes the low social status of most converts three times in 27 and 28—**the foolish things of the world . . . the weak things of the world . . . the base things of the world.** Adam Clarke suggests that **foolish things** refer to illiterate men who confounded the greatest of Greek philosophers; **weak things** to those without secular power or authority; and **base things** to those "who were considered base and despicable in the eyes of the Jews, who counted them as no better than dogs."[20]

Thus the very nature of the converts indicated **that no flesh should glory in his presence** (29). The wise, the powerful, the well-born may boast about their social distinctions. In contrast, the Christians may glory in Christ because in Him they have experienced true wisdom, riches, and power. They may be counted as nonentities, but they represent God's highest wisdom and power. Because they are actually *in Christ* they participate in all that God is.

Thus **Christ** is the Christian's **wisdom, and righteousness, and sanctification,**[21] **and redemption** (30). Christ became everything to the Christian because of His incarnation, death, and resurrection. Christ is **wisdom** in that He reveals and imparts the counsel, purpose, and effects of God's redemptive work. One commentator summarized the totality of the meaning of Christ in these words: "What we are and have we are and have received from God through Christ. United to Christ we are righteous and holy, since all those blessings are founded in His work. . . . *Redemption*, often used of the liberation of slaves through .he payment of a ransom, indicates the way Christ delivers us

---

[19]*Ibid.*, p. 24.   [20]*Op. cit.*, II, 196.

[21]"Procuring for and working in us, not only an external and relative *holiness* . . . but . . . true and eternal *holiness*, Eph. iv. 24, wrought in us by the Holy Spirit" (*ibid.*).

... by His sacrifice, His death on the cross. In surrendering Himself He brings us knowledge, righteousness and holiness."[22]

The grand Object of all preaching is Jesus Christ. He should be the central Figure in all of our worship. Thus there can be no reason to be proud or conceited about any human talents or abilities. What had grieved the apostle most was the divisions caused by extolling human names alongside the name of Christ. The knowledge that "we are indebted to the Lord for every good thing should keep us from glorying in self or anyone else."[23] **He that glorieth, let him glory in the Lord (31).**

C. PERSONAL KNOWLEDGE VERSUS DIVINE REVELATION, 2:1-16

Paul had made a choice in his method of preaching. No doubt his mind was as active and alert as were his physical labors. He was a man of broad scholarship and wide learning. But somewhere along the line of his ministerial apprenticeship he had made a choice between framing the gospel message in human, personal wisdom or stating it according to divine revelation. Because of this deliberate choice to proclaim the gospel as a divine revelation, Paul's preaching had a number of significant characteristics.

1. *His Preaching Was Simple* (2:1)

When Paul preached, he **came not with excellency of speech or of wisdom,** but simply proclaimed the message given to him. Simplicity does not mean shallowness. Nor does it indicate an absence of mental ability or of arduous study and careful preparation. Simplicity means stating truth in clear, direct, and understandable language. Paul avoided a display of distracting oratorical tricks. His preaching was devoid of subtle philosophical suggestions. There was no theological double-talk and nothing mysterious or hidden. God had given him a message and he delivered **the testimony of God.**

2. *His Preaching Was Christ-centered* (2:2)

Paul deliberately excluded from his message everything except the revelation of the atoning work of Christ. In his preaching "he intentionally set aside the different elements of

---

[22]F. W. Grosheide, *Commentary on the First Epistle to the Corinthians* (Grand Rapids: Wm. B. Eerdmans, 1935), p. 54.

[23]Vine, *op. cit.,* p. 32.

human knowledge by which he might have been tempted to prop up the preaching of salvation."[24]

The apostle fulfilled the ideal of preaching suggested by Morris: "Preaching the gospel is not delivering edifying discourses, beautifully put together. It is bearing witness to what God has done in Christ for man's salvation."[25] When he preached **Jesus Christ, and him crucified** Paul selected the one point that was the most criticized by the Jews and Greeks.

3. *Concern, Power, and Purpose* (2:3-5)

Paul makes a rather puzzling statement regarding his feelings when he first came to Corinth. He says, **And I was with you in weakness, and in fear, and in much trembling** (3). Paul did not have a craven fear of physical violence or an overly sensitive attitude toward popular opinion. Rather, he came to Corinth with a sense of utmost concern because of the gigantic task of preaching the gospel in a completely corrupt city. Coupled with the overwhelming task of evangelizing Corinth there may have been an awareness of the personal physical ailment to which he refers in II Cor. 12:7 or he may have been somewhat apprehensive about his unimpressive physical appearance (II Cor. 2:10). At any rate, Paul was neither reluctant to come to Corinth nor was he ashamed of the gospel. But he was mightily concerned about the seriousness of his mission. He had a "trembling anxiety to perform a duty."[26]

Paul's preaching was powerful. It **was not with enticing words of man's wisdom, but in demonstration of the Spirit and of power** (4). His use of words, his arrangement of ideas, and his content were not designed to gain mere assent or applause. He knew the reputation of Corinth, where the "spurious art of persuading without instructing"[27] was held in such high repute. The word **demonstration** (*apodeixis*) is used only here in the NT. Literally, a demonstration is a "showing forth" or "a proof."[28] As Paul uses the term, "it has the force of a proof, not an exhibition, but that which carries conviction."[29] In reality it is God's "power to save man and give a new direction to his life."[30] Paul

[24]Godet, *op. cit.*, pp. 125-26.   [25]*Op. cit.*, p. 51.
[26]Barclay, *op. cit.*, p. 27.   [27]Findlay, *op. cit.*, p. 776.
[28]Thayer, *op. cit.*, p. 60.   [29]Vine, *op. cit.*, p. 35.
[30]Robertson and Plummer, *op. cit.*, p. 33.

wanted results—converts. He knew that a spiritual work must be done by spiritual means. So he simply preached the gospel.

The purpose of Paul's preaching was to establish the converts in faith, to ground them in divine power. An experience based only upon moving speeches or clever arguments may be removed by the same kind of message from another person. But he who accepts the gospel of the cross of Christ is established in divine love and power by the Holy Spirit.

4. *Human Knowledge Versus Divine Revelation* (2:6-9)

Paul was certain that he spoke the truth when he preached the gospel. He consistently showed the practical benefits of divine wisdom and the emptiness of human wisdom. For him the **wisdom** (understanding) that came from God was knowable only by personal experience. In this sense wisdom is more than knowledge, insight, or prudence regarding the cross of Christ.

Paul referred to speaking **wisdom among them that are perfect (6)**. Most writers translate the word **perfect** in this statement to indicate mature Christians. Trench says: "This image of full, completed growth, as contrasted with infancy and childhood, underlies the ethical use of *teleioi* [**perfect**] by St. Paul."[31] Godet makes a sharp distinction between the **perfect** man and the believer in general when he writes: "The word *perfect* has therefore a meaning much narrower than *believer*. It denotes the state of the *mature man*, in opposition to the infant."[32]

Paul had no faith in man's wisdom in relation to redemption. So the gospel message was **not the wisdom of this world, nor of the princes (rulers) of this world, that come to nought.** The wisdom of God reveals His purposes and plan in redemption, while the wisdom of human leaders inevitably becomes ineffective and inoperative. Man's knowledge cannot bring about the redemption of the race, nor can it achieve peace, prosperity, and permanent security for us.

When Paul referred to **the wisdom of God in a mystery (7)**, he was not referring to a puzzle or to an event which man finds difficult to solve. In Paul's vocabulary God's **wisdom** was a **mystery** (*mysterion*) in the sense that human reason was unable to penetrate or to discover it. Paul also used the term **mystery** in the sense of something hidden from the person not initiated into

[31]*Op. cit.,* p. 75.   [32]*Op. cit.,* p. 132.

the group. Once initiation has taken place, all the things formerly unknown are now crystal-clear. Thus **the wisdom of God** is a **hidden wisdom,** meaning that men who reject Christ cannot understand it.

Moreover, God's wisdom was **ordained before the world.** He had marked out beforehand the method of man's redemption. It was not a hasty postscript added because of unexpected circumstances. This divine wisdom was something which **none of the princes of this world knew** (8). Despite their eminence as leaders in society, the men of authority and honor did not discern the true nature of redemption.

If the leaders had been aware of who Christ really was, **they would not have crucified** Him (8). **Lord of glory** is a unique and wonderful title. It suggests both the essential nature of Jesus Christ and the environment He creates. At this point Paul presents a sharp contrast between the humiliation of the Cross and the "intrinsic majesty and glory of the Crucified."[33] This exalted title shows Paul's understanding of the centrality of Christ in man's redemption.

Not only do believers find true wisdom and personal spiritual power in Christ. The best is yet to be. For no human powers of sense or of imagination are able to conceive of the **things which God hath prepared for them that love him** (9). The word **love** (*agapao*) refers not only to love expressed in affection but love shown in unselfish service, love in harmony with the nature of Christ.

5. *Spiritual Man Versus the Natural Man* (2:10-16)

One of the unique aspects of the Christian gospel is its simple yet sharp classification of men as spiritual and natural. The natural man lives according to human reason or human impulses. The spiritual man is given life by the Holy Spirit and is directed by the Holy Spirit.

a. The spiritual man (2:10-13). The only person who can tell us the truth about God is the Holy Spirit. Regarding spiritual facts Paul writes: **But God hath revealed them unto us by his Spirit** (10). The statement, **The Spirit searcheth all things,** does not mean that He investigates or inquires into all things. The phrase means that the Holy Spirit possesses "complete and accu-

[33]Vine, *op. cit.*, p. 39.

rate knowledge."[34] The revelation of God is made by the Holy
Spirit. "The *deep things of God* designate God's essence, then
His attributes, volitions, and plans."[35] Vine states that they are
"the counsels and purposes of God, as well as all that pertains to
His nature and attributes."[36]

Paul presents two kinds of truth and two kinds of people.
There is spiritual truth which comes through the Holy Spirit,
and is understood by spiritual people. Then there is natural wisdom which is opposed to spiritual truth. Spiritual men accept
and understand spiritual truth, which the natural man does not.
**Now we have received, not the spirit of the world, but the spirit
which is of God** (12). This **spirit of the world** is man in his
natural state; it is the principle which pervades mankind in its
alienation from God. In contrast to the spirit of the world is **the
spirit which is of God**; that is, the Holy Spirit, who is given by
God to believers,[37] or "the spirit of true faith and trust toward
God, the spirit of humility and love."[38] The Spirit of God is given
to man, that he might understand and experience the blessings
of salvation.

The person who has received the Spirit of God does two
things. First, he teaches the things God has revealed to him, **not
in the words which man's wisdom teacheth, but which the Holy
Ghost teacheth** (13). As God has revealed himself to man, He
now enables man to present the revealed truth to other men.
Thus divine truth does not depend upon human contrivance in its
presentation. Moreover, God gives words as well as ideas. Godet
interprets the statement as a contrast between divine revelation
and human inspiration when he writes: "By revelation God communicates Himself to man; inspiration bears on the relation of
man to man."[39] The Holy Spirit enables all who minister the
gospel to do so effectively.

The spiritual man also makes a practice of **comparing spiritual things with spiritual.** Commentators have given two meanings to this phrase: (1) joining or combining spiritual things
(ideas, revelations) with spiritual words; (2) interpreting, adapt-

---

[34]T. T. Shore, "First Epistle to the Corinthians" (*Commentary on the
Whole Bible*, ed. C. J. Ellicott; Grand Rapids: Zondervan Publishing House,
n.d.), VII, 294.

[35]Godet, *op. cit.*, p. 148.   [36]*Op. cit.*, p. 40.

[37]Morris, *op. cit.*, p. 58; Vine, *op. cit.*, p. 40.

[38]Lenski, *op. cit.*, p. 109.   [39]*Op. cit.*, p. 153.

ing, or applying with discernment spiritual teachings to spiritual men. In either case, Paul wants to make the point that human learning and human salvation are not sufficient to present the gospel. Salvation truth is a revealed message which is taught under the direction of the Spirit.

Verses 1-13 suggest "How to Have Spiritual Victory in Difficult Times." (1) Be faithful in witnessing, 1-3; (2) Rely on the Spirit, 4-5; (3) Be sure that you speak for God, 6-13.

b. *The natural man* (2:14). In contrast to the spiritual man is **the natural man.** The word for **natural** (*psychikos*) always denotes "the life of the natural world and whatever belongs to it, in contrast to the supernatural world, which is characterized by *pneuma* (spirit)."[40] Thus the natural man is "one who possesses . . . simply the organ of purely human cognition, but has not yet the organ of religious cognition in the . . . spirit."[41] The natural man has only the common powers of man separated from God; as such he **receiveth not the things of the Spirit of God . . . neither can he know them, because they are spiritually discerned.**

Since the natural abilities of man "are altogether corrupt because of sin, every activity of his soul and mind will be darkened accordingly."[42] Spiritual things are foolishness to the natural man, for such a man lives as if the totality of life were in physical things; he lives only for this world. His values are based on the material and the physical, and he judges everything in the light of these terms. Such a man simply cannot understand spiritual things. He who thinks only in terms of sexual gratification cannot understand the meaning of chastity; a person dedicated to piling up material possessions cannot grasp the meaning of generosity; a man motivated by a lust for power cannot know the meaning of sacrificial service; an individual whose life is directed by worldly attitudes cannot appreciate inner, spiritual impulses. Because the natural man does not open his life to the Holy Spirit, he counts all spiritual life and values as foolishness.

c. *The mind of Christ* (2:15-16). Because of the presence of the Holy Spirit, **he that is spiritual judgeth all things, yet he himself is judged of no man** (15). This passage does not grant

[40]Arndt and Gingrich, *op. cit.,* p. 902.

[41]Marvin R. Vincent, *Word Studies in the New Testament* (Grand Rapids: Wm. B. Eerdmans Publishing Co., 1957), III, 198.

[42]Lenski, *op. cit.,* pp. 114-15.

a license for the Christian to sit in judgment on the activities of others. Nor does it mean that a spiritual man is immune to criticism or evaluation by the world. The passage means that the Christian has a spiritual capacity to sift, to investigate, to examine, to discern all things within the framework of the divine revelation of redemption. On the other hand, the natural man does not have an ability to subject the Christian way of life to examination and judgment, for he is completely unacquainted with the meaning of spiritual life.

In v. 16, Paul adapts a quotation from Isa. 40:13, which also appears in modified form in Rom. 11:34. God's ways and methods are beyond the understanding of man. It is thus futile for the natural man to attempt to understand the operation of divine redemption. What supreme egotism it would be for a man to attempt to instruct the Lord! In contrast, the indwelling Spirit reveals Christ and the power of God to redeem. The spiritual man, because he has **the mind of Christ,** does not evaluate things from the point of view of the world. The Christian sees things in the light of the revelation of God in Christ.

D. CARNAL CHILDREN VERSUS SPIRITUAL TEMPLES, 3:1-23

Paul delicately, yet relentlessly, presents the claims of the gospel to the Corinthians. In his contrast of the spiritual man and the natural man he had written in broad, general principles. Now he becomes direct and specific. For Paul knew well that finally the truth must be driven home and ultimately basic issues must be faced if Christianity is to be significant in man's life. So he presents the issue: Are the Corinthians to remain as carnal children or will they become spiritual temples?

1. *The Carnal Christian* (3:1-9)

Paul could not speak to these people as Spirit-filled believers. Thus a distinction is made within the ranks of the church. All believers receive the Holy Spirit when they have faith and believe (Eph. 1:13). Spiritual life is possible only in and through the Holy Spirit. But not all Christians are Spirit-filled and Spirit-directed. Some Christians are carnal. But even though he labels the Corinthians as being carnal, Paul is quick to remind them that they should be God's temples.

a. The reality of the carnal Christian (3:1-3a). Paul is about to level a most severe charge at the Corinthians. Yet he does so in a spirit of love, for he identifies himself with them by calling them **brethren,** or "fellow-Christians."[43] **And I, brethren, could not speak unto you as unto spiritual, but as unto carnal, even as unto babes in Christ** (1). Paul was not able to speak to these people as Spirit-filled because, even though converted, they were **carnal** (*sarkinos*). The word means "people still fleshly in their way of thinking and acting and not able, like a truly spiritual man, to judge aright all things."[44] Another scholar interprets this word **carnal** as "what a man cannot help being, but a state to be subordinated to the higher law of the Spirit, and enriched and elevated by it."[45]

The presence of original sin does not involve personal guilt. Only after the Christian is enlightened by the Holy Spirit does he bear guilt for the continued presence of this state of sin.

These Christians were **babes;** they were "still weak in grace, although eminent in gifts."[46] In the beginning they were called "saints"; they were **in Christ,** and were expected to develop and grow. Thus Paul, in his first ministry among them, could not teach or treat them as mature Christians.

Looking back on their early, infantile state of grace, Paul said: **I have fed you with milk, and not with meat** (2). Milk and meat are both nourishing foods. But normally milk is for the infant of delicate and undeveloped body, while meat is for the strong and mature person who needs strength to do rugged work. Paul was not referring to two sets of doctrine, one for weak Christians and another for mature Christians. His gospel was the same for all. But there are different methods and varying purposes in preaching. **Milk** thus is a symbol of the simple declaration of the gospel to sinners. It is missionary or evangelistic preaching. **Meat,** on the other hand, suggests the kind of preaching which shows the possibilities of grace, which lays out the obligations and duties of the Christian life, which presents the grand scope of personal redemption and the worldwide ministry of the Holy Spirit. Paul, in the beginning, dealt gently with the Corinthians, like a nursemaid with a baby. His reason for the

[43]Alexander Souter, *A Pocket Lexicon to the Greek New Testament* (Oxford: The Clarendon Press, 1960), p. 6.

[44]Lenski, *op. cit.,* p. 120.

[45]Robertson and Plummer, *op. cit.,* p. 52.

[46]John Wesley, *Explanatory Notes upon the New Testament* (London: Epworth Press, 1958 [reprint]), p. 592.

nursemaid approach was that **ye were not able to bear it.** The deficiency was in the people's ability to receive the full gospel menu, not in Paul's inability to present it.

But Paul was not willing to remain a nursemaid. He was a prophet. So he levels a severe charge at them in the words: **Neither yet now are ye able.** The Corinthians had not grown. Instead of developing in grace and humility, they were proud of their gifts and abilities; instead of expressing a strong spirit of unity, they were full of discord and dissension; instead of a sharp sensitivity to sin, they were tolerating the worst sins in their group; instead of glorifying Christ, they were bickering among themselves; they were misusing the Lord's Supper and denying the resurrection. While Paul did not attach serious blame to their initial state of weakness because of their natural carnal tendencies, he now makes a direct charge, telling them that the reason for their actions is the persistence of the carnal mind: **For ye are yet carnal** (3).

The word for **carnal** in this indictment is *sarkikos,* a severe term, "signifying sensual . . . under the control of the fleshly nature instead of being governed by the Spirit of God."[47] Another interpretation of the term is, "Under the dominion of sinful flesh."[48] They were carnal by act. This is the persistent threat to spiritual growth. In the beginning of the Christian life people are carnal because of "the hurtful persistence of the state of nature."[49] But the Christian life is not static. One either develops into a mature Christian through the elimination of carnal tendencies or he invariably settles down to a state of deliberate babyhood. Godet describes the difference between the normal carnal weakness of new Christians and the prolonged state of carnal living: "The matter in question is no more a simple state of weakness which continues in spite of regeneration, but a course of conduct which attacks the new life and tells actively against it."[50] The problem of the church at Corinth was the glaring reality of a carnal spirit. All their problems grew out of this.

b. *The characteristics of the carnal Christian* (3:3b-9). Paul lists several characteristics of the carnal state in vv. 3-9. This list does not exhaust all the expressions of such a state. But it helps Paul to get to the first of the major problems at Corinth, that of divisions.

[47]Vine, *op. cit.,* pp. 44-45.   [48]Grosheide, *op. cit.,* p. 80.
[49]Godet, *op. cit.,* p. 166.   [50]*Ibid.,* p. 168.

(1) *Envy* (3:3) The word for **envying** (*zelos*) is usually rendered "jealousy." It is that spirit which makes a person tear down another in order to exalt himself. Jealousy refuses to recognize the talents or gifts of others, yet boasts of these same things when one possesses them himself.

(2) *Strife* (3:3). Jealousy and envy lead to **strife** (*eris*). In classical Greek the word was very powerful. In this context it is used to suggest the nature of a person "when hate takes hold upon him."[51] Jealousy and strife point to unhealthy and unchristian rivalries. Barclay writes: "If man is at variance with his fellow men, if he is a quarrelsome, competitive, argumentative, trouble-making creature, he may be a diligent church attender, he may even be a church office-bearer, but he is not a man of God."[52] The Corinthians were walking **as men**; that is, they were living like people who had never experienced the grace of God.

(3) *False loyalties* (3:4-5). Another characteristic of the carnal man is false loyalties. The result of jealousy and strife is usually an open and practical expression. In this case it was manifested in a misplaced loyalty to human leadership: **For while one saith, I am of Paul; and another, I am of Apollos; are ye not carnal?** (4) The exaltation of human personality to a point of divisions is an act of fallen humanity. "Their divisions were a standing witness to their worldly mentality, not to their spiritual perception."[53] The apostle asks: **Who then is Paul, and who is Apollos, but ministers by whom ye believed, even as the Lord gave to every man?** (5) Apollos and Paul were not little gods to be served; they, like all Christians, were the servants of the Lord. They were to be the instruments, not the objects of faith.[54] What God gave to Paul and to Apollos, He gave to every man— a witness to the living power of the gospel of Christ.

(4) *False loyalty rebuked* (3:6-9). By using an illustration from agricultural practices Paul rebuked false loyalty to human leadership: **I have planted, Apollos watered; but God gave the increase** (6). Paul was the missionary who first preached to the Corinthians. He had founded their church. Apollos was a fellow preacher who succeeded Paul as the pastor at Corinth. He nourished and sustained the Christians with the preaching of the gos-

---

[51]Moulton and Milligan, *op. cit.,* p. 254.   [52]*Op. cit.,* p. 34.

[53]Morris, *op. cit.,* p. 64.   [54]Lightfoot, *op. cit.,* p. 187.

pel. Both the verbs, **planted** and **watered,** are in the aorist tense, indicating a past action completed and done with. The third verb, **gave,** is in the imperfect tense, indicating a continual action, or a process going on all the time. So it was God who was causing the increase. Men come and go in God's work. Each makes a contribution to the process of planting or nourishing. But God works throughout the entire process.

Since God produces the growth, it follows that **neither is he that planteth any thing, neither he that watereth** (7). Paul and Apollos were servants and instruments of God's salvation. They neither desired nor deserved personal devotion. Planting and watering are necessary in the growing process, but without the fruit these activities are meaningless. And it is God who produces the fruit. Moreover, **he that planteth and he that watereth are one** (8). Paul and Apollos were themselves unified. They were not quarreling with each other about credit for success or about the number of followers they had. To consider them rivals was absurd as well as carnal. Yet God would reward them. For **every man shall receive his own reward according to his own labour.** But their reward is not human loyalty; it is, rather, divine approval. The word for **reward** (*mysthos*) was used primarily of wages paid for work, but came to mean any reward or recognition for services. **Labour** (*kopos*) suggests difficult work involving weariness and intense exertion.

In finishing this section on the nature of growth in the Christian community Paul states: "For we are fellow workmen for God; you are God's field, God's building" (9, RSV). God alone calls men. These men are His servants and work for Him. But the Church also belongs to God. Thus the Corinthians are like a field or a vineyard which God owns and which is planted and cultivated by God's workers. If the Corinthians are in fact God's vineyard, they have a double motive to deter them from false loyalties: "(1) they are misusing God's ministers who because of their very office belong to God; (2) they are thereby untrue to themselves who as the very product of this ministry also belong to God."[55] The Church is God's **building** (*oikodome*). The word is used in two ways. It sometimes describes a finished structure (Matt. 24:11); it may also be used for the process of building, as a building in the course of construction. It is this second meaning that Paul uses here. It is out of this figure of God's people as a

---

[55]Lenski, *op. cit.,* p. 131.

building in the process of construction that the question arises:
Are the Corinthians going to be carnal babes or spiritual temples?

2. Christ as the Foundation (3:10-15)

From 11-15, Maclaren preached on "The Testing Fire."
(1) The patchwork structure—**wood, hay, stubble,** 12; (2) The
testing fire, 13; (3) The fate of the two builders, 14-15.

The carnal man tends to build on human wisdom. He proceeds by purely human designs. He hopes to do all the work and
receive all the credit. A true servant, on the other hand, realizes
that God designs the building program and each man makes a
contribution. Paul regarded himself as an evangelist-missionary.
As such he started churches, that is, laid the foundations upon
which others built. He suggests four things in this short passage
about the Christian and the churches as God's buildings.

a. Paul laid only the foundation (3:10). The apostle writes,
**According to the grace of God which is given unto me, as a wise
masterbuilder, I have laid the foundation, and another buildeth
thereon.** Paul was the skilled craftsman, the **masterbuilder**
(*architekton*), who laid the foundation. He was not the designer,
for God was that. Neither was Paul an overseer, directing the
activity of other workmen. He did the work himself. Moreover,
Paul was a **wise** builder. As such, however, he did not claim
any particular or unique wisdom for himself. He was wise in
the sense that he preached the gospel of Christ and centered the
experience of the Corinthians squarely upon the crucified
Saviour.

Paul realized that, in the very nature of the life of the church,
someone else would build on the foundation. The foundation is
laid once and for all—in Christ—but the building process continues. The expression **buildeth thereon** means that another "does
the up-building." When Paul said that he **laid** the foundation, the
aorist tense is used to indicate a completed act. When referring
to building, he uses the present durative "to indicate the work of
building which goes on indefinitely and is going on even now as
Paul writes these lines."[56]

b. Christ the only Foundation (3:11). The master craftsman
is a servant. As such he does not select the type, shape, or the

[56]*Ibid.,* p. 134.

material of the foundation. All these are settled once and for all—
**For other foundation can no man lay than that is laid, which is
Jesus Christ.** No man may begin anywhere else than in Christ
Jesus. No man may improve on Christ as the Foundation. And
no man may end anywhere else than in Christ. Jesus Christ was
the Foundation, the only true Gospel.

c. *The test of building* (3:12-15). In reference to the testing,
or inspection of the building, several things are clear. *First,* there
are alternative materials that may be used. Paul mentions **gold,
silver, precious stones, wood, hay, stubble** (12). The material is
of two distinct and opposite kinds, "rich and durable or paltry
and perishing."[57] One type suggests maturing, stable Christians
grounded on sound doctrines and rich experience. The other
type is the flimsy straw of human opinion, the random bits of
wooden human wisdom. This suggests immature, unstable church
members.

Second, Paul states that **every man's work shall be made
manifest . . . and the fire shall try every man's work of what sort
it is** (13). The result and true nature of every man's work will
be openly exhibited in the great day of judgment so often mentioned by Paul. Three verbs are used to indicate the nature of the
open manifestations of man's work—**declare, revealed,** and **try.**
To **declare** is to make plain or evident. To reveal is to disclose or
to uncover. To **try** (test) is to determine whether it is genuine
or false.

The method of testing is **by fire.** This does not mean a pur-
gatorial or disciplinary period for the Christian. It is the work
that is tested, not the character of the worker. Man's work will
be reviewed in the light of the judgment—that is, in relation to
the holiness of God. To remind these carnal Christians that all
man's work would be judged by God was to remind them that
their quarreling and disputing about human leadership was
wrong.

Third, Paul states that, if a man's gospel work is of a character that can endure the evaluation of God, **he shall receive a reward** (14). The nature of the reward is not indicated, but it
seems evident that the reward is not personal salvation or eternal
life, for these are given to all believers. Some particular reward

[57]Findlay, *op. cit.,* p. 791.

of sharing the honor and glory of God seems to be indicated for the faithful servant who builds eternally by building on Christ and Him crucified (cf. Rev. 3:31; 22:5).

On the other hand, it is possible to build with materials that are not lasting. In this case a man loses his reward: **If any man's work shall be burned, he shall suffer loss; but he himself shall be saved; yet so as by fire (15)**. A careless builder will not receive the reward of his work, in personal satisfaction, divine approval, or divine honor. The faithless builder is like a workman who is either denied the normal compensation or is fined for faulty construction. It is possible for a slovenly workman to be saved personally, but only like someone who escapes from a house on fire. Paul is presenting the danger of attempting to do spiritual work with carnal, selfish, or inferior motives. Good men who work with tainted motives or twisted methods may be saved, but their work crumbles. Those who try to build only upon natural talents, human skills, or personal charm will see their work go up in smoke.

The doctrine of purgatory is not taught in the passage under consideration. One writer gives an acceptable explanation of the idea of a man's work being tried by fire in these words: "The fire . . . is not *purgatory* . . . but *probatory,* not restricted to these who die in venial sin: not the supposed *intermediate class* between those entering heaven at once and those dying in mortal sin who go to hell, but *universal,* testing the godly and ungodly alike (2 Cor. 5:10; cf. Mark 9:44)."[58] Godet summarized the objections to any reference to purgatory in these passages as follows: "1. that the fire is allegorical like the building; 2. that it is only teachers who are in question; 3. that the trial indicated is a means of valuation, not of purification; 4. that this fire is lighted at Christ's coming, and consequently does not yet burn in the interval between the death of Christians and that advent; 5. that the salvation of the worker, of which Paul speaks, takes places not *by,* but *in spite of* the fire."[59]

In 3:1-15, Paul draws a disturbing picture of "The Carnal Christian." (1) Infantile appetites, 1-2; (2) Juvenile attitudes, 3-4; (3) Faulty activities, 10-15.

---

[58]Robert Jamieson, A. R. Fausset, and David Brown, *Commentary Critical and Explanatory on the Whole Bible* (Grand Rapids: Zondervan Publishing House, n.d.), VI, 291.

[59]*Op. cit.,* p. 190.

3. *Spirit-filled Temples Versus Carnal Men* (3:16-23)

For Paul, Christians are not only buildings; they are a particular kind of building—temples. All religious groups in Paul's day spoke of the temple of a god. But the pagan temple featured an *image* of a god. The Jewish Temple pointed to a symbol of God's presence in the ark of the covenant, the altar, and the incense. Paul made a drastic contrast to both of these temples when he asked: **Know ye not that ye are the temple of God, and that the Spirit of God dwelleth in you?** (16) The question is either a gentle reminder or a mild rebuke, for the Corinthians should have been aware of their spiritual status. **Temple** (*naos*) points to the shrine of the Temple, the inner sanctuary. The Church, the body of Christian believers, is God's temple, and God's Spirit dwells in it (cf. Eph. 2:20-22). However, here as elsewhere (6:19; II Cor. 6:16) the reference is also clearly to the individual believer.

There is stern warning in that, **if any man defile the temple of God, him shall God destroy** (17). If any man "destroys"—so reads the best Greek text—the Church of God by corrupt practices, or by false doctrines, then that man will be destroyed by the judgment of God. God's holiness is to be reflected in His Church—**the temple of God is holy.** The Church is thus to be separated from the world and be free from the dissensions and moral laxity so evident in the church at Corinth.

The Corinthians could be either temples or foolish, carnal men. Paul relentlessly warns those who assume a role of being "wise with this world's wisdom" (Moffatt). The reference may be to human pride in mere debating skill. To those who pretend to be worldly-wise Paul issues a blunt challenge: **Let him become a fool, that he may be wise** (18). The man who is conceited or has fallen into self-deception is to make a true evaluation of human wisdom. When he sees this wisdom in relation to divine revelation, let him renounce human wisdom and cast it aside insofar as personal redemption is concerned. When he discards the deceptive wisdom of this world, he will appear to be a fool. In reality, though, he has become wise. For only by this act of turning from worldly wisdom to divine power can a man actually attain true wisdom. To drive home the idea of the inability of human planning to redeem man, Paul repeats the now familiar phrase: **For the wisdom of this world is foolishness with God** (19).

Paul's low estimate of human wisdom is not a private opinion. He quotes the ancient scriptures to support his conviction. His first citation is from Job 5:13, in a variation of the text, as follows: **He taketh the wise in their own craftiness.** Literally, the verse means that He closes His fist upon men of unscrupulous conduct or of slippery manipulations. The second quotation is from Ps. 94:11, which Paul uses to suggest that God knows the patterns of thought, the processes of reasoning, the very essence of human thinking. Knowing such thinking completely, God regards it as **vain (20).** Human thought is fruitless in the sense that it is unable to produce anything of spiritual value that redeems man from sin.

Since human wisdom is foolishness with God, it is a waste and a folly to quarrel about the fancied superiority of one human leader over another. **Therefore let no man glory in men (21).** To boast of supreme loyalty to men as the Corinthians were doing was wrong, because it led to the exaltation of man instead of the exaltation of Christ. This practice of making a fetish of man was not only wrong; it was self-defeating. Paul said: **For all things are yours (21).** As all things belong to Christ and are under Him, so the Christian enjoys a joint ownership with Christ. Why then settle for less? Why limit their spiritual potential by an unchristian devotion to one man?

For whether Paul, or Apollos, or Cephas, or the world, or life, or death, or things present, or things to come; all are yours (22). All that Paul taught, all that Apollos preached, all that Peter witnessed to, were part of the rich heritage of the Christian. But Paul did not stop at this point. He expanded the realm of the Christian to include an understanding and appreciation of **the world** as God's creation. All the blessedness of spiritual **life** is theirs also. Even **death,** the last enemy to be faced, is in reality a blessed end in that the Christian falls asleep in Jesus.

Paul's eyes are not dim nor is his mind cloudy. He soars beyond the limits of time and space to declare that both **things present** (contemporary happenings) and **things to come** (future events) are under the sovereign control of Christ. And since the Christian is Christ's, all things belong to him. **And ye are Christ's; and Christ is God's (23).** The petty quarrels of the Corinthians were reduced to insignificance in the light of the possibilities of grace through Christ. Since Christ was God revealed, He would unite all believers in God.

337

E. STEWARDSHIP VERSUS HARSH LEADERSHIP, 4:1-21

Paul soared to the heights of spiritual understanding in presenting the unlimited possibilities of life in Christ. But he was not one to get lost in oratorical and inspirational ecstasy. He descended abruptly from the heights to wrestle with the problem at hand. The problem facing the Corinthians was their insistence on evaluating preachers from a human standpoint rather than regarding them as servants and stewards. All except the last verse of this chapter deals with the nature of apostolic stewardship. In the closing verse the option is given—dedicated stewardship or harsh leadership. Paul's concern was to present the proper evaluation of an apostolic leader.

1. *The Mission of the Apostle* (4:1-5)

The mission of Paul and of all who were called to preach the gospel was built upon four elements: service, stewardship, faithfulness, and a sensitivity to the judgments of God. While all of these are related, there are shades of difference between them.

a. Service (4:1). Paul and Apollos were not to be regarded as leaders of different gospels. They were both **ministers of Christ**. The word **ministers** (*hyperetas*) means "servants." Originally the term referred to the oarsmen who helped propel boats through the waters of the sea. The word suggests the toil and sustained labor involved in the work of the gospel.

b. Stewardship (4:1). Paul and Apollos were also **stewards of the mysteries of God**. A steward (*oikonomos*) was literally a "house-manager." Often he was a respected and efficient slave to whom the businessman or landowner had turned over the management of the estate. As such, the steward had authority over the helpers or the staff. He assigned work and distributed supplies. He was the superintendent over the operation of the entire enterprise. Yet he was always aware that he was a slave and was under obligation to initiate and to carry out the desires of the owner.

The term **mysteries** refers to the whole plan of salvation (cf. comment on 2:7). Paul and Apollos did not possess secret knowledge hidden to all but a choice few. They were teachers and preachers of the revealed truth about salvation in and through Jesus Christ.

c. *Faithfulness* (4:2). This is the prime qualification of an apostle: **Moreover it is required in stewards, that a man be found faithful.** When all is said and done, the main requirement for a man who teaches or preaches is faithfulness to God and to the truth. Not eloquence in words, not brilliance in thinking, not magnetism in appearance—but day-by-day faithfulness is the demand.

d. *Man's judgment, self-judgment, and God's judgment* (4: 3-5). Paul stated that it mattered little what evaluation the Corinthians made of him. He was always compassionate, considerate, and courteous. But he was almost totally indifferent to the reactions of men to him personally when it came to the issue of preaching the gospel. Such judgments had no influence upon his belief or conduct. The reason was simple: as a steward he was directly responsible to Christ.

Nor did Paul depend upon self-judgment. He did not omit self-criticism (cf. 9:15; 15:9), and he was painfully aware of his shortcomings. Yet he said: **I judge not mine own self** (3). Self-judgment is dangerous because a person so easily sanctions his own views, approves his own conduct, or rationalizes his own mistakes. **For I know nothing by myself** (4) is better rendered, "I know nothing against myself." Paul could recall nothing in his Christian life which condemned him. Nor was he aware of anything that was held against him or his ministry. However, he did not feel acquitted because of a clear conscience. He knew full well that often an unaccusing conscience does not indicate freedom from guilt. In Paul's case, his clear conscience and the absence of private condemnation came as a witness from the Lord —and the Lord was the final Judge.

Further, if Jesus Christ is the final Judge, the Corinthians should **judge nothing before the time, until the Lord come, who both will bring to light the hidden things of darkness, and will make manifest the counsels of the hearts** (5). The idea was that the Corinthians should not "anticipate the great judgment . . . by any preliminary investigation . . . which might be futile and incomplete."[60] In the time of the final judgment God would reveal the things kept secret in this life, including the inner feelings and motives which determine the true quality of an act. At the final judgment **shall every man have praise of God.** Thus people

___
[60]Lightfoot, *op. cit.*, p. 198.

should be careful neither to heap premature praise on favorite preachers nor to pour scorn upon people who were not to their particular liking. God is the only One qualified to judge. He alone can dispense well-founded praise or punishment.

In vv. 3-5, Maclaren finds "The Three Tribunals." (1) The lowest—man's judgment, 3*a*; (2) The higher court of conscience, 3*b*-4*b*; (3) The supreme court of final appeal, 4*c*-5.

2. Carnal Pride Versus Apostolic Humility (4:6-21)

Up to this point Paul had been as diplomatic and courteous as possible, although he had taken every avenue to show the Corinthians the error of their practice. But now diplomacy is laid aside. Paul levels a frontal attack. He charges the Corinthians with a display of carnal pride.

a. A fourfold object lesson (4:6-8). Because of their carnal pride, Paul used himself and Apollos as a kind of object lesson: **And these things, brethren, I have in a figure transferred to myself and to Apollos for your sakes** (6). Instead of naming outright those who were responsible for the quarreling and divisions in Corinth, Paul had changed the form of his approach. But this veiled allusion to himself and Apollos still carried a pointed message to the unnamed party leaders who were the center of difficulty at Corinth.

The message in this illustration had several features. First, that they might **learn . . . not to think of men above that which is written.** Some commentators interpret this phrase as a warning against going "beyond the terms of the commission entrusted to a teacher."[61] Others think that Paul is using a general reference to the OT, which consistently elevates God, not man.[62] The Corinthian emphasis on the importance of teachers meant they were placing too much confidence in man.

A second note was a warning against being **puffed up for one against another.** In the original Greek the word for **puffed up** means to "make proud or arrogant, or conceited," or "groundlessly inflated by his fleshly mind."[63] God-anointed leadership is a wonderful and necessary part of the church. But attachment to leadership should never result in the formation of cliques nor degenerate into undue loyalty. To select a leader and to elevate

---

[61]Vine, *op. cit.*, p. 61.   [62]Morris, *op. cit.*, pp. 77-78; Lenski, *op. cit.*, p. 175.
[63]Arndt and Gingrich, *op. cit.*, p. 877.

him to the point of opposing him to other leaders is the result of carnal pride.

A third part of Paul's object-lesson message is contained in three sharp questions. These questions were designed to shock proud and foolish people into a sense of Christian humility. The first question is: **For who maketh thee to differ from another?** (7) The verb **maketh . . . to differ** (*diakrinei*) means two things: "to put a difference between" and "to regard as superior." In either case the question here is: "Who gives you the exalted powers of discrimination so that you put one teacher against another?" The obvious answer is that such a claim arises from carnal pride. A second question: **What hast thou that thou didst not receive?** is a rhetorical one which reminds them that all gifts and abilities come from God. If man owes everything he has to God's grace, self-conceit is ruled out. A third question completely punctures their proud bubble of conceit: **Why dost thou glory, as if thou hadst not received it?** Since the grace of God is the source of all spiritual gifts, boasting is completely out of place.

The final phase of this object lesson contains severe irony and biting sarcasm. Hear Paul as he assails these proud, carnal Corinthians: **Now ye are full, now ye are rich, ye have reigned as kings without us (8).** The verb **ye are full** is one which is normally used in reference to food. It means to satisfy. The Corinthians felt a sense of spiritual preeminence. They did not "hunger and thirst after righteousness" (Matt. 5:6). They were not "poor in spirit," but were already "rich," and acting like kings.

They had achieved this self-exalted spiritual state without the help or the presence of Paul. He had preached to them and nourished them, but they had forgotten this. In their carnal state they acted as if they had far surpassed their spiritual guide. Paul comments sadly: **And I would to God ye did reign, that we also might reign with you.** The apostle thus shows his continuing spiritual concern for them. He looks toward the day when all divisions among them will be cured, when God's people will be united in the presence of Christ.

b. *Apostolic humility* (4:9-13). Paul's severity was always followed by tenderness. Because his bluntness grew out of compassionate concern, he tempered his direct challenge with a sobering picture of apostolic humility. This was not a pious pose of public self-effacement. The attitude Paul spoke of was a principle of his ministry that was reflected in both public and private activity. It is found only in the pure in heart, who seek first God's kingdom and righteousness.

Paul presents first a contrast between true apostolic humility and the smug self-satisfaction and rivalries of the Corinthians. **For I think that God hath set forth us the apostles last, as it were appointed to death** (9). The verb **hath set forth** (*apodeiknumi*) literally means "to display" or "to show publicly." In its technical sense, the word was used in reference to the spectacle of exhibiting gladiators in the arena for the entertainment of the people. It was also used in regard to the public execution of criminals for the entertainment of a bloodthirsty mob.

Another picture which rebuked the carnal pride of the Corinthians was Paul's statement: **For we are made a spectacle unto the world, and to angels, and to men.** The word **spectacle** means "theatre." While it was often used of the place of an exhibition, it was also used of persons exhibited. Here Paul uses the word to depict the humble role of the apostle. The picture is that of a Roman general who had won a great military victory. On such occasions the victorious general paraded through the city, displaying all the booty and plunder he had taken. The whole procession was called a "triumph." The end of the triumphal parade was made up of a band of bound captives who were doomed to die. The procession ended at the arena, where the prisoners were thrown into the pit to fight with the beasts until they died. Not only had **the world** heard of the tragic end of the doomed apostles, but even the **angels** were aware of the sufferings of the servants of God.

A third contrasting picture between Corinthian pride and apostolic humility is etched in a series of penetrating observations. The first is drawn in these words: **We are fools for Christ's sake, but ye are wise in Christ** (10). Paul was regarded as foolish and stupid because he preached the gospel of a crucified Redeemer. The Corinthians regarded themselves as extremely prudent. In their proud self-estimate they thought of themselves as possessing extraordinary powers of wisdom and gifts. Another etching is found in the declaration, **We are weak, but ye are strong.** Paul refused to modify the gospel by cheap means which impress men. He was content to rely upon the power of God. But the Corinthians felt that their display of worldly wisdom and their exhibition of personal gifts made them stronger than the apostle who preached the gospel of Christ. A third etching is: **Ye are honourable, but we are despised.** The word **honourable** (*endoxos*) means "enveloped in glory." In this picture Paul suggests that the Corinthians act as if they already had halos on their heads, with men bowing before them and accepting their teaching without question. The apostles, on the other hand, are like men disgraced, deprived of even normal human respect.

The fourth picture is a series of graphic glimpses of the apostolic ministry. Paul does not need to apply the truth to the Corinthians. The pictures speak sharply enough without personal application.

Of the apostles Paul says: **We both hunger, and thirst** (11). In contrast to the Corinthians, who seemed to have arrived at a superior state of spirituality as well as a secure status of material prosperity, the apostles still suffer without respite. In their extensive travels they often went hungry and thirsty. **Are naked** (*gymniteuo*) means to be scantily clad. Because of their traveling and the lack of funds, their sandals were often tattered and their clothing frayed.

Are buffeted (*kolaphizo*) means beaten with the fists or lashed with a whip. Such cuffing, striking, and lashing was usually reserved for slaves. It refers to "uncalled-for, vulgar, physical abuse."[64] **And have no certain dwellingplace** indicates that they had no security. They were not welcomed in many places but were regarded as vagrants. Their wandering, however, was not the aimless wandering of a tramp, but was the deliberate forsaking of the comforts of home for a cause.

In the statement, **And labour, working with our own hands** (12), the word **labour** (*kopiao*) suggests not only the idea of work, but of prolonged labor to the point of weariness. The idea of working for a living is particularly significant in view of the fact that the Greeks despised all manual labor, regarding it as the duty of slaves or of those who were mentally unfit for anything else. The apostle referred to his work, not as a mark of shame, but as a matter involved in his commission.

Paul had gone from generalities (vv. 9-10) to specific details about the physical hardships of the apostolic ministry (11-12a). Now he paints the most graphic picture of all—a portrayal of the inner response to the ill treatment they received. **Being reviled, we bless.** Being sneered at and treated with contempt, they

[64]Lenski, *op. cit.*, p. 186.

wished their tormentors well. **Being persecuted, we suffer it.** When they were mistreated and abused, the apostles maintained their poise and did not yield to either discouragement or retaliation. This idea of patient endurance without revenge was a sharp thrust at the petty quarreling of the Corinthians. **Being defamed, we intreat (13).** When the apostles were the object of evil speaking, they responded with a gentle request for fair treatment instead of replying by violent rebuttal or stinging denunciation.

In summarizing this unforgettable picture of apostolic humility Paul refers to the early preachers as the **filth of the world, and . . . the offscouring of all things.** The word **filth** denotes the scum and refuse, the rubbish of humanity. **Offscouring** refers to the accumulated dirt which is removed by scrubbing a filthy object. In the minds of the worldly-wise the apostles represented the litter of sweepings, the rubbish to be removed, the filth to be rubbed off. And this treatment was not temporary, for Paul said it continued **unto this day.**

c. *Father in the faith* (4:14-21). Paul was a man of deep emotions as well as of strong convictions. Thus the mood of his letters often changes rapidly. He passes quickly from stern rebuke to tender encouragement to the Corinthians.

The first expression of fatherly concern was the assurance, **I write not these things to shame you, but as my beloved sons I warn you** (14). The verb **warn** (*noutheteo*) conveys the ideas of criticism in love, or admonishing. Paul does not speak as a stern stranger or an impersonal critic. He speaks with the tenderness of a father who is concerned with the welfare of his son.

Another expression of fatherly concern is found in the distinction between teacher and father: **For though ye have ten thousand instructors in Christ, yet have ye not many fathers** (15). The **instructors** (*paidagogous*) were slaves who directed the learning and conduct of the child. The tutor took the child to school, sometimes taught him, and generally looked after him. He was a guardian. But a guardian can never have the same love for a son as does a father. Paul regards himself as the spiritual father of the Corinthians. Two things were included in the idea of this spiritual fatherhood. First, his affection for them was great. Second, they owed more to Paul than to anyone else. Thus he could say: **Wherefore I beseech you, be ye followers** (lit., imitators) **of me** (16).

Paul's fatherly concern is indicated also by his intention to send Timothy to them (17). Timothy stood in a comparable relationship to Paul as did the people at Corinth. But there was one difference. Timothy was loyal to the apostle and to the gospel that he preached. So Timothy would be sent to be a personal reminder of Paul's early ministry and also would call their attention to Paul's **ways which be in Christ.** Timothy would show them Christian humility and would dissipate the idea that Paul was the leader of a party in opposition to other church leaders.

A final expression of Paul's fatherly spiritual concern is the announcement of his intention to visit them. Some of the Corinthians assumed that he was afraid to face them and they had become **puffed up** (18, arrogant) in their reaction to him. But he declares that all such claims are groundless: **I will come to you shortly, if the Lord will** (19). Paul's hesitation in coming to Corinth was not a matter of personal reluctance to face them. He had delayed his visit because he felt subject to divine direction and was not free to come at the time of this writing. A man under divine instructions must exercise restraint.

But Paul assures them that when he comes he will not ignore their proud pretensions and their conceited interpretations of the gospel. His speech will not be the speech of the worldly-wise, but will be in the prophetic **power** which produces spiritual results and Christlike character. **For the kingdom of God is not in word, but in power** (20). God's kingdom is a spiritual Kingdom and uses spiritual power. Its energies and activities are not based on human logic, brilliant discourses, or emotional eloquence. God's kingdom is spiritual truth presented in a spirit of humility and producing spiritual results.

Finally, Paul faced them squarely with the issue. It is not *when* he will visit them, but *how* he will come. **Shall I come unto you with a rod, or in love, and in the spirit of meekness?** (21) The **rod** stands as a symbol of rebuke and discipline administered by a tutor. The phrase **in love** indicates the parental approach that Paul prefers to take.

"God's Standards for Effective Service" are: (1) Faithful stewardship, 1-2; (2) Charitable judgment, 4-5; (3) Humble sacrifice, 9-13; (4) Spiritual power, 17, 20.

Section **III** *The New Faith and a*
New Morality

I Corinthians 5:1-13

Paul was vitally concerned about a new morality. He felt that the old code of conduct led to despair and self-destruction. This old morality was in the process of decay in both individuals and nations. The Christian gospel presented a new religious faith and a new ethical outlook. The new faith was grounded on the revelation of God in Christ. The new morality also was founded on the life and teachings of Jesus. This new ethic was not an attempt to make the demands of the gospel acceptable to man. It grew out of the direct challenge of God's claims upon life.

A. THE BOLDNESS OF SIN, 5:1

The pride of learning and of gifts in the church at Corinth did not produce a corresponding strength in ethical and moral matters. In fact, the Corinthian church had degenerated to the level of public scandal. The cause was a weak toleration of sin.

1. *The General Knowledge of the Sin* (5:1a)

Paul asserts: **It is reported commonly that there is fornication among you.** Perhaps through Chloe or Stephanas the report had come to Paul of this shocking situation. **It is reported** is taken from the verb "to hear." The meaning is not so much that a report had come to the apostle nor even that the situation was common knowledge in churches in other cities. The truth was that the incident was generally known within the church at Corinth. The matter was a topic of frequent conversation, and Paul might have said, "Among you one hears of fornication."

The word **commonly** (*holos*) means "altogether," "most assuredly," "incontrovertibly."[1] These people who were so proud of their knowledge now had a personal knowledge of another kind —a firsthand acquaintance with sin in its rawest form. The Corinthians were quick to parade their intellectual achievements and to argue the fine points of theological issues. They could quarrel

[1]Robertson and Plummer, *op. cit.*, p. 95.

over nonessentials and split the church over the importance of various leaders. These carnal Christians could exalt their gifts and exult in their ecstatic experiences. But their knowledge, their ardor for debate, their gifts, and their ecstatic experiences seemed powerless to deal with a glaring sin which shamed the entire church. The ultimate test of spirituality is not knowledge or gifts; it is the ability to deal effectively with the sin problem.

2. The Reality of the Sin (5:1b)

Fornication (*porneia*) originally meant prostitution, "but came to be applied to unlawful sexual intercourse generally."[2] It is possible, even after people have been saved from sin, for such things to erupt occasionally in the church. The Corinthian man involved probably had joined the church as a true believer, and had fallen into this sin after becoming part of the church fellowship. The problem at hand was not so much that one of the converts had fallen into sin. The big problem that caused such concern on the part of Paul was the reaction of the church to the situation.

Paul was well aware of the sensual and licentious attitudes in Corinth. Here vice existed in every form. Some descended to the bestial level and became brutish in their actions. Others, more refined and sophisticated, tended to regard sex as a casual method of entertainment or recreation. Still others associated sexual intercourse with religion and made it a part of pagan worship.

Paul wanted to be relevant in his preaching. But he realized that making the gospel relevant was not a matter of softhearted tolerance or of softheaded compromise. To him the gospel was relevant when it dealt adequately with sin. The apostle's concept of Christianity centered in the Cross and in the Christ who died to make men holy. Thus any situation which encouraged sin and threatened or contradicted the life of holiness was regarded as a perversion of the gospel. For Paul it was a denial of the power of God to profess to be a Christian and to live in open immorality.

3. The Nature of the Sin (5:1c)

The flagrant nature of this sin was something that even the easygoing heathen would not permit—it was **such fornication as is not so much as named among the Gentiles.** The sin was incest.

---

[2]Moulton and Milligan, *op. cit.*, p. 529.

A man was living in sin with **his father's wife.** It is not clear whether the man had seduced his stepmother, whether the affair had caused a divorce between the father and the woman, or whether the father had died. Whatever the details, it was commonly regarded as a particularly foul situation.

Such a degrading domestic arrangement was contrary to both social standards and religious practices. The marriage of a son with his stepmother was, among Jews, forbidden under penalty of death (Lev. 18:8; Deut. 22:30). Even Roman law did not permit unions of this kind.[3] In the phrase **have his father's wife,** the verb suggests that the relationship between the man and the woman was continuing. To Paul the situation was unbearable, and it illustrates the boldness and the deceit of sin. Vine writes: "This case shows that the natural conscience of an unregenerate man can act on a higher level than the seared conscience of a carnal believer."[4]

B. Weak and Carnal Tolerance, 5:2-5

It is not clear why the guilty person had not been called to account. Perhaps he was a prominent man whom the members felt reluctant to challenge, or he may have claimed superior knowledge or displayed exciting gifts that seemed to clothe the situation with respectability. Perhaps the church was so engrossed in its quarrels that it ignored the sin. Finally, the Corinthians may have tolerated this immorality in order to gain a license for other vices or non-Christian attitudes. Whatever the causes, the apostle speaks to the matter directly.

1. *Carnal Pride Versus Humble Mourning* (5:2)

Paul writes, **And ye are puffed up, and have not rather mourned, that he that hath done this deed might be taken away from among you.** The verb **are puffed up** is in the perfect tense, indicating a permanent condition of carnal pride. The church was proud of its knowledge and of its gifts. But "no intellectual brilliance, no religious enthusiasm, can cover this hideous blot."[5] In the church at Corinth "the sin of pride had dazzled them so that they did not see things as they really were."[6]

Instead of living in blind pride, the church should have been in tearful mourning. The verb form **have not . . . mourned** is

---

[3]Lenski, *op. cit.*, p. 207.
[5]Findlay, *op. cit.*, p. 807.
[4]*Op. cit.*, p. 71.
[6]Grosheide, *op. cit.*, p. 120.

an aorist, pointing to an act which should have been completed in the past. As Kling stated it, a truly spiritual church would have mourned "that a member of their body had sunk so low, and the Church of the Lord, which ought to have been kept, had been thus defiled and dishonored."[7] The word **mourned** (*epenthesate*) denotes funeral mourning. The picture is that of a public demonstration of grief because a member of the family has died.

The church at Corinth is not blamed because one of its members sinned. The indictment is because they tolerated the situation. The church should have either sorrowfully expelled the guilty man from its number or prayed for God to remove him. Godet suggests that, if the church had gone into mourning, perhaps God would have removed him as He did Ananias and Sapphira.[8] But in spiritual smugness the church did neither. Instead, it continued to boast of its knowledge and gifts, to manifest a weak tolerance toward an infamous sinner, and to display a proud spirit at the same time, making the entire congregation share the guilt of the sin.

2. The Apostolic Judgment (5:3-5)

Since the church was unduly tolerant of the situation, Paul was forced to proceed with his own recommendation, which involved a threefold judgment.

a. The decision of Paul (5:3). The apostle writes, **For I verily, as absent in body, but present in spirit, have judged already . . . concerning him that hath so done this deed.** The Corinthians were present on the spot and could have taken disciplinary action against the offender, but they did not. Paul was absent and could have excused himself from immediate responsibility, but he stood in the prophetic succession and was more concerned about the holy state of the church than about avoiding difficult issues. Even though he was in another city, he felt this problem as keenly as though he were sitting in their congregation. And his decision was exactly the same that he would have made if he had been at Corinth.

In v. 3, Paul said, in effect: "I have already decided and passed sentence, as if I were present in the church." The verb

[7]"I Corinthians," *Commentary on the Holy Scriptures,* ed. J. P. Lange (Grand Rapids: Zondervan Publishing House, n.d.), pp. 108-9.
[8]*Op. cit.,* p. 243.

have judged is in the perfect tense, indicating a note of finality
regarding the decision. Paul's judgment may appear to be severe,
but the case was a clear-cut violation of the Christian ethic. The
man had openly entered into a relationship knowing full well that
it defied all social custom in general and the new morality of the
Christian faith in particular. In addition, the man persisted in
his state without shame or remorse. He was a spot of cancer on
the body of the church. Paul prescribed immediate surgery to remove the affected part.

b. *Congregational procedure* (5:4). Verse 4 indicates the
basis for the apostolic judgment. **In the name of our Lord Jesus
Christ, when ye are gathered together, and my spirit, with the
power of our Lord Jesus Christ.** Paul identified himself with
them even though he had just rendered a strong personal pronouncement. But he recognized that his personal authority could
not be imposed on the congregation. More importantly, he was
alert to the truth that human authority never has priority over
divine power. He appealed to them on the basis of a congregational procedure involving both spiritual and legal principles.

The spiritual principle was that they should consider the
matter **in the name of our Lord Jesus.** Paul's **spirit** (presence)
would be unseen but would exert a definite influence. However,
in such a situation "a *third Supreme Presence* is necessary to
make the sentence valid."[9] The gravity of the situation required
that any action taken be done in the name of the Lord. Such a
procedure was not designed to open the door to false claims of
ecclesiastical power to punish or to torture. What unspeakable
crimes and how much injustice have been done under the pretense of executing punishment in God's name! The presence of
the Lord is needed to sanction any disciplinary procedure. All
such actions should be in harmony with NT teachings and with
the spirit of Christ.

Paul also recommended a legal principle—a formally called
meeting of the congregation to consider the matter. The words
gathered together mean an officially assembled group.[10] That
such a meeting was held may be inferred from II Cor. 2:6, where
reference is made to punishment decided upon by the majority.
Both the divine guidance and the officially called meeting were
to operate within **the power of our Lord Jesus Christ.**

In other words, the basis for any decision was to be the gospel

[9]Findlay, *op. cit.,* p. 808.   [10]Lenski, *op. cit.,* p. 213.

of Christ. Only this gospel can form a valid criterion of judging those who are joined to Christ and those who are not.

c. *Ecclesiastical pronouncement* (5:5). Paul has progressed from personal judgment to congregational procedure, all under the direction of Jesus Christ, the Lord. Now the climax is reached in the official pronouncement by the church.

First, Paul suggests that the church **deliver such an one unto Satan.** Several interpretations have been given of the earlier statement of v. 2, "That he . . . might be taken away from among you," and of this figure of delivering the offender to Satan. John Calvin thought that v. 5 established the power of excommunication in the church.[11] Others feel that Paul was issuing a pronouncement of a personal penal sentence which would take effect immediately, as in the case of Ananias and Sapphira (Acts 5:1-11) and of Elymas (Acts 13:6-11).[12] Still others interpret this action as simply placing the offender outside the bounds of the church, where Satan rules as "the god of this world" (II Cor. 4:4). "He was for a time separated from spiritual influences, and was . . . handed over to Satan."[13] This last explanation appears to be the most acceptable.

A second aspect of this pronouncement was its purpose—**the destruction of the flesh.** The word for **destruction** (*olethron*) means "to ruin" rather than "to destroy" or "to annihilate." The suggestion is that, if the man is thus given over to evil, he will exhaust his physical powers and ruin his opportunities for happiness. Having done this, he will, like the prodigal son, recognize his spiritual poverty, and desire to return to the fellowship of Christ and the church. The sentence of Paul is remedial rather than punitive. A similar incident is contained in I Tim. 1:20, where Hymenaeus and Alexander are delivered over to Satan "that they may learn not to blaspheme."

This ecclesiastical pronouncement contains also spiritual concern for the offender. The reason for the action was not only to protect the church from the infiltration of sin, but also **that the spirit may be saved in the day of the Lord Jesus.** The idea is

[11]John W. Frazer (trans.), *The First Epistle of Paul the Apostle to the Corinthians*, "Calvin's Commentaries" (Grand Rapids, Mich.: Wm. B. Eerdmans Publishing Co., 1960), p. 106.

[12]Lightfoot, *op. cit.*, p. 204.

[13]Farrar, "I Corinthians" (*The Pulpit Commentary*, ed. H. D. M. Spence and Joseph S. Exell; Grand Rapids: Wm. B. Eerdmans Publishing Company, 1950 [reprint]), p. 167.

that, if the man is at all sensitive to God's redeeming grace, the discipline of rejection from the church may bring him to his senses and he may be saved. The man was doomed if he continued in his state of sin. Even if he experienced physical death under the judgment of God, such a death would be a blessing if its imminence caused the man to repent before he died.

Paul's view of sin was solemn and serious. He was tolerant of mistakes and realized the awful grip of sin upon the human personality. But he preached that the grace and power of God were designed to lift people to a life of holiness and of purity. Anything which threatened the holy life of the church had to be eliminated. Paul would not quibble about the fine points of the ceremonial law. Nor did he get unduly exercised about the external rituals of Christianity. But when it came to sin in the church he was adamant. A church that tolerates sin is carnal and is ripe for destruction, so Paul proceeds to the larger area of the whole attitude of the Corinthian church in this regard.

C. The New Faith and a New Power, 5:6-13

To the Apostle Paul the salvation offered freely in Christ Jesus was a truly revolutionary force in man's life. The new faith produced a new power. This power was an inward, spiritual force with unlimited potential for spiritual progress. In his discussion of the spiritual life of the church, Paul states a principle, declares an imperative, presents a potential, makes an exhortation, and issues a warning.

1. *A Spiritual Principle* (5:6)

The spiritual law stated by Paul has a negative aspect and a positive one. The negative element is found in the expression: **Your glorying is not good.** The term **glorying** (*kauchema*) does not denote an exhibition of boasting. It points rather to the attitude of pride and conceit. The abundance of knowledge and gifts should have produced a higher type of spiritual life in the church. But it had the contrary effect. The people were smug about a self-assumed spiritual superiority, yet blind to an open act of shame.

The positive aspect of the spiritual law stated here is sobering indeed: **Know ye not that a little leaven leaveneth the whole lump?** To be indifferent to the presence of sin does three things to a congregation. It makes them share part of the responsibility and guilt; it lowers the standards of biblical faith and conduct;

and it encourages a gradual spread of other sins in the congregation.

The trouble with the church of Corinth was that it was either unaware of or indifferent to the seriousness of its spiritual decline. The **leaven** was not only the presence of an unpunished offender in their fellowship, "but the general laxity and impurity displayed by their whole bearing in the matter."[14] A sin so poisonous, if permitted to remain, "held an indefinite power of corruption; it tainted the entire community."[15] Since one bad member can infect the whole church, there was a "danger of future contagion."[16] A spiritually proud church can be gradually infected by sin until the entire church is caught up in either guilty toleration or actual participation in sin.

2. The Spiritual Imperative (5:7a)

Because of the danger to the whole church Paul issues a ringing command: **Purge out therefore the old leaven.** The reference to leaven is taken from Exod. 12:18-20 and 13:6-7, where each Jewish family was commanded to get rid of all leaven in preparation for the Passover. The word **purge** is a strong one meaning to "cleanse thoroughly, purify . . . to eliminate."[17] **The old leaven** was the spiritual evil that permitted the church to tolerate the incestuous person. It is called **old** because "it was the remains of their former unregenerate state, which, like leaven, was still at work vitiating their character."[18] Paul indicates that the reluctance of the Corinthians to deal with the glaring sin in their church was because all the Corinthians had **the old leaven** in them —"the old worldly and fleshly disposition that was carried over in their hearts from their former life."[19] To **purge out . . . the old leaven** meant that each member should apply the purging process to himself, "in order to leave in the church not a *single* manifestation of the old man, of the corrupt nature, undiscovered and unchecked."[20] Each Christian is exhorted to be delivered, not only

---

[14]*Ibid.*   [15]Findlay, *op. cit.*, p. 809.

[16]Robert Jamieson, A. R. Fausset, and David Brown, *A Commentary Critical, Experimental and Practical on the Old and New Testaments* (Grand Rapids: Wm. B. Eerdmans Publishing Co., 1961), VI, 296.

[17]*The Analytical Greek Lexicon* (New York: Harper and Brothers, n.d.), p. 124.

[18]Lange, *op. cit.*, p. 114.   [19]Lenski, *op. cit.*, p. 220.

[20]Godet, *op. cit.*, p. 263.

by ridding himself of all sin, but also by living the kind of holy life that is potentially his in Christ Jesus.

3. *Spiritual Potential* (5:7*b*)

The reason for Paul's concern regarding the cleansing of the old leaven of "heathenish and natural corruption"[21] was that the Corinthians might realize their spiritual potential in Christ: **that ye may be a new lump.** The removal of this remnant of natural corruption would result in a fresh, new kind of Christian life. **New** (*neos*) means new in the sense that the thing or condition did not exist before.

Another word for **new** (*kainos*) means new in the sense of differing from what is old. The Corinthians were already new in the sense of differing from their old way of life. But now they were to be new in a distinct sense—"Their Christian life and character are to be like an entirely fresh start."[22] Kling writes of the new lump: "There is no leaven, hence a complete whole, morally renewed by purification—a church holy and free from sin, evincing its early love and zeal."[23]

Paul reminds the Corinthians of their potential by a reference to the Christian ideal: **Ye are unleavened,** i.e., without the old leaven of sin. It is the method of Scripture to refer to Christians in their ideal rather than their actual state.[24] Such a reference serves as a reminder that they should "come up to their true ideal."[25] This spiritual potential is realized through the power of Christ. What the Christian needs to do is to become in reality what he already is in potential. "He must become holy in fact, as he is in idea."[26]

The basis of the spiritual potential of the church is found in the words: **For even Christ our passover is sacrificed for us.** The verb **is sacrificed,** or "has been sacrificed," is an aorist, indicating a definite, completed act. The benefits of the completed sacrifice still linger and apply to the Christian, both of Paul's day and of the present day.

4. *Spiritual Exhortation* (5:8)

In v. 8, Paul spiritualized the Passover feast for the church. **Therefore let us keep the feast, not with old leaven, neither with**

[21]Jamieson, Fausset, and Brown, *op. cit.*, 296.   [22]Lenski, *op. cit.*, p. 221.

[23]Lange, *op. cit.*, p. 114.   [24]Farrar, *op. cit.*, pp. 167-68.

[25]Lange, *op. cit.*, p. 115.   [26]Godet, *op. cit.*, p. 264.

the leaven of malice and wickedness; but with the unleavened
bread of sincerity and truth. Thus the church is called upon to
"break with all the evil dispositions of the natural heart, or that
which is elsewhere called the old man."[27] The phrase let us
keep the feast means to observe a festival. Keeping the feast suggests the continuous life of the Christian, a day-by-day walk in
holiness, strength, and joy.

But the Christian cannot make his life a daily festival of the
Spirit while the old nature remains, because that old nature works
against the Spirit. Two features of this nature are malice (*kakia*)
and wickedness (*poneria*). Malice means "a desire and effort to
injure a neighbor" or a deliberate vice, while wickedness means
"the performance of evil with persistency and delight."[28]

The new morality which Paul associates with the revelation
of God in Christ is expressed by sincerity (*elikrineias*), which
means pure, unalloyed, or consisting of unmixed substances. According to Godet the word originally meant "to judge by the light
of the sun," thus denoting transparency, and "so the purity of a
heart perfectly sincere before God."[29] Truth means reality, or
that which is in harmony with the revelation of God in Christ.
Sincerity and truth are the constant source of nourishment in the
building of a holy life in Christ.

5. *Spiritual Warnings* (5:9-13)

a. *The warning repeated* (5:9). In a previous letter (perhaps a lost epistle) Paul had warned the Corinthians not to company with fornicators. The term to company with carries the
idea of mingling freely, or of living in an intimate and continuous relationship with those who were obsessed with sex. Apparently the Corinthians had either ignored Paul's warning or
had bypassed it with subtle double-talk. So he repeats the warning.

b. *The warning explained* (5:10-11). Verse 10 explains that
to refrain from all contact with people of loose morals would be
impossible. Especially in a city dedicated to sexual license it
would be impossible to isolate oneself from sinful society. The
only way to avoid mixing with sinful people is to go out of the
world—to exile oneself from society. But the impossibility of
avoiding incidental social contact with immoral people was no
excuse to condone such association in the church.

[27]*Ibid.*, p. 263.   [28]Lange, *op. cit.*, p. 116.
[29]*Op. cit.*, p. 267.

In v. 11, Paul repeats his warning against association with such fornicators. Necessary incidental contacts are not to become intimate associations. With such people Christians are **not to eat.** Here the Oriental idea of inviting or permitting a man to eat at the table as an honor or gesture of friendship is indicated. To eat with a man was to put a personal stamp of approval on him.

Paul presents a list of those who should be excluded from free and open domestic and social association. There is, of course, the **fornicator.** The person who practices illicit sexual behavior does not grace the table of the Christian. The **covetous** person, goaded by greediness and motivated by self-interest, makes a poor companion for the man who desires to serve God. The **idolater,** with his deference to false gods and materialistic concepts, is not a congenial dinner partner for one who accepts and honors Christ. The reviler, who uses violent and abusive language against God and man, will scarcely add flavor to the table conversation. The **drunkard,** with his idiotic prattle or belligerent arguments, will edify no one and will embarrass all. The **extortioner** who has cheated a gullible woman or exploited a naive man can add nothing to the food and drink of love and charity.

c. *The warning limited to believers* (5:12-13). Paul was not commissioned **to judge them . . . that are without** (12). This is what the Jews called the heathen. Paul borrows the term and uses it to include both heathen and Jews—all those who had not accepted Christ. To the unregenerate, Paul had only one obligation—to preach the gospel. He was aware that his influence in apostolic discipline extended only to those who professed a common faith in Christ. The duty of both Paul and the Corinthians was to exercise discipline upon those **within** the church.

God deals with the unregenerate: but **them that are without God judgeth** (13). Of course, the unfaithful Christian is also judged by God. But the Christian has an obligation to exercise a valid discrimination in regard to conduct within the fellowship of believers. So Paul's verdict still stands: **Therefore put away from among yourselves that wicked person.** The church should manifest a concern over the action of its members.

"A Disciplined Church" (1) Does not sanction immoral conduct, 1-5; (2). Is a purified church, 6-7; (3) Reflects sincerity and truth, 8; (4) Recognizes that different treatment is appropriate for sinners in the church and those outside the church, 9-13.

Section IV The New Faith and a New Fellowship

I Corinthians 6:1-20

To Paul the gospel of Jesus Christ was a new and vital force in life. In the first four chapters the apostle emphasized the truth that the new faith in Christ should result in a sense of unity and purpose. He pointed out in precise terms the fact that the divisions and quarrelings in the church were contrary to the new faith. In c. 5, Paul pinpointed the principle that the new faith produced a new morality. This new morality was not based on human wisdom, but was the result of God's revelation in Christ.

In c. 6 the apostle discusses the problem of lawsuits among the members of the church. He asks them to settle their problems within the church fellowship rather than submitting the cases to unchristian courts. After showing the folly of Christians taking each other before heathen tribunals, Paul warns them against the danger of a lapse back into sin. He is particularly concerned about the sin of fornication, which seemed to be an acute problem in Corinth. He ends this section by reminding the Corinthians of the inspiring truth that they were, in reality, temples of the Holy Spirit.

A. FELLOWSHIP VERSUS CARNAL LITIGATION, 6:1-11

Paul felt that the church at Corinth was losing its spiritual balance within, and dissipating its missionary influence without. Among the several reasons for loss of vitality and influence was the spectacle of Christians parading their differences before the civil courts.

1. *Lawsuits Unworthy of the Church* (6:1-4)

To Paul the church was a union of believers in Christ. The union should be characterized by fellowship with man as well as worship before God. But the church at Corinth seemed to prefer carnal litigation to Christian fellowship.

a. Christian arbitration is better than pagan verdicts (6:1). To Paul, public lawsuits involving Christians were unthinkable.

357

Thus he writes: **Dare any of you, having a matter against another, go to law before the unjust, and not before the saints?** This abrupt question "marks an outburst of indignant feeling."[1] One commentator suggests that Paul's language indicates that he regards public lawsuits as "treason against Christian brotherhood."[2]

The apostle did not deny the possibility of real differences between Christians. The phrase **having a matter against another** means "a cause for trial, a case."[3] But the thing Paul opposed was the increasing number of Christians who were submitting their differences to the heathen courts. To **go to law** (*krino*) is an attempt to have a verdict rendered, to seek for judgment. The verb form used here (*krinesthai*) indicates that the parties involved took the initiative in taking their problems to court. And these lawsuits were between fellow believers, not between Christians and those outside the church.

Jesus had already laid down the principle that His followers ought to settle their differences between each other (Matt. 5: 39-40). The example of the Jews should also have been a lesson to the church. Rabbinical literature prohibited lawsuits before idolatrous judges. To the rabbis such action was in the same category as blasphemy.[4] The Roman government permitted the Jews autonomy in matters of disputes between themselves. In the Jewish community the house of judgment (Bethdin) was almost as common as the synagogue (Beth-keneseth). So it was probably not Jewish converts who were involved in these lawsuits. The Greeks, however, were fond of disputings and litigations, and they may have been involved.

The term **unjust** (unrighteous) does not necessarily mean that it was impossible to secure justice in the civil courts. The Romans were proud of their sense of justice and their record of legal tolerance. Paul himself had appealed to Roman justice (Acts 28:19). But Paul's case in that instance was not made against a fellow believer. However, the trial of Jesus before Pilate and the record of the public courts regarding the Christians was a rather sad picture of justice (Acts 12:1-2; 16:19-24; 24:27).

Christian fellowship would call for a hearing in matters of everyday life before the saints. Christians here are given a title

---

[1]Findlay, *op. cit.*, p. 813.   [2]Jamieson, Fausset, and Brown, *op. cit.*, p. 297.
[3]Robertson and Plummer, *op. cit.*, p. 110.
[4]Findlay, *op. cit.*, p. 814.

of honor and dignity—**the saints** (*hoi hagioi,* "the holy ones").
God had separated them from the world and He had provided
for them a holy life in Christ. He had given them wisdom and
power. Then why should those whom God has so honored be
called to appear before men who recognized no God, or only
heathen gods? Further, the whole procedure of civil courts
operates according to impersonal evidence and technical details.
The Christian Church, on the other hand, operates as a personal,
united group which lives according to the motives of mercy, love,
and kindly concern for one another. Thus Christian arbitration was better than pagan verdicts.

b. *Christian potential versus carnal procedure* (6:2). The
Corinthians faced a choice of measuring up to their spiritual
potential or descending to carnal procedures. The potential of
the Christian is breathtaking indeed, as Paul points out in these
words: **Do ye not know that the saints shall judge the world?
and if the world shall be judged by you, are ye unworthy to
judge the smallest matters?** The question **Do ye not know?** is
used 10 times in the Corinthian letters, but only three times elsewhere in Paul's writings (Rom. 6:3, 16; 7:1). The Corinthians
were either carnally indifferent to their spiritual potential or
were ignorant of their unique destiny.

In Paul's thinking, the believers are to participate as associates of Christ in the rulership of the entire world. Jesus said of
the apostles that they should "sit upon twelve thrones, judging
the twelve tribes of Israel" (Matt. 19:28). This is extended here
to all the followers of Christ. Lightfoot comments: "Just as the
faithful shall reign with Christ as kings (2 Tim. ii:12, Rev.
xxii:5), so shall they sit with Him as judges of the world."[5]

The inspiring spiritual potential of the people of God as
future rulers and judges of the world appears in Dan. 7:22; Ps.
49:14; Matt. 19:28; Rev. 2:26-27; 3:21; 20:4. The term **world**
here includes all those who have rejected the appeal of the gospel.[6] Another way of stating the meaning of v. 2 would be: Don't
you realize that you, the future judges of final destinies and the
arbiters of eternal matters, are able to make decisions regarding
routine matters of life?

The truth Paul is trying to impress upon the Corinthians is
that ultimately the heathen will come under the divine judgment,

---

[5]*Op. cit.,* p. 210.   [6]Godet, *op. cit.,* p. 286.

in which all Christians participate. How strange, then, that these same heathen are called upon to settle the disputes of the Christians!

c. *Celestial power versus earthly confusion* (6:3). Not only will the redeemed believers assist Christ in the rulership of the world. They also will participate in the judgment pronounced on **angels.** The angels are the highest order of beings under God, as things now exist, yet they are part of the universe in general. Christ will rule over the entire universe and the believers in Christ "shall share in His regal exaltation, which exceeds any angelic dignity."[7]

Whether good angels or bad angels are indicated in this passage is not specified. Tertullian, Chrysostom, and other Early Church writers regarded them as fallen angels. Later commentators, such as Alford, regarded them as good angels.[8] But the meaning is the same in either case. Even an exalted order of beings like the angels will be subject to the judgment of the Christians, because of the Christians' unique relationship to Christ. If, then, these Corinthians expect to assist in the judgment of angels, they ought to be competent to settle disputes regarding life on the earth. If they are to exercise celestial power, they should be able to eliminate earthly confusion.

d. *Christian perspective on worldly authority* (6:4). Paul was concerned for the spiritual influence of the church. He felt that Christians should avoid lawsuits entirely. But if they found it necessary to establish tribunals to deal with the everyday affairs of this life, then let them set as judges the lowest in the churches.

There are various interpretations given to the phrase **least esteemed in the church.** Some have interpreted this as a touch of irony in Paul's speech, and interpret the words to refer to the most simple among the church—that any, "however low in the church, rather than the heathen,"[9] should judge. Others feel that the words refer to "persons of proved inferiority of judgment."[10] Still others regard the words as a reference to the unbelievers, who pass for nothing in the church and enjoy no confidence or authority there.[11] The RSV thus interprets the verse, "If then

[7]Robertson and Plummer, *op. cit.*, p. 112.   [8]*Op. cit.*, p. 512.
[9]Jamieson, Fausset, and Brown, *op. cit.*, p. 298.   [10]Farrar, *op. cit.*, p. 192.
[11]Lenski, *op. cit.*, p. 239.

you have such cases, why do you lay them before those who are least esteemed by the church?" Christian arbitration is superior to pagan verdicts.

2. Lawsuits a Disgrace to the Church (6:5-6)

Paul was concerned for the spiritual development of the church and for the impact of the church on the world. He realized that lawsuits between members of the church were a sign of spiritual weakness—and a symbol of disgrace. Thus Paul wrote: **I speak to your shame** (5). He may have added this comment "to account for the severe irony of the last remark,"[12] or to actually humiliate them by the question he is about to ask.[13] The question was double-barrelled. First Paul asked: **Is it so, that there is not a wise man among you?** Can it really be that this church, which was so proud of its wisdom, of its gifts, and of its superior spirituality, could not find anyone wise enough and fair enough to settle disputes?

The second part of the question would be equally embarrassing to the Corinthians. **Was there not even one that shall be able to judge between his brethren?** The nature of the problems causing these lawsuits appeared to be such that a person was needed to decide between conflicting ethical practices (*diakrinai*) rather than **to judge** (*krinai*) legal crimes. The reason for these questions was to bring the Corinthians to their senses. "Considering how wise they were in their own conceit, the question is a very cutting one."[14]

The climax to Paul's indictment of shame came in the next statement: **But brother goeth to law with brother, and that before the unbelievers** (6). It is dismal when sharp differences arise between church members. But when professed believers persist to the point of parading these differences in a pagan court, it is a scandal before the world.

The magistrates and judges of these pagan courts are called "unjust" (*adikia,* unrighteous) in v. 1. Now they are called **unbelievers** (*apistia*)—devoid of faith. These pagan officials decided legal cases according to technical details, debating skill, or the weight of evidence. Christians, on the other hand, must

---

[12]Farrar, *op. cit.,* p. 192.

[13]Alford, *op. cit.,* pp. 513-14; Robertson and Plummer, *op. cit.,* p. 114.

[14]Lange, *op. cit.,* p. 124.

consider problems in the light of God's grace and of personal fellowship, as well as in the light of legal procedure.

3. *Warning Against Spiritual Degeneration* (6:7-11)

The outbreak of lawsuits among the Corinthians was actually a sign of spiritual degeneration in the church. In rapid-fire order Paul listed their spiritual failures. Then, as was his custom, he softened the charge with a reminder of their spiritual heritage.

a. *Spiritual loss and defeat* (6:7a). Looking at the problem as a whole, Paul stated, **There is utterly a fault among you, because ye go to law one with another.** The word **fault** (*hettema*) is given various shades of meaning. It may mean "the spiritual loss sustained by the assembly because of their disputes and habits of going to law."[15] Another writer interprets **fault** as a falling short of their "inheritance of the kingdom of God."[16] Still another says that it means more than a defect, or a loss— it is a clear spiritual defeat for those who go to court.[17] Any of these interpretations reveal that this church was in a state of spiritual degeneration and was living far below its Christian potential.

b. *The Christian method of settling problems* (6:7b). Paul had pointed out the proper method of solving disputes when he had first preached to them. He here repeats the Christian method of solving differences: **Why do ye not rather take wrong? why do ye not rather suffer yourselves to be defrauded?** A Christian need not be a pawn, nor should he permit himself to be misused. But, in Paul's thinking, it was better to endure an injustice or to sustain a financial loss than to suffer spiritual damage. Jesus himself teaches that the Christian should not resist evil (Matt. 5:39). The church was suffering a loss in dignity and honor; it was experiencing a decline of influence and respect; it was sapping its evangelical strength. The Christian method of avoiding lawsuits was to suffer instead of retaliating.

c. *Fraud instead of charity* (6:8). Not only had these Corinthians refused to suffer injustices and losses; they also were aggressively exploiting their fellow Christians. Paul states the situation in these words: **Nay, ye do wrong, and defraud, and**

---

[15]Vine, *op. cit.*, p. 83.   [16]Alford, *op. cit.*, p. 514.
[17]Findlay, *op. cit.*, p. 816.

that your brethren. They were not spiritual enough to endure wrong for the sake of the gospel. But they were carnal enough to inflict injury on others. And those being wronged were not outside the church; they were fellow believers. Such action was contrary to the Sermon on the Mount (Matt. 5:38-40); it was contrary to the unity of believers in Christ (I Cor. 12:12-13); it was contrary to the idea of regarding oneself as the temple of the Holy Spirit (I Cor. 6:19). Thus there was more than the absence of love; there was the presence of injustice. Instead of displaying Christian unity, they were guilty of outright fraud.

d. A solemn warning (6:9-10). Paul insists that they already know the proper course of action. They knew, or should have known, that unrighteousness was sin, that **the unrighteous shall not inherit the kingdom of God** (9). The word **unrighteous** put their actions on a level with the heathen. "But here the word denotes the immoral generally, those who offend God and man by iniquities of every kind."[18] The warning of Paul included a sharp note: **Be not deceived.** The verb shows that "seductive arguments are in circulation by which the vicious succeeded in quieting their consciences."[19]

In order that he make himself absolutely clear, Paul presented a list of sins which apparently were special temptations to the Corinthians. Any of these sins would break a man's relationship in Christ and would disqualify him as an heir to the kingdom of God. The tenfold list is representative rather than exhaustive. The sins are associated with personality response, thus making them more specific. (1) **Fornicators** generally means those "who practice sexual immorality."[20] (2) **Idolaters** are those who follow false religions or who are totally irreligious. (3) **Adulterers** are married persons who indulge in sexual activity outside the married relation, which violates the divine commandment as well as disregards the rights of the married partner. (4) **Effeminate** means soft or voluptuous, and is used by Paul "to signify general addiction to sins of the flesh."[21] Godet translates it "those who pamper the body,"[22] while Arndt and Gingrich render it "men and boys who allow themselves to be misused homosexually."[23] (5) **Abusers of themselves with man-**

---

[18]Lange, *op. cit.*, p. 125.
[19]Godet, *op. cit.*, p. 296.
[20]Arndt and Gingrich, *op. cit.*, p. 700.
[21]Findlay, *op. cit.*, p. 817.
[22]*Op. cit.*, p. 296.
[23]*Op. cit.*, p. 489.

kind—the sin of sodomy was widely practiced by the Greeks. (6) **Thieves** were the swindlers, cheaters, and robbers. (7) The **covetous** are those who are greedy for gain, with an insatiable desire to have more. (8) **Drunkards** refers to those who drink freely and habitually, who become intoxicated. (9) **Revilers** would be persons guilty of using abusive speech, slanderers; perhaps the "scoffer" of the OT who brazenly rejected the claims of God. (10) **Extortioners** are those who rob or confiscate property during a persecution. Here it may mean those who take unfair legal advantage of others.

Paul's direct statement is that such people **shall not inherit the kingdom of God.** The Corinthians may have thought that they would be saved by the mere fact of making an open profession or by being publicly baptized. The apostle warns them that "faith without works is dead, and privileges without holiness are abrogated."[24] Paul is giving rather bitter medicine at this point. But he sweetens the bitterness with a reminder.

e. Spiritual heritage of the Corinthians (6:11). Paul does not accuse all of the Corinthians with being involved in the sins he has presented. Instead, he reminds them that **such were some of you.** The word translated **such** means literally "these things." Some of them had been identified with these sins in the past. However, they had experienced a radical change. The triple use of the word **but** in this verse stresses the contrast between their present life in Christ and their past life of sin. These people had known a religious experience which Paul describes in a threefold fashion.

First, he says, **But ye are washed.** The construction of the verb in the aorist middle voice calls attention to the fact that the Corinthians were actively involved in the process. In response to the gospel message, they had deliberately and voluntarily sought to get rid of the filth of their old life. In presenting themselves for baptism their faith found open expression. They had desired to be baptized; so it was not a formal gesture. Thus being **washed** "refers to the putting away of sin in repentance, of which water baptism is the sacramental seal (Acts xxii:16.)."[25]

Second, Paul asserts, **But ye are sanctified.** Here the word "sanctify" does not mean the removal of inherited impurities which hinder Christian development. In this instance it means

---

[24]Farrar, *op. cit.,* p. 193.   [25]Jamieson, Fausset, and Brown, *op. cit.,* p. 298.

"the initial act whereby the believer passed from his previous state of corruption to that of holiness."[26] This is what John Wesley called "initial sanctification," the setting aside of the regenerated person to God's way of living.

Third, Paul writes, **But ye are justified.** To "justify" means to declare to be just or right. Because they had thus been set apart to serve God, they were righteous before God. This kind of sanctification and justification is the work of the Spirit of our God.

Each of these three verbs—**washed** (baptized), **sanctified,** and **justified**—is a strong reminder of the past experiences of the Corinthians. They had experienced dramatic conversions. Now it would be tragic indeed if they returned to their old manner of living.

B. LIBERTY VERSUS SPIRITUAL DISCIPLINE, 6:12-14

Paul had fought for liberty from the law of the Judaizers, who wanted to impose the OT ceremonial law on Christianity. But carnal Christians seem prone to seize any point as an excuse to turn liberty into license. Apparently some of the Corinthians were defending their low living by the principle of Christian liberty. Paul does not retract his position on spiritual liberty, but he defines its proper application to the Christian life. This application has two major aspects.

1. *Liberty Limited by Spiritual Expediency* (6:12a)

Paul here gives his famous spiritual emancipation proclamation: **All things are lawful unto me.** He did not refer to things which are known to be wrong in either civil practice or in Scripture. He would not become a spiritual anarchist, rebelling against helpful law and attempting to annul all restrictions. Paul applied the principle mainly in reference to food, stating that he felt at liberty to satisfy his hunger by any foods available. This attitude contradicted the Jewish ceremonial law, which regarded some food as unclean (cf. Lev. 20:25; Acts 10:13-14). The Corinthians had broadened Paul's idea to include the free satisfaction of all bodily hungers, but the missionary leader closed this loophole once and for all.

---

[26]Godet, *op. cit.*, p. 298.

To the apostle all things may be **lawful . . . but all things are not expedient.** Thus liberty is not the final measure of Christian conduct. Liberty must be exercised in the light of all the facts. The verb "to be profitable" (*sumphero*, lit. "to bring with" or "bring together") means to be helpful or advantageous. Thus all use of Christian liberty must be beneficial—to ourselves and to others. A Christian has no right to participate in activities which may appear innocent to him but which may be harmful to others.

2. Liberty Is Subject to Self-discipline (6:12b)

In addition to helpfulness, Paul limited liberty by the idea of self-discipline: **I will not be brought under the power of any.** All things are permissible, but Paul refused to be dominated by even legitimate things. Self-discipline is actually the greatest liberty of all. In self-discipline the Spirit directs, and the Christian lives free from the tyranny of either sinful deeds or the domination of things that in themselves are not wrong. Liberty becomes a snare when it weakens characters, saps spiritual vitality, or reduces the effectiveness of the Christian witness.

In vv. 1-12, Paul gives the essence of "Christian Liberty." (1) Charity in personal relationships, 1-7; (2) Vitality in personal experience, 9-11; (3) Discipline in personal outlook, 12.

3. Illustrations of Spiritual Liberty (6:13-14)

Paul had a genius for illustrating profound spiritual truth with simple ideas. In this instance he uses the normal appetites of eating and sex to illustrate the nature of liberty.

a. *Liberty and food* (6:13a). To show the nature of Christian liberty Paul spoke of one of the most common of all human practices—eating. He writes: **Meats for the belly, and the belly for meats.** Both false asceticism and unnecessary ceremonialism regarding food are rejected by Paul. Food and the stomach are made for each other. Food is essential to the natural functions of the body.

However, since the physical body represents a temporary aspect of existence, its functions will stop at death. **God shall destroy both it** (the stomach) **and them** (foods). In and of themselves the natural bodily functions have no moral or spiritual meaning. Such functions acquire spiritual significance only by the motivation and circumstances in which they take place.

b. *The glory of the body* (6:13b-14). Paul persists in warning against sexual looseness. He drives home the truth that **the body is not for fornication, but for the Lord** (13). Paul thus makes a valid distinction between the need of the body for food and for the expression of sex appetite. The body cannot exist without food, but it can exist without sexual indulgence. The body, unlike the meats and the stomach, will not be eliminated, but will be transformed and glorified. Not only is the body **for the Lord,** but **the Lord** is **for the body.** The Lord Jesus and sensual appetites both attempt to dominate the personality. When their claims are in conflict, to accept one is to reject the other. Christ is to be Lord over the total being. Though it is sometimes hard to realize, the lordship of Christ is meant for—and best for —the body.

To strengthen the Corinthians in their struggle to develop holy character Paul declared that the resurrection of Jesus points to the resurrection of the body. **And God hath both raised up the Lord, and will also raise up us by his own power** (14). The same divine power that caused the resurrection of the Lord will bring about the resurrection of the body. The raising of Christ from the dead and the coming resurrection of God's people are the supreme manifestations of God's power.

C. A WARNING AGAINST FORNICATION, 6:15-18

Paul repeats his favorite question: **Know ye not?** (15) It is a rhetorical question, for the answer is obvious. Like many of the questions of Christ and Paul, it is used as an unanswerable approach. Its purpose is to drive home spiritual truth. In warning against fornication Paul suggests two ideas.

1. *The Body of the Christian Belongs to Christ* (6:15)

Paul declares, **Your bodies are the members of Christ.** Every believer is a part of the body of which Christ is the Head (12: 12-27; Rom. 12:4-5; Eph. 4:15-16; 5:30). The body is a living organism "fitted to carry out His purpose through grace."[27] The believer's relationship with Christ includes the fact that his body is an instrument through which the Lord acts.

The Greeks taught that man's body was a drag or a lower part of nature that identified man with the beasts. They thought

[27]Vine, *op. cit.,* p. 89.

that only man's intelligence and reason were in harmony with the higher realms of truth and reality. The Romans generally regarded the body as the instrument of power or pleasure. But in the NT the entire person, including his body, is a member of the body of Christ. The body is sacred and belongs to the Lord.

2. Fornication Cuts One Off from Christ (6:16-18)

All sin is a severing of our spiritual ties to God. Sin either directly denies or indirectly rejects the principle of spiritual union with Christ. The sin of fornication, in Paul's view, certainly severed this relationship. The apostle declares that sexual intercourse with a harlot, unlike union with a wife, separates one from Christ.

Sexual union constitutes a permanent bond between two parties. The act is incorporated into their lives and can never be removed. Paul writes, **He which is joined to an harlot is one body, for two . . . shall be one flesh** (16). To be thus identified with a harlot was harsh language, for often the man feels contempt for her and uses her only as a lump of flesh, with no respect for her as a person. Paul will have none of this. A man united to a harlot is reduced to her level both physically and spiritually. To Paul the sexual relationship is more than an animal response—it is the complex and mystical union of two personalities. Thus the fornicator becomes one with the harlot he uses. The apostle does not debate the issue. He issues a pronouncement. Whether they believe it or not, accept it or not, know it or not—it is so.

In direct opposition to the corrupt union of a man with a harlot is the spiritual union of the believer with Christ. Where the fornicator joins himself to a harlot in lust and corruption, the believer joins himself to the Lord in faith and love. The man who is **joined unto the Lord is one** (in) **spirit** (17) with the Lord. Here is man's highest privilege, his unique opportunity. The believer enters into a mystical union with Christ. Not only the body but the total person is involved. This union with Christ does not nullify man's nature nor minimize his personality. He remains man, but becomes more than man because his spirit is one with Christ.

After presenting the contrast between the union of a man with a harlot and the union of a believer with Christ, Paul again flashes the warning: **Flee fornication** (18). The verb here is a present imperative. **Flee** means to run from it, get out of danger. The command suggests the danger of thinking, reasoning, or arguing about it. Some sins may be faced, fought, and overcome. Other sins may bring a shock or a recoil which drives the person from them. But fornication is too subtle to discuss or to debate. The Christian's course of action should be like that of Joseph in Pharaoh's house (Gen. 39:12). The only sure way to guarantee abstinence from immorality is to immediately and decisively remove oneself from the possibility of it.

The reason for Paul's drastic condemnation of sexual sin is its effect on human personality. **Every sin that a man doeth is without the body; but he that committeth fornication sinneth against his own body** (18). Other sins may be harmful to the body, but this one is more. In fornication people lower themselves, shed their dignity and honor, become completely carnal and corrupt. The harlot has already denied her intrinsic worth by placing a price tag on her body and selling it as merchandise. But she always loses, for money is a poor exchange for human value. Likewise the man involved regards his body as something to be bartered, abused, or destroyed.

Other sins, such as murder or theft, are projections or misuses of the powers of the body. But fornication involves the body as the very center, the motive as well as the seat of sin. All sin is a destructive force, and fornication is no exception. It cripples the entire personality, defies God, degrades others, and corrupts oneself.

D. THE CHRISTIAN'S BODY AS A SANCTUARY, 6:19-20

There are several ways a person may regard his body. He may pamper and idolize it. He may regard it with disgust or shame. He may use it like a machine to produce work. He may use it as a weapon to gain power. He may dedicate it to carnal pleasures and use it as an instrument of vice. Or with Paul, he may look upon it as a **temple** (*naos*, sanctuary). **Know ye not that your body is the temple of the Holy Ghost which is in you, which ye have of God?** (19)

Jesus referred to His body as a temple when He said: "Destroy this temple, and in three days I will raise it up." John presented the interpretation of this statement when he said that Jesus spoke of "the temple of his body" (John 2:19-21). Paul had also referred to the local congregation as a temple (I Cor. 3:16). The temple was regarded by the Jews as the special residence of God. So the body as a temple becomes a special place of residence for the Holy Spirit.

When the Holy Spirit resides in a temple, it belongs to God. Thus Paul says: **Ye are not your own.** The Christian has entered into a transaction, signed a deed, and turned over possession to God. This indwelling Spirit is a Gift from a holy God and cannot dwell in a polluted sanctuary.

A further reason for placing a spiritual evaluation on the body is that each person has been **bought with a price** (20). The word means a payment which results in a change of the ownership. Paul inevitably pictures every phase of life against the background of the Cross. The sacrifice of Christ was the purchase price for man's personal redemption. Paul next adds a positive note: **Therefore glorify God in your body.** It is absolutely necessary to keep the body from immorality. To do this, more than a negative legalism or passive submission is required. The positive idea of glorifying God in one's body is both an obligation and a sign of gratitude and devotion. The believer is also to **glorify God . . . in your spirit.** Both body and spirit belong to God. Thus in act, in motive, in conduct, and in response the Christian is to glorify his Maker and Redeemer.

Looking back on all of c. 6 it is clear that, if the Christian is dedicated to glorifying God, both shameful lawsuits and fornication will disappear from the church. The new faith has produced a new fellowship which swallows up petty differences. Fellowship in Christ brings unity and peace to the believer.

In "The Christian Understanding of the Body" we see that: (1) The body belongs to God, 13-15; (2) The body is a temple, 19; (3) The body may glorify God, 20.

Section V *The New Faith and Marriage*

I Corinthians 7:1-40

The church at Corinth had written to Paul concerning a number of problems existing within the membership.[1] Paul had used his answer to deal with additional problems which the inquiry had not mentioned. Thus the first six chapters of this letter may be considered a "literary bonus" or a "spiritual extra." In the first four chapters Paul dealt with the matter of divisions in the church. In c. 5 he had shown that faith in Christ produced a new morality. In c. 6, Paul had discussed the nature of Christian liberty, in relation to both permissible and non-permissible areas. In c. 7 he begins to answer questions which were the occasion of the letter. Here the concept of Christian liberty appears again, but now the problem centers in domestic relationships.

A crucial question at Corinth was the Christian concept of marriage. Paul's idea of marriage as stated in this chapter is not a general statement which may be applied universally, but must be understood against the peculiar background of the Corinthian church. Charles R. Erdman writes: "It seems certain, at least, that some Christians regarded marriage as an absolute duty. Others considered the marriage state as an inferior moral condition, a weak concession to the flesh. Still others held that by accepting Christ all existing social relationships, including marriage, were dissolved."[2]

A. Marriage and Celibacy, 7:1-2

Paul interprets the institution of marriage from a practical rather than from a moral point of view. He looks at the single state from the angle of expediency rather than from the standpoint of the rightness or wrongness of being married. In the apostle's thinking, the practical benefits of remaining single were significant. However, if a person married, he neither enhanced his spiritual life nor did he mar his religious experience. But marriage brought obligations which the Christian could not

[1] See Introduction, "Occasion and Purpose of the Letter."
[2] *The First Epistle of Paul to the Corinthians* (Philadelphia: Westminster Press, 1928), p. 65.

371

ignore. These obligations were especially difficult in times of distress.

1. *Benefits of Remaining Single* (7:1)

In his opening remark, **It is good for a man not to touch a woman,** Paul does not present a low estimate of marriage. Nor does he attempt to downgrade it. Paul's basic concept of marriage is a lofty one, for in Eph. 5:23-28 he uses it as an illustration of the relationship of Christ to the Church. The view of marriage reflected here was a specific answer to this particular church, in response to **the things whereof ye wrote unto me.**

Some of the church members in Corinth may have been influenced by a type of Greek thought which regarded the single state as superior to marriage. Others may have placed a wrong interpretation on the words of Jesus, "But they which shall be accounted worthy to obtain that world, and the resurrection from the dead, neither marry, nor are given in marriage" (Luke 20: 35). Again, some may have spiritualized the single state, making celibacy seem superior because they were disgusted with the extreme emphasis on sex in Corinth.[3]

On the other hand, the Jewish element in the church may have disparaged or criticized the single state. The Jews regarded marriage as a sacred obligation and the family as the center of society. This idea of marriage is traced back to Gen. 2:18, "And the Lord God said, It is not good that the man should be alone; I will make him an help meet for him."

Paul speaks to defend the single state. "He proclaims aloud that the state of celibacy in a man is absolutely becoming and worthy, has nothing in it contrary to the moral ideal."[4] According to Lenski, the phrase **to touch a woman** refers "to sexual contact and intercourse in marriage."[5] The word **good** (*kalon*) does not indicate morally good, for there is no question of sin or of wrongdoing. The word means that it is for man's best interest in some circumstances to remain single. However, the words of the apostle do not state a general principle for every age of the Church. "Paul writes for the Corinthians and for their specific circumstance at the time."[6] Nor do the words of the apostle refer to "abstinence from intercourse in the already married."[7] Paul is

---

[3]Godet, *op. cit.,* p. 318. [4]*Ibid.,* p. 320.
[5]*Op. cit.,* p. 273. [6]*Ibid.*
[7]Alford, *op. cit.,* p. 520.

simply stating a practical concept of the benefits of remaining single. The ideas of spirituality and morality are not included in his statement.

2. Practical Necessity of Marriage (7:2)

The loose attitude in the city of Corinth made **fornication** a persistent temptation. Marriage would thus be a safeguard against sin. Here again Paul is not depreciating the romantic aspect of marriage, nor does he make marriage a concession to fleshly appetites. He does not regard marriage as an escape mechanism for those too weak to bridle the passions. Elsewhere he speaks of it as "honourable" (Eph. 5:25-27). Here Paul only points out that a practical result of marriage is that one could avoid temptation in the area of sex.

In his statement Paul included "an incidental prohibition of polygamy,"[8] which was common at this time. Even some Jewish rabbis encouraged a plurality of wives. Paul took this occasion to remind the Corinthians indirectly of the words of Christ, "And I say unto you, Whosoever shall put away his wife, except it be for fornication, and shall marry another, committeth adultery: and whoso marrieth her which is put away doth commit adultery" (Matt. 19:9). Thus, while celibacy is honorable, it should not be the rule for the Christian.

B. THE CHRISTIAN ATTITUDE TOWARD SEX, 7:3-6

Marriage involves certain practical obligations which husbands and wives owe to each other, especially in matters of sex.

1. The Obligation of Reciprocity (7:3-4)

Paul frankly states that intercourse between married people is not only a valid aspect of marriage, but is also an obligation in accord with need and desire. The verb translated **render** "signifies not the granting of a favour, but the discharge of an obligation, here from husband to wife and wife to husband."[9] Godet says: "This verse confirms us in the idea that among some of the Corinthians there existed an exaggerated spiritualistic tendency, which threatened to injure conjugal relations, and thereby holiness of life."[10] In its deepest sense the verb **render** (*apodidomi*) means to give what one owes or is under obligation to give. The

---

[8]Lightfoot, *op. cit.*, p. 221.   [9]Vine, *op. cit.*, p. 93.
[10]*Op. cit.*, p. 324.

apostle puts the sexual aspect of marriage in its proper perspective, avoiding both a loose attitude and also a rigid asceticism.

In v. 4, Paul expands the idea of mutual reciprocity to include all of life when he states that married partners have power over the bodies of each other. The words **hath not power** refer to the exercise of authority. Mutual understanding eliminates two extremes in the married state—separate ownership of oneself and the subjection of one party to the other. In marriage each partner has a legitimate right on the person of the other.

In other writings Paul regards the husband as the head of the household, stating that the wife should be subordinate (Eph. 5:22-23). But in the sexual area both are on the same level. The main teaching here is that husbands and wives have the same rights. Both should act as Christians. Thus any excessive or abusive conduct is prohibited. But extreme asceticism—in which one partner might feel that sexual relations are out of harmony with spiritual living—is also eliminated.

2. *Temporary Abstinence* (7:5-6)

There are exceptions to the rule of mutual reciprocity in sexual relations. At times one party may desire to pursue a course free from sexual activity. Under the pressure of a spiritual burden or driven by an impulse toward extraordinary spiritual activity, one may wish exemption from fulfilling the marital obligation. Where such a situation rises, three conditions must be met: (1) there must be mutual **consent**; (2) the situation must be temporary (**for a time**); (3) it must be for purposes that are higher than even our highest physical joys. Alford calls them "seasons of urgent supplication."[11] When the reason for the extraordinary time of **prayer** is past, the couple should **come together again**, i.e., resume normal relations.

Paul's views on marriage here stated are mainly **by permission, and not of commandment** (6). He has no direct command from God, but presents a bit of personal advice. When he says, **But I speak this by permission, and not of commandment,** he refers to v. 5 and includes the possibilities suggested there.

C. Personal Preference and Peculiar Gift, 7:7-9

From a practical point of view Paul would have preferred that all Christians remain single in order to permit complete and

[11]*Op. cit.*, p. 521.

unbroken work in preaching the gospel of Christ. But he realized that this was both impossible and impractical. The apostle recognized that he had a special gift in this area, and that a person could and should marry if his natural inclinations made it desirable.

1. Paul's Marital Status (7:7a)

Paul said: **For I would that all men were even as I myself** (7:7a). The words imply "with certainty that Paul was not married, and quite as certainly that he was not a widower. For how could he have expressed the desire that all men were widowers?"[12]

Some have suggested that the reference to Paul's voting in Acts 26:10 indicates that he was a member of the Sanhedrin, and that such membership was limited to married men. However, a distinction existed between the Great Sanhedrin and lesser Sanhedrins. Paul could have voted as a member of a lesser Sanhedrin without having been married. Moreover, it was only a maxim of later rabbis, not a rule of eligibility, that a man must be married to sit in judgment. Paul never refers to wife or to children. The entire approach of the apostle is that of one who has never been married.

2. Paul's Peculiar Gift (7:7b)

Paul's preference that all men remain single is not a common or natural reaction. There is a difference among men which must be taken into consideration. Jesus had previously pointed out (Matt. 19:10-12) that some men have a tendency not to marry. They may be too restless or too highly motivated in a certain direction. When spiritual zeal is added to such a tendency, there is apparently little struggle with the natural desire to marry.

Such complete self-mastery is a gift of God. It is not given to everyone. Man's natural inclination as well as God's revealed plan for man includes marriage. So one person has a God-given aptitude for celibacy. Another person follows the normal pattern and marries. There is no spiritual superiority of one state over the other.

[12]Godet, *op. cit.*, p. 327.

3. *Both Marriage and Celibacy Permitted* (7:8-9)

The phrase **to the unmarried** (8; *tois agamois*) refers to those who had never married.[13] Paul suggests to them, men or women, and also to the woman who had lost her husband, that they remain single **even as I.** It should be restated that Paul was here answering questions in a particular situation. It should be stated also that Paul's ideas were matters of personal conviction rather than of divine command, and that these ideas were stated under a strong sense of urgency regarding the task of the Christian to serve Christ fully and completely.

Yet marriage was also permissible (9). It is not a sin to desire a marriage partner, for this is man's natural state. Marriage was initiated by God, sanctioned by Christ, and used by the apostle to express the relationship of Christ to the Church (Eph. 5:22-29).

Paul here presents only one reason for marriage when he writes: **But if they cannot contain, let them marry: for it is better to marry than to burn** (9). The compound verb **contain** (*egkratevomai*) means "to possess in oneself the power of controlling oneself."[14] When used with a negative it means the lack of power, the absence of self-control. If people lack this power, let them marry. It is permissible for people who lack the power of control in matters of sex to marry and thus solve the problem related to sex impulses. It must be stated again that Paul is answering a question about a specific situation in Corinth, and not presenting a universal principle for all Christians. To encourage Christians to marry for purposes of sex alone would be absurd, but it is one of the factors to consider. It is better to marry than to continually struggle with the fire of sexual desire or, worse yet, to suffer the guilt of yielding to such a desire outside the married relationship. In a very real sense, **to burn** means "to be consumed with passions which would hold the upper hand if there was no continence."[15]

D. Christian Obligations in Marriage, 7:10-16

In dealing with the obligations involved in marriage Paul speaks with authority. In all cases people are to accept their station in good grace.

---

[13]Godet, *op. cit.*, p. 329.   [14]*Ibid.*, p. 330.
[15]Grosheide, *op. cit.*, p. 162.

1. *Obligations in Christian Marriages* (7:10-11)

In dealing with marriages between Christians, Paul can speak with authority: **And unto the married I command, yet not I, but the Lord.** In essence he transmits a command given by the Lord Jesus Christ. Paul appears to have in mind the words of Jesus in Matt. 5:32; 19:9; Mark 10:11; and Luke 16:18. These commands of Jesus, repeated by Paul, simply state that Christians ought to remain loyal to their marriage vows, and remain together as man and wife.

The basic reference in regard to separation and divorce is addressed first to the wife: **Let not the wife depart from her husband** (10). The command may have been directed to the woman because "the Christian *women* at Corinth may have been the most ready to make the separation."[16] Or the woman may have been forced to leave, since the husband normally controlled the property. If for some reason the Christian wife left her husband, she had only two options—to **remain unmarried** (11) or to effect a reconciliation.

The husband had an equal obligation, for he was commanded not to **put away his wife.** Divorce was a free and easy matter in Corinth, as in all cities under Roman rule. The Roman legal system granted either party the right to take the initiative in dissolving a marriage. The Jewish law also permitted a man to give a woman a statement of divorce for insignificant reasons. In addition, marriages between slaves were not considered binding, and marriages between a freeman and a slave had a very low standing. All these factors combined to make Corinthian marriages rather insecure and temporary arrangements.

2. *Obligations in Religiously Mixed Marriages* (7:12-16)

Many in the church had become Christians after they were already married. Unless the other partner was won to Christ, the Christian was faced with the problem of living with a heathen. Since Jesus left no direct command on this subject, the apostle speaks as he feels directed (12). However, Paul did not make his declaration regarding mixed marriages a matter of indiscriminate personal opinion. He was not an ecclesiastical dictator, but he was an apostle. Therefore his words were to be authoritative in the Church. Two examples of mixed marriages are discussed.

[16]Alford, *op. cit.*, p. 523.

a. *A Mixed Marriage Where the Partners Are Content* (7: 12-14). The first example of a mixed marriage is one in which the unchristian partner is willing to remain with the partner who has become a Christian. In such a case the Christian was obligated to remain with the unchristian partner. Such a directive from Paul would make it clear that a Christian could not leave or divorce a partner on the grounds that the partner refused to become a Christian. Christianity cannot become an excuse for unchristian conduct. So if the unchristian partner is content, the believer is obligated to remain married

There is no spiritual stigma attached to a new convert who remains with an unconverted mate. On the contrary, the unconverted partner receives some spiritual benefit from the Christian. Regarding the spiritual blessings which the unsaved share, Paul writes: **For the unbelieving husband is sanctified by the wife, and the unbelieving wife is sanctified by the husband (14).** This does not mean that the unbeliever undergoes a moral or spiritual change. The verb **is sanctified** "cannot mean holy in Christ before God, because that kind of holiness cannot be predicated of an unbeliever."[17] Paul uses **sanctified** here with a ceremonial meaning rather than in an ethical or spiritual sense.

The unbelieving husband or wife of a Christian believer is set apart or dedicated to God by the life of the believer. As Lenski interprets it, "Through the believing spouse the blessings of a sanctified marriage are bestowed upon the unbelieving spouse and thus more is given to him than his unbelief deserves."[18] Even the children of such a marriage are benefited in that **now are they holy (14)**. Here again the idea is that the children of mixed marriages are acceptable within the church and that in both home and church they are surrounded with the blessings related to the believer. Notwithstanding any spiritual blessings coming from the parent, "the Christian child is individually born in sin and a child of wrath; and individually needs the washing of regeneration and the renewing of the Holy Ghost."[19]

In mixed marriages where the unbelieving partner is content to remain together, the Christian is under obligation to be

---

[17]Grosheide, *op. cit.*, p. 164.   [18]*Op. cit.*, p. 292.
[19]Alford, *op. cit.*, pp. 524-25.

loyal to the marriage contract. A difference exists, however, when the unbelieving partner chooses to leave.

b. A Mixed Marriage Where the Unbeliever Is Not Content (7:15-16). The situation here is the opposite of a mixed marriage where the partners remain together by mutual consent. If the unbeliever refuses to remain with the believer, the Christian is free from obligation to sustain the marriage: **But if the unbelieving depart, let him depart** (15). In this way the believer comes into **peace.** Under these circumstances the Christian is not committed to a lifetime of persecution, abuse, and agony because of his relationship to a heathen partner. But the separation must be initiated and completed by another. The Christian should neither encourage dissension nor promote separations. Peace and love should always be the trademarks of Christian living.

There is no contradiction between Paul's permission to allow the breakup of a marriage with a heathen unbeliever and the command of Jesus in Matt. 5:32. The Lord's words were directed to those who professed to be loyal subjects of God. The words of Paul are addressed to those who are married to unbelievers. The directive does not grant permission for a believer to marry an unbeliever. The guidance is for a married person who becomes a believer after his marriage. In such a situation the Christian is free to let the unbeliever depart, rather than insist on continuing a union which survives in an atmosphere of tensions, bickerings, and fear.

Marriage is never to be undertaken as a "missionary institution."[20] When one is already married, as in this instance, there is no way of knowing whether or not the other party will be saved (16). Nevertheless, the Christian wife or husband is under obligation to try to win the other partner (I Pet. 3:1). Paul also urges that the Christian partner sacrifice much in the hope that the unbelieving husband or wife might be saved eventually. But if the unbelieving partner is hostile and antagonistic to Christianity, he will not be apt to become a Christian. A person's salvation is ultimately a matter between himself and God. The Christian partner is obligated to do all he can to persuade the unchristian husband or wife to come to Christ. But finally the person stands at the crossroads of decision. So no one can guarantee

[20]Grosheide, *op. cit.*, p. 167.

the salvation of another. If the unbelieving partner initiates the separation, the Christian should not condemn himself for the failure of the departed spouse to become a Christian.

E. PRINCIPLE OF SPIRITUAL CONTENTMENT, 7:17-24

The Christian is under obligation to fulfill all the duties of the particular relationship in which he is involved at the time of his conversion. This principle of obligation is more than a mere duty; it is a matter of spiritual contentment.

1. *The principle* (7:17)

Paul writes, **But as God hath distributed to every man, as the Lord hath called every one, so let him walk** (17). The apostle ordained that people should place spiritual matters foremost in their lives. The word **ordain** (*diatasso*) means to prescribe or to appoint. Such an ordination indicates a summary decision and suggests apostolic competency. This principle of spiritual contentment means that "every believer ought to remain in the earthly situation in which the call to salvation found him."[21] The mandate from Paul does not mean that one should not seek to improve himself through education or that he should not seek to advance himself by diligent effort. The point that the apostle makes is that a new convert should not use the gospel as an excuse to free himself from an unfortunate situation. Nor should the believer use the gospel as a springboard for unnecessary personal change or for social anarchy.

2. *The Illustration of Circumcision* (7:18-20)

The Christian state does not depend upon or call for external rites. If a Jew was converted to Christ, let him remain **circumcised** (18). If a convert was a Gentile, he did not need to be circumcised. Thus circumcision, which played so decisive a role in Judaism, was shown to be meaningless in Christianity. "The coming of Christ inaugurated a new era, in which holiness alone remains."[22] The meaning is that both Jew and Gentile should be content to remain in the particular physical state, regarding circumcision, as they were when they were converted.

Since both the former Jews and the former pagans are now Christians, **circumcision is nothing, and uncircumcision is noth-**

---

[21]Godet, *op. cit.*, p. 353.   [22]*Ibid.*, p. 355.

ing (19). Paul's own personal actions supported his teaching at
this point. He had encouraged the circumcision of Timothy as
the child of one Jewish parent (Acts 16:3), and had refused to
seek the circumcision of Titus (Gal. 2:3). The principle Paul
presents condemns those who insist on the absolute rejection of
former conditions as well as those who insist on returning to
them. Lightfoot writes that in this instance circumcision is used
as "a symbol of a much wider application . . . the observance of
sabbaths, festivals, etc."[23]

While observing external forms was of little importance to
Paul, it is of utmost importance that a Christian have a concern
for the keeping of the commandments of God. The Christian
ought to be careful in fulfilling the requirements of the gospel;
he ought to be concerned about "faith working by love."[24]

Rather than lose spiritual victory because of undue concern
for external status or conditions, a Christian should **abide in the
same calling wherein he was called** (20). The word **calling** may
mean three things: a designation of a calling or vocation, an invitation to attend a supper, or an official summons to appear as
a witness or advocate in court. Here the meaning is "the summons to the knowledge of God, to membership in the Church, to
the kingdom of Christ."[25] Another writer suggests that the term
calling should not here be interpreted "in the sense of a man's
profession, position, or life work, for this is the standard apostolic
term for the effective gospel call which makes a man a true Christian."[26] The apostle simply presents the truth that the gospel is
designed primarily to change one's spiritual life, not his social
status. The change in status may come later, as a result of personal improvement or a change in society.

3. The Illustration of Slavery (7:21-24)

If the believer was **a servant** (slave, 21) when he was converted, he should not react to his situation so that he loses his
spiritual peace and victory. At this point Paul did not condone
slavery. The apostle was neither a rigid reactionary nor an anarchist. To him the important thing was personal redemption. The
slave should not lose his spiritual balance because he was a slave.
Freedom in Christ elevates a man above his social status. In an

---

[23]*Op. cit.*, p. 228.
[25]Lightfoot, *op. cit.*, p. 228.
[24]Wesley, *Notes*, p. 605.
[26]Lenski, *op. cit.*, p. 302.

ideal society there would be no slavery of any kind. But Paul was a realist who knew that the Roman Empire was not an ideal society.

A man may have spiritual victory in a social situation which he cannot control. But if a legitimate opportunity for freedom comes, the Christian should take advantage of it: **If thou mayest be made free, use it rather.** The free man can be of more service to Christ than a slave. No Bible command and no Christian ethic forbids any man to improve his social or economic status by rightful means. In the days of the Early Church, a slave could be freed (*a*) by the death of a master who left a legal will freeing him, (*b*) by a reward for service given to a generous master, or (*c*) by an act of worship on the part of the master, who gave the price of the slave as an offering to his god. In the latter case, no one could enslave him again, for he was the property of the god.

Whether a man is free or a slave, he **is Christ's servant** (22). Christ has paid the purchase price to free man from the mastery of sin. Paul writes, **He that is called in the Lord . . . is the Lord's freeman.** According to Roman law, a person freed from slavery by a generous benefactor was obligated to take his patron's name, live in his house, and consult him on business affairs. The Christian likewise owes a debt to Christ that he can never fully pay.

The man who is a slave is free in Christ, and the man who is free is the servant of Christ. Thus both men are free and both men are slaves. As Alford puts it, "The (actual) slave is (spiritually) free: the (actually) free is a (spiritual) slave."[27]

Since Christ has freed us, the Christian should guard his liberty: **Be not ye the servants of men** (23). Some regard the command as a warning against selling oneself into slavery. In any case, the idea is that Christ has freed the believer, and the believer should not allow social relations or social status to rob him of spiritual victory.

The Christian should **abide with God** (24), and live in the atmosphere of the Spirit. Such spiritual freedom is true freedom. The word **with** (*para*) suggests the idea of being by God's side in peace and rest, regardless of physical or social conditions. In this emphasis on spiritual freedom Paul does not condone slavery. In writing to Philemon about the treatment of a runaway slave the apostle had said: "Knowing that thou wilt do even beyond what

[27]*Op. cit.*, p. 528.

I say" (Philem. 21). Godet declares that "this passage may certainly be called the first petition in favour of the abolition of slavery."[28] It is the genius of Christianity to apply Christian principles to social situations and to change them for the better. The Christian practice, then, is "accepting everything to transform everything, submitting to everything to rise above everything, renewing the world from top to bottom while condemning all violent subversion."[29]

F. MARRIAGE AND CHRISTIAN SERVICE, 7: 25-38

Apparently the church at Corinth had asked Paul's opinion regarding unmarried daughters and the responsibilities of parents in such instances.

1. *Apostolic Advice* (7:25)

Paul writes that he has **no commandment of the Lord** but that he would give his own personal opinion. He had received no direct revelation from the Lord, nor did he know of any direct teachings of Christ in the matter. Yet he felt qualified as an apostle and steward to speak on the subject. The word "virgins" appears in Rev. 14: 4 in relation to unmarried people of both sexes. But here it refers to unmarried daughters and the father's role in assenting to or prohibiting marriage. The question must be understood in the light of the Oriental practice which permits the daughter to marry only if the father agrees. There are three aspects in the apostle's reply.

2. *The Single State Better in Times of Distress* (7:26-31)

Paul stated that in his judgment the unmarried state was **good for** (because of) **the present distress**. The word **good** (*kalos*) denotes something that is intrinsically good in its nature, something well-adapted to its purpose or condition. **Present** (*enestos*) in some cases means imminent, and here alludes to the "painful and terrible experiences which the confession of Christ may at any time bring upon a believer."[30] **Distress** refers to the tensions or the situations caused by external events beyond one's control. A person who was single would eliminate the heartache that married people face in times of physical disaster. Because of the perilous times which were coming, neither the married nor the unmarried should seek a change (27).

---

[28]*Op. cit.*, p. 361.   [29]*Ibid.*, p. 365.   [30]Lenski, *op. cit.*, p. 313.

However, if a person does **marry** even in the face of imminent danger, he has **not sinned** (28). Marriage in such cases "is not a matter of right and wrong but of expediency and personal choice."[31]

But those who marry may expect **trouble in the flesh.** Such trouble will not be the result of any personal wrongdoing, but rather it will be because trouble is inevitable in times of social upheaval. Perhaps Paul was thinking of the distress of the Jews who were carried into captivity or of the agony of certain families during the wars of the Maccabbees. Or more to the point, the apostle may have seen the inevitable tensions and unavoidable conflict between the Roman state and the Christian Church. He was trying to spare his converts from heartache and tragedy.

In his intense concern for the welfare of both the people and the gospel Paul wrote: **But this I say, brethren, the time is short** (29). The word **say** (*phemi*) means to declare, while the word **time** (*kairos*) indicates a season or a period providing an opportunity. Here it refers to the return of Christ.

Because the time of opportunity to work for Christ has been shortened, all believers should become detached from the things of the earth, which are about to come to an end (29-30). While it is impossible to escape the domestic and other functions completely, such activities should be viewed in the light of the coming of Christ. Thus marriage, sorrow, joy, and business transactions, all should be put into an eschatological setting. The believer may **use** the things of **this world** (31) but he should never allow secular affairs to interfere with spiritual life. The word **abusing** "appears here to imply that intense and greedy use which turns the legitimate use into a fault."[32] The apostle declares that **the fashion of this world passeth away**—that the old arrangement of things was changing. Because of the drastic changes to come it was better to be unmarried.

3. *Advantages of the Unmarried Life* (7:32-35)

Paul wanted both men and women to be free from care. The term **careth** (32) is used to denote "special attention and effort to some person or some thing."[33] In this sense, the unmarried man has only one concern—to please the Lord. The married man, on the other hand, has specific obligations that tend to divide his

---

[31]Erdman, *op. cit.*, p. 72.   [32]Alford, *op. cit.*, p. 531.
[33]Lenski, *op. cit.*, pp. 320-21.

interests. While the married man is not necessarily worldly in his outlook, often he acts as though he were, because of the responsibility of the married life (33). In times of distress he cannot escape the anxieties associated with his family.

Similarly, there is a difference between the service given to the Lord by **the unmarried woman** and the **virgin** (34). Like the unmarried man, **the unmarried woman** has only one dominant concern—to please the Lord. Thus she is **holy both in body and in spirit. The unmarried woman** is separated **in body,** and dedicated **in spirit** to the Lord. The married woman, like the married man, has a double obligation—one to her family and one to her Lord. These two sets of obligations are not antagonistic or mutually exclusive. But a simple fact of arithmetic dictates that two sets of obligations are more difficult to fulfill than one, especially in times of emergency or distress.

Paul speaks for the benefit of the Corinthians (35). The word **profit** suggests that which contributes to a person's best interests. The apostle does not intend to put a spiritual **snare** upon the Christians to deprive them of their liberty. Instead, he wants to point out the life that seems best suited to believers in their circumstances. The purpose of remaining unmarried is that one may apply himself diligently to the work of the Kingdom, **without distraction.** Thus the entire matter is lifted out of the area of the moral and ethical into the arena of spiritual advantage.

4. *Duty to Unmarried Daughters* (7:36-38)

This passage has always presented problems. The traditional approach has been to interpret it as a matter of the father's reaction to an unmarried daughter who has reached the age of maturity.[34] Vine suggests that the reference is to a father who may have refused to allow his daughter to marry. The father finally decides that he is acting in an unfair and unwise fashion by refusing to give his consent. The father has decided that his rigid refusal might drive the daughter to rebellion, or possibly to immorality. The daughter may have indicated a desire to marry, and was not gifted in the powers of self-denial. In this case her father should **let them marry** (36).

Another interpretation of the passage under consideration is that it refers to a couple who may not have been married for-

[34]Vine, *op. cit.,* p. 107; Lenski, *op. cit.,* pp. 326-27.

mally. They decide to live together, to share the same problems, but refrain from entering into sexual relations. Barclay suggests that the couple was actually married,[35] but had agreed upon a "spiritual union," which was never consummated in a physical sense. However, their original decision is overcome by a desire to consummate their marriage. This they may do, without any sense of having done wrong (36).

Most commentators accept the traditional view, interpreting it as a father-daughter situation. Either way, the idea is that it is not sinful to marry and to live together as man and wife. However, if the father, or the couple, decide to remain firm, it is also within the bounds of practical Christian ethics.

Four things should determine the father's decision if he refuses to permit his daughter to marry (37). First, he should be convinced that the single state is better for the daughter—**he will keep his virgin.** Second, the father should know that the daughter is not especially interested in marriage or is not bothered by sexual impulses—"having . . . desire under control" (RSV). Third, he is free to make his decision as he will—**having no necessity.** Finally, he should make a decision and hold to it—**standeth stedfast in his heart**—rather than keep the matter in a state of indecision.

Whether the daughter marries or remains single involves only practical results, not spiritual superiority. The words **doeth well** and **doeth better** (38) sum up the whole chapter. **Well** indicates that marriage is neither defiling nor unholy. **Better** is a kind of apostolic judgment that the single state is expedient because in it one avoids suffering and gains more time to serve the Lord.

G. Christian Remarriage, 7:39-40

Paul held a lofty concept of marriage, although in some instances he recommended the single state. To the apostle marriage was a lifelong arrangement: **The wife is bound by the law as long as her husband liveth** (39). However, in the event the husband dies, the widow is completely free to remarry. The only reservation Paul places upon such a remarriage is that it be with a Christian man, i.e., one who is **in the Lord.** However, even in

---

[35]*Op. cit.*, p. 75.

such a case Paul adds that according to **my judgment** (40) she would be **happier if she so abide** (remained single).

Paul has been accused of being "a narrow ascetic who despised women and discouraged marriage."[36] Actually, he advised marriage as a general rule for most Christians and never placed any superior ethical or spiritual evaluation on celibacy. His views here expressed on marriage must be interpreted in the context of the problems presented to him by the church at Corinth. Paul wrote to discourage an extreme asceticism which had placed a spiritual priority on remaining single. He also wrote that in times of distress or of emergency the single person had fewer obligations and less concern for the ordinary affairs of this world. This chapter should be understood as a commonsense approach to decisions regarding marriage and remarriage. Paul leaves them as decisions of personal preference, not of spiritual strength or weakness.

[36]Erdman, *op. cit.*, p. 66.

Section **VI** *The New Faith and Spiritual Liberty*

I Corinthians 8:1—11:1

Up to this point Paul has dealt primarily with personal or individual problems. Now he broadens the scope of the discussion to show how the new faith in Jesus Christ includes obligations and responsibilities to the Church as a whole. The Christian has an obligation to be an example of the grace of God.

A. The Principle of Spiritual Liberty, 8:1-13

In theory Paul is the champion of Christian freedom. In practice he imposes rather severe restrictions on the exercise of freedom. He was adamant in his insistence that spiritual life in Christ freed one from the ceremonial law of Judaism. When it came to personal redemption, Paul was clear that salvation was primarily a matter of a mystical union with Christ through faith. But Christian liberty, to Paul, was never a vague and abstract idea that permitted complete freedom in personal conduct. To him, Christian freedom had to be exercised not only from the standpoint of knowledge and rights, but also from the standpoint of love and its obligations to others.

1. *Love as the Guide in Christian Liberty* (8:1)

The church at Corinth had, no doubt, requested Paul to give some direction concerning the matter of Christians eating meats offered to idols. Thus Paul begins: **Now as touching things offered unto idols, we know that we all have knowledge.**

a. *The problem explained* (8:1a). The eating of meats offered to idols was far more than a matter of diet. It involved a basic part of heathen customs in the pagan religious and social practices of the day. When a man offered an animal as a sacrifice to an idol, a part of the animal was placed on the altar to be consumed by fire, a part was given to the officiating priest, and the remainder was given to the man who offered the sacrifices. The part retained by the worshiper could be eaten at a feast in the temple in honor of the idol, or it could be eaten at home as part of a private festive occasion, or it could be disposed of by sale in the public market. Since the priest received more than he could consume personally, he would dispose of his extra meat at the public market also.

The questions regarding the propriety of Christians eating meat probably arose at two points. One would have been the rightness of eating such meat either in one's own home or in the home of a friend. A greater problem would have been the question of participation by Christians in banquets at the heathen temples or in other festivals in honor of the idol.

The eating of meals, which included meat offered to idols, was, as Moffatt says, "all part and parcel of the formal etiquette in society."[1] Since many of these converts at Corinth had worshiped heathen idols prior to their conversion to Christ, they would have friends and relatives among the unconverted. At times the Christians would be invited to celebrate a festive occasion with their former associates or relatives who were still idolaters. One writer suggests that "as the sacrifice usually took place in connection with some joyful circumstances, relatives and friends were invited to the feast, among whom it might easily happen that there were Christians."[2] Thus the problem became one that involved social relationships. "To have nothing to do with such gatherings was to cut oneself off from most social intercourse with one's fellows."[3]

This meat offered to idols may have been sold in the public market "as ordinary butcher's meat, without any notification that it had ever formed part of a sacrifice."[4] Paul states that all enlightened Christians know that no spiritual defilement can come from eating meat under such circumstances.

b. The danger of knowledge (8:1b). That Christ was the only true and living God was admitted by all Christians. Some therefore reasoned that, since they knew an idol was unreal, they could eat idol offerings with a clear conscience. Such knowledge, however, was not the solution to this particular problem. These problems are solved on the basis of love, rather than knowledge—**Knowledge puffeth up, but charity edifieth.** Anyone who insists

---

[1]Quoted by Morris, *op. cit.*, p. 123.   [2]Godet, *op. cit.*, I, 401-2.
[3]Morris, *op. cit.*, p. 123.

[4]James C. Gray and George M. Adams, *Gray and Adams Bible Commentary* (Grand Rapids: Zondervan Publishing House, n.d.), V, 128.

on acting solely on the basis of what in theory is permissible has not yet learned the basic principle of Christian liberty. "In the Christian life, love and not knowledge is the safest guide."[5] The Christian needs knowledge, but there is always a degree of danger in it. As Barclay writes, knowledge "tends to make a man arrogant; it tends to make him feel superior and to look down on the man who is not as far advanced as himself."[6]

The word **edifieth** translates a verb *oikodomei,* which refers to the erection of a building. Paul frequently uses it as an illustration of building up Christian character (cf. I Thess. 5:11). Knowledge builds up pride in the individual, while love builds up the church. Godet makes the following comparison of knowledge and love: With the "idea of personal inflation the apostle Paul contrasts that of edification, that is to say, of a solid and growing building."[7] Thus love is the true guide to Christian liberty.

2. *The Nature of True Knowledge* (8:2-3)

The man who is confident **that he knoweth any thing** perfectly really has not learned the essential aspects of knowledge: **He knoweth nothing yet as he ought to know** (2). This statement of Paul was designed "to condemn that vain conceit of knowledge, or self-confidence, which would lead us to despise others, or to disregard their interests."[8] The "assumption of omniscience" is obnoxious in any person. In the Christian such an assumption is contrary to humility and love as well as ruinous in the area of personal influence. For one to have supreme confidence in his knowledge means that he thinks he knows things perfectly "as to nature, consequence, and personal duty and relations."[9]

The nature of knowledge is to be understood in terms of love. For love is the basis of a personal relationship to God. Such love is both the way to understanding God and the way to recognition by God. Paul writes: **If any man love God, the same is known of him** (3). To be **known of him** means that one "is approved by God; is loved by him; meets with his favour."[10] Since the Corinthians placed such a high value on knowledge, they needed

[5]Erdman, *op. cit.,* p. 78.   [6]*Op. cit.,* pp. 84-85.

[7]*Op. cit.,* I, 408.

[8]Albert Barnes, *Notes, Explanatory and Practical, on the First Epistle of Paul to the Corinthians* (New York: Harper and Brothers, 1844), p. 154.

[9]Gray and Adams, *op. cit.,* p. 128.   [10]Barnes, *op. cit.,* p. 155.

to be reminded that love took priority. God meets a person on the basis of love, which becomes the focal point of God's response to man. As Godet writes, "In a residence, every one knows the monarch; but every one is not known by him. This second stage of knowledge supposes personal *intimacy* . . . a character which is foreign to the first."[11] In vv. 1-3, Paul has indicated that one can place too high a value on assumed personal knowledge. Love, not knowledge, should determine Christian conduct.

3. *Christian Liberty as God-centered* (8:4-6)

An idol is the creation of man's imagination; therefore Paul writes: **An idol is nothing** (4). "In all this ordered universe there is no reality corresponding to idols."[12] The Christian knew that the carved block of wood and the finely chiseled slab of stone possessed no real intelligence capable of receiving worship or of contaminating meat. Yet, "the great mass of the heathen world *did* regard the dumb idols as the proper objects of worship, and supposed that they were inhabited by invisible spirits."[13]

The question presented to Paul was, Is it right for the Christian to eat the meat of animals that had been slain as sacrifices to such idols? The act of **eating** (*brosis*) "has in it something disdainful; it emphasizes the lower and material character of the act in question."[14] The issue of Christian liberty in relation to eating such meat had both a negative and a positive aspect. The negative factor was the nonexistence of the false deities represented by the idols. The positive aspect was the existence of God, for **there is none other God but one.**

However, not all men shared this knowledge of the one God. Some heathen believed in the reality of the deities represented by the idols. Beet writes, "The fancy of the Greeks peopled with deities the *heaven*, visible and invisible, and the mountains, woods, and rivers of *earth*."[15] There were the celestial gods who occasionally visited the earth, such as Juno, Jupiter, Mercury, Apollos, and Mars. Then there were gods who were supposed to rule the earth, e.g., Neptune and Ceres. There were even gods inside the earth, such as Pluto.

---

[11]*Op. cit.*, I, 410.
[13]Barnes, *op. cit.*, p. 156.
[12]Morris, *op. cit.*, pp. 125-26.
[14]Godet, *op. cit.*, I, 411.

[15]*A Commentary on St. Paul's Epistle to the Corinthians* (New York: Thomas Whittaker, n.d.), p. 138.

Paul admits that in the minds of the pagans **there be that are called gods** (5). And in some cases, "this name *lord* was often given to their idol gods."[16] But Christians acknowledge only **one God** (6). He alone has the right of rule over man. He alone is worthy of worship. Moreover, He is the **Father** of **all things**, the Designer and Creator of the world. **All things** evidently refers to the whole work of creation.[17] While God is the Source of all things, Christ is the Agency **by whom are all things, and we by him.** The words **But to us** are an emphatic statement which declares that Christians are different from idolaters. The Christian is not a syncretist, who attempts to harmonize the teachings of all religions. He is different because his liberty is centered in God as the Creator and Father. Since the Christian's liberty is thus God-centered, it follows that there would be some related limits to his liberty.

4. Restrictions on Christian Liberty (8: 7-11)

Paul was the champion of Christian liberty in the area of personal decisions, but in practice he placed a number of restrictions upon the exercise of such liberty.

a. Weak consciences restrict Christian liberty (8:7). Paul recognized that not all Christians were in a state of intellectual understanding or spiritual vigor where they could, without hurt to themselves, attend a feast in an idolatrous atmosphere. When these people had become Christians, they accepted the God of the Christian faith as the only true God. But this concept was limited. One scholar wrote: "This monotheistic knowledge possessed by . . . all has not yet unfolded in the consciousness of all its full consequences."[18] Some perhaps still had the remains of their former superstition in them, and feared the power of idols. Such people would not regard the idols as equal with God, but as "intermediate beings, good or bad angels, and . . . it was proper to seek their favour or avert their wrath."[19] Thus there were **some with conscience of the idol**, "which in such persons . . . survived their conversion."[20] Not having matured to the point of a complete rejection of the reality of false gods, these Christians would feel a sense of guilt if they ate meat offered to idols.

[16]Barnes, *op. cit.*, p. 157.　　[17]*Ibid.*, p. 158.　　[18]Godet, *op. cit.*, I, 419.
[19]Barnes, *op. cit.*, p. 159.　　[20]Godet, *op. cit.*, I, 421.

The result was that **their conscience being weak is defiled.**
A **weak** conscience does not mean one that is easily persuaded,
but rather one that is unenlightened or oversensitive. If such a
person participated in a heathen festival, he would be doing what
his conscience forbade, and his conscience would be **defiled.**

b. *Christian liberty may become a stumbling block* (8:8-11).
There was no merit in eating or in not eating **meat** (8). It was
a matter of ethical and spiritual indifference whether or not one
ate. He was not thereby recommended "to the favour of God."[21]
Thus the Christian had liberty. Nevertheless a moral and spiritual issue was involved because of the influence one might have on
others.

The Christian would **take heed lest by any means this liberty
of yours become a stumblingblock to them that are weak** (9).
Christians should seriously consider their actions, as "opposed to
the lightness with which the Corinthians used their right."[22] Paul
agreed with the Corinthians that there was nothing wrong with
eating meat. Yet the principle of loving concern remained. It is
more important that a weak Christian brother be kept from temptation than for a strong person to express his freedom.

Liberty (*exousia*) means the right or authority to do a thing.
Some in Corinth had claimed the right to do as they pleased in
regard to eating meat offered to idols. But no Christian is free
to do entirely as he pleases if his actions become a hindrance to
the weak. The strong must not use his strength indiscriminately,
but wisely. The object of the Christian is to serve God and win
others, not to live by a personal bill of rights.

Conscience must always be obeyed. "Its demands may be
absurd but they cannot be disregarded."[23] If the fully informed
went to eat in the temple festival, they might be presumed by
others "to be partaking of this feast in honour of the idol."[24] **To
sit at meat** (10) meant to recline at the table, or to enjoy a leis-
urely meal, including the social atmosphere. The weak Christian
would be encouraged to do the same. But because his outlook
was different, his reaction would be different. He would pay a
certain respect to the idol or be attracted by the idolatrous atmosphere.

Thus the unrestrained use of freedom could cause the down-

---

[21]Barnes, *op. cit.*, p. 160.
[23]Erdman, *op. cit.*, p. 79.

[22]Godet, *op. cit.*, I, 424.
[24]Barnes, *op. cit.*, p. 161.

fall of a weak Christian. The unwise use of freedom would have brought another to spiritual disaster. But **Christ died for the weak** (11). If Christ died to save a man, should not a "strong" Christian be willing to forego a social meal to help accomplish the same end?

5. *Christian Liberty May Lead to Sin* (8:12-13)

The exercise of liberty can actually become a sin. If a Christian, by the unwise exercise of his freedom, causes the spiritual collapse of another, he has not only harmed the person, but has also sinned **against Christ.** Barclay writes: "A pleasure or an indulgence which may be the ruin of someone else is not a pleasure but a sin."[25] The word **wound** (12) means to strike vigorously, or to beat. Every such violence done to a brother's conscience "is a sin committed against Christ, whose work so painfully accomplished we compromise."[26]

The apostle's concluding principle is that even valid "indulgence may imperil the weak; therefore liberty must be regulated by love."[27] Eating meat is a matter of comparative insignificance. It really is not important in the overall Christian perspective. But "even if a thing is harmless for you, if it hurts someone else, it must be given up, for a Christian must never do anything which causes his brother to stumble."[28] The Christian must be careful **lest I make my brother to offend** (13). The word **offend** (*skandalizei*) comes from *skandalon,* which "refers to the moveable stick . . . of a trap."[29]

For the Christian, "The Limits of Spiritual Liberty" are determined by: (1) Our love for God, 3; (2) Our knowledge of man, 7; (3) Our influence on the weak, 9-13.

B. CHRISTIAN LIBERTY AND DEDICATION, 9:1-27

After discussing in c. 8 the nature of Christian liberty in relation to the eating of meat offered to idols, Paul here pursues the subject further. The principle of self-denying love in Christian living is so important that the apostle emphasizes it. Apparently Paul inserted the defense of his apostleship into the matter of "his treatment concerning Christian liberty, using his

---

[25]*Op. cit.,* p. 85.
[27]Erdman, *op. cit.,* p. 80.
[29]Thayer, *op. cit.,* p. 576.

[26]Godet, *op. cit.,* I, 427.
[28]Barclay, *op. cit.,* p. 84.

personal conduct as an example."[30] The Corinthians acted as if they had achieved a special position which entitled them to act without regard for other men. But Paul declares that Christian liberty must be limited by spiritual dedication.

The logic of Paul was unassailable. If he could forfeit valid claims to material assistance as a preacher of the gospel, the Corinthians ought to be willing to forego some personal expression of liberty also. The question was not one of personal salvation, but one of Christian effectiveness.

1. *Paul's Apostleship and His Rights* (9:1-14)

Paul wanted to show the Corinthians that Christian liberty was always subject to another and a higher law. He uses his exercise of personal liberty as an example.

a. Paul's apostleship (9:1-3). Paul first asserts that he was not bound by the ceremonial law. "Am I not free? Am I not an apostle?" (1, RSV) In matters of Christian action he had complete freedom within the limits of the ethical and spiritual law. In this respect he had the freedom of all Christians, whose personal redemption is based on faith in the Lord Jesus Christ. But Paul had an even greater freedom, that of an apostle. His claim to all the privileges of that office was supported by two facts.

(1) He had **seen Jesus Christ our Lord** (1). By definition "an *apostle* is one sent immediately by the Lord, who alone can confer such a mandate."[31] This does not mean that he saw Christ as part of a crowd or in a vision but "can only designate the positive historical fact of the appearing of Jesus on the way to Damascus."[32] This personal acquaintance with Christ was the essence of apostleship (Acts 1:22; 2:32; 3:15; 4:33).

(2) Paul's second validation as an apostle was the success of his work among the Corinthians. He had balanced doctrine with practical results. **Are not ye my work in the Lord?** was a question that could be answered only in the affirmative. And such an answer would support his claim, for he had come to them as an apostle of the Lord Jesus Christ. Thus the Corinthians should be the last to question the validity of his commission. They were his **seal . . . in the Lord** (2).

---

[30]Grosheide, *op. cit.*, p. 202.   [31]Godet, *op. cit.*, II, 3.   [32]*Ibid.*

The **seal** or signet was an emblem of ownership and security. As used here the "word stands for the impression made by the seal, and is used metaphorically of the converts at Corinth as an authentication of Paul's apostleship."[33] All other congregations founded by Paul would be similar seals.

The word **examine** (3) "signifies the critical investigation of his claims to apostleship."[34] The use of the present tense suggests that some at Corinth were making a continuing practice of challenging Paul's apostolic credentials. Alford holds that **Mine answer to them that do examine me** refers to the previous verses.[35] Lenski feels that vv. 1-2 are preliminary and that Paul's real defense of his apostleship begins in v. 4.[36]

b. *Apostolic rights and apostolic dedication* (9:4-14). The problem discussed here is the apostle's right to expect material support and the church's obligation to give such support. Paul's approach is presented in a series of rhetorical questions which could be answered only with an emphatic yes.

The first question is: **Have we not power** (no right) **to eat and to drink?** (4) Paul does not refer to either idol-meat or to normal eating and drinking. At this point he "is speaking about the right of the apostles to be supported with food and drink by the congregations they founded and served."[37] Although Paul had personally declined "entertainment at the cost of those to whom he ministers, yet he has a right to it."[38] His dedication had led him to bypass a right which he had every reason to exercise.

The second question expands the right of personal support to include one's **wife** (5). Paul means that an apostle has the right to have his wife accompany him and that "they have a right to maintenance at the cost of the Church."[39] Some have suggested that **a sister** may refer to a companion other than a wife, but the idea seems absurd. "The apostle is not contending that a missionary had a right to take about with him a woman who was not his wife."[40] One scholar has commented that to regard the **sister** as "a woman assistant in missionary work, or merely a companion for the sake of company and to help with cooking, etc., is even morally preposterous."[41] To reinforce his

[33]Vine, *op. cit.*, p. 119.

[34]*Ibid.*

[35]*Op. cit.*, p. 541.

[36]*Op. cit.*, p. 354.

[37]*Ibid.*, p. 355.

[38]Robertson and Plummer, *op. cit.*, p. 179.

[39]*Ibid.*, p. 180.

[40]*Ibid.*

[41]Lenski, *op. cit.*, pp. 355-56.

idea of an apostle's right to support, Paul refers to **the brethren of the Lord, and Cephas.** "There is nothing in Scripture which forbids the natural interpretation that they [these **brethren of the Lord**] were the children of Joseph and Mary born after the birth of Christ."[42] The most noted of these was James (Gal. 1:19; 2:9), the resident bishop of the mother church at Jerusalem.

The third question (6) suggests that **Barnabas** had followed Paul's example and had refused compensation for his services. "It is possible that there had been an agreement between them that on their missionary journey (Acts xiii. 3) they would not cost the churches anything."[43] **Working** refers to manual labor. Paul's willingness to earn his own living was especially significant in view of the fact that the Greeks despised such labor. Their philosophers regarded the men who performed menial tasks as inferior to the soldier, the businessman, and the man of reason.

Verse 7, which continues the discussion of the apostle's right to support, is actually three questions in one. All three are illustrations which have points of similarity with the work of a missionary. The nation or city provides a soldier with the necessary equipment for warfare, and pays him to fight. The husbandman who plants **a vineyard** is the first to taste the grapes. In fact, according to Jewish scripture, a part of the harvest belonged to him (Deut. 20:6). The shepherd **who feedeth a flock** also lives off it. The principle involved is that "the man who consecrates his labour to a work, ought to be able to live by that work."[44] From the logic of the situation it becomes more and more evident that the churches were under obligation to provide material sustenance for the ministers who served them.

A fifth question raises the level of discussion to a scriptural point of view: **Say I these things as a man? or saith not the law the same also?** (8) "In these matters the natural and the Christian life coincide."[45] The law commanded that a pawned garment be restored to a needy man immediately after sunset (Deut. 24:10-13); that the worker be paid his wages each day (Deut. 24:14-15); and that the farmer leave some grain untouched in the harvest process (Deut. 24:19-22). Concern and compassion were to be exercised in every area of life.

[42]Robertson and Plummer, *op. cit.,* p. 181.   [43]*Ibid.,* p. 182.
[44]Godet, *op. cit.,* II, 9.   [45]Lenski, *op. cit.,* p. 358.

The law even provided for the care of animals which helped supply man's needs. Thus **the ox** (9) that drew the heavy sled over the threshing floor was not to wear a muzzle, but to be permitted to eat some of the grain he helped thresh. The Gentiles normally muzzled such oxen, but the Jews regarded animals as part of God's creation and therefore as worthy of humane treatment. However, the welfare of the beast was not the primary reason for the law concerning the care of the oxen. Paul asks, **Doth God take care for oxen? Or saith he it altogether for our sakes?** (9-10) "The good done to man's immortal spirit by acts of humanity and justice, infinitely outweighs the mere physical comfort of a brute which perishes."[46]

Further, the man who engages in the exhausting work of plowing needs the encouragement of a future reward. Those involved in threshing and plowing do so in hope of sharing in the results of their labor—and so should apostles and ministers. The gift of the apostle in **spiritual things** (11) was incalculable. Therefore if he asked a little material sustenance, what did it matter? The term **carnal things** does not here refer to anything sinful. It means earthly or material, and is used in contrast to spiritual things.

In v. 12, Paul reasons that **if others**, such as the Jewish teachers, have the privilege of being supported by their congregations, he has an even greater right to support. **Nevertheless**, he had never exercised this power. Paul's reason for not exercising his option was that he did not want to **hinder the gospel of Christ**. The term **hinder** means literally an incision, or a violent break. "It is perhaps a metaphor from breaking bridges or roads to stop the march of an enemy."[47] Paul had the fullest liberty according to nature, reason, practice, and scripture to demand support, and yet he voluntarily forfeited his liberty. "He was concerned to exalt the dignity of his message by making it gratuitous."[48] Had Paul exercised his right in this matter, he might have been accused of preaching for personal gain and thus have weakened his influence.

A final question relates directly to congregational support for the ministry. Both Jewish history and Gentile practice show that the priests who officiate **at the altar** (13) live by gifts. **They**

---

[46]Alford, *op. cit.*, p. 544.   [47]Robertson and Plummer, *op. cit.*, p. 186.
[48]Godet, *op. cit.*, II, 20.

which minister about holy things is a general expression including all the personnel devoted to the Temple service. **To wait at the altar** applied only to the priests, who alone offered the sacrifices. The verb **wait** means "to sit steadily beside." The priests were always on call; thus they needed support. Christianity has replaced the Temple, and it requires no less of the minister than the old system.

The final conclusion is **that they which preach the gospel should live of the gospel** (14). When Paul states, **So hath the Lord ordained,** he refers to the OT practice in general and to the words of Christ in particular (Matt. 10:10; Luke 10:7). Because some have received a specific call and have devoted themselves fully to the spiritual task, turning away from secular gain, "the Church to which they thus consecrate their life is bound to provide for their material support."[49] The expression **live of the gospel** could be applied, "according to time or place, to free gifts or to a regular salary."[50] Paul has shown that he was a true apostle and that all apostles and ministers have a right to material support from the congregation. He next proceeds to explain why he had not accepted the support which he so vigorously claimed as an apostolic right.

2. Dedication Has Priority over Liberty (9:15-27).

In discussing the problem of eating meats offered to idols Paul had shown that love should be a guiding factor in the expression of Christian liberty. Now he adds another guideline.

   a. Principle of apostolic dedication (9:15-18). Paul had the right to make full use of the church's obligation to provide support but he did not exercise the right—**I have used none of these things** (15). The perfect tense, "I have not used," indicates that Paul still maintained this practice at the time he was writing to the Corinthians. Nor did the apostle write this letter in hope of getting help from the church. He had no intention of changing his course. In fact, he was so far committed to the idea of self-support that he would prefer to die of privation than to accept support from the congregation. Paul's **glorying** should not be interpreted as an egocentric whim, but rather as a deep-seated personal conviction. The Greek term for **glorying** (*kauchema*) does not mean a reason for boasting, but the "joyous feeling of

---

[49]Godet, *op. cit.*, II, 23.   [50]*Ibid.*

the moral worth of one's own actions."[51] *Living Letters* renders
it, "I would rather die of hunger than lose this glorious privilege
of preaching to you without charge." There is a sharp contrast
here between the voluntary sacrifice of Paul and the self-inter-
ested Corinthians who insisted on exercising their right to eat
meat offered to idols (c. 8).

The apostle next indicates that he deserves no credit for
preaching the gospel. One does not deserve credit when he does
what he must do. Paul writes, **Necessity is laid upon me; yea,
woe is unto me, if I preach not the gospel!** (16) He doubtless
refers to the special commission received on the way to Damascus
(Acts 9:6). He had been "a chosen vessel" to bear Christ's "name
before the Gentiles, and kings, and the children of Israel" (Acts
9:15); and had been separated by the Holy Spirit for this particular work (Acts 13:2). It was therefore impossible for him to
do anything other than to preach the gospel without directly
rebelling against God (Rom. 1:14; Gal. 1:15).

Preaching was Paul's whole life, and "he could no more stop
doing it than he could stop breathing."[52] The word rendered **is
laid** means "to press heavily upon." Preaching was "a task which
he is *forced* to discharge."[53]

Living Letters clarifies v. 17 thus: "If I were volunteering
my services of my own free will, then the Lord would give me
a special reward; but that is not the situation, for God has picked
me out and given me this sacred trust and I have no choice."
Since Paul preached from a sense of compulsion, he could say
that **a dispensation of the gospel is committed unto me** (17). The
term **dispensation** means a stewardship or appointment to ad-
minister. "Among the ancients, stewards belonged to the class of
slaves . . . Now a slave, after completing his task, has no recompense to expect; he would simply have been punished had he
not done it."[54] **What,** then, is Paul's **reward** (18)? It is the work
of preaching itself. "And this is so because he only receives his
reward if he is willing to do the work the Lord has committed to
him."[55] Since Paul feels he is performing a duty in preaching,
he must exercise his liberty in another direction. This he does by
refusing any assistance. "He wishes at any price to pass from

[51]Godet, *op. cit.*, II, 29.   [52]Barclay, *op. cit.*, p. 91.
[53]Godet, *op. cit.*, II, 28.   [54]*Ibid.*, p. 31.
[55]Grosheide, *op. cit.*, p. 211.

the servile state to that of a freeman acting from gratitude."[56] Dedication goes beyond duty. Spiritual dedication takes priority over spiritual liberty.

b. *Examples of apostolic dedication* (9:19-27). In relation to personal redemption Paul was free from all external ceremonies and from all humanistic systems of salvation. But in relation to winning men to Christ he said: **I made myself servant unto all, that I might gain the more (19).** He was not guilty of double-talk or of hypocrisy. He simply pushed his own ideas and desires aside in order to meet men on their level. "So far from doing what he had the abstract right to do, he made every necessary concession wherever he saw a possibility of bringing souls to Christ."[57] If one is to follow the apostle's example "many innocent practices must be renounced because of the prejudices and opinions of others."[58] Paul accommodated himself to several groups in order to be a more effective preacher.

(1) Servant to the Jews. In v. 20 the apostle writes, **And unto the Jews I became as a Jew, that I might gain the Jews.** He observed the Jewish law only as a matter of social living and as a method of personal influence, not as a matter of salvation. He refused to antagonize the Jews by openly disregarding their prejudices. Paul felt that he was free from all external restrictions. Yet "he was infinitely less afraid of sacrificing his liberty than of using it so as to compromise the salvation of one of his brethren."[59]

(2) Submission to the Gentiles. When dealing **with them that are without law (21,** the Gentiles) Paul ignored the ceremonial and nationalistic laws of the Jews. **Without law** (*anomos*) does not mean " 'lawless' in the sense of disregarding and transgressing law."[60] These persons were not anarchists or outlaws, but rather those with no privilege of the moral and spiritual law (Rom. 2:14). While indicating his submission at certain points to Gentile ideas or practices, Paul is careful to point out that at all times he is **under the law to Christ.**

(3) Consideration for the weak (9:22-23). The apostle next writes, **To the weak became I as weak, that I might gain the weak (22).** The term **weak** denotes Christians who were re-

[56]Godet, *op. cit.*, II, 33.   [57]Erdman, *op. cit.*, p. 85.
[58]*Ibid.*, p. 86.   [59]Godet, *op. cit.*, II, 35.
[60]Robertson and Plummer, *op. cit.*, p. 192.

cently converted, extra sensitive, lacking strong convictions, or deficient in understanding. Paul's approach did not involve a "sacrifice of principle, but a readiness to approach men on their most accessible side."[61] Godet writes of Paul, "No observance appeared to him too irksome, no requirement too stupid, no prejudice too absurd, to prevent his dealing tenderly with it in the view of saving souls."[62] The same author added this significant comment: "Free in respect of everything, he made himself the slave of all from love."[63] Saving souls was more important than personal liberty.

But Paul had a twofold reason for his approach to the ministry. One was for the sake of effectively preaching the gospel. The other was that he might experience the highest Christian life himself—**that I might be partaker thereof with you** (23).

(4) Example of the athlete (9:24-27). Paul was motivated by a desire to win others to Christ. However, he realized that private, personal experience cannot be divorced from public expression and declaration. So the apostle presents an illustration of discipline and self-sacrifice that includes both public effectiveness and personal spiritual development.

Every two years the Isthmian games were held at, or near, Corinth. These ranked among the great athletic events of Greece. They generally consisted of five events—leaping, discus throwing, racing, boxing, and wrestling. In any of these contests at least four qualities were necessary to win.

First, a winner must exert himself to the fullest extent: **So run, that ye may obtain** (24). Second, a winner must accept the rigors of training—**Every man that striveth . . . is temperate** (25). For a Greek athlete, this period of intense training lasted 10 months.[64] During these months the competitors lived a life of consistent exercise and rigid self-discipline in which they abstained from everything that would weaken or fatten the body. The reference is not to refraining from criminal acts and immoral practices, but from valid self-expression and gratification. Paul points out that these athletes receive as a reward only **a corruptible crown**—a wreath of pine, ivy, or parsley leaves, which soon faded. The Christian, on the other hand, sought **an incorruptible crown**.

[61]Vine, *op. cit.*, p. 126.   [62]*Op. cit.*, II, 40.
[63]*Ibid.*   [64]Robertson and Plummer, *op. cit.*, p. 194.

A third feature of the winner was certainty of direction. The Christian did not **run . . . as uncertainly** (26), nor did he fight **. . . as one that beateth the air.** In the Christian race Paul "knew the goal quite well, and he knew the road which led to it."[65] In spiritual fighting, he "uses his fists as one in deadly earnest, and does not miss: he plants his blow."[66] To Paul the Christian life was not an exercise in religious shadowboxing, but a raging combat which demanded one's best.

A fourth and final condition for winning is a consistent self-mastery. The apostle writes: **I keep under my body, and bring it into subjection** (27). The greatest hindrance to winning the race is one's own person. Paul does not say *flesh*. It is the total organism, the entire person, which is brought under control. He uses a strong term. Literally the word "buffet" (*upopiazo*) means "to strike heavily in the face so as to render black and blue."[67] The phrase **bring it into subjection** means to "lead captive." Paul was not only a herald to summon others to toe the mark—he was a competitor himself. He knew well how tragic it would be for "one who had instructed others as to the rules to be observed for winning the prize, should he himself be rejected for having transgressed them."[68]

The Christian lives on a spiritual level "Beyond Personal Liberty" when: (1) He is driven by a great call, 16-18; (2) Motivated by a grand compassion, 19; (3) Disciplined by a master plan, 24-26; (4) Overshadowed by a wholesome fear, 27.

C. CHRISTIAN LIBERTY: DANGERS AND LIMITS, 10:1—11:1

Paul has shown (c. 8) that an excessive stress on freedom may present a spiritual stumbling block to weak or underdeveloped Christians. He has also pointed out that insistence on personal liberty can be a detriment to the effective ministry of God's Word (c. 9). Now he writes that an undue display of personal liberty may cause spiritual decay and actually imperil one's Christian experience.

1. *Danger of Self-confidence* (10:1-13)

Paul had ended the previous paragraph with a challenge to rugged discipline in the Christian life. Now he presents a warn-

---

[65]*Ibid.*, p. 196.   [66]*Ibid.*
[67]Alford, *op. cit.*, p. 551.   [68]Robertson and Plummer, *op. cit.*, p. 197.

ing in the form of an example from the spiritual history of Israel. God's chosen people had experienced a miraculous deliverance and had received many advantages from God. Yet they fell into sin and almost all of them perished in the wilderness.

   a. Deliverance of Israel (10:1-4). Paul begins, **Moreover, brethren, I would not that ye would be ignorant** (1). The first word, **Moreover,** may be translated "for," showing the close connection to the previous verse. The apostle was not speaking in vague abstractions nor was he merely dispensing information. He uses a historic tragedy to demonstrate the truth that present spiritual blessings may be canceled by smug self-confidence.

   (1) All were delivered by a miracle. **All our fathers were under the cloud** means that "they were *under the shelter* of the Divine presence manifested by the cloud."[69] The cloud was their means of divine guidance. The verb **were** (*esan*) in the imperfect tense denotes a state which was continuing and prolonged. The verb in **all passed** (*dielthon*) **through the sea** is in the aorist, indicating a completed act.

   (2) All were baptized. Baptism is primarily a public testimonial or a personal declaration of identification. The statement, **Were all baptized unto Moses in the cloud and in the sea** (2), is here only a figure, for the people neither entered the cloud nor were they immersed in the sea. But they passed under both, as the one who is baptized passes under the water. By accepting the leadership of Moses and by participating in the events surrounding the Exodus, the people identified themselves with him. But submission as well as identification is involved in baptism. "Just as baptism has as one effect, the bringing of a man under the leadership of Christ, so did the participation in the great events of the Exodus bring the Israelites under the leadership of Moses."[70]

   (3) All were sustained in a supernatural way. Manna, the basic diet of the people, was a **spiritual meat** (3) because it was provided by a supernatural means (Exod. 16:1-36). Here **meat** means food, not meat in the common use of the word.

   Water was also supplied by supernatural means; they **drank of that spiritual Rock that followed them: and that Rock was Christ** (4). This statement may have been an allusion to the

[69]Godet, *op. cit.,* II, 52.   [70]Morris, *op. cit.,* p. 141.

smiting of the rock to obtain water (Exod. 17:6). It is farfetched, however, to interpret this reference as a repetition of the Jewish legend that a rock followed the Israelites throughout the wilderness wanderings.

The preexistence of Christ is clearly suggested, for "Paul understands Christ to have been the source of all the blessings the Israelites received as they journeyed."[71] Vine also writes: "The description of the rock as spiritual and as following them is a distinct testimony to the pre-existence of Christ."[72] Our Lord is thus represented as the Divine Being who accompanied the people of God on their journey in the wilderness and the One who provided the means of their deliverance.

The practical meaning for the Corinthians would be obvious. Christ dwelt among the people of Israel, and did wondrous and unique miracles for them. Yet they perished because of unbelief and sin.

b. *Disaster in the wilderness* (10:5). In spite of God's miraculous provision for His people, He eventually was forced to punish them. Because of their self-complacency and rebellion, **God was not well pleased.** Most of them failed. Only Joshua and Caleb entered the land of Canaan (Num. 14:30-32). All the rest failed to obtain the prize, **for they were overthrown in the wilderness.** The verb **overthrown** means literally "to strew, scatter, or spread out." **The wilderness** was strewn with corpses. These disobedient people died there because of God's displeasure. The pictorial image of the desert littered with corpses was meant to jar these smug, self-satisfied groups of Christians at Corinth.

c. *Similar disaster threatens the disobedient* (10:6-10). The rejection and punishment of Israel were offered "as examples, as object lessons to us, to warn us against doing the same things" (11, LL). The example of Israel was a warning regarding what could happen to the Corinthians if they became overconfident and misused their liberty. To make himself crystal-clear, Paul listed five sins of Israel which apparently were threatening the church at Corinth.

(1) **Lust after evil things.** The word **lust** (6, *epithymia*) means "to desire" either good things or bad things. Generally, as here, it is associated with illicit or harmful desire. In this more

---

[71]*Ibid.*, p. 142.   [72]*Op. cit.*, p. 132.

common meaning it expresses "the motive of the soul (*thymos*) toward (*epi*) a good thing which God does not give, egotistical and discontented aspiration."[73] The lusting of the Israelites is recorded in Num. 11:4, where the people expressed a strong desire for the things left behind in Egypt. The lust for these things was due in part to the mixed nature of the people, who were not all fully committed to the way of life directed by Moses. Commenting on the results of a group with mixed motives, Vine wrote: "If God's people do not tread a path of complete separation, they will inevitably find themselves led astray by evil associations."[74] The warning against illicit desires was especially relevant to the Corinthians. *"The history of the Jewish nation is a mirror for all mankind."*[75] It was a mirror for Corinth in a special way.

(2) Idolatry. The Israelites were recorded as having **sat down to eat and drink** (7) at the idol feast of the golden calf in Horeb. By associating with the heathen in their festivals, the Israelites became actual **idolaters.** The Corinthians were in danger of doing the same. Paul warned against the degeneracy often involved in the festivals in which "men's lowest passions might be, and often were, unleashed in the very act of worship."[76]

(3) **Fornication.** The apostle next warns, **Neither let us commit fornication, as some of them committed** (8). Sexual looseness was a constant threat to Corinth, as indicated by II Cor. 12:21. It was also a continual danger in Israel. The incident of Israel's adultery here referred to is found in Numbers 25. Those destroyed because of fornication are given in 25:9 as 24,000. Paul states that 23,000 were destroyed. In explaining this difference Vine writes: "The Apostle may be giving the immediate result here, while the record given by Moses mentioned the full result."[77] The lesson Paul presents is that sensual indulgence among people who are spiritually enlightened is worse than among the heathen and brings greater punishment.

(4) Tempting God. The next admonition is, **Neither let us tempt Christ** (9). The verb **tempt** (*ekpeirazo*) is an intensive form of the more common *peirazo* and is used to suggest the idea of challenging God. "To tempt God is to endeavor to put Him to

---

[73]Godet, *op. cit.*, II, 60.   [74]*Op. cit.*, p. 132.
[75]Lange, *op. cit.*, p. 207.   [76]Morris, *op. cit.*, p. 143.
[77]*Op. cit.*, p. 133.

the test as if to see how long His longsuffering will continue."[78]
The source of discontentment at Corinth was "evidently the dis-
content which they . . . [felt] on account of the self-denial required by their Christian call."[79] They were tempting God by
pushing their Christian liberty to the limits in regard to idol
feasts.

In Num. 14:22 the Israelites actually tempted God 10 times,
"daring Him, in trying His patience by rebellious conduct and
sin."[80] Because of this disobedience the people were destroyed
by serpents. In our dispensation "the serpents which will destroy us are the gnawings of a guilty conscience."[81]

(5) *Murmurings and unbelief.* To **murmur** (10) means "to
complain" or "to find fault." Such "murmuring has its roots in
unbelief. It is a denial of the goodness and mercy of God."[82] In
the OT most of the complaint was directed at Moses and Aaron
(Num. 14:2, 36; 16:11, 41). Paul compares the murmurings of
the Corinthians to this lament of the Israelites. Because murmuring is an openly expressed distrust of God's providence, and a
denial of His wisdom and goodness, it often results in swift retribution. **The destroyer** here means death (Amp. NT).

d. *Application to the Corinthian church* (10:11-13). The OT
is not merely a history of secular events. It contains the revelation of God's dealing with man. Thus OT history is used to show
a pattern of behavior to be followed or avoided. The example of
Israel is written **for our admonition** (11). The word **admonition**
means a "putting in mind" or a "training by word." In II Tim.
3:16-17 it carries the idea of a rebuke or a correction. **Upon
whom the ends of the world have come** means we who live in
the last era of time, the Christian dispensation.

The application is plain and direct. The overconfident and
egotistical Corinthians were warned that at the very time they
felt most secure they might **fall** (12). The figures of standing and
falling represent a state of faithfulness and a state of disobedience. "The fall of others should make us more careful about
ourselves."[83]

Paul softens the severity of his words by assuring them that

[78]*Ibid.*
[80]Alford, *op. cit.*, p. 555.
[82]Vine, *op. cit.*, p. 134.

[79]Godet, *op. cit.*, II, 62-63.
[81]Lange, *op. cit.*, p. 207.
[83]Lange, *op. cit.*, p. 207.

the peculiar temptations of the Corinthians are **such as are common to man** (13). Nothing unusual had happened to the Corinthians. All men experience temptation. Thus if they fail they have no excuse. Paul also declares that God acts consistently and always provides strength for those who trust and follow Him. As Alford writes: "He *has entered into a covenant* with you by *calling* you: if He suffered temptation beyond your power to overcome . . . He would be violating that covenant."[84] God is fully aware of the circumstances surrounding every temptation and **will with the temptation also make a way to escape, that ye may be able to bear it.**

The term **way to escape** (*ekbasis*) was used for a mountain pass. The picture is that of an army or a group of travelers trapped in the mountains. A pass is discovered and the group escapes to safety. The phrase **that ye may be able to bear it** indicates the sustaining power of the Holy Spirit, which all men may experience. Victory over temptation is possible through humble trust. But smug self-confidence when temptation comes is an avenue to certain defeat.

2. *Danger of Idolatry* (10:14-22)

In addition to the danger of self-confidence, the Corinthians were threatened with a relapse into idolatry.

a. A warning (10:14-15). Paul never loses his tenderness. Thus he writes: **Wherefore, my dearly beloved, flee from idolatry** (14). The verb **flee** is a present imperative, which suggests that the Corinthians should make a practice of flying from the presence of sin. While the reference here may be directly to partaking in idol feasts, it may also be applied "to everything which might be set up by a believer in his heart which would take the place of devotion to Christ and His service."[85] The addition of the preposition **from** (*apo*, away from) emphasizes that they are not only to flee from idolatry itself, "but to flee far from all that approaches it or might lead them into it."[86]

However, even in this warning, Paul would not impose his will on them. He says, **I speak as to wise men; judge ye what I say** (15). The word **wise men** (*phronimois*) suggests the posses-

[84]*Op. cit.*, p. 557.   [85]Vine, *op. cit.*, p. 136.
[86]Godet, *op. cit.*, II, 74.

sion of a practical wisdom which would enable them to under-- stand the meaning and force of Paul's words.

b. *The cup of fellowship* (10:16-18). **The cup of blessing** **(16)**, i.e., the Lord's Supper, prohibits any type of idol worship. The word **communion** (*koinonia*) means "having in common" and frequently denotes "the share which one has in anything."[87] Thus **the cup of blessing which we bless** and **the bread which we break** represent an actual sharing in the redemptive work of Christ.

Blessing (*eulogia*) means literally "good speaking." It is used in the Scriptures in various ways, such as praise (Rev. 5:12); benediction (Heb. 12:17); a benefit (Rom. 12:29); or of giving thanks, which is the meaning of this verse. The **cup of blessing** was part of the paschal feasts. In these festive meals the father of the family passed the cup as part of the sacrificial ritual. Each member of the family was thus involved in the rite. This was also the cup which Jesus had initiated. It indicated particularly the benefits of the death of Christ. There were no reservations in Paul's mind about the focal point of redemption. To him the basis of all spiritual blessing was **the blood of Christ.**

Similarly, the breaking of bread was a personalized partici- pation in the redemptive benefits, for Christ was the Living Bread. **We are all partakers of this one bread** (17) probably reflects the practice of each believer breaking off a piece of the loaf for himself, indicating both individual blessing and corporate fellowship. Communion with the Lord brings fellowship with each other. The communicants, by all receiving a piece of the same loaf, are made into **one** spiritual **body.** When **Israel after the flesh** (18), i.e., an Israelite, had eaten a part of the sacrifice to Jehovah, identifying himself with the covenant people, he could not afterwards take part in a heathen ceremony. So the Christian who took the cup and broke the bread could no longer participate in idol worship.

c. *The sin of idolatry* (10:19-22). Paul opens this section with the question, **What say I then? that the idol is any thing?** **(19)** His answer is, No. The meat offered to idols was no differ- ent from other meat. The idol to which the sacrifice was made was no god. And yet there were demonic forces associated with idol worship—**The things which the Gentiles sacrifice, they sacri-**

---

[87]Vine, *op. cit.*, p. 137.

fice to devils (20). Paul means that "heathen religions emanate from . . . malignant spirits, and that consequently the man who takes part in such worship puts himself under their influence."[88]

From this point of view, the meat offered to the idols was not the important question. The essence of the matter lay in participation in idol worship, which was a reversion to heathenism. Alford writes: "Heathendom being under the dominion of Satan . . . he and his angels are in fact the powers honored and worshipped by the heathen, however little they may be aware of it."[89]

It is a moral impossibility to **drink the cup of the Lord, and the cup of devils (21)**. The cup of demons was the climax of heathen banquets, in which a threefold toast was made in honor of the gods. A believer could not take part in such a pagan rite without violating his conscience. Any attempt to have fellowship with God while deliberately participating in idolatrous practices will **provoke the Lord to jealousy (22; Deut. 32:21)**.

3. *Limits of Spiritual Freedom* (10:23—11:1)

Faith in Christ had brought a wonderful freedom to Paul. The mystical union in Christ resulting from faith and grace cleared away forever the external trappings and mechanics. Thus he could say: **All things are lawful for me (23)**. The **all things** refers to those activities in which the Christian has freedom, such as eating a particular kind of food. Paul was free, in that his personal redemption caught up and far excelled legalistic and humanistic religious practices. Yet he again placed specific limitations on his spiritual freedom.

a. Expediency and edification (10:23). The apostle states that the final justification for individual conduct is not personal freedom, but expediency and edification. The word **expedient** refers to benefit in general, including one's own spiritual good. Edification means building up, strengthening, or nourishing. Vine writes: "A freedom which is enjoyed at the expense of detriment to others cannot be really beneficial to oneself."[90] Paul declares that a Christian has the abstract and theoretical right to do whatever is not in itself sinful, "but considerations of expediency and of the welfare of others place practical limits upon this liberty."[91]

[88]Godet, *op. cit.*, II, 89.   [89]*Op. cit.*, p. 560.
[90]*Op. cit.*, p. 140.   [91]Erdman, *op. cit.*, p. 94.

b. The interests of others (10:24). Paul writes, **Let no man seek his own, but every man another's wealth** ("good," NASB). The highest principle of conduct and of Christian liberty is not self-expression, but consideration for the good of others. If the Christian seeks the best interest of others, he will not put his own judgment or interests ahead of theirs. Alford writes of such a lofty approach to Christian freedom: "This ought to be our object: the bringing of one another to perfection, not the pleasing ourselves."[92]

c. A clear conscience (10:25-30). Ordinarily the Christian is free to follow his Spirit-sensitized conscience. Thus when he shops for meat **in the shambles** (25, market) he should purchase it and eat it asking no question about its origin. The attitude of the Christian should be that **the earth is the Lord's and the fulness thereof** (26). This quotation from Ps. 24:1 means that the Christian is free to regard everything from the standpoint of God's glory and man's good. "The misuse of a thing by the worldling need not hinder a believer from using it for the Lord."[93]

Individual conscience should also guide a person in the matter of eating a social meal in the house of a nonbeliever. There is no restriction on accepting such an invitation. At the meal the Christian should eat **whatsoever is set before** (27) him, **asking no question** involving questions of **conscience**. But there is one exception to eating entirely according to personal conscience. If another is present, and makes it known that **this is offered in sacrifice unto idols** (28), the believer should not eat the meat. The Christian is under obligation to forfeit his own personal freedom in order to give a clear Christian witness, or to help the weaker Christian who is not enlightened in these matters. "The abstention was to be out of regard for the informant himself and for his conscience."[94] This attitude is another way to recognize that **the earth is the Lord's, and the fulness thereof**. Because all that we have comes from God, we ought in every circumstance to do the thing that will best advance His kingdom.

In vv. 29-30, Paul writes as though he hears an objection from one of the "enlightened" Corinthians. *Living Letters* para-

[92]*Op. cit.*, p. 561.   [93]Vine, *op. cit.*, p. 141.
[94]*Ibid.*, p. 142.

phrases it thus: "But why, you may ask, must I be guided and limited by what someone else thinks? If I can thank God for the food and enjoy it, why let someone spoil everything just because he thinks I am wrong?" In v. 31, Paul replies, "Well, I'll tell you why."

d. *Liberty for God's glory* (10:31—11:1). In activities which are not specifically good or evil but left to Christian conscience, the primary question should not be: What is most satisfying or desirable to me? The question should be: What will bring honor to God's cause? **Whether therefore ye eat, or drink, or whatsoever ye do, do all to the glory of God** (31). Paul wanted to remove all possible hindrances to an effective ministry. He specifically mentioned three classes of people whom he was eager to help. He avoided antagonizing **the Jews** (32), who were religious, but not converted. He gave careful and courteous thought to **the Gentiles**, who were heathen and unconverted. But he was especially concerned about the members of **the church of God.**

Paul was a leader in the experience of freedom in Christ. But he was a self-disciplined and dedicated servant in his approach to personal conduct. He refused to do anything which might hinder men outside the church or alienate those already saved. For this reason he said: **Even as I am not seeking mine own profit, but the profit of many, that they may be saved. Be ye followers of me, even as I also am of Christ** (10:33—11:1). Christ came as a Servant. He was the Sovereign of the universe, yet accepted the role of a slave. The lesson is clear. It is not the exercise of personal liberty that attracts men. It is the submission of the Christian to God and the exercise of the "liberty of service" to man.

Paul's "Guidelines for Christian Living" are: (1) Recognize the destructive power of sin, 10:1-12; (2) Accept the victorious possibilities of grace, 10:13; (3) Live in the consistent strength of fellowship, 10:15-17; (4) Choose the inspiring freedom of love, 10:23-24, 31-33; 11:1.

Section **VII** The New Faith and
Public Worship

I Corinthians 11:2-34

In the first 10 chapters Paul has discussed a series of subjects related to the spiritual and moral life of the Christian believer. He now passes to considerations related to public worship.

A. APPEARANCE OF WOMEN IN PUBLIC WORSHIP, 11:2-16

1. *Preliminary Commendation* (11:2)

As an introduction to the discussion Paul expresses his appreciation: **Now I praise you, brethren, that ye remember me in all things, and keep the ordinances, as I delivered them to you.** While the church had questioned some of Paul's instructions, they had not rebelled against him and still regarded him as their spiritual advisor. For this Paul was thankful. Further, the Corinthians, in the main, still retained the **ordinances** given to them by Paul. An ordinance, as Paul used the term, "is any deliverance, any bit of instruction, any principle, and any rule of conduct which Paul handed over to the Corinthians when he was in their midst."[1]

2. *A Matter of Practical Priorities* (11:3-6)

Ordinarily women who appeared in public wore a veil over their heads to indicate both modesty and subordination. The question of Christian women continuing to observe this Oriental custom is the point at issue in this section. It is not clear how the question arose, though it may have had its origin in the apostle's own teachings. Paul himself had said that in Christ all things are made new: "There is neither Jew nor Greek, there is neither bond nor free, there is neither male nor female: for ye are all one in Christ" (Gal. 3:28). With the spirit of freedom prevalent in the church, some may have assumed that the custom of wearing the veil was no longer necessary. Further, if a woman was inspired to speak in public, would not the "fact of her inspiration

[1]Lenski, *op. cit.*, pp. 431-32.

413

release her from that obligation, and make it proper that she should lay aside her veil, and appear as public speakers did among men?"[2] But Paul felt strongly that women should cover their heads in a public service. He therefore limits freedom in worship by some practical priorities.

a. A threefold hierarchy of relationships (11:3). To support his teaching that women should wear a veil in public worship, Paul suggests three levels of relationship. Lowest in the scale is the completely human relationship of husband and wife—**The head of the woman is the man.** Next, and higher, is the divine-human relationship—**The head of every man is Christ.** Highest in the scale is the divine relationship—**The head of Christ is God.** Two ideas are involved in this scale: "community of life and inequality within this community."[3] Thus Christ, the Saviour, is also the Master of those who serve Him. The husband is coequal with the wife but is the director of the home. Even in the redemptive relationship, Christ subordinated himself to God and was obedient in all things.

b. The unveiled man (11:4). The Jews always wore a head covering in the Temple or synagogue as a sign of reverence. Among the Greeks only slaves wore a head covering, and the uncovered head was a sign of freedom. Paul at this point simply tells the Corinthian men to follow their custom, which was to appear without a head covering. For them to worship with the head uncovered indicated respect and reverence for God as Ruler and King.

c. The veiled woman (11:5-6). Because the Ruler of the man is Christ, the man can appear in worship with an uncovered head. The opposite is true of the woman. Because the husband is the head of the wife, for a woman to appear without the veil would be an act of rejection or rebellion against the husband. Further, it was a common custom among ancient people that a woman of good character did not appear in public without a veil. On these two grounds, Paul ruled that if a woman prayed or delivered a revelation from God in public, she should keep her head covered.

The apostle was concerned both to retain the proper relationship in the home and to sustain the good reputation of the Christian woman. Thus he compares the woman who appears in

[2]Barnes, *op. cit.*, p. 218.   [3]Godet, *op. cit.*, II, 108.

public **with her head uncovered** to one whose head was **shaven** (5). The shaved head "was never found among the Greeks, except in the case of women who were slaves; among the Jews, only in the case of the woman accused of adultery by her husband (Num. v. 18)."[4] To make his teaching even more emphatic Paul makes a ruling in case **the woman be not covered** (6, veiled). The verb here has a double meaning that is not apparent in our English translation. It is in the present continuous tense, suggesting a habitual attitude of indifference to modesty and custom. It is also in the middle voice, indicating that the act is persistent and deliberate. In this case Paul would apply a severe penalty, **Let her also be shorn.** Since this would be a disgrace no woman would desire, she would agree to wear the veil.

3. *Priorities in Creation* (11:7-10)

Man's appearance in public with his head uncovered reflects a priority of divine origin. By creation **he is the image and glory of God** (7). The word **image** means a visible representation. As such, "man was designed to be the representative of his Creator to display the attributes of God."[5] Moreover, because man is the image of God he is sovereign over all creation and thereby "visibly reflects the sovereignty of the invisible Creator over all things."[6] As God's image and glory, man's **head** should be uncovered—"his head because it is the noblest part of his body and most expressive of his personality."[7]

In the case of a woman the situation is different, for **the woman is the glory of the man.** She was created to be a helpmate to the man (8-9). Because of the sequence in the creation of man and woman, all customs which symbolize these facts ought to be followed in the worship of God. **For this cause ought the woman to have power on her head because of the angels** (10). The term **power** refers to the veil or covering as "a symbol of authority" (NASB). Because the woman was formed from man and for man, she was obligated to openly wear a symbol of her subordination to her husband. The phrase **because of the angels** reflects Paul's belief that all of God's creation somehow participates in an act of true worship. An act of impropriety would offend these invisible attendants and cast a shadow over the service.

[4]*Ibid.*, p. 118.
[6]Godet, *op. cit.*, II, 119-20.

[5]Vine, *op. cit.*, p. 148.
[7]Lenski, *op. cit.*, p. 442.

4. The Practical Equality (11:11-12)

The apostle is careful to eliminate any ground for the mistreatment of a woman under the guise of religious teachings. Her role is a subordinate one in the order of creation, and this role is to be indicated by a modest and discreet wearing of the veil in public. In practice and in private, however, man and woman are equal and interdependent. They are one **in the Lord** (11).

Further, from the natural point of view, man cannot be independent of the woman. **For as the woman is of the man, even so is the man also by the woman** (12). Vine explains, "Man is the initial cause of her being, she is the instrumental cause of his."[8] On a personal basis man and woman are equal, although for administrative purposes the woman is subordinate to the man. Ultimately **all things** are **of God**, so all ranks and all levels disappear in His grace and service.

5. Personal and Natural Lessons (11:13-16)

One additional point is presented to complete the discussion regarding the head covering for women during worship. Paul had presented the matter from the standpoint of divine authority and natural creation. He now appeals to the instinctive good sense of the Corinthians when he says: "Judge for yourselves; is it proper for a woman to pray to God with her head uncovered?" (13, RSV) In a public meeting, "when the woman's voice is uttering the deepest impressions and the holiest emotions of adoration and love . . . a feeling of holy modesty ought to constrain her to secure herself from every indiscreet and profane look."[9]

On the other hand, **if a man have long hair, it is a shame unto him** (14). Generally, **long hair** has been regarded as unnatural in man. Especially in Corinth, with its sexual perversion, "such long hair will make a man seem much like a woman and will thus bring a corresponding 'dishonor' upon him."[10] The situation is just the opposite with a woman. **Long hair . . . is a glory to her: for her hair is given her for a covering** (15). By nature woman is given a covering which is in effect a veil. Godet comments that this long and rich hair "is a natural symbol of reserve and modesty, woman's most beautiful ornament."[11]

---

[8] *Op. cit.*, p. 150.
[10] Lenski, *op. cit.*, p. 449.

[9] Godet, *op. cit.*, II, 127-28.
[11] *Op. cit.*, II, 129.

An added factor was that in Corinth there was a social custom which supported Paul's case for Christian modesty. This being the case, the Christian should conform to the custom in order to manifest a Christian character. Paul ends the discussion by a reference to the general practice of the Church. To those who might disagree with him on this matter, he states simply, **We have no such custom, neither the churches of God** (16). The apostle "means that neither he, nor the Christians formed by him, nor in general any of the Churches of God, either those which he had not founded or those properly his own,"[12] have the custom of women worshiping without a veil of some kind. In this matter it should be stated that the exact length of a woman's hair is not prescribed, and that Paul was sanctioning a custom of the day.

B. DISORDERS AT THE LORD'S SUPPER, 11:17-34

The problem of feminine modesty in relation to public worship was a small matter in comparison with some problems which had developed in the observance of the Lord's Supper. The rejection of a head covering for women may have arisen from lack of knowledge or from a misunderstanding about the nature of Christian liberty. But the deliberate perversion of the sacred Communion service betrayed a disregard for basic Christian teachings. Thus Paul's tone is severe as he denounces the gluttony and bickering associated with this symbol of fellowship.

1. *A Stern Rebuke* (11:17-22)

In v. 2, Paul had praised the Corinthians for their general loyalty to teachings and practices he had given them. Now he writes, **I praise you not** (17). The situation is serious. The verb **declare** (*parangello*) means to level an authoritative charge. He commands them to straighten out the matter. The occasion for Paul's severe accusation is one of the most shocking developments that can occur in a group holding a worship service: **Ye come together not for the better, but for the worse.** Instead of building up the spiritual life of the church the Communion was a time of spiritual decline.

a. Divisions in the church (11:18-19). Paul writes, **I hear that there be divisions among you** (18). The word for **divisions**

---

[12]*Ibid.,* p. 132.

(*schismata*) was used earlier (1:10) to describe the spirit which was tearing the church apart. When the people convened for the worship of God, they revealed this spirit of division and exclusiveness even at the most sacred of Christian rituals.

The word **heresies** (19) is derived from a term stressing the idea of choosing between alternatives. In biblical and church language the word usually means a wrong choice, and hence a false doctrine. It can be one of the "works of the flesh" (Gal. 5:20). Here the meaning seems to be parallel to the **divisions** of 18. The RSV translates it, "There must be factions among you." The meaning of the last part of 19 seems to be in the form of satire: You must keep divisions among you so that those who insist that they are right can prove it by separating themselves from the rest of the church.

b. Misuse of the Lord's Supper (11:20-21). The divisions at Corinth were so serious that when the people assembled for the service it was **not** really **to eat the Lord's supper** (20). Their carnal divisions had in reality changed the service into a kind of dissipation that made it something other than the Lord's. At Corinth the Communion service was not simply symbolic with token food and drink. It was an actual meal. Each member apparently brought food to the service. Such sharing of food in religious festivals was common among heathen religions, being called *eranio*. Also the Early Church apparently shared a common meal on certain occasions, which was called a *love feast* or *agape* (II Pet. 2:13; Jude 12). However, at Corinth the meal did not express Christian love or even the goodwill of the heathen feasts. Paul writes concerning it, **For in eating every one taketh before other his own supper: and one is hungry, and another is drunken** (21).

At the Corinthian Communion each person apparently placed the food before himself and proceeded to eat **his own supper.** The picture is that of a greedy scramble to eat the provisions before it became possible "to make a general distribution of them, and without sharing them with your neighbors."[13] As a result the poor who could not bring much, or those who could bring nothing and who were late in arriving, would go hungry. Thus **one is hungry, and another is drunken.** The verb **is drunken** (*methuein*) usually means "to be intoxicated." But it also

---

[13]Godet, *op. cit.*, II, 143.

means to eat and to drink to one's complete satisfaction, which could be the meaning here. At any rate, the Corinthians had completely distorted the meaning of the Communion. The Lord's Supper is the symbol of sacrifice, love, and fellowship. At Corinth it had come to mean selfishness, intemperance, and indifference to the needs of others.

c. *Sins in the misuse of the Lord's Supper* (11:22). Paul points out three specific wrongs committed by the Corinthians. First, they had changed a spiritual observance into a kind of holiday feast. The purpose of the Communion was to remind the believers of the death of Christ and of the redemptive results of His suffering. If the people wanted to satisfy their hunger or to have a festive meal, they should do so on another occasion. Second, the Corinthians had shown lack of reverence and respect for the church of God. To make the church a place for holiday celebration "is to degrade it, hence to look down on it, to despise it."[14] Third, by their selfishness the more wealthy members embarrassed and humiliated the poor among the believers. This combination of sins led Paul to the simplest yet most complete statement of condemnation: **What shall I say to you? shall I praise you in this? I praise you not.**

2. *Meaning of the Lord's Supper* (11:23-26)

Paul's understanding of the Lord's Supper was a direct revelation from God. The apostle presents "on an immovable foundation the authority of his narrative."[15] As he had received the gospel directly from Christ (Gal. 1:11-12), and not from man, even so he had received the instructions concerning the Lord's Supper. Moreover, he had carefully and faithfully transmitted this information to the church. Thus he could say with finality and authority, **I have received of the Lord that which also I delivered unto you** (23).

The Supper represented the establishment of a new covenant of grace and was to be observed as a memorial. Both the "broken body" and the "shed blood" are to be regarded as symbolical rather than actual references to the body of Christ. When Jesus said, **This is my body, which is broken for you** (24), He was not physically at the table. Any ideas of a miraculous change in either the bread or the wine is contrary to the biblical account.

---

[14]Lenski, *op. cit.*, p. 460.   [15]Godet, *op. cit.*, II, 147.

Finally, the Eucharist was to be observed as a memorial or reminder, not as a means of salvation. The statements, **This do in
remembrance of me,** and, **Ye do shew the Lord's death till he
come** (26), both support the idea of the Supper as a spiritual reminder or symbol of the death of Christ.

3. Observance of the Lord's Supper (11:27-34)

The Lord's Supper is a spiritual memorial to our Lord's act
of redemption, and a public testimony to our faith in Jesus Christ.
It should therefore be celebrated in a solemn, yet thankful
fashion.

a. *Unworthy participation* (11:27). Paul asserts that it is
possible to **eat this bread, and drink this cup of the Lord, unworthily.** The adverb **unworthily** refers to a balancing of weights
and so means "of unequal weight" or "improperly balanced."
The attitude of the person does not balance with the importance
of the occasion. If a person partakes of the Lord's Supper in a
light and frivolous manner, without reverence and gratitude, or
while indulging in sin, or while manifesting bitterness against a
fellow believer, he is partaking unworthily.

To thus partake **unworthily** is to **be guilty of the body and
blood of the Lord.** The word **guilty** (*enochos*) means to be "liable
to the penal effect of a deed; here it . . . [involves] the guilt of
His death."[16] Instead of coming to the table with a wrong or sinful attitude, the believer should come "in faith, and with a due
performance of all that is fitting for so solemn a rite."[17]

b. *Spiritual examination* (11:28). Before taking part in this
sacred service **let a man examine himself** with a rugged self-
study. The word means to test. So the believer should examine
his motives and actions. Certainly no one can earn the grace and
forgiveness of God. But on the other hand, an honest self-examination will indicate whether or not one comes to the sacred table
with proper motives and in active obedience to the Lord. Paul's
instruction is wholesomely positive. He does not say to examine
oneself and leave the Lord's table in despair. Rather he counsels
a man to search his heart and then in honest faith **let him eat of
that bread, and drink of that cup.**

c. *Dangers of irreverence* (11:29-30). The RSV renders
v. 29, "For any one who eats and drinks without discerning the

---

[16]Vine, *op. cit.*, p. 160.   [17]Morris, *op. cit.*, p. 163.

body eats and drinks judgment upon himself." The word *krima* which the KJV translates **damnation** means "condemnation." Paul does not intend to state that a person who comes to the table without the proper spiritual qualifications will be eternally damned. He means that such an act will bring condemnation and guilt. **Not discerning the Lord's body** means that the worshipper has failed to distinguish between the sacred memorial of the Lord's Supper and other kinds of meals.

The apostle indicates that as a result of the misuse of the Lord's Supper **many are weak and sickly among you, and many sleep (30)**. It is too strong to state that eternal damnation is the result of a misuse of the Lord's Supper, but Paul issues a warning that God's judgment could come, bringing sickness and even physical death. **Weak** (*asthenes*) means sickness; the term **sickly** (*arrostos*) means infirmity and decay, while the word **sleep** (*koimaomai*) is used most frequently in the NT to indicate the "death of those who belong to Christ."[18] Godet says that Paul is writing of "a warning judgment, specifically inflicted by God, such as He sends to awaken a man to salvation."[19]

d. *Reverent participation* (11:31-34).

The way to avoid God's judgment is to voluntarily and truthfully **judge ourselves (31)**. But even when God sends judgment upon the believer, he is **chastened of the Lord (32)**. God's judgments in these cases are not harsh punishments, but symbols of His love. "They are sent to bring us back from the wrong way, so that we shall not share in the condemnation of the world."[20]

The proper way to observe the sacrament is to **tarry one for another (33)**. They should wait until all are assembled, then considerately and with brotherly affection conduct the love feast. The final injunction of v. 34 is again a warning not to regard the Lord's Supper as an ordinary meal. If a man is hungry, **let him eat at home.** The purpose of the Communion is to remind the believers of the redemptive work of Christ and to bring a spirit of unity and love in the church.

Some other points in this matter still required attention. Speaking of these Paul wrote: **And the rest will I set in order when I come (34).** These matters were not seriously affecting

---

[18]Vine, *op. cit.*, p. 161.   [19]*Op. cit.*, II, 168.
[20]Morris, *op. cit.*, p. 165.

the life of the church and could be postponed. What were the rest of the concerns that Paul had in mind? Perhaps he wanted to separate completely the idea of a love feast from the observance of the Lord's Supper. We know that about A.D. 150 the custom of eating a meal in connection with the Communion was discontinued.

For the Christian there is "Strength Through Sacraments." (1) They are given by the Lord, 23*a*; (2) They are reminders of Christ's sacrifice, 23*b*-26; (3) They demand self-examination, 27-29; (4) They produce concern for others, 33-34.

I Corinthians 12:1—14:40

The Corinthians had lost their sense of values in regard to the various gifts of the Holy Spirit. They had come to look upon ecstatic utterances as the choicest of spiritual gifts, and tended to minimize other ministries of the Spirit. In c. 12, Paul states two simple truths. First, all gifts come from the same Holy Spirit and cannot be in opposition to each other. Second, the apostle illustrates the importance of all gifts by comparing the members of the Church to the structure of the human body.

A. THE VARIETY OF SPIRITUAL GIFTS, 12:1-7

Paul first presents some general ideas, then shows that all gifts come from the same Spirit, and finally mentions a list of specific gifts.

1. Spiritual Gifts in General (12:1-3)

The words **now concerning** indicate that Paul is about to introduce another matter which the Corinthians had mentioned in their letter to him. Whether the word **gifts** should be inserted is a much debated question. **Spiritual** (*pneumatika*) is usually accepted as referring to "spiritual things"[1] or to **spiritual gifts**. The common NT term for "gifts" is *charisma*. The word does not occur in the text, but since the entire context deals with this subject, it is correct to interpret *pneumatika* as meaning **spiritual gifts**.

The apostle introduces this discussion by noting the importance of spiritual gifts, yet warning against their misuse.

a. *The importance of a true understanding of spiritual gifts* (12:1). When Paul writes, **I would not have you ignorant**, he points out the importance of the whole matter. These Corinthians were recent converts to Christianity. "With their ideas of Christian morality but imperfectly shaped, little acquaintance with the

---

[1] The word is clearly neuter in 14:1, and should be treated as such here.

Old Scriptures, and the New not as yet having been fully written, it is no wonder the Corinthians were ignorant."[2]

An understanding of the place and nature of spiritual gifts was important because the Corinthians had a background of idolatry. Paul was anxious to "efface from their minds some traces of their old polytheism by impressing them with the truth that all their variety of gifts is from *one Spirit,* the Infinite Unity."[3]

In Corinth the whole idea of the gifts of the Spirit had degenerated. As a natural consequence, "those gifts were most highly honoured, not which were most useful, but which were most astonishing. Amongst these the gift of tongues rose preeminent, as being in itself the most expressive of the new spiritual life."[4] Most of the gifts listed by Paul in c. 12 were ignored. The one stressed above all others was speaking in tongues. Interest seemed to center in acquiring a power to do miraculous things and to create astonishment in non-Christian minds. The Holy Spirit was exploited for sensational results. "His receiving, sanctifying function seems to have been left very much in the background. He was thought of as the author, not of grace . . . but of Charisms [gifts,] and 'spiritual' in the vocabulary of the period was an attribute ascribed to the effects of a spirit of *power,* not to those of a spirit of *holiness.*"[5]

In this manner the gift of the Holy Spirit came to mean, in the common mind, not the power to believe, to hope, to love, to be pure, but the power to speak ecstatically and to perform sensational deeds. Of this type of religion the same author declared:

> The whole fraternity of people who can be religious and at the same time false, greedy, sensual, bending like reeds before the swollen stream in a time of enthusiasm without radical change of heart soon began to swarm. They appeared everywhere, tares among the wheat of the Kingdom, they were unusually abundant in the Corinthian Church, where everyone could speak in one way or another, and virtue was at a discount—a church mostly gone to tongues.[6]

[2]Whedon, *op. cit.,* p. 91.   [3]*Ibid.*

[4]Arthur Penryhn Stanley, *The Epistles of St. Paul to the Corinthians* (London: John Murray, 1876), pp. 210-11.

[5]A. B. Bruce, *St. Paul's Conception of Christianity* (New York: Charles Scribner's Sons, 1898), p. 245.

[6]*Ibid.,* p. 247.

Because of the dissension and friction caused by the loss of perspective regarding spiritual gifts, the Corinthian church faced serious difficulties, even spiritual extinction. As Hayes has remarked, "It is a proof of the surpassing genius of the apostle Paul that he was able to save this church and all his churches from fanaticisms and dissolution and to build out of them a world-conquering Christianity."[7]

b. *The impotence of idolatry* (12:2). To puncture any pride in their present state and to forestall possible argument, Paul reminds them of the helplessness of their former condition. **Ye know** suggests that "they knew very well the situation they were in when they were still pagans."[8] In their state of heathenism they had been **carried away unto these dumb idols.** Literally, they were led about like a condemned prisoner. The heathen here are pictured, "not as men freely following the gods their intellects have fully approved, but as under constraint, as helpless, as men who know no better."[9] As heathen, the Corinthians had been "bandied about among a multitude of dead and dumb gods, knowing nothing of the living, speaking One."[10] Instead of hearing the personal voice of a divine Father these people had bowed down before a god who could neither speak nor act. The point the apostle wants to make is that abandonment of oneself to an excessive display of ecstasy under the guise of spirituality might be as fruitless as their former abandonment in idolatry.

c. *The immediate supervision of the Holy Spirit* (12:3). Apparently the Corinthians were concerned as to whether or not all their utterances came from the Spirit of God. Paul's answer at this point was specific: **No man speaking by the Spirit of God calleth Jesus accursed.** "It is impossible that one who speaks in the Spirit of God would say *Jesus is anathema*, for there is in the Christian faith one firm principle, one work of the Spirit which always remains the same . . . and never turns away from Jesus Christ."[11]

Accursed (*anathema*) means something "devoted to the divinity,"[12] or that which is set apart or devoted to a god. Thus the word came to mean something totally lost to the giver, some-

---

[7]*Op. cit.*, p. 211.
[9]Morris, *op. cit.*, p. 167.
[11]Grosheide, *op. cit.*, p. 280.

[8]Grosheide, *op. cit.*, p. 279.
[10]Whedon, *op. cit.*, p. 91.
[12]Arndt and Gingrich, *op. cit.*, p. 53.

thing in reality destroyed. So the meaning passed over to "the object of a curse," which is the usual meaning in the NT. To say, "Jesus is accursed," may have been the test of renouncing loyalty to Christ, before a Jewish tribunal or in the Jewish synagogue. On the other hand, to say, "Jesus is Lord," would indicate loyalty to Christ.

At this point Paul states clearly that even in the excitement of ecstatic utterance no one can claim that the Holy Spirit inspired him to say that Jesus Christ was accursed. On the other hand, **no man can say that Jesus is the Lord, but by the Holy Ghost.** This does not mean that it would be impossible to speak the words. But it would be impossible for one to state personally and experientially that Christ is Sovereign without the direct assistance and revelation of the Holy Spirit.

2. *God Reveals Himself in Many Ways* (12:4-7)

In this paragraph there is an indirect presentation of the Trinity but there is no conflict of interests in the various manifestations of the Triune God. The God of the Christian faith reveals himself in both gifts and services in man.

a. A variety of gifts (12:4). The word **diversities** conveys the idea of distribution, apportionment, or division. The Holy Spirit does not oppose himself. Thus any gifts which the Spirit bestows on one person would not stand in opposition to a gift given to another. Nor would one gift be superior or inferior to another. All gifts come from God and are used for God's redemptive work among men.

Gifts (*charisma*) comes from the same root as the great Christian word grace (*charis*). The idea is that of something bestowed. In this sense all Christians receive gifts from God, insofar as love and grace and the totality of the Christian life are given to man. But in a special sense, some in the Church receive gifts in addition to those directly related to personal salvation. These special gifts are varied in number, but all come from the same Spirit.

b. A variety of services (12:5). In addition to a wide variety of gifts which are direct expressions of the Holy Spirit, there is a wide distribution of **administrations** ("services," RSV). The way the gifts are used is called *services* or **administrations** (*diakonia*). The Greek word denotes "every service to the good of the church."[13] Paul apparently adds the idea of "services" to that of **gifts** to minimize the importance of gifts and to magnify the unity of the Spirit.

c. *A variety of results* (12:6). In the Church there are also **diversities of operations.** The word **operations** (*energematon*) suggests a "thing wrought"[14] or an effect produced. There are different forces working in and through the Church which produce various results. There is evidence everywhere, in creation and in the Church, of the ways in which God works. But He never works against himself. Here again the apostle draws a contrast between the harmony in God's manifestations and the dissension and divisions of the Corinthians.

d. *The Holy Spirit works for a single purpose* (12:7). The gifts, services, and results produced all work toward a single purpose—to benefit the entire Church and to glorify God. Thus the gifts should not foster rivalry or generate jealousy. The spiritual gifts are **to profit withal,** that is, to benefit others. They are for the common good.

B. THE GIFTS OF THE HOLY SPIRIT, 12:8-11

The various gifts are all given by the Spirit, which indicates that they are all useful. They are bestowed on man according to God's sovereign will, not according to man's desires. Verses 8-10 present a list of nine gifts. All are given *through the Spirit.* God grants the gifts, but He does this through the Holy Spirit, who was the special Director of the Church after Pentecost. The Holy Spirit also determines the character of the gifts (Rom. 5:5; 8:12; Eph. 4:4; I Thess. 4:8).

1. *The Word of Wisdom* (12:8a)

Word signifies an utterance or something spoken. **Wisdom** (*sophia*) means "Good judgment in the face of the demands made by human and specifically by the Christian life."[15] It is this practical wisdom that James regards as a gift of God (Jas. 1:5). In this sense "wisdom is the capacity for applying our knowledge in judgments or practice."[16]

---

[13]Grosheide, *op. cit.,* p. 283.   [14]Thayer, *op. cit.,* p. 215.

[15]Arndt and Gingrich, *op. cit.,* p. 767.   [16]Whedon, *op. cit.,* p. 92.

2. *The Word of Knowledge* (12:8b)

Knowledge (*gnosis*) "implies . . . research and investigation, although knowledge too should not be taken in a purely intellectual sense; it has an existential character."[17] Paul also associates **knowledge** with a kind of supernatural mystical awareness, and relates it to mysteries, revelations, and prophecy (13:2; 14:6). While wisdom comes *through* the Spirit, knowledge comes *according* to the Spirit.

3. *Faith* (12:9a)

By the term **faith** the apostle here means a "faith that has special, visible results, a faith that enables one to do miracles."[18] This is the type of faith that Paul pictures in 13:2—the faith that could move mountains. Whedon suggests a different idea when he writes that this kind of faith is "that realization of divine realities by which a powerful and heroic Christian character is formed, shown in maintaining truth resistlessly, and suffering for it unshrinkingly."[19] The gift of faith enabled the Christians to become uninhibited witnesses and fearless martyrs.

4. *Healing* (12:9b)

The power to perform miracles of dramatic restoration to health was one of the gifts given by the Spirit to the Primitive Church. Adam Clarke states that this gift "simply refers to the power which at particular times the apostles received from the Holy Spirit to cure diseases."[20] He points out that the apostles did not have this power as a permanent gift which was effective on all occasions.[21] Paul could not effect a cure in Timothy, nor could he remove his own thorn in the flesh. **Healing** is plural in the Greek text, which would indicate that there were different "healings" for various kinds of sickness and disease.

5. *Working of Miracles* (12:10a)

Miracles (*dynameon*) emphasizes the element of power. It may refer to the ability to perform extraordinary physical exertion (II Cor. 11:23-28). John Calvin relates this type of miraculous power to such events as the smiting of Elymas with

---

[17]Grosheide, *op. cit.*, p. 285.   [18]*Ibid.*, p. 286.
[19]*Op. cit.*, p. 92.   [20]*Op. cit.*, II, 259.
[21]Grosheide, *op. cit.*, p. 287.

blindness (Acts 13:11) and the sudden deaths of Ananias and Sapphira (Acts 5:1-10).

6. Gift of Prophecy (12:10b)

In the OT, prophecy contained both prediction and proclamation. To many people, the element of prediction overshadows that of proclamation. Others tend to minimize the element of prediction, regarding prophecy as only a declaration of God's message for one's own time. Both elements are present, although the major emphasis of prophecy, even in the OT, was the direct presentation of God's message for the people of the day in which the prophet lived. In the NT prophecy might be occasional (Acts 19:6), or a permanent office (I Cor. 12:28).

Prophecy in the NT "is that special gift that calls and enables certain persons to convey revelations of God to His church."[22] Another scholar interprets it as "delivering inspired exhortations, instructions, or warnings."[23] Whedon gives a comprehensive definition: "Inspired preaching; either predicting the future, unfolding mysterious truth, or searching the secrets of men's hearts and characters."[24] Paul holds the office of prophecy in high regard, as indicated by the comparison of prophecy and speaking in tongues in c. 14.

7. Discerning of Spirits (12:10c)

Every Christian must have, to a certain degree, the ability to "try the spirits" (I John 4:1). Otherwise he becomes a victim of false impressions from without or of ruinous pressures from within. The original text here speaks of discernings, which means that the Christian must continually be alert to the direction of the Holy Spirit. But apparently some have the gift of special spiritual insight and knowledge, having the ability to distinguish between prophetic utterances, to know whether they proceed from true or false spirits.

Paul believed that there were evil **spirits** working in the Gentile churches and among the Gentile Christians (I Thess. 2:2). In some instances these spirits manifested themselves not only in false prophecies but also in the performing of miracles (Acts 19:13-16). "In general there was a devilish imitation of the charismata and of the work of Christ."[25] An excellent de-

---

[22]*Ibid.*
[24]*Op. cit.*, p. 92.

[23]Vincent, *op. cit.*, III, 256.
[25]Grosheide, *op. cit.*, p. 287.

scription of the **discerning of spirits** is: "The power of detecting the hypocrite, as Peter did Ananias; of distinguishing true and false gifts; of recognizing genuine inspiration."[26] The problem of the Early Church was not that of a secularized society but of paganized religions. With so many claims to divine direction, it was essential that the Church distinguish between true and false claims.

8. *Speaking in Tongues* (12:10d)

The excessive concern for the gift of **divers kinds of tongues** was the core of the whole problem in this section. **Tongues** (*glosson*) is given various interpretations: the speaking tongue, or the tongue in action;[27] rare, provincial, poetic, or archaic words; a spiritual language, unknown to man, uttered in ecstasy;[28] a known language or dialect.[29]

Among the older commentators it was customary to interpret both the tongues at Pentecost and the tongues at Corinth as known languages. Such writers as Lange,[30] Calvin,[31] Adam Clarke,[32] and Matthew Henry[33] held this position. Recent writers tend to make a distinction between the two kinds of tongues. One who accepts the tongues of Pentecost as spoken languages writes of the tongues at Corinth: "Others possessed a strange gift called the gift of tongues. It is not clear what it was; but it seems to have been a kind of tranced utterance, in which the speaker poured out an impassioned rhapsody by which his religious feeling received both expression and exaltation."[34] A contemporary writer states that "the lack of any need for interpretation [at Pentecost] makes it difficult to identify the situation with that which Paul seeks to regulate in the Corinthian Church."[35]

It appears from Paul's discussion of the Corinthian situation that the problem was that of ecstatic utterance. From Paul's

[26]Whedon, *op. cit.*, p. 92.　　　　　　[27]Grosheide, *op. cit.*, p. 288.

[28]Jamieson, *op. cit.*, p. 288.　　　　　　[29]Vincent, *op. cit.*, III, 257.

[30]*Commentary on the Holy Scriptures, Corinthians* (Grand Rapids, Zondervan Pub. House, n.d.), p. 252.

[31]*Commentary on the Epistles of Paul the Apostle to the Corinthians* (Edinburgh; Calvin Translation Society, 1848), I, 417.

[32]*Op. cit.*, II, 259.　　　　　　[33]*Op. cit.*, VI, 571.

[34]James Stalker, *The Life of St. Paul* (New York: Fleming H. Revell Co., 1912), p. 106.

[35]Blaiklock, *op. cit.*, p. 57.

treatment it is certain that the gift was not to be regarded as part of the evangelistic work of the Church. Nor was it to be regarded as highly significant, when compared with other gifts. While the entire matter is a delicate one, it is the author's opinion that there was a valid gift of languages in the Early Church, and that Paul was aware of the true Pentecostal gift of speaking in known languages. But the tongues known in Corinth were not of this kind. It is quite possible that the genuine gift of languages related to Pentecost could have degenerated into unintelligible utterance in the lives of the unstable Corinthian Christians.

9. *The Interpretation of Tongues* (12:10e)

Two explanations are given for the special gift of **interpretation of tongues.** One idea is that "this was the gift whereby God made intelligible what was hidden from all in the ecstatic utterances."[36] Another view is suggested by Adam Clarke: "It was necessary that while one was speaking the deep things of God in a company where several were present who did not *understand,* though the *majority* did, there should be a person who could immediately interpret what was said to that part of the congregation that did not understand the language."[37]

Verse 11 again emphasizes the main point of the whole discussion, namely, that all the gifts come from one Spirit. The verb **worketh** is present tense and "implies that the Spirit gives these gifts continually."[38] The unity and consistency of divine purpose are revealed in the expression **that one and the selfsame Spirit.** Different gifts do not indicate different divine purposes. God does not oppose himself nor does He cause friction in the way He distributes gifts. **Every man severally** indicates that God deals with man on a personal, individual basis. **As he will** means that the sovereign God bestows the gifts in harmony with His purpose. It is God, not man, who selects the gift to be given. Therefore man should not dictate which gift he would choose, though Paul admonishes us to "covet earnestly the best gifts" (12:31). Certainly no one gift should be regarded as an evidence of superior spirituality. Nor should any particular gift be selected as the exclusive manifestation of the Holy Spirit. To do so would be to distort the work of the Spirit and to disrupt the divine unity.

[36]Morris, *op. cit.,* p. 173.   [37]*Op. cit.,* II, 259.
[38]Grosheide, *op. cit.,* p. 289.

C. Diversity in Unity (12:12-31)

The Church is a unit. It is the body of Christ, and the same Spirit works in the entire body. But the Church, like the physical body, is a unity which also contains differences.

1. *The Unity of the Church Is a Vital Unity* (12:12)

The human body is a living organism that has many members. Each member is different, yet each makes a specific contribution to the entire body. But despite its different members the body contains a common life that operates in every member. Thus Paul writes that **the body is one, and hath many members.** The many and different members form **one body.** The apostle concludes, **So also is Christ.** The unity of the Christians, like the unity of the physical body, is vital. "The same spiritual life exists in all Christians, derived from the same source, supplying them with similar energy, and prompting them to the same habits and aims."[39]

2. *Common Experiences Shared by the Church* (12:13)

Because the Church is a unity in diversity, it shares in the same experiences. Paul stresses two which are shared by all.

a. All are baptized (12:13a). The word **baptized** "relates to the actual act of baptism"[40] which is the common experience of all in the Church. Therefore none should be puffed up. This emphasis was stated earlier by Paul (1:13-17). The common baptism may also refer to the Spirit's coming at Pentecost. As one writer observed, "The descent of the Pentecostal Spirit, like the outpouring of baptismal water, consecrated its subjects into the living church."[41] On either interpretation, Paul attempts to eliminate tensions and rivalries by pointing to the essential unity of believers in Christ. The unity of the Church transcends all distinctions. Thus **Jews or Gentiles . . . bond** (slaves) **or free,** all share in the common experiences of the one body, the Church.

b. All Christians share in the fellowship of Christ (12:13b). **All** have been **made to drink into one Spirit.** These words do not refer to any specific act or activity on the part of the Christian Church. Used in a figurative sense, **to drink** (cf. John 6:53)

---

[39]Dods, *op. cit.,* p. 285.   [40]Hering, *op. cit.,* p. 130.
[41]Whedon, *op. cit.,* p. 93.

suggests a close communion, or the idea of an inner presence which works in every part of the Christian's personality. The phrase **made to drink** (*epotisthemen*) was sometimes used of irrigating a field and suggests an abundant supply. Paul's meaning is that members of the Church are united as closely as possible with the one Spirit of God who dwells in all.

3. *Bodily Efficiency Depends on Variety* (12:14-26)

The lowest forms of life have no variety of members or, at best, very few. But in higher levels the organism is more complex. The body of Christ represents the highest sphere of living and therefore is certain to have innumerable ways of expressing itself. Now Paul has arrived at the heart of the illustration.

a. The body is the totality of its members (12:14). The essence of the human body is its unity in diversity. It has many parts. If the body had only one part, it would not be the marvelous organism that we know. Since it would be absurd to regard the body as only one member, it is also ridiculous to exalt one member of the Church above another.

In 12:1-14 we find Paul's teaching regarding "Spiritual Gifts." (1) All spiritual gifts come from the same Holy Spirit, 1, 4-6; (2) There are different kinds of gifts, 7-10; (3) All gifts are given to contribute to the unity and well-being of the body, 11-14.

b. Each member contributes to our well-being (12:15-17). Apparently the aggressive few with sensational gifts had made some of the Corinthians feel inferior or unnecessary. Paul suggests that the **foot** (15) is necessary to run races and carry burdens, even though it cannot perform the creative work of **the hand**. The **ear** (16) may not flash with fire like the **eye**, nor serve as a camera to record the panorama of life. But the ear is an amazingly efficient servant in recording sound, receiving messages, and listening to the words of man. However, even the ear cannot perform the function of **smelling** (17).

c. The parts of the body are ordained by God (12:18-20). The apostle makes the highest possible appeal for unity by the statement that all parts of the body are the result of God's sovereign activity. For **God set the members . . . in the body, as it hath pleased him** (18). Set (*etheto*) is in the aorist, referring to the completed act in the creation of man. God created the body as it is and bestowed upon each member a particular function. God did this **as it hath pleased him**—at His own good pleasure.

Without members there would be no human **body;** it would be a shapeless lump of flesh (19). The lump would have unity, but no variety of functions. It is the existence and interaction of the various members that give the body meaning. Thus Paul comes back to his theme: **But now are they many members, yet but one body** (20).

d. Members of the body are interdependent (12:21-26). When members of the church lose their sense of unity, they face a double hazard. Those who feel inferior may leave the church. The ones who feel superior may lose their spiritual values and become hypocrites. In v. 15, Paul had referred to those who might feel inferior. Now he deals with those who have an unchristian, exalted concept of their own importance.

(1) *The feeble member* (12:21-22). No member of the body is unimportant. Even **those members of the body, which seem to be more feeble, are necessary** (22). **Feeble** (*asthenes*) means basically "sick," and so "weak, feeble, miserable."[42] It is difficult to say which bodily members Paul has in mind. Hering states that "only the digestive organs can be intended, here presented as especially despised."[43] Vincent thinks that "the allusion is probably to those which seem to be weaker in their original structure, naturally."[44] Still others interpret these "feeble members" as those which on occasion seem to be weaker, as when a particular member is diseased. At any rate, the idea is that all members of the body, both seen and unseen, are necessary.

(2) *The less honorable member* (23). **Less honourable** members are not the same as the "more feeble." By the words **we bestow more abundant honour,** Paul probably had in mind the use of clothing. Hence some writers think that here he refers to the organs of excretion and reproduction.[45] Certainly there are parts of the body which seem to be **less honourable.** These members receive more attention and are given a **comeliness** which they lack by nature because they are necessary for the life of the body.

(3) *The comely parts* (24-26). **Our comely parts** (24) are the presentable members, those we accept because they are

[42]Arndt and Gingrich, *op. cit.,* p. 115.   [43]*Op. cit.,* p. 131.
[44]*Op. cit.,* III, 259.
[45]Hering, *op. cit.,* p. 131; Grosheide, *op. cit.,* p. 296.

attractive or good-looking. They **have no need** of extra attention or adornment.

At this point Paul again presents the thought that the body is structured according to God's will—**God hath tempered the body together.** He has blended the bodily organs so that there are harmony and interdependence. As a result there is no division. The body functions as a unit and all **the members . . . have the same care one for another** (25). When one member **suffer[s], all the members suffer with it** (26). On the other hand, all parts of the body share in the good feeling that results from the wholesome operation of all parts of the body.

4. The Church Is Unified, Yet Diversified (12:27-30)

Paul now makes his application: **Ye are the body of Christ** (27). "The Corinthian church as such is a *corpus Christi,* an organism made by Christ and maintained by Him, having the complete character of a body as that was described."[46] Since the Church is in reality a spiritual organism, individuals are **members in particular.** Each of them belongs to the body. Therefore none can rightfully claim to be of greater importance than others, nor should anyone regard others as inferior.

a. The unified Church has many different offices and gifts (12:28). Paul now advances from general ideas to specific issues. He shows that in the body of Christ men do not choose this or that office. Nor do men select their gifts. It is God who **hath set some in the church** to do particular things.

These offices and gifts are listed as follows: (1) **apostles,** (2) **prophets,** (3) **teachers,** (4) **miracles,** (5) **gifts of healings,** (6) **helps,** (7) **governments,** (8) **diversities of tongues.** "The order in which the . . . list of ministries is named is deliberate. The apostles have received the highest and the speakers in tongues the lowest."[47] Another echoes a similar idea: "In Corinth . . . it required an interpreter to explain the tongue to those who knew it not. Hence Paul placed this gift lowest of all. It created wonder but did little real good."[48] Still another author writes: "Instead of a mere enumeration, Paul prefers an arrangement in

[46]Grosheide, *op. cit.,* p. 297.

[47]Clarence Tucker Craig (exegesis), *The Interpreter's Bible,* X (New York: Abingdon-Cokesbury Press, 1953), 163.

[48]Robertson, *op. cit.,* IV, 170.

order of rank."[49] The offices and gifts and their significance may be stated briefly.

(1) **Apostles.** These were men called and commissioned directly by Christ to be His witnesses.

(2) **Prophets.** The prophets were those called to predict the course of redemptive history, to proclaim God's message, and to exhort.

(3) **Teachers.** Teachers were regarded as highly essential and necessary to the welfare of the Early Church. When books were scarce, the teacher was a key figure in presenting and interpreting the teachings of the OT and the doctrines of the Church.

(4) **Miracles.** Paul passes from "endowed *persons* to abstract *gifts.*"[50] To some, God apparently gave unusual powers to perform feats that would be impossible from the standpoint of human ability (cf. v. 10).

(5) **Gifts of healings.** The Early Church witnessed dramatic healings and instantaneous restorations (Acts 3:1-11; 9:32-42).

(6) **Helps.** Some in the Church were given special concern, compassion, and ability to assist the needy. Or the reference may have been to persons who acted as church secretaries, treasurers, or assistant pastors.

(7) **Governments.** The word governments (*kyberneseis*) "denotes the activity of the steersman of a ship, the man who pilots his vessel through the dangerous shoals and brings her safe to port."[51] Thus the term probably refers "to administrators of church government, as presbyters."[52]

(8) **Diversities of tongues.** Regarding this gift Clarke writes: "The power to speak, on all necessary occasions, languages which they had not learned."[53] Some scholars feel that the charismatic gift here includes the gift of intelligible languages as at Pentecost, as well as that of the *pneumatika* of 14:2 ff. Others hold that the gifts (*charismata*) are different from the *pneumatika.*

b. *The reality of diversity in the Church* (12:29-30). Paul now asks a series of rhetorical questions. **Are all apostles? Are all prophets?** These questions are all introduced with the parti-

---

[49]Findlay, *op. cit.,* pp. 894-96.   [50]Vincent, *op. cit.,* III, 260.
[51]Morris, *op. cit.,* p. 179.   [52]Vincent, *op. cit.,* III, 260.
[53]*Op. cit.,* II, 262.

cle *me*, which indicates that a negative answer is expected. No gift can be despised and no gift should be unduly exalted above others. The Christian way is to accept diversity in the Church and to honor and respect all members as important and essential.

5. The Best Gifts (12:31)

a. Desire the best gifts (31*a*). At this point Paul seems almost to contradict himself. In v. 11 the apostle had stated that the Spirit was at work in the Church, "dividing to every man severally as he will." Again in v. 28 he had declared that it was God who "set some in the church." Both of these statements indicate that the gifts are sovereignly bestowed at God's will. Yet now Paul tells the Corinthians to **covet earnestly the best gifts.** Here are reflected the parallel truths of the sovereignty of God and the free will of man.

To **covet** (*zeloute*) means to be "burning with zeal, a zealot."[54] The exhortation to desire the **best gifts** points to a difference between these bestowments of the Spirit. Paul had earlier shown that all of the spiritual gifts were needed. But this does not deny that some are more important than others. The fault of the Corinthians was that they exalted a lesser gift to a place of prominence. The apostle's aim is to direct the Corinthians away from a distorted interest in speaking in tongues to other more significant gifts. He reminds them of all of God's gifts and urges them to seek the greater ones. The Church must always leave it to God to determine which gifts are most necessary, but the Church must also always seek to be guided by God's priorities.

b. The greatest gift (12:31*b*). At this point Paul lifts the entire matter into proper perspective by presenting a gift that was available to all and which was the most Christlike of all— the gift of love. This gift is called the **more excellent way.**

Commentators generally agree that Paul is referring to love as a distinct gift rather than to the other gifts expressed with or without love. This love is a gift of the Spirit, which is available to all; and "that is precisely the reason why love can be called the highest of all the charismata (cf. Gal. 5:22)."[55] Paul has arrived at the point where he wants to show that "there is a more excellent way to edify the church than even to exercise

---

[54]Thayer, *op. cit.*, p. 271.   [55]Grosheide, *op. cit.*, p. 301.

apostolic gifts; this is the way of love, which he proceeds to celebrate."[56]

The apostle does not digress from the discussion of the gifts of the Spirit by introducing the "hymn of love" in c. 13. He returns in c. 14 to a detailed discussion of the gifts. His purpose here is to encourage the Corinthians to seek love rather than gifts. For it is only when viewed in the light of love that gifts can be seen in proper perspective.

D. THE GREATEST OF SPIRITUAL GRACES (13:1-13)

The NT word for **love** is *agape.* The term was not common before the birth of the Christian Church, but it was known. The Septuagint (LXX) uses the word frequently. The Christians of the first century adopted it to designate a love differing from both *eros* (selfish, desiring love) and *philia* (natural sympathy, or friendship).

Agape is love which is completely in harmony with the character of the person expressing it. Thus *agape,* in the NT, expresses concern and compassion for the utterly unworthy. It was love poured out upon others without any thought of personal benefit or reward. Such love seeks only the good of the loved one. It is ultimate, redemptive, and can come only from God. Its highest expression was revealed in the cross of Christ. It was to be the unique trademark of all Christians.

"The Greatest Gift" is love because: (1) It is the most essential gift, 1-3; (2) It is the most Christlike gift, 4-6; (3) It is the most comprehensive gift, 7; (4) It is the most permanent gift, 8-13.

1. *Love Is Essential* (13:1-3)

Gifts have a place in the Church and are useful. But love is the essence of the Christian life and is absolutely necessary. It will find a way even without charismatic gifts. But gifts without love are like a body without a soul.

a. Love is greater than speaking ability (13:1). Paul begins by presenting a hypothetical possibility: **Though I speak with tongues of men and of angels.** If a person has the gift of golden-tongued oratory or of angelic utterance, but does not have love,

---

[56]Dods, *op. cit.,* p. 295.

he amounts to nothing. Without love one's gifts of speaking become hollow and brassy—he becomes as **sounding brass, or a tinkling cymbal.** The **sounding brass** ("noisy gong," RSV) signifies either a piece of unwrought metal or a gong used to attract attention. **Tinkling** (*alalazon*) means "clashing" or a loud, harsh sound. The **cymbal** consisted of two half-globes which were banged together. The idea is that of the unmeaning clash of metal instead of music.

The apostle's aim here is to show that a man who professes the gift of glossolalia as practiced at Corinth but who has no love is in reality no more than an impersonal, metallic instrument. However, the purpose "of this verse is not to place glossolalia without love over against glossolalia with love but rather to compare glossolalia as such with love."[57] In Christianity, there is no substitute for love.

b. Love is more necessary than prophecy, knowledge, or faith (13:2). Paul has ranked **prophecy** next to apostleship (12:28) and does not minimize its significance. But as inspiring as prophecy is and as vital as it is to the progress of the Church, it is not as necessary as love. **Mysteries** are truths which cannot be known by human reason; they are given by divine revelation. These mysteries are spiritual truths which relate to redemptive history, especially the truths of an eschatological nature, i.e., relating to future events in God's plan for the world. **Knowledge** is more than intellectual comprehension. Because such knowledge is a gift it contains a mystical element which is based on personal experience and personal relationship. **Faith** here refers to the extraordinary power to perform miracles. As such it is a gift. **All faith** indicates the possibility of having this gift in its fullest sense.

The church at Corinth placed much importance on the people who had a knowledge of both human and divine affairs and who could fascinate others with their feats of faith. Yet Paul issues a sweeping declaration that one may have all these gifts—and be **nothing.** Love makes the difference. Even without gifts, love is still of supreme value. Without love, all gifts are meaningless.

c. Love is more important than self-sacrifice (13:3). Paul has compared love to dramatic acts of speaking and to dynamic activities of the mind and spirit. Now he turns to deeds of mercy and sacrifice. He writes: **And though I bestow all my goods to**

[57]Grosheide, *op. cit.*, p. 304.

**feed the poor, and though I give my body to be burned, and
have not charity, it profiteth me nothing.** The word **bestow**
(*psomiso*) means to "break off, and to distribute in small portions; to feed by morsels; and may be applicable even to distributing one's property in small portions."[58] The verb is in the
aorist tense, indicating that the action is over and the distribution
made.

Even beyond selling possessions and giving the proceeds
away in a single sweeping gesture, one may offer his **body to
be burned.** This expression may refer to the act of punishing a
Christian like a criminal by branding his body with a hot iron.
Or it may have referred to martyrdom, in which the person
experienced an agonizing death by being fastened to a stake,
having wood piled high around him and ignited. Others think
the meaning may have been the voluntary selling of oneself
into slavery in order to secure money to help the cause of Christ.
At any rate, no matter how much of a sacrifice a person has made,
if he doesn't have love, he is not benefited.

2. Love Is Christlike (13:4-6)

a. Christlike in its affirmation (13:4a). Love is the parent
of patience and kindness. Paul declares, **Charity suffereth long**
(*makrothymia*). This item means patience to bear injustice
without anger or despair. "Love has an infinite capacity for endurance."[59] This patience involves people more than circumstances. To be **kind** (*chrestotes*) is a type of "goodness and
courtesy coming from the heart and represents the active counterpart of forbearance."[60]

b. Christlike in its negations (13:4b-6). Love manifests
itself positively in patience and kindness. It also reveals itself
negatively by the restrictions it places on itself. Thus love can
be depended upon for both what it does and what it does not do.

(1) *Love does not envy* (13:4). **Envieth** is a verb which is
used sometimes in a favorable sense, as in 12:31: "Covet earnestly
the best gifts." The word basically means "to be *zealous* for or
against any person or thing."[61] When used in an unfavorable
setting, it means to be *zealous* against a person; hence to be
jealous, or to feel displeasure at the success of another.

[58]Barnes, *op. cit.*, p. 262.   [59]Morris, *op. cit.*, p. 184.
[60]Hering, *op. cit.*, p. 139.   [61]Barnes, *op. cit.*, p. 264.

(2) *Love does not exalt itself* (13:4). **Vaunteth not itself** introduces a vivid word which means "braggart or windbag."[62] It is "used of one who sounds his own praises."[63] This warning was especially needful to the Corinthians, who were inclined to be proud of their gifts.

(3) *Love is not puffed up* (13:4). **Puffed up** (*physioutai*) means to blow, to puff, to pant. Hence the meaning is "inflated with pride, vanity, and self-esteem." It differs from **vaunteth** in that it denotes the active expression of the feelings of pride and egotism. A man may feel a sense of self-exaltation and be clever enough to mask it under the guise of piety. Thus he would not expose himself to the criticism of being **puffed up**. Love eliminates both the inner feeling of self-exaltation and the outer expression of it.

(4) *Love does not behave improperly* (13:5). Paul here speaks of perfect love and of its operation in the Christian life. The "more excellent way" is the way of holiness. The apostle does not refer merely to an ideal to be sought. He points to an experience in love which is in the present tense. The time is now. Such love does not **behave** in **unseemly** fashion. It does not do anything which is "disgraceful, dishonourable, indecent."[64] Love has proper respect for those in authority and proper regard for those over whom authority is exerted. Love "prompts to all that is fit and becoming in life; and would save from all that is unfit and unbecoming."[65]

(5) *Love is not self-seeking* (13:5). Jesus had described the basic approach to Christian living when He spoke of the grain of wheat falling to the earth and dying that it might live (John 12:24). This is Christian love. It is the direct opposite of self-seeking. Selfishness and love cannot reside in the same human spirit. Love cannot find its own happiness at the expense of others. This does not mean that a man should have no concern for his own welfare. Nor does it mean that he should disregard his personal health, property, happiness, or salvation. It means that a man does not make his personal happiness and welfare the chief motivation of his life. Love prompts the Christian to seek the well-being of others even at the cost of toil, self-denial, and personal sacrifice.

[62]Arndt and Gingrich, *op. cit.*, p. 659.   [63]Vincent, *op. cit.*, III, 264.

[64]Morris, *op. cit.*, p. 184.   [65]Barnes, *op. cit.*, p. 266.

(6) *Love is not irritable* (13:5). Love is not provoked. "*Easily* is superfluous, and gives a wrong coloring to the statement, which is absolute: *is not provoked or exasperated.*"[66] When used in an unfavorable sense the word means to "provoke to wrath, to irritate."[67] Hence love is not touchy, nor hypersensitive, and does not take offense. Love alone can overcome the real or fancied aggravations that a person experiences in life.

(7) *Love does not record evil* (13:5). The word translated **thinketh** (*logizetai*) means to take into account, to charge, to calculate, or to record. Love does not add up, or assign evil intentions and wrong designs to a man. Love does not credit other people with evil motives. As Godet puts it, "Love, instead of entering evil as a debit in its account book, voluntarily passes the sponge over what it endures."[68]

(8) *Love finds no joy in evil of any kind* (13:6). Love does not participate in any personal sins or acts of unrighteousness. Nor does love rejoice over the vices of other men. It finds no pleasure when others are proved guilty of crime. Love never derives satisfaction when another falls into sin. Rather, love rejoices with the **truth** and finds joy in the virtues of others. Love and truth are twins in the household of faith. Such love cannot be indifferent or neutral. It must take sides. Love shrinks from injustice but it embraces truth.

3. *Love Is the Most Comprehensive of All Graces* (13:7)

The apostle here shifts his theme from resounding negatives to thrilling positives. The charismatic gifts, especially glossolalia, were confined to a few and accomplished little of practical value. Love, on the other hand, is as wide and as inclusive as God's grace can make a man's spirit.

a. Love covers and endures (13:7a). In classical literature **beareth** (*stego*) meant "to cover, pass over in silence, keep confidential."[69] An excellent rendering of Paul's idea here is "love that throws a cloak of silence over what is displeasing in another person."[70] The word also contains the idea of enduring. So love may conceal what is displeasing or it may endure what is un-

---

[66]Vincent, *op. cit.*, III, 265.   [67]Arndt and Gingrich, *op. cit.*, p. 634.
[68]*Op. cit.*, II, 247.   [69]Arndt and Gingrich, *op. cit.*, p. 773.
[70]*Ibid.*

pleasant in another. Whedon comments: "So does a mother seek to *cover* the faults of her child; so would Paul rather cover than expose the errors of his Corinthians."[71] Love keeps out resentment and expects the best of people, even when appearances are against them.

b. *Love generates confidence in others* (13:7b). The Corinthians were a suspicious crowd. They had difficulty in placing confidence in each other. Their rivalry over the various gifts had produced a gap in their trust. Paul reminds these spiritual problem-children that love **believeth all things.** The verb **believeth** (*pisteuei*) means to have confidence in others, to put the best construction on their actions and motives. Certainly Paul did not suggest that a Christian filled with love would be a person of naive credulity who would believe everything presented to his mind. He means that love is eager to believe the best about others, and to make allowance for circumstances.

c. *Love produces perpetual hope* (13:7c). Love never gives up—it follows a man to the edge of the grave, always expecting the best. Love does not produce a kind of sentimental optimism which blindly refuses to face reality, but it refuses to take failure as final. Rather than accept the failure of another, "love will *hold on to this hope* until all possibility of such a result has vanished, and it is compelled to believe that the conduct is not susceptible of a fair explanation."[72]

d. *Love remains steadfast* (13:7d). Love bears up under disappointment, is courageous under persecution, and does not murmur. **Endureth** (*hypomeno*) means to "stand one's ground, hold out, endure."[73] Thus when the Christian can no longer believe or hope, he can love. This enduring is not a mere passive acquiescence. It is rather a quiet, stable reaction to people and events which do not merit patience. Love is steadfast.

4. *Love Is the Most Complete Grace* (13:8-13)

Paul now reaches his climax. Three of the most highly regarded gifts are spoken of as temporary. Over against this temporary character of all other virtues stands the permanence of love. Charismatic gifts are partial, while love is perfect.

---

[71]*Op. cit.*, p. 99.   [72]Barnes, *op. cit.*, p. 270.
[73]Arndt and Gingrich, *op. cit.*, p. 853.

a. *Love is eternal* (13:8). When the redeemed stand before God, there will be no further need of **prophecies.** The **tongues,** so highly regarded by the Corinthians, will **cease,** since man will be delivered from all that separates him from God and from others. **Knowledge,** both the learning acquired by man and the mysteries revealed by God, will **vanish away** in the perfect light of the knowledge of God.

b. *Love is perfect and complete* (13:9-12). Knowledge and prophecy were highly esteemed by the Corinthians, but the apostle states that all such earthly knowledge is partial. Man can never fully understand God. Both sin and finitude make this impossible. Paul adds that **we prophesy in part.** While man can grasp some truths, he never receives the full measure of God's revelation.

In the final consummation of redemptive history all imperfections will be replaced by the perfect—**When that which is perfect is come, then that which is in part shall be done away** (10). In that day all imperfections will vanish. All that appears obscure and dim here will be made plain.

(1) *The imperfection of partial understanding* (13:11). Man's present knowledge compared with that which he will have in heaven is like the knowledge of the infant compared with the mature man. **Child** (*nepios*) denotes a baby, an infant, though without any specific age limit. It refers to the first period of existence before boyhood or youth.

The verb **understood** (*ephronoun*) refers here "to the earlier undeveloped exercise of the childish mind; a thinking which is not yet connected reasoning."[74] **Thought** (*logizomai*) denotes a progression over **understood;** from *logizomai* comes the meaning of reasoning things out or relating concepts. The idea here is that when Paul matured in Christian love he put away childish things with deliberate decision and finality.

(2) *The imperfection of partial vision* (13:12). Paul writes, **For now we see through a glass, darkly.** The word **glass** (*esoptron*) means a mirror. Because of the nature of the mirrors of Paul's day, the reflection would be vague or obscure. The mirror of the Greeks and Romans was a thin disk of metal polished on one side, the other side being left plain or containing some design.

---

[74]Vincent, *op. cit.,* III, 266.

Glass mirrors were also made at this time, but were not widely used.

The word **darkly** (*ainigmati*) actually means a "riddle," and thus suggests an enigma or an obscure intimation. Hence the word as the apostle uses it means obscurely, darkly, or imperfectly. The expression **but then face to face** indicates a bright prospect. When man stands before God, his vision will be perfect, with nothing between to obscure the presence of God.

As it will be with seeing, it will also be with knowing. Paul has already stated that our earthly knowledge is partial (9) even when it is a special gift. Over against this partial knowledge the apostle sets the perfect knowledge of the redeemed in God's presence. The TEV renders the meaning, "What I know now is only partial; then it will be complete, as complete as God's knowledge of me."

(3) *The perfection of love* (13:13). In contrast to the temporary gifts that so occupied the attention of the Corinthians, the permanence of the three cardinal Christian graces is asserted: **And now abideth faith, hope, charity.** According to Paul **faith** is essential to salvation (Rom. 3:28; Gal. 2:20). It is impossible to live without **hope.** When hope dies the spirit dies. But of these three basic Christian graces—the greatest is love.

Faris D. Whitesell titles his exposition of c. 13 "The Excellency of Love Demonstrates Its Excellency." (1) Love makes life's gifts profitable, 1-3; (2) Love makes life's relationships beautiful, 4-7; (3) Love makes life's contributions eternal, 8-13 (*Sermon Outlines on Favorite Bible Chapters*).

E. PROPHECY SUPERIOR TO SPEAKING IN TONGUES, 14:1-40

In c. 12, Paul had presented a general discussion of spiritual gifts. There he did not pinpoint the problem that speaking in tongues presented to the church at Corinth. He followed the general discussion of spiritual gifts with the hymn of love found in c. 13. Love, as Paul presents it, is the greatest of all spiritual values. Now, lest someone might still miss the direction of his thinking, Paul comes to grips with the problem introduced in 12:1. He selects prophecy, which is also a gift of speaking, to show that speaking in tongues, no matter how it is understood, occupies an inferior position. As such it can never be regarded as the necessary or indisputable evidence of either the baptism in or with the Holy Spirit.

1. *Limitations of Speaking in Tongues* (14:1-25)

a. *Prophecy is the most important gift* (14:1). In his opening words Paul uses two verbs that are significant: **Follow after charity . . . and desire spiritual gifts.** The verb **follow after** (lit., pursue) "indicates a never terminating action while 'to desire earnestly' stresses the intensity rather than the continuity of the action."[75] Love is to be followed with persistence, but it is also right to **desire** gifts. Of these Paul gives first place to prophecy, which is closely related to preaching. The essential element is the utterance of a message directly inspired by God. Several comparisons between speaking in tongues and prophesying follow, each one pointing out the weaknesses and limitations of the glossolalia as practiced at Corinth.

b. *Prophecy Is Understood* (14:2-3). Paul intends to magnify prophecy but he does so by first pointing out the limitations of "strange sounds" (TEV).

(1) *No one understands the man speaking in tongues* (14:2). One reason that speaking in tongues is inferior to prophecy is that it is not understood by others. **For he that speaketh in an unknown tongue speaketh not unto men, but unto God.** The word **unknown** is in italics, indicating that it is not in the original text. However, the KJV translators caught the meaning of Paul's words correctly, so its use does not distort the meaning of the sentence. **No man understandeth him** suggests that the gift discussed here is not the same as the speaking in other languages at Pentecost (Acts 2:4). The man exercising this gift is not speaking **unto men** but is involved in a personal expression of praise to **God.**

In the spirit probably means the spirit of the person himself, carried away in excitement and emotion.[76] In this condition he speaks mysteries which neither he nor anyone else understands, except someone interprets. Since such speaking in tongues is unknowable to men, it is vastly inferior to prophecy.

(2) *Prophecy is understood by men* (14:3). In contrast to the unknown nature of ecstatic utterances, prophecy serves the purpose of **edification, and exhortation, and comfort.** The word

[75]Grosheide, *op. cit.*, p. 316.

[76]See Morris, *op. cit.*, p. 191; Hering, *op. cit.*, p. 146; Godet, *op. cit.*, p. 266. Contra RSV, Berk., Moffatt, TEV, where **spirit** is capitalized.

edification (*oikodomen*) means "building as a process, construction."[77] Paul uses it in the sense of building up Christian character. **Exhortation** means "admonition, encouragement."[78] **Comfort** is the translation of *paramythia*, which in classical Greek meant "any address, whether made for the purpose of persuading, or of arousing and stimulating, or of calming and consolation."[79] Prophecy is thus an inspired utterance which all men understand; it serves to build up Christian character, to encourage, to strengthen, and to comfort or console.

c. *Prophecy builds up the church* (14:4-6). Because prophecy is understood by men it **edifieth the church** (4). Speaking in unknown tongues serves only to strengthen the individual. However, Paul does not completely forbid this practice: **I would that ye all spake with tongues** (5). The verb **would**, or wish (*thelo*) "does not express an order, but a concession in the form of a wish unlikely to be fulfilled (cf. 7:7)."[80] Regarding the statement Bruce writes: "Possibly Paul fears that he has gone too far in rejecting tongues. Hence, he makes it clear that he is not forbidding tongues, but is insisting on the superiority of prophecy."[81] Because it was difficult to distinguish the valid gift of languages or the legitimate expression of ecstatic spiritual desire from an invalid expression of personal exultation, Paul would not forbid speaking in tongues. However, he quickly and distinctly points out that the gift of prophecy is superior: **but rather that ye prophesied.**

The criterion of any gift is its value to the Church. Even where Paul makes a concession to speaking in tongues, he immediately insists that its value is less than prophecy unless it be interpreted, so **that the church may receive edifying** (5). The words **except he interpret** do "not refer to a particular interpretation of a message spoken in tongues, but to a permanent gift of interpretation. . . . Paul has in view a person who has received two gifts, that of speaking in tongues and that of interpretation."[82] Thus the apostle indicates that any glossolalia should be interpreted to strengthen the congregation.

When Paul alludes to a coming visit to Corinth, he again makes edification of the Church the criterion of value for the

---

[77]Arndt and Gingrich, *op. cit.*, p. 561.   [78]Thayer, *op. cit.*, p. 483.
[79]*Ibid.*, p. 485.   [80]Hering, *op. cit.*, p. 146.
[81]*Op. cit.*, p. 207.   [82]Grosheide, *op. cit.*, p. 320.

gifts of the Spirit: **What shall I profit you, except I shall speak to you either by revelation, or by knowledge, or by prophesying, or by doctrine? (6)**

d. *Speaking in tongues leads to confusion* (14: 7-12). In this section Paul continues to drive home the superiority of prophecy over speaking in tongues.

(1) *The realm of music* (14: 7). The apostle first selects an illustration to show that indistinct sounds lead to confusion. **Even things without life,** such as a **pipe or harp,** must make a **distinction in the sounds.** Otherwise an aimless jangle is the result. The **pipe** (*aulos*) was a flute, and represents wind instruments, while the **harp** (*kithara*) stands for the stringed instruments. None of these produces meaningful music unless it is played according to some form or order.

(2) *The realm of the soldier* (14: 8). **The trumpet,** in ancient days, called the people to arms and conveyed the directions in fighting. But if the war-trumpet gives merely a blare of noise rather than a recognized military command to men at a distance, **who shall prepare himself to the battle?** Random blasting on the trumpet would neither rally the people to fight nor give adequate directions in battle. If the signals are **uncertain,** confusion and disorder are the result.

(3) *The realm of religion* (14: 9-12). Paul now makes the application to the problem at hand—the wrong emphasis placed on speaking in tongues. **Except ye utter . . . words easy to be understood . . . ye shall speak into the air** (9), i.e., speak entirely in vain.

In v. 10, Paul continues, **There are . . . many kinds of voices in the world.** "By *voices* are meant *languages*."[83] All the different languages have **signification,** for the entire purpose of language is to communicate. It is therefore necessary to know **the meaning of the voice** (11). The word **meaning** (*dynamis*) indicates power, resources, or capability. Speech that is not understood has no power to communicate.

According to Paul, if one does not understand what is spoken, he becomes a **barbarian.** The term was probably used originally of those who uttered harsh or guttural noises. Later it was "applied to all who did not speak Greek."[84] Thus the word came to mean one whose language did not make sense. So the "ecstatic

---

[83]Vincent, *op. cit.,* III, 268.   [84]*Ibid.*

speech which seemed to the Corinthians a matter for such pride turns out to be the means of making them nothing more than barbarians."[85]

In v. 12, Paul relentlessly comes back to his point of chief emphasis: **Forasmuch as ye are zealous of spiritual gifts, seek that ye may excel to the edifying of the church.** The primary aim of the Christian is to build up the Church and to strengthen its members. If a person desires to promote the well-being of the Church, he will test his gifts by that criterion.

e. Speaking in tongues has little practical value (14:13-25). Since the gift of speaking in tongues, as practiced at Corinth, had little practical value, Paul urges a course of action that will be more beneficial to the Church.

(1) *The gift of interpretation needed* (14:13). Paul here urges: **Let him that speaketh in an unknown tongue pray that he may interpret.** The one who pours out his words in impassioned utterance should also pray that he be given the ability to interpret his utterance to the church.

(2) *Understanding important* (14:14-15). A man who prays **in an unknown tongue** is not using his **understanding** (14; *nous*). The word signifies the mind. Christian living does not depend entirely upon the intellect, but the Christian needs the intellect for full enjoyment of the Christian experience. To omit the intellect is to be unfruitful. Speaking or praying in tongues furnishes nothing for others. In v. 15, Paul asserts that he will both **pray** and **sing with the spirit, and . . . with the understanding also.** He will praise God in prayer and song with both mind and spirit. Man reaches the acme of spiritual life when emotions and intellect are both stretched to the limit in an act of worship. Praying and singing in tongues may be an emotional release and make one feel inspired, but it adds nothing to an understanding of the gospel.

(3) *Unknown tongues do not help the congregation* (14:16-17). In the Christian congregation there would be **the unlearned** (16; *idiotes*). The term indicates either inquirers who were not yet committed to Christ or Christians in the church who as yet had received no gifts. In either case these people would not be able to understand the words and thus could not confirm or **say Amen** to the prayers. It is well to give **thanks** (17), but

[85]Morris, *op. cit.*, p. 193.

even in such praise meetings one should seek to strengthen the church.

(4) *Plain words better than numberless noises* (14:18-20). Paul's admonitions here are gentle. He identifies himself with those who spoke in tongues: **I thank my God, I speak with tongues more than ye all** (18). Jerome, in his *Notes*, says that Paul is exulting in his ability as a linguist.[86] It appears logical to accept Jerome's idea of Paul's ability to speak many languages, for his training and background would have made him an excellent linguist, a master of languages. However it is also certain that Paul was rich in emotional experiences. Whether or not he would use tongues in one sense as applied to the Corinthians and in another sense as applied to himself is an open question.

But even if it is granted that Paul may have spoken in unknown tongues, this admission means little, for Paul immediately makes two statements that empty speaking in tongues of all significance. First, he devalues the practice in public worship: **In the church I had rather speak five words with my understanding . . . than ten thousand words in an unknown tongue** (19). Five words clearly stated are worth more than an infinite number which no one knows. Then, secondly, the apostle points out that all the commotion about tongues was so much childishness, and chides the Corinthians accordingly: **Brethren, be not children in understanding** (20). Godet interprets the meaning thus: "It is indeed the characteristic of the child to prefer the amusing to the useful, the brilliant to the solid. And this is what the Corinthians did by their marked taste for glossolalia."[87] Yet **in malice** they were to be as **children** (*nepiazete*, childlike). Moffatt renders v. 20, "Brothers, . . . in evil be mere infants, but be mature in your intelligence."

(5) *Strange tongues were once a punishment* (14:21-22). Paul now introduces an extremely sober note. Whereas the Corinthians regarded speaking in tongues as something to be desired, Paul points out that it might be a sign of God's displeasure and punishment. The apostle paraphrases a warning found in Isa. 28:11 when he writes to the Corinthians: **With men of other tongues and other lips will I speak unto this people; and yet for all that will they not hear me, saith the Lord** (21). Vincent writes: "The point of the quotation is that speech in

---

[86]Findlay, *op. cit.*, p. 908.　　　　　　[87]*Op. cit.*, II, 287.

strange tongues was a chastisement for the unbelief of God's ancient people, by which they were made to hear His voice 'speaking in the harsh commands of the foreign invader.' "[88]

When Paul quoted this verse from Isaiah, he was reminding the Corinthians of their childishness and rebellion, not encouraging them to speak in tongues. He wanted to remind them that the simple, intelligible good news of God's revelation in Christ had not been received properly. With this warning in mind he asserts that **tongues are for a sign . . . to them that believe not** (22). He means that the unbeliever can understand and thus be benefitted by the judgment of God. **Prophesying**, on the other hand, is not for the unbeliever, **but for them which believe.** Prophecy brings the true message of God to the church.

(6) *Speaking in tongues does not help unbelievers* (14:23-25). Now Paul presents a hypothetical case for the Corinthians. What would happen if **the whole church be come together into one place, and all speak with tongues?** (23) If the gift is as desirable as the Corinthians indicate, the entire church has a right, even an obligation, to seek it. But what would happen if **the unbelievers** came into such a church? **Will they not say that ye are mad?** Paul was not concerned about ecclesiastical popularity polls. Nor was he trimming the gospel message to fit the mold of public opinion. His idea was that the task of the Church is to attract unbelievers and win them to Christ. He was alarmed that, instead of helping to convert sinners, speaking in tongues would arouse only derision and scorn from unbelievers.

The result of prophecy is different. **If all prophesy, and there come in one that believeth not . . . he is convinced . . . he is judged of all** (24). The word **convinced** (*elenchetai*) means convicted or reproved of his sins. It is used in John 16:8 in reference to the Holy Spirit's work in convicting "the world of sin, and of righteousness, and of judgment." **Judged** (*anakrinetai*) implies inquiry, or heart-searching utterances which reveal the unbeliever's condition to himself. Even the things long hidden or remote from public scrutiny are paraded before his conscience, for now **are the secrets of his heart made manifest** (25). Prophecy thus produces the redemptive results that the Church of God seeks, for the unbeliever falls **down on his face** and will

[88]*Op. cit.,* III, 271.

worship God. To the unbeliever, then, tongues are a token of madness. But prophecy leads men to God.

2. *Restrictions in the Church* (14:26-40).

In dealing with the excessive interest of the Corinthians in the gift of speaking in tongues, Paul did not openly challenge nor disallow the practice, but he did place severe restrictions on it.

a. The rule of edification (14:26). Paul's first guideline was, **Let all things be done unto edifying.** When the Corinthians assembled for worship, every part of the service should contribute to the building up of the church. The **psalm** (song), the **doctrine** (Christian teaching), the **tongue** (some utterance not in the commonly understood language), a **revelation,** an **interpretation** of the **tongue**—all were for the purpose of strengthening the church.

b. Only two or three permitted to speak (14:27a). Paul places a limitation on the number of people permitted to **speak in an unknown tongue** in any public gathering. **Let it be by two, or at the most by three.** Such a restriction would eliminate the confusion and bafflement that would occur if much of the service was given to such activities.

c. Must speak in turn (14:27b). Not only was there a limit placed on the number of people who could speak in tongues in one service, but also they were to speak **by course,** that is, in turn. This restriction would eliminate confusion arising from several speaking at the same time in a public service.

d. Must have an interpreter (14:27c-28a). Paul's third rule was, **And let one interpret; but if there be no interpreter, let him keep silence in the church.** All speaking in tongues must be accompanied by an interpretation. According to Morris, this restriction "shows us that we must not think of 'tongues' as being the result of an irresistible impulse of the Spirit, driving the man willy-nilly into ecstatic speech. If he chose he could *keep silence,* and this Paul instructs him to do on occasion."[89]

e. Prophesying subject to regulation (14:29-33a). Just as speaking in tongues was subject to regulation, so was prophecy: **Let the prophets speak two or three** (29). Here again the apostle is concerned that no one group and no single gift become domi-

[89]*Op. cit.*, pp. 199-200.

nant. Even though he had deliberately rated prophecy superior to tongues, he would not permit an excessive display of even a superior gift. Further, the one who prophesied might be subject to error. Thus Paul says: **And let the other judge** (29b). The word **judge** (*diakrinetosan*) means to discern, to discriminate. "It was the duty of all to examine whether that which was uttered was in accordance with truth."[90]

A further regulation eliminated rivalry for a favored position in the prophetic sequence. It appears that certain members of the church, **the prophets**, could be appointed as speakers for the worship services. But if someone else, **another that sitteth by** (30), desired to speak, the appointed speaker should yield the floor to him. In this way there would be time enough for all to **prophesy one by one** (31). In this way all would contribute, there would be no confusion, no one would dominate the meeting, and all would be edified.

In v. 32, Paul states again that the working of the Holy Spirit does not produce uncontrollable bursts of speech. Man is never more his true self than when under the influence of the Holy Spirit. Thus Paul writes: **And the spirits of the prophets are subject to the prophets** (32). The TEV interprets v. 32, "The gift of speaking God's message should be under the speaker's control.

Paul "lays down the principle that, in true prophecy, self-consciousness, and self-command are never lost."[91] Prophecy is a means of spiritual illumination, but a prophet can remain silent if he chooses. While the Holy Spirit will be directly operative in the Church, He **is not the author of confusion, but of peace** (33).

f. Women should not disturb the worship service (14:33b-36). The last part of v. 33 belongs rather with 34 as in the Greek text (cf. Berk., RSV). Paul wanted the Corinthians to observe the customs which prevailed **in all churches of the saints** (33). The particular custom he referred to was that of women remaining quiet in the church. **Let your women keep silence in the churches: for it is not permitted unto them to speak** (34).

There are two possible ways to interpret this statement. It may be applied generally to exclude women from all vocal participation in a church service. But in a previous statement (11:5) Paul had written of women praying and prophesying with their

---

[90]Barnes, *op. cit.*, p. 292.   [91]Vincent, *op. cit.*, III, 272.

heads uncovered. In this instance Paul's concern was for the preservation of modesty, which at that time was associated with coverings on the head. The apostle apparently sanctioned public prayer and public speaking by women if the head was covered.

A second explanation is that women should not speak in tongues nor ask controversial questions in church. This is the more probable explanation, for the prohibition appears in the center of a discussion on the value of tongues and prophecy. Rather than speak in tongues or question the utterance of the prophets, the women should seek information from **their husbands at home** (35). Barnes writes: "The sense evidently is, that in all those things which he had specified, the women were to keep silence; they were to take no part. . . . These pertained solely to the male portion of the congregation."[92] The last part of 34 has been interpreted, "They are not allowed to speak; as the Jewish law says, they must not be in charge" (TEV).

The Corinthians were next reminded that they were part of an organism called the Church. As such they were not permitted to make their own rules. **What? came the word of God out from you? or came it unto you only?** (36) Here Paul states very pointedly, by means of questions, that the gospel did not originate with the Corinthians. Nor was it given to them alone. Thus they could not regard themselves as an exclusive group which traveled its own way and set up its own spiritual principles.

g. *Conclusion* (14:37-40). In summarizing the whole matter Paul emphatically states that he has written divine truth. In doing this he puts the Corinthians squarely on the spot. They have professed to be super-spiritual and have been proud of their gifts. The apostle therefore writes, **If any man think himself to be a prophet, or spiritual, let him acknowledge that the things that I write unto you are the commandments of the Lord** (37). If the Corinthians possess such gifts, let them demonstrate this by recognizing inspiration when they come face-to-face with it. More drastically, Paul states, "If anyone does not recognize this, he is not recognized" (38, NASB).

In vv. 39-40, Paul makes a final reference to spiritual gifts. In regard to prophecy he is positive and affirmative. **Covet to prophesy** (39). If a man wishes to speak in the church, let him speak under the direction of the Holy Spirit in such a manner as

[92]*Op. cit.*, p. 294.

to strengthen the church. On the other matter Paul is cautious: **Forbid not to speak with tongues.** This gift was not to be forbidden or despised. For in its own place and in its proper time it may be a valuable endowment.

The discussion of the place of prophecy and speaking in tongues ends with a notable principle. Worship is essential to the building up of the body of Christ. But sometimes worship which seeks or stresses the presence and power of the Holy Spirit tends to be confused or chaotic. Here the Pauline principle is important: **Let all things be done decently and in order** (40).

Decently (*euschemonos*) means "everything is to be done properly and in good order."[93] **Order** (*taxin*) carried a similar meaning—"in an orderly manner."[94] Adam Clarke writes: "Where *decency* and *order* are not observed in every part of the worship of God, no spiritual worship can be performed."[95] Paul wanted the presence and power of the Holy Spirit; and he knew that the Holy Spirit worked in a way to produce harmony, peace, order, and edification.

---

[93]Arndt and Gingrich, *op. cit.*, p. 327.   [94]*Ibid.*, p. 811.
[95]*Op. cit.*, II, 279.

Section **IX** *The New Faith and*
the Resurrection

I Corinthians 15:1-58

I Corinthians runs the full gamut of problems in the Christian Church. Beginning with matters of a personal and ethical nature, Paul had passed to liturgical questions, then to the dynamic expression of the place and nature of spiritual gifts. The last problem discussed is in the area of doctrine. Perhaps the apostle reserved it until last because of its importance.

The Church is, in a sense, the practical expression of doctrine. Any significant corruption in doctrine immediately "vitiates the body of Christ."[1] The apostle opens this letter by stating that the foundation of his preaching is Christ crucified (1:23; 2:2). He ends by declaring that the crown and climax of his message is the resurrected Christ. As Godet remarks: "In these two facts, applied to the conscience and appropriated by faith, there is concentrated indeed the whole of the Christian salvation."[2]

The doctrine of the resurrection of an individual believer was either doubted or rejected by some in Corinth. Since most of the problems among them had risen from their Greek background, it is probable that the problem concerning the resurrection came from the same source. The teachings of the popular Greek religions and philosophies "envisaged the disembodied spirit of man passing through the planetary spheres finally sloughing off every part of man's flesh-and-blood existence, even self-consciousness and reason."[3]

This Greek approach was based on the idea that matter, or material substance, was the source of all evil. Thus the resurrection of the body was a thing with little appeal to those influenced by Greek thought. For these people the immortality of the soul, and the soul alone, was the object of their faith and hopes. Others apparently taught that the resurrection had already taken place

[1]Godet, *op. cit.*, II, 321.   [2]*Ibid.*
[3]James L. Price, *Interpreting the New Testament* (New York: Holt, Rinehart and Winston, 1961), p. 382.

(II Tim. 2:18). To Paul this was heresy. Some taught that it actually took place in the act of baptism. Moule writes, "These heretics maintained that by baptism they were already made partakers of the risen life and that there was nothing further to follow."[4]

Paul taught, as did all the apostles, that the resurrection of Christ was "the firstfruits" or the initial evidence of the resurrection of the Christian. Redemption in Christ is total, including the body. To the Early Church the death and resurrection of the believer was not an escape from the body nor oblivion in a great "oversoul." They looked for an event in the future, which involved a complete transformation of the body. As Moule says, "They affirmed corporate redemption as against individualistic escape."[5]

Paul acknowledges that "flesh and blood cannot inherit the kingdom of God" (15:50). But he proceeds to show them a mystery. The resurrection of the believer is not simply a transition from death to a state of bliss and eternal life; it is "a change from a 'physical body' to a 'spiritual body' involving both continuity and change."[6] Paul founded his entire experience in Christ on the hope of a personal resurrection.

A. CERTAINTY OF THE RESURRECTION, 15:1-34

The certainty of the resurrection of the believer rests squarely upon the fact of the resurrection of Christ. Paul has already shown that the Church is a living organism, with Christ as its Head (c. 12). If Christ as the Head of the organism arose, the body will rise also.

1. Results of Paul's Preaching (15:1-2)

The best argument for any preaching is the results it produces. The very core of Paul's message was the death and resurrection of Jesus. This gospel the Corinthians had believed and were saved. They now doubted what the apostle had formerly preached to them. Thus Paul is constrained again to declare . . . **the gospel which I preached unto you** (1). Godet suggests that

[4]*The Birth of the New Testament* ("Harper's New Testament Commentaries"; New York: Harper and Row, 1961), p. 101.
[5]*Ibid.*   [6]Price, *op. cit.*, p. 382.

the word **declare** "is chosen with the intent of humiliating the readers."[7]

In the time between the original preaching and this letter, the Corinthians had permitted some basic elements of the gospel to slip. Paul reminds them that they had received this teaching at first, and that they still remain in a **saved** (2) condition because they had received it. If they will stop to consider their state of salvation, they will realize that faith in Christ crucified and risen is impossible unless this crucified and risen Christ is a reality. If He is not a reality, they **have believed in vain.** That is, they had accepted Paul's preaching "heedlessly, at random, without serious apprehension, without realizing the facts involved."[8] But the gospel which saved them was valid and should not be rejected.

2. Testimony of History (15:3-11)

The testimony of history includes the writings of Scripture and personal witness.

a. Declaration of the Scriptures (15:3-4). Paul stated that "his teaching was no invention of his own, that he was but the channel through which it came to the Corinthians."[9] One of the sources of his ideas was the **scriptures** (3). Since the NT was not in existence at this time, **the scriptures** referred to would be the OT. The passages that Paul probably had in mind were Isaiah 53; Psalms 16; and Hos. 6:2. The verb **was buried** (4) is an aorist, indicating a completed past event. The verb **rose** (*egegertai*) is in the perfect tense, indicating a continuing process —for the risen Christ is continuously central in life.

b. Testimony of personal witnesses (15:5-11). The appeal to scriptures would carry weight with Jewish Christians, but individual witnesses might impress the Gentile Corinthians more. The number of witnesses to the resurrection of Christ is impressive.

(1) *Cephas* (15:5). Since there was a party of Corinthians loyal to Peter (cf. 1:12), they would appreciate his testimony. Thus the apostle writes of Christ that **he was seen of Cephas.**

---

[7]*Op. cit.,* II, 601-2.   [8]Findlay, *op. cit.,* p. 919.
[9]Beet, *op. cit.,* p. 265.

Paul had no doubt received the report from Peter himself, for he had spent 15 days with him in Jerusalem (Gal. 1:18).

(2) *The Twelve* (15:5). **The twelve** is the official name for the original apostolic body. Actually only 10 were present the first time Christ appeared to the disciples. Judas had committed suicide and Thomas was absent (John 29:24). That the 11 saw Christ personally is stated in Luke 24:33. The fact that all of the apostles saw the Lord after the Resurrection would carry weight among these people who were desirous of signs.

(3) *Five hundred witnesses* (15:6). If by chance the Corinthians might doubt Peter and the other apostles, they could look to a larger group, for, **after that, he was seen of above five hundred brethren at once.** The occasion of this appearance is not mentioned elsewhere in the Bible. Apparently it was well enough known at the time that Paul could use it as convincing evidence. A number of this group were still alive, and available for questioning, even though some had **fallen asleep.** Here Paul speaks of "actual death as a sleep."[10]

(4) *James* (15:7). Three years after his conversion Paul met James in Jerusalem. James was the presiding officer of the church at Jerusalem and therefore is mentioned as an authority among those who saw the Lord after the Resurrection. He was not a believer during Jesus' lifetime (John 7:5). Apparently the Resurrection convinced him of the truth about Christ, for he was among the group in the Upper Room after the Ascension (Acts 1:13).

(5) *All the apostles* (15:7). This appearance probably occurred immediately prior to the Ascension. On such an occasion, as Godet put it, "The apostolic college must be there in full and Jesus had provided that none of the apostles should be wanting."[11]

(6) *The Apostle Paul* (15:8-11). Paul includes himself among those who saw the resurrected Christ: **And last of all he was seen of me also** (8). Paul did not believe that he had seen Christ only in a vision. He regarded his Damascus road experience as a valid personal appearance of the risen Lord. The apostle knew of no later appearances of Christ to anyone—that of Christ to John on Patmos took place after Paul's death. Paul here refers

[10]Robertson and Plummer, *op. cit.*, p. 337.   [11]*Op. cit.*, II, 337.

to himself as **one born out of due time** (*ektroma*). This strange phrase means an abortion, or an untimely birth and "denotes a child born in a violent and premature way."[12]

This reference to Paul's conversion is a description of "the suddenness and violence of the transition . . . while he was still in a state of immaturity."[13] In contrast, the 12 disciples were called, nourished, trained, and then commissioned. They were learners, or disciples, before they became apostles. Paul's change was dramatic and unusual. Yet he saw the risen Lord as really as they did.

Not only had Paul seen the Lord, but this experience had completely revolutionized his life. He was well aware that he was **the least of the apostles** (9) and was not worthy to bear the title, because of his intense persecution of the Church. But in spite of his lack of merit and fitness, **the grace of God** (10) had made him equal to the task. That abundant **grace which was bestowed** upon Paul **was not in vain,** for it was fruitful and worthwhile.

Paul declares of the other apostles: **I laboured more abundantly than they all.** This may mean that Paul lived longer and therefore worked longer, or it may mean that he was more successful than the others in establishing churches. While Paul is human enough to enjoy his success as a steward of the Lord, he knew his achievements were not due to his talents, but to **the grace of God which was with me.**

The conclusion is that all the apostolic leaders and several hundred other believers in the Early Church accepted the fact of the resurrection of Christ. Moreover, this fact had been preached to the Corinthians and they had accepted it. With finality Paul could say in regard to the Resurrection: **Therefore whether it were I or they, so we preach, and so ye believed** (11).

3. Results of Rejecting the Resurrection (15:12-19)

Paul has shown that both scripture and the personal witness of reliable believers support the actual resurrection of Christ. Now he turns to the negative side. By using a method of reasoning called *reductio ad absurdum,* he shows that without the doctrine of the Resurrection the Christian faith collapses.

The evidence for the resurrection of Christ is overwhelming. Paul reasons, therefore, If even one person has indeed been raised

---

[12]*Ibid.,* p. 338.   [13]Robertson and Plummer, *op. cit.,* p. 339.

from the dead, **how say some among you that there is no resurrection of the dead?** (12) To question this basic fact is to start a chain reaction that in effect nullifies the entire gospel.

a. *Denies the resurrection of Christ* (15:13). The Corinthians may have accepted the resurrection of Christ as a unique event because of His divine nature. But they felt that a similar resurrection was not possible or probable for all believers. Paul's answer is emphatic: **If there be no resurrection of the dead, then is Christ not risen.** In essence, "If Christ has risen, it must be admitted that others can be raised, and *vice versa*, a denial that others will rise involves a denial that Christ has been raised."[14]

b. *Makes void apostolic preaching* (15:14). The resurrection of Christ was a pivotal point. Not only Paul's **preaching,** but the preaching of the other apostles made the Resurrection an essential element of the gospel. If the Resurrection is not a fact, then both Paul's **preaching** and that of the other apostles was fiction and a farce.

c. *Makes Christian faith unreal* (15:14). Christianity rises or falls with the resurrection of Christ. As the apostle writes, without the Resurrection **your faith is also vain** (*kene*). The word denotes a reference or witness to an event that was unreal or imaginary. If the Resurrection is fictitious, then so is the faith of the Corinthians.

d. *Makes the apostles false witnesses* (15:15-16). All the apostles had declared repeatedly that Christ had risen. They met on the first day of the week to celebrate His resurrection. Without the Resurrection they would all be **found false witnesses of God** (15). The expression **we are found** means "we are caught out" or "we are detected." These men had staked their lives on the reality of the Resurrection. They had **testified of God that he raised up Christ.** They were not expressing personal opinions, presenting good advice, or spinning fanciful yarns. The phrase **testified of God** actually means "testified against God." If Christ was not truly risen, all the apostles had presented false claims about God, and in fact had spoken against Him.

The apostles had associated the resurrection of believers with the resurrection of Christ. Paul repeats the idea in 16. There can be no other conclusion: **For if the dead rise not, then**

---

[14]Vine, *op. cit.*, p. 207.

is not Christ raised. The issue is simple and clear. To deny personal resurrection is to deny the resurrection of Christ.

e. *Man would still be in sin* (15:17-18). Here is a solemn repetition and expansion of the idea presented in v. 14. Without the reality of the Resurrection their **faith is vain** (*mataia*); it is fruitless, futile, and barren in results. Even worse than a futile faith is their spiritual state, for without the Resurrection they were still in their **sins** (17). "If Christ had not risen, they would still be living in their original heathen wickedness, for baseless credulity could never have delivered them."[15] It was faith in a living Christ which had transformed them.

If there is no Resurrection, the state of the Christians who died believing in the Resurrection is tragic. Instead of being redeemed saints, they have **perished** (18, *apolonto*). The word means "utter loss consequent upon dying in sin."[16] These saints had died in the hope that they were simply falling asleep. Christ was supposed to have conquered death, taking the sting out of it. Paul had spoken elsewhere of death as gain (Phil. 1:21) and of his desire to depart, in order to be with Christ (Phil. 1:23). If there was no Resurrection, the death of Stephen, of James, and of others was a tragedy of the highest order. "If such monstrous conclusions be true, Christians are most to be pitied of all men."[17]

f. *No hope without the Resurrection* (15:19). If the Christian has **hope** only in the present life, then he is **of all men most miserable.** To have renounced all the possible benefits of earth because of a faith in heaven, to have sacrificed the inferior pleasures of this life because of the anticipation of the joys of heaven, to hope to live eternally with Christ, and then to find all these aspirations a delusion, would make a man more pitiable than the pagan who never nourished such hopes. As Godet remarks, "To the sufferings accumulated during this life there would come to be added the most cruel deception after this life."[18] But this is not the case. Verses 19-20 have been translated: "Ah, if in this life we have nothing but a mere hope in Christ, we are of all men to be pitied most! But it is not so! Christ did rise from the

---

[15]Robertson and Plummer, *op. cit.*, p. 350.   [16]*Ibid.*

[17]P. B. Fitzwater, *Preaching and Teaching the New Testament* (Chicago: Moody Press, 1957), p. 430.

[18]*Op. cit.*, II, 350.

dead, he was the first to be reaped of those who sleep in death."[19]
Our real hope is in His resurrection.

4. Future Resurrection of Believers (15:20-28)

The future resurrection of the believers is as certain as the
past resurrection of Christ. The risen Christ is the Firstfruit of
the great harvest of believers whose ingathering is essential to
the completion of redemption in the kingdom of God.

a. Christ, the Firstfruits (15:20-22). Christ was the first to
rise from the dead. Prior to His resurrection none had returned
from the grave as He returned. To be sure, some, such as Lazarus, came forth as a result of His command. But in these instances the spirit returned to the same body that was laid in the
grave. As such it was destined to return to the grave.

Christ is the firstfruits of them that slept (20). He continues permanently in His position and role as the risen Lord. **Firstfruits** suggests two things: (*a*) the first blade or sheaf of the
harvest, which was brought to the Temple and offered (Lev. 23:
10-11); (*b*) more fruit to follow later. In other words, "Christ
risen is to the multitude of believers who shall rise again at His
advent what a first ripe ear, gathered by the hand, is to the
whole harvest."[20]

There is in the expression **firstfruits** (*aparche*) the further
idea of a vital, living relation between Christ and the believer.
Even as the natural head of the human race was responsible for
the imposition of **death** on all members of the human family, so
the spiritual Head of the body of believers imparts **the resurrection from the dead** (21) to those who accept Him. There is
here no hint of universal salvation for all men, for the whole
idea of the resurrected Christ is directed to the believers—with a
warning that unbelief can bring spiritual death. Because of Adam
all men became subject to **death**. Because of Christ, all men
who believe become objects of eternal life (22).

b. The order of the resurrection (15:23-28). This passage
presents a graphic picture of the sequence of the resurrection,
as indicated by the words: **but every man in his own order** (23).
The word **order** (*tagma*) signifies the particular place assigned
in a series to each individual or group.

---

[19]Moffatt, *ad loc.*   [20]Godet, *op. cit.*, II, 351.

(1) *First was Christ* (15:23). **Christ the firstfruits** stands alone and supreme. It is He who is the Captain of man's salvation, the Conqueror of death, and the Deliverer from sin. He opens the door to the life of glory.

(2) *The dead in Christ follow* (15:23). At this point those who are to be raised from the dead are divided into two groups. Those that are in Christ arise **at his coming.** The clause **they that are Christ's** points to a "special resurrection, in which only *true* believers will participate."[21] The phrase **at his coming** (*parousia*) refers to the Second Advent. *Parousia* ordinarily means "coming" or "presence." However, "it came to be used among the Christians as the technical term for the Lord's return."[22] Thus the second coming of the Lord will bring about a distinction between the true and false members of the Church.

(3) *The final resurrection and judgment* (15:24-28). In the clause **Then cometh the end** (24), the word **then** (*eita*) does not mean "immediately after," but refers to some unspecified event in the future. **The end** means the ultimate aim, the final goal of Him who has authority over all events, things, and activities (25). *The Berkeley Version* renders it "the completion"; a footnote explains it as the completion "of the number in Christ." Even **death** will be banished and have no power over man (26). The sovereign rulership of Christ shall subdue and subject all things (24). Yet Christ shall continue to be obedient to the Father (27-28). The point the apostle makes here is that the risen Christ is actively involved in a historic redemptive process that will reach a sweeping climax under the rulership of God, who shall **be all in all** (28).

In 15:3-28 we see "The Keystone of the Christian Faith." (1) The Bible witnesses to the Resurrection, 3-7; (2) Paul's personal experience gives evidence of the Resurrection, 8-11; (3) New Testament preaching was based on the Resurrection, 12-16; (4) Personal redemption depends on the Resurrection, 17; (5) Our hope for the future rests on the Resurrection, 19-28.

5. *Practical Questions and Warnings* (15:29-34)

At this point the apostle presents several questions and answers related to the moral consequences of denying the doctrine of the resurrection.

---

[21] *Ibid.*, p. 356.   [22] Morris, *op. cit.*, p. 215.

a. *Baptism for the dead* (15:29). Some scholars interpret the clause **they . . . which are baptized for the dead** to mean an actual ritual carried out by the living in the hopes of achieving salvation for men after death. According to one author, "Paul presupposes that the potency of intercessory baptism of the dead reaches even to Sheol and there benefits men who in this mortal life have not been sealed with the name of Christ."[23] Tenney interprets the question as a reference to "a local custom in the Corinthian Church which was not necessarily approved, but which was used by Paul as a practical point of appeal in his argument for the resurrection."[24]

Godet states that about 30 different explanations are given for the expression.[25] He himself suggests that to be **baptized for the dead** refers, "not to the baptism of water, but to the baptism of blood, by martyrdom."[26] He bases his interpretation on the words of Jesus in Luke 12:50 and Mark 10:38. Lenski regards the reference under consideration as a general symbol of the baptism of all believers, which "connects us with death and with the resurrection. Rom. 6:3-5 tells us that baptism joins us to Christ's death, burial, and resurrection."[27] These latter views appear more in harmony with both Paul's lofty concept of personal redemption and with the practices of the Early Church. "Such practice, whether right or erroneous, involved faith in immortality" (Berk., fn., *ad loc.*).

b. *Threat of constant danger* (15:30). Baptism may have been suggested as a rite which placed the convert to Christianity in danger of martyrdom. This led to Paul's question, **And why stand we in jeopardy every hour?** Even when there was no threat of death, the Christian was in constant danger. The subject **we** included Paul, Apollos, Silas, and Timothy, all of whom preached at Corinth. It also included apostles other than Paul. Because Christians were a "people without a country," they were always on the threshold of disaster, living their lives at the edge of the grave. If there was no resurrection, to suffer and die for one's faith was absurd.

---

[23]Ethelbert Stauffer, *New Testament Theology*, trans. John Marsh (New York: The Macmillan Company, 1955), p. 223.

[24]*New Testament Survey* (Grand Rapids: Wm. B. Eerdmans Publishing Co., 1961), p. 298.

[25]*Op. cit.*, II, 383.   [26]*Ibid.*, p. 389.

[27]*Op. cit.*, p. 689.

c. *Personal danger* (15:31-32). In the Greek text v. 31 begins, "Daily I die." The TEV renders the verse, "Brothers, I face death every day! The pride I have in you in our life in Christ Jesus our Lord makes me declare this." Paul's past history was well-known to the Corinthians. They knew that he placed his life in jeopardy every time he entered a city to preach. The expression may have included the physical perils and dangers he constantly experienced for the gospel. But the risk was worthwhile, in that the Corinthians were an example of the results of Paul's preaching.

The apostle presents an example of his constant danger when he asks: **If after the manner of men I have fought with beasts at Ephesus, what advantageth it me?** (32) In other words, If I risked my life for purely human motives, what have I gained? As a Roman citizen Paul would not have been subjected to exposure to wild beasts in the arena. The statement, **I have fought with beasts,** may mean that he struggled with an infuriated mob calling for his blood. Whether it was a bloodthirsty mob or a hungry lion, the results were equally perilous. Paul was always only one step ahead of sudden death.

If there is no resurrection, all such exposure to danger and death is preposterous. If there is no resurrection, **let us eat and drink; for to morrow we die.** Vine reminds us that "rejection of the doctrine of resurrection opens the way for unbridled sensuality."[28] On the other hand, assurance of the resurrection was a constant source of balance and loyalty in Paul's ministry.

d. *Warnings* (15:33). Apparently some in the Corinthian church were in danger of being corrupted by their heathen friends. Perhaps they had become apologetic, or even openly defiant, about the doctrine of the resurrection in order to please their pagan friends. So Paul writes: **Be not deceived** (33, *me planasthe*). This phrase does not mean to be misled by others. It means, "Do not deceive yourselves (by false reasonings)."[29]

Another warning is added: **Evil communications corrupt good manners.** The word **communications** means "fellowship," "companionship," or "company." "The point of Paul's citation is that keeping the wrong kind of company (that of men who deny the resurrection) may well corrupt your Christian habits, and turn men away from the true position."[30]

---

[28]*Op. cit.*, p. 216.   [29]Godet, *op. cit.*, II, 395.
[30]Morris, *op. cit.*, p. 221.

e. A strong exhortation (15:34). Paul fairly shouts, **Awake to righteousness and sin not.** The term **awake** (*eknepsate*) in its original meaning carried the idea of becoming sober after drunkenness. The use of the aorist imperative signifies a deliberate, energetic act. The strong language indicates that Paul considered the Corinthians' doctrinal wanderings to be serious. As one commentary says, "He addresses them . . . as if they were drunk or mad."[31] The same writers continue: "It is possible that these sceptics claimed to be sober thinkers, and condemned the belief in a resurrection as a wild enthusiasm."[32] Vine suggests that this strong warning "is against fellowship with any whose influence is contrary to the Holy Spirit."[33]

The reason that believers should avoid such company is that they **have not the knowledge of God.** This lack is not merely a harmless void. Its results are disastrous. Godet writes: "It is not merely a deficiency, the lack of a good thing, it is the possession of a real evil. It involves not only inanition, but poisoning."[34] The word **some** evidently refers to members in the church itself. "Otherwise the mention of them would not put the church to shame."[35]

In all this discussion Paul has dealt with a doctrinal problem—the resurrection. Doctrine may seem to be remote and unnecessary. But what one believes eventually leads to conduct, "and unsound doctrine in the end must lead to sinful behaviour."[36] Paul was not fighting a battle of words. To deny the resurrection was to negate the gospel and open the door to sin. To affirm the resurrection was to validate the gospel and open the highway to holiness.

B. NATURE OF THE RESURRECTION BODY, 15:35-58

The apostle had effectively demonstrated the importance of the resurrection in the total pattern of redemption. But establishing the *fact* of the resurrection of Christ and showing the *reality* of the resurrection of the Christian would still leave some questions in the minds of the Corinthians. These questions concerned the nature of the resurrection body.

---

[31]Robertson and Plummer, *op. cit.*, p. 364.
[32]*Ibid.*   [33]*Op. cit.*, p. 216.
[34]*Op. cit.*, II, 397.   [35]Beet, *op. cit.*, p. 286.
[36]Morris, *op. cit.*, p. 221.

1. *Illustrations of the Resurrection Body* (15:35-44)

Paul was aware that some would ask: **How are the dead raised up? and with what body do they come?** (35) The apostle answers by presenting some illustrations from nature and by showing the harmony of the resurrection with the divine nature of things.

a. *Planting grain* (15:36-38). Paul introduces his illustration with a strong reproof, **Thou fool** (36). This "mode of address strikes a blow at the self-conceived acuteness of the questioner."[37] The common experiences of sowing and reaping should have been enough to convince the doubters about the resurrection. The truth should be self-evident: **That which thou sowest is not quickened, except it die.** The death of the seed is the condition of the growth of the plant. The term **is quickened** does not apply strictly to a grain of wheat, but it is an example of the resurrection power producing the new body of the Christian.

What a man sows is not what springs up out of the ground as a new plant (37). Morris describes the difference: "A dead-looking, bare, dry seed is put into the ground, but what comes up is a green plant, vigorous and beautiful."[38] It is God who governs the process of sowing and growing. In the statement, **God giveth** (38), the verb is in the present tense, indicating that God continually exercises power over the whole process.

b. *Differences among living beings* (15:39). From the area of agriculture Paul turns to that of beings with animal life. **All flesh** is not of the same kind. **Flesh** (*sarx*) denotes the material substance of the organism. It is obvious that there is a distinct difference between the flesh of man, cattle, birds, and fish. Paul's reasoning is that "in creation God was not restricted to one kind of flesh; how can he then be restricted in the resurrection?"[39]

c. *Natural bodies* (15:40-41). Various **bodies**—plants, planets, and natural formations—have diverse beauty and attraction. Each of these has its own peculiar **glory** (*doxa*). Here the word means brightness or manifestation. The **celestial bodies** are the sun, moon, and stars. The **terrestrial** bodies are mountains, trees, and rivers of the earth. Each aspect of nature has its own particular beauty and attractiveness. God is not limited to any type

---

[37]Vine, *op. cit.*, pp. 217-18.   [38]*Op. cit.*, p. 224.
[39]Lenski, *op. cit.*, p. 708.

or kind of creation. Thus the resurrection is simply another aspect of God's creative work.

  d. *The illustrations applied to the resurrection* (15:42-44). The constant display of death and life, and of variation and degree in nature, should affirm that God will perform the same work, on an infinitely higher plane, in the resurrection of the Christian. Paul states four things about the resurrected body.

  First, **It is sown in corruption; it is raised in incorruption** (42). The term **corruption** (*phthora*) usually refers to the natural condition of creation. Here it describes "the effect of the withdrawal of life and thus of the condition of the human body in burial."[40]

  Second, **It is sown in dishonour; it is raised in glory** (43). According to Godet **dishonour** "embraces all the miseries of this earthly life, which precede and go to produce the dissolution of the body, all the humiliating conditions to which our body is now subjected."[41] The resurrection body will experience a perfect environment without any of the things which constantly threaten man's earthly existence. This is the **glory** to which **it is raised.**

  Third, the **body is sown in weakness; it is raised in power.** From the time of birth man's physical frame is subject to weakness. No matter how he cultivates his health, disciplines his powers, or pampers his person, the body remains a comparatively frail and weak instrument. When death comes, the body is the ultimate symbol of weakness. The resurrection body will be exempt from the mortal ills that plague us in this life, and will be characterized by **power.**

  Finally, **it is sown a natural body; it is raised a spiritual body** (44). **Natural** (*psychikon*) is the material body of this life, "formed by and for a soul, destined to serve as an organ to that breath of life . . . which presided over its development."[42] As Paul uses the term here, **natural** "signifies that the body we now have is a body suited for the present life."[43] The resurrection body will be a **spiritual** (*pneumatikon*) **body.** This does not mean a body composed of spirit. Rather, it means "a body formed by and for a principle of life which is a spirit, and fully appropriated to its service."[44]

[40]Vine, *op. cit.*, p. 219.
[41]*Op. cit.*, II, 411.
[42]*Ibid.*, p. 413.
[43]Morris, *op. cit.*, p. 228.
[44]Godet, *op. cit.*, II, 413.

2. Resurrection Versus Natural Generation (15:45-49)

The apostle presses the comparison of the natural body and the spiritual body back to the origin of each. Thus the comparison is between Adam, the first of the physical race, and Jesus, the Source of the new spiritual race. The development of the two bodies is traced to the two successive heads of the race. Thus Paul directs attention to Gen. 2:7, **And so it is written, The first man Adam was made a living soul** (45). God himself made man so that his body is animated by the soul. All of Adam's descendants resemble him in this essential feature—in every body there is a living soul.

a. *The first Adam and the last Adam* (15:45). While the first Adam passed death on to his descendants, **the last Adam was made a quickening spirit.** Adam and Christ "differ here not as the sin-committing and sin-abolishing . . . but as the rudimentary and finished man respectively, with their physique to match."[45] Adam was the founder of the human race, while Christ initiated a new order of men—spiritual men. The true and final nature of the spiritual life produced by Christ is the resurrected life. "By rising from the dead Christ . . . entered on the spiritual and ultimate form of human existence."[46]

b. *First the natural man, then the spiritual man* (15:46-49). Human life begins with the physical and ideally ends as the spiritual. **First comes that which is natural; and afterward that which is spiritual** (46). Physical life may be created freely by the hand of a bountiful God—because natural life is the measure of man's opportunity; but spiritual life, the life of holiness, cannot be given indiscriminately, for it depends on a man's choice. Holiness, the highest expression of spiritual life, cannot be imposed on us. It must be received voluntarily.

Man was therefore created in a probationary state in which freedom is an indispensable element. With this power of choice the natural man faces two options: to remain on a purely natural level or to rise into a higher life of the spirit. When this principle is applied to mankind generally, it follows that **the first man is . . . earthy, while the second man is heavenly** (47-48). The word **earthy** (*choikos*) means "made of dust." Thus Adam and all his successors have bodies adapted to this earthly mode of existence.

---

[45]Morris, *op. cit.*, p. 228.   [46]*Ibid.*, p. 938.

Over against the **earthy** type of man identified with Adam is the **heavenly** man identified with Christ.

That the Christian is **earthy** no one would deny. As such, man shares the inevitable fate of all members of the race who are subject to the natural physical aging which results in death. But the Christian is more than **earthy**. He is also **heavenly** because of his relationship to Christ. For the apostle this fact had far-reaching consequences. To be **heavenly**, or spiritual, has great import for life here and now. But something more is involved, for **as we have borne the image of the earthy, we shall also bear the image of the heavenly (49)**.

The word **image** (*eikon*) carries the meaning of representation and manifestation. The application is twofold. All men are representations and manifestations of the original prototype, Adam. Even so shall all true believers become representatives and manifestations of Christ. The phrase **the image of the heavenly** means that all Christ's people will be like Him. That is, they will be resurrected to a new spiritual life (Phil. 3:21; I John 3:2). The resurrection body of Christ shows the believer something of the new life he will experience after his own personal resurrection. Paul waš as certain of the future image of Christ in the resurrection as he was of his own present image of Adam.

3. The Conquest of Death (15:50-58)

Paul has shown that the resurrection of the body is an essential part of God's redemptive plan and that "the transformation of the earthly into the heavenly, of the psychic into the pneumatic form of being, is involved in the present constitution of things and ascends with the lines of development traceable in nature and revelation."[47] He now comes to a magnificent climax. In a burst of unbounded joy the apostle exults in the triumph over death.

a. The principle (15:50). The principle of heavenly inheritance is simply **that flesh and blood cannot inherit the kingdom of God**. They comprise the perishable and temporary aspect of man. Nothing transient can enter into a full possession of the eternal kingdom of God. **Flesh and blood** is a common way of referring to the life of this world. Thus all crude and magical ideas of the resurrection are eliminated.

b. The presentation of a mystery (15:51-53). The term **mystery**, as Paul often uses it, is not something hidden or difficult

---

[47]Findlay, *op. cit.,* pp. 939-40.

to understand. Rather, a **mystery** is something which cannot be discerned by human reason, but is the result of revelation. The **mystery** of which Paul speaks here is the dramatic change that will take place at the second coming of Christ.

The apostle says that some will be living when Christ comes again: **We shall not all sleep** (51). Not all men will pass through death, but all will be instantly transformed. This dramatic change in man's essential nature will take place **in the twinkling of an eye** (52). The signal for this climactic redemptive event will be the sounding of a celestial **trumpet** which shall send its clarion call around the world. The echoes will have scarcely faded away when the dead in Christ shall be resurrected, with a new and incorruptible body.

This change is not a renovation or mere strengthening of the body which now exists. "In the resurrection the body is reorganized, the house built up again. In the rebuilding of the body, such parts and functions as are no longer needed are left out, and the whole is organized upon a different basis adapted to the heavenly life."[48] But personal identity is not lost. It must certainly be true that redeemed saints will recognize each other in heaven.

c. The end of sin and death (15:54-57). The resurrection is the ultimate victory over sin and death. These twin evils have haunted man from the Garden of Eden to the present. But the resurrection will make real and experiential the final redemptive work of God. With the appearance of this new body, **death is swallowed up in victory** (54).

In the victory of the resurrected body, the sting of death is removed, because **the sting of death is sin** (56). Sin produced death, and sin also added to it the poison and bitterness of despair. Paul declares that **the strength of sin is the law.** Law intensifies sin in that it makes man aware of sin, increases its power and guilt, yet makes no provision for victory over it (Rom. 7:7-13; 8:2-3). But **God . . . through our Lord Jesus Christ** (57) has given **victory** over sin and death. The whole redemptive plan was designed to provide this total triumph.

Victory over sin is so interwoven with the resurrection that to deny one is to deny the other. If there is no resurrection, there is no possibility of victory over sin. If there is to be a total and

[48]Fitzwater, *op. cit.,* 432.

absolute victory over sin, the resurrection is a necessity. To Paul, victory over sin and the reality of the resurrection were the towering peaks of redemption.

d. An exhortation (15:58). In view of the hope based on the resurrection, Paul exhorted the Corinthians to be **stedfast, unmoveable, always abounding in the work of the Lord.** To be **stedfast** refers "to personal faithfulness, sticking to it."[49] Being **unmoveable** suggests faithfulness in times of opposition, or the ability to withstand false teachings. **Abounding** means going beyond minimum requirements, and gladly doing more than the situation demands.

Paul encourages Christians to loyal service, **forasmuch as ye know that your labour is not in vain in the Lord.** Wesley wrote: "Whatever ye do for His sake shall have its full reward in that day."[50] He then adds his characteristic emphasis: "Let us also endeavour, by cultivating holiness in all its branches, to maintain this hope in its full energy."[51]

For Paul, certainty of conviction and loyalty to the doctrine of the resurrection were sure defenses against assaults on the faith and life of the Christian. Assurance of eternal life is the foundation of all who are united to Christ, who is the Head of a new, victorious order of redeemed humanity.

---

[49]G. Campbell Morgan, *The Corinthian Letters of Paul* (New York: Fleming H. Revell Company, 1946), p. 206.

[50]*Notes,* p. 640.   [51]*Ibid.*

Section **X** *Fellowship in the New Faith*

I Corinthians 16:1-24

In cc. 1—15, Paul has attempted to correct certain unchristian practices, and to restate specific doctrines in which the Corinthians were becoming either truant or indifferent. In the last verse of c. 15 the apostle made his throbbing appeal for loyalty and steadfastness to the fundamentals of the Christian faith. In this final chapter, he discusses some practical matters, all of which are framed in the circle of Christian fellowship and Christian unity.

A. CHRISTIAN LIBERALITY, 16:1-4

Paul's sudden shift in emphasis from the glory of the resurrection to the mere taking of a collection may seem abrupt. For him, however, taking an offering for the needs of the church was as much a part of the Christian fellowship as was the thrill of a coming resurrection. The instructions concerning the collection were directed to the needs of the church at that time, but they contain principles of giving that may well be applied to our day also.

1. *Collection for the Saints* (16:1)

Paul worked with his hands to earn his own way lest he be a burden to others. But he was never reluctant about asking for money to meet the needs of the church. The offering he was asking from the Corinthians was for the members of the church at Jerusalem. Apparently they had become poverty-stricken, for when Paul wrote his Roman letter he had referred to "the poor saints which are at Jerusalem" (Rom. 15:26).

Clarke suggests that the reason for their poverty was the persecution of the Jews: "The enmity of their countrymen to the Gospel of Christ led them to treat those who professed it with cruelty, and spoil them of their goods."[1] G. Campbell Morgan attributes this poverty to a failure to carry out the Great Commission: "That commission was given at the beginning of the Acts. They never did this until they were driven out by persecu-

[1]*Op. cit.*, II, 296.

tion. They hugged the church, and hugged their privileges, and lost their real spiritual power."[2]

Whatever the reason for their condition, the mother church was in need of financial help. Paul, the Apostle to the Gentiles, was well-aware that the total Church was indebted to the saints in Jerusalem. Further, he realized that the circle of Christian fellowship included more than sympathy and prayers. He knew that at times fellowship must be expressed in concrete terms. So he asked for an offering for the saints.

2. The Offering a Mandate (16:1b)

To Paul, expressing liberality toward a distressed church was a privilege and a matter of Christian fellowship. But it was more—it was a mandate: **As I have given order to the churches of Galatia, even so do ye.** Of this command Joseph S. Exell comments: "An inspired apostle is the highest human authority in all that related to Christian duty."[3] The Christian is under obligation to give whenever a need arises.

3. Based on Stated Principles (16:2)

Paul was gifted with the "talent of the specific." He did not leave things dangling on vague generalities. There was no question regarding the manner of giving.

a. To be regular (16:2a). The apostle stated that the offering was to be taken **upon the first day of the week.** This appointed time kept the duty constantly before the people. In addition, the Christian would be reminded that he should give on the Lord's Day. Christian giving is not a hit-or-miss matter. Nor is it a once-and-for-all proposition. A Christian gives systematically and consistently.

Adam Clarke attached an additional meaning to these instructions. He writes: "It appears from the whole that *the first day of the week,* which is the Christian Sabbath, was the day on which their principal religious meetings were held in *Corinth,* and the churches of Galatia; and consequently in all other places where Christianity had prevailed."[4] Paul's words here add to the

[2]*Op. cit.,* p. 208.

[3]"I Corinthians." *The Biblical Illustrator* (Grand Rapids: Baker Book House, 1958 [reprint]), II, 563.

[4]*Op. cit.,* II, 296.

evidence that the Early Church, in tribute to the resurrected Christ, had made the first day of the week its regular day of worship.

b. *Personal and all-inclusive* (16:2b). Each person was obligated to give. Paul writes: **Let every one of you lay by him in store.** All were included in the giving. As Wesley remarks, it was "not the rich only: let him also that hath little gladly give of that little."[5] Many giving a little is more significant than one giving much.

c. *According to individual prosperity* (16:2c). The Christian at Corinth was to increase his giving as God increased his substance. **In store** means "in keeping with his gains."[6] Wesley calls this the "lowest rule of Christian prudence."[7] To give **as God hath prospered** is surely a minimal guideline to the expression of Christian gratitude.

d. *The spiritual above the material* (16:2d). Paul wanted the taking of these offerings done systematically and regularly, so **that there be no gatherings when I come.** He was coming to them for a spiritual purpose "and he wanted all the material things out of the way. He did not want them going around trying to whip up a collection."[8] The apostle felt that his time and energies should be spent in preaching the gospel rather than in raising offerings. The gifts were an important and necessary part of the Christian fellowship, but the church itself should take care of this matter. Then Paul could come to them to preach and raise the spiritual level of the congregation.

4. *To Be Dispensed Immediately* (16:3)

The apostle writes, **Whomsoever ye shall approve by your letters, them will I send to bring your liberality unto Jerusalem.** It is not clear why Paul would ask for letters of approval for those who would take the money to Jerusalem. Adam Clarke suggests that Paul here refers to recommendations which the Corinthians had sent to him,[9] and that the apostle agrees to appoint these persons. Here Paul shows his genius. While he was dogmatic about the necessity of taking the offering, he was com-

---

[5]*Notes*, p. 640.   [6]Arndt and Gingrich, *op. cit.*, p. 362.
[7]*Op. cit.*, p. 640.   [8]Morgan, *op. cit.*, p. 209.
[9]*Op. cit.*, II, 296.

pletely democratic about the method of dispatching it. No doubt he wanted those who were leaders in promoting the offering to experience the thrill of personally turning it over to the Jerusalem Christians.

In vv. 1-3, Paul presents a practical and efficient "Formula for Christian Giving." (1) It should be widely applicable, 1; (2) Regular, 2*a*; (3) Proportionate in amount, 2*b*; (4) Church-centered in interest, 2*c*; (5) Unselfish in outreach, 3.

5. *To Be Personally Supervised* (16:4)

There was no limit to Paul's concern for the welfare of the church and for unity in methods of procedure. He was genuinely concerned about the offering, and was fully aware of all the delicate problems involved in the distribution of the money. If it was necessary for him to personally supervise the distribution in Jerusalem, he would go, but these recommended people **shall go with me.** Thus the apostle insured himself against possible criticism.

B. PAUL'S EVANGELISTIC CONCERN, 16:5-12

G. Campbell Morgan writes that this sixteenth chapter "is a page that illustrates the fellowship of the Church in the work of the Lord."[10] In vv. 5-12, Paul presents himself, along with Timothy and Apollos, as an evangelist attempting to work and to share in the missionary task of the Church.

1. *An Evangelistic Interlude* (16:5-9)

Paul was the NT "man on the go." Almost always his life reveals intense activity and specific purpose. But at this time he seems to be a little uncertain as to what his future plans would be. Even a spiritual giant like Paul had times of uncertainty regarding the future when he simply waited for directions from the Holy Spirit. But even though he was not completely clear about his time schedule, Paul was positive about his purpose and his goal.

a. Proposed visit (16:5). The apostle wrote: **I will come unto you, when I shall pass through Macedonia** (see map 1). Clarke comments: "St. Paul was now at *Ephesus;* for almost all allow, in opposition to the subscription at the end of the epistle that states it to have been written from *Philippi,* that it was from

10*Op. cit.,* p. 210.

Ephesus."[11] Paul was not certain when he would leave for Macedonia, but when he left, he would come to the Corinthians. Even though Corinth was not on the direct route from Ephesus to Macedonia, the apostle intended to go out of his way to visit them.

b. *Possibly a long visit* (16:6-7). Paul suggested that he might remain at Corinth all **winter** (6). If he stayed on at Ephesus until Pentecost, he would be spending the entire spring there. Then he possibly would go on to Macedonia for the summer, and from thence come to Corinth to spend the winter. The statement **that ye may bring me on my journey whithersoever I go** means that Paul expected them to furnish the money for his traveling expenses to the next field of evangelistic work. He wasn't certain where this place of preaching would be. But he knew that, if the Corinthians provided the material means, God would supply spiritual direction.

Paul did not intend to spend a casual visit at Corinth, as indicated by his words: **For I will not see you now by the way** (7). He did not want to visit Corinth briefly, though he could have done this easily. It was only a short trip across the Aegean Sea from Ephesus (see map 1). Rather he wanted to **tarry a while—** but only if God permitted. The apostle's life was lived under the motto, **if the Lord permit.**

c. *Evangelistic prospects* (16:8-9). Paul planned to stay **at Ephesus until Pentecost** (8), one of the three great Jewish feasts. This feast was associated in the Early Church with the descent of the Holy Spirit. Paul had two reasons for staying in Ephesus.

(1) *Open door for evangelism* (16:9). The apostle never bypassed an opportunity to preach the gospel of Christ. At Ephesus the prospects seemed especially good. Paul regarded this opportunity as **a great door and effectual . . . opened unto me.** The number of people coming to hear the gospel was large and the effect upon them was encouraging. Ephesus was a center of pagan worship, a banking and commercial metropolis, and the political center of the Ionian confederacy. Since God had opened this door for Christian service, Paul wanted to use it to full advantage.

(2) *Many adversaries* (16:9). A second reason Paul wanted to remain in Ephesus was that **there are many adversaries.** The door was open wide, but the opponents were great. The steadfast

[11]*Op. cit.,* II, 297.

Paul stayed because the opposition was intense. Perhaps he enjoyed the spiritual struggle. But more likely the apostle chose to face the opposition himself rather than have someone else do it. Probably Paul felt that the presence of adversaries indicated a vital spiritual work was being accomplished. G. Campbell Morgan wrote: "If you have no adversaries, you had better move out and find the places where you get them."[12] Most people do not invite opposition, but the loyal servant of Christ will not run from it.

2. Brotherly Concern (16:10-12)

Paul was concerned for the welfare of his fellow evangelists, Timothy and Apollos.

a. Timothy, the young pastor-evangelist (16:10-11). Paul was especially interested in Timothy, who was like a son to him. Nevertheless the apostle's words, **See that he may be with you without fear,** were designed as much to protect Corinth from wrongdoing as to save Timothy from hurt. Paul knew that these Corinthians were a difficult group to serve, being critical of preachers. They were divided into groups centering around Peter, Apollos, and Paul (cf. 3:3-6). The Corinthians were learned, given to philosophical speculation, and they loved oratorical preaching. Clarke interprets Paul's meaning as follows: "That he may be treated well, and not perplexed and harassed with your divisions and jealousies."[13]

Because Timothy was in the Lord's work Paul wrote, **Let no man therefore despise him** (11). The fact that a man has been called by God to the ministry should create a courteous and respectful attitude toward him on the part of those to whom he is sent. To freeze out, snub, or disdain a messenger of the Lord is carnal and unchristian. The Corinthians were to accept Timothy as having full authority from God to do the work of an evangelist.

Verse 11 indicates that Paul expected Timothy to join him a little later. *The Berkeley Version* translates, "Whenever he returns to me, see him off safely." Clarke believes that the last part of the verse should be understood as if Paul and the brethren that were with him were expecting Timothy, "I, with the brethren, am looking for him."[14]

[12]*Op. cit.*, p. 213.   [13]*Op. cit.*, II, 297.
[14]*Ibid.*

b. Apollos, a brother beloved (16:12). Paul calls Apollos **our brother.** He was well aware of the dissensions in Corinth centering around himself and Apollos. The apostle wanted to show the Corinthians that there was perfect fellowship between the two of them. The quarreling factions at Corinth had not been able to drive a wedge between these evangelists.

Paul wanted Apollos to go to Corinth immediately, **but his will was not at all to come at this time.** Here one gains insight into Paul's democratic attitude in matters of procedure. He had no criticism of Apollos for not coming to Corinth immediately. He gave in to the desires of his co-worker, stating that Apollos would visit them when it was **convenient** for him to go. Paul was more concerned with fostering Christian fellowship than with forcing his will on a fellow evangelist, or with criticizing Apollos for not following his recommendations.

C. Conclusion, 16:13-24

The last paragraph of the letter divides itself into three parts. First there is a list of exhortations, then some personal references, and finally the closing salutations.

1. *Exhortations* (16:13-14)

a. Watchfulness (16:13a). **Watch ye** means: keep awake, do not go to sleep, do not take a vacation from the work of the Lord. Paul was not speaking against taking time to rest and relax one's body and mind. Rather, the idea is that a person can never let down, or turn aside even briefly from the holy calling of the Christian life. There were many glaring evils and weaknesses in the Corinthian church, such as dissensions, heresies, immorality, and intemperance. Little wonder that Paul exhorted them to be alert and watchful!

b. Stability (16:13b). The carnal mind produces a vacillating Christian life. Holiness produces stability. Thus the Corinthians were to **stand fast in the faith.** Exell writes that Paul was saying: "Strike the roots of your faith deep into the soil of eternal truth."[15] Both sound doctrine and vital experience are essential to spiritual stability.

c. Manliness (16:13c). Courage is a by-product of experiential Christianity. Genuine Christian faith does not produce timid,

---

[15]*Op. cit.,* p. 572.

apologetic, insipid personalities. Christianity is a religion of strength; it produces heroes. When Paul exhorted the Corinthians, **Quit you like men,** he simply asked that they should conduct themselves in a courageous way. Morgan states that the exhortation means, "Grow up, do not be children, do not be babes, be able to stand up."[16]

d. Strength (16:13*d*). To **be strong** requires that we drink deeply at the fountain of God's love and eat consistently at God's table. To **be strong** means to exercise oneself in the Lord. It indicates the ability "to do and suffer all His will."[17] Christianity would never have made an impact upon the pagan society of the first century without strong men and women, people who were mightily strengthened through the Holy Spirit.

e. Love—the integrating principle (16:14). Love is the unifying force that makes all other Christian qualities work in harmony. Love triggers the desire for watchfulness, for spiritual alertness. Love anchors man's faith and produces stability. Love generates a manly spirit that fears no foe and yields to no sin. Love nourishes strength in the Christian warfare. Therefore the apostle exhorts, **Let all your things be done with charity.**

2. *Personal References* (16:15-18)

Paul was aware that the gospel centers in individuals, not in movements. He never lost sight of the importance of persons. He appreciated all men, regardless of state or station. Here he names three associates who had meant much to him—**Stephanas and Fortunatus and Achaicus** (17).

The Berkeley Version renders the parenthesis of v. 15, "You know the Stephanas family, how it is the first fruits of the Achaia [see map 1] converts, and how they have devoted themselves to the service of the saints." A footnote reminds us that "there were converts in Athens (a port of Achaia) previous to the work in Corinth, but Achaia is here used in the narrow sense."[18]

Paul had baptized **Stephanas** and his household (1:16). Little is known of **Fortunatus** except that Clement, possibly the writer referred to in Phil. 4:3, states that Fortunatus was the messenger who carried this letter of Paul to Corinth.[19] **Achaicus** is mentioned nowhere else in the NT.

[16]*Op. cit.*, p. 217.   [17]Wesley, *Notes*, p. 641.
[18]Fn., *ad loc.*   [19]Clarke, *op. cit.*, II, 298.

These unknown men had done a service for Paul: **That which was lacking on your part they have supplied** (17). What these men gave to him is uncertain. They may have brought news from Corinth in addition to the letter which the Corinthians sent to the apostle. They may have provided money or provisions for the support of Paul in his ministry. Of this service Paul writes, **They have refreshed my spirit** (18). In helping Paul they had helped the Church, including the congregation at Corinth. Because of this personal contribution the Corinthians were to pay these men special respect and esteem. They were to recognize them as fellow laborers with Paul.

3. *Closing Salutations and Benediction* (16:19-24)

Paul adds a note of cordial fellowship at the end. He wants the churches to feel a sense of kinship, of belonging to each other. The apostle had already laid down some basic doctrines regarding Christian unity. But he knew that little courtesies as well as great doctrines contribute to church unity. The greetings came from several different sources.

a. The churches (16:19a). **The churches of Asia salute you** refers to the churches of Asia Minor, which included Ephesus (see map 1). Paul did not have a special greeting from each church but he was speaking for them. In this simple statement the apostle presented the idea of the universal bond that unites Christians.

b. Fellowship in the church (16:19b). To be more specific in his greetings, Paul selects two outstanding Christians, **Aquila and Priscilla.** Aquila was a tentmaker who had been forced into exile in Corinth. He had been driven out of Rome because he was a Jew (Acts 18:2). He and his wife, Priscilla, were able to teach the eloquent Apollos the deeper things of the Scriptures (Acts 18:26). They now joined Paul in sending greetings to the Corinthians. Later they returned to Rome (Rom. 16:3). **The church** which met in the home of this loyal lay couple also sent greetings to the Corinthians.

c. A holy greeting (16:20). Most ancient people, including the Jews, usually greeted each other with a kiss on the cheek. This was a sign of peace and friendship, indicating the absence of malice and ill will. Hence Paul wrote, **Greet ye one another with an holy kiss.**

d. A personal greeting (16:21-24). Paul had sent greetings from churches and individuals. Now he wanted to make the letter as personal as possible, so he took the pen and wrote, **The salutation of me Paul with mine own hand** (21). It is probable that the letter, up to this point, had been dictated to a secretary or to an associate.

Verses 8-24 give us "A Warrior's Challenge." (1) An awareness of spiritual opportunities, 8-9; (2) An exhortation to spiritual alertness, 13-14; (3) A plea for spiritual unity, 15-18; (4) An appreciation for spiritual activity, 19-24.

Paul's personal greeting contained several sobering thoughts. First, he said, **If any man love not the Lord Jesus Christ, let him be Anathema Maranatha** (22). The Greek word **Anathema** means "accursed, devoted to destruction." This is not meant as a threat or a hope on Paul's part, but as a simple statement of historic fact. "Whoever does not love the Lord, he shall be accursed" (Berk.). **Maranatha** is a Syriac term which means, "Our Lord is coming." The apostle here warns the Corinthians that the love of Christ is their only hope in the future. If they reject the Christ whom they have accepted, they will be swallowed up in destruction when the Lord returns.

But Paul is too tender to end his letter on a stern note of warning. As always, the apostle makes Christ the center of his thinking. Thus he prays, **The grace of our Lord Jesus Christ be with you** (23). He then adds the guarantee of his own affection: **My love be with you all in Christ Jesus** (24). Paul's last word to the church at Corinth was **Jesus.** We can only join him in his glad **Amen.**

Bibliography

I. COMMENTARIES

ALFORD, HENRY. *The Greek Testament*, Vol. II. London: Rivingtons, 1871.

BEET, JOSEPH A. *A Commentary on St. Paul's Epistles to the Corinthians.* New York: Thomas Whittaker, n.d.

CLARKE, ADAM. *The New Testament of Our Lord and Saviour Jesus Christ,* Vol. II. New York: Abingdon-Cokesbury Press, n.d.

DODS, MARCUS. "The First Epistle to the Corinthians." *The Expositor's Bible.* Edited by W. ROBERTSON NICOLL. London: Hodder and Stoughton, n.d.

DUMMELOW, J. R. (ed.). *A Commentary on the Holy Bible.* New York: The Macmillan Co., 1956 (reprint).

EXELL, JOSEPH S. "I Corinthians." *The Biblical Illustrator.* Grand Rapids, Mich.: Baker Book House, 1958 (reprint).

FARRAR, F. W. (exegesis). "I Corinthians." *The Pulpit Commentary.* Chicago: Wilcox and Follett Co., n.d.

FINDLAY, G. G. "St. Paul's First Epistle to the Corinthians." *The Expositor's Greek Testament.* Edited by W. ROBERTSON NICOLL. Grand Rapids, Mich.: Wm. B. Eerdmans Publishing Co., 1951.

FRAZER, J. W. (trans.). *The First Epistle of Paul the Apostle to the Corinthians.* "Calvin's Commentaries." Grand Rapids, Mich.: Wm. B. Eerdmans Publishing Co., 1960.

GODET, F. *Commentary on the First Epistle of St. Paul to the Corinthians,* Vols. I and II. Grand Rapids, Mich.: Zondervan Publishing House, 1957 (reprint).

GRAY, JAMES C., and ADAMS, GEORGE M. *Gray and Adams Bible Commentary.* Grand Rapids, Mich.: Zondervan Publishing House, n.d.

GROSHEIDE, F. W. *Commentary on the First Epistle to the Corinthians.* "The New International Commentary on the New Testament." Grand Rapids, Mich.: Wm. B. Eerdmans Publishing Co., 1951.

JAMIESON, ROBERT, FAUSSET, A. R., and BROWN, DAVID. *Commentary Critical and Explanatory on the Whole Bible.* Grand Rapids, Mich.: Zondervan Publishing House, n.d.

LANGE, JOHN PETER (ed.). "I Corinthians." *Commentary on the Holy Scriptures.* Grand Rapids, Mich.: Zondervan Publishing House, n.d.

MOFFATT, JAMES (ed.). *The First Epistle of Paul to the Corinthians.* "The Moffatt New Testament Commentary." New York: Harper and Brothers, n.d.

MORRIS, LEON. *The First Epistle of Paul to the Corinthians.* "Tyndale New Testament Commentaries." Grand Rapids, Mich.: Wm. B. Eerdmans Publishing Co., 1958.

ROBERTSON, ARCHIBALD, and PLUMMER, ALFRED. *A Critical and Exegetical Commentary on the First Epistle of St. Paul to the Corinthians.* "The International Critical Commentary." Edinburgh: T. and T. Clark, 1911.

SHORE, T. T. "First Epistle to the Corinthians.' *Commentary on the Whole Bible.* Edited by C. J. ELLIOTT. Grand Rapids, Mich.: Zondervan Publishing House, n.d.

————. *The Pulpit Commentary: Corinthians.* Edited by H. D. M. SPENCE and JOSEPH S. EXELL. Grand Rapids, Mich.: Wm. B. Eerdmans Publishing Co., 1950 (reprint).

WESLEY, JOHN. *Explanatory Notes upon the New Testament.* London: Epworth Press, 1958 (reprint).

WHEDON, D. D. "I Corinthians—II Timothy." *Commentary on the New Testament.* New York: Phillips and Hunt, 1875.

II. OTHER BOOKS

Analytical Greek Lexicon, The. New York: Harper and Brothers, n.d.

ARNDT, W. F., and GINGRICH, F. W. *A Greek-English Lexicon of the New Testament and Other Early Christian Literature.* Chicago: University of Chicago Press, 1957.

BAIRD, WILLIAM. *The Corinthian Church. A Biblical Approach to Urban Culture.* New York: Abingdon Press, 1964.

BARCLAY, WILLIAM. *The Letters to the Corinthians.* Philadelphia: The Westminster Press, 1954.

BARNES, ALBERT. *The Apostle Paul.* Grand Rapids, Mich.: Baker Book House, 1950.

BETTESON, HENRY (ed.). *Documents of the Christian Church.* London: Oxford University Press, 1963.

BLAIKLOCK, E. M. *The Acts of the Apostles.* Grand Rapids, Mich.: Wm. B. Eerdmans Publishing Co., 1959.

BRUCE, A. B. *St. Paul's Conception of Christianity.* New York: Charles Scribner's Sons, 1898.

CHADWICK, HENRY, and OULTON, JOHN E. L. *Alexandrian Christianity.* "The Library of Christian Classics." Philadelphia: The Westminster Press, 1954.

CONYBEARE, W. J., and HOWSON, J. S. *The Life and Epistles of St. Paul.* Hartford, Conn.: S. S. Scranton Co., 1904.

CRAIG, CLARENCE TUCKER. *The Beginning of Christianity.* New York: Abingdon Press, 1943.

CREMER, HERMANN. *Biblico-Theological Lexicon of New Testament Greek.* Edinburgh: T. and T. Clark, 1962 (reprint).

DEISSMANN, ADOLPH. *Paul: A Study in Social and Religious History.* Translated by WILLIAM E. WILSON. New York: Harper and Brothers, 1957.

EARLE, RALPH, et al. *Exploring the New Testament.* Kansas City: Beacon Hill Press, 1955.

ERDMAN, CHARLES R. *The First Epistle of Paul to the Corinthians.* Philadelphia: The Westminster Press, 1928.

FINEGAN, JACK. *Light from the Ancient Past.* Princeton, N.J.: Princeton University Press, 1946.

FITZWATER, P. B. *Preaching and Teaching the New Testament.* Chicago: Moody Press, 1957.

GREENSLADE, S. L. (ed. and trans.). *Early Latin Theology.* "The Library of Christian Classics." Philadelphia: The Westminster Press, 1956.

HAYES, D. A. *Paul and His Epistles.* New York: The Methodist Book Concern, 1915.

HERING, JEAN. *The First Epistle of Saint Paul to the Corinthians.* Translated by A. W. HEATHCOTE and P. I. ALLCOCK. London: The Epworth Press, 1962.

HURD, JOHN C. *The Origin of I Corinthians.* New York: Seabury Press, 1965.

LENSKI, R. C. H. *The Interpretation of St. Paul's First and Second Epistles to the Corinthians.* Minneapolis, Minn.: Augsburg Publishing House, 1963.

LIGHTFOOT, J. B. *Notes on the Epistles of St. Paul.* Grand Rapids, Mich.: Zondervan Publishing House, 1957 (reprint).

MATHEWS, H. F. *According to St. Paul.* New York: Collier Books, 1962.

MORGAN, G. CAMPBELL. *The Corinthian Letters of Paul.* New York: Fleming H. Revell Co., 1946.

MOULE, C. F. D. *The Birth of the New Testament.* "Harper's New Testament Commentaries." New York: Harper and Row, 1961.

MOULTON, JAMES HOPE, and MILLIGAN, GEORGE. *The Vocabulary of the Greek New Testament.* London: Hodder and Stoughton, 1949.

PRICE, JAMES L. *Interpreting the New Testament.* New York: Holt, Rinehart and Winston, 1961.

REDPATH, ALAN. *The Royal Route to Heaven.* Westwood, N.J.: Fleming H. Revell Co., 1966.

SOUTER, ALEXANDER. *A Pocket Lexicon to the Greek New Testament.* Oxford: The Clarendon Press, 1960.

STALKER, JAMES. *The Life of St. Paul.* New York: Fleming H. Revell Company, 1912.

STANLEY, ARTHUR PENRYHN. *The Epistles of St. Paul to the Corinthians.* London: John Murray, 1876.

STAUFFER, ETHELBERT. *New Testament Theology.* Translated by JOHN MARSH. New York: The Macmillan Company, 1955.

TAYLOR, WILLIAM M. *Paul the Missionary.* New York: Harper and Brothers, 1882.

TENNEY, MERRILL C. *New Testament Survey.* Grand Rapids, Mich.: Wm. B. Eerdmans Publishing Co., 1961.

THAYER, JOSEPH HENRY. *A Greek-English Lexicon of the New Testament.* New York: American Book Co., 1889.

TRENCH, RICHARD C. *Synonyms of the New Testament.* Grand Rapids, Mich.: Wm. B. Eerdmans Publishing Co., 1963 (reprint of ninth ed.).

VINCENT, MARVIN R. *Word Studies in the New Testament.* Grand Rapids, Mich.: Wm. B. Eerdmans Publishing Co., 1957.

VINE, W. E. *I Corinthians.* Grand Rapids, Mich.: Zondervan Publishing House, 1961.

WEISS, JOHANNES. *Earliest Christianity: A History of the Period A.D. 30-150.* New York: Harper and Brothers, 1937.

WRIGHT, G. ERNEST. *Biblical Archaeology.* Philadelphia: The Westminster Press, 1957.

The Second Epistle of Paul

to the

CORINTHIANS

Frank G. Carver

Introduction

A. A Personal Document

None of Paul's other letters carries us so deeply into the heart of the man and the apostle as this letter to the church at Corinth. "Here," writes Hanson, "broken sharply off, with none of the jagged edges filed down, is a chunk of Paul's life—authentic, uncensored, bewilderingly complicated, but amazingly interesting."[1] As Philippians amazes us with its unveiling of the quality of Paul's commitment as a Christian, II Corinthians astounds us by its revelation of the radical caliber of his commitment as an apostle. Open to view in this letter is the heartthrob of that gospel ministry which belongs to every member of Christ, laity and clergy alike—its commitment, its content, its resources, its character. Witness is borne to the inescapable truth that the mission of the Church as the body of Christ is the carrying on of the self-giving, sacrificial, suffering ministry of Jesus.

Humanly the letter is designed to complete the personal reconciliation of Paul as a spiritual father with his impertinent children in the faith.[2] They had been seduced for a time by severe criticisms leveled at the integrity of Paul's apostolic ministry by some in their midst. Paul meets this attack on his personal calling by an appeal to the character of the gospel itself. Interestingly, in Galatians, when some had attempted to attach a legalistic compromise to the gospel of grace, Paul had argued in reverse manner, from the divine origin of his apostolate to the integrity of his gospel. The message and the manner of its communication were inseparable for Paul. The manner of his ministry was determined by the nature of his message. So as Paul defends his ministry we are confronted again with an effective witness to the reality and import of the coming of God into the world "in Christ."

Apart from the more personal sections (1:1-11; 6:11-16; 13:11-14) and his concern for the collection project (8:1—9:15) the

[1] *The Second Epistle to the Corinthians* ("Torch Bible Commentaries"; London: S.C.M. Press, 1954), pp. 7-8.

[2] See R. H. Strachan, *The Second Epistle of Paul to the Corinthians* ("The Moffatt New Testament Commentary"; New York: Harper and Brothers, 1935), pp. xxix-xxxviii, for a portrayal of the apostle's personality as sketched from II Corinthians.

letter falls into two main sections. The first (1:12—6:10) contains Paul's defense of his apostolic integrity in regard to his motives and methods of operation in relation to the Corinthians. The second (10:1—13:10) deals with the vindication of his apostolic authority in the light of the attacks which had been made against it. The necessity of defending the integrity of his total existence in such personally excruciating circumstances reveals the fundamental drives of the man. Out of this situation has come to us a penetrating witness to the all-pervading dynamic of the gospel of Christ in the life of the apostle.

B. LITERARY INTEGRITY

1. *Authenticity*

The letter claims to come from the hand of Paul: "Paul an apostle of Jesus Christ . . . unto the church of God which is at Corinth" (1:1). All indications within the letter itself confirm this claim. There was no doubt as to its Pauline authorship in the Ancient Church and it remains undisputed in the reputable scholarly circles of the Modern Church.[3]

Some, however, view 6:14—7:1 as a non-Pauline interpolation into the letter. The arguments include (1) the large number of words not found elsewhere in Paul or in the NT, (2) word combinations unusual for Paul (cf. 6:14; 7:1), and (3) close conceptual relationship with the Qumran community.[4] While these objections cannot be proved invalid, neither do they constitute decisive proof that Paul could not have written the passage.[5] Until conclusive evidence is forthcoming there is no commanding reason to deny the authenticity of 6:14—7:1. The phenomenon that demands explanation is the poor connection of the passage with its context, discussed next.

[3]For a listing of the internal and external evidence see Alfred Plummer, *A Critical and Exegetical Commentary on the Second Epistle of St. Paul to the Corinthians* ("The International Critical Commentary"; Edinburgh: T. and T. Clark, 1919), pp. xi-xii.

[4]J. Z. Fitzmyer, "Qumran and the Interpolated Paragraph in 2 Cor. 6:14—7:1," *Catholic Biblical Quarterly*, XXIII (1961), 271 ff. K. G. Kuhn, "Les Rouleaux de Cuivre De Qumran," *Revue Biblique*, LXI (1954), 203, note 2, suggests that Paul Christianized an Essene text.

[5]See Paul Feine, Johannes Behm, and Werner Georg Kuemmel, *Introduction to the New Testament*, trans. A. J. Mattill, Jr. (14th ed., rev., New York: Abingdon Press, 1966), p. 211, for a few of the factors which militate against any overweighting of these objections.

2. Unity

In spite of the fact that there is no supporting evidence in the history of the transmission of the text many scholars hold that II Corinthians is a collection of letters or fragments of letters which the apostle wrote to Corinth at various times.[6] Some go so far as to include not only 6:17—7:1 and cc. 10—13 but also 2:14—7:4 and c. 9 as coming from one or more other letters of Paul.[7] Kuemmel rightly insists that a convincing motive for a secondary combination must be recognizable before the unity of the letter is abandoned. He finds none which he would accord that status among the proposals of those who would reconstruct the letter.[8] Only two passages have been sufficiently challenged to merit our attention here: 6:14—7:1 and cc. 10—13.

Because 6:14—7:1 appears to interrupt the thought connection between 6:13 and 7:2, it is often held to be an interpolated fragment of an earlier letter known as the "previous letter" (I Cor. 5:9).[9] The contents, however, do not appear to agree, for that letter warns against fellowship with a fornicator "that is called a brother" (I Cor. 5:11). Here the warning is against being "unequally yoked together with unbelievers" (6:14). Also, as Filson suggests, "7:2 does not follow 6:13 as smoothly as some have said. It reads like a resumption of an appeal after an interruption."[10] Paul could have paused, after asking the Corinthians to open their hearts wide to him, to warn them against being too free in their friendships. But even if a connection with the context is not discerned, there is no reason why this could not be an example of the apostle's tendency to digress, due perhaps to his having written the letter at several sittings.[11]

[6] For the gamut of the proposals see Donald Guthrie, *New Testament Introduction: The Pauline Epistles* (London: The Tyndale Press, 1961), pp. 62-64.

[7] Guenther Bornkamm, "The History of the Origin of the So-called Second Letter to the Corinthians," *The Authorship and Integrity of the New Testament* (London, S.P.C.K., 1965), pp. 13-81; J. T. Dean, *St. Paul and Corinth* (London: Lutterworth, 1947), pp. 40-42.

[8] Feine, Behm, Kuemmel, *op. cit.*, p. 214.

[9] So Strachan, *op. cit.*, p. xv. See S. M. Gilmour, "Corinthians, Second Letter to the," *The Interpreter's Dictionary of the Bible*, ed. George Buttrick (New York: Abingdon Press, 1962), *A-D*, 694-95; hereafter cited as IDB.

[10] "The Second Epistle to the Corinthians" (Exegesis), *The Interpreter's Bible*, ed. George A. Buttrick, *et al.* (New York: Abingdon-Cokesbury Press, 1953), X, 270.

[11] Guthrie, *op. cit.*, pp. 48-49.

Very widespread is the assumption that cc. 10—13 were written earlier than cc. 1—9 and constitute part of what has been called the "sorrowful" or "intermediate letter" (2:3-9).[12] This letter written "out of much affliction and anguish of heart" (2:4) had made possible the reconciliation of the church as a whole with Paul (7:6-16).

The problem arises primarily out of a change from the sense of an accomplished reconciliation (cc. 1—9) to a renewed attack against "some" (10:2) in the church whom Paul calls "false apostles" (11:13). He fears that when he comes he will not find them as he would like (12:20), and if so he "will not spare" (13:2). To this, many supporting arguments have been added.[13]

The decisive question is whether or not it is possible for cc. 10—13 to have stood in the same Epistle with cc. 1—9.[14] Two basic considerations remove the supposed impossibility. The first is that, although Paul does appear to change his position in respect to the church in the latter section, there are indications in the previous chapters that all is not right with the church. There are defenses against a misinterpretation of the conduct of his ministry (4:2-6; 5:11-15; 7:2) and a polemic against other traveling preachers (2:17—3:1; cf. 4:2-5). Since it is mentioned in 2:6 that the majority punished the offender, there may have been a minority who opposed Paul's judgment in the matter. Second, the polemic of 2:17 is expanded in cc. 10—13, where Paul indicates that it is only specific persons in the church who are attacking him (10:2; 11:5, 12:15, 21; 13:2). Paul is writing to the majority, who are reconciled with him, to support them in their handling of the dangerous minority, at whose center are the "false apostles" (11:13).

Further it is difficult to maintain the identity of cc. 10—13 with the intermediate letter. Nothing is said in 10—13 about the

[12]The classical arguments for this position are given by Plummer, op. cit., pp. xxvii-xxxvi. See also Filson, op. cit., pp. 270-71, and Gilmour, op. cit., p. 695.

[13]For evaluation of these arguments against the unity of the letter see Guthrie, op. cit., pp. 47-64; Philip E. Hughes, Paul's Second Epistle to the Corinthians ("The New International Commentary on the New Testament"; Grand Rapids; Wm. B. Eerdmans Publishing Co., 1962), pp. xxi-xxv; R. V. G. Tasker, The Second Epistle of Paul to the Corinthians ("The Tyndale New Testament Commentaries"; London: The Tyndale Press, 1958), pp. 23-25; A. M. G. Stephenson, "A Defence of the Integrity of 2 Corinthians," The Authorship and Integrity of the New Testament (London: S.P.C.K., 1965), pp. 82-97.

[14]See Feine, Behm, Kuemmel, op. cit., 212-15.

event mentioned in 2:3-9. Also nothing is said in cc. 1—9 about the reaction of the congregation to the polemic against the false apostles of cc. 10—13. In 12:18, Paul looks back to the sending of Titus with the letter. Hughes concludes that

> the difficulty of the change of tone and content of the final four chapters is more imaginary than real . . . it can be demonstrated that they harmonize with the pervading *theme* of the epistle—the theme, namely, of strength through weakness. In this theme is bound up the whole argument for the genuineness of Paul's apostolic authority, which has been impugned by his adversaries in Corinth. . . . It is by the amazing contrast between his own frailty and the all-conquering strength of God manifested through him that his apostleship is unshakably authenticated to the world.[15]

C. HISTORICAL SITUATION

1. City of Corinth and Founding the Church

Corinth, the capital of the Roman province of Achaia, was a prosperous commercial city located on the Isthmus of Corinth (see map 1). Through it passed the mainland route between East and West as well as several sea routes. Its population was a cosmopolitan mixture of Romans, Greeks, Orientals, and Jews. Although it was not the cultural match of Athens, it prided itself on its intellectual sophistication. But its fame was more as a city of pleasure. The Isthmian games were held every other year. It was the center of worship for the goddess Aphrodite, whose temple women were also entertainers in the city's night life. All this produced a city filled with vice and licentiousness under a veneer of sophistication. Corinth became so notorious for its loose morals that its very name became an expression for such behavior—to Corinthianize.

To this strategic center the apostle came on his second missionary journey after a somewhat disappointing visit to Athens (Acts 18:1-22). In Corinth he made his home with two exiled Jews from Rome, Aquila and Priscilla, and worked with them at their common trade of tentmaking. Every Sabbath, Paul was in the synagogue persuading the Jews and Greeks that Jesus was the Christ. Opposition soon arose from the Jews. So he turned to the Gentiles, continuing his evangelistic activity in the house of Titius Justus next door to the synagogue. Crispus, the leader of the synagogue, along with many of the Corinthians, believed in the Lord. Thus the church was composed of both Gentile and

[15]*Op. cit.*, p. xxx. He lists the passages which demonstrate this unity of theme.

Jewish believers. Silas and Timothy became co-workers with Paul in Corinth (II Cor. 1:19). During his stay Paul was brought by the Jews before the Roman proconsul Gallio. He, however, refused to indict Paul, securing him for the most part from further open attacks from the Jews. Aided by direct divine encouragement Paul remained in Corinth for a year and a half, establishing the church. When the apostle left he returned to Antioch by way of Ephesus, having no further contact with the church at Corinth until his three-year mission in Ephesus during his third missionary journey.

The church in Corinth, a cross section of the local inhabitants, was affected by the moral laxity and intellectual pride of its pagan environment. It gave Paul more problems and severely anxious moments than any other church. In his letters extant, as Paul deals with these problems (I Corinthians) and his own relation to them (II Corinthians), we are afforded a rare glimpse into the heart of a primitive Christian community.[16]

2. Paul's Relations with the Church

In I Cor. 5:9, Paul alludes to a "previous letter" which he had written warning them not to associate with immoral persons within the fellowship of the church. This they had misconstrued, deliberately or otherwise, to mean immoral men in general (I Cor. 5:10-11). This letter has not been preserved, due perhaps to the repetition of its substance in I Corinthians.

A second letter, our I Corinthians, was written in response to this misunderstanding as well as to several other matters. For Paul had heard of divisiveness (1:11), immorality (5:1-2), and lawsuits (6:1-8) within the church. Also a letter had come to him possibly by a delegation (16:17) asking questions in regard to marriage (7:1), meat sacrificed to idols (8:1), spiritual gifts (12:1) and the resurrection (15:1-58). This letter was sent in the spring of 55 or 56.

I Corinthians, sent perhaps by Timothy (I Cor. 4:17; 16:10), did not produce the desired results. The report came back that conditions in the church were becoming worse. So Paul left his work at Ephesus and paid what is described as "the painful visit" (II Cor. 2:1) to Corinth. It appears that some particular person, a ringleader, rose up in arrogant defiance to Paul (II Cor. 2:5-8;

[16]For a picture of the church at Corinth based on I Corinthians see William Baird, *The Corinthian Church—A Biblical Approach to Urban Culture* (New York: Abingdon Press, 1964).

7:12);[17] the church sided with him, and Paul was forced to retreat in haste.

II Corinthians gives evidence that the polemic against the apostle had been stepped up. The charges and slurs against his person were many. The integrity of his motives, of his behavior, and even of his apostolic ministry were all brought into question (1:13; 3:1; 4:2-5; 5:11-12; 6:3; 7:2; 10:2, 7, 13; 11:5, 7-9; 12:11-13; 13:3). Even his courage (10:1, 10) and abilities were attacked (10:11; 11:6). Paul's critics appear to have been a minority (2:6), centering in a few Jewish Christians (2:6) who had made their way into the congregation with letters of recommendation and self-commendation (3:1; 10:12, 18). According to Kuemmel they were not "'Judaizers,' but Palestinian opponents of the Pauline mission and apostolic dignity"[18] who had joined themselves with the somewhat Gnostic-like opposition to Paul already evident in I Corinthians.[19]

On returning to Ephesus from the "painful visit" Paul wrote the "sorrowful letter" (2:3-4) and dispatched Titus (7:6) to take it to Corinth and attempt to restore the church to Paul. After Titus' departure, Paul's troubled concern would not let him continue his work, so he proceeded to Troas and on to Macedonia (2:12-13; 7:5; see map 1) to await the return of Titus. When Titus came with word that the church had dealt with the offender and that it had re-submitted itself to the authority of the apostle, Paul was comforted (7:6-12).

So from Macedonia, within a year (8:10; 9:2) after the writing of I Corinthians, Paul wrote to the church of God in Corinth. He included "all the saints which are in all Achaia" (1:1) and asked them to prepare the way for his third visit. In the letter he expressed his relief at the success of Titus' mission of reconciliation and answered the derogatory charges of his critics. Throughout the entire letter, but especially in cc. 10—13, he found it necessary to defend the legitimacy of his apostleship.[20] Although proper relations between the apostle and the church as

[17]Hughes would identify the man in II Cor. 2:5-8 and 7:12 with the incestuous man of I Cor. 5:1 and would make I Corinthians the "sorrowful letter" (op. cit., pp. 59-61, xxvii-xxxv). But see Guthrie, op. cit., pp. 47-62.

[18]Feine, Behm, Kuemmel, op. cit., p. 209.

[19]See Dieter Georgi, Die Gegner des Paulus im 2. Korintherbrief, Wissenschaftliche Monographien zum Alten und Neuen Testament, ed. G. Bornkamm and G. Von Rad (Neukirchen-Vluyn: Neukirchener Verlag, 1964), for a thorough treatment of the nature of Paul's opponents in Corinth.

[20]Ernst Kasemann, "Die Legitimat des Apostels, Zeitschrift zum Neuen Testament Wissenschaft, XLI (1942), 33 ff.

a whole were restored, some opposition to Paul still remained in Corinth. He hoped to heal fully the situation there.

With the restoration of normal relations Paul was also concerned that the collection project be reactivated and carried to completion (cc. 8—9). When he visited Corinth for the third time (12:14; 13:1-2), he spent the winter, before continuing on to Jerusalem with the offering for the poverty-stricken Christians there.

The three well-defined sections of the letter (cc. 1—7; 8—9; 10—13) reflect the perspective of the apostle in the successive phases of his relations with the church. As he is writing, cc. 1—7 look back to his anxiety and relief in relation to the mission of Titus; cc. 8—9 reflect his present position as he seeks to motivate their generosity; and cc. 10—13 look ahead to some factors that still need attention in the church.[21]

[21]Everett Harrison, *Introduction to the New Testament* (Grand Rapids: Wm. B. Eerdmans Publishing Co., 1964), p. 272.

Outline

Section I An Apostolic Introduction

II Corinthians 1:1-11

The very words with which Paul begins this intensely personal letter to the church at Corinth indicate his central concern. Even as he greets the church (1-2; cf. I Cor. 1:1-9; Phil. 1:1-11) and pauses to give praise to God (3-11), Paul touches that nerve which sensitizes the entire letter—the actuality, integrity, and character of his apostleship.

A. PAUL GREETS THE CHURCH, 1:1-2

Paul . . . unto the church . . . grace . . . and peace follows the prevalent form of ancient letter writing—the writer, those addressed, and the greeting (Acts 15:23; 23:26).[1] The apostle expands the salutation in I Cor. 1:1-3 with a distinctly Christian accent.

Paul, the writer, focuses the attention of his readers upon his office as **an apostle of Jesus Christ**[2] **by the will of God** (1). **Timothy our brother** (cf. Acts 16:1-3; 17:14-15; 18:5; I Cor. 4:17; 16:10-11) is mentioned both from courtesy (Phil. 1:1; Col. 1:1; I Thess. 1:1; II Thess. 1:1; Philem. 1) and as a Christian **brother**[3] of the Corinthians. As one who has worked with Paul in Corinth (1:19) he supports the apostle in what he has to say. The apostolate originated in the decision of Jesus to select 12 of His disciples and "send them out" (*apostellein,* Mark 6:7) as bearers of His own authority to preach and heal (Matt. 10:1-7; Mark 6:7-30;

---

[1]Adolf Deissmann, *Light from the Ancient East*, trans. L. R. M. Strachan (New York: Harper and Brothers, 1927), p. 188: "Antonis Longus to Nilus his mother many greetings. And continually do I pray that thou art in health." This second-century letter illustrates as well Paul's normal custom (Galatians and Titus are exceptions) of following the greeting with a prayer of thanksgiving.

[2]The Greek word order is "Christ Jesus" with a possible emphasis on the Messianic significance of the title "Christ."

[3]The Greek word *adelphos* in the Early Church designated a "fellow Christian," replacing the term "disciple" (*mathetes*), used so often in the Gospels. *Adelphos* was used in that time by members of any select community for one another (see Deissmann, *op. cit.,* p. 107).

Luke 6:13; 9:1-6). These apostles sent out by Jesus were as Jesus himself: [4] "The one who listens to you listens to Me, and the one who rejects you rejects Me; and he who rejects Me rejects the One who sent Me" (Luke 10:16, NASB). The sense of identity between Jesus and those He commissions in respect to the will and activity of God is such that when they proclaim the gospel in His name they actualize His presence. Following the death and resurrection of Jesus the apostolic office was renewed by the personal commission of the risen Lord. The command is to bear witness to Jesus and the Resurrection in utter reliance upon the Holy Spirit as revealed at Pentecost (Acts 1:6-8, 15-26; 2:4, 32-33; 4:33; 5:29-32).

Paul knew himself to be an apostle by virtue of his personal encounter with the risen Lord. He equated the appearance of the Lord to him with the appearances of the risen Lord to the other apostles (I Cor. 9:1-2; 15:5-8). Paul had been directly commissioned by Jesus to bear witness of Him to the Gentiles (Acts 9:1-9, 15-16; 22:12-21; 26:15-18, 22-23; I Cor. 15:9; Gal. 1:15-16). Munck suggests that Paul viewed God's call to him as "a renewal of God's will for the salvation of the Gentiles, giving him a place in the history of salvation"[5] in continuity with Isaiah and Jeremiah.[6] Although Paul was not a witness of the earthly life of Jesus in exactly the same sense as the Twelve (Acts 1:21-22; Luke 1:2), he entered wholeheartedly into the stream of early Christian tradition concerning Jesus (I Cor. 11:2, 23; 15:1-11).[7] He became one with the original apostles in his "inner commitment

---

[4]The Rabbis said of the Jewish *shaliach*, "The one sent by a man is as the man himself." Quoted from K. H. Rengstorf, *"apostello," Theological Dictionary of the New Testament,* ed. G. Kittel, trans. G. W. Bromiley, I (Grand Rapids: Wm. B. Eerdmans Publishing Co., 1964), 415. Hereafter cited as TDNT.

[5]*Paul and the Salvation of Mankind,* trans. Frank Clarke (Richmond, Virginia: John Knox Press, 1959), p. 26.

[6]Cf. Gal. 1:15-16 with Isa. 49:1-6 and Jer. 1:4-5, and Acts 26:12-18 with Jer. 1:7-8; Isa. 42:6-7, 16, and 61:1 (*ibid.,* pp. 24-27).

[7]This is the reason Paul felt it mandatory to live in fellowship with the apostles of Jerusalem. See Gal. 2:1-10. "Paul makes this visit to them precisely because he finds it indispensable that the authentic character of his apostleship, and consequently the authentic Christian character of the churches he founded, be established" (Philippe H. Menoud, "Revelation and Tradition, The Influence of Paul's Conversion on His Theology," *Interpretation: A Journal of Bible and Theology,* VII [1953], 138-39).

to the history of Jesus as the only foundation and content of his proclamation."[8] His apostleship was thus somewhat unique in character: "one untimely born . . . the least of the apostles" (I Cor. 15:8-10, RSV). Paul's apostolic sense of mission originated for him solely in **the will of God** (cf. Gal. 1:1). The call came by divine revelation uncorrupted by men (cf. Gal. 1:11-17). If his apostolic authority was questioned, the issue became not his own person but the cause of God, who commissioned him "through Jesus Christ" (Gal. 1:1, ASV). Paul as **an apostle** was the servant of his message—"the word of the cross" (I Cor. 1:18, NASB). So whenever he found it necessary to speak authoritatively to his churches, he stressed his apostolic authorization by Christ[9] at the beginning of his letters.

Those addressed include **the church of God which is at Corinth,** the localized manifestation of the body of Christ (I Cor. 12:13-27), and **all the saints** in the Roman province of **Achaia** (Greece), of which Corinth was the capital city (see map 1). **All the saints** (*hagios*, lit., "the holy ones") indicates simply "all Christians" (Phillips; cf. Acts 9:13; Rom. 8:27; I Cor. 6:1; Heb. 6:10). The background of the term in the OT is cultic. In the NT it designates those who belong to the new covenant community (cf. Dan. 7:18) in virtue of the sacrificial death of Christ (Heb. 13:12). They are a holy people only "in Christ Jesus" (I Cor. 1:2, 30; Phil. 1:1). Their vocation is to belong wholly to God (Rom. 1:7; I Cor. 1:2; Col. 3:12) and to serve Him utterly (Rom. 12:1). The effective Agent is the Holy Spirit (Rom. 15:16; I Cor. 3:16-17; I Pet. 1:2).

Purity of relationship with God in Christ is the emphasis. Procksch concludes that the basic reference of *hagios* is to "the static morality of innocence rather than to ethical action."[10] But these go together in the actual lives of those who belong to God, for the ethical quality of their relationship to Him must answer to what God is (I Pet. 1:14-16). This is nothing less than Christlikeness (I John 2:6; 3:2-3). Paul, however, does not address his readers as **saints**[11] because they have realized in life the full

---

[8]Rengstorf, *op. cit.*, p. 437.   [9]*Ibid.*, p. 440.

[10]"*Hagios,*" TDNT, I, 109.

[11]*Hagioi* is never applied in the NT as a synonym for individual Christians. But *hagios* is applied to the incarnate Christ (Mark 1:24; Luke 1:35; 4:34; John 6:69; Acts 3:14; 4:27, 30; I John 2:20; Rev. 3:7).

implications of the name, but simply because they authentically belong to Christ as a body of believers.

The greeting proper, **Grace be to you and peace from God our Father, and from the Lord Jesus Christ** (2),[12] is Paul's favorite. It unites the usual Greek (Acts 15:23) and Hebrew (Dan. 4:1) forms of greeting. But Paul has immersed them in Jesus Christ. "Grace is the first and last word of the Gospel" (cf. II Cor. 8:9), writes Denney, and "peace—perfect spiritual soundness—is the finished work of grace in the soul"[13] (cf. Col. 3:15). The order is first **grace**, then **peace**.

These two opening verses afford us an authentic insight into the essential character of (1) God's messenger, (2) God's people, and (3) God's message.

B. PAUL PRAISES GOD FOR HIS COMFORT, 1:3-11

The thanksgiving which normally follows the greeting in Paul's letters is here quite different from that of the first letter (I Cor. 1:4-9). There he speaks of the Corinthians' rich experience of the grace of God in Christ Jesus. Here his thoughts flow from a perilous personal experience in Asia (8-11) to the role of such affliction[14] in his ministry to them as an apostle (3-7). Paul's words evidence the depth of his devotion to the Corinthians and suggest the place of suffering in the life of a genuine apostle.[15] Implicit even in his expression of praise is the problem of Paul's personal relation to the church at Corinth.

1. *Comfort Through Christ* (1:3-7)

Typical of Paul (cf. Rom. 15:1-7; I Cor. 1:18-31; 4:9-10; Phil. 2:5-11) and particularly characteristic of this letter (4:7-12; 6:

---

[12]It is possible that this greeting may have been a formula of introduction to the primitive Christian worship service. See Gerhard Delling, *Worship in the New Testament*, trans. Parey Scott (Philadelphia: The Westminster Press, 1962), pp. 48 ff. These titles for Jesus are theologically significant and should be researched further by the reader who is unaware of their full biblical connotation.

[13]"The Second Epistle to the Corinthians," *The Expositor's Bible*, ed. W. Robertson Nicoll, V (Grand Rapids, Michigan: Wm. B. Eerdmans Publishing Co., 1947), 721.

[14]The words **tribulation, trouble,** and **afflicted** (3-11) are basically the same word in the original (see ASV, RSV, NASB). The root meaning is "pressure."

[15]Cf. NASB, v. 5, "The sufferings of Christ are ours."

4-10; 7:5-7; 11:30; 12:5-10; 13:2-9) is the interchange of opposite experiences in Christ.[16] Here it is the interchange of comfort[17] and affliction that permeates Paul's words of praise. The thought which links the two opposites is **the sufferings of Christ** (5), for Paul describes his own sufferings in relation to those of our Lord.

The One whom he praises as "the God and Father of our Lord Jesus Christ"[18] (NASB) he has experienced also as **the Father of mercies** (Ps. 103:13; Rom. 12:1), **and the God of all comfort** (3). The continuity which Paul emphasizes by his inverted repetition of **God** and **Father** is at the heart of his concept of Deity. **The Father of mercies, as the God of all**[19] **comfort,** comforts Paul and thus enables him to comfort others (4). He is the "God and Father" of that One whose **sufferings abound in** (*eis*) **us** (5). The Father[20] is the **God of our Lord Jesus Christ** (3), for the consequence of Jesus' becoming genuinely human (John 1:14; Heb. 2:14) was that it became necessary for Him to live in complete dependence upon God for spiritual strength (Mark 15:34; John 20:17; Heb. 10:7). God is **the Father** of Jesus Christ, for Jesus was also the divine Son, who lived in perfect obedience to His Father (John 5:30). The key to Paul's perspective is the Son of God's actual obedience as man even to suffering and death for mankind (Phil. 2:8; Heb. 5:8).

It is because Paul's afflictions are so vitally related to **the sufferings of Christ** that his "comfort also aboundeth through [*dia*] Christ" (5, ASV) to the Corinthians. Paul's thought is well-expressed by Phillips' translation: "Indeed, experience shows that the more we share Christ's suffering the more we are able to give of his encouragement." So both Paul's afflictions and his experiences of comfort are for the sake of the Corinthians (4:15;

[16]See Hanson, *op. cit.,* pp. 29, 32-35.

[17]Both **comfort** and **consolation** are used to render *parakaleo* and *paraklesis,* which together are used 10 times in 3-7. The basic idea of the verb is "to call alongside to help." The relation is close to *parakletos* in John 14:16, 26; 15:26; 16:7; and I John 2:1.

[18]Although the translation, **God, even the Father of our Lord Jesus Christ,** is possible, it is not likely. See Eph. 1:3 and I Pet. 1:3 where the Greek wording is identical. See also Rom. 15:6; II Cor. 11:31.

[19]Note the threefold use of *pas* (all, all, any) in 3-4.

[20]Paul's thinking of God as Father may be traced back to his conversion (Gal. 1:16), for "his recognition of the risen Christ as the Son of God was a new consciousness of the nature of God as Father" (David Michael Stanley, *Christ's Resurrection in Pauline Soteriology* [Romae: E. Pontificio Instituto Biblico, 1961], p. 256).

12:15), whose sufferings are of the same kind as his (6).[21] Just as they share in the sufferings which are Paul's lot as a servant of Christ, in the same measure they will be able to partake of the comfort (7) which finds its source in Christ (4-5). This comfort, as Filson interprets it, "is more than consolation in sorrow or trial; it includes encouragement, and implies the divine gift of strength to meet and master life's crises."[22]

Paul finds the source of mutual comfort in the character of God as revealed in Jesus Christ. He does this by uniting the sufferings of the Church—apostle and people—with the sufferings of Christ. But upon what basis can Paul make this identification? What precisely does he mean by it? This identification of the sufferings of Christ and the Church arises out of the redemptive participation in the life and death of Christ (6:5) which Paul finds at the heart of being "in Christ." Involved in the earthly ministry of Jesus which culminated in the Cross were the Messianic afflictions (Mark 13:19, 24) which Paul links with the life of the Christian in Rom. 8:17-18. The sufferings of the Christian can partake of the nature of Christ's sufferings because the Christian is redemptively united with Christ in both His death and life (Rom. 5:10). For Paul, participation in the afflictions of this age, which may in a sense be styled the Messianic sufferings, is an indispensable part of the ongoing life of the Church (Acts 14:22; Phil. 1:29-30).

Even discipleship during Jesus' lifetime appeared to lead to a sharing in His life and ministry, to a participation in His Servant destiny. In Eduard Schweizer's words, "As Jesus' own way, by divine necessity leads to rejection, suffering and death, and only so to glory, so also the way of those who follow him"[23] (cf. Matt. 16:21; Mark 8:31-38; 10:35-45). On the basis of a comparison of Paul's writings with the Servant Songs of Isaiah, D. M. Stanley suggests that Paul found in the Suffering Servant figure the pattern for his own ministry.[24]

[21]Greek, *ton auton pathematon.* The better MSS do not contain the second *and salvation* in 6 and have a different word order (see ASV, RSV, NASB).

[22]*Op. cit.,* p. 280.

[23]*Lordship and Discipleship* (London: SCM Press, 1960), p. 20.

[24]"The Theme of the Servant of Yahweh in Primitive Christian Soteriology, and Its Transposition by Saint Paul," *Catholic Biblical Quarterly,* XVI (1954), 385-425. Cf. Phil. 2:6 with Isa. 49:4; Rom. 10:15 with Isa. 52:7 and 53:1; II Cor. 5:20 with Isa. 52:7; Acts 26:12-18 with Isa. 42:1-16.

The verses before us (3-7) indicate that in his own life most specifically Paul experienced those afflictions which he looked upon as a necessary part of God's redeeming activity. (He uses here the editorial **we** and **us** in reference to himself.) By **the sufferings of Christ** (5), "Paul means not only the endurance of persecution, but all that the struggle with sin cost him, both within and without."[25] For him such sufferings were integral to Christian service in general and an essential element of his apostolic ministry in particular (Acts 9:15-16). When Paul writes to the Colossians that through his sufferings he is completing in his flesh what is lacking in Christ's afflictions (Col. 1:24), he is viewing his own actual sufferings as a real participation in the sufferings of Christ. This is because they are endured for Christ's sake and in vital fellowship with Him; the Spirit of Christ is the life-principle of Paul's service for Christ.

In Phil. 3:10-11 suffering is a part of the perfecting path which leads to the resurrection from the dead. These sufferings, which include the actual afflictions of Paul's life, comprehend the lifelong state of death ("being made conformable unto his death" —see 4:11-12; Rom. 8:36) inaugurated through the power of the Spirit. Thus through the bond of the resurrection Spirit, Paul can call them "His sufferings" (NASB). At the heart of the sharing in the sufferings of Christ lies the experience of union with Christ in His death and resurrection. For Paul this intimacy with his Lord is so close that he can regard his apostolic career as an inner participation in His sufferings. This is so vital for the apostle that he proclaims to the Corinthians, in the words of Ahern, that "the glorious Savior claims as his own the sufferings which the dynamic presence of his Spirit occasions in his members."[26] Such a view of his afflictions gives to Paul (a) a new revelation of God (3, 5) and (b) a new power to comfort others (4-7).[27]

2. Affliction and Deliverance (1:8-11)

The thanksgiving continues. Paul accounts for its peculiar nature (cf. I Cor. 1:4-9) by reference to an incident of extreme

[25]R. H. Strachan, *The Second Epistle of Paul to the Corinthians* ("The Moffatt New Testament Commentary"; New York: Harper and Brothers, 1935), p. 48.

[26]"The Fellowship of His Sufferings (Phil. 3:10), A Study of St. Paul's Doctrine of Christian Suffering," *Catholic Biblical Quarterly*, XXII (January, 1960), 32.

[27]Denney, *op. cit.*, pp. 722 ff.

personal peril which had happened to him in the Roman province
of Asia (see map 1). Through this experience of affliction and
deliverance, most especially, Paul was able to encourage the Corinthians in the manner that he did (3-7).

The reference to the **trouble** (8) [28] is obscure as to place and
kind. Paul was relating it only as an occasion for testifying to the
mercies of God. The language fits best a situation due to mob
violence, possibly at Ephesus, but hardly the one described in
Acts 19:23-41. Other suggestions include Paul's anxiety concerning the Corinthians (2:13; 7:5), a serious illness, Paul's thorn in
the flesh (12:7), and his fighting with wild beasts in Ephesus
(I Cor. 15:32). [29]

The affliction was **so great** (10) [30] that Paul **despaired even
of life** (8). As far as he could see he, like Isaac (Heb. 11:17-19),
had received the **sentence of death** (9). But the divine purpose
(*hina*) of such deep despair, Paul learned, was "to prove to him
his own helplessness" [31] and to teach him, like Abraham (Rom.
4:17), to rely utterly on the **God which raiseth the dead.** Here is
a chord which reverberates throughout the entire letter (2:13-14;
4:7-12, 16; 12:7-10; 13:4). The God who delivered Paul and on
whom he had set his hope [32] for future deliverance (10) [33] is the
God who raised Jesus from the dead—the God of the Resurrection (Rom. 1:4; 8:11; I Corinthians 15; Eph. 1:19-20). This is
his proclamation (Acts 17:18). This is his testimony!

Involved in the gift (*charisma*) of God's deliverance are the
prayers of the Corinthians for Paul (11). [34] He asks that their
prayers continue in order that "thanks may be given by many

[28]The **to us** is not found in the better MSS.

[29]This last would demand a literal interpretation of I Cor. 15:32, which is
highly improbable.

[30]V. 8: "We were burdened excessively, beyond our strength" (NASB).

[31]Plummer, *op. cit.*, p. 18. Stanley suggests that, "given Paul's character,
the realization of his total dependence upon God was perhaps the most
difficult supernatural truth he ever had to assimilate" (*Christ's Resurrection in Pauline Soteriology, op. cit.*), p. 130.

[32]**We trust** (*elpikamen*) is lit. "we have set our hope."

[33]The **doth deliver** reads "will deliver" in the better MSS. The **that**
should probably also be omitted and the untranslated *kai* made the beginning of a new sentence: "And he will yet deliver *us,* ye also helping . . ."

[34]Although the general meaning is clear, the exact translation of the
verse is difficult. **Persons** is literally "faces." The RSV renders the verse:
"You also must help us by prayer, so that many will give thanks on our
behalf for the blessings granted us in answer to many prayers."

persons on our behalf" (ASV). Although it is God who freely delivers, Paul values highly the intercessory prayers of other Christians. The function of such prayer is twofold. It emphasizes the utter dependence of man and the absolute sovereignty of God; and it both expresses and promotes the fellowship of the saints.[35]

In his introduction (1-11) Paul witnesses effectively out of his own experience that "the God and Father of our Lord Jesus Christ" (NASB) is the God who comforts us (4) and the **God which raiseth the dead** (9).[36] The connection between the two is both real and significant. Thus we see how Paul can set affliction before us as a school of sympathy (4), of encouragement (5), and of hope (10).[37]

[35]Philip E. Hughes, *op. cit.*, p. 23.

[36]Both phrases contain a "timeless present participle expressing a permanent attribute" (Plummer, *op. cit.*, p. 18).

[37]*Ibid.*, p. 19.

Section II The Apostolic Ministry

II Corinthians 1:12—7:16

Paul opens the main body of the letter with a brief defense of his conduct in relation to the Corinthian church (1:12—2:17). This moves him to discuss at length the character of his apostolic ministry (3:1—6:10). A few words about his attitude towards the church and his relationship to them concludes the section (6:11—7:16).

A. Paul Reveals His Intentions, 1:12—2:17

In this portion of the letter Paul's main concern as he explains his motives and conduct to the Corinthians is to assure them that "in holiness and godly sincerity . . . we have conducted ourselves . . . toward you" (12, NASB). He has not been insincere (1:12-14). The reason that he did not come (1:15-22) was out of consideration for them (1:23—2:4) and for the one whom they are to forgive (2:5-11). He did in fact come as far as Macedonia (2:12-13). Through it all he has reason to praise God (2:14-17).

1. The Sincerity of His Correspondence (1:12-14)

These verses are transitional. Paul can ask for the help of the Corinthians in prayer (11), because (for, 12), contrary to the accusation of his opponents, his life has been pure and his purposes transparent among them. This assertion of integrity also prepares the way for the further defense of his conduct (cf. v. 15).

Paul's **rejoicing** (12, lit., boasting;[1] "exultation," Berk.), based on **the testimony** given by his **conscience**, is that his **conversation** (behavior) has not been, like that of his adversaries, in the realm of (*en*) "a wisdom dominated by human motives"[2]

---

[1]Here *kauchesis* is "act of boasting," and in v. 14 *kauchema* is probably "reason for boasting" or the "completed boast" (see Plummer, *op. cit.*, p. 24). With the verb *kauchasthai* these words occur altogether 29 times in this letter, more than in all the rest of the NT.

[2]William Barclay, *The Letters to the Corinthians* ("The Daily Study Bible"; Edinburgh: The Saint Andrew Press, 1954), p. 193. Hereafter cited as Barclay in the text.

(I Cor. 1:20; 2:6; cf. 3:1-3). Rather it has been in (*en*) the realm of **the grace of God** with (*en*) the "holiness[3] and sincerity of God" (ASV). Both are divine qualities[4] which as God's gifts are able to characterize the conduct of Paul. "Holiness" stresses the "moral purity"[5] of Paul's outward behavior, **sincerity** the transparency (2:17; I Cor. 5:8) of his inner motives.

This sincerity extends also to his letters, for what they **read** (13) from him is consistent with what they **acknowledge** ("understand," RSV; cf. 6:9; 13:5) him to be. There are no hidden undertones. Paul hopes that they "will understand fully" (RSV), just as they have understood **in part** (14) already. He desires that they may be able to boast of him as he of them (I Thess. 2:19) at **the day of the Lord Jesus** (the day of judgment; cf. I Cor. 1:8; 5:5; I Thess. 5:2).[6] Paul's main point in view of the criticism is that their knowledge of him might be such that they may be as proud of him as he of them in the day when all secrets are open (14).

Thus Paul rests the general defense of his personal integrity in these verses, first on the witness of his conscience (12), and second in the partial acknowledgment by the Corinthians of the genuineness of his apostolic ministry to them (13-14).

2. The Integrity of His Travel Plans (1:15-22)

Because he had not carried through his announced itinerary (I Cor. 4:19; 16:5-6), certain of the Corinthians had challenged Paul's integrity. Before he explains the actual reason for his change of plans Paul first denies the charge of fickleness and then

---

[3]Reading with the better MSS *hagiotes* rather than *haplotes* (**simplicity**). Otto Procksch, "*hagiotes*," TDNT, I, 114, on internal criteria prefers *haplotes*. *Hagiotes* occurs in the NT only here and in Heb. 12:10, "partakers of his [God's] holiness." See I Pet. 1:15.

[4]Jean Hering, *La Seconde Epitre de Saint Paul aux Corinthians* ("Commentaire du Nouveau Testament"; Paris: Delachaux and Niestle, 1958), p. 24, points out that **sincerity** (*eilikrineia*, perhaps "examined by the sun") is used in LXX, Wisdom of Solomon 7:25, as a divine attribute. The genitive *tou theou* ("of God") most probably qualifies both nouns, though most scholars go along with the **godly sincerity** of the KJV (see RSV and NASB).

[5]William F. Arndt and F. Wilbur Gingrich, *A Greek-English Lexicon of the New Testament and Other Early Christian Literature* (Chicago: The University of Chicago Press, 1957), p. 10.

[6]See Isa. 13:6, 9; Jer. 46:10; Ezek. 30:3; Joel 1:15; 2:10-11, 31; Zech. 14:1; Acts 2:20.

proceeds to ground his integrity as a minister of Christ in the integrity of God himself: "God is faithful" (18, ASV, KJV marg.).

On the basis of the **confidence** (15) which Paul expressed in 12-14 he had wished to visit them both on his way to and on his way from **Macedonia** (16), and by them to be helped on his journey[7] to **Judaea** (see map 1). He desired that they should have "the benefit of a double visit" (15, NEB; lit., "have a second grace"[8]). The expression is peculiar. Wendland notes that "a tremendous awareness of power comes to light in these words: The apostle is the bearer of divine grace, and his presence in the church signifies a time when grace is at work (see Rom. 1:11; 15:29)."[9] Paul wanted to be a blessing to them both going and coming.

In the meantime, however, as a result of a very "painful visit" (2:1, RSV; cf. 13:1-2) to the church, Paul had felt it best to alter his intentions. Such change of plans, according to his critics in Corinth, was evidence of the **lightness** ("levity"[10]) of Paul's character (17). This inference the apostle finds incredible. "Therefore [appealing again to **this confidence**, v. 15], I was not vacillating when I intended to do this, was I?" (NASB) The form (*meti*) of this question and the more comprehensive one which follows anticipates a negative answer. He does not dispute the fact that he has changed his plans. But he does emphatically deny that he makes his plans "as a worldly man might make them, so that I say yes and no at the same time" (Barclay; cf. Matt. 5:37; Jas. 5:12). To make his decisions **according to the flesh** (5:16; 10:2; 11:18) would be in direct opposition to the life "according to the Spirit" (Rom. 8:4-8, RSV) or "by [*en*] the grace of God" (12), which he professes and which the church has experienced in him. Thus Paul makes his final appeal for the integrity of his relations with the Corinthians an appeal to the integrity of God

---

[7]I.e., with food, money, companions, means of travel (see Acts 15:3; Rom. 15:24; I Cor. 16:6, 11; Arndt and Gingrich, *op. cit.*, p. 716).

[8]*Chara* "joy" is as well supported in the Greek MSS as *charin*, "grace." So RSV has "a double pleasure." Both terms come from the same root and are not always clearly distinct from one another in meaning (Arndt and Gingrich, *op. cit.*, p. 885). See Hughes, *op. cit.*, pp. 30 ff., fn. 6.

[9]*Die Briefe an die Korinther* (7th ed., rev.; "Das Neue Testament Deutsch," ed. Paul Althaus; Gottingen: Vandenhoeck and Ruprecht, 1954), VII, 147.

[10]Arndt and Gingrich, *op. cit.*, p. 248.

himself: "But as God is faithful,[11] our word to you is[12] not yes and no" (18, NASB).

Paul proceeds in vv. 18-20 to vindicate his character with an argument, writes Denney, that "might be *repeated* by a hypocrite, but no hypocrite could ever have *invented* it."[13] His underlying assumption is that a man's character is transformed by that to which he gives his life. It was **the Son**[14] **of God**, Christ Jesus,[15] **who was preached** (19) among the Corinthians, not alone by Paul, but also by **Silvanus** (Acts 15:22, 27; I Thess. 1:1; II Thess. 1:1; I Pet. 5:12) **and Timothy.** This Christ has proved himself in their midst once and for all (*gegonen*) to be the grand "Yes" of God (Heb. 13:8). Paul the servant must be as his Master, and the Master is the true Son of His Father, the faithful God. Thus Paul's **word** (18) to them can hardly be untrustworthy.

It is God's "Yes" which Paul proclaims in Christ Jesus (cf. Rom. 15:18), for He is the "Yes" to **all the promises of God** (20). The OT Messianic promises of salvation are all realized in the person of Christ. "Wherefore also through him"[16] (ASV) is the **Amen**[17] (Rev. 3:14) which the Corinthians say in their public worship[18] (I Cor. 14:16) to **the glory of God** through Paul and

[11]Or with Plummer (*op. cit.*, p. 35) as a plain statement: "But God is faithful in that (*oti*) our word ..." See I Cor. 1:9; 10:13; I Thess. 5:24.

[12]The MS evidence favors the reading "is" over **was.**

[13]*Op. cit.*, p. 728.

[14]The Greek order *ho tou theou gar huios*, placing **God** (*theou*) in a prominent position, indicates the sequence of thought. For Paul's use of the title **Son** see Rom. 1:3-4, 9; 5:10; 8:3, 29, 32; I Cor. 1:9; 15:28; Gal. 1:16; 2:20; 4:4, 6; Eph. 4:13; Col. 1:13.

[15]Again as in v. 1 this is the Greek order, though some MSS have the KJV order.

[16]The better MSS do not contain **and in him,** but the meaning is not altered by its omission.

[17]**Amen** comes from a Hebrew root meaning "to be firm or faithful." In both the OT and NT **Amen** is "the acknowledgement of a word which is valid, and the validity of which is binding for me and then generally in this acknowledgement" (Heinrich Schlier, "amen," TDNT, I, 335 ff.). See Deut. 27:15; I Chron. 16:36; Neh. 5:13; Ps. 106:48; Jer. 28:6. The key words of this passage—**true** (18), **yea** (19-20), **he which stablisheth** (21), and **faith** (24)—may all be associated with this root. (See Hughes, *op. cit.*, p. 38, fn. 38.)

[18]By the spoken **Amen** the congregation is not only assenting to the Yes that God has spoken to His promises in the Christ-event, "but a placing of oneself under what has previously been said, a knowing of oneself to be bound by what has previously been stated" (Delling, *op. cit.*, p. 74).

his co-workers. It is due to Paul's ministry that they through their experience of Christ are able to praise God openly for the proof of His faithfulness to them in Jesus Christ. "How illogical, then," as Hughes puts it, "while by their 'Amen' attesting the trustworthiness of God, to suspect the trustworthiness of the Apostle who taught them to do so!"[19] Paul in a very subtle manner confronts the Corinthians with their own charge of inconsistency.

We see next the final phase of Paul's affirmation of the integrity of his travel plans. It is an appeal to a present, progressive experience confirmed by three decisive, simultaneous acts of the Holy Spirit in his life (21-22). In practice Paul grounds his reliability as an apostle in his dynamic union with Christ: it is **in** (*eis*) **Christ** (21) that **God** continuously establishes (makes firm; I Cor. 1:8; Col. 2:7) Paul **with** the Corinthians. As members of the body of Christ, His personal qualities are transmitted to them and they are able to reproduce in their own lives the actions of Jesus.[20] **Stablisheth** (*bebaion*) is a legal term which represents the relationship as one that is legally indisputable or indestructible.[21]

Paul applies the decisive action of the Spirit expressed by the three aorists **anointed . . . sealed . . . given** primarily but not exclusively to his own calling and commission (Acts 9:15-18). He has been **anointed** by the Spirit as was Christ (lit., Anointed One; Isa. 61:1-3; Mark 1:10-11; Luke 4:18-19; cf. Acts 26:17-18) with power for an effective witness (Acts 1:8; 5:32; see John 3:34; 15:26-27). In the OT prophets (I Kings 19:16), priests (Lev. 16:32) and kings (I Sam. 15:1) were anointed for the task of their office. Anointing carries with it the concepts of authenticity and reliability (cf. I John 2:20, 27). Paul has been **sealed** (22) by the Spirit of Christ (3:17; Rom. 8:9), who stamps His own image (Rom. 8:29; Col. 1:15) on the human personality. This seal of the Holy Spirit guarantees the genuineness of his relation to God (Eph. 1:13; II Tim. 2:19; Rev. 9:4; cf. Rom. 4:11; I Kings 21:8) and protects him in that relationship (Eph. 4:30; see Dan. 6:17).

---

[19]*Op. cit.,* p. 38.

[20]Margaret E. Thrall, *The First and Second Letters of Paul to the Corinthians* (Cambridge: Cambridge University Press, 1965), p. 126.

[21]G. Adolf Deissmann, *Bible Studies,* trans. A. Grieve (Edinburgh: T. and T. Clark, 1901), pp. 104 ff.

Sealing is the mark of identification and security (Ezra 9:4; Esther 3:12; Jer. 32:10-14).

Thirdly, Paul has been **given the earnest**[22] **of the Spirit** in his heart. He speaks of the gift of the Spirit (Acts 2:38; 15:8-9) under the legal figure of the first installment which guarantees the full payment. It is "the same in kind,"[23] "the firstfruits of the Spirit" (Rom. 8:23; cf. 5:5). A piece of the future has already become present and as such is the pledge of the future. By the use of the term **earnest** Paul links the Spirit to the fulfillment of God's promises (22), to the resurrection life of the redeemed (5:5), and to the inheritance of redemption (Eph. 1:14).[24] Lightfoot suggests that the metaphor **earnest** contains another related idea:

> The recipient of the earnest-money not only secures to himself the fulfillment of the compact from the giver, but he *pledges himself* to accomplish his side of the contract. By the very act of accepting the part payment, he has bound himself over to a certain reciprocation. The gift of the Spirit is not only a *privilege,* but also *an obligation* . . . The Spirit has, as it were, a lien upon us.[25]

Paul's case for the integrity of his intention as a minister of Christ is now complete. The faithfulness of God (18) certified by Christ (19-20) is verified in his life and ministry by the Spirit (21-22),[26] whom the Corinthians have also experienced. In view of the integrity of God thus realized, surely they can see how groundless are their accusations.

3. *The Reason He Did Not Come* (1:23—2:4)

Paul now returns to his original intention to visit Corinth (1:15-16), which he had not felt free to carry through. This change of plans was not due to a defect in his personal integrity, but rather to his deep concern for them. As Paul lays bare his

[22]*Arrabon,* "first installment, deposit, pledge, down payment," is a Semitic loan word (see Gen. 38:17-20; Arndt and Gingrich, *op. cit.,* p. 109).

[23]J. B. Lightfoot, *Notes on Epistles of St. Paul from Unpublished Commentaries* (New York: Macmillan and Co., 1895), p. 323.

[24]Neill Q. Hamilton, *The Holy Spirit and Eschatology in Paul, Scottish Journal of Theology Occasional Papers No. 6* (Edinburgh: Oliver and Boyd Ltd., 1957), p. 20.

[25]*Op. cit.,* p. 324.

[26]See G. Campbell Morgan, *The Corinthian Letters of Paul* (New York: Fleming H. Revell Company, 1946), p. 230.

motives, we are granted a revealing insight into the heart of a true minister of Jesus Christ.

The apostle undergirds the truth of his explanation with a solemn oath: **Moreover I call God for a record** (lit., witness) **upon my soul** (23). He is calling upon God to support his testimony, to add His witness to Paul's in line with the scriptural principle that an unsupported testimony does not stand (cf. John 5:31-37). In v. 19 he has named two witnesses besides himself. Paul's statement could also mean that, conscious of God's scrutiny of the secrets of his heart, he would not dare to lie (cf. 11:31; Rom. 1:9). The actual reason that "he came no more" (NASB)[27] was to **spare** them an unpleasant exercise of his apostolic authority. He wanted to give them time to repent, so that his coming might result in joy (cf. I Cor. 4:31).

But for fear that a possible inference from his explanation might offend these touchy Corinthians, Paul hastens to assure them that he does not dictate ("lord it over," RSV) their **faith** (24; cf. 4:5). Faith has to be free. Ministers are rather **helpers of** their **joy:** "The kingdom of God is . . . joy in the Holy Ghost" (Rom. 14:17). Furthermore he has no need to dominate them, **for** it is **by faith that** they **stand.** This expression, however, may more likely imply that they are standing firm in their faith. What is significant from these verses concerning the character of Paul's ministry is that "he was not one of those who love to be censors of the faults of others" nor "one of those who love to rule."[28]

It was not only to spare them, but perhaps also for his own sake (2:1) that Paul **determined** (*ekrina,* cf. I Cor. 2:2) **not to come again** to them **in heaviness** (1).[29] A second visit to Corinth made previous to this writing, but not recorded in Acts, had turned into a very painful experience for both Paul and the church. He had no desire to precipitate such a situation again unless apostolic duty absolutely demanded it. For in the light of his conviction that the prime function of the Christian ministry is the promotion of mutual joy (cf. 1:24), how could his heart be

---

[27]Rather than **came not as yet**, which would imply only one visit of Paul to Corinth previous to this writing. See Introduction.

[28]F. W. Robertson, *Expository Lectures on St. Paul's Epistles to the Corinthians* (London: Smith, Elder, and Co., 1859), pp. 330 ff.

[29]"Grief, sorrow, pain," Arndt and Gingrich, *op. cit.,* p. 438. In vv. 1-7 the words rendered by **heaviness, sorry, sorrow,** and **grief** are derived from the same Greek root.

cheered by those whom[30] he had **made sorry** (2)? And as their spiritual father (I Cor. 4:14), why should he have **sorrow** from those who **ought to** make him **rejoice** (3)?

So rather than visit them at such an inopportune time Paul had sent instead a "sorrowful letter" (3-4), written **out of** (*ek*) **much affliction and anguish of heart . . . with** (*dia*) **many tears.**[31] Any grief the letter would cause was transcended by its twofold purpose. Its first design was the prompting of joy in both apostle and people. For if it accomplished its purpose of inciting repentance towards Paul—and that it did (cf. 7:8-9)— Paul could rejoice. And he wrote with the **confidence** that his **joy** would be shared by the Corinthians. Second, he intended to reveal the only valid basis for his authority over them as a minister, **the love**[32] which he had especially for them.

Anguish and love course together in the heart of him whose ministry is one in spirit with His who was "a man of sorrows, and acquainted with grief," who has "borne our griefs, and carried our sorrows" (Isa. 53:3-4). Those who wish a share in Christ's ministry among men must pursue His method. "Depend upon it, we shall not make others weep over that for which we have not wept; we shall not make that touch the hearts of others which has not first touched our own."[33] This is God's work principle in the world, one to which He himself submitted in His Son. He who would minister to men in Christ's name cannot escape it.

4. Forgiveness for the Offender (2:5-11)

The "sorrowful letter" was occasioned by the offense of a particular person in the church at Corinth. This one is to be freely forgiven by all concerned. But Paul in his delicate regard for the dignity and feelings of the individual does not name either the offender or the offense. He says only what is actually needed for his relations with the church. The Corinthians knew what he meant, but it is difficult for us to be certain. The offender has been traditionally identified with the incestuous man of I Cor.

---

[30]The Greek is singular (*tis ho*), referring possibly to the **man** of vv. 5-11, but more probably used here in a general sense. See Plummer, *op. cit.*, p. 48.

[31]See Introduction.

[32]For love (*agape*) in Paul see Rom. 5:5; 13:8; I Cor. 13:1-13; Gal. 5:6, 22; Col. 13:14. See E. Stauffer and G. Quell, "*agapao*," TDNT, I, 21-55.

[33]Denney, *op. cit.*, p. 735.

5:1-5.[34] It suits the situation better, however, if he is viewed with more recent interpreters as one who had been guilty of a personal insult to Paul. When the apostle made his second visit to Corinth to deal with the difficulty prompted by hostile intruders (11:4, 20), this man acted as the ringleader for the opposition and turned the occasion into a very distressing one for Paul (2:1). So these verses hint at the heart of the dissension between Paul and the Corinthians.

Although the offense was very personal, Paul refused to consider it on this level (5). As a modern version paraphrases the verse, "Any injury that has been done, has not been done to me; to some extent, not to labour the point, it has been done to you all" (NEB). The words **in part** belong with **you all;** thus the RSV has "in some measure . . . to you all." The phrase **that I may not overcharge**[35] is parenthetical. The affront was really to the integrity of the entire church, although a part of the church did not see it that way.

Since the church in response to Paul's letter had taken steps to punish the offender, Paul's plea is for mercy on the man who was his enemy (6). The **punishment** inflicted by the **many** ("the majority," RSV) has been **sufficient** for the situation. "The majority" suggests a minority who did not assent to the disciplinary measures, or possibly who felt that the church had not been severe enough. Paul's point is that the proper repentance is in evidence which enables the church now to turn from discipline, and to **forgive** (cf. Col. 3:13), and **comfort** the offender (7). The goal of punishment was not vengeance but restoration. The man must be reinstated before his excessive **sorrow** drives him to despair and thus from the redeeming fellowship of the church. So Paul's urgent plea is that they **confirm** ("reaffirm," NASB) their **love** for him (8). But Paul does not command forgiveness on the basis of his apostolic authority. Rather he urges it as a fellow Christian in keeping with the character of Christian love.

Such a demonstration of discipline and love was indeed the very reason Paul had written the "sorrowful letter" (9). His

---

[34]For a modern defense of this view, see Hughes, *op. cit.*, pp. 59 ff. For the contrary, see Plummer, *op. cit.*, pp. 54 ff.

[35]*Epibareu,* lit., "weigh down, burden," with the probable meaning here "in order not to say too much." Other possibilities are "exaggerate, be too severe with" (Arndt and Gingrich, *op. cit.*, p. 290).

purpose as he expressed it was to **know the proof of you** ("put you to the test," NASB), **whether ye** are (*este*) **obedient in all things** (cf. 7:15; 10:6). At stake in their response to his letter was the proper recognition of Paul's apostolic authority as well as their integrity as a "church of God" (1:1).

Since the Corinthians had joined Paul in the expression of condemnation, he joins them in the granting of forgiveness (10). His words are literally, "But to whom you forgive anything, I also; for what I also have forgiven (if I have forgiven anything) was for your sakes in the presence of Christ."[36] In "a gracious parenthesis"[37] Paul indicates the depth of his Christlike spirit (cf. Luke 23:34), for he speaks of the offense as merely hypothetical. Forgiveness has been in his heart from the first. He has forgiven and forgotten it **for** their **sakes** as one who lives in the presence of Christ (cf. 2:17; 4:2; I Cor. 4:5; Gal. 2:20).

What Paul precisely has in mind by **for your sakes** is **lest Satan should get an advantage of** (outwit) **us** (11). For if he and the church were to withhold their forgiveness from the offender, Satan could very well regain control of their Christian brother through his excessive sorrow (cf. v. 7). But just as damning would be the presence of a harsh, unforgiving spirit in their own hearts. By such a spirit Satan would have defrauded them of their "joy and peace in believing" (Rom. 15:13) and of the bond of love (Col. 3:14) which must characterize the Church as a saving fellowship. For such an outcome they would be personally accountable to Christ, for He is the all-comprehending motive for the exercise of forgiveness. Paul knew that the enemy would take an advantage of a strict sense of justice and of the sorrow of the repentant man. He therefore warns, **We are not ignorant of his devices** ("designs," RSV). He would say, "Let us not be hesitant with our forgiveness and assurances of love, lest Satan use what is our good against us for evil." To promote disunity within the congregation is one of Satan's ways of thwarting the purposes of Christ.

Within the context of the church "Forgiveness Is a Must": (1) For the sake of the one who does wrong, 5-7; (2) For the spiritual well-being of those whose part it is to forgive, 8-10; and (3) For the integrity of the fellowship of the church, 11.

---

[36]This rendering follows the older and better MSS.

[37]Plummer, *op. cit.*, p. 62.

5. *The Trip to Troas and Macedonia* (2:12-13)

As he returns to the theme of his itinerary, Paul provides the Corinthians with further proof that his change of plans did not indicate a vacillating character or a lack of love for them on his part. He had come to the seaport town of **Troas** (see map 1) with the primary purpose to preach **Christ's gospel** (12). There he discovered that the **door** (cf. Acts 14:27; I Cor. 16:9; Col. 4:3) of evangelistic opportunity had been opened wide for him in (*en*) the service of **the Lord**: "There was free liberty to speak, and many were willing to hear."[38] Augustine comments that this is "a most manifest demonstration that even the very beginning of faith is the gift of God."

Paul intended to occupy himself with this mission until **Titus** (13), his Greek "partner and fellowhelper" (8:16, 23; cf. 7:6-7; Gal. 2:1; II Tim. 4:10; Titus 1:4), returned from Corinth with the news of the situation there (7:6-15). But he was so overwhelmingly concerned for the spiritual welfare of the Corinthians that he could find no **rest** ("relaxation, relief"[39] from affliction; cf. 2:4; 7:5) for his **spirit**. So he "said good-bye" (Goodspeed) to his new converts and proceeded on **into Macedonia**, hoping to meet Titus on the way. So great was his anxiety for the Corinthians that for their sakes he would abandon a promising missionary opportunity. Certainly they could not now question the integrity of his attachment to them. He had robbed others out of concern for them, a fact on which they ought to reflect with shame.

Paul was certainly not an insensitive Stoic with a calm spirit that nothing could disturb. He was a thoroughly human person, a Christian who for the sake of the church could get emotionally involved (cf. 2:4). Paul experienced grief, shed tears, and anxiety overtook him.

6. *Thanksgiving for Triumph in Christ* (2:14-17)

Praise to **God** (14) bursts forth from Paul's heart at the thought of the **triumph** of the gospel in Corinth. This outburst begins a digression which continues until 7:5. There Paul again resumes the narration of his anxiety concerning the Corinthians

---

[38]John Wesley, *Explanatory Notes upon the New Testament* (London: The Epworth Press, 1950), p. 648.

[39]Arndt and Gingrich, *op. cit.*, p. 64.

which was relieved by the encounter with Titus. Although it interrupts the narrative, this digression with its soaring insights provides living flesh for the structural bones of the argument.

Paul unites two pictures to depict the triumphal course of the gospel through the apostolic ministry: "But thanks be to God, who always leads us in His triumph in Christ,[40] and manifests through us the sweet aroma of the knowledge of Him in every place" (NASB). The first metaphor is that of a triumphal procession of a victorious Roman general.[41] It is difficult to be certain whether the use of the metaphor is only general, with Paul occupying a place of honor, or if he views himself specifically as a conquered captive in the procession. The resultant meaning is much the same either way. If a captive, the nature of the captivity is such that it is in the deepest sense also triumph for Paul—triumph in Christ because it is God who triumphs over him! The victory of the gospel is Christ's and the apostle is privileged to share in it.

> *Make me a captive, Lord,*
> *And then I shall be free.*
> *Force me to render up my sword,*
> *And I shall conqueror be.*[42]

The second metaphor is that of an offering burning on an altar of sacrifice, sending up a pleasing aroma to God (cf. Gen. 8:20; Exod. 29:18; Ezek. 20:41; Mal. 3:4; Eph. 5:2; Phil. 4:18). This **savour** (*osmen*) is the **knowledge** of Christ which has been made **manifest** through the apostolic ministry **in every place**. The reason for the sweetness is that "we are a fragrance [*euodia*] of Christ" (NASB), pleasing to God both "among those who are being saved and among those who are perishing" (15, RSV). Being "in Christ" was the character of their ministry, whether men received or rejected the gospel they proclaimed. And this gospel was a fragrance of Christ!

The effect of the gospel ministry is twofold. Those who resist it find it "a savour [*osme*] from [*ek*][43] death unto [*eis*] death"

---

[40]For a treatment of the phrase "in Christ" in the writings of St. Paul see John B. Nielson, *In Christ* (Kansas City, Mo.: Beacon Hill Press, 1960).

[41]For a description of a Roman triumph see Barclay, *op. cit.*, p. 205.

[42]George Matheson.

[43]The preposition is omitted in the text underlying the KJV. For this combination of prepositions (*ek . . . eis*) see Rom. 1:17.

(ASV), and those who respond to it discover it "a savour [osme] from[43] life unto life" (16, ASV). There is a rabbinical concept of the Law as a drug whose effect could be either fatal or vitalizing, depending on how it is approached.[44] Similarly, Paul's view of the ministry of the gospel of grace is that it is inevitably a sentence of death to some and an opportunity of life for others (cf. 4:3; Luke 2:34; I Cor. 1:18; Phil. 1:28). The same act of salvation which has destroyed death for the saved has made death irrevocable for those who **perish**. The responsibility entailed in a proclamation which would be "from beginning to end"[45] an occasion of death or life for men overwhelmed Paul. He could only utter, **Who is sufficient for these things?** (16) What kind of ministry could be adequate for such a task?

"Ours is!" Paul replies. **For** (gar) **we are not as many, who corrupt** (adulterate)[46] **the word of God** (17; cf. 11:13). The figure is originally that of a tavernkeeper who mixes poor wine with good to increase his profit (cf. Isa. 1:22, LXX).[47] This figure contains two ideas. The first concerns motives; they make apostleship a business for personal gain. The second implies method; they adulterate the gospel with more palatable demands and limited perspectives to further their own interests. The first leads to the second. In fact to approach the ministry with motives of personal profit, ambition, or vanity is already to adulterate it. He who makes the Word serve his advantage rather than being a servant of the Word changes the very character of the gospel.

Quite contrary to these "peddlers" (RSV) "who try to get what price they can and shape the Word of God accordingly"[48]

[44]Herman L. Strack and Paul Billerbeck, *Die Briefe des Neuen Testaments und die Offenbarung Johannis* ("Kommentar zum Neuen Testament aus Talmud und Midrash"; München: C. H. Beck'sche Verlagsbuchhandlung [Oskar Beck], 1926), III, 498 ff.: "He who occupies himself with the teaching of the Law for its own sake, for him it is a life-giving medicine. But whoso does not occupy himself with the teaching of the Law for its own sake, for him it is a deadly poison." The preceding translation is quoted from Strachan, *op. cit.*, p. 76.

[45]Denney, *op. cit.*, p. 741.   [46]Arndt and Gingrich, *op. cit.*, p. 404.

[47]Adam Clarke, *The New Testament of Our Lord and Saviour Jesus Christ, A Commentary and Critical Notes* (New York: Carlton & Phillips, 1854), II, 322.

[48]R. C. H. Lenski, *The Interpretation of St. Paul's First and Second Epistle to the Corinthians* (Columbus, Ohio: Wartburg Press, 1937), p. 904.

is the absolute **sincerity** of Paul's ministry (cf. 1:12; 12:19). He speaks "as from [*ek*] God" (NASB) and **in the sight of God** (cf. 4:2; 12:19); he speaks **in Christ** (cf. 1:14; 5:17). "He is one," comments Plummer, "who teaches with the openness and fullness which come from the God who inspires him; and in God's presence he works as befits a member of Christ."[49] In this lies his sufficiency (cf. 3:5-6), which he is soon to expound more clearly (3:1—6:10). It is the character of the gospel which qualifies both the motive and the method of his ministry. In these verses Paul has presented us with "The Apostolic Ministry": (1) The secret, 14-15*a*; (2) The solemnity, 15*b*-16*a*; and (3) The sincerity, 16*b*-17

As the apostle reveals his intentions to the Corinthians (1:12—2:17), the integrity of the man of God is seen (1) in his own conscience, 1:12; (2) by his conduct when among his converts, 1:13-14; (3) in the character of the God whom he proclaims, 1:15-22; (4) by his concern for those whom he serves in the gospel, 1:23—2:11; and (5) in the conquest of the gospel through his ministry, 2:14-17.

B. PAUL CHARACTERIZES HIS MINISTRY, 3:1—6:10

This new section of the letter, part of the digression of 2:14—7:4, bursts enthusiastically from Paul's dictation as he contemplates the great things that God has accomplished by means of an instrument as feeble as he (2:14-17). **We have this ministry** (4:1) is his theme as he delineates its character more precisely as a ministry of the Spirit (3:1—4:6), a ministry of suffering (4:7—5:10), and a ministry of reconciliation (5:11—6:10). A right view of Paul's ministry is necessary for the restoration of the right relation between the Corinthians and the apostle.

1. *A Ministry of the Spirit* (3:1—4:6)

The nature of Paul's apostolic ministry is such that he has no need of a letter of recommendation to the Corinthians (3:1-3). It is a ministry of a new covenant whose adequacy as the covenant of the life-giving Spirit surpasses that of the old (3:4-11), and whose liberty is that of the transforming Spirit of the Lord

[49]*Op. cit.,* p. 75.

(3:12-18). A ministry thus grounded in the mercy of God is completely open to men and before God (4:1-6).[50]

a. *Paul's letter of recommendation* (3:1-3). These verses look back to 2:17 and anticipate 3:4-6; they are transitional and introduce Paul's defense of his apostolic ministry, i.e., of himself, his office, and his message. In them he states that the recommendation of his ministry is simply the evident character of the Corinthians themselves. They are like a letter written by Christ himself with Paul as the scribe or courier.

Paul is fearful that the insistence on his sincerity (2:17) would be again turned into an accusation of self-praise by his enemies (cf. 4:2-5; 5:12; 6:4; 10:12), so he deftly fields the anticipated charge: "Do we need, as some do, letters of recommendation[51] to you, or from you?" (1, RSV) The question implies a negative answer, and with neat, almost sarcastic irony returns the charge to Paul's opponents. **Some** (cf. 2:17; 10:2; I Cor. 4:18; 15:12) had actually invaded the Corinthian church on the strength of "these bills of clearance for the profitable marketing of their merchandise in spiritual things."[52] The phrase **epistles of commendation** is a technical expression for a type of letter current in Paul's day[53] and commonly used by the Early Church. Philemon and Romans 16 are examples (cf. 8:16-19; Acts 9:2; 18:27; I Cor. 4:17; 16:3, 10-11; Col. 4:10). While letters of recommendation could be misused, they were often a necessity in the Early Church.

But Paul had no need to flourish such letters written on parchment or papyrus. Rather the Corinthians themselves constituted his apostolic credentials: **Ye are our epistle written in our hearts** ("your hearts," RSV),[54] **known and read of all men** (2). The unmistakable transformation that had taken place in the lives of the Corinthians through the power of the gospel (cf. Acts

---

[50]For devotional comments on this chapter see A. F. Harper, *Holiness and High Country* (Kansas City: Beacon Hill Press, 1964), pp. 338-40.

[51]The better Greek MSS have **commendation** only once in v. 1.

[52]Hughes, *op. cit.*, p. 85.

[53]William Baird, "Letters of Recommendation: A Study of II Cor. 3:1-3," *Journal of Biblical Literature*, LXXX (June, 1961), 168 ff. For a secular example see Deissmann, *op. cit.*, pp. 170 ff.

[54]In an effort to harmonize the metaphors of 3:1-3, RSV translates *humon* rather than the better supported *hemon* (KJV). See Baird, "Letters of Recommendation," *op. cit.*, p. 168.

4: 13-16) continually evidences (present participles) to all who know them the genuineness of Paul's apostleship (I Cor. 9:2; cf. Rom. 15:16). It is a deep, personal, and enduring love (**written** is a perfect participle) for these folk (2:4; 6:11-13; 7:2) that Paul carries about with him in his heart (not a letter in his luggage). This is in contrast to the **some** (1) whose ministerial motives were highly questionable (2:17; 11:13). For the apostle an authentic ministry is impossible apart from sincere motives and an intense concern for people.

Paul's letter of recommendation which has been **written** (*engegrammene*) in his heart (2) has been **written** (*engegrammene*) by **Christ** himself, **not with ink, but with the Spirit of the living God,** "not on tablets of stone, but on tablets of human hearts"[55] (3, NASB). The reference to the writing of the new covenant (Jer. 31:33; Ezek. 11:19; 36:26) in contrast to that of the old (Exod. 31:18; Deut. 9:10) has led most commentators to interpret the **heart** of 3:3 as that of the Corinthians. But it may be more plausible to identify **heart** in v. 3 with the use of **hearts** in 2 as the heart of Paul (cf. 1:21; 4:6). The stress, in line with the central concern of the letter, would then be on the character of his apostolic commission (cf. 3:6; 5:18-20). Thus Paul does not view himself as the amanuensis or scribe of the letter.[56] The letter is rather **ministered,** that is, "delivered" (RSV, cf. 8:19-20; Rom. 15:25) by him. Baird, whose interpretation we have been presenting, concludes that, though Paul does mix his metaphors, the figure of the new covenant is "introduced in order to expand the figure of the letter of recommendation. This letter is no literal epistle; the Corinthian church is its content; Christ is its author; Paul is its courier; indeed, it is written on his heart by the Spirit of God. Ultimately, that which commends the apostle is his divine commission which is symbolized by his reception of the ministry of the new covenant."[57] And it is this ministry of the Spirit, written first in his own heart and then delivered to

---

[55]Literally, "hearts of flesh," following the better MSS.

[56]Deissmann, *op. cit.,* p. 374. Plummer feels the metaphor cannot be pressed in detail either way. He paraphrases, "a letter composed by Christ and published by me." That is, "St. Paul and his colleagues were Christ's ministers in bringing the letter of recommendation into existence by converting the Corinthians" (*op. cit.,* pp. 76, 81). See NASB, "cared for by us."

[57]Baird, "Letters of Recommendation," *op. cit.,* p. 172. For the more common interpretation see commentaries such as Clarke, Denney, Hughes, or Plummer.

others, that he proceeds to enlarge upon by the contrast between letter and spirit in v. 6.

b. *The adequacy of the new covenant ministry* (3:4-11). Paul continues to guard himself against a misinterpretation of the triumphant description of his apostolic ministry (2:14-17). His motives have been pure, for he really has no need to commend himself to the Corinthians (3:1-3). Now in 4-11 the ground of his confidence is not in himself, for it is God who has made him adequate as a minister of the new covenant. This he has already intimated by his imagery in 3. As a ministry of the Spirit and not of the letter, the ministry of the new covenant transcends that of the old covenant. This Paul illustrates with an allusion to the shine on Moses' face, which he covered with a veil on account of the people after he returned to them from Mount Sinai (Exod. 34:29-35).

The **trust** (4; "confidence," ASV) Paul expresses refers primarily to his conviction that the Corinthians themselves constitute an irrefutable witness to the validity of his apostolic calling. He was convinced of the truth of the gospel and of the reality of his vocation. Hodge comments that "it is easy to determine whether such confidence is self-inflation, or the strength of God in the soul. If the former it has its natural concomitants of pride, arrogance, indifference, contempt of others. If the latter, it is attended by self-abhorrence, meekness, long-suffering, a willingness to be the least and lowest, and by all other graces of the Spirit."[58] **Such** confidence came to Paul **through Christ** from God, to whom he looked as its ultimate Source. It was not a human confidence, but one in a sense spoken face-to-face (*pros*) with God, one that could stand the test of the judgment.

Thus he further explains, it is **not that we are sufficient** (*hikanos*) **of ourselves** (5) even "to conceive a single thought on our own initiative"[59] (lit., "to think out from [*ek*] ourselves") in relation to the gospel and its ministry, **but our sufficiency** (*hikonotes*) **is of** (*ek*) **God** (cf. 4:7; 5:18; 6:4; 7:5-6; 11:23; 12:9-10; 13:3-4; I Cor. 15:10). Paul's grasp and mastery of his apostolic ministry did not stem from his own resources. He can lay

---

[58] *An Exposition of the Second Epistle to the Corinthians* (New York: Robert Carter and Brothers, 1868), p. 53.

[59] F. F. Bruce, *The Letters of Paul, An Expanded Paraphrase* (Grand Rapids: Wm. B. Eerdmans, 1965), p. 131. Hereafter cited in the text as Bruce.

no personal claim to his **sufficiency** in the gospel. By the same language with which he first raised the question in 2:16, "Who is sufficient?" Paul is developing his answer in 5 and 6 (cf. NASB, "adequate").

So with an allusion to his call (Acts 9:3-18; 22:14-16; 26:16-18; I Tim. 1:12), Paul insists that "our adequacy is from God, who also made us adequate [*hikanosen*] as servants[60] of a new covenant" (5-6, NASB). From the total biblical perspective "covenant"[61] is more suitable than **testament** as a translation of *diatheke* in the NT with the possible exception of Heb. 9:15-20. "Covenant" in the Bible refers to an agreement, not between equals, but between God and His people. It is constituted by God's gracious offer of His saving presence and confirmed by the grateful response of His people in the fulfilling of its obligations. Paul is a minister of a **new** covenant (Jer. 31:31-34; Matt. 26:28; Mark 14:24; Luke 22:20; I Cor. 11:25; Heb. 7:22; 8:6-13; 9:15-22), in contrast to the old (3:14; Exod. 24:3-8; Gal. 4:24). It is a newness (*kaines*) not only in time but also in kind—"fresh and effective . . . in contrast to worn out and obsolete"[62]—for it is **not of the letter, but of the spirit** (cf. Rom. 2:28-29).

By **letter** Paul views the old covenant as set down in an outward "written code" (RSV). By **spirit** he is characterizing the dispensation of the new covenant in Christ in terms of an inner dynamic, spiritual as contrasted to legal. Although the reference is not yet directly to the Holy Spirit (**spirit**, 6, 8; "Spirit," 17-18),[63] certainly the presence of God's Spirit is involved in a brand-new way. So while Paul's use of **spirit** is general in a qualitative sense, what he means cannot be understood apart from the operation of the Holy Spirit. The glory (cf. 7-11) of the ministry of the new covenant as a ministry of the spirit (cf. 8) is set in bold relief by the fact that **the letter killeth, but the spirit giveth life** (cf. Rom. 7:6). God's will and purpose expressed only in the form of written prohibitions could only incite and

---

[60]**Ministers.** This word with its cognates occurs significantly in vv. 3, 6-9.

[61]The LXX translates the Hebrew *berith* (covenant) by *diatheke*. See Arndt and Gingrich, *op. cit.*, p. 182; Gottfried Quell and Johannes Behm, *"diatheke,"* TDNT, II, 104-34; G. E. Mendenhall, "Covenant," IDB, *A-D,* 714-23.

[62]Plummer, *op. cit.*, p. 85.   [63]So Lenski, *op. cit.*, pp. 920 ff.

condemn sin (cf. Rom. 7:7-25);[64] for it was powerless due to the weakness of the flesh (Rom. 8:3). Thus it could lead only to death. But "the Spirit of life in Christ Jesus" (Rom. 8:2; cf. 3: 17; I Cor. 15:45) is able to engrave the will of God on the heart (3:3; Acts 15:9), enabling the Christian to fulfill the righteous requirements of a holy God (3:9; Rom. 8:4). The Law, however, was not invalidated, for "the law is holy" (Rom. 7:22). Rather it is established (Rom. 3:31) or fulfilled (Rom. 13:8-10; Gal. 5:14) when by the power of the constant presence of the Spirit of Christ (Rom. 8:2-9) faith operates through love (agape) in the ethical concern of the Christian (Gal. 5:6). The sufficiency of Paul's calling is that it is anchored in a superior ministry, the ministry of a transforming Spirit (3:18).

The apostle now brings out clearly what he has only alluded to previously (cf. 3, 6)—the contrast between the dispensations (cf. RSV) of the Law and of the Spirit, between the ministry of Moses and that of Paul. The ministry of **Moses** (7) is characterized by the **glory** ("brightness," RSV) of Moses' face. "Fading as it was" (NASB), it was yet so bright that **the children** (huious, "sons") **of Israel could not** "look intently" (NASB) at it (Exod. 34:29-30). Paul's emphasis is on the glory[65] or splendor of Moses' ministry as a revelation of the eternal will of God. Thus if **the ministration of death,**[66] "in letters, and engraven on stones"[67] (cf. Rom. 7:7-8; I Cor. 15:16) "came with such splendor" (RSV), isn't it obvious (ouchi), asks Paul, that **the ministration of the spirit**[66] (8) which gives life (3:6; cf. Gal. 3:5) "should . . . be attended with greater splendor" (RSV)?

So in the second phase of his contrast he explains further

[64]A very helpful discussion of Romans 7 can be found in Richard N. Longenecker, *Paul, Apostle of Liberty* (New York: Harper & Row, 1964), pp. 86-97, 109-16.

[65]**Glory** with its cognates is a key word in this passage which Paul made use of in view of its use by the LXX for the shine on Moses' face in Exod. 34:29 ff. It is used to express the awful holiness of the Divine Presence as unapproachable Light (Exod. 24:16-18), or of any revelation of God's will and purpose (4:4). God is most glorified when His holy character is recreated in human lives (3:18). See Strachan, *op. cit.*, pp. 85 ff., or Gerhard Kittel and Gerhard von Rad, *"doxa,"* TDNT, II, 233-53.

[66]Objective genitives, ministries which bring death and life, respectively.

[67]Plummer, *op. cit.*, p. 89, following the better MSS. **Engraven** is perfect tense with the import of engraved forever, i.e., the Law as a **ministration of death.**

that "if the ministry of condemnation[68] [Deut. 27:26; Gal. 3:10] has glory, much more does the ministry of righteousness[68] [Rom. 1:17; 5:17; 8:1-4; I Cor. 1:30] abound in glory" (9, NASB). "The office of the law," comments Calvin, "is to show us the disease, in such a way as to show us at the same time, no hope of cure; the office of the gospel is, to bring a remedy to those who were past hope."[69] The latter exceeds the former "because it is a greater matter to acquit the condemned sinner than to condemn him."[70] The one takes only the letter of the law on stones, the other the blood of God's own Son and the power of the Spirit. The righteousness[71] upon which Paul bases the superiority of his ministry is "the righteousness of God" revealed in "the gospel of Christ" (Rom. 1:16-17), which he expounds in terms of justification and sanctification in Rom. 3:31—8:39.

This contrast between ministries can even be considered so radical that the first, **which was made glorious** (10) as an instrument of God's self-revelation, now "in this case has no glory on account of the glory" (NASB) of the second, which so far surpasses it (cf. John 1:17; Rom. 10:4; Gal. 3:21-25). "Its glory is now dimmed like the shine of lamps when dawn comes" (R. A. Knox).[72]

Paul develops his final point of contrast (11) from the brightness of Moses' face (3:7), which was fading according to Jewish tradition even as he was coming down from Mount Sinai. He saw this as indicative of the transitory nature of the old covenant which Moses represented. The contrast is with the permanency of the dispensation of the Spirit. **For if that which is done away was glorious** (*dia doxes*), **much more that which remaineth is glorious** (*en doxe*).

So the adequacy of Paul's apostolic ministry is its superiority as a ministry of a new covenant—a ministry of the Spirit— (1) superior as life is more glorious than death, (2) as righteousness is more glorious than condemnation, and (3) as that which is permanent is more glorious than that which fades away.

---

[68]Once more objective genitives.

[69]*Commentary on the Epistles of Paul the Apostle to the Corinthians,* trans. John Pringle (Grand Rapids: W. B. Eerdmans, 1948), II, 178.

[70]Lenski, *op. cit.,* p. 930.   [71]See comment on 5:21.

[72]Quoted from Tasker, *op. cit.,* p. 63.

c. *The liberty of the new covenant ministry* (3:12-18). With such a ministry Paul, unlike his opponents, is able to speak out boldly, concealing nothing. Paul's ministry, unlike that of Moses, who personifies the Law, possesses the liberty of the Spirit of the Lord which enables all to behold the glory of the Lord in a life-transforming manner.[73]

Paul declares that the **great plainness of speech** (*parresia*) with which he conducts his ministry is based on the **hope** that he has (12). He speaks of the ministry of the new covenant as a **hope** first in view of its permanence (cf. 11); it has a glorious future (cf. 8, *estai*). Second, it is a **hope** because the glory of God's future age is authentically present in the ministry of the Spirit (cf. 1:21-22; Rom. 8:24). Such an adequate **hope** (cf. 1: 5-6) allows, indeed demands, a ministry that is courageous and outspoken (for *parresia,* cf. Mark 8:32; John 7:4; Acts 4:29, 31; 28:31; Col. 2:15; Heb. 4:16; 10:35).

To illustrate this assertion of great openness Paul returns to the contrast of his ministry with that of Moses, which was characterized by concealment. The KJV translation of Exod. 34:33 gives the impression that Moses covered his face in order to avoid frightening the Israelites by the glory of his countenance. This interpretation seems consistent with the whole OT account. However, the Hebrew text of this verse in Exodus and Paul's interpretation of the event indicate a further fact. Moses' practice was to **put a veil over his face** (13) *after* he had delivered God's message to the people (cf. Exod. 34:33-35, RSV, Berk., Amp. OT). This was done so **that the children of Israel could not stedfastly look to the end** of "what was fading away" (NASB). *The Berkeley Version* translates it, "to keep the sons of Israel from gazing at something that faded." Paul's point here is that the Israelites were not permitted (v. 13) to gaze on Moses' glory while it passed away.[74] In v. 7 he had made the point that they were not permitted to look at that glory uninterruptedly. The limitations

---

[73]Although the general sense of vv. 12-18 is plain, the interpretation of some of the details is difficult. The writer can only present his best exegetical judgments.

[74]Interpreting *eis to telos* with Hughes, *op. cit.*, p. 109, fn. 6, as "right on to the end" rather than "on the end." See pp. 107 ff. for a full discussion of the interpretation of v. 13 followed in this paragraph. For the two alternative interpretations see Plummer, *op. cit.*, p. 97, and R. V. G. Tasker, *The Second Epistle of Paul to the Corinthians* ("The Tyndale New Testament Commentaries"; London: The Tyndale Press, 1958), pp. 64 ff.

of that dispensation were such that its ministry had to conceal even a transient glory. Paul's ministry is just the opposite. He uses, not a veil, but **great plainness of speech.** His is a message, not of condemnation and death, but of grace, mercy, and life. By faith the Christian can gaze intently on his Lord without interruption.

The reason for the veil over Moses' face was that **their minds were blinded** (14; "hardened," RSV) because of their moral rejection of light (cf. Acts 28: 27; Rom. 1: 21). Further, and in verification of what he has just said, this **same veil** "remains unlifted" (NASB) **until this day, when Moses** (the old covenant) **is read** (14-15). This is true because the veil "is removed (only) in Christ"[75] (NASB). Paul is now speaking of the present spiritual blindness of Israel, which was identical to that of their ancestors. The proper reception of the message of Moses would have prepared the way for Christ (cf. John 5: 46-47). But the veil remains, since they are not in any great measure returning to Christ (cf. Romans 9—11). **Nevertheless,** whenever the **heart** of Israel **shall turn to the Lord, the veil shall be taken away** (16), just as Moses removed the veil from his face in the presence of the Lord (Exod. 34: 34). They will then be able "in Christ" to gaze steadfastly at the glory of the Lord, as Moses did. This was Paul's own personal experience as "an Hebrew of the Hebrews" (Phil. 3: 5). When he met the risen Jesus on the Damascus road, he began to see the true significance of the new covenant as fulfilled in Jesus Christ (Acts 10: 4). The veil had been removed from his spiritual understanding. The cross of Jesus, once so utterly despicable, was now bathed with the very glory of God himself.[76]

When it shall turn to the Lord is better rendered, "Whenever one turns to the Lord" (Berk.). **The Lord** to whom Paul turned for the veil to be taken away was Jesus, the risen Christ (14): "God hath made that same Jesus, whom ye have crucified, both Lord and Christ" (Acts 2: 36; cf. Ps. 110: 1; Mark 12: 35; Rom. 10: 9; I Cor. 12: 3; Phil. 2: 9-11). Here Paul, in line with the confession of the Early Church, identifies the resurrected and exalted Jesus as **the Lord**[77] of the OT before whom Moses appeared.

---

[75]See 2: 14, 17; 3: 14; 5: 17 for the phrase **in Christ,** so significant in Paul.

[76]Menoud, *op. cit.,* pp. 134-44.

[77]**Lord** (*Kyrios*) is the LXX translation of the sacred name Jehovah, or better Yahweh, for God in the OT.

Verse 16 is a direct quotation of Exod. 34:34. The God of the OT has revealed himself in Jesus Christ. There is no discontinuity or contradiction between the old and new covenants.

Now the Lord,[78] Paul goes on to make clear in terms of his argument, is **that** (the) **Spirit** (17). The word **that**, not actually present in the text, was inserted by the translators to bring out the connection with v. 6. **Spirit** is here capitalized in distinction to "spirit" (6), indicating the progression in Paul's thought. The Holy Spirit is now distinctly in view but not in terms of any personal identity with Christ. Rather Paul speaks of an identity occurring in redemptive action[79] by which he explains concretely why the veil concealing the glory of God is removed in Christ. From one perspective the Messianic revelation of the Spirit of God has taken place in Jesus Christ. From another, the total benefits of the new covenant are actually communicated to men by the Spirit. The Spirit is only where Christ is; and where the Spirit is, there is Christ.[80]

Paul's Christo-centric conception of the Spirit has been determined by his faith in Jesus Christ, and his experience of the Spirit (cf. 3) has convinced him of the spiritual nature of the new covenant ministry. The emphasis here is not on the personality of the Holy Spirit, for the Spirit is self-effacing in His presentation of Christ, so as not to detract from our Lord (John 15:26; 16:13). Paul's stress is rather on the power of the Spirit, for the quality of the redemptive action of the Spirit supremely characterizes the new dispensation in Christ (cf. John 4:24). He refers to the function of the Holy Spirit in order to more fully clarify the basic character of his ministry as one "not of the letter, but of the spirit" (6).

Thus Paul can boldly assert that, **where the Spirit of the Lord is, there is liberty.** This **liberty** is essentially freedom from the Law, release from the limitations of the old covenant (Rom. 7:5-6; Gal. 4:5-6; 5:1), by the purification of the heart. Freedom from the Law[81] as effected by the life-giving presence of the Holy

---

[78]The NEB identifies the threefold appearance of **Lord** in 16-17 with the Lord of the OT only: "Now the Lord of whom this passage speaks is the Spirit." See Thrall, *op. cit.*, p. 137. But this misses the point of Paul's transition from the old to the new covenant inherent in the passage.

[79]Hamilton, *op. cit.*, p. 6.   [80]Wendland, *op. cit.*, pp. 158 ff.

[81]It is this point and its implications that Paul is concerned to expound in Galatians 3—5 and in Romans 6—8.

Spirit comprehends freedom from sin (Rom. 6:6-7), from death (Rom. 6:21-23; 7:10-11), and from condemnation (Rom. 8:1, 17-21, 28-39): "There is therefore now no condemnation for those who are in Christ Jesus. For the law of the Spirit of life in Christ Jesus has set me free from the law of sin and death" (Rom. 8:1-2, RSV). It is the freedom of sonship (Rom. 8:14-16), the possession of the prospect of "the glorious liberty of the children of God" (Rom. 8:21; cf. John 8:36).

Paul crowns his contrast between Moses' ministry of the old covenant and his own ministry of the new as he reflects on the privilege of all Christians. All who are in Christ, who are now "with unveiled face beholding as in a mirror the glory of the Lord, are being transformed into the same image from glory to glory, just as from the Lord, the Spirit" (18, NASB). Formerly only Moses could thus gaze upon the glory of the Lord, for a veil hid even its fading reflection from the people of Israel, typifying the state of those under the law (13-15). But the veil has been removed from the hearts of all who have turned to the Lord and they are able by faith to behold Christ, "who is the image of God" (John 1:14; 14:9; II Cor. 4:4; Col. 1:15). And thus "beholding as in a mirror the glory of the Lord" (ASV),[82] the quality of their Christian lives is in the continual process of being **changed** (*metamorphoumetha*, Rom. 12:2; cf. Matt. 17:2; Mark 9:2, "transfigured") **into the same image**[83] (Gen. 1:26-27; Rom. 8:29; I Cor. 15:49; Col. 3:10). For just as a mirror reveals the physical features in order that one may be correctly groomed, so the constant faith-vision of Christ reveals the shortcomings of Christian character and inspires their correction. The transformation which results is a transformation **from glory to glory**, that is, into the likeness of Christ (Eph. 4:13). This transformation penetrates to the inner life of man (cf. 3; 4:16; Heb. 4:12-13), and will not cease until that day when we shall see "face to face" (I Cor. 13:12). Then we "shall be like him; for we shall see him as he is" (I John 3:2; cf. Rom. 8:18). The new covenant liberty of the Spirit includes not only the crises of forgiveness of sins and the cleansing of the heart, but also stresses the continuing sanctification of all

---

[82]*Katoptrizomenoi* can also mean "reflect as in a mirror" (NEB). See Wilfred L. Knox, *St. Paul and the Church of the Gentiles* (Cambridge: At the University Press, 1939, pp. 131 ff.) for an interpretation of the passage which assumes this meaning. The interpretation followed above appears correct because it suits better the main point of the context.

[83]See comment on 4:4.

of life (7:1; I Thess. 5:20-23; Heb. 12:14). This process reaches completion only at glorification in full conformity to the image of the Son of God (Rom. 8:28-30).[84]

Such a glorious freedom is **by the Spirit of the Lord,** or "from the Lord, the Spirit" (NASB). This spiritual liberty can be the actual experience of all who turn to the Lord, for the power of God's great future has been released among men through the person and work of Jesus Christ—in the ministry of the new covenant. Thus it is the practical presence of the Holy Spirit undergirding Paul's ministry that moves him to speak of it as a "hope" (12). This fact makes for utter openness in his access to God in Christ, and in his proclamation of the gospel. For in the gospel of Christ there is a liberty (1) which is actually present among men, (2) which can penetrate to the core of the personality, and (3) which is thrillingly promising in its future perspectives. In Christ the Christian has freedom of access (1) to the presence of God, (2) to the deep needs of his own heart, and (3) to the sure hope of the glory of God forever for his life (cf. Rom. 5:1-5).

> *Take time to be holy. The world rushes on;*
> *Spend much time in secret with Jesus alone.*
> *By looking to Jesus, like Him thou shalt be;*
> *Thy friends in thy conduct His likeness shall see.*
>
> (W. D. Longstaff)

d. *The openness of the apostolic ministry* (4:1-6). With direct application to the practical character of his own ministry, Paul continues the theme of 3:12, the frankness of his preaching (cf. vv. 5-6). It is a boldness, an openness issuing from the ministry of the Spirit (3:4-18). As in the intervening verses (12-18), Paul again has three subjects: (1) the splendor of the new covenant ministry (1-2), (2) the condition of those who are unable to see that splendor (3-4), and (3) the divine source of the splendor of the gospel ministry (5-6).[85]

Paul's courage as an apostle is rooted in the caliber of **this ministry** (1) that he possesses. It is one that he has just described as a ministry of life, righteousness, liberty, and glory. On

---

[84]For a masterful application of this verse to spiritual growth under the title "The Gaze That Transfigures," see Paul T. Culbertson, *More like the Master* (Kansas City, Mo.: Beacon Hill Press, 1966), pp. 156-66.

[85]Plummer, *op. cit.,* pp. 95, 109.

this basis he himself has **received mercy** (cf. I Cor. 7:25; I Tim. 1:16). It is only to and by that which has become the essence of his own life that Paul bears witness in his preaching. His integrity as a minister is the integrity of mercy, the mercy of God that undergirds the entirety of his own existence. Mercy is his only boast, his only ground of confidence as an apostle (cf. 3:4). On this basis alone he writes, **We faint not** (cf. v. 16; Luke 1:18). Here is the heart of his outspokenness (3:12) and the compulsion of his unceasing activity for men (7-15).

The phrase **but** (*alla*) **have renounced** (2) points emphatically to what is excluded from such a ministry. When Paul entered the apostolate he disowned once and for all[86] any method which he would be ashamed to make public. **Dishonesty** (*aischunes*) is more accurately "shame." This policy he unfolds as twofold. First, Paul's ministry had never been and was not now party to **walking in craftiness** (*panourgia*). He was not, like Satan (11:3) and his ministers (11:14-15; 12:16), ready to adopt any means to achieve his ends. Nor, second, was he guilty of **handling the word of God deceitfully** (cf. 2:17; I Thess. 2:3). It was not his practice to adulterate his message "by any additions or alterations, or by attempting to accommodate it to the taste of the hearers."[87] This, writes Lenski, is the most dastardly "of all the dastardly deeds done in the world."[88] These go together always—integrity in one's ministerial methodology, and honesty with the Word. Could it be said then that he who would surrender scripture to doctrine would also surrender love to legalism? Or vice versa?

But (*alla*), on the contrary, Paul's method above all is **by manifestation of the truth commending** (cf. 3:1-6; 5:11; 6:4) **ourselves to every man's conscience in the sight of God** (cf. 1:12; 2:10, 17). Paul seeks simply to make **the truth** known, for he somehow dares to believe that the saving truth of God needs nothing added to it to effect its ends (cf. Jer. 23:29). It needs not the cleverness but the utter honesty of men. So Paul submits his claim not only **to every man's conscience,** but also to Him on whose mercy his ministry rests and who scrutinizes every conscience (cf. I Cor. 4:4; Heb. 4:13). Paul's appeal has reached a climax. In this verse he appears to have been answering and

---

[86]Plummer would make the aorist **renounced** timeless rather than give it the same reference as **received mercy** (also aorist), *ibid.,* p. 111.

[87]Wesley, *op. cit.,* p. 652.   [88]*Op. cit.,* p. 955.

accusing his detractors. These first muffled rumblings of polemic prepare the way for what will come in cc. 10—13.[89]

Paul's opponents appear to have objected that, if his proclamation were so straightforward, why was the **gospel** (3) still veiled (3:15) for so many of his hearers? He concedes ("and even if," ASV) that for some it is veiled. But **it is hid**[90] only in the case of "those who are perishing" (RSV). The fault is not that of the gospel, but of its hearers. As Tasker observes, Paul is "stating in different language the teaching of Jesus in the parable of the sower."[91]

The minds of them which believe not (4) have been **blinded by the god of this world** (cf. Mark 3:22; John 12:31; 14:30; Eph. 2:2; 6:12; I John 5:19). Satan, who is against God, exercises a limited and temporary, but very real, lordship (Matt. 4:9; Luke 4:6) during "the present evil age" (Gal. 1:4, RSV).[92] This dominion extends to all who give wholehearted allegiance to any cause which compromises God's eternal purpose of grace. Thus even the Law, misconceived and misused by the Jewish legalist, could become a demonic force (3:15) and drive a zealous Saul of Tarsus to persecute the Church of God (I Cor. 15:9). In the same way "the princes of this world . . . crucified the Lord of glory" (I Cor. 2:6).[93] Such "world-forces of this darkness" (Eph. 6:12, NASB), over whom Christ has triumphed (Col. 2:15), keep those who have refused to believe "from seeing the light of the gospel of the glory of Christ" (RSV),[94] **who is the image of God.** Thus, since they are blinded to Christ, God remains hidden from them (cf. 6).

[89]P. E. B. Allo, *Seconde Epitre aux Corinthiens* (2nd ed.; "Etudes Bibliques"; Paris: Librairie Le Coffre, 1956), p. 99.

[90]*Kekalummenon* (veiled) is cognate to *kalumma* (veil) in 3:15.

[91]*Op. cit.*, p. 70.

[92]The two ages, as perceived by Jewish thought, overlap in time for the NT Christian, but are qualitatively distinct. The sovereignty of Satan as "the god of this age" (NASB) is utterly broken for those who through faith in Christ are partakers of the Messianic age (cf. Luke 18:30; Eph. 2:1; Heb. 6:5).

[93]See G. B. Caird, *Principalities and Powers* (Oxford: Clarendon Press, 1956), pp. 51-53, 84.

[94]The KJV makes *augasai* intransitive, translating **lest the light . . . should shine upon them.** The better MSS, however, do not contain **upon them** (*autois*), making the RSV and NASB rendering preferable. Also "the gospel of the glory of Christ" (ASV) is to be preferred to **the glorious gospel of Christ.**

The commanding peak of the passage is scaled with the mention of Christ as **the image of God**. Here is the glory of Christ, for it is the nature of Christ as "the image of the invisible God" (Col. 1:15; cf. John 12:45; 14:9) to radiate the very glory of God among men (cf. Heb. 1:3). The emphasis is on the equality of **the image** (*eikon*) with the original (cf. Phil. 2:6); *eikon* does not imply a feeble copy of something, but "the illumination of its inner core or essence.[95] Christ, the Man from heaven, fulfills in himself the divine destiny of the image of God in man (Gen. 1:26-27; cf. Heb. 2:6-9). Through Him the Christian is "being transformed into the same image from glory to glory" (3:18, NASB).[96] Thus in Christ the Christian is restored to the image of God (cf. 5:17).

Paul is now prepared to make very plain to his critics (cf. 3:1) what he meant in v. 2 by "manifestation of truth." With such a "gospel of the glory of Christ" (RSV) "we do not advertise ourselves" (Bruce), our ideas, our gifts, or our personalities, but **we preach . . . Christ Jesus the Lord** (5). The only exaltation that the apostle could indulge in was that of "Christ Jesus as Lord" (ASV, Acts 2:36; I Cor. 12:1; Phil. 2:9-11). The lordship of Christ governs completely the methodology of Paul's ministry (1:24; I Cor. 2:2). The only legitimate self-proclamation worthy of the ministry according to Paul is **ourselves your servants** (*douloi*) **for Jesus' sake.** This was a service motivated (5:14) and characterized by that of the great Servant who left His exaltation to God (Phil. 2:5-9; I Pet. 2:23; 5:6). "The unkindest thing that a congregation has in its power to do to its pastor," writes C. E. B. Cranfield, is "to indulge in a personality cult . . . for it tempts him to betray his ministry."[97] To preach oneself would tempt one to use "craftiness"—any method—to put oneself over. It would in fact be adulterating the Word of God, and would

[95]Herman Kleinknecht and Gerhard Kittel, *"eikon,"* TDNT, II, 389, 395. Phil. 2:6 and Heb. 1:3, though employing different terms, speak of Christ in much the same way. See Ralph P. Martin, *The Epistle of Paul to the Philippians* ("The Tyndale New Testament Commentaries"; London: The Tyndale Press, 1959), pp. 95-109; and H. Orton Wiley, *The Epistle to the Hebrews* (Kansas City, Mo.: Beacon Hill Press, 1959), pp. 38-43.

[96]Oscar Cullman, *The Christology of the New Testament,* trans. S. C. Guthrie and C. A. M. Hall (Philadelphia: The Westminster Press, 1959), pp. 176 ff.

[97]"Minister and Congregation in the Light of II Corinthians 4:5-7," *Interpretation* (April, 1965), p. 164.

sooner or later cause one to leave the ministry discouraged and disillusioned.

For Paul self-exaltation was excluded entirely from the gospel ministry by the very nature of his conversion encounter with the risen Christ (6). In that experience, the God of creation, who by a word had dispelled the **darkness** with the light (Gen. 1:3; Isa. 9:1; John 1:5), had himself more wonderfully shone[98] into Paul's darkened life, **to give the light of the knowledge of the glory of God in the face of Jesus Christ** (Acts 9:3; 20:13; 22:6; Gal. 1:15-16). Denney observes, "In that light which God flashed into his heart, he saw the face of Jesus Christ, and knew that the glory which shone there was the glory of God."[99] In the abiding reality of this experience lay Paul's unique qualification to be a minister of Christ. The light of God illumined his life that he might also illumine others (Acts 26:16-18) with the knowledge of God's glory in Jesus' face. The anchor of the apostle's ministry was certainly not in himself.

The bold confidence of Paul's apostolic ministry, received from God through Christ (Gal. 1:1), is seen in its methodology, which, first, is utterly open to the scrutiny of man and God and, secondly, seeks only to manifest Jesus Christ as its supreme content. Christ himself is the ultimate measure of both the hearer and the preacher of the gospel, for God can be adequately known only in Him. To refuse the gospel of the glory of Christ is to invite spiritual darkness; to exalt self in the presentation of Jesus is to betray the ministry.

Paul grounds the integrity of his ministry in its basically spiritual character: (1) its proof is in transformed people (3:1-3); (2) its dynamic is the life-giving quality of the new covenant (3:4-11); (3) its boldness resides in the transforming presence of the Spirit of the Lord (3:12-18); and (4) its openness flows out of the fullness of the revelation of the glory of God in Christ as received by the apostle (4:1-6).

2. A Ministry of Suffering (4:7—5:10)

Due possibly to the reproaches of his critics, Paul now turns from the sublimity of his mission to the actual misery of his

---

[98]The aorist *elampsen* indicates that it is primarily the time of his conversion that Paul has in mind. The better MSS indicate that the first part of the verse should read, "For it is the God who said, 'Light shall shine out of darkness,' who shined in our hearts."

[99]*Op. cit.*, p. 754.

physical existence. The frail apostle was continually exposed to suffering and death. But it was a suffering that revealed the resurrection life of Jesus to the Corinthians (4:7-15). Even the apostle himself in the midst of outer decay was experiencing inner renewal (4:16-18). The sure hope for the heavenly home was at work in his life (5:1-10). The boldness of the new covenant ministry is enhanced rather than hampered by the weakness of its ministers (cf. 13:4).

a. *The life of Jesus revealed in affliction* (4:7-15). From Paul's perspective, suffering and glory belong inseparably together in a kind of paradoxical polar tension. For if the glory of Christ is revealed in His passion and death, must not also the glory of the apostolic office be revealed through suffering?[100] Thus the very "act of God which the gospel is, is an act of suffering."[101] Through his actual physical hardships and dangers Paul had reenacted the sufferings of Christ (cf. 1:5) and thus confronted men with the resurrection power of the living Christ. Here we meet in the letter a second interchange of opposite experiences (cf. 1:3-7), the interchange of life and death.

Paul is entrusted[102] with **this treasure** (7) of the gospel, "the light of the knowledge of the glory of God" (6). But he has it in a personality which he compares to a common and fragile clay vessel (cf. Isa. 29:16; 64:8; Jer. 18:6; Acts 9:15). The allusion may either be to an earthen jar in which precious treasures were often hidden,[103] or to a small, inexpensive pottery lamp. The minister possesses a frailty which includes the total person (cf. 1:8; 7:5). But the weakness of the man only serves to magnify the message (cf. 12:9). It is the message that possesses the value. The lowliness of the human vessel demands and proves that the **excellency** ("surpassing greatness," NASB) **of the power** belongs to **God** (*tou theou*) "and does not proceed from us" (*ex*

[100]Wendland, *op. cit.*, p. 164.

[101]William Baird, *Paul's Message and Mission* (Nashville: Abingdon Press, 1960), p. 69.

[102]The affirmation **we have** (*echomen* or *echontes*) occurs significantly throughout the discussion of the ministry (3:4, 12; 4:1, 7, 13; 5:1; 6:10; 7:1).

[103]Hughes, *op. cit.*, p. 136, points out that it was customary in Roman triumphal processions for gold and silver to be carried in earthen vessels. Paul is fond of this graphic simile (cf. 2:14 and I Cor. 4:9) and he may be suggesting "a picture of the victorious Christ entrusting His riches to the poor earthen vessels of His human followers."

hemon, Bruce). In the true apostle the power is "transcendent" (RSV).

With a series of four contrasts (8-9) the apostle illustrates from his daily experience (present participles) of human necessity (cf. 6:4-5; 11:23-27; I Cor. 4:11-13) that the excess of the power in his ministry is clearly God's. The metaphor is that of "a mortal chase and flight."[104] The order is climactic as the persecution becomes ever more intense. But the redeeming factor of the Lord's presence (cf. Matt. 28:20) is decisively expressed by emphatic negatives (*ou* rather than the expected *me*). Paul and his helpers **are troubled on every side** (afflicted; cf. 1:4, 6, 8), but not hopelessly hemmed in (crushed); they **are perplexed** (*aporoumenoi*), **but not in despair** (*exaporoumenoi*); **persecuted** (pursued or hunted), **but not forsaken;** caught and "struck down" (RSV), **but not destroyed** (8-9; cf. Acts 14:19).

As Paul moves to his climax, he interprets the four aspects of suffering as the **dying of . . . Jesus,**[105] and the four aspects of deliverance as **the life . . . of Jesus** (10). His thought is that as a minister of the gospel he carries around with him **always . . . in the body** that same process of dying which culminated in the passion of Jesus. But that was a death which gave way to the resurrection of Jesus. Thus the same resurrection life is now **made manifest** in Paul's **body,** i.e., in a life that bears the marks of Jesus (cf. Gal. 6:17). Because the apostle shares "the death that Jesus died" he shares also "the life that Jesus lives" (NEB).

In Paul's life the dying of Jesus means Paul's "constantly being delivered over to death for Jesus' sake" (11, NASB; cf. Mark 9:31; 10:33; 14:10). But it was only as his suffering was **for Jesus' sake** that the apostle could view his continual exposure to death (cf. Rom. 8:36; I Cor. 15:31) as the same kind of suffering that Christ endured (cf. 1:5). The remarkable recurrence (four times) of the name of **Jesus** in 10-11 indicates how closely Paul linked the career of Jesus with that of his own as a servant of the Servant. The mark of a true apostle (and minister?) is that "he is, like Jesus, a suffering and dying figure, whose work and power and victory arise from his weakness and infirmity and

---

[104]R. C. H. Lenski, *op. cit.,* p. 977. Clarke, *op. cit.,* p. 330, sees the contrasts as arena metaphors. The third alludes to a race and the fourth to a wrestling contest.

[105]The better MSS do not contain **the Lord,** but the sense of the passage is not changed by its omission.

defeat."[106] Thus in the apostle as in his Lord "the tension between this age and the age to come shows itself at its sharpest."[107]

The life . . . of Jesus is inevitably **made manifest** in the **mortal flesh** of the minister who can so identify with Christ's death. The union between Christ's death and resurrection is absolute. They cannot be separated, either in the life of the Christian or in the pattern of the ministry (cf. Rom. 6:4, 8, 17; Gal. 2:20; Phil. 3:10). Participation in one is participation in the other. So the life of Jesus presented by the life of the apostle to the Corinthians is the resurrection life of the Jesus who was crucified (cf. Acts 2:42). It is the life that the once earthly Jesus now lives at God's right hand, effective in the Church through the presence of the Holy Spirit (1:22; 5:5), who communicates the resurrection life of Jesus as Lord (3:17; Rom. 1:4).[108]

From this perspective of the nature of the Christian witness, particularly as it is operative in his own apostolic ministry, Paul can speak to the Corinthian church. He says to those who are tempted to despise the character of his ministry, **So then death worketh** ("is at work," RSV) **in us, but life in you** (12). Paul exposes himself to the forces of death that the Corinthians might be exposed to the force of life. What is in him the sign of the Cross is in them the sign of the Resurrection!

Such a perspective is possible for Paul only because of the particular character of his faith. He professes **the same spirit of faith** as the Psalmist (116:10), who speaking in the face of the opposition of men declared, **I believed, and therefore have I spoken**[109] (13). This psalm is a song of thanksgiving for deliverance from death, and Paul uses the text to bring the import of the whole psalm to bear on his own declaration, **We also believe, and therefore speak.** The apostle's disposition of faith is one that must proclaim—that finds it impossible to keep silent (cf. 4:2, 5). Here according to G. Campbell Morgan is "the principle, faith creating testimony," which "is one secret of power" in

---

[106]Munck, *op. cit.*, p. 184.

[107]W. A. Beardslee, *Human Achievement and Divine Vocation in the Message of Paul* (Naperville, Ill.: Alec R. Allenson, 1961), p. 114.

[108]Hamilton, *op. cit.*, pp. 12-15.

[109]Paul's quotation follows the LXX, which renders the Hebrew in one of at least three possible ways. See the English versions of the OT. The Jewish Targum interestingly paraphrases in Aramaic, "I have confidence that I will speak in the congregation of the righteous" (Strack-Billerbeck, *op. cit.*, III, 517).

the ministry. He adds, "If you do not believe, shut your mouth."[110]
A minister must be honest enough to proclaim only what he himself really believes. Any message is unauthentic and hollow if
the messenger himself is not risking the integrity of his own existence at the moment of proclamation.

From the biblical perspective, preaching partakes of the
character of witness, and witnessing by its very nature consists
of more than mere correctness and enthusiasm—it demands authenticity. The communication of Christianity ultimately ends
in bearing witness, and one does not bear witness without a
measure of self-exposure. Thielicke reminds us that "people today are not generally asking the question: 'Where shall I learn
to believe?' . . . People are rather asking, 'Where can I find
credible witnesses?' "[111]

The faith, which transforms Paul's present, is the hope of the
final transformation of the resurrection. Paul is certain (*eidotes*,
a casual participle) that God, who **raised up the Lord Jesus shall
raise up us also** (14). The content of his faith is the certainty of
the future resurrection from the dead as guaranteed by the prior
resurrection of Jesus (cf. I Cor. 15:1-8). Christ is "the firstborn
from the dead" (I Cor. 15:20; Col. 3:15-18; Heb. 1:6), "the firstborn among many brethren" (Rom. 8:29). The hope is sealed
by the experiential presence through the Holy Spirit of the actual
resurrection life of Jesus with the apostle and his converts (1:22;
5:5; Rom. 8:11; Phil. 3:10-11). For it is "with [*syn*] Jesus"
(ASV)[112] that they are raised up (cf. 13:4; Rom. 8:17; Col. 3:
3-4; I Thess. 4:14, 17; 5:10). The solidarity of the Christian "with
Christ"[113] includes all the decisive moments in His life for men—
His death, resurrection, and final triumph. It is in this relationship that they will be presented approved (cf. 11:2; Acts 23:33;
Eph. 5:27; Col. 1:22, 28; Jude 24) before the throne of God. Verse
14, by its explicit reference to the Resurrection, furnishes the
bridge between this section (7-15) and that which follows (4:16—
5:10).

---

[110]*Op. cit.*, p. 239.

[111]*The Trouble with the Church: A Call for Renewal* (New York: Harper & Row, Publishers, 1965), p. 15.

[112]The KJV **by Jesus** is based on the poorly attested *dia* rather than the
syn of the better MSS.

[113]For the meaning of this phrase in Paul see Ernest Best, *One Body in
Christ* (London: S.P.C.K., 1955), pp. 44 ff.

Filson[114] points out that Paul is supported in his perilous and demanding calling by the reassurance of the Psalmist (13) and his conviction of the certainty of a triumphant future (14). He is held steady, third, by his concern for his converts (15). The **all things are for your sakes** explains the addition of **with you** in the preceding verse. Paul's suffering is "a calling or gift which he shares with all the Church"[115] (cf. 1:3-6). The fourth factor in the steadfastness of his ministry is its absorption in the execution of God's purpose for the world. For the ultimate goal of it all is the **glory of God**. The means is the **grace** of God which, as it reaches more and more people, enables that many more thanksgivings to rise to the greater glory of God. The NEB renders 15, "As the abounding grace of God is shared by more and more, the greater . . . the chorus of thanksgiving that ascends to the glory of God."[116]

The presentation in vv. 7-15 of the gospel as a treasure in earthen vessels is illuminating. The weakness of the human vessel demands the intervention of divine power for the very preservation and usefulness of the vessel (7-12). Further, the character of that intervening divine life convinces those who share it of the resurrection perspective of the gospel (13-15). From such an assured vantage point of faith Paul was willing to suffer, first **for Jesus' sake** (11), then for the sake of men (15), but most of all for the eternal **glory of God** (15).

b. Outer decay but inner renewal (4:16-18). The connection of these verses with what has preceded is seen in the reiteration of **we faint not** (16) from v. 1. There the reference was to Paul's confidence in the character of his ministry. Here it is to the ground of his courage as he faces the depletion of his physical and mental resources by the hardships of his ministry (cf. 8-11).

Paul does "not lose heart" (RSV) in spite of the deadly process at work in his **outward man**.[117] Even though his "out-

---

[114]*Op. cit.*, pp. 321 ff.   [115]Beardslee, *op. cit.*, pp. 114 ff.

[116]The translation of this verse, like 1:11, is difficult. The general sense, however, is clear. See Plummer, *op. cit.*, pp. 134 ff., for a discussion of the various possibilities.

[117]The **outward man** is not to be identified as the "old man" of Rom. 6:6; Eph. 4:22; and Col. 3:9. It is Paul's life "viewed in its physical external relation to this age" (E. Earle Ellis, *Paul and His Recent Interpreters* [Grand Rapids: Wm. B. Eerdmans, 1961], p. 37). See Oscar Cullmann, *Immortality of the Soul or Resurrection of the Dead?* (London: The Epworth Press, 1958), pp. 28-39.

ward humanity" (NEB) is steadily "decaying" (ASV), the inward man (cf. Rom. 7:22; Eph. 3:16) is renewed day by day.[118]
Both verbs are in the present tense, indicating a continuing process. Paul is supremely optimistic. His life in its relation to
Christ[119] consists of the reception of fresh spiritual resources
each day (cf. Rom. 12:2; Titus 3:5). It is constantly on the increase. Although the one process must inevitably end in death,
the other will just as certainly result in life which is eternal. Contrary to the godless man, in whom "the decay of the outward man
. . . is a melancholy spectacle, for it is the decay of everything,"[120]
the Christian is on a "path . . . like the light of dawn, which shines
brighter and brighter until full day" (Prov. 4:18, RSV; cf. v. 6).
Ellis suggests that, while this renewing finds its ultimate goal at
the Parousia (Rom. 8:29), its process in this life, as "effected by
the Spirit is solely moral and psychological. It affects one's outlook on life and what the body *does,* not what the body *is;* this
latter awaits the resurrection."[121]

Paul explains his paradoxical affirmation with a series of
startling contrasts (17). His **affliction,** borne "for Jesus' sake"
(11), is actually producing "an ever-increasing excess"[122] (cf. 7)
of **glory.** In comparison with the **affliction** which is **light** and
for a moment, the **glory** is a **weight** which is **eternal** (cf. 3:18;
5:1-6). Humanly we would tend to reverse the adjectives. But
Paul knows that suffering in the likeness of the Cross results in
glory. It so far outweighs and outlasts the suffering that there
can be no real comparison (cf. Rom. 8:17).

This perspective is effective in the life of the apostle and
his co-workers **while** ("because," RSV) they are concentrating
their attention, **not on the things which are seen, but on the
things which are not seen** (18; cf. Col. 1:16). Paul's **affliction**

[118]Hering, *op. cit.,* p. 45, comments that vv. 16-18, if one disregards the
context, could have been written by Philo or any other Platonist. But Paul's
thoroughly Christian use of the terminology in an eschatological context
would have been completely unacceptable to the current Hellenistic theology. See Hughes, *op. cit.,* pp. 154 ff.

[119]The **inward man** can be defined as "the renewed being of the Christian" (Werner Georg Kuemmel, *Man in the New Testament,* trans. J. J. Vincent [Philadelphia: The Westminster Press, 1963], p. 43). W. David Stacey
suggests that "the inward man is the real self that passes from the body of
flesh to the body of the resurrection" (*The Pauline View of Man* [London:
Macmillan & Co., 1956], p. 211).

[120]Denney, *op. cit.,* p. 759.   [121]*Op. cit.,* p. 38.
[122]Hughes, *op. cit.,* p. 158.

and the decay of the **outward man** are only **temporal** (temporary), but those unseen values on which he has set his heart (Rom. 8:38-39; Phil. 3:14) are **eternal,** and thus more real to him (5:7; Heb. 11:1). So what does it matter if his life of daily deliverance from death should in some moment end in death? He possesses a certain future beyond death, a future which has broken into his present with assurance (cf. 14; 5:5).

This present transformation (cf. 3:18) is the narrowing of the gap between the Christian's individual and corporate existence. It is in Paul's perspective the actualization in the life of the individual Christian of what he is "in Christ" (2:14, 17; 3:14; 5:17). This process is twofold. As articulated by Ellis it is (1) "a progressive moral conformity to the character of Christ," and (2) the individual actualization of the reality of the new age "in a psychological or *weltanschaulich* transformation in which the Christian mystery is increasingly apprehended and increasingly determinative for one's world and life view."[123]

c. *The hope for the heavenly home* (5:1-10). The chapter division here is purely arbitrary, for this paragraph belongs more to what precedes than to what follows. Paul's courage as he faces his failing faculties and the inevitability of suffering and death is grounded in his assurance of the unseen and the eternal (4:18), in the certainty of his final heavenly home.[124]

By the revelation of God in Christ, Paul is certain[125] that **if our earthly house** is pulled down (*kataluthe*), **we have a building** (*oikodomen*)[126] from **God** (1). The transitory character of

---

[123]*Op. cit.,* p. 39.

[124]This passage is one of the most difficult in the letter to interpret precisely. The view is presented by Tasker, *op. cit.,* pp. 77 ff., that Paul is speaking of the heavenly shelter which awaits him immediately after death, irrespective of when he dies in relation to the Lord's return in glory and his reception of the resurrection body. The more traditional interpretation, that includes Paul's dread of the intermediate state in case he should die before his assumption of the resurrection body at the coming of the Lord, is given with some variation by Filson, *op. cit.,* pp. 326 ff.; Hughes, *op. cit.,* pp. 160 ff.; Plummer, *op. cit.,* pp. 140 ff.; and Geerhardus Vos, *The Pauline Eschatology* (Grand Rapids: Wm. B. Eerdmans Publishing Company, 1930), pp. 186 ff.

[125]**Know** (*oidamen*) means to know a truth by intuition or revelation as the result of perceiving or seeing. This is in contrast to *ginoskein,* to acquire knowledge by instruction or research (Hughes, *op. cit.,* p. 160).

[126]This word is used often of the body of Christ, the Church (I Cor. 3:9; Eph. 2:21; 4:12, 16).

life on earth is expressed by the familiar metaphor of a tent which may be dismantled at any time (cf. Heb. 11:8-10). When this happens Paul already possesses **by faith** (7) **an house not made with hands** (*acheiropoieton*), **eternal in the heavens** (cf. Col. 2:11; Heb. 9:11). The language of Mark 14:58 is amazingly similar: "We heard him say, I will destroy [*kataluso*] this temple that is made with hands [*cheiropoieton*], and within three days I will build [*oikodomeso*] another made without hands [*acheiropoieton*]." To this statement of Jesus as it appears in John's Gospel the Evangelist adds, "He spake of the temple of his body" (2:21). Paul links the resurrection of Christ with the Church as the body of Christ,[127] and uses the temple figure for the latter (6:16; I Cor. 3:16). Therefore **a building of God** and **an house not made with hands** may belong to the same circle of ideas. If so, Paul's hope is expressed in terms not exclusively of the resurrection body (cf. I Cor. 15:44). His ideas may fall within the larger framework of the "corporate solidarities which inhere . . . in Christ . . . in whom the new aeon has been fully actualized and who alone is individually present in the heavenlies."[128] If this be correct, Paul has in view the final actualization at the Parousia **in the heavens** of that mode of existence which is his "in Christ." This is the "eternal weight of glory" (4:17).

Coextensive with this assurance is the fact that **in this** present life with all of its limitations and imperfections **we** continue **to groan, earnestly desiring** ("longing," ASV) **to be clothed upon with our house which is from heaven** (2; cf. v. 4; Rom. 8:23). With a change of metaphor Paul now speaks of putting on the heavenly existence[129] over the old like a garment (*ependusasthai*). He is "sure that [*ei ge kai*], when we have put it on" (Weymouth), **we shall not be found naked**[130] (3). **Naked,** like **unclothed** (4) along with "shame" in both the Old (Gen. 3:10;

---

[127]See J. A. T. Robinson, *The Body* (Chicago: Alec R. Allenson, 1952), pp. 49 ff. Some of his interpretations, however, need qualification.

[128]Ellis, *Paul and His Recent Interpreters*, pp. 41-42. For a recent study of corporate solidarity in Pauline thought see R. P. Shedd, *Man in Community* (Grand Rapids: Wm. B. Eerdmans Publishing Co., 1959).

[129]**Our house** (*oiketerion*) denotes a permanent home. It differs from *oikia* (v. 1) in that it implies an inhabitant (Plummer, *op. cit.*, p. 145).

[130]Hughes, *op. cit.*, pp. 168 ff., interprets this of an intermediate state between the Christian's death and the Parousia, but is forced to make **being clothed** (*endusamenoi*) quite distinct from *ependusasthai* (2, 4) and refers the former to the earthly body. Vos, *op. cit.*, p. 196, to avoid the obvious difficulty, takes the less attested *ekdusamenoi*.

Isa. 20:4; Ezek. 16:37, 39; 23:26, 29; Hos. 2:3) and New Testaments (Rom. 10:11; I John 2:28; Rev. 3:17-18), is used of the guilty before the judgment of God. Here both **naked** and **unclothed** have the judgment scene in view (10). As Ellis writes, it is "at the parousia that those without the wedding garment (Matt. xxii. 11), the spiritual body (I Cor. xv. 44, 53 f.), the heavenly house (II Cor. v. 1 f.) to put on will be discovered stripped and naked (II Cor. v. 3 f.)."[131]

Thus, as Paul himself restates it: "For indeed while we are in this tent, we groan, being burdened, because we do not want to be unclothed, but to be clothed [*ependusasthai*], in order that what is mortal may be swallowed up by life" (4, NASB). The last assertion, like I Cor. 15:53, "For this corruptible must put on incorruption, and this mortal must put on immortality," has reference primarily to the Parousia. Death itself cannot be a redeemer, for death too must be "swallowed up in victory" (I Cor. 15:54). Irrespective of whether or not he dies before the Parousia, Paul's longing is for full and final redemption: We ourselves, who have the firstfruits of the Spirit, groan inwardly as we wait for adoption as sons, the redemption of our bodies (see Rom. 8:23; cf. Phil. 3:10-15). It is a tension shared by all of creation, for all are awaiting anxiously the final actualization of the new creation in Christ at His coming.

To God belongs all the credit[132] for the certainty of such a hope. God himself is the One who has **wrought** ("prepared," RSV) **us for** this very **thing,** for He has **given unto us the earnest of the Spirit** (5).[133] The presence of the Holy Spirit prepares us for the final swallowing up by eternal life of what is mortal, in that He is God's "pledge" (NASB) or "guarantee" (RSV) of the consummation of His purpose for us (Phil. 1:6; I Thess. 5:24): "If the Spirit of him who raised Jesus from the dead dwells in you, he who raised Christ Jesus from the dead will give life to your mortal bodies also through his Spirit which dwells in you" (Rom. 8:11, RSV; cf. Eph. 1:13-14, 19-20). The Spirit of Christ is "a first installment of the life to come" (Barclay). Through "the firstfruits of the Spirit" (Rom. 8:23) Paul possesses in mortal life the authentic beginning of that perfect life (Phil. 3:12) which will comprise the totality of his existence at the end of the age.

[131]*Op. cit.,* p. 45.

[132]As in 1:22, **God** occupies an emphatic position in the sentence.

[133]For the metaphor of **earnest** see comment on 1:22.

The connection is real, personal, and spiritual. So his longing is no illusion, for it is grounded in God's own preparation in Paul's present life. The hope gives certainty! Sanctification is security, and security is sanctification (Rom. 8:1-39)!

Paul faces the realities of his ministry with what Wendland calls "the 'dialektic' of Christian existence (groaning—being of good courage)."[134] His attitude toward the consummation (I Cor. 15:28) is twofold, that of longing and assurance. Because of the Spirit's presence, **therefore** (6), he can be not only confident of the future, but also courageous in the present. He is **always confident** ("of good courage," ASV), **knowing** (*eidotes*) **that, whilst we are at home in the body, we are absent from the Lord.** The figures of the tent, building, and house (1-2) now reappear in a new form. **At home in the body** means "in the solidarities and securities of earthly existence."[135] It is not the body as such, but the same general state of life as indicated by the "natural body" in I Cor. 15:44.[136]

To be in our earthly existence is to be **absent from the Lord,** which Paul hastens to clarify with the parenthetical **For we walk by faith, not by sight** (7; cf. Rom. 8:24; I Cor. 13:12). The object of reference is the heavenly Christ. On earth the Christian lives in relation to his Lord, not by what is seen (*eidous*) or by appearance (cf. 16), but by faith in "the things which are not seen" (4:18; cf. Heb. 11:1). Paul is painfully aware that earth is not heaven, that a faith vision of Jesus is not to be compared with the direct vision of the Lord in His glory (Rom. 8:16-18; cf. I John 3:2).

This fact the apostle emphasizes[137] as he resumes his sentence, **We are confident** (8) in the midst of present circumstances. Then with an interesting exchange of terms from v. 6 he adds that he "prefers"[138] **to be absent from the body, and to be present** (at home)[139] **with the Lord.** He prefers sight (v. 8) to

---

[134]*Op. cit.,* p. 170. Cf. 2 and 4 with 6 and 8.   [135]Robinson, *op. cit.,* p. 29.

[136]See W. David Stacey, *op. cit.,* p. 190.

[137]The verb *tharrein* is in the emphatic position in 6 and 8, replacing *stenazein* in 2 and 4.

[138]Arndt and Gingrich, *op. cit.,* p. 319. The literal is "well-pleasing rather."

[139]The words **present** and **absent,** used in 6-9, are *endemein* and *ekdemein,* from *demos,* and mean " 'to be among one's own people,' a pilgrim or stranger in alien surroundings, i.e., away from home" (Lenski, *op. cit.,* pp. 1008 ff.).

faith (v. 6). Paul is **willing rather** to be "out" (*ek*) of the body than "in" (*en*) the body, and "face to face with" (*pros*) the Lord than "away from" (*apo*) the Lord. His preference as previously stated (vv. 1-4) is for that final manner of life, involving the "spiritual body" (I Cor. 15:44), which he will possess at the Parousia. That will be the day when for Paul faith will become sight, and he will realize in the entirety of his individual existence the consummation of that justification, sanctification, and redemption (I Cor. 1:30) which are now his "in Christ."

This preference rules all of Paul's circumstances. He is not only "of good courage" (8, RSV), but "therefore also we have as our ambition" (NASB), **whether present or absent, to be accepted of him** (9). It is Paul's love "as a point of honor"[140] (*philotimoumetha*), whether he is at home in heaven or away from home on earth, "to be pleasing to Him" (NASB, cf. Rom. 12:2; Eph. 5:10). This is the consuming passion of his life (cf. 14).

The motivation for such an "honor aim"[141] is at least in part the fact of Paul's final and absolute responsibility to God (10). **For we must all** (all of us Christians) be publicly exposed for what we are (I Cor. 4:5; cf. Heb. 4:13; *phanerothenai*) **before the judgment seat of Christ** (10; cf. Acts 17:31; Rom. 14:10). The true reality of one's character will be openly and fully revealed. The nature of the judgment is interesting if not fascinating. Each one will receive as his own (*komisetai*) to carry away the very **things done in his body, according to** ("facing," *pros*) what **he hath done, whether . . . good or bad** (lit., "worthless").

God's judgment even on the godless is not arbitrary, but natural retribution (cf. 11:15). Their punishment is fundamentally what they are (Gal. 6:7-8). But here the reward of the Christian, although he is saved by sheer grace (Eph. 2:8), is the resultant quality of his own life viewed as a whole[142] (Eph. 6:8; cf. Luke 19:16-27; I Cor. 3:10-15). Paul wanted to keep the worthless in his life of service to Christ at an absolute minimum, for there is a direct and definite continuity between this earthly existence and the heavenly one to come. His point is that the

---

[140]Lenski, *op. cit.*, p. 1013. **We labour** does not do justice to the word which means "to love honor."

[141]*Ibid.*

[142]*Ta dia tou somatos pros ha epraxen.* The aorist is constative and conceives the idea as a whole. See Hughes, *op. cit.*, p. 181, fn. 58; Lenski, *op. cit.*, p. 1015.

Christian is fully answerable to God for the quality of his present life. There is a real sense in which a holy character will ever be its own reward in the presence of a holy God. In fact, what more could God give than a life like His?

Paul's passionate courage in the face of a ministry that is characterized by the dying of Jesus in his body (4:10) is doubly motivated. First (1-5) is his assured certainty that the Parousia-resurrection will usher him into a fully redeemed existence. Then flesh, the power of death, will have lost its grasp even on the outer man, as it has already over the inner man, and all will be made new by the Spirit of the Lord.[143] Second (6-10) is his intense concern to be pleasing to the Lord, not only now, but supremely then. And how pleasing he will be when "at home with the Lord" cannot be separated from how pleasing he is now "at home in the body." Here was a man not satisfied merely to make heaven, but an apostle with an insatiable longing to possess all the privileges of heaven, and to utterly please the Lord with the positive quality of his character and service.

According to the preceding explanation, II Cor. 5:1-10 is not concerned with the intermediate state. The overall contrasts are throughout "between this age and the age-to-come and are completely within the framework of Paul's parousia eschatology and his concept of corporate solidarity."[144] The two types of existence now overlap, but Paul's assured hope is for that life in which his corporate existence in Christ shall be individually and fully actualized at the Parousia. Although the possibility of death is assumed (4:16; 5:1), nothing is said about what happens at death before the Parousia. That is not his point, for his view is the long one. Any intermediate state, however, would not be construed by Paul "as an anticipated fulfillment at death of the parousia consummation,"[145] but more in terms of "an altered or suspended time factor for the dead."[146] Those who die in the Lord are "with Christ" (Phil. 1:23). They "have fallen asleep in Jesus" (I Thess. 4:14, NASB) and await the consummation when death, the last

---

[143]See Cullmann, *Immortality of the Soul or Resurrection of the Dead?* pp. 28-39.

[144]Ellis, *op. cit.*, p. 48.   [145]*Ibid.*

[146]*Ibid.* See Cullmann, *Immortality of the Soul or Resurrection of the Dead?* pp. 48-57. The intermediate state can be linked with the "paradise" of 12:4 and Luke 23:43. See also Luke 16:22.

enemy, will be destroyed (I Cor. 15:26). Paul's hope is in the abiding Christ; he believes not in the immortal soul of Platonism, but in the "God who raises the dead" (1:9, NASB).

Paul thrills to his ministry of suffering (4:7—5:10) because (1) the afflictions which he courageously endures as he proclaims the gospel (a) partake of the nature of the sufferings of Jesus and (b) therefore have been broken into by the power of the resurrection of Jesus, 4:9-11. Thus (2) the resurrection life of Jesus by the Spirit is the dynamic of Paul's ministry (a) authentically confronting men with Jesus and (b) preparing him for the full consummation of his resurrection hope with the Lord, 4:12—5:10.

3. *A Ministry of Reconciliation* (5:11—6:10)

The third characteristic of Paul's ministry is that of reconciliation as he proceeds to reassert the sincerity of his labors among the Corinthians (cf. 1:12; 2:17; 4:2). The selflessness of his motives is guaranteed equally by the fear of the Lord and by the love of Christ (5:11-15). His perspective is that of the reconciliation of God in Christ (5:16-21); and his manner of life as an apostle is consistent with his message (6:1-10). Such is the answer that the Corinthians can give to those who would impugn the character of Paul's ministry.

a. *The fear of the Lord and the love of Christ* (5:11-15). Contrary to what some at Corinth appear to insist, Paul is not self-seeking in his labors among them. Not only is he accountable to God for the quality of his ministry, but also the very nature of Christ's love for him excludes such motives.

Paul has the fact and character of the judgment in mind (cf. 10) and is thus fully conscious of his awesome responsibility[147] to God. He **therefore** (11) is persuading men, when necessary, of the integrity of his ministerial motives. Their security against any insincerity on his part is that he has been **made manifest unto**

---

[147]**Terror,** or better "fear" (ASV), is "the wholesome reverential awe and respect" with which Paul faces the Lord, from whom he will receive "what he has done in the body" (RSV). Cf. Filson, *op. cit.,* p. 330. Morgan suggests that "the old way of defining the fear of the Lord is that I used to be afraid that God would hurt me. Now the fear is, or should be, that I should hurt Him, that I should grieve Him" (*op. cit.,* p. 242).

God.[148] His appeal is to what God knows about him, which is everything (cf. Heb. 4:12-13). But that is not all: **I trust** (lit., hope) **also that we are made manifest in your consciences.** Has he not been as transparent with them as he has been with God (cf. 4:2)? His appeal is to their moral consciousness (1:12; 4:2; 5:11), not to their proud intelligence (cf. I Cor. 1:18-31). Paul believes that in their hearts they know he is genuine.[149]

Lest his adversaries interpret this affirmation of openness as arrogant boasting (cf. 2:17; 3:1), Paul hastens to make himself clear. He is not beginning to **commend** himself **again** to them.[150] Rather, his purpose is to **give** them an **occasion to glory on** his **behalf** (12). He wants to furnish them with an incentive and the resources to adequately answer those who are attacking him.[151] They are in a position to defend the apostle (1:14) and ought to be at it against "those who take pride in appearance and not in heart" (NASB). **Heart** in Paul's usage describes "the *whole* man to his very depths."[152] Kuemmel writes that here **appearance** (*prosopon*) "indicates man centered on himself and *kardia* man centered on God."[153] The boast of Paul's opponents is only a pretense, designed to impress men and gain a material advantage. That they care nothing for the realities of the ministry is evident from their opposition to Paul as a suffering apostle. Their "pride is all in outward show and not in inward worth" (NEB).

The Corinthians may well defend the sincerity of the apostle (13), based on the fact that "in Paul self-interest is completely overcome, for his life stands under the two-fold rule: for God— for you."[154] As Bruce paraphrases Paul's claim, "Are we mad, as some think? Well, let God be glorified. Are we sober and sensible? That is for your advantage." Paul has been charged with

---

[148]This clause belongs more closely to what precedes than to what follows. The antithesis is that "God knows all about us through and through, but we have to persuade men to believe in our integrity" (Plummer, *op. cit.*, p. 168).

[149]The perfect tenses indicate that "his character has been, and still is, laid bare" (Plummer, *op. cit.*, p. 169).

[150]Indicating that perhaps his detractors had interpreted an earlier letter as egotistical self-commendation (cf. 3:1).

[151]**Occasion** (*aphorme*; cf. 11:12; Gal. 5:13) "means both a starting point for an operation and the resources with which an operation can be launched" (Tasker, *op. cit.*, p. 84). Bruce translates it "opportunity."

[152]Kuemmel, *op. cit.*, p. 171.   [153]*Ibid.*

[154]Wendland, *op. cit.*, p. 176.

being **beside** himself (*exestemen*), just as Jesus was: "They said, He is beside himself" (*exeste*, Mark 3:21). The reference is to the constant spiritual tension in which Paul lived and worked. The apostle's

> enthusiasm, his absolute superiority to common selfish considera-
> tions . . . his resolute assertion of truths lying beyond the reach of
> sense, the unearthly flame which burned unceasingly in his bosom
> . . . all these constitute the temper which is described as being "be-
> side oneself," a kind of sacred madness . . . The disciple and the
> Master alike seemed to those who did not understand them to be in
> an overstrained, too highly wrought condition of spirit; in the
> ardour of their devotion they allowed themselves to be carried be-
> yond all natural limits.[155]

Consider the impulsive reaction of Festus to Paul's defense before Agrippa: "Paul, you are mad; your great learning is turn-ing you mad" (Acts 26:24, RSV).[156] When Paul's behavior is exceptional by normal human standards, as he insists, **it is to God**; and when his behavior is ordinary, **it is for your cause.** There-fore, in contrast to his critics, the entirety of his conduct is free from self-seeking.

What restrains Paul from such motives is **the love of Christ (14).** The verb **constraineth** refers to "the pressure which con-fines and restricts"[157] (cf. Phil. 1:23). He is controlled, held within bounds by Christ's love for him. The genitive **of Christ** is exclusively subjective[158] (cf. Rom. 8:35, 39). This is indicated by the immediate reference to Christ's death: **One died for all.** For Paul the death of Christ is "the self-giving of Christ without limit."[159] It genuinely manifests the love of God: "God demon-strates His own love toward us, in that while we were yet sin-ners, Christ died for us" (Rom. 5:8, NASB). The practical result is that "the love of God has been poured out within our hearts

---

[155]Denney, *op. cit.*, p. 764.

[156]Some, like Filson (*op. cit.*, p. 333), interpret *exestemen* as ecstatic or notable spiritual experiences. See 12:1-4; Acts 9:3-6; I Cor. 14:18. Plummer suggests that it "refers to his self-commendation, which his critics said amounted to a mania" (*op. cit.*, p. 172).

[157]Plummer, *op. cit.*, p. 173. See Luke 8:45; 12:50; 19:42; Acts 18:5. The meaning could also be "confined as between walls to a concentration or in-crease of activity," i.e., "urge on, impel" (Arndt and Gingrich, *op. cit.*, p. 797).

[158]C. F. D. Moule, *An Idiom Book of New Testament Greek* (Cam-bridge: Cambridge University Press, 1959), p. 41.

[159]T. W. Manson, *On Paul and John* (London: SCM Press, 1963), p. 53.

through the Holy Spirit who was given to us" (Rom. 5:5, NASB). This is the love that holds Paul captive, a "love which originates and ends with God in Christ"[160] (cf. Rom. 8:28-30).

Paul goes on to explain the reason the love of God in Christ has such a controlling grip on his motive life. He had reached some vital conclusions—**we thus judge**[161]—probably soon after his conversion. Basic is the fact that Christ **died for all** (cf. 15). From this, two things follow which demonstrate why "the love of Christ ... leaves us no option" (Bruce).

His first conviction is that, since **one died for all, then were all dead**. This result implies two facts in relation to man. (1) When Christ died, the whole human race was involved; for He is "the incorporated Head of the human race ... the personified principle of its existence."[162] Thus in Him "all are regarded as dead"[163] and in utter need of redemption, or Christ would not have needed to die. (2) As indicated by the **for** (*hyper*), not only are men identified with Christ in what He did for them (i.e., **died**), but also in that same event He identified himself with their sin (v. 21; cf. I Pet. 2:24). Involved is the thought of substitution. As Tasker writes, "Christ's death was the death of all, in the sense that He died the death they should have died."[164] In view of Christ's death, all men *are* dead in respect to any spiritual self-sufficiency. The simplest interpretation is that the fact that Christ died for all proves that all were dead.

This leads us to Paul's second conviction that excludes self-seeking from the life of one who is "controlled by the love of Christ" (Moffatt). **He died for all, that** those who live in the world should "live no longer for themselves but for him who for their sake died and was raised" (15, RSV; cf. Rom. 14:7-9; I Cor. 3:21-23; Gal. 2:20). The Resurrection and the Crucifixion are inseparably joined in the atoning work of Christ (Rom. 4:25; I Cor. 15:17). Identification by faith with Christ in His death involves union with Him in His resurrection life (Rom. 5:10). The old un-

---

[160]Hughes, *op. cit.,* p. 192. See also TDNT, I, 49 ff.

[161]**Judge** is an aorist participle. The phrase is better rendered, "having concluded this" (NASB). See Tasker, *op. cit.,* p. 85.

[162]Hanson, *op. cit.,* p. 50.

[163]Rudolf Bultmann, *Theology of the New Testament,* trans. Kendrick Grobel, I (London: SCM Press, 1952), 296.

[164]*Op. cit.,* p. 86. See Denney, *op. cit.,* p. 765.

regenerate life with self as the focus of interest[165] gives way to a new life centered on One who **died for them, and rose again.**

This "means that the root of sin is dug out of his life."[166] So justification reaches out to involve sanctification. In Paul's own words: "Our old self was crucified with Him . . . that we should no longer be slaves to sin . . . Now if we have died with Christ, we believe that we shall also live with Him. . . . For the death that He died, He died to sin, once for all; but the life that He lives, He lives to God. Even so consider yourselves to be dead to sin, but alive to God in Christ Jesus" (Rom. 6:6-11, NASB). For Paul, "to live is Christ" (Phil. 1:21). In such a life there remains no room for self-centered living (cf. Phil. 2:5-18).

Paul never seeks merely to exalt and advance himself, (1) for he is absolutely transparent to the God to whom he must give an account for the integrity of his ministry. His real self (*a*) is open to his converts, 11, (*b*) in contrast to the duplicity of his critics, 12. Paul does not commend himself, (2) for he is held in check by the amazing reach of Christ's love for him. This love, effected in Christ's death on his behalf, can radically control his motives because (*a*) he is aware of the desperate helplessness of the death from which it has delivered him, 14, and because (*b*) he is captured by the transcendent quality of the life it has set him free to live, 15. Paul is constrained by his awesome responsibility to God and by his gratifying life in Christ.

b. The perspective of reconciliation (5:16-21). Paul's sincerity is supported by the very character of his message. He proclaims God's reconciling act in Christ, an event that has furnished the final criterion for his view of himself and others.

In a parenthetical statement (16) which is linked with the thought that "all have died" (14, RSV) Paul asserts his changed way of regarding men. Ever since his discovery of the significance of the death of Christ ("from now on," NASB), he does not "know anyone in terms of a relationship which is purely of this world" (Bruce). **After the flesh** (cf. 1:17; 10:2; 11:18) has reference to the typical worldly distinctions—race, social status, wealth, and title—by which men estimate one another.[167] The values of Paul's critics were similar (12). But Christ's death has

---

[165]This is the "old self" (NASB) or "old man" which Paul speaks of in Rom. 6:6; Eph. 4:22; Col. 3:9.

[166]Manson, *op. cit.*, p. 54.   [167]Hughes, *op. cit.*, p. 197.

robbed such standards of significance (14), for they are contrary
to the resultant reality of the Spirit (Rom. 8:5; cf. I Cor. 3:1-4).[168]
Even though Paul once viewed Christ by the fleshly criteria of
his culture (Phil. 3:4-6; cf. Gal. 1:13-14), he does so no longer.[169]
For it had led him to judge Jesus' claim to Messianic sonship as
blasphemous and to persecute His followers (I Tim. 1:13). Now
he knows Christ as He really is—the risen, exalted Lord (Phil.
2:5-11). Paul may have had contact with Jesus during His
earthly ministry, but that is not what he is saying here.

As a direct consequence of vv. 14-15 comes one of the most
fascinating verses in the letter with its "grandiose anticipation."[170]
Out of death has come the new life that one lives to the Lord, "a
new life in a new context,"[171] which Paul describes by his most
characteristic phrase **in Christ** (17). To be **in Christ** is to be a
new creature (cf. Gal. 6:15; Eph. 2:10; 4:24). Through Christ a
brand-new situation has been created (cf. Isa. 43:19; Rev. 21:15).
A new order of affairs has come into being bringing with it a new
man. Man is a distinctively **new creature** "in virtue of the new
relation to God."[172] All the former relationships, though honored
with age,[173] **are passed away**, for "behold, new things have
come"[174] (NASB). The apostle is jubilant at the thought. His
ministry is based on the fact that "everything is superceded . . .
and loses all value before that single perspective in which from
now on everything converges."[175] Denney suggests that "to be
guided by worldly distinctions is to know only a few people, and

---

[168]"Flesh" and "Spirit" are ethical opposites in Paul's thought. They
belong to different realms or relations. See Rom. 8:1-11; Gal. 5:16-24.

[169]Paul is not referring to a post-conversion, deficient view of Christ.
Neither is he depreciating the significance of the earthly life of Jesus, that
is, exchanging the "historical Jesus" for a "kerygmatic Christ." See Plummer, *op. cit.*, pp. 177 ff., or Hughes, *op. cit.*, pp. 199 ff., for a detailed discussion of these and other alternatives.

[170]Hering, *op. cit.*, p. 52.   [171]Manson, *op. cit.*, p. 77.

[172]TDNT, III, 1034. New (*kainos*) "is what is new in nature, different
from the usual, impressive, better than the old, superior in value or attraction" (TDNT, III, 447). See Roy A. Harrisville, *The Concept of Newness in
the New Testament* (Minneapolis: Augsburg Publishing House, 1960),
pp. 90-91.

[173]Old (*archaios*) is "from the beginning," that which is older than
palaios and "confers a romantic aura of dignity" (TDNT, I, 486).

[174]All things (*ta panta*) is not found in the better MSS.

[175]Michel Bouttier, *Christianity According to Paul*, trans. Frank Clarke
(London: SCM Press, 1966), p. 17.

to know them by what is superficial in their nature; but to see that such distinctions died in Christ's death, and to look at men in relation to Him who is Redeemer and Lord of all, is to know all our brethren, and to know them not on the surface, but to the heart."[176]

Significant for Paul's thought here as well as for his total perspective is the phrase **in** (*en*) **Christ**.[177] By it he vividly portrays his conviction that it is in intimate personal relationship to the risen Christ that the salvation of God is continually realized; **in Christ** is in direct contrast to "in law"[178] (cf. Rom. 6:14; 8:2). To be **in Christ** is to be taken up into the sphere of God's total redemptive activity (5:21; I Cor. 1:30). This results from a realistic identification with the person of Christ, both crucified and risen, a dying and rising with Christ (Rom. 6:1-12; Gal. 2:20). The concept is social[179] as well as individual (I Cor. 1:2); to be **in Christ** is a sharing-together (*koinonia*) in Christ (I Cor. 1:9). Paul conceived Christ in virtue of the Resurrection as the Second Adam (Rom. 5:12-21; I Cor. 15:45) and the Head of a new humanity of which He was the "firstfruits" (I Cor. 15:20, 23), the "firstborn" (Rom. 8:29; Col. 1:18), and the "life-giving spirit" (see I Cor. 15:45). Christ is realistically and intimately bound up with the new humanity as its constitutive Head. In his key phrase, **in Christ,** Paul appears to have made use of the Hebrew idea of corporate personality by which a community can be thought of in terms of its representative head.[180]

This new situation in which men are new creatures in Christ is due to God's creative act (cf. 4:6; Rom. 3:25; 11:36). **All things are from Him,** testifies the apostle, because **He has reconciled us to himself through Christ**[181] (18-19). Reconciliation involves the

[176]*Op. cit.,* p. 768.

[177]The *en* is usually local (Best, *op. cit.,* pp. 1, 5, 19, 21). For the meaning of this phrase in Paul see Neilson, *op. cit.,* and the bibliography given there.

[178]Fritz Neugebauer, *In Christus* (Goettingen: Vandenhoeck and Ruprecht, 1961), p. 92.

[179]W. D. Davies, *Paul and Rabbinic Judaism* (London: S.P.C.K., 1948), p. 86.

[180]Best, *op. cit.,* p. 263. See Walter Bartling, "The New Creation in Christ," *Concordia Theological Monthly,* XXI (June, 1950), 412 ff.

[181]Jesus is missing in the better MSS, but its omission does not alter the meaning. The Son as the Word of God is the Agent in the new creation, even as He was in the old (John 1:3; Col. 1:16).

overcoming of personal alienation (Eph. 4:18) or hostility (Col. 1:21) caused by man's rebellion against his rightful Sovereign. The result is a new condition of peace (Rom. 5:1; Gal. 5:22; Eph. 2:12-17; Phil. 4:7) and the restoration of fellowship.

It is man who must be reconciled, not God, as in Judaism,[182] for God does the reconciling. Involved certainly is the wrath of God against the sin of men (Rom. 1:18; 2:5), or else their trespasses would not be counted against them. But God in holy love took the initiative. In the cross of Christ, He became the Aggressor and invaded estranged human life with forgiving love: "While we were enemies we were reconciled to God by the death of his Son . . . God's love has been poured into our hearts" (Rom. 5:10, 5, RSV). The "largest possible change has taken place *in man* . . . his whole nature and life"[183] is altered because of the change of relation between God and man. Sin is adequately dealt with (21) in regard to both what it has done to man (Rom. 7:5-25; 8:2) and what it means to God's holiness (Rom. 3:21-26).

For Paul and the Corinthians reconciliation is accomplished. The way is open now to all, and the apostle has been given **the ministry of reconciliation.** This is the climax of the passage and the final reason he cannot live to himself (13-15). His task is to announce to men the news, **to wit** ("to the effect"),[184] **that God was in Christ, reconciling the world unto himself.** No comma should be placed after **Christ** (cf. ASV, RSV), for Paul's point is what God did in Christ.[185] The link (Rom. 5:9-10) between reconciliation and justification (12) is brought out in the word **imputing** ("reckoning," ASV; cf. Rom. 4:3-8). The work of reconciliation, however, is not completed as far as the world is concerned,[186] for God has **committed** ("deposited," Weymouth) to Paul **the word**[187] of reconciliation (cf. I Cor. 1:18). **The word** (*logos*), according to Cullmann, "is the final definitive revelation

---

[182]Manson, *op. cit.,* p. 51. See Alan Richardson, *An Introduction to the Theology of the New Testament* (London: SCM Press, 1958), p. 217, for the OT emphasis.

[183]Manson, *op. cit.,* p. 52.

[184]Nigel Turner, *Syntax,* Vol. III of James Hope Moulton, *A Grammar of New Testament Greek* (Edinburgh: T. & T. Clark, 1963), p. 137.

[185]See Plummer, *op. cit.,* p. 183.

[186]TDNT, I, 257. The participle is aorist in v. 18 and present in v. 19. But see Denney, *op. cit.,* pp. 769 ff.

[187]Or "message" (RSV). One papyrus MS, P 46, has "the gospel."

as such."[188] The **word of reconciliation** is the essence of the **ministry of reconciliation**. The **word** absolutely qualifies all phases of the **ministry**. This ministry is not primarily giving good advice, but communicating to men the good news of what God has done **in Christ** for **the world**.

Paul is thus the servant of his message. As **ambassadors for Christ** (cf. Isa. 52:7; Eph. 6:20), Paul and his helpers serve as representatives of (*hyper*) Christ (20). His apostolic office is likened to that of the powerful legate of an ancient emperor.[189] His dignity and authority are those of his Sovereign. It is not **as though,** but "seeing that[190] God is making entreaty through us" (Weymouth), which is the basis of his urgent, compassionate appeal. He urges the world on behalf of Christ to **be ... reconciled to God.** Here are the value and the dynamic of the ministry. God by the Spirit of Christ stands behind the preaching of Paul and actually speaks through him. His word is God's word[191] (cf. I Thess. 2:13). A theology of the Christian ministry can be found in these verses.

The reconciliation of men has two efficient causes: (1) what God has done in Christ—**made him to be sin for us;** and (2) what, as a result, Christ means for us—**the righteousness of God in him** (21). Bengel suggests that "He was made *sin* in the same way that we are made *righteousness.*"[192] The **in him** (*en auto*) corresponds to the **for us** (*hyper hemon*). Both parties embraced that which is not deservedly theirs. Christ, who "was innocent of sin" (NEB), entered a sphere utterly alien to Him, that we might enter that sphere from which we have alienated ourselves. Christ, an absolute Stranger to any rebellion against the Father (John 8:46; Heb. 4:15; I Pet. 2:22), was treated as fully responsible for man's rebellion against God (Isa. 53:6; I Pet. 2:24). He suffered "what

---

[188]*Christology of the New Testament,* p. 261.

[189]Deissmann, *op. cit.,* p. 374. See the earlier discussion on "apostle" in relation to 1:1. The repeated *hyper christou* characterizes the official authority of an apostle as of the highest. Plummer, *op. cit.,* p. 186.

[190]See Plummer, *op. cit.,* p. 185, and Turner, *op. cit.,* p. 168, on the force of *hos* here.

[191]Wendland, *op. cit.,* pp. 182 ff. See the final chapter in Robert H. Mounce, *The Essential Nature of New Testament Preaching* (Grand Rapids: Wm. B. Eerdmans Publishing Co., 1960).

[192]*Gnomon of the New Testament,* trans. James Bryce (7th ed., Edinburgh: T. and T. Clark, 1895), III, 385. See Thornton, *op. cit.,* p. 45.

God does to sin, and makes visible what happens when man has God against him."[193] Christ became "a curse for us" (Gal. 3:13; cf. Deut. 21:23; Isa. 53:12; Luke 22:37; Rom. 8:2). He . . . made him indicates the unity of the Father and Son in the identification with sin (John 10:30; Phil. 2:8; Heb. 9:1-14). In the ultimate sense it is God who suffers in himself the consequences of man's sin for the sake of forgiving love (Rom. 13:8).

The result is "forgiveness in the fullest sense,"[194] the restoration of a right relation to God with the deliverance and newness of life which that requires. The **righteousness of God** is an activity of God (Rom. 1:17) by which He vindicates His cause or accomplishes His purposes among men.[195] Stemming from God as righteous it is a regal act, not of acquittal, but of amnesty or pardon (Rom. 3:24-26). Justification is a forensic action, but the image of mere words is shattered, for it is not "a mere word, but it is God's word that works and creates life."[196] So man is taken up into the **righteousness of God,** into a new condition of life (15, 17) whose merit is the cross of Christ and whose substance is the Spirit of Christ. The resultant righteous character of man is that of the rightness of his new relation to God (Phil. 3:9) and his possession of that right Spirit, the transforming Holy Spirit (3:18), who has been given to him (Rom. 5:5). Again justification reaches out to involve sanctification, for it is a righteousness **in him** (17) who has become to us "righteousness, and sanctification, and redemption" (I Cor. 1:30).[197]

Paul's approach to his ministry is supremely "in Christ." (1) As a new creature "in Christ," he looks out on the world of men (16-17). As such (2) he has been entrusted with the message of God's reconciling act "in Christ" (18-19), in order that (3) he

[193]Adolf Schlatter, *Paulus, Der Bote Jesus, Eine Deutung Seiner Briefe an die Korinther* (Stuttgart: Calwer Verlag, 1956), p. 568.

[194]Joachim Jeremias, *The Central Message of the New Testament* (New York: Charles Scribner's Sons, 1965), p. 66.

[195]See C. H. Dodd, *The Epistle of Paul to the Romans* ("The Moffatt New Testament Commentary"; New York: Harper and Brothers, 1932), on Rom. 1:17 for documentation of the righteousness of God as God's saving action. See also Richardson, *op. cit.,* pp. 79 ff.

[196]Jeremias, *op. cit.,* p. 64.

[197]See TDNT, II, 203-10. To understand the meaning of **righteousness,** here, Rom. 3:21-28; 5:1-11; and 8:1-39 should be read as a unity expounding what Paul has in mind by the gospel as the revelation "of the righteousness of God . . . from faith to faith" (Rom. 1:17).

might offer men the free opportunity "in Christ" to become the righteousness of God (20-21).

c. *The life of an apostle* (6:1-10). The chapter division here is quite arbitrary. Paul is still defending the character of his ministry from the viewpoint of his conduct and experiences as an ambassador of Christ.

The thought of 5:20 is resumed as Paul, on the basis of his message (5:21), urgently entreats the weak believers in Corinth not to receive[198] **the grace of God in vain** (6:1). His fear is that they will not allow God's salvation in Christ to really produce the required fruit of a holy walk—a life which properly answers to the death of Christ (5:14-15) and which can face the judgment unashamed (5:10; cf. I Cor. 3:10-15). The new relationship with God brought into being by Christ does not automatically maintain itself. Thus they are urged not to "let it go for nothing" (NEB). Paul makes his appeal **as workers together** with God (5:18, 20; I Cor. 3:9). Beardslee concludes that the apostle is very cautious in speaking of God and man as working together. He suggests that "it would be truer to Paul's thought to say that all real human work is God's work than to say that God and man work together."[199] This is in line with the declaration of Isa. 26:12: "O Lord . . . thou hast wrought for us all our works" (RSV).

Verse 2 is a parenthesis which reveals one of the fundamental assumptions of Paul's gospel; the urgency of his appeal is reinforced by the interjection of Isa. 49:8. There the Servant of the Lord is promised help in the day that salvation will be offered to the Gentiles (Isa. 49:1-12). To his readers Paul therefore announces, **Behold, now is the accepted time; behold, now is the day of salvation** (2). What the Corinthians have experienced through the proclamation of the apostle is the actual fulfillment of prophecy. God's final salvation action is taking place in the present; the last things are not just a far-off event. Today is the time **accepted** by God for men to partake freely of His reconciliation in Christ: "The devil's time is always tomorrow; God's time is always today."[200]

The exhortation of Paul and his helpers is not inconsistent

[198]The aorist infinitive *dexasthai* may be either timeless (present) or it may have the force of a past tense, "to have received."

[199]*Op. cit.,* p. 60.

[200]Alan Redpath, *Blessings out of Buffetings: Studies in II Corinthians* (Westwood, N.J.: Fleming H. Revell, 1965), p. 112.

with the quality of their lives. **Giving** (3) and **approving** (4) are coordinate participles with "working together" (1, RSV). The apostle's conscience is clear, for he seeks always to give "no cause for offense in anything, in order that the ministry be not discredited" (NASB). No real cause for the rejection of his message could be found in his conduct. This is the character of the Christian ministry.

But since his Corinthian detractors apparently felt that the honor of appointment by God meant success and preeminence, Paul had to point out that even his sufferings were demonstrations of the genuineness of his apostleship (4-5).[201] In everything —possibly on every occasion—Paul and his fellow laborers were **approving** (commending, cf. 3:1; 4:2; 5:12) themselves as **ministers** (servants; cf. 6:4; Matt. 20:26; Mark 10:43) **of God.** Redpath suggests that all the conditions mentioned in 4-10 "provide a platform for the display of God's grace" in the lives of His servants.[202]

Paul commends his ministry first **in much patience** ("great endurance," RSV). This quality, greatly stressed by Jesus (Matt. 10:22; 14:13; Luke 8:15; 21:19) and certainly significant for Paul (1:6; 11:23-30; Rom. 5:3; I Thess. 1:3), is placed at the head of three groups of trials. The first triplet, placed in climactic order in v. 4, presents Paul's sufferings in general terms. These may refer to those hardships which are independent of human agency. They include **afflictions** (cf. 1:3-10; 2:4; 4:8, 17; Acts 14:22; 20:23), all experiences of physical, mental, or spiritual pressure which might possibly be avoided; **necessities** ("hardships," NEB), which could not be evaded; and **distresses** ("dire straits," NEB, 4:8), from which no escape is possible.

The second triplet (5) specifies particular sufferings which are inflicted by men. Paul endeavors to commend himself as a true servant of God, "showing the utmost patience amid" (Bruce) **stripes** (11:23; Acts 16:23), **imprisonments** (11:23; Acts 16:23-24), and **tumults** (Acts 13:50; 14:19; 16:19; 19:29; 21:30). The third triplet consists of those disciplines which he imposed upon himself in the furtherance of his mission: **in labours, in watchings, in fastings.** The great apostle for the sake of the gospel often (1) pushed himself to the point of weariness, (2) shortened his hours of rest in order to devote more time to the ministry of

---

[201]Beardslee, *op. cit.*, p. 89.   [202]*Op. cit.*, p. 114.

the Word and prayer, and (3) bypassed his meals when his work was urgent.

Having finished with the nine conditions which indicate the sphere of endurance, Paul now takes a fresh breath. He enumerates nine spiritual characteristics, coordinate with the virtue of **patience,** which God has enabled him to exhibit as a minister of Christ (6-7). The apostle kept his life pure and his motives single. He possessed the **knowledge** of what God had done in Jesus Christ (cf. 8:7; 11:6; I Cor. 2:6-16) both in his own life and in its implications for all men. He was **longsuffering,** in that he could endure the injuries, insults, stubbornness, and stupidity of people without anger or revenge (cf. Col. 3:12). But beyond endurance, he was sympathetically kind and sweet-tempered in his relation to such people (cf. Luke 6:35; I Cor. 13:4; Gal. 5:22). The Holy Spirit, himself the Dynamic of all Paul's virtues, was on display in his ministry (I Cor. 2:4; I Thess. 1:5). The primary fruit of the Spirit, which is genuine **love** (cf. Rom. 12:9; I Tim. 1:5; I Pet. 1:22), reflects the very attitude of Christ (cf. 5:14; I Cor. 13:1-13) in the life of the apostle.

The word of truth (objective genitive) refers to Paul's proclamation of the truth of the gospel (cf. 5:19; Eph. 1:13; Col. 1:5). All this he has done in (*en*) **the power of God** (cf. 4:7-11; 12:9-11; I Cor. 2:3-7). His ministry is the very activity of God (5:20). With a change in prepositions (*dia* replacing the *en* of 4-7a), Paul states that his weapons (cf. 10:4) consist of the **armour** (cf. Isa. 59:17; Rom. 13:12; Eph. 6:13-17; I Thess. 5:8) "which divine righteousness provides"[203] (5:21; cf. Rom. 6:13). From the resources of his relationship to God he is fully equipped with both offensive and defensive armor. For his **right hand** there is "the sword of the Spirit" (Eph. 6:17) and for his **left,** "the shield of faith" (Eph. 6:16).

Now comes a list of nine contrasting conditions which Paul suffers cheerfully for the sake of his calling (8-10). This is the third interchange of opposite experiences in Christ that he has listed in the letter (1:3-7; 4:7-12).[204] The same paradox of humiliation and glory that characterized the career of Jesus is an integral part of Paul's ministry. This is already evident in the

---

[203]Turner, *op. cit.,* p. 207.

[204]See 7:5-7; 11:30; 12:5-10; 13:2-9.

contrast between vv. 4-5 and 6-7. The first four pairs (8-9a) present the ways Paul is thought of by various persons:

By [205] honour	and dishonour,
by evil report	and good report:
as[206] deceivers,	and yet true;
as unknown,	and yet well known.

The last five pairs (9b-10) present the actual facts of the apostle's ministerial existence in relation to Jesus Christ. This relation was a state of affairs "determined by crucifixion and resurrection, and by the subordinate position deliberately taken by the exalted Christ."[207] Paul actually lives:

as dying,	and, behold, we live;[208]
as chastened,	and not killed;[209]
as sorrowful,	yet alway rejoicing;
as poor,	yet making many rich;[210]
as having nothing,	and yet possessing all things.[211]

Thus as a minister of God's reconciliation in Christ, Paul can exhort the Corinthians for two reasons not to frustrate the grace of God in their lives. First is the fact that his ministry is God presently at work in last-day redemptive action (1-2). Second, the quality of his life of service does not hinder acceptance of the grace of God (3). Rather, Paul's life displays that grace (a) in the endurance of severe trials, 4-5; (b) by manifesting the actual traits of the new man in Christ, 6-7; and (c) through a ministry which shares in the paradox of Jesus' own life, 8-10.

The essence of Paul's task as an apostle is the ministry of reconciliation (5:11—6:10). It is a mission (1) whose motives are found in God's act in Christ, 5:11-15; (2) whose perspective is God's act in Christ, 5:16-21; and (3) whose conduct partakes of the nature of God's act in Christ, 6:1-10.

Looking back briefly over Paul's characterization of his ministry (3:1—6:10), it is evident that he defends his office by the

[205]*Dia* now designates state or condition rather than instrument (7). Honour (8) is more accurately "glory."

[206]As is *hos*. The change of prepositions throughout the passage is interesting, *en* (4-7a), *dia* (7a-8a), and *hos* (8b-10).

[207]C. K. Barrett, *From First Adam to Last* (London: Adam & Charles Black, 1962), p. 107.

[208]See 1:8-10; 4:8-12; 11:23-30; Acts 14:19; I Cor. 15:30-31.

[209]See Ps. 118:17-18   [210]See 8:9.

[211]See I Cor. 3:21-23; Phil. 4:12.

nature of the message which has been committed to him and experienced by the Corinthians. (1) His ministry is supremely one of spirit because of the working of the Holy Spirit, 3:1—4:6; (2) This can be so because all that Paul endures for Jesus' sake is the dying of Jesus, which releases to his hearers the Holy Spirit —the resurrection life of Jesus in which Paul will fully share in the future, 4:7—5:10; (3) But both are true only in that Paul's ministry consists of God's act of reconciliation in Christ for the world, 5:11—6:10.

C. PAUL HAS CONFIDENCE IN THE CHURCH, 6:11—7:16.

Paul has now finished with the characterization of his ministry and its implications for the integrity of his attitude toward his converts. He resumes directly the matter of his relationship with the Corinthians. His appeal to them is based on the attitude "Great is my confidence in you" (7:4, NASB; cf. 7:16). He interrupts for some reason the call for renewed affection (6:1—7:4) with an exhortation to separated living (6:14—7:1). The section closes with a consideration of the effect of Titus' role in the reconciliation of Paul with the church at Corinth (7:2-16; cf. 2:12-13).

1. *An Appeal for Fellowship* (6:11-13)

The apostle is surprised at himself for having so frankly opened to the Corinthians the essence of his life as an apostle. He therefore attempts to capitalize on the significance of this opening of himself to them.

Paul was deeply affected by what he had just dictated, and in rare fashion he addressed his converts directly, **O ye Corinthians** (11; cf. Gal. 3:1; Phil. 4:15). The very fact that his **mouth** stands so **open**—that he has spoken so freely—should be evidence to them that his **heart** also is **enlarged** (open wide)[212] to them (cf. Ps. 119:32). Such spontaneous, uninhibited expression could flow only from a warm, trusting heart: "Out of the abundance of the heart the mouth speaks" (Matt. 12:34, RSV).

There are no restrictions or restraints in the feelings of Paul. Any barriers to intimate fellowship are in the affections of the Corinthians: **Ye are straitened in your own bowels** (12). Like **heart** (*kardia*), **bowels** (*splachnois*) is used to denote the seat

[212]Arndt and Gingrich, *op. cit.*, p. 672.

of the emotions. The reference is to the vital organs—the heart, liver, and lungs—in distinction from the lower organs. The Corinthians are the ones who are cramped in their affections.

So speaking to them as his **children** (13) in the faith (cf. I Cor. 4:14, 17; Gal. 4:19; I Tim. 1:2, 18; II Tim. 1:2; 2:1; Titus 1:4), he appeals for **a recompence in the same**—"a like exchange" (NASB). They should also be **enlarged** in their love and openness to him as their spiritual father.

The fact that the apostle by his language (2:14—6:10) has put his heart into his mouth (1) indicates the largeness of his love for them and (2) furnishes an adequate motivation for them to remove all the littleness from their attitude toward him. There must be this openness of love and confidence between minister and people for the free operation of the grace of God in the midst of the people.

2. *An Exhortation to Holy Living* (6:14—7:1)

Abruptly after the burst of affection from the heart of the apostle comes an admonition for a radical ethical separation of the church from its pagan environment. Kling suggests that "it is the very nature of a love so ardent, so aroused at the moment, and now touched with some jealousy, to make sudden transitions."[213] The necessity for separation lies in the very nature of the Church as the temple and family of God. The ethical character of the Church is "to be marked, not by external rules, but by inward purity."[214]

Paul may be tying his leading exhortation of 6:17 and 7:1 to his plea to "receive not the grace of God in vain" (6:1). It is a call to the Corinthians not to become **unequally yoked together with unbelievers** (14). The theme of both is the holiness of life which must result from the reception of the word of reconciliation (5:20-21). The apostle is no doubt using as a figure the OT prohibitions against plowing "with an ox and an ass together" (Deut. 22:10) and against crossbreeding animals of different

---

[213]"Corinthians," *A Commentary on the Holy Scriptures,* ed. John Peter Lange (Grand Rapids: Zondervan Publishing House, n.d.), p. 117. See Introduction for a discussion of the relation of this passage to the letter.

[214]L. S. Thornton, *The Common Life in the Body of Christ* (3rd ed.; London: Dacre Press, 1950), p. 12.

kinds (Lev. 19:19). Included in the sweep of his metaphor are marriage (I Cor. 7:12-15) and at least all the ethical problems dealt with in I Corinthians (6:5-10; 10:14; 14:24). The call is to avoid those close relationships with the heathen which compromise Christian consistency in worship and ethics (cf. I Cor. 5:9-13). No pharisaical exclusiveness is intended. For the sake of winning men, Paul would seek to conform to the pattern of the culture in which he found himself (I Cor. 9:19-23)—not, however, at the expense of the integrity of the Christian faith and its moral standards.

With the rhetoric of a preacher Paul reinforces his injunction by a series of antithetical questions. The first four (14-15) are arranged in pairs with the last question concluding the series and stating the premise for what follows.[215] The incongruity is absolute between the **righteousness** of the Christian (5:21) and the **unrighteousness** (lit., lawlessness) of the pagan (cf. Ps. 45:7; Heb. 1:9). The contrast is between the realm of **light** and the realm of **darkness** (cf. 4:6; Eph. 5:7-11). The second series of contrasts is more concrete and personal; first the leaders of the two realms, **Christ** and **Belial**,[216] are contrasted, then the subjects "believer" and "unbeliever" (RSV). There is no **fellowship** (*metoche*), no **communion** (*koinonia*), no **concord** (*symphonesis*)—nothing at all "in common" (RSV) between that which is peculiar to the respective domains.

The final antithetical question is, **What agreement** (*sygkatathesis*) **hath the temple of God with idols?** (16) Paul appeals to Judaism's complete break with idolatry (cf. Rom. 2:22), which the Gentile believers are to emulate (cf. Acts 15:20; I Cor. 6:9; 10:14; I Thess. 1:9). They must make this rupture because the Church[217] is **the temple of the living God.** The term **temple** (*naos*) refers to the inner sanctuary where the Divine Presence was located in distinction from the entire Temple area (*hieron*). Paul demonstrates his supporting point by an OT quotation which combines Lev. 26:11-13 and Ezek. 37:26-27, describing God's presence with His people and His covenant relationship

---

[215]Plummer, *op. cit.,* p. 207.

[216]**Belial** ("the prince of lawlessness and darkness," Hughes, *op. cit.,* p. 248) was mainly a descriptive term in the OT (Deut. 13:13). It became personalized in the intertestamental literature (but cf. Nah. 1:15) and by NT times was used as a synonym for Satan.

[217]The better MSS read "we are" in place of **ye are.**

with them.[218] The Church is now the **people** of God and to them belong all the promises of the OT. Idolatry and its attendant moral corruption are thus utterly irreconcilable with the life of the Church.

The NT Church as the temple of God is a familiar figure (I Cor. 3:16-17; Eph. 2:20-22), related to the Church as the body of Christ. We saw this underlying 5:1-4. We saw there too that Paul's use was related to Jesus' own use of "temple" for His body, which was to be resurrected (John 2:21; cf. Acts 6:13; 7:48; 17:24). New Testament Christians are construed as "a spiritual house, an holy priesthood, acceptable to God by Jesus Christ" (I Pet. 2:5). The ethical response of the Christian is viewed as "a living and holy sacrifice, acceptable to God, which is your spiritual service of worship" (Rom. 12:1, NASB).[219] Thus in Robertson's words, to anticipate 7:1, "Christian sanctification . . . is nothing less than presenting the whole man a sacrifice to Christ."[220]

Even the obvious conclusion (17-18) can be expressed in Scripture quotation. In v. 17, Paul combines Isa. 52:11 and Ezek. 20:34, where the Jews in Babylon are called out of exile (cf. Jer. 51:45; Rev. 18:4). Verse 18 is II Sam. 7:8, 14 with some reflections of Isa. 43:6 (cf. Jer. 3:19; Hos. 1:10; 2:1). The break is to be decisive, for the tenses are aorist: **come out . . . be ye separate . . . touch not.** The promise is just as decisive that God will "welcome" (RSV) them. They are now God's family, which may necessitate leaving their own homes and families (cf. Matt. 10:34-37). **Daughters** is added by Paul to the OT text, reflecting perhaps the new dignity of women in Christ. **Lord Almighty** (all-powerful), used only here and in Revelation (1:8; 4:8; 11:17; 15:3; 16:7; 19:6; 21:22), imparts confidence in God's power to fulfill His promises.

On the basis of these promises (7:1) Paul makes one final

---

[218]In the quotations of 6:16-18, the variations from the OT text (LXX and Heb.) are due to Paul's use of a Jewish hermeneutical method known as *Midrash pesher.* He incorporates his NT interpretation into the body of the text itself. Here the deviations "are evidently designed for a Messianic-Age interpretation of the prophecies" (Ellis, *Paul's Use of the Old Testament,* p. 144). See pp. 90 ff., 139-49.

[219]See Theodore Gaster, *The Dead Sea Scriptures* (New York: Doubleday and Company, 1957), p. 57, for a similar application of the figure of the Temple and its sacrifices to a community and its ethic.

[220]*Op. cit.,* p. 436.

exhortation to his **beloved** Corinthians which sums up the preceding appeals (6:14, 17; cf. 6:1). The emphasis is on the ethical life: **Let us cleanse ourselves** (cf. Rom. 6:13; 12:1; Jas. 1:27). For this they must apply for the grace of the transforming Spirit (Rom. 12:2).[221] But it is something for which they are responsible. The ethical cleavage with the old way of life is to be both decisive (aorist tense) and comprehensive: **all filthiness of the flesh and spirit.** The terms **flesh** and **spirit** are not used here in the technical Pauline sense of opposite ethical principles (Rom. 8:1-11; Gal. 5:16-24), but in the popular manner of the day to comprehend all the facets of a man's existence (cf. 2:13; 7:5; I Cor. 7:34; I Thess. 5:23).[222] All acts and attitudes which would compromise the singleness of their devotion to the will of God are to be avoided once and for all. Wesley speaks here of all outward and inward sin.[223]

The break is not only decisive (6:17) but is also to characterize[224] all of their living (6:14; cf. Rom. 12:2); **Let us cleanse ourselves** is further interpreted by the nominative present participle, **perfecting holiness in the fear of God.** The term **perfecting** (*epitelein*) means "to bring to a goal," and the durative tense should be taken as repetitive: "We cleanse ourselves effectively when in every instance that presents itself we turn from the stain of flesh and spirit."[225] We are to continue moment by moment to attain the goal of the proper ethical response to a holy God. Clarke would define this process of completing sanctification as "getting the whole mind of Christ brought into the soul ... [which is] the grand object of a genuine Christ pursuit."[226]

The term **holiness** or "sanctification" (*hagiosune*, elsewhere only in Rom. 1:4 and I Thess. 3:13) refers to a quality of ethical life resulting from the reconciliation of man with God in Christ (5:18-21). The cognate term *hagiasmos*, which is more frequent

---

[221]See Clarke, *op. cit.*, p. 344.   [222]See Stacey, *op. cit.*, pp. 135, 171 ff.

[223]*Op. cit.*, p. 661. For the use of **cleanse** (*katharizo*) in the NT in the religious and moral sense, see Matt. 23:26; Acts 15:9; Eph. 5:26; Titus 2:14; Heb. 9:14, 22; I John 1:7, 9. See TDNT, III, 413-26.

[224]Lenski, *op. cit.*, p. 1091, calls it an effective aorist, "the aorist to express a cleansing that actually cleanses." For an aorist similar to **let us cleanse**, cf. Rom. 13:13: "Let us walk." Indicated is a decisive course of action. See Turner, *op. cit.*, pp. 76 ff. But see Olive M. Winchester and Ross Price, *Crisis Experiences in the Greek New Testament* (Kansas City: Beacon Hill Press, 1953), pp. 72 ff.

[225]*Ibid.*, p. 1093.   [226]*Loc. cit.* See Wesley, *loc. cit.*

in the NT, indicates a "sanctifying action" with an ethical import (cf. Rom. 6:19, 22; I Cor. 1:30; I Thess. 4:4, 7; II Thess. 2:15; I Tim. 2:15; Heb. 12:14; I Pet. 1:2).[227] In this Corinthian passage the present participle **perfecting** emphasizes the practical ethical progress toward the full likeness of Christ (cf. 3:18; I John 3:2). This is to be a continuing part of the daily lives of those who live **in the fear of God** (cf. 5:10-11). There is a paradox here. Those who have been brought into a sanctified relationship to God in Jesus Christ (cf. I Cor. 1:2, 30; Heb. 2:11; 10:10, 14, 29; 13:12) must ever reach for the ethical ideal of that relationship; holiness is both a gift and a task. It means, Become what you are! Such an actualized attitude to life (cf. Phil. 3:12-15) is the respect and reverence that we owe to God.

Although the focus of the passage is not on the crisis of entire sanctification as such,[228] the holiness ethic certainly presupposes the crisis. As Strachan so aptly puts it, "To be 'holy' . . . means that we belong to God. The moral demand of this relationship is determined by our conception of God, and the extent of our surrender to His will."[229]

Paul has made an impassioned outcry against worldliness of every form in the body of Christ. A Church conformed to the world will never lead it. If the Church is to be truly in the world ministering to the needs of men, it must cleanse itself from the world inside and out, even to the weapons of its warfare (10:4). Verses 6:14—7:1 present us with (1) The demand, 14-16a; (2) The necessity, 16b; and (3) The motivation for that quality of life which is actually **perfecting holiness in the fear of God**, 6:17—7:1.

3. *Renewed Appeal for Fellowship* (7:2-4)

The thought of 6:11-13 is now resumed. **Receive us** (2) goes back to "Be ye also enlarged" (6:13). What the latter means is made clear as Paul seeks to complete his reconciliation with the Corinthians.

Receive us is literally, "Make room for us." So, "Open your hearts to us" (ASV), is certainly Paul's meaning. His heart is already opened wide to them (6:11), but they must reciprocate

---

[227] TDNT, I, 113-15. See comments on 1:1 in regard to "saint."

[228] But see George Allen Turner, *The Vision Which Transforms* (Kansas City, Mo.: Beacon Hill Press, 1964), 118, 122, 259.

[229] *Op. cit.*, p. 6.

if there is to be genuine fellowship. For this the way is open, because he has never at any time (aorists) **wronged, corrupted** (injured), or **defrauded** ("taken advantage of," RSV; cf. 2:11; 12:17) any of them. Such charges may have been made against him (cf. 1:24; 5:5; 12:16-19), but he is not finding fault with them. On the contrary his desire for mutual love and confidence is so intense that he can say, "We hold you so close in our hearts that nothing in life or in death can part us from you" (3, Knox; cf. 1:6-7; 3:2; Phil. 1:7). Paul may even mean that he is willing to share either life or death with them. Wendland points out that "the bond (*Verbundenheit*) between the apostle and the church is a portrait of the fellowship in destiny (*Schicksalgemeinschaft*) between Christ and Christian (4:10-12)."[230] Even death, therefore, cannot destroy their fellowship (cf. Rom. 8:38-39).

Rather than **condemn** them, he has **great** confidence[231] in them (4). He even boasts about them with **great** pride (cf. 1:14; 7:14; 8:24; 9:2-4). The news of the Corinthians brought by Titus (6) enables Paul to say in regard to them, "I have been comforted to the full; in all the affliction I have to endure I bubble over with joy" (Bruce, cf. 1:4-8; 4:8, 17; 6:4). This verse, which marks the end of the digression that began at 2:14, is a transition to the resumption of Paul's account of his meeting with Titus in Macedonia (2:13). The apostle has kept the door open to personal reconciliation by (1) the integrity of his behavior, 2; (2) the depth of his devotion, 3; and (3) the positiveness of his attitude in regard to the Corinthians, 4. "Love bears all things, believes all things, hopes all things, endures all things" (I Cor. 13:7, RSV).

4. The Coming of Titus (7:5-7)

Paul had left off this subject out of an irresistible urge to give praise to God (2:14). This in turn led him into a discussion of the character of the apostolic ministry as he was reminded of the reproaches against its integrity. To Paul's digressions we owe some of our richest biblical treasures (I Corinthians 13; Phil. 2:5-11). This digression (2:14—7:4) indicates that Paul was writing spontaneously in his capacity as apostle and pastor.[232]

[230]*Op. cit.,* p. 189.

[231]**Boldness of speech** (cf. 6:11) may be the right translation here but *parresia* often has the general meaning of confidence, as in Eph. 3:12; I Tim. 3:13; Heb. 3:6; 4:16; 10:19; I John 2:28; 3:21; 4:17; 5:14. Most commentators prefer the latter sense.

[232]Hughes, *op. cit.,* p. 264.

When the apostle went to Troas in search of Titus and did not find him, he was so anxious ("no rest in my spirit") that he had to turn away from an excellent opportunity to preach, and go on into Macedonia (2:12-13; see map 1). There likewise, his **flesh had no rest**, for he was **troubled** (afflicted) **on every side** (5). "Spirit" and **flesh** (cf. 7:1) are again used by Paul in the popular sense to indicate the sphere of his suffering and anxiety caused by "conflicts without" and "fears within" (NASB). Tasker observes: "It is a part of the frailty of human nature that it is subject to tensions and strains which have both mental and physical repercussions; and such strains are most acutely felt by hypersensitive souls such as Paul."[233] Grace intensifies love. Genuine concern, such as Paul had for the Corinthians, increases the capacity for suffering.

The One "who comforts the downcast" (RSV, Isa. 49:13), that is, "the God of all comfort" (1:3), has **comforted** Paul **by the coming**[234] **of Titus** (6). It was not just the fact of reunion with a beloved companion but the **consolation** (comfort) of the news he brought that rejuvenated the apostle (7). Titus too must have been in low spirits, for **he was comforted** over the Corinthians as he told Paul of their "longing" (ASV), **mourning,** and "zeal" (ASV) in relation to the apostle. Thus "the joy of Titus" (13) and the knowledge that his own feelings in regard to them were now shared by them (note the threefold **your**) caused Paul to rejoice all **the more.** These verses indicate (1) that human affairs had power to depress the apostle, but (2) the God who has "compassion on his afflicted" (Isa. 49:13, RSV) was (3) also sovereignly able through human agency to lift his depression: "Blessed be . . . the God of all comfort" (1:3).

5. *The Repentance of the Church* (7:8-12)

In a most delicate manner Paul attempts to perfect his reconciliation with the church. If all the misunderstandings, suspicions, and bitterness are to be removed from their relationship, the past must be opened up, not just covered over only to rise again in some future circumstance. Love that is spiritual seeks a reconciliation so real that the relation can actually be the same again

---

[233]*Op. cit.*, p. 103.

[234]*Parousia*, "presence" or "coming . . . as the first stage in presence." Used mainly in NT of Christ's second advent, e.g., I Cor. 1:8. See Deissmann, *op. cit.*, pp. 369-73.

even though the healed wound will ever bear a scar. Paul indeed has the Corinthians in his heart to die and live together (3).

The sorrowful **letter** (8), written "out of much affliction and anguish of heart" (2:4), had caused them pain and grief.[235] It had been sent by Titus that the Corinthians might know the abundance of Paul's love for them (2:4). There were times before Titus' return that the apostle regretted[236] sending the letter. He shared the feelings of a father compelled to severely punish his son (cf. 2:9). But he does not now regret it, "seeing" that the letter **made** them **sorry,** "though only for a little while" (RSV).

So **now I rejoice** (9), not because of their grief, but because of the fruit of their grief—**repentance.**[237] They felt "a grief such as God wants."[238] Their difficulty with Paul was placed in its proper context, that of their own relation to God. Because Paul's painful words resulted in a grief "according to the will of God" (NASB; cf. Rom. 8:27) the Corinthians would not "suffer loss" (ASV) in their stewardship of the grace of God (cf. I Cor. 3: 10-15).

For, writes Paul, there are two kinds of **sorrow** (10). One is the mere **sorrow of the world,** a remorse only over the exposure of sin and the dread of its painful consequences. Such a halfhearted dissatisfaction with sin leads the sinner only to spiritual death (cf. Rom. 6:23; 7:13). The other sorrow is that of the Corinthians, a **godly sorrow,** which produces a **repentance to salvation** that is not to be regretted. Such **repentance** is a change of attitude which is itself a sign of the operation of the Spirit of God (Acts 11:18) in His long-range salvation action (Rom. 5:9; 8:18-25). Mackintosh writes:

> Repentance, like every religious act, concerns the three cardinal modes of being conscious—knowing, feeling, willing. Sin is recognized, it is disliked, it is disowned. Recognition of sin by itself is

[235]*Lupeo,* which along with its cognates is translated in the KJV as **made sorry** (8-9), **sorrowed** (9, 11), **sorrow** (10).

[236]**I did repent**(*metamelomai*) is to be distinguished from **repentance** (*metanoia*) in vv. 9-10.

[237]**Repentance** (*metanoia,* "a change of mind, turning about") is a rare word in Paul (7:9-10; Rom. 2:4; II Tim. 2:25). The verb occurs only in II Cor. 12:21. "Faith" was Paul's big word to describe man's approach to God in a Gentile world, while the Early Church in its Jewish environment favored "repentance" (Matt. 3:11; Luke 24:27; Acts 2:38; 3:19; 5:31; 11:18).

[238]Filson, *op. cit.,* p. 359.

not repentance; it may be defiance. Nor is sorrow for sin repentance, if it be alone in the mind; it may be remorse or despair. Abandonment of sin, by itself, may be no more than prudence. The regenerating fact is all three, as a unity, baptized in a sense of God's personal grace to the sinful.[239]

The apostle is thrilled as he points out to the Corinthians that they truly exemplify the kind of sorrow for wrong which God can build upon: **Behold . . . what carefulness** (11; "earnest care," ASV) it has produced in them in regard to the situation (cf. 7). Indeed they are now concerned to clear themselves; they are indignant with themselves;[240] they are spiritually alarmed;[241] they long to be fully reunited with the apostle; they are zealous for the honor and authority of Paul against those who would dishonor him; and they have punished the one who had so grievously offended him (2:6). In every instance they have **approved** (shown) themselves **clear** (innocent) **in this matter.**

Paul's main reason for writing such a letter was that the "earnest care" (ASV, cf. 11) of the Corinthians—their real feeling for Paul[242]—might come to light **in the sight of God** (12). Their spiritual integrity was at stake, for they had let the troublemakers in the church cast a cloud of disloyalty and disrespect over their attitude toward their spiritual father.[243] Secondary motives in Paul's writing involved both the offender and himself as the offended. All aspects of the wrong needed attention.

As their father in the faith, Paul is so concerned for their total spiritual well-being that (1) he does not hesitate to cause them pain, even though he is not less pained, 8-9. (2) Such pain when used of God effects the repentance that leads (a) to salvation and (b) to the correction of the difficulties within the church, 10-12.

6. The Experience of Titus in Corinth (7:13-16)

Picking up again the thought of v. 7, the apostle tells the Corinthians of his comfort in regard to them. He also writes of

[239]*The Christian Experience of Forgiveness* (Glasgow: William Collins Sons & Co. Ltd., 1961), p. 202.

[240]In mind could be the chief offender (2:5) or the "false apostles" (11:13).

[241]Possibly by the fear of Paul ready to come with stern discipline (I Cor. 4:21).

[242]Instead of **our care for you** the best MSS read "your care for us."

[243]Hughes,*op. cit.*, p. 276.

his rejoicing in **the joy of Titus** (13) occasioned by his visit to them.

The statement, **Therefore we were** ("and are," perfect tense) **comforted**, correctly belongs to v. 12 and concludes the preceding paragraph. The **and** is placed before **in your**[244] **comfort** in the best MSS. It opens a new clause, as in RSV: "And besides our own comfort we rejoiced still more at the joy of Titus" (cf. ASV, NASB). Titus, too, had been deeply concerned about the kind of reception he would get in Corinth. So Paul's joy was doubled when he learned that Titus' **spirit was refreshed by . . . all** the church. Titus was happy because the church had "set his mind completely at rest" (NEB).

The reason for Paul's joy over and above his comfort was that he had not been "put to shame" (14, ASV) by his previous boasting to Titus about the expected behavior of the Corinthians. The vindicated **truth** of the apostle's Spirit-inspired insight of love pierced their rebellious attitude of the moment. It penetrated to the genuineness of their care for him (11-12). Paul was not a man to despair of the grace of God in his converts. The truth of his boast about them was in line with the fact that he had always spoken **all things** to them in **truth.** Their conduct "was a further testimony to the consistency of the Apostle's character and the reliability of his work, which he had been constrained to defend in the early part of this epistle."[245]

The affection of Titus is overflowing when he thinks of the **obedience** (cf. 2:9) of the Corinthians, of **how** they **received him . . . with fear and trembling** (15). They had accepted him as the authoritative representative of the apostle. The beginning of Paul's ministry in Corinth was "in fear, and in much trembling" (I Cor. 2:3), due to the sense of his awesome responsibility before God (cf. Ps. 2:11; Eph. 6:5; Phil. 2:12). Now it was appropriate that **fear and trembling** should characterize a hesitant congregation when it faced up to its responsibility to those who proclaimed the will of God to them.

The reconciliation is now complete: **I rejoice . . . that I have confidence in you in all things** (16).[246] Paul may be saying, **I rejoice** because "I am of good courage concerning you" (ASV).

---

[244]The better MSS read "our" (*hemon*) in place of **your** (*humon*).

[245]Hughes, *op. cit.,* p. 279.

[246]Some ancient scribes added **therefore** (*oun*) to emphasize the concluding nature of the verse.

This verse concludes not only the paragraph but the whole first section of the Epistle (1:12—7:16). As Hughes writes, "It is the delicate pin around which the whole of the epistle pivots,"[247] for it serves as a perfect transition to what follows in the rest of the letter. In the light of his vindicated confidence in the Corinthians, Paul has the courage to bring up the matter of their responsibility to Christians in need (cc. 8—9) and to denounce those false apostles who had been undermining his authority in the church (cc. 10—13).

The apostle's sense of joy (13-16) is intimately tied to the total well-being of those with whom he is lovingly concerned, whether it be (1) his fellow worker, 13-14, or (2) his converts to the faith, 15-16.

His confidence in the Corinthians (6:11—7:16) arises from (1) the openness of his heart and life to them, 6:11—7:4; (2) the continued operation of the grace of God in the lives of the Corinthian believers, 7:5-12; and (3) his conviction of their real attitude towards him when undisturbed by outside influence, 7:13-16.

On Paul's side the reconciliation (1:12—7:16) has been effected by completely laying open (1) the details of his relations with them, 1:12—2:14; (2) the motives of his ministry among them, 3:1—6:10; and (3) the depth of his affection toward them, 6:11—7:16.

[247]*Op. cit.*, p. 282.

Section III The Grace of Christian Giving

II Corinthians 8:1—9:15

Paul's attention now turns to the collection which he organized among his missionary churches in Galatia, Achaia, and Macedonia (see map 1) for the relief of the Jerusalem Christian community (cf. Rom. 15:22-28; I Cor. 16:1-4). This offering appears to have been very significant in Paul's apostolic ministry, for he persisted in its personal delivery in spite of the dangers he knew awaited him in Jerusalem (Acts 20:3, 23; 21:4, 10-15; Rom. 15:30-32). Further, it was accompanied by a delegation (8:16-24; Acts 20:4; I Cor. 16:3) that far outweighed the size of the offering, judging by the poverty of the churches from which it came. The theological significance of the collection has been summed up as

> (1) an act of Christian charity among fellow believers motivated by the love of Christ; (2) an act expressing the solidarity of the Christian fellowship by presenting irrefutable evidence that God was calling the Gentiles to faith; (3) an eschatological pilgrimage of the Gentile Christians to Jerusalem by which the Jews were to be confronted with the undeniable reality of the divine gift of saving grace to the Gentiles and thereby be themselves moved through jealousy to finally accept the gospel.[1]

This collection project was in continuity with the OT covenant ethic (Lev. 19:17-18 and Mic. 6:8) and the charity of Judaism[2] (Matt. 6:2; Acts 3:2). It was also in agreement with Jesus' teaching on assistance to the poor (Matt. 5:42; 6:2; 25:43-46; Mark 10:21; Luke 19:2-9; John 13:29). This teaching, along with the nature of the inner disciple relationship (Matt. 20:24-25; Mark 10:42-45; Luke 22:24-27), came to striking fruition in the "all things common" spirit and action of the earliest church (Acts 2:44; 4:32; cf. 6:1-8). Such spontaneous brotherly love, effected by a new relation to God through the Holy Spirit, was kept by

[1]Keith Nickle, *The Collection, A Study of Paul's Strategy* (London: SCM Press, 1966), p. 142. This is the most recent thorough study of the collection. Its general conclusions are sound, although a few of the supporting positions in regard to historical reconstruction and the nature of the literary sources can be questioned. The discussion which follows owes much to it.

[2]George Forte Moore, *op. cit.*, pp. 93 ff.

Paul at the heart of the Christian ethic (Rom. 12:8-13; 13:8-10; Gal. 6:6; Phil. 4:14-17). For him, "concern for the needs of a Christian brother was a direct expression of the peculiar organic fellowship which Christians enjoyed 'in Christ' "[3] (Rom. 5:5).

An offering raised among the Gentile churches for Jewish Christians—"the poor saints which are at Jerusalem" (Rom. 15:16)—would testify to the solidarity of the Church as "one body in Christ" (Rom. 5:5; I Cor. 10:17; 12:12-27; Gal. 3:28). If the Gentiles who have shared in the spiritual blessings of the Jews sense an obligation to be of service to them in material blessings (Rom. 15:26-29), the Jews will be moved to glorify God (9:12-41) for the genuineness of the Gentiles' faith in Christ. They will see the reality of the bond of fellowship between them as equally privileged members of the body of Christ.[4] Paul asked the Romans to pray with him that the offering would be accepted in this spirit (Rom. 15:30-31). He knew that if the Jerusalem church refused such a service they would be denying the lordship of Christ over the Church (cf. I Cor. 1:13; 10:17; 11:29; 12:27).[5]

As the anticipation of Christian eschatology, the collection project was bound up with Paul's desire for the conversion of Israel (Rom. 9:1-5). The dominant view of the OT was that Israel would first be restored to the divinely intended relationship and then God through them would call the Gentiles to salvation on an equality with the Jews. Jesus, in opposition to Judaism, which would subject the Gentiles to Israel in the scheme of salvation, revitalized the OT position.[6] Paul, faced with the problem of the conversion of the Gentiles and the unbelief of Israel in relation to the gospel, saw the order of redemption

[3]Nickle, *op. cit.*, p. 103. It is noteworthy that the Corinthians had never contributed to Paul's support as had the churches of Macedonia (11:8-9; 12:2; I Cor. 9:11-12; Phil. 4:14-17).

[4]Nickle goes beyond the evidence to posit a serious rift between the two segments of the Church that needed to be healed. If the incident between Paul and Peter at Antioch (Gal. 2:11-14) took place after the Jerusalem Council (Acts 15), this would be plausible, but certainly not mandatory. It is quite possible, however, that the incident took place before the council which settled the Jewish-Gentile issue in the Church.

[5]Because of its symbolism for the unity of dispersed Judaism, Paul seems to have patterned the organization of his collection after the Jewish Temple tax (*ibid.*, pp. 99, 74-93).

[6]See Joachim Jeremias, *Jesus' Promise to the Nations* (London: SCM Press, 1958), pp. 19 ff., 25 ff., 46 ff.

reversed for an unbelieving Israel (Romans 9—11). He saw the Gentile Christians as authentically the new Israel (Rom. 9: 6-11; 15: 15-19), which was now to be the instrument of God for the salvation of Israel according to the flesh (Rom. 11: 11-24).

The offering and the witness of the Gentile delegates would be concrete evidence that salvation had come to the Gentiles (9:10) and would, Paul hoped, provoke the Jews to jealousy, so that God might save some (Rom. 11: 11-14). The delegates from the churches would be going to Jerusalem as a sign of the Gentiles' thank offering and the nations' pilgrimage to Zion in fulfillment of prophecy (Isa. 2: 2-4; 60: 5-12).[7] According to Hahn, "Paul sees himself, as an apostle to the Gentiles, called at least indirectly to the service of Israel. This expectation of Paul's was not fulfilled; the Jews did not open their minds to the gospel, but used this journey of Paul and his Gentile Christian delegation as an opportunity to take him prisoner."[8]

A. PAUL COLLECTS AN OFFERING, 8: 1-15

When Paul's mission to the Gentiles had been recognized by the pillar apostles in Jerusalem as of equal validity with theirs to the Jews, he had been given "the right hands of fellowship" (*koinonias*) and asked only to "remember the poor" (Gal. 2: 9-10). Because of a famine in Jerusalem, Paul had already, along with Barnabas, brought a relief contribution from Antioch to Jerusalem. This was either before or at the time of the visit for the Jerusalem conference (Acts 15: 1-31; Gal. 2: 1-10).[9] Now on his third journey Paul undertakes a much more widespread offering occasioned, though not solely motivated, by the need among the Christians in Judea. Probable factors in their condition of poverty were (1) the continuing results of the famine, (2) economic persecution, (3) very few rich and many poor in the composition of the church, and (4) their dissipation of what capital resources they possessed.

---

[7]*Ibid.*, pp. 129-43; Munck, *op. cit.*, pp. 285-303; Ferdinand Hahn, *Mission in the New Testament*, trans. Frank Clarke (London: SCM Press, 1965), p. 109.

[8]*Op. cit.*, pp. 109-10.

[9]Which it is would depend on whether the visit of Gal. 2: 1 is identified with Paul's Jerusalem visit of Acts 11 or 15. See Nickle, *op. cit.*, pp. 23-32, for an attempt to bring out the significance of this offering. He finds it quite anticipatory of the one at hand.

At least a year prior to the writing of this Epistle, Paul had asked the Corinthians to contribute to the offering week by week and to have delegates ready to accompany him to deliver the offering (I Cor. 16:1-4). Due to the difficulty between them, the church had not much more than made a start (8:10; 9:2), so he seeks to reactivate the project among them.

In what has been called "A Philosophy of Christian Giving," Paul first bases his appeal (1) On "the grace of partaking in the ministry to the saints," 8:3;[10] (2) On the example of other churches, 1-7; and (3) On the example of their mutual Lord, 8-15.

1. *The Liberality of the Macedonians* (8:1-7)

Delicately the apostle moves to the touchy subject of money. His perspective is that of **grace** (*charis*, vv. 1, 4, 6, 7; cf. 9, 16, 19; 9:8, 14, 15). The churches in Philippi, Thessalonica, and Beroea had been highly motivated in their giving and so ought the Corinthians to be. **We do you to wit** (1) is, "We must inform you" (KJV, marg.).

Paul wants the **brethren** in Corinth to know the nature of **the grace of God** which has been given to **the churches of Macedonia**. This **grace** or free favor **of God** in Christ to men (8:9; Rom. 3:24) is the heart of Paul's theology from which all else flows. The Macedonian response to divine grace was such that in the midst of severe **trial** (testing) **of affliction** (Phil. 1:29; I Thess. 1:6-7; 2:14; II Thess. 1:4-10) **the abundance of their joy** and "their down-to-depth poverty"[11] "overflowed in the wealth of their liberality" (2, NASB). This was a kind of paradox of grace (cf. v. 9). Under persecution and in poverty grace had produced in the Macedonians "two of the loveliest flowers of the Christian character, **joy** and **liberality**."[12] **Liberality** (*haplotetos*, simplicity, sincerity[13]) refers here, not to the size of their contribution, but to the attitude of concern which prompted their participation (cf. 9:11, 13; Rom. 12:8). It was their uncalculating spirit of generosity, as vv. 3-5 indicate. Here was unquestionable evidence of the genuineness of grace and of their likeness to Christ (v. 9; cf. Mark 12:41-44).

---

[10]Literal translation.   [11]Plummer, *op. cit.,* p. 234.

[12]Tasker, *op. cit.,* p. 11.

[13]Arndt and Gingrich, *op. cit.,* p. 85. The word is peculiar to Paul's writings: cf. 8:2; 9:11, 13; 11:3; Rom. 12:8; Eph. 6:5; Col. 3:22.

The liberality of the Macedonians was evidenced in three ways (3-5). These verses are one sentence in the original: "For in accordance with their ability, I testify, indeed, contrary to their ability, of their own accord, with much entreaty beseeching of us the favour, namely, fellowship in the ministry to the saints, and not just as we had expected, but they gave their own selves first to the Lord and to us by the will of God."[14]

The verb **gave** (5) governs the whole sentence. First they gave **beyond** the limits of the normal precautions for their own necessities of life, and they did it "of their own free will" (RSV). Although the apostle had asked them for the gift, he had not pressured them. Second, they had themselves earnestly begged Paul for the favor[15] of **fellowship** (participation, *koinonian*) in the ministry **to the saints** (cf. 1:1). Paul's use of *koinonia* for the collection is significant (cf. 9:13; Rom. 12:13; 15:26-27; Gal. 6:6; Phil. 4:15). Implied in the use of this expression is the common participation in the resurrection life of Christ which constitutes the Christian community (cf. 13:14; Acts 2:42; I Cor. 1:9; 10:16; Phil. 1:5; 3:10; Philem. 6; I John 1:3-7).[16] As applied to the offering, the term would indicate not only a common participation in the offering, but a deeper relationship "in Christ" of which taking part in the offering is an essential expression. Added to this short line of spiritually significant words (*charis, koinonia*) with which Paul describes the collection is **the ministering** (*tes diakonias;* cf. Acts 6:1-5; 11:29; 12:25). This was Paul's favorite designation for his own ministry (3:6; 4:1; 5:18; 6:3-4; 11:8, 23; cf. Mark 10:43-45). By **ministering** (*diakonia*) he was regarding the collection "as an essential act of Christian fellowship fulfilled in the service of the Lord"[17] (cf. 9:1, 12).

The third evidence of Macedonian liberality was that, more than Paul had **hoped** or expected, they **first gave their own selves to the Lord** and then had put themselves at Paul's disposal. Their spontaneous response to the offering was a direct

[14]Hughes, *op. cit.*, pp. 289 ff.

[15]**That we would receive** (4) is not in the better MSS. **Gift** (*charis*) is "grace" or "favor."

[16]See Thornton, *op. cit.*, pp. 5-33; C. E. B. Cranfield, "Fellowship, Communion," *A Theological Wordbook of the Bible,* ed. Alan Richardson (London: SCM Press, 1957), pp. 81-83; Nickle, *op. cit.*, pp. 105 ff.

[17]Nickle, *op. cit.*, p. 109. See his discussion, pp. 106-9, for the total background of the word in relation to its use here.

result of their commitment to Christ. This was according to **the will of God** as it is made known in the grace of God in Christ (v. 1; cf. v. 9). This was as it ought to be.

The appeal to the Corinthians (6-7) is twofold. As a consequence of the liberality of the Macedonians, Paul encouraged Titus to complete in the Corinthians **the same grace** (gift, *charis*) **also**—"this gracious work as well" (NASB). Titus had begun the collection possibly with the delivery either of I Corinthians (cf. 16:1-4) or "the sorrowful letter" (2:3-10). Paul has now applied *charis* directly to the offering itself. He never uses the ordinary word for "collection" in this letter, as he had in the first (16:1). Strachan suggests, he "uses all the resources of language to dispel any merely commercial atmosphere."[18]

But a stronger reason why the Corinthians should respond is that they too are abundantly supplied with the gifts of divine grace (9:14; I Cor. 1:4-5; cf. cc. 12—14). Listed are **faith** (I Cor. 12:9; 13:2), **utterance** (I Cor. 1:5; 12:10), **knowledge** (I Cor. 1:5; 12:8), and **all diligence.** This **diligence** ("earnestness," RSV) is probably not one of the Corinthian charismatic gifts as the former three, but a moral quality which has been renewed among them (7:11); it is one that should characterize all Christians. The last characteristic of grace is **your love to us.** According to the preferred reading in the MSS it should be "the love from us which is in you," i.e., "the love we inspired in you" (NASB). Paul's open affection to them had found its answer in their own hearts (6:13; 7:2-7). Love for one another as members of the body of Christ had not been one of the most cultivated gifts among the Corinthians (I Cor. 8:1; 13:1). Paul's boast was that they abounded **in every thing,** so certainly they will **abound in this grace also.**

If one includes the use of *charis* in 9 and 19, it can be observed with Nickle that **grace** as applied to the collection was, *first,* "the divine gift which made genuine Christian participation possible" (8:1-6; 9:8, 14-15). *Second,* incorporated in the collection, **grace** was a "direct expression of Christian brotherly fellowship" (8:4, 7) and "an integral component of Paul's ministry, stimulated and justified by the example of the grace of Christ" (8:9, 19; cf. 9:1).[19]

<hr />

[18]*Op. cit.*, p. 134.

[19]*Op. cit.*, pp. 109 ff. In I Cor. 16:3 *charis* (liberality) designates the offering itself.

2. The Challenge of the Liberality of Christ (8:8-15)

The challenge to the Corinthians to complete the offering continues. The manner in which Paul seeks to motivate them is thoroughly Christian. Hughes speaks of Paul's "affectionate diplomacy."[20]

Although he had the right by virtue of his authority as an apostle (1:1), Paul does not enforce the offering by **command-ment** (8). That would contradict its nature as a gift of love. Rather he is using the **forwardness** (lit., earnestness; cf. v. 7; 7:11-13) of the Macedonians to **prove** (put to the test) the **sincerity** of the **love** of the Corinthians. "Genuine" love (RSV) is love in action.

Paul does not need to dictate, for he can crown all other incentives (7-8) with appeal to the ethic of the Incarnation (9). In James Stewart's words, this is using "a sledgehammer to crack a nut!"[21] The "grace of God" (1) is now defined in **our Lord Jesus Christ.** The Corinthians **know** that **for** their **sakes**[22] the One who was **rich** in preexistent splendor (John 1:1-5; 10:30; 17:5; Col. 1:15-17; Heb. 1:3) **became poor**[23] (cf. Matt. 8:20). Bruce's translation of Phil. 2:6-8 sharpens this radical contrast:

Though He existed in the form of God,
He did not exploit equality with God for His own advantage,
But emptied Himself and took the form of a slave,
Appearing in the likeness of men.
And thus appearing in human shape,
He humbled Himself and became obedient—
Obedient to the hour of death,
Even death upon a cross.[24]

Our Lord descended from the height of riches to the depth of poverty. And this was not just a general display of the essence of divine grace. It was a personal example to the Corinthians that they **through his poverty might be rich** (cf. I Cor. 1:5). Such grace, likewise at the heart of Paul's own ministry (6:10), should certainly be adequate to motivate the Corinthians. Only Christ's love could truly make man's love genuine in such a project. Paul knew of no distinction between dogma and ethic; for him the

---

[20]*Op. cit.,* p. 297.   [21]From class notes.

[22]The Greek places this phrase first for emphasis.

[23]The aorist tense indicates the crisis of the Incarnation and all that it involved.

[24]*Loc. cit.* On Phil. 2:5-11 see R. P. Martin, *An Early Christian Confession* (London: The Tyndale Press, 1960).

most difficult doctrines of all, the Incarnation and the atonement, belonged at the heart of the practical ethic of every Christian. The center of our faith must be applied to its every circumference or we are unfaithful servants.

Thus Paul needs only to give **advice**, for his counsel is in the best interest of the Corinthians. **A year ago** (I Cor. 16:1-4) they "began not only to do but to desire" (RSV) to **perform** that which there was a **readiness to will** (10-11). Forward would be "willing" (KJV, marg.). They should **now** complete the offering, in order that their original enthusiasm of which Paul had boasted to the Macedonians (9:2-5) might be proved by their **performance also out of** their ability. They were not asked to give as the Macedonians, "beyond their power." If **a willing mind** (12) is present, their contribution is acceptable (cf. 6:2; Rom. 15:16, 31; I Pet. 2:5). God judges **according** to what a man has, **not according to that he hath not** (cf. Mark 12:43-44). It is not the size of the offering that counts, but the sense of stewardship from which it actually comes. The amount is determined not so much by a certain proportion of what a man has, but according to the measure of his grace.

The intent of the offering was not to ease others to the impoverishment of the Corinthians (13-14). The principle is that of **equality.** One section of the Church was not to burden itself for the luxury or indolence of another section (II Thess. 3:10). But the Corinthians in **this time** of their **abundance** were to **supply** the **want** of the Jerusalem Christians. The time might come when the positions would be reversed and they would be the ones in **want.** The **equality** has as its object "the relief of want, not an artificial equalization of property."[25]

This mutual reciprocity of resources which expresses the true nature of the Church, Paul illustrates by the daily gathering of the manna in the wilderness by the Israelites: **He that had gathered much had nothing over; and he that had gathered little had no lack** (15; Exod. 16:18). All wealth is as manna from the Lord, intended not for intemperance and luxury but for the relief of the necessities of the brethren.[26] Wealth enjoyed at the expense of those in want soon corrupts like hoarded manna and

---

[25]Hughes, *op. cit.,* p. 306. Nickle, *op. cit.,* p. 121, feels that **their abundance** refers to "the 'spiritual blessings' of the Jerusalem Christians" rather than to possible reciprocal financial aid.

[26]See the apt comments of Calvin, *op. cit.,* p. 297.

leads to inequalities that are contrary to the nature of the Christian community. There is probably no place for elegance in the fellowship of the Church; it is certain that there is no room for hunger and nakedness that can be relieved (cf. Prov. 3:27-28; Matt. 25:31-46; Acts 4:34). Hanson refers here to the "self-adjusting love of Christ in His members which supplies the need of each without deficiency or embarrassment."[27]

"The Criteria of Christian Giving" that Paul applied in these verses include: (1) The magnitude of the grace of Christ, 1-9; (2) The extent of material blessing, 10-12; and (3) The measure of the needs of the body of Christ, 13-15.

B. PAUL CHOOSES MESSENGERS, 8:16—9:15

The spiritual nature of the offering continues to be emphasized in the apostle's appeal to "the grace of partaking in the ministry to the saints" (8:4, lit.). However, the basis of his request to the Corinthians now moves to include the safeguards surrounding the collection (8:16-25) and the results of the gift for both the givers and the recipients (9:1-15).

1. *The Recommendation of Titus* (8:16-24)

Three men were sent to collect the offering in Corinth. These verses constitute a letter of commendation (cf. 3:1) for Titus and the two "brothers" who are to safeguard the integrity of the offering.

Paul gives **thanks** (*charis*) for the way in which God has used **Titus** in relation to the church at Corinth (16-17; cf. 2:13; 7:6, 13-16). Even at the time of writing He is graciously putting[28] **the same earnest care** into Titus' **heart** for the Corinthians as Paul had. Titus' concern in coming is far more than just the material needs of the Jerusalem poor. His Spirit-motivated care is such that **he accepted** (actually "welcomes," epistolary aorist) **the exhortation** (appeal) of Paul. In fact, **he went** ("is going," epistolary aorist) actually **of his own accord** (cf. 3).

The brother (18) whom Paul **sent** ("is sending," epistolary aorist) with Titus is one already famous in the work of **the gospel throughout all the churches.** Further, he has been **chosen** (19)[29]

---

[27]*Op. cit.,* p. 71.

[28]The participle is present in the better MSS.

[29]*Cheirotonetheis* meant originally "to elect by raising hands" (Arndt and Gingrich, *op. cit.,* p. 889).

by the Macedonian (?) **churches** to accompany them in[30] **this grace** (*charis,* cf. 6-7), **which is** being **administered . . . to the glory of the . . . Lord** himself. Generous giving manifests the very glory of God (cf. 9). All of these arrangements show the **ready mind** of Paul and his fellow workers in the matter (cf. Gal. 2:10). The best attested reading is "our" rather than **your;** a scribe could have made the substitution in the light of 8:11 and 9:2.

The identification of **the brother** is problematic. Luke has most frequently had this honor in the minds of exegetes but the reasons are far from conclusive.[31] Nickle, interpreting **the churches** (19) as the churches of Judea, identifies the two brethren respectively as "Judas surnamed Barnabas, and Silas, chief men among the brethren" (Acts 15:22). He feels that these men, appointed to carry the apostolic decree to the Gentile churches, were also selected to assist with the collection among the Gentiles.[32] This identification is plausible, but again far from certain.

When it came to money, Paul was extremely cautious (20-21). He shared with others the responsibility of its being **administered** (*diakonoumene*) in order **that no man should blame** (or "discredit," NASB; cf. 6:3) **us in this abundance.** The abundance ("liberal gift," RSV) implies that Paul expected their giving to be generous. He thus is indirectly motivating them not to disappoint his expectations. The ASV translates 21, "For we take thought[33] for things honourable not only in the sight of the Lord, but also in the sight of men" (cf. 4:1). This verse indicates that Paul recognized the importance not only of *being* honest, but also of *appearing* honest before men. Hodge comments that "it is a foolish pride which leads to a disregard of public opinion."[34] Paul's language reflects Prov. 3:4, which, as Nickle points out, "was used to justify the elaborate care exercised at the appropriation from the Temple treasury."[35] The care which Paul was taking may have been due in part to criticism from some in Corinth (cf. 12:16-18).

---

[30]The MSS tradition is divided between **with** (*syn*) and "in" (*en*).

[31]See Hughes, *op. cit.,* pp. 312-16, for the arguments for Luke and the others mentioned in the history of interpretation.

[32]*Op. cit.,* pp. 18-22. His arguments are subjective and at times even objectionable.

[33]Reading *pronooumen gar* with the better MSS rather than *pronooumenoi.*

[34]*Op. cit.,* p. 210.   [35]*Op. cit.,* p. 89.

The second delegate, **our brother** (22), who was to accompany Titus to Corinth, Paul had "often tested and found diligent in many things" (NASB). This **brother** was now all the **more diligent**[36] in the face of his assignment in Corinth, due to the **great confidence** he had in the Corinthians. Although the Greek does not specify, the **confidence** is more naturally the envoy's (cf. marg. reading; also RSV, ASV, NASB) rather than Paul's, as in KJV.

Titus (23) the apostle can commend as his full **partner** (*koinonos*)[37] in the gospel ministry. He had shared with Paul in his work in the service of the Corinthians. As for the **brethren**, they are **the messengers** (lit., apostles) **of the churches**—ones who come with the full authority of those who have commissioned them (cf. 5:20; Phil. 2:25).[38] Further, to those who would raise a question, Paul presents them as **the glory of Christ**, men in whose ministry the light of the gospel shines out (cf. 3:4-11; 4:4, 6; 8:19; 9:13). They are men who are "a credit to Christ" (Bruce).

The Corinthians should therefore demonstrate to these messengers the **proof** (24) both of their **love** (cf. 8) and of Paul's reason for **boasting** about them (cf. 9:2). This consideration is to be shown **before the churches** (lit., "in the face of the churches"). Plummer suggests, "as if the congregations to which they belong were present,"[39] for the delegates will report back to their respective churches.

Paul has encouraged the Corinthians to full participation in the offering (1) by his handling of the project in a manner which leaves no room for suspicion. This he did (2) by delegating a share of the responsibility for the collection and its oversight to others, (3) to spiritual men duly qualified to adequately represent Paul and the churches who sent them.

2. The Sending of the Brethren (9:1-5)

These verses are not a misplaced fragment, for the connection in thought is close with the preceding verses.[40] The apostle

---

[36]*Spoude* and its related forms occur significantly in the chapter; vv. 7-8, 16, 22; cf. 7:11-12.

[37]See comments on 4 where *koinonia* is used.

[38]TDNT, I, 42 ff. See comments on 1:1.   [39]*Op. cit.*, p. 251.

[40]Hughes, *op. cit.*, pp. 321 f., has a discussion of this issue.

here intensifies the urgency of his appeal to the Corinthians to complete the offering.

It is superfluous (1) for Paul to write more about the ministering to the saints (cf. 8:4); what they need is to get on with the project. He is aware of their willingness—forwardness of your mind (2)—for he boasts continually to the Macedonians that Achaia (Corinth) was ready a year ago (cf. 8:10-11). The tense (perfect) implies only that the beginning was made. The result was that the Corinthians' zeal had provoked (stirred up) "most of them" (RSV).

So Paul is sending (epistolary aorist) the brethren (3) that his boasting of the Corinthians should "not be made empty in this case" (NASB); that is, that their completion of the offering would bear out what he had been saying about them. Again his reference is to the preparation that had been made a year ago (2).[41] If some Macedonians come with (4) Paul on the heels of Titus and the two brethren,[42] there is danger that they might find the Corinthians unprepared. If so, Paul and his companions—to say nothing of the Corinthians—would be put to shame by their supposition[43] or confidence in the church.

Prudently (cf. 8:20-21) Paul has exhorted the brethren (5) to go on ahead and arrange beforehand for the bounty (*eulogia*, gift of blessing) which had been promised.[44] The apostle wanted the offering to be ready as indeed a "blessing" and "not as something grudgingly parted with" (Bruce, cf. 7). Covetousness (*pleonexia*) is the opposite of bounty (*eulogia*). Because of the character of its purpose and the quality of the motives behind it, Paul, with a play on words from I Cor. 16:1 (*logia*, collection), now labels it *eu-logia*, a "really fine collection" which will be a blessing.[45] The term ordinarily reflects the relationship between man and God (cf. Eph. 1:3). Here it relates to motivation, for "only if their participation was a free act of Christian love could

[41]Lenski, *op. cit.*, p. 1164.

[42]This verse gives some credence to the view of Nickle that the two brethren were appointed by the Jerusalem church (*op. cit.*, pp. 19 ff.).

[43]So Hering translates *hypostasis*, *op. cit.*, p. 74. Lenski, *op. cit.*, p. 1165, favors "assurance." Boasting is not in the better MSS.

[44]Whereof ye had notice before is based on an alternative reading which has no support in the earliest MSS.

[45]Hans Windisch, *Der zweite Korintherbrief, Kritisch-exegetischer Kommentar uber das Neue Testament* (Gottingen: Vandenhoeck & Ruprecht, 1924), p. 274.

their gift be a vehicle for the blessings of God."[46] This is the thought that is developed in the next section.

Paul sought to insure the appropriate response to the mission of the brethren (1) by reminding the Corinthians that he had staked the integrity of his word on their performance, 1-4; and (2) by the use of language that highlights the spiritual character of the undertaking, 5.

3. The Blessings of Liberality (9:6-15)

The theme touched on in the last clause of v. 5 is now expanded to show how giving, when done in the proper spirit, can be a fountain of blessing to all concerned—to others, to God, and to ourselves.

The apostle first explains that the Christian giver is "one who sows." There is no fear of destitution in giving, for "to give is to sow," and to sow is to expect a harvest. The world enriches itself by depriving others; the Christian enriches himself by giving to others. In one of his contrasting expressions (cf. 2:16; 4:3; 6:8; 10:11-12; 13:3) Paul suggests that there are two ways of sowing— **sparingly** and **bountifully** (6)—with the appropriate harvests. "One man gives freely, yet grows all the richer; another withholds what he should give, and only suffers want. A liberal man will be enriched, and one who waters will himself be watered" (Prov. 11:24-25, RSV; cf. 19:17; Gal. 6:7-10). He who sows **bountifully** (*ep eulogias*) sows "on the principle of blessings,"[47] and on this basis he reaps. The idea of blessings is the principle of Christian stewardship (cf. Luke 6:38).

Consistent with this principle is another. Each **man** (7) is to give only as he has freely decided in his heart ahead of time[48] (8:3; cf. Acts 4:32). Giving is not to be done **grudgingly** (lit., from grief) or **of necessity** (compulsion). Giving that is motivated primarily by external compulsion is done with pain and regret. Such giving cannot be reconciled with the mind of Christ (cf. I Cor. 2:16; Phil. 2:5). It is the **cheerful giver** that **God** loves (Prov. 22:8, LXX). The Greek puts the emphasis on **cheerful** (*hilaron*) and on **God**. It is from *hilaron* that we get our word "hilarious." This verse implies that tithing merely as a legalistic duty is sub-Christian. Christian giving is adequately motivated— giving that stems from grace (8:1; 9:8) and aims at blessing.

[46]Nickle, *op. cit.*, p. 122.   [47]Lenski, *op. cit.*, p. 1170.
[48]The better MSS read "has purposed" rather than **purposeth.**

God is able (8) to furnish both the motivation and the means for generous giving. The big word is **grace,** the concept that underlies Paul's entire treatment of the collection.[49] It is **every grace** that **God is able ... to make ... abound.** Thus the Christian in everything with **every sufficiency ... may abound to every good work.**[50] The term **sufficiency** or "self-sufficiency" is the ability to be independent of external circumstances in the sense that one can view what he has as sufficient for his needs. The man who has the grace to get along with less has more for others. God by His gifts of divine grace can supply all that a man needs—spiritual and material—to be a blessing to others. God's grace is a giving grace, able to fatten the leanest and meanest of souls.

Paul illustrates his point from Ps. 119:9, where the man who serves the Lord scatters his wealth like the farmer scatters his seed, giving **to the poor: his righteousness remaineth for ever** (9; cf. 1, 3). The man who expresses his righteousness in acts and gifts of kindness will never lack the means to do it. **Righteousness** would then mean here "almsgiving" (cf. Matt. 6:1-4). If **righteousness** is primarily a godly quality of life,[51] it will stand the test of judgment. Both ideas are probably present here as in Matthew 6.

His point reinforced by scripture, Paul **now** (10) nails it down. He calls attention to God in the descriptive words of the prophet Isaiah as "he who furnishes seed to the one sowing and bread for eating"[52] (55:10). Even the seed and the strength to sow are from God (cf. I Cor. 4:7). The verbs that follow are future in the better MSS, and thus the parenthesis of the KJV around vv. 9-10 is unnecessary. Such a God, Paul promises his readers, "will supply (lavishly) and multiply your seed for sowing and increase the harvest of your righteousness" (NASB). The last phrase is taken from Hos. 10:12.[53] The apostle has paint-

---

[49]8:1, 4, 6, 7, 9, 16, 19; 9:8, 14, 15; I Cor. 16:3.

[50]Note the "every's" (*pan*)—*pasin ... panti pantote pason ... pan.*

[51]See comment on 5:21. Righteousness received is the fountain of righteousness displayed: "as we have received mercy" (4:1).

[52]Lenski, *op. cit.*, p. 1177.

[53]Nickle (*op. cit.*, p. 137) feels that Paul's use of these two OT quotations in the light of their original contexts supports the idea "that Paul had embodied his desire for the conversion of Israel within his collection project." Thus the "harvest" here would be the hoped-for "conversion of Jews." But this is perhaps straining at the meaning.

ed the generosity of Christians in a vivid picture of the farmer as he plants and harvests.

Thus, to sum it all up, the Corinthians will be **enriched in every thing to all bountifulness** (11; *haploteta,* liberality; cf. 8:2). The "harvest of righteousness" is a single-minded spirit of generosity from which comes selfless giving for the needs of others. This kind of giving—in the concrete form of the collection raised and delivered through Paul and his helpers to the saints in Jerusalem—will produce **thanksgiving to God.**

The offering will have a twofold result. It **not only supplieth** (in full) **the want** (cf. 8:14) **of the saints** (12), but also causes an overflowing through **many thanksgivings** to God. Paul interestingly calls it **the administration** (*diakonia;* cf. 8:4; 9:1, 13) **of this service** (*leitourgias;*[54] cf. Rom. 15:27; Phil. 2:17). He is using the language of sacrifice (cf. Luke 1:23; Heb. 8:6), as he often does for Christian work (Rom. 12:1; 15:16). What is done in the name of Christ partakes of the character of His sacrificial service.

Literally translated, vv. 13-14 show the profoundest result of the collection. "By means of the test of this ministry (*diakonia*), they will glorify God for the submissiveness of your confession in regard to the gospel of Christ, and for the singlemindedness of your sharing-out attitude (*haploteti ten koinonias*)[55] towards them and all others; while they also, with supplication on your behalf, are longing for you because of the surpassing grace of God upon you."

The offering will cement the ties of mutual recognition and love between Gentile and Jewish believers. God will be glorified because the genuineness of the Gentiles' confession of Christ will be evidenced by the **grace of God** (14) which the collection so beautifully displays. It is a long way from Jerusalem to Corinth, but the distance can be spanned by prayer and intercession. Perhaps too, Israel can be provoked to jealousy as the Gentile delegates witness in Jerusalem to the reality of their reception of redemption (cf. Rom. 11:11-14).[56]

---

[54]The word is used in the LXX of the function of priest and Levites in the sanctuary. It can also mean "public service." See Hughes, *op. cit.,* p. 337.

[55]See 8:4; Rom. 15:25. *Koinonia* by itself never means "contribution." In Rom. 15:25 it is *koinonian tina* (a certain sharing-out), which together means "contribution." On **liberal,** see comment on 8:2.

[56]See Nickle, *op. cit.,* pp. 136 ff.

The subject of the collection is closed by Paul with an outburst of gratefulness: **Thanks** (*charis*) **be unto God for his unspeakable gift** (15). The **gift** (*dorea*) is supremely God's indescribable gift of himself in His Son. Here is the source of all the grace and love and blessing that will flow through the churches as a result of the offering (cf. Rom. 8: 32). The apostle's appeal proved successful, for a few months later he wrote from Corinth to the Romans: "Macedonia and Achaia have been pleased to make a contribution for the poor among the saints in Jerusalem" (15: 26, NASB).

Paul gives us (6-15) three "Valid Motives for a Generous Attitude and Joyous Giving": (1) To give with a right spirit is a sowing that guarantees a harvest, 6-7; (2) God is able and willing to grant all that a man needs within and without for a loving sharing with others, 8-10; (3) What is given does more than meet material needs; it has thrilling spiritual implications—blessings all around, 11-15.[57]

If one puts together all the significant terms that Paul applies to the collection in cc. 8—9, Christian giving is (1) an expression of grace (*charis*, 8:1, 4, 6-7, 9; 9:8, 14); (2) freely and sincerely motivated (*haplotetos*, 8:2; 9:11, 13); (3) the implementation of Christian fellowship (*koinonia*, 8:4; 9:13-15; Rom. 15:26-27); (4) an indispensable part of a Christian ministry (*diakonia*, 8:4, 19-20; 9:1, 12-13); (5) a generous gift (*hadrotes*, 8:20); (6) a means of spiritual blessing (*eulogia*, 9:5-6); and (7) a sacred service (*leitourgia*, 9:12).

[57]Plummer, *op. cit.*, p. 257.

With an abrupt change of subject Paul moves into the theme of the legitimacy of his apostleship. He seeks to answer the personal attacks of the false apostles and to counteract the ill effects of their influence in the church. A stern note of warning resounds throughout the passage. As he prepares the way for his third visit to the Corinthians, the character of a true apostolic ministry is further expounded.[1]

A. PAUL ANSWERS HIS OPPONENTS, 10:1-18

The men who opposed Paul were Jews (11:22) who claimed to be apostles of Christ (11:13).[2] They came into the church at Corinth, worked there a short time, and proceeded to take the credit for all that had been accomplished (10:12-18). They were arrogant, tyrannical, and boastful men (10:12; 11:18, 20). The apostle faced their charges fundamentally with his assertion that "we do not war after the flesh" (3, ASV). His weapons are spiritual (1-6), his authority is consistent (7-11), and his boasting legitimate (12-18).

1. *The Spirituality of Paul's Weapons* (10:1-6)

The apostle is imploring the Corinthians, asking that it not be necessary for him to assert his authority boldly when he comes. His critics had made the charge that his personal presence did not answer to the authority he had assumed in his letters. They had misinterpreted Paul's reticence to exert his apostolic authority because they did not adequately discern the nature of apostolic warfare.

Now I Paul myself (1) fairly rings with the overtones of authority (cf. Gal. 5:2). It is related to the difference he made between himself and Timothy (1:1). He personally faces head on the challenge to his authority as an apostle: "It is the very person whose authority is in dispute who puts himself forward

[1]See Introduction for the role of these chapters in the letter.
[2]See Munck, *op. cit.*, pp. 168 ff.

deliberately in this authoritative way."[3] But it is an authority affectionately exercised in the spirit of Christ, by whom Paul has been commissioned to serve. **Meekness** (*prautetos;* cf. Isa. 42: 2-3; Zech. 9:9; Matt. 5:5; 11:29; 21:5; I Cor. 4:21; Gal. 6:1) is that grace-imparted disposition by which we accept without resistance the disciplines of God (cf. Heb. 12:10), just as Jesus submitted to the disciplines of His suffering Servant ministry (cf. Heb. 5:7-9; I Pet. 2:21-23).[4] **Gentleness** (*epieikeias;* cf. Acts 24:4; Phil. 4:5) is that consideration issuing from a position of dignity and authority which can set aside the strict letter of the law to accomplish a higher good[5] (cf. 10:8; 2:6-7; Matt. 18:23). Paul's severity in the exercise of his ministry, like that of his Lord, rises out of his compassion for those whom he serves (4:5).

Behind the apostle's appeal is the accusation that he is **base** (lowly) "when face to face" (RSV) with the Corinthians, but **bold** (*tharro*) in his approach when **absent**. His enemies in usual fashion have distorted a truth (cf. I Cor. 2:1-5) into an untruth —Paul's gentleness being interpreted as weakness.

The apostle literally "begs"[6] (2) the Corinthians to set things in order so that he will not need to be **bold** (*tharesai*) when he comes. He had decided "to challenge decisively"[7] (*tolmesai*) those who regard him as if he **walked according to the flesh** (cf. 1:12; 5:12). It is difficult to know whether **flesh** is meant in a sinister, sinful sense (Rom. 8:4-8) or in a merely human manner (5:16). In this context the two cannot be separated neatly, for the term refers to the supposed contradiction in Paul's behavior as motivated by purely personal concerns. It is acting in dependence on human abilities according to external worldly criteria for reasons of expediency and self-seeking. To conduct one's ministry thus would be sinful.

In answer to the charge the apostle admits that **we walk in the flesh** (3); that is, his life is in the world and subject to human

---

[3]Denney, *op. cit.,* p. 787.

[4]For **meekness** and **gentleness** see Richard C. Trench, *Synonyms of the New Testament* (Grand Rapids: Wm. B. Eerdmans Publishing Co., 1880, 1953), pp. 152-57.

[5]Herbert Preisker, *"epieikeia,"* TDNT, II, 589.

[6]**Beseech** (*deomai*) here is not the same as **beseech** (*parakalo*) in 1. Also in this verse **be bold . . . be bold** translates two very different Greek words.

[7]Lenski, *op. cit.,* p. 1201.

weakness. But he and his helpers **do not war**[8] **after the flesh.** Paul does not conduct his ministry with **weapons** (4) like those the world would use: "human cleverness or ingenuity, organizing ability, eloquent diatribe, or reliance on charm or forcefulness of personality."[9] These when relied upon become **carnal** (fleshly) or sinful in the context of the ministry. They are powerless "for the demolition of" (Bruce) the **strong holds** of the enemy in the hearts of men. The enemy cannot be defeated on his own level of warfare. Paul's **weapons** (*hopla*, cf. Rom. 13:12, "the armour [*hopla*] of light") are **mighty** before **God**; they are "divinely powerful."[10] He is armed with the "tremendous sense of what the Gospel was—the immensity of grace in it, the awfulness of judgment; and it was this which gave him his power, and lifted him above the arts, the wisdom, and the timidity of the flesh."[11]

Paul has sought only to declare the truth openly (4:2). He comes with weapons that are utterly dependent on the power of the Spirit rather than the power of the human (4:7; I Cor. 2:1-5). The apostle defines the **strong holds** when he declares that "we demolish sophistries and all that rears its proud head against the knowledge of God" (5, NEB). The defiant walls and towers of the intellect (cf. I Cor. 1:18-25; 8:1) and will of man must be torn down by the gospel. The inner loyalty of men cannot be won by fleshly or shortcut means (cf. Matt. 4:1-11). But by spiritual warfare **every thought** must be led **into captivity . . . to the obedience of Christ** (cf. I Cor. 2:16). The power of God is able to break down barriers in the minds and hearts of men by means of a truly gospel ministry. The capture then becomes a radical liberation in virtue of the character of the King (cf. 2:14).

A readiness to revenge (6) conveys a wrong impression to the modern reader. Still within the language of the military, Paul affirms that in consistency with the nature of his warfare he is "prepared to court-martial" (Moffatt) or "bring to justice"[12] **all disobedience** yet remaining in the Corinthian church. But such are his patience and his method of meeting difficulties that he will come only "to punish" (RSV) **when the obedience** (2:9; 7:15) of the majority **is fulfilled.** The apostle believed in giving the congregation time to solve its own problems before exercising his

---

[8]For Paul's use of the **war** metaphor for the Christian life and ministry, see 6:7; Rom. 13:12-13; Eph. 6:11-17; I Thess. 5:8; I Tim. 1:18; II Tim. 2:3-4.

[9]Tasker, *op. cit.*, p. 134.   [10]Hughes, *op. cit.*, p. 351.

[11]Denney, *op. cit.*, p. 788.   [12]Lenski, *op. cit.*, p. 1210.

apostolic prerogatives of excommunication from the fellowship of the church (cf. 13:2; Matt. 16:19; 18:18; I Cor. 5:5).

Whether he was moved to act with bold authority or to suffer in humiliation, Paul did not hesitate to ground his ministry in the power of the gospel. It alone was able to destroy the towering walls with which men fortify themselves against obedience to Christ. To fight the Christian warfare with spiritual weapons was (1) never to rely solely on the methods the world uses to capture the minds of men, 3-5; and (2) always to act in submission to the Spirit of Christ in the defense of the right, 1-2, 6.

2. *The Consistency of Paul's Authority* (10: 7-11)

The apostle insists that, once the Corinthians take proper account of the spiritual quality of his authority, they will discover that he is in person what he appears to be in his letters. As an apostle of Christ there is no inconsistency between his written and spoken word, regardless of how men mistakenly judge him by their worldly criteria. In response to their charge he gives an answer and a warning.

The question, **Do ye look on things after the outward appearance?** (7) can correctly be translated as a simple statement, "Ye look at . . ." (ASV), or even as an imperative: "Look at what is before your eyes" (RSV). Though any one of the three could be correct, the last seems to satisfy best the flow of the apostle's thought. Having pointed out to his readers the nature of his warfare, he now exhorts them to "take a look at what is obvious" about his ministry among them (cf. 12:6).

First of all, **if any** one of them "is confident in himself" (NASB) **that he is Christ's** (cf. Mark 9:41; Rom. 8:9; I Cor. 1:12; 3:23; 15:23; Gal. 3:29), **let him . . . think this again with**[13] **himself . . . that, as he is Christ's, just so is Paul.**[14] Perhaps those of the "Christ" party (I Cor. 1:12), or more likely some unduly influenced by Paul's opponents, had become convinced of a superior spirituality which by their criteria would discredit even the apostle.[15] But the plain fact before their face (*prosopon*)

---

[13]Reading with the better MSS *eph* instead of *aph*, which the KJV translates **of.**

[14]The Greek does not repeat **Christ's** (*christou*) the third time, as does KJV.

[15]Paul may be referring in this verse to his opponents in line with the "some" in vv. 2 and 12. Lenski, *op. cit.*, p. 1213, emphatically thinks not; but see Tasker, *op. cit.*, p. 137.

was that he had as much right to claim to belong to Christ as they. If personal conviction was valid for them, it was also valid for him. And was it not his ministry which first brought the gospel to them? The genuineness of their relationship to Christ in a sense then really validated his. Bengel speaks here of "the condescension of Paul, inasmuch as he merely demands an equal place with those whom he had begotten by the Gospel; for he himself must previously [have] belonged to Christ, or been a Christian, by whom another was brought to belong to Christ."[16] Of first importance with Paul in this question of the legitimacy of his apostleship is the integrity of his relationship to Christ.

The facts of his ministry among them, writes the apostle, speak for themselves. Even if he does **boast** "a little too much" (RSV) of his **authority,** he will **not be ashamed** (8). He will not be embarrassed "as having said more than I can make good."[17] The source and practice of his **authority** back up his boast. His **authority** has been given by the **Lord**[18] (5:18-21), **for edification, and not for . . . destruction.** The end result of his ministry has been a building up (12:19; I Cor. 8:1; 14:26) and not a tearing down. Here is the proof which is right before their eyes. Paul, according to v. 5, attempts only to tear down[19] "the conceits of men, every barrier of pride which sets itself up against the true knowledge of God"[20] (cf. Jer. 1:10; 24:6). His opponents, in contrast, tear up the fellowship of love which is the Church (12:20), the body of Christ.

With the term **boast** (cf. 11:16; 12:6) we encounter one of the key words in cc. 10—13. But the apostle is a little uneasy about the fact that the situation has driven him to **boast somewhat more** than he would normally feel proper. Even so, the quality of his labors will protect him from being put to shame.

Even though he has to discuss his authority, he does not wish to **terrify** them by his **letters** (9). This reflects the charge (cf. 10-11) of a discrepancy between the tone of his letters and his actual conduct among them. Paul writes again with a touch of irony. **Terrify** (*ekphobein*, to scare them out of their wits) is

---

[16]*Op. cit.*, p. 412.   [17]Wesley, *op. cit.*, p. 668. See 12:6.

[18]The better Greek MSS do not contain **us,** but this meaning seems obvious.

[19]The word in 5 and 8 is the same, *kathairesin*.

[20]R. A. Knox, *The New Testament* (New York: Sheed and Ward, Inc., 1944), cited in the text from this point on as "Knox."

a strong expression. As Hughes notes, "The picture of Paul . . . acting the part of a distant despot terrorizing them by his correspondence must have struck the Corinthians as altogether ridiculous."[21]

The criticism which was being circulated against the apostle in Corinth, he now quotes: "His letters are impressive and telling, but his personal appearance is insignificant and as a speaker he amounts to nothing"[22] (10). As Bruce pictures it: "He won't say 'Boo' to a goose when he is here himself . . . but when he is away he pretends to be bold and fearless and writes strong letters; if he were sure of his authority, he would show some of his letter-writing severity when he is dealing with us face to face."[23] Whatever else this criticism was, it was a testimony to the effectiveness of Paul's letters[24] to them (cf. II Pet. 3:16). They were mighty **and powerful.** But the charge was one of inexcusable inconsistency. In contrast to his letters his "personal presence is unimpressive" (NASB)—a reference, not to his physical appearance,[25] but to "the meekness and gentleness of Christ" (1), by which Paul always sought to conduct himself. This their worldly hearts had no way to comprehend. Also they considered Paul's **speech contemptible.** His delivery did not come up to their standards of Greek rhetoric—he was not a polished orator (11:6) —and his message (*logos*) was quite beneath their dignity. The fact that Paul had come to Corinth "not with excellency of speech or of wisdom" but only with "Jesus Christ, and him crucified" (I Cor. 2:1-2) had not impressed them: "The word [*logos*] of the cross is folly to those who are perishing" (I Cor. 1:18, RSV).

Paul's answer to his critics is straightforward. **Let such an one think** (consider) **this** (11). Bruce interprets it, "When I come to you I will be as resolute in action as I am resolute in the letters I write when I am away from you." Paul's patience

---

[21]*Op. cit.*, p. 361.

[22]E. J. Goodspeed and J. M. Powis Smith, *The Bible, An American Translation* (Chicago: The University of Chicago Press, 1928, 1948), cited in the text from this point on as "Smith-Goodspeed."

[23]*Paul and His Converts* (New York: Abingdon Press, 1962), p. 73.

[24]Fresh in their minds may have been the "sorrowful letter." See Introduction.

[25]For an apocryphal description of Paul see "The Acts of Paul," in M. R. James, *The Apocryphal New Testament* (Oxford: Clarendon Press, 1924), p. 273.

and gentleness will not prevent him from bold, decisive action, if need be, when he visits them again (cf. 1; 13:2, 10).

Paul's consistency which ought to be obvious to them all can be seen (1) in his commitment to Christ, 7; (2) in his commission from the Lord to build up and not to tear down, 8; and (3) in his conduct among the Corinthians, 9-11.

3. The Legitimacy of Paul's Boasting (10:12-18)

Because his opponents had implied that they were vastly superior to him, Paul, for the sake of the church, felt forced to resort to the somewhat dubious defense of boasting (8). But now as he does so, the boast of false apostles is sent crashing down with one neat blow. At the same time the limits of the apostle's own boasting are carefully fixed.

With a bit of sarcasm, Paul admits to the charge that he is a coward—at least in one matter. He does not have the courage to class[26] himself **with** those who **commend themselves** (12)— "certain people who write their own references"[27] (cf. 3:1; 5:12). Paul cannot compete with the kind of boldness that rests its authority on self-commendation. Such people are completely out of his class.

Paul's point is that their self-praise is really dispraise,[28] for they have refused any worthy standard of comparison. They are **measuring themselves by themselves, and comparing themselves among themselves.** Their own standards applied within their sectarian circle as the only criterion of measurement indicates plainly that they are "without understanding" (ASV). Such persons are impostors who are ignorant of the real character of a servant of Christ and what it means to be commissioned by Him. Thus, Hughes concludes, "the very accusation of self-commendation which . . . they had maliciously hurled at Paul (cf. 3:1; 5:12) recoils with crippling force upon the heads of these intruders."[29] Yet the sad fact is that there are always those who fall for the arrogant, the bigoted, and the dogmatic.

---

[26]Arndt and Gingrich, *op. cit.,* p. 215. There is a play on words here which Plummer brings out with " 'pair' and 'compare,' " *op. cit.,* p. 286. See Hughes, *op. cit.,* p. 364, fn. 21.

[27]Alexander Jones, ed., *The Jerusalem Bible* (Garden City, New York: Doubleday and Company, Inc.), cited in the text hereafter as "Jerusalem."

[28]Tasker, *op. cit.,* p. 140.   [29]*Op. cit.,* pp. 364 ff.

The apostle, for his part, is not going to **boast** in regard to **things without . . . measure** (13), i.e., "things that nobody can measure"[30] (*ta ametera*). These fellows who make themselves "100 percent fit so that when they measure themselves, they always rate 100 percent,"[31] preclude all valid measurement. Paul's criterion, however, is valid (*kanonos*). It is the **measure of the rule** (cf. Rom. 12:3) that **God** has apportioned to him. **Rule,** from which we get our English word "canon," refers here to "sphere of action or influence."[32] The apostle describes it in relation to the Corinthians, **to reach even unto you.** Like a runner in the Isthmian games, Paul stays within the lane marked out for him, in vivid contrast to his opponents, whom God "had not admitted to any lane, let alone one which led to Corinth."[33]

The **rule** or limits are not primarily geographical, as if these interlopers actually possessed an allotted territory for a genuine apostolic ministry. It is perhaps more the specific task and the particular grace presented to Paul (Rom. 15:15-16; Gal. 2:9) which had been demonstrated and confirmed by the fruitfulness of his missionary labors (cf. I Cor. 15:10).[34] He was commissioned an apostle to the Gentiles (Acts 9:15; Rom. 1:5; Gal. 2:9) and was not to build on other men's foundations (Rom. 15:20). Within these limits he had worked as a pioneer missionary to the heathen, even at Corinth.

So, in his boast Paul says, "We are not overextending ourselves, as if we did not reach to you, for we were the first to come even as far as you in the gospel of Christ" (14, NASB). **We are come** (14, *ephthasamen*) keeps here its full meaning "to arrive first," which is well-attested in the NT period. Instead of exaggerating in his boast, Paul may mean here that he is not overstretching his commission (NEB). The fact that he was the first to arrive at Corinth with **the gospel of Christ** (I Cor. 3:6) makes that evident. He had laid the foundation (I Cor. 3:10) and had become their father in the gospel (I Cor. 4:15). Thus with sharp irony Paul has pointed out that his opponents are in effect disqualified as competitors to the apostle. They were nothing but proselyters, who, like all their stripe, make it their business to invade other men's work rather than open up new territory in which to spread their error.

---

[30]Lenski, *op. cit.*, p. 1222. RSV translates "beyond limit."

[31]*Ibid.*, p. 1225.

[32]Arndt and Gingrich, *op. cit.*, p. 403.   [33]Hughes, *op. cit.*, p. 367.

[34]Wendland, *op. cit.*, p. 206.

So Paul will not boast **of things** beyond **measure,**[35] that is, in **other men's labours** (15; cf. Rom. 15:20). This is a reference to those "who, while they had put forth their hand in the reaping of another man's harvest, had the audacity at the same time to revile those, who had prepared a place for them at the expense of sweat and toil."[36] The very fact that Paul's mission had prospered in Corinth was proof that he had been within his **rule** (sphere; cf. 13) in his ministry among them.

The apostle has **hope** that, in spite of the attention given to the impostors, the church's **faith** will increase to the point that he can safely trust its stability. Then he and his helpers, as Paul puts it, will **be enlarged by you according to our rule abundantly.** It is not praise that he is after, but by the encouragement of their full obedience to the gospel he hopes to have his pioneer ministry expanded. The ministry of the great apostle is limited by the faith of his converts. They have the power to set him free to a greater usefulness, or to keep his ministry tied up by their foolish immaturity in the gospel.

The **enlarged . . . abundantly** of v. 15 is **to preach the gospel** (16) "in the lands that lie beyond."[37] Paul wants to evangelize those fields that lie beyond Corinth. As he later indicates, he wanted to visit Rome en route to a mission to Spain (Acts 19:21; Rom. 15:22-24). Thus there would be no cause for him **to boast in another man's line**[38] **of things made ready to our hand.** The words are again scornfully stinging. "Another man's sphere of work already done by him"[39] was the only boast these conceited proselyters could muster. Surely what they really were was plain to the Corinthians (cf. 7a). "We should notice," writes Allo, "that he utters no reproach against the community, to the contrary, Paul is counting on them for the unlimited extension of his apostolate."[40] His controversy in these chapters is primarily with the intruders.

The apostle has been led into the matter of boasting against his personal wishes and now seeks to keep the emphasis properly

---

[35]Or "the things that nobody can measure." The expression is the same as in 13. See Lenski, *op. cit.,* p. 1223.

[36]Calvin, *op. cit.,* p. 335.   [37]Arndt and Gingrich, *op. cit.,* p. 848.

[38]Greek, *kanoni,* translated **rule** in 13 and 15.

[39]Charles B. Williams, *The New Testament* (Chicago: Moody Press, 1937). Cited in the text hereafter as Williams.

[40]*Op. cit.,* p. 253.

placed: **But he that glorieth** (lit., boasts), **let him glory** (boast)
in the Lord (17). Paul must have kept Jer. 9:23-24 close to the
heart of his ministry, for he had used the same citation before in
I Cor. 1:31. Even now, when in a sense he has to boast, he wants
it understood that it is strictly **in the Lord** (cf. 12:2). He never
took credit for the successes of his labors, but kept the words of
the prophet between him and the applause of men:

> *Let not the wise man boast of his wisdom,*
> *Nor the strong man boast of his strength,*
> *Nor the rich man boast of his riches!*
> *But if one must boast, let him boast of this,*
> *That he understands and knows me.*
>   (Jer. 9:23-24, Smith-Goodspeed)

The basic principle of the apostle's ministry was that **not he**
who commendeth himself is approved, but whom the Lord com-
mendeth (18; cf. 5:9; I Cor. 4:15). Strachan suggests that "it is
as though he said, 'After all, apostolic authority is not really safe
in my hands. God's recommendation is the only mark of genuineness.' Paul boasts, not that he is an apostle, but that God made
him one."[41] The servant of Christ can boast only of what God
has done, what He is doing, and what He has promised to do.
Paul's great desire was to have God's approval always. The
standards a man applies to himself may be faulty or even dishonest, but God can see all the way through him.

A threefold criterion is given in these verses which discredits
the boast of Paul's opponents and sets the limits to one's legitimate
boast as a servant of Christ: (1) a standard external to one's
own immediate frame of reference, 12; (2) the nature of the commission personally received from Christ, 13-16; and (3) the approval of the Lord himself, 17-18.

Paul's answer to his opponents in 10:1-18 defines the process
of victory in a ministry for Christ. Redpath comments on these
verses: "Resist, counterattack, deal with the situation upon the
same level that the world deals with it, and you are defeated."[42]
A ministry to men, whether by laymen or clergy, should be in
spiritual continuity with that of the apostle, an imitator of Christ
(I Cor. 11:1). "Consistent Christian Service" is (1) Consistent
with the principle of the Cross in its methodology and techniques,

---

[41]*Op. cit.,* p. 16.   [42]*Op. cit.,* p. 176.

1-6; (2) Consistent with the integrity and quality of one's calling in Christ, 7-11; and (3) Consistent in an attitude of humility which labors only in obedience and gives all credit for its successes to the Lord, 12-18.

B. PAUL BOASTS IN HIS FOOLISHNESS, 11:1—12:13

All that Paul has formerly said is just the prelude. He now begins the sharpest polemic to be found in his writings. He wields masterfully the weapon of irony here sharpened by a holy anger and, as always with Paul, tempered by the supremacy of the truth.[43] The apostle puts on a mask to play the role of his opponents.

The catchword "boast," which appeared in 10:12-18, continues to dominate Paul's approach. But his boasting is a foolishness which he asks the Corinthians to endure (11:1-6, 16-21a). His boast, however, is not an empty one (11:7-15). As an apostle of Christ he can ultimately sum up that boast (11:21b—12:10) in terms of the Christlike declaration, "When I am weak, then am I strong" (12:10; cf. 13:4). His conduct in Corinth (12:11-13) is the basis upon which he has demonstrated the authenticity of his apostleship.

In a form of self-glory—imitating his opponents—Paul really boasts in Christ, his Lord. The contradiction between the mask of his boasting and what he is really saying gives this whole passage a unique literary charm and captivating force. But more important, it reveals to us Paul's sufferings and the personal revelations given to him. These were wrung from him in the struggle[44] with the opposition at Corinth; without that struggle we would have missed his testimony.

1. *An Appeal to Bear with Paul's Foolishness* (11:1-6)

As the apostle moves into a type of defense for which he has no real appetite, he begins with an apology. He wants the Corinthians to understand that the necessity for his boasting results from his affectionate concern for them. He fears lest they should be seduced by the false apostles from their fidelity to Christ. It is the church that he is addressing as he begs them to put up with his brand of self-commendation.

[43]Wendland,*op. cit.,* p. 208.   [44]*Ibid.*

With the word **folly** (1; nonsense[45]) Paul warns his hearers (cf. 16-17, 19, 21; 12:6, 11) that he is now arguing as if "he had the same selfish motives and worldly outlook as his opponents."[46] His boasting is just "a little foolishness" which he is hoping they will be able to see through and endure. And of this he is confident as he adds, "But indeed you are bearing with me" (NASB).[47] It is as if the apostle were expressing his thanks for what he knows they will be gracious to do. Paul believes in the Corinthians that they are already those who bear with him and who will not misinterpret his motives. Again he is giving voice to his underlying confidence in the church at Corinth (cf. 7:4, 14, 16; 8:24; 9:2).

The apostle's "foolishness" is prompted by the fact that he is **jealous** (deeply concerned[48]) **over** them **with godly jealousy** (2), or better, with "the jealousy of God himself" (Knox, cf. Deut. 5:9; 6:15). Bruce paraphrases this, "My jealousy is like God's desire for His people's single-hearted devotion." The expression is a strong one, as the imagery of the rest of the verse indicates.

The metaphor that Paul employs to explain further his **jealousy** is a familiar one in Scripture—**I have espoused** (betrothed) **you to one husband, that I may present you as a chaste** (pure) **virgin to Christ.**[49] God is pictured often in the OT as the Bridegroom of Israel (Isa. 50:1; 54:3, 6; Jer. 3:1; Hos. 2:19-20), illustrating the nature of the bond between them. The figure probably comes more directly from Jesus himself, who spoke often of the Messianic consummation in terms of a marriage feast (Matt. 22:2; 25:1; cf. Rev. 19:7-10) and of himself as the Bridegroom (Mark 2:18-20). Thus the apostle's image of Christ as the Bridegroom, not only of the whole Church (Eph. 5:32), but also of each par-

---

[45]J. H. Bernard, "The Second Epistle to the Corinthians," *The Expositor's Greek Testament*, ed. W. R. Nicoll (Grand Rapids, Mich.: Wm. B. Eerdmans Publishing Co., 1951), p. 99.

[46]Hanson, *op. cit.*, p. 78.

[47]The indicative is preferable to the imperative, **And indeed bear with me.** To take *anechesthe* as indicative fits better the preceding *alla kai*. Further, an imperative following a wish for the same thing would be redundant.

[48]Arndt and Gingrich, *op. cit.*, p. 338.

[49]While not substantially affecting the meaning, the word orders of RSV and Moffatt are not true to the most natural arrangement of the original.

ticular local congregation,[50] stresses both the intimacy and the inviolability of the relation between Christ and the Corinthians.

Paul thinks of himself as a father who in true Oriental manner has arranged the marriage of his daughter to the noblest of bridegrooms. As Lenski translates, he has betrothed the Corinthians "to One as husband."[51] Now it is his responsibility to guard the conduct of the promised bride until the time when he will present her as a pure virgin to the Bridegroom at the marriage.[52] Three things are suggested here: (1) The bride does not betroth herself; (2) Betrothal is more than a modern engagement, for the formal legal vows were taken,[53] leaving only their consummation to the time of the marriage festivities; and (3) Paul's point is the preservation of the chastity of the bride, which he guards with a **godly jealousy.**

In keeping with the figure, the consummation at which Paul is to present the Corinthians **as a chaste virgin to Christ** is no doubt the day of Messianic fulfillment, the Parousia.[54] The apostle's concern here is one he often expressed: that his converts "may be pure and blameless for the day of Christ" (Phil. 1:10, RSV; cf. I Cor. 1:8; Eph. 5:27; Col. 1:22; I Thess. 5:23). The Church and the Christian are to live "in between the times" with the loyalty and the purity of an eager bride. Paul's function is to preserve this fidelity.

Thus in line with the responsibility for them he is afraid lest they should be completely deceived (*exepatesen*) by Satan, as was **Eve** by the craftiness of **the serpent** (3). The serpent prefigures the false apostles (13-15), who are Satanic in their methods, doing the devil's work. **Subtilty** (*panourgia*) is "an extreme malignity

---

[50]Paul may also have this image in mind in I Cor. 6:13-17 for the relation of Christ and the individual Christian. But see Denney, *op. cit.*, p. 729.

[51]*Op. cit.*, p. 1235.

[52]Strachan suggests that the thought may be: "God created Eve and brought her to Adam. Paul, by the power entrusted to him, brought this community into being and betrothed it to Christ" (*op. cit.*, p. 17).

[53]This is seen in Joseph's resolve "to divorce her quietly" when he discovered that Mary had become pregnant between the time of betrothal and the consummation of the marriage (Matt. 1:18-19). The word "divorce" is the same as in Matt. 5:31-32; 19:9; and Mark 10:11-12. See George Foot Moore, *Judaism* (Cambridge: Harvard University Press, 1944), II, 121.

[54]See comments on 5:1-10.

which is capable of everything."[55] For the Corinthians to be influenced by such men would be to violate their betrothal pledge to Christ, for their **minds** (thoughts, *noemata*) would be "led astray"[56] **from the simplicity** (sincerity)[57] **that is in Christ.** Many of the earlier MSS contain after **simplicity** "and the purity" (*kai tes hagnotetos*),[58] which continues the marriage metaphor. It would then be *"that* single mindedness and *that* purity,"[59] as the Greek articles emphasize. It is this attitude which must characterize their relation to Christ that concerns Paul. The RSV translates the meaning well: "a sincere and pure devotion to Christ."

In v. 4, Paul brings up a second reason why they should bear with his folly. **For** (*gar*) connects the thought with v. 1. When one of the boastful interlopers comes to Corinth preaching **another Jesus,** chides the apostle, "you manage to put up with that well enough"[60] (NEB). The unspoken thought in Paul's mind which his readers could not miss is added by Bruce, "Why should you not put up with me then?" If they could tolerate so beautifully one who preaches **another** (*allon*) **Jesus,** a Messiah other than the Son of God, crucified and risen, and **receive another** (*heteron*) **spirit**[61] and **another gospel** (cf. Gal. 1:6) than that which they **accepted** from Paul's ministry, surely his "little foolishness" would be no burden to them. The preaching of the false apostles is probably not to be identified with that of the Judaizers in Gal. 1:6-9.[62] The false teaching was rather an interpretation of the ministry of Jesus which would discredit the ministry of the apostle as a "strength . . . made perfect in weakness" (12:9; cf. 11:21-30). The result would be **another** (different) **gospel.** A ministry whose methodology was not grounded in the weakness of the Cru-

---

[55]Hering, *op. cit.,* p. 84. *Panourgia* is the "craftiness" which Paul renounced in 4:2. See 12:16.

[56]Arndt and Gingrich, *op. cit.,* p. 865.

[57]*Haplotes.* See comments on 1:12; 8:2; 9:11, 13. **In Christ** should be "toward [*eis*] Christ" (ASV).

[58]**So** (*outo*) is absent from the better MSS, though its addition does not essentially change the meaning.

[59]Lenski, *op. cit.,* p. 1239.

[60]**Ye might well bear with him** is based on a less attested reading. *Anechesthe* should be read in place of *aneichesthe.*

[61]See 3:17; Rom. 8:15; 14:17; I Cor. 2:12; Eph. 3:20; Col. 1:11; 5:1, 22; II Tim. 1:7.

[62]See Introduction for the identification of Paul's opponents in Corinth.

cifixion and the resultant power of the Resurrection (cf. 13:4) would not produce "good news" disciples. They would not follow Jesus with the self-denial of His cross (Mark 8:34; cf. II Cor. 4: 7-15; 6:4-5), and they would be essentially worldly in their outlook (cf. 10:3-4; I Cor. 2:12).

Hanson suggests that Paul gives us a three-word summary of Christianity—*Jesus, spirit,* and *gospel.* Christianity for him consists of "Jesus—the New Creation; Spirit—the new Life in which to live in this Creation; Gospel—the instrument for spreading this life in this Creation."[63]

The Corinthians "submit . . . readily enough" (RSV) to those who come with a presentation of Jesus that suits better the egos of the worldly-minded. The apostle therefore considers himself "not a single bit inferior to those superior apostles" (5, Williams; cf. 12:11). **The very chiefest apostles** (lit., super-apostles) is a sarcastic description of those whom Paul later designates "false apostles" (13). The reference is clearly not to the pillar apostles in Jerusalem (Gal. 2:9). The reasons why Paul does not think himself **a whit behind** "these superlative apostles" (RSV) constitute the rest of this section (11:6—12:13; cf. Acts 9:16; I Cor. 4:10-13; 15:10).

He immediately qualifies the assertion in v. 5. **Though** (6) he is not "a polished speechmaker" (Jerusalem; cf. 10:10; I Cor. 2:1-4), he knows what he is talking about. **Rude** (unskilled) **in speech** does not mean that Paul was a poor speaker but that he was untrained (*idiotes*) in Greek rhetoric, just as Peter and John were *idiotai* in regard to rabbinic training (Acts 4:13). Paul's critics in Corinth had resorted to the cheap trick of calling attention to the exterior wrapping in order to divert attention from the true value of the contents.

The apostle is emphatic that he is not in any way inferior when it comes to his **knowledge** of Christ and the gospel. The mystery of God in Christ had been revealed to him and fully proclaimed by him (I Cor. 2:6-16; Gal. 1:11-17; Eph. 3:3-4). He knows Christ, "in whom are hid all the treasures of wisdom and knowledge" (Col. 2:3). This fact Paul **throughly** (in every way, *en panti*) had **made manifest**[64] to them **in all things.** Through the

---

[63]*Op. cit.,* p. 81.

[64]*Phanerosantes* rather than *phanerothentes* is the preferred reading; that is, not "having been made manifest," but "having made manifest." An object is understood.

faithfulness of his witness to them of the gospel of Christ (I Cor. 2:1-5) they have the evidence of the true character of his apostleship (cf. 12:12).

The rationale for the foolishness in which Paul felt he must indulge in view of the situation in Corinth confronts us with "A Stewardship of the Gospel." It is (1) Cognizant of its human limitations, 6; (2) Confident in its conviction of divine truth, 5-6; and (3) Concerned for the spiritual welfare of those it has fathered in the faith, 2-3.

In vv. 2-3 the jealousy of God furnishes us with (1) the dynamic of a proper concern for others in the gospel and (2) the imperative for a pure personal loyalty to Christ.

2. *The Self-support of Paul's Mission* (11:7-15)

Another matter in which Paul feels himself not in the least inferior is his refusal to be financially dependent on those whom he serves in the gospel. The self-appointed apostles who had invaded the church at Corinth took pay for their services. They did their best to use this fact to degrade Paul in the minds of his Corinthian converts (cf. 3). A clear contrast is drawn by the apostle between his motives and those of the false apostles.

He admits preaching the **gospel of God** (7) to the church **freely,** i.e., "free of charge" (Bruce, cf. I Cor. 9:18). This was his practice always in his missionary enterprises. He fully recognized that "the Lord commanded that those who proclaim the gospel should get their living by the gospel" (I Cor. 9:14, RSV; cf. Deut. 25:4). But Paul's preaching did not incur a debt; it discharged one: "I am debtor" (Rom. 1:14). Freely he had received; freely he would give (Matt. 10:8). The gospel was a commission which had been entrusted to him: "For if I preach the gospel, that gives me no ground for boasting. For necessity is laid upon me. Woe to me if I do not preach the gospel!" (I Cor. 9:16, RSV). He did not take it up voluntarily; therefore his reward could not be in mere obedience (cf. Luke 17:10). His reward must be "just this: that in my preaching I may make the gospel free of charge, not making full use of my right in the gospel" (I Cor. 9:18, RSV; cf. vv. 15-18). For this he had been criticized in Corinth.

So he asks, **Have I committed an offence** (lit., a sin) **in abasing myself that ye might be exalted?** The fact that Paul made his living with his own hands (Acts 18:1-3; I Thess. 2:9; II Thess.

3:8) laid him open in a place like Corinth to the charge of being nonprofessional (cf. 6). The Greek professional teachers of the Hellenistic period always lived by their art. It was beneath their dignity to soil their hands. To refuse pay was to admit that one's teaching was of little value.[65] The accusation of the false teachers would be that Paul was not genuine: "His teaching is so worthless that he does not accept payment for it; a man . . . who so obviously declares himself to be the unskilled amateur, is unworthy the credence of intelligent people."[66] But the apostle is only following the example of the Carpenter (Mark 6:3) and humbling himself for the exaltation of others. Paul did it for the church, lest they think he was motivated by material gain and so miss the impact of his message. His question was a forceful one, "Was this a sin to degrade myself to exalt you?"

To make the truth smart he adds, **I robbed other churches . . . to do you service** (8). He had allowed others to contribute to his support while he labored to bring the gospel to the Corinthians (Phil. 4:15). Hughes points out that the metaphor is military. The **wages** (army pay)[67] which were due to Paul as an apostle in Corinth he had obtained by plundering other places which he had already conquered for the gospel in the course of his missionary campaigns.

It was not a matter of extortion, for it was freely brought by **brethren . . . from Macedonia** (9; cf. Acts 18:5) as an expression of the bond between them. The implication is that the Corinthians were indebted to the Macedonians and the latter were once again an example of earnestness (8:8) to the Corinthians. While Paul was in Corinth he **wanted,** his "resources failed" (Weymouth), but even then he was **chargeable to no man** ("did not burden any of you," Smith-Goodspeed). The idea of numbness caused by heavy pressure is fundamental to the verb.[68] **That which was lacking** to Paul was "fully supplied" (NASB) by the Macedonians. He is not rebuking the Corinthians for not having supported him. He would not let them do this, for he had in the past kept himself from being **burdensome** to them (cf. 12:14-15), and intended to do so in the future. He will not let slander alter his principle. The reception of support from Macedonia was not a

---

[65]See Plummer, *op. cit.*, p. 302.   [66]Hughes, *op. cit.*, p. 383.

[67]Deissmann, *Bible Studies, op. cit.*, p. 266. See Arndt and Gingrich, *op. cit.*, p. 606: *"ration (money)* paid to a soldier."

[68]The verb comes from *narke*, a fish that shocks its victim into numbness. From *narke* and *narkao* we get the English word "narcotic."

violation of Paul's stand because he was not laboring for them at the time. He was not too proud to accept help when he was in want.

Paul saw himself as a special case—an apostle by abortion (I Cor. 15:8),[69] "unfit to be called an apostle" (I Cor. 15:9, RSV). The compulsion to apply to himself such a unique stringency arose from his Damascus appearance—"necessity is laid upon me" (I Cor. 9:16).[70] Thus he declares to the Corinthians, **As the truth of Christ is in me, no man shall stop me**[71] **of this boasting in the regions of Achaia** (10; i.e., Corinth; see map 1). In a former letter he had told them that he would rather die than have any man make this boast an empty one (I Cor. 9:15). Now it is linked up with the integrity of his apostleship—**the truth of Christ** in him (cf. I Cor. 2:6). The boasting that he will not allow to be blocked off "is in the resolution to ensure that the gospel, which he had received at no cost to himself and which he was under the obligation of debt to proclaim to others, should be ministered by him to others without cost."[72] Paul is not idly boasting; it is the integrity of his own calling that he will not allow to be compromised away.

No wonder that his rivals in Corinth criticized his practice, for it put them at a disadvantage and cast doubt on their motives. Was their use of the gospel mercenary? (Cf. 2:17; 4:2.) So they suggested that his independence was really unconcern. But Paul replies that the reason for his determination is that he does truly **love** them (11). "And why," cries the apostle from the heart, "because I do not love you? God knows I do" (Smith-Goodspeed). He leaves his vindication to God, to whom he has always been open (5:11). Human persuasion is now useless. If they do not know his love, God does. This is his assurance.

The apostle's reason in relation to his opponents for continuing the stand that he has already taken in Corinth in regard to his support is not to give them a new "point of departure" for their mischief. He wants to **cut off occasion** (12), or "cut the ground from under those who would seize any chance to put their vaunted apostleship on the same level as ours" (NEB).[73] That is, by

---

[69]Lenski, *op. cit.*, pp. 638 ff., 1252.   [70]Munck, *op. cit.*, p. 22.

[71]*Eis eme*, "in regard to me."   [72]Hughes, *op. cit.*, p. 389.

[73]The RSV interprets the meaning of the verse even more clearly: "And what I do I will continue to do, in order to undermine the claim of those who would like to claim that in their boasted mission they work on the same terms as we do."

their insistence that it is a sign of apostolic dignity to receive support from the congregation they hope to induce the apostle to accept payment for his services. Then he would be on an equality with them and his advantage would be gone. They would no longer be hard put to explain why they took money and Paul did not. But they were too mercenary to rise to his level. Paul knew the spot he had them in and he meant to keep them there. He was not deceived by their tactics to drag him down to their level.

What Paul has been implying he now plainly states. He maintains his difference from them because they are **false apostles, deceitful workers, transforming** (cf. Phil. 3:2) **themselves into the apostles of Christ** (13). They were "pseudo-apostles" (cf. 26; Mark 13:22), claiming a category which did not belong to them. Therefore the message they preached, the spirit they spread, and the gospel they offered did not ring true (4). As "sham apostles" (Weymouth) their activities in Corinth were deceitful, treacherous, and cunning. Lenski points out that the noun *dolos,* cognate to *dolios* (**deceitful**), originally meant "bait."[74] They put out bait to catch victims; the idea is that of a deception that kills.[75] These men were "masquerading as" (Bruce) **apostles of Christ.** They were projecting the image of an apostle, but Christ had not sent (*apesteilen*) them. They were counterfeit.

And there is nothing incredible about this, the apostles goes on, **for Satan himself** "masquerades as" (Phillips) **an angel of light** (14). They are only like their master, as already hinted in 3. Paul had no doubt discovered through his own experience that Satan, whose realm is darkness (Eph. 6:12; Col. 1:13; cf. Acts 16:18), never comes as Satan, but always in the garb of light. How else could he get his lies across?

Therefore it is no great thing if his ministers[76] **also be transformed** (masquerade) **as the ministers of righteousness** (15).[77] It is neither "strange" (RSV) nor "surprising" (NASB) that men who are really agents of Satan's realm should attempt to sell themselves as agents of "the righteousness of God" (Rom. 1:16) in Christ. Paul labels their self-seeking approach to the gospel just what it is—Satanic! Strong words, but true; words that deserve meditation by some of us who "live of the gospel" (I Cor. 9:14)! Of those who sell the gospel for money (cf. 2:17)

---

[74]See Arndt and Gingrich, *op. cit.,* p. 202, on *dolos* and *dolios.*

[75]*Op. cit.,* p. 1256.   [76]*Diakonoi.* See 3:3, 9; 4:1; 5:18; 6:3.

[77]See comments on 5:21.

the apostle can only say, their **end shall be according to their works.**[78] Could it be said that a man's ministry turns out according to his motives?

Integral to Paul's ministry was a principle of operation, a personal conviction resulting from his particular commission by Christ. From this principle he could not be separated, even by treacherous means.

To apply the matter of masquerading to the professed Christian, Barclay quotes the four tests drawn up by the Synod of the Church in Uganda by which a man may examine the reality of his own Christianity.[79]

(i) Do you know salvation through the Cross of Christ?
(ii) Are you growing in the power of the Holy Spirit, in prayer, meditation, and the knowledge of God?
(iii) Is there a great desire to spread the Kingdom of God by example, and by preaching and teaching?
(iv) Are you bringing others to Christ by individual searching, by visiting, and by public witness?

Such criteria, honestly applied, would tear away the masks with which some of us today are deceiving ourselves.

3. *Renewed Appeal to Bear with Boastings* (11:16-21a)

Paul turns again to his request of v. 1: indulgence in the foolishness of his boasting. Verses 16-21a introduce the second part of the apostle's "senseless discourse"[80] relating to 11:21b—12:10 as 11:1-6 relates to 11:7-15.

The apostle **again** talks about acting the **fool** (16; cf. v. 1; 10:8; 12:6). The reference is the boasting to which he feels the situation compels him. He does not really want to be thought **a fool,** but if they insist on putting him on the same level as his opponents, he asks only for the same indulgence that the Corinthians have granted them: "Then treat me as a fool and let me do a little boasting of my own" (Jerusalem). Paul indicates his embarrassment at the whole procedure. Nevertheless, in view of the necessity to commend himself in some measure (cf. 11:2-5), he is willing to be misunderstood if need be to make the issues clear in this relation to them.

The apostle declares that when he thus boasts he is speaking **not after** (*kata*) **the Lord,** but **after the flesh** (17-18). However,

[78]Ps. 62:12; Prov. 24:12; Matt. 16:27; II Tim. 7:14; I Pet. 1:17.
[79]*Op. cit.,* p. 279.   [80]Hering, *op. cit.,* p. 87.

since with a full awareness he labels as "foolishness" **this confidence of boasting,** he is not "stooping to sin." Nevertheless he "is ethically on a lower plane than the one on which Jesus moved."[81]

In his **boasting,** conceding that the matter really has to degenerate to this level, Paul appears to be affirming "the certainty that I have something to boast about" (Jerusalem).[82] On the other hand, the expression could indicate the false confidence which dares such an undertaking.[83]

The apostle views his **boasting** as a form of self-justification; thus it is in accord with the norm of "earthly distinctions" (NEB; cf. 5:12). This **after the flesh** (5:16; cf. Phil. 3:4; Gal. 6:13) norm of worldly externals is the principle followed by the **many** who are Paul's opponents in Corinth. Since they glory[84] by such criteria, he **will glory also** (18). But he speaks of his **boasting** in a way that reveals its sharp contrast to that of his opponents. He characterizes it by **flesh** in opposition to **Lord,** a contrast which corresponds to his more usual opposing of "flesh" and "Spirit" (cf. Rom. 8:1-11).

But Paul has yet more pungent words to use. He is foolish (*aphrona,* 16) and they **are wise** (*phronimoi,* 19). Yet they who are so smart "bear with the foolish [*aphronoi*] gladly" (NASB). The first implication is that they should have no difficulty putting up with what Paul is about to impose upon them since in this matter he has joined the ranks of those whom they so amazingly tolerate. But with the second implication comes the sting, as Lenski expresses it, "that such smart people are bigger fools than the fools they indulge; and that, by getting such indulgence from people who think themselves so smart, these fools are smarter than the smart people on whom they impose."[85]

These sharp words are reinforced by five examples of the actual impositions of the false apostles. In this passage "all of the 'ifs' denote reality" and the conditional form "implies that they are ready to have it repeated again and again."[86] First they **suffer** ("bear it," RSV) if anyone brings them **into bondage** (20) or enslaves them to his will. Second, they allow these men to **devour** (lit., eat down; cf. Matt. 12:40; Luke 20:47) their resources like parasites. Third, they **take** them captive as birds in a

---

[81]Lenski, *op. cit.,* p. 1261.   [82]See Hering, *loc. cit.*

[83]Lenski, *loc. cit.*

[84]From the same root as **boasting.** See comment on 1:12.

[85]*Op. cit.,* p. 1263.   [86]*Ibid.*

trap. Further, these "super-apostles" **exalt** themselves; they "are presumptuous"[87] in their arrogant treatment of the Corinthians. In fact the Corinthians put up with these foolish boasters even when they slap them **on the face**—"a daring description of violence and contempt."[88]

Paul may be using only figurative language in the last example, but Hughes feels that he is alluding to instances of actual physical assault. In that time those in authority, even those in ecclesiastical authority (Acts 23:2; cf. I Cor. 4:11), considered themselves free to strike offenders for their insolence and impiety. Paul himself felt it necessary to declare plainly that bishops were not to be pugnacious (I Tim. 3:3; Titus 1:7). Hughes notes that "the fault of the Corinthians was that they had accepted this indignity as though coming from men of apostolic authority, without discerning how utterly incongruous it was with the true spirit of Christ and His apostles, and thereby dishonouring Paul, whom in their hearts they knew to be Christ's genuine apostle, and the gospel which he had preached to them."[89]

With these examples Paul seems to be saying to them, You who "let other people tyrannize over you, prey upon you, take advantage of you, vaunt their power over you, browbeat you" (Knox), surely you cannot object to a little boasting from me. For I would never dream of inflicting such personal indignities upon you as you have suffered from those self-appointed apostles.

About all this, he says with the deepest thrust of his irony, **I speak as concerning reproach** (*atimian*; 21). "Disgrace"[90] (lit., dishonor) is the norm[91] he is now using. Thus it is "to my shame" he says "that we have been weak" (NASB) in comparison with the abusive bullies the Corinthians had submitted to so meekly. If what his opponents have displayed is the mark of true apostolic authority, then he is indeed a weak failure. He admits the **reproach** (cf. 10:10, 12). Although **weak**, Paul is bold enough to counterattack effectively.

In the course of his embarrassing apology for his boasting which is to follow, Paul finds its legitimacy in (1) the realization of its true character—foolishness; and in (2) the recognition of

[87]Arndt and Gingrich, *op. cit.*, p. 281.

[88]J. A. Beet, *A Commentary on St. Paul's Epistles to the Corinthians* (5th ed., London: Hodder and Stoughton, 1892), p. 448.

[89]*Op. cit.*, p. 401.   [90]Arndt and Gingrich, *op. cit.*, p. 119.

[91]See vv. 17-18 for the other two norms indicated by **concerning** (*kata*).

the particular nature of the situation which has made it necessary.

4. The Boasting of the Apostle (11: 21b—12: 10)

The apostle now boldly engages in that "foolishness of boasting" in which he has been so hesitant to indulge. As he presents his credentials as an apostle (11: 21b-33) and brings to light his visions and revelations from the Lord (12: 1-10), he sweeps from the field his opponents with their meager bragging.

a. The credentials of an apostle (11: 21b-33) This section reminds us of 6: 4-10, but it is a richer, more comprehensive and passionate presentation. To the emphasis on the privileges of his birth and training Paul adds a full account of all the sufferings and perils he had undergone as an apostle of Christ. With a formidable list he overwhelms the Corinthians and smothers every contradiction.[92]

Paul is now on the attack, matching boldness with boldness. **I speak foolishly** (21) indicates that his mood of irony continues. It reveals too that he is not indulging in behavior that merits emulation by his readers. Rather he has been forced into it for the sake of the **Corinthians.**

The invaders in Corinth were no doubt Aramaic-speaking Palestinian Jews. They were attempting to use their descent and heritage to put the apostle, who came from foreign soil—Tarsus in Cilicia (Acts 22: 3)—in an unfavorable light. They were boasting "after the flesh" (18)—of language, religion, and race.[93] Now Paul will also boast, **Are they Hebrews? so am I** (22). In Acts 6: 1, this term designated the Hebrew- or Aramaic-speaking Jews in distinction from those who could speak only Greek.[94] Paul, as well as any Jew and better than most, could read and study the Jewish Scriptures in the languages in which they were written. Moreover, he handled the Aramaic dialect with such mastery that he commanded the attention of a hostile mob in Jerusalem as he stood on the steps leading to the fortress Antonia (Acts 21: 39— 22: 3). On that occasion he declared, "I am a Jew, born in Tarsus

---

[92]Wendland, *op. cit.*, p. 215.

[93]Hering, *op. cit.*, p. 88. Or the terms may be roughly synonymous, all variants of the same idea. So Lenski, *op. cit.*, p. 1269.

[94]Ralph Earle, "The Acts of the Apostles," *Beacon Bible Commentary*, ed. A. F. Harper, *et al.*, VII (Kansas City, Mo.: Beacon Hill Press, 1965), 323.

of Cilicia, but brought up in this city, educated under Gamaliel"
(Acts 22:3, NASB). In a careful study W. C. van Unnik concludes that "although Paul was born in Tarsus, it was in Jerusalem that he received his upbringing in the parental home just
as it was in Jerusalem that he received his latter schooling for
the rabbinate."[95] The tongue of Paul's youth at home and in
school may well have been Aramaic. He was indeed a "Hebrew
of the Hebrews" (Phil. 3:5).

Are they Israelites? so am I. He too was a son of Jacob
(Gen. 32:28), "of the people of Israel, of the tribe of Benjamin"
(Phil. 3:5, RSV; cf. Rom. 11:1). Paul thrills at his involvement
with those people chosen as God's particular instrument of His
purposes for all of mankind. They were "Israelites, to whom belongs the adoption as sons and the glory and the covenants and
the giving of the Law and the temple service and the promises,
whose are the fathers, and from whom is the Christ according to
the flesh" (Rom. 9:4-5, NASB). The faith of Israel was fully his,
too; for, like Nathanael, Paul was "an Israelite indeed" (John
1:47).

Are they the seed of Abraham? so am I. Paul was not only
by race a member "of the seed of Abraham" (Rom. 11:1), to
whom the promises were given (Gen. 12:1-2; Rom. 9:4; Gal. 3:8,
16); he was a member also by faith. The Seed of Abraham was
Christ (Gal. 3:16), and in Christ the blessing of Abraham had
come upon all, wrote Paul, "that we might receive the promise of
the Spirit through faith" (Gal. 3:14). As a Christian he remained
more than ever a member of Abraham's race.

The apostle's opponents had nothing on him. He was a Jew
in the fullest sense of the term: "According to the strictest party
of our religion I have lived as a Pharisee" (Acts 26:5, RSV; cf.
Phil. 3:5-6). Yet he could count it all loss in view of the greater
privilege of "the knowledge of Christ Jesus my Lord" (Phil. 3:8).

Are they ministers[96] of Christ? (23) This fourth question,
although similar to the three preceding, transcends them and contains the central issue. All four designations are terms that Paul
had taken from the boasts of his opponents in Corinth. Indicative

---

[95]*Tarsus or Jerusalem,* tr. George Ogg (London: The Epworth Press,
1962), p. 52. But see Longenecker, *op. cit.,* pp. 22-27, who is of the opinion
that Paul did not come to Jerusalem from Tarsus until he was in his teens.
Acts 22:3 can be punctuated as in RSV, "brought up in this city at the feet
of Gamaliel, educated according . . ."

[96]*Diakonoi.* See 3:3, 6-9; 6:4.

of the preeminence of the final claim is Paul's reply: not, "So am I" (*kago*, 22), but, **I am more** (*hyper ego*). He is more a minister of Christ than they: "I am a better one" (RSV). But to talk in this way is for him to "speak as if insane" (NASB). **I speak as a fool** (*paraphroneo*, to be beside oneself) [97] is a stronger word than *aphron*, which was rendered "fool" in vv. 16 and 19. The apostle's thought, as Plummer suggests, is that "to glory about so sacred a matter as the service of Christ is downright madness." [98]

Paul now proceeds to define his superiority as a minister of Christ. In short "they are servants of Christ far less than he himself, because they have had far fewer 'weaknesses' " [99] (cf. 11:23 —12:10; I Cor. 4:10-13). If there are apostolic credentials "after the flesh" (18), they are to be found, not in the strength of the flesh according to human criteria, but in its infirmities (12:5). By the proper measure of an apostle, Paul is "not at all inferior to these superlative apostles" (12:11, RSV). His ministry was in fulfillment of the words spoken by the Lord of him to Ananias, "I will shew him how great things he must suffer for my name's sake" (Acts 9:16; cf. Matt. 10:24). [100]

How utterly Paul is beyond his opponents is brought out by an advance guard of four *en* phrases coupled with adverbs. [101] Lenski notes that "these four are used to indicate rhetorical completeness and are arranged in an ascending scale: " [102] **labours . . . prisons** [103] **. . . stripes . . . deaths.** The words **more abundant** and **more frequent** translate the same adverb, the comparative *perissoteros* used with a superlative force. Thus it is possible that after **I am more** the thought of comparison is dropped. [104] But Lenski would make all the adverbs modify **I am more,** and in this way he maintains the idea of comparison throughout. [105] Paul would then be indicating why he is beyond them, and not detailing the particular items in which he may have surpassed them.

As a minister of Christ the apostle surpasses his opponents altogether because of the excessiveness of his **labours,** i.e., his numerous and arduous evangelistic campaigns; because of the excessiveness of his imprisonments; in view of his **stripes above**

---

[97]Arndt and Gingrich, *op. cit.,* p. 628.   [98]*Op. cit.,* p. 321.
[99]Munck, *op. cit.,* p. 184.
[100]See comments on 1:5-10; 4:7-12; and 6:4-5.
[101]Lenski, *op. cit.,* p. 1271.   [102]*Ibid.*
[103]The better Greek MSS have this order. See RSV.
[104]Plummer, *op. cit.,* p. 322.   [105]*Op. cit.,* p. 1272.

measure (cf. 6:5); and due to the fact that he had been "often in danger of death" (NASB, 1:9-10; 4:11; I Cor. 15:32). These experiences from Paul's life as poured out for the gospel were no doubt foreign to the so-called ministry of his opponents. They probably had hardly worked, much less labored. And it is doubtful if they had ever been in prison or beaten or faced death for Christ's sake. These pretenders to be ministers of Christ are now shown up for what they are. They might have been able to claim equality with Paul in the first three boasts (22) but here it ends: "Paul moves into a different category. Where the ministry is concerned, his is something beyond their horizen."[106] The expression **in deaths oft** is enlarged upon in 24-25.

From the hands of **the Jews** (24) Paul records that **five times** he received 39 lashes. The Jewish law (Deut. 25:1-3) allowed a maximum of 40 stripes to be administered to a convicted man. So the Jewish practice was to stop at 39 lest a miscount should lead to infringing the law. This scourging could be brutal, and its administration took place in the synagogues. Christ had warned His disciples that they would be scourged by the Jews in their synagogues (Matt. 10:7; Mark 13:9; Luke 12:11). Paul had himself fulfilled this prophecy by his own persecution of the first Christians (Acts 22:20; 26:11). The precise occasions of the five scourgings suffered by Paul cannot be identified, but their mention reflects the persistent and bitter hostility of the Jews toward him.

Three times Paul was **beaten with rods** (25). One such instance was at the Roman colony of Philippi (Acts 16:22-23). Normally, as a citizen of Rome, Paul was protected from such treatment at the hands of the authorities, but occasionally as in Philippi he may have been beaten before it was discovered who he was. It is possible, too, that local Roman magistrates under pressure from an aroused populace could have disregarded Paul's privilege as a citizen.[107]

The one time that Paul was **stoned** is recorded for us in Acts 11:19-20, where he was given up for dead at Lystra. Shortly before this he had barely escaped at Iconium (Acts 11:5-6). Stoning was the normal Jewish procedure for carrying out the death penalty. Perhaps the pretext was blasphemy (cf. Acts 6:11; 7:56), for which the Mosaic law prescribed death by stoning (Lev. 24:16).

---

[106]Hughes, *op. cit.*, p. 405.

[107]Plummer, *op. cit.*, p. 325. But see Lenski, *op. cit.*, p. 1274.

No mention is made in Acts of the three shipwrecks which the apostle suffered prior to the writing of II Corinthians. His movements by sea, however, gave ample opportunity for such to have happened.[108] As a result of one of these shipwrecks Paul spent **a night and a day** "adrift in the open sea" (Jerusalem). Verses 24-25 form "a parenthesis of particularity,"[109] for they are both preceded and followed by more general descriptions of the apostle's hardships.

In journeyings often (26) introduces the dangers which Paul faced in the course of his frequent missionary travels in the Mediterranean world of the first century. These journeys were all the "more hazardous because he was subjected to the hatred of all men, to whatever region of the world he might go for Christ's sake"[110] (cf. Matt. 10:22). Lenski comments that the emphasis is on the fact of Paul's travels, for **journeyings** (*hodoiporias*) depends on **I am more** (23) and is thus parallel to the *en* clauses of v. 23.[111] Every time the apostle went forth in obedience to his apostolic commission, he took his life in his hands.

He faced **perils** from unbridged rivers which he may have had to ford at floodtimes. **Robbers** often infested the uninhabited areas which he had to pass through. His life was in danger both from his **own countrymen**, who hated him for his acceptance of a crucified Messiah, and from **the heathen** when he was brought before their courts. Nowhere was he free from peril. **In the city** mobs were incensed against him. **In the wilderness** there was the savagery of man and beast. On **the sea**, storms could break the calm and wreck the small vessels of that day. But worst of all, in a class by itself were **perils among false brethren** (cf. 13). As Plummer comments, "The other dangers threatened life and limb and property, but this one imperilled, and sometimes ruined, his work."[112] Under the mask of **brethren** these men could insinuate themselves into the Christian community and without warning undermine the ministry of the apostle. The Christian Church has never been free from treachery within. Even Christ had a Judas.

At v. 27 the characterization of the apostle's ministerial life appears to move to his experiences in a city while founding and

---

[108]See Acts 9:30; 13:4, 13; 14:25-26; 16:11; 17:14; 18:18.

[109]Hughes, *op. cit.*, p. 408.   [110]Tasker, *op. cit.*, p. 163.

[111]*Op. cit.*, p. 1276. The repetition of **often** (*pollakis*) from the end of 23 brings out this continuity of thought.

[112]*Op. cit.*, p. 327.

establishing a church. The basic description is **weariness and painfulness,**[113] for the phrase is parallel to **in journeyings often** (26) and **in deaths oft** (23). It depends like them on **I am more** (23) and is qualified by the *en* phrases in the rest of the verse.

The first phrase, translated as "labor and hardship" (NASB; cf. I Thess. 2:9; II Thess. 3:8), refers to the manual toil by which Paul supported himself during his evangelistic endeavors. **Weariness** (*kopo;* cf. 23) is passive, indicating the fatigue resulting from prolonged exertion; while **painfulness** (*mochtho*) is active, denoting the actual struggle involved in the exertion. It was not beneath the dignity of the great apostle to work with his hands.

Paul's labors took place in the midst of **watchings often;** that is, sleepless nights due most probably to his long hours of activity. He worked **in hunger and thirst,** due to his inability at times to obtain proper food and drink. **Fastings often** refers probably not to religious discipline but to going without meals in order not to interrupt his work as a minister of Christ. Like his Master, his meat was to do the will of Him who had sent him (John 4:34). The mainspring of Paul's life was the conviction that "man shall not live by bread alone" (Matt. 4:4). Finally in the course of his ministry he had to endure **cold and nakedness** when adequate clothes and shelter were denied to him. One observes with awe the things which the apostle sets forth as the authenticating marks of his ministry. Is not the conclusion inescapable in our time and culture "that less self-concern and less love of present security would mean greater apostolicity?"[114]

But these were not all of the burdens Paul bore. **Besides those things that are without** (28) may refer to "these external things" (NEB) just enumerated,[115] or more probably to a list of things that he has not even mentioned.[116] The RSV translates: "Apart from other things." The chief burden which Paul had to bear was "the daily pressure" (NASB) of his **care of all the churches.** The translation **that which cometh upon me** is based on the inferior reading (*he episustasis mou*) rather than the better attested (*he epistasis moi*), which the NEB renders "the responsibility that weighs on me." The "responsibility" is defined by the phrase which follows—Paul's anxious concern for the **churches** he has established. All his other sufferings were inci-

---

[113]**In** (*en*) is not found in the better MSS.
[114]Hughes, *op. cit.,* p. 414.   [115]So ASV and Lenski, *op. cit.,* p. 1280.
[116]See Hughes, *op. cit.,* pp. 414 ff.

dental to the weight of this concern. This his opponents could not share; in fact they contributed to its occasion (cf. Matt. 18:7; Luke 17:1; Acts 20:29-30).

According to the most frequent interpretation v. 29 presents the cause of the apostle's intense concern. It is his identifying pastoral love for his converts (cf. 2). This compassion which Paul feels for his spiritual children has two complementary aspects.[117] First is sympathy with the weak: **Who is weak, and I am not weak?** (Cf. I Cor. 9:22.) By **weak,** Paul may have in mind the overscrupulous (Rom. 14:1) or those oversensitive to others. But most probably he means those who are weak in relation to their spiritual responsibilities. He not only feels their weakness as his weakness, but he actually considers himself weak with them in contrast to his opponents who boast of their great strength.

Second is indignation at those who would seduce any of his converts into sin: **Who is offended, and I burn not?** The sense is made clear by the NEB: "If anyone is made to stumble, does my heart not blaze with indignation?" The figure is that of being caught in a trap (*skandalizetai*). Tasker notes that "while all Christians would agree that sympathy is of the essence of Christian love, it is not so generally recognized that without moral indignation that love is imperfect."[118]

But there is a strong possibility that the two rhetorical questions in 29 are more synonymous than complementary.[119] Lenski would take them both quite literally with the second forming a climax to the first. The sense of the second would then be: "Is anyone getting himself into a fatal trap, and I on my part am not doing even far worse, getting myself into the fire?"[120] The context of Paul's two affirmations about himself would then be the work and burden of his ministry. The fire would be the fire of the suffering thus involved. Origen preserves a saying of Jesus which reads: "He that is near me is near the fire."[121]

[117]Tasker, *op. cit.*, p. 166.   [118]*Ibid.*

[119]Plummer, *op. cit.*, p. 331, interprets **burn** in the sense of the shame that Paul would feel with the fallen one. So *The Jerusalem Bible* has it: "When any man is made to fall, I am tortured." Plummer would keep the two questions parallel, with the second "a studied advance on the first." Both would present Paul's identifying sympathy with his converts.

[120]*Op. cit.*, p. 1282.

[121]This saying echoes Mark 9:49 and 12:34 and may be genuine. It is quoted from Joachim Jeremias, *Unknown Sayings of Jesus*, trans. R. H. Fuller (London: S.P.C.K., 1958), p. 54.

In view of the context this interpretation perhaps has the most to commend it, for it contributes to the particular presentation of his ministry to the Corinthians that Paul is making in the entire passage (11:21b—12:10). The import of the verse, then, is not the description of the identifying sympathy which gave rise to the apostle's anxiety. The verse rather lays emphasis on the weaknesses that he has been delineating as the credentials of a true apostle.

So with the next verse the thought comes clear: **If I must needs glory, I will glory of the things which concern mine infirmities (30)**. Paul had entered the realm of his opponents in order to counter their claims. But his boast is in that which they despise—his "weakness" (RSV). This boast they cannot and will not match. Paul's "principle of boasting" is paradoxical. His pride is in the utter weakness of the human instrument. In his humiliations and sufferings he can indeed boast, for they become the occasion of the display of the grace and power of the God of the resurrection (cf. 1:8-10; 4:7-12; 13:4). The letter now begins to move rapidly to its climax, which comes with 12:9-10. The theme of divine power through human weakness threads itself through the entire Epistle.

All that he has said and is going to say in relation to his boast in weakness Paul solemnly affirms to be the truth: **God . . . knoweth that I lie not (31;** cf. 11 and 1:13). As always when faced with those who might doubt his veracity, Paul appeals to God, before whom he lives an utterly open life (cf. 1:23; Rom. 9:1; Gal. 1:20; I Tim. 2:7). The God to whom he appeals is the **God and Father of our Lord Jesus.**[122] He is a God whom Paul knows intimately through that Man who is also the Son of God, **Jesus.**[123] Because God has "in Christ" made his way into Paul's life, He **is blessed for evermore** (cf. Mark 14:61; Rom. 1:25; 9:5).

In what seems at first a strange manner, Paul drops in at vv. 32-33 an account of his escape from Damascus. At the instigation of the Jews (Acts 9:23) the **governor** (ethnarch) **under Aretas IV,** king of the Nabataeans, A.D. 9-40,[124] "was guarding the city of the Damascenes in order to seize" (NASB)[125] the fledgling

---

[122]The better MSS do not contain **Christ,** but its omission does not change the meaning.

[123]See the interpretation of this phrase in connection with 1:3.

[124]On the problem of Aretas' authority over Damascus at this time see Hughes, *op. cit.,* pp. 424 ff.

[125]The better MSS do not contain **desirous.**

apostle. Hughes suggests, "It is not unlikely that the ethnarch was himself a Jew and that the guard appointed by him was composed entirely of men of the Jewish race."[126] In order to get away with his life, Paul **was let down by the wall.** His friends lowered him **through** (*dia*) an opening in the wall and he **escaped** the **hands** of the ethnarch.

There is no doubt that this experience held a particular significance for the apostle. Its place after both the list of his sufferings in the service of Christ and the statement of principle which led to their listing appears to have been deliberate. Hughes outlines three reasons: [127] First "this persecution was," in Calvin's words, "Paul's first apprenticeship,"[128] his initiation as a raw recruit into the front line of gospel warfare. Second, it emphasized for him the frailty and the humiliation that were to characterize his total apostolic ministry. The contrast between the mighty Saul of Tarsus who arrogantly approached Damascus, but who entered it weak, stricken, and blind, and the apostle who fled for his life under cover of night from that same city was never forgotten by him. Third, Paul may be presenting it "as an effective and contrasting prelude to the experience which he is now about to describe"[129] (12:2-4). The rapturous ascent into the third heaven was experienced by the same man who suffered the ignominious descent through the Damascus wall. The reference to his high spiritual experience is kept between the narration of an unpretentious escape and the mention of his humiliating "thorn in the flesh" (12:7-10). Paul intends to keep himself and his ministry in true perspective—a weak instrument utterly dependent on the transcendent power of God.

Out of necessity Paul was forced to present his credentials as an apostle of Christ, 21b-33. They can be viewed as "The Credentials of a Christian Ministry." They consist of, (1) not primarily a privileged heritage, 22; but rather (2) in part those indignities and hardships most contrary to human exaltation, comfort, and ease, 23-27; and (3) most centrally, a burdened concern for those for whom he is responsible before God, 28. These all flow from the principle that (4) the human foundation of a true ministry of Christ is the recognition and acceptance of weakness, 29-33.

---

[126]*Op. cit.*, p. 424.   [127]*Ibid.*, p. 422.

[128]*Op. cit.*, p. 363.   [129]Hughes, *op. cit.*, p. 422.

b. Paul's revelations from the Lord (12:1-10). The second phase of Paul's "foolishness of boasting" begins as he moves from the description of his sufferings for Christ's sake to the mention of the heavenly experience given to him. But, as his thorn in the flesh reminds him, his boast must continue to be only in his weakness, so that his confidence may be only in the power of Christ.

The apostle continues: "I am obliged[130] to boast. It does no good;[131] but I shall go on to tell of visions and revelations granted by the Lord" (NEB). Once again he calls attention to the fact that he is forced to boast (cf. 11) both by his opponents and by the church that has listened to them. Hesitatingly he speaks of his ecstatic experiences to a Greek congregation that was tempted to overplay the significance of such manifestations (cf. I Cor. 14: 1-5).[132] The genitive **of the Lord** (1) is subjective, indicating that Paul's **visions and revelations** originated from a divine source. They are not of the same level as his encounter with the risen Christ on the road to Damascus, but are perhaps more in continuity with his experiences recorded in I Cor. 14:18-19.

The reticence with which Paul speaks of his extraordinary religious experiences is instructive. He deliberately discounts them as an argument and describes such use of them as boasting. It is not that Paul belittles religious experience but that he attempts always to keep it in proper perspective and balance as "a sign, a consequence and, within clearly understood limits, a guarantee of what has happened to those who have been brought into redeemed relation with God."[133] The yardstick of all ecstatic experiences and emotional demonstrations is, as Schweizer puts it, "whether they proclaim Jesus as Lord, or in other words, whether they build up the church."[134]

Egocentric language is carefully avoided as Paul writes, I

[130]Rather than *de*, reading *dei* with the better MSS. So RSV: "I must boast."

[131]**For me** (*moi*) is omitted by the better MSS. NASB translates the verse quite literally: "Boasting is necessary, though it is not profitable; but I will go on to visions and revelations of the Lord."

[132]Some feel that Paul is here distinguishing himself "from opponents who preen themselves on the ecstatic experiences and seek to supplant him on this ground" (Rengstorf, *op. cit.*, p. 440). But see Hughes, *op. cit.*, p. 428.

[133]Hanson, *op. cit.*, p. 90. See his expanded "Note on St. Paul's Conception of the Function of Religious Experience," pp. 88 ff.

[134]*The Church as the Body of Christ* (London: S.P.C.K., 1965), p. 31.

knew (rather, "I know," *oida*) **a man in Christ**[135] . . . **caught up to the third heaven** (2). He speaks of himself simply as a Christian, **a man** overwhelmed in a gracious moment by the power of Christ (cf. 10:17). By the phrase **in Christ** the apostle is disclaiming all credit for what happened to him. Calvin refers it to the disposition which intimates "that Paul has not here an eye for himself, but looks to Christ exclusively."[136] There is a sense, we could perhaps call it existential, in which Paul here distinguishes two men in himself—the man in Christ and the natural, earthly man of flesh (cf. 5).[137] Only when he views himself from the standpoint of the latter will he boast; when he speaks of himself as the former, the "I" has been eclipsed by Christ. Could we not have here a pattern for personal witness?

So far from taking to himself that which God has given him, the apostle openly admits that he did not really know precisely what had happened to him: **Whether in the body, I cannot tell; or whether out of the body, I cannot tell** (*oida*): **God knoweth** (*oiden*). Further, so little did he intend to exploit it that for **fourteen years** he had kept it a secret, until it was forced from him. Here is "the rarest of all examples: a boastless boast."[138] **Fourteen years** previous would be approximately A.D. 44, probably the year that Paul spent in Antioch (Acts 11:26). To connect this experience to his commissioning at Antioch as apostle to the Gentiles is only conjecture.[139]

The nearest description that Paul gives is **caught up to the third heaven**. The same verb is used of Philip in Acts 8:39 and of the Parousia in I Thess. 4:17. Although Jewish literature speaks of seven heavens,[140] the NT does not; so the third of seven heavens is hardly in view. Bengel suggests that Paul thinks of three heavens: one of the earth's atmosphere, a second of outer space, and the third of the spiritual realm where God dwells.[141] But more likely is the suggestion of Calvin that "the number *three* is made use of . . . *by way of eminence,* to denote what is highest and

---

[135]See comments on 5:17. Plummer points out that *en christo* belongs to *anthropon harpagenta* (*op. cit.,* p. 340).

[136]*Op. cit.,* p. 367.   [137]See Wendland, *op. cit.,* p. 219.

[138]Lenski, *op. cit.,* p. 1292.   [139]See Plummer, *op. cit.,* p. 341.

[140]See *The Testaments of the Twelve Patriarchs,* "Testament of Levi," Chapter 3. Clarke, *op. cit.,* p. 236, lists the seven. Only here does the NT speak of the third heaven, but Eph. 4:10 speaks of "all the heavens" (RSV).

[141]*Op. cit.,* p. 426: "The first heaven is that of the clouds; the second is that of the stars; the third is spiritual."

most complete."[142] Indicated would be the most sublime condition conceivable, the heavenly presence of Jesus. It would have been an experience comparable to that of Peter, James, and John on the Mount of Transfiguration. Paul, like them, would be getting a glimpse of the glory that is yet ahead at the Parousia (cf. 4:14—5:10) and by it be strengthened for the sufferings which awaited him in the course of the mission to the Gentiles: "I consider that the sufferings of this present time are not worth comparing with the glory that is to be revealed to us" (Rom. 8:18, RSV; cf. II Tim. 4:8). It is only the *man in Christ* who has this anticipation.

In a manner similar to the ancient prophets the apostle describes again in 3-4 the same revelation:[143] **And I knew** (lit., know) **such a man, (whether in the body, or out of the body, I cannot tell** [*oida*]: **God knoweth** [*oiden*]. The verb is the same but now "the third heaven" is identified as **paradise**. In the only other NT occurrences of this word Jesus says to the thief on the Cross, "To day shalt thou be with me in paradise" (Luke 23:43), and the church of Ephesus is promised: "To him that overcometh will I give to eat of the tree of life, which is in the midst of the paradise of God" (Rev. 2:7). The word is used in the Septuagint of the Garden of Eden (Gen. 2:8; 13:10; Isa. 51:3) and of the abode of God (Ezek. 28:13; 31:8). Barclay illuminatingly writes of this word: "*Paradise* comes from a Persian word which means *a walled-garden*. When a Persian king wished to confer a very special honour on someone who was specially dear to him he made him a *companion of the garden,* and gave him the right to walk in the royal gardens with him in close and intimate companionship."[144]

Paul was granted for an indescribable moment intimate companionship with the Lord within the courts of heaven itself. For an instant he was "at home with the Lord" (5:8, RSV). But he did not know if he was **in** or **out of the body,** so rapturous was the event that briefly parted the mists of earthly existence and transported him into the ultimate heavenly glory of the presence of the Son of God. There is no adequate reason to distinguish between the meanings of the three NT occurrences of **paradise**.

The influence of this and other like experiences upon Paul's

---

[142]*Op. cit.*, p. 368.

[143]Some see two experiences here (e.g., Plummer, *op. cit.*, p. 344). See v. 7. See also Hughes, *op. cit.*, pp. 435 ff.

[144]*Op. cit.*, p. 286.

ministry must have been incalculable, as the words which he heard were **unspeakable.** Could not the secret of his power lie somewhat in his reticence to speak of such personal revelations?

What Paul heard in paradise was both **unspeakable** and **not lawful for a man to utter.** It was to be kept sacred between him and God. It was meant for his sake alone; "for one who had such arduous difficulties awaiting him, enough to break a thousand hearts, required to be strengthened by special means, that he might not give way, but might persevere undaunted."[145] Paul communicated all that had been delivered to him to communicate. While heaven is not fully described for us, it is enough to know that we shall share the glory of Christ's exalted presence, and that we are to be like Him now (3:18). We are "not to seek to know anything, but what the Lord has seen it good to reveal to his Church."[146]

In order to introduce what he has to say in v. 6, Paul again (cf. 11:30) declares that he will boast only in his weakness (5). He will not boast in the fact that he has been to paradise. **Of such an one,** or "on behalf of such a one" (ASV), **will I glory: yet of myself I will not glory.** This indicates again the distinction that Paul makes between two aspects of his existence.[147] Of his experience "in Christ," an undeserved act of grace, he will boast, for the credit goes only to the Lord. Moffatt translates it: "Of an experience like that I am prepared to boast, but not of myself personally." When his boast turns away from Christ to himself, Paul can boast only of his **infirmities.**[148] His real boast is only of "a man in Christ," not of *himself* as a Christian, but of himself as a *Christian.*

Lest the Corinthians should wonder why the apostle seems to undervalue so legitimate a subject for boasting, he furnishes them with the motive for his discretion in regard to his revelations. If he **would desire to glory** (6), he would **not be a fool;** such boasting would be in accord with the **truth.** Only a fool boasts beyond the truth. But the real reason that he refrains from boasting about his elevation to paradise is that he does not want anyone to form an estimate of him which goes beyond what he sees in Paul or hears from (*ex*) him. He does not want to be judged "by his report of his own spiritual experiences, but by his

---

[145]Calvin, *op. cit.*, p. 370.   [146]*Ibid.*, p. 371.

[147]Hering, *op. cit.*, p. 95. See comments on v. 2.

[148]The better MSS omit **mine**, but the sense is not changed.

laborious and painful life in the service of the Gospel."[149] The apostle has discovered that, no matter how highly the Lord favors and blesses him, it is the Lord's will that he remain utterly humble; also that no man think more of him than can be gained from normal personal contact. As the Lord was lowly in His ministry among men, so the vessels dare be earthen only, if they are to transmit the gospel (4:7).[150] This must be the attitude of all who would seek to minister to others in Christ's name.

Paul now mentions his **thorn in the flesh** (7) to enforce the point just made. The Lord wants His vessels kept earthen, "to make it clear that such an overwhelming power comes from God and not from us" (4:7, Jerusalem). We see now that the reason behind the apostle's disclosure of his rapturous experience was that he might expose and explain his greatest disability.[151] Hughes writes: "It is most remarkable how, by a kind of condign paradox, the explaining of his deepest humiliation requires the revealing of his highest exaltation, so that the very point where his adversaries hold him to be most contemptible is linked with an ineffable experience far outshining the tawdry tinsel of their vaunting."[152] Thus the hypocrisy of the position of Paul's opponents is revealed to the gaze of all.

The purpose of the **thorn** is doubly indicated by the repetition of **lest I should be exalted above measure.** It was **given** to him as **the messenger of Satan to buffet** him, in order that his ministry might be exercised in deepest humility. The higher his privileges of grace and apostleship, the more necessary was his realization of utter dependence on the Lord. God would need only to withdraw His hand and Paul would be completely in Satan's power. Paul expresses himself somewhat paradoxically: that which Satan used as a torture-instrument against him in the providence of God could serve the divine purpose in his life.[153]

Although the primary and classical meaning of *skolops* **(thorn)** is "stake," a sharpened wooden shaft, it is used mostly in the Septuagint (Num. 33:35; Ezek. 28:24; Hos. 2:6) and the papyri for thorn, splinter, or sliver.[154] Pillai suggests that the

---

[149]Bernard, *op. cit.,* p. 110.   [150]Lenski, *op. cit.,* p. 1298.

[151]Hughes, *op. cit.,* p. 441.   [152]*Ibid.*

[153]See Neil Gregor Smith, "The Thorn That Stayed, An Exposition of II Corinthians 12:7-9," *Interpretation,* XIII (October, 1959), 411 ff.

[154]J. H. Moulton and G. Milligan, *The Vocabulary of the Greek New Testament* (Grand Rapids: Wm. B. Eerdmans Publishing Co., 1949), p. 578. See Arndt and Gingrich, *op. cit.,* p. 763.

picture is that of a barefoot plowman who gets a thorn in his foot. Due to the lack of modern methods of sterilization, he finds it safer to leave it in than to pull it out. So he limps along for a couple of weeks until a thick layer of skin has formed around it; then he will cut it out safely with a knife.[155] The picture then that Paul draws is that of something sharp stuck painfully deep in the flesh which cannot be pulled out but continues to cause aggravating difficulty. The verb **buffet** in the present subjunctive presents the idea of the continual repetition of blows struck with a closed fist (Matt. 26:67; cf. I Cor. 4:11).

But can we specifically identify that to which Paul is referring? He calls it a **thorn in the flesh** (*skolops te sarki*). The **in** is not literally expressed by an *en* but stems from a locative interpretation of the dative *te sarki*. Such a construction would denote most naturally something embedded in the flesh, a physical malady. However, if the apostle had meant this, it would seem more natural for him to have said *en te sarki,* as in Gal. 4:14. Therefore the expression is better interpreted as a dative of disadvantage, "for the flesh," i.e., for its inconvenience. This neither limits it to nor excludes a physical affliction.

Many of the medieval commentators, encouraged by the rendering of the Latin Vulgate, *stimulus carnis,* assumed that Paul was speaking of fleshly temptations to impurity. The Reformers broadened this to spiritual temptations of all kinds designed to prick the bubble of any arrogance that may have survived in the life of the converted Pharisee.[156] Calvin locates the sphere of such temptations in the fleshly nature which remains active in the regenerate;[157] but even modern Calvinistic commentators, while they mention the possibility, do not contend for this as the meaning here.[158]

Some present-day interpreters follow the general trend of the exegesis of the Chrysostom, supported by the Greek fathers generally and by Augustine. These interpreters felt that the reference was to "Alexander the coppersmith" (II Tim. 4:14), the party of Hymenaeus and Philetus (II Tim. 2:17), and all the adversaries of the Word who were doing Satan's business.[159]

[155]*Light Through an Eastern Window* (New York: Robert Speller and Sons, 1963), p. 109.

[156]Tasker, *op. cit.,* p. 175.   [157]*Op. cit.,* pp. 373 ff.

[158]Tasker, *op. cit.,* p. 176; Hughes, *op. cit.,* p. 448.

[159]Chrysostom, *Homilies on II Corinthians,* Hom. XXVI

Munck, for example, accepts the judgment of the Danish commentator, Koch, to the effect that "the 'messenger of Satan' refers
to acts of violence, annoyances, and popular tumults . . . the
apostle's incessant persecutions, the 'sufferings of Christ.' "[160]
R. A. Knox renders *skolops te sarki* as "a sting to distress by
outward nature" in line with his judgment, expressed in a footnote, that it is Paul's persecution by the Jews which permanently
irritates him by humiliating him before the Gentile world.

"When used as a figure of speech," comments Pillai, "a thorn
in the flesh always refers to irritating or bothersome people."[161]
This is seen in Num. 33:55, where Moses warns the Israelites as
they are about to enter Canaan: "But if you do not drive out the
inhabitants of the land from before you, then those of them whom
you let remain shall be as pricks in your eyes and thorns in your
sides, and they shall trouble you in the land where you dwell
(RSV; cf. Josh. 23:13; Judg. 2:3).

This interpretation would fit well with Paul's designation of
a **messenger of Satan.** Paul pictures Satan in other places as the
adversary who interferes with the spread of the gospel. In Acts
13:10, "Elymas the sorcerer" is called "thou son of the devil"
when he attempts "to turn away the deputy from the faith." In
I Thess. 2:18, Paul wrote that Satan had hindered him from
coming as often as he had wanted to Thessalonica.[162] And this
opposition came most often from his "kinsmen according to the
flesh" (Rom. 9:3). Tasker writes, when coming down on the
side of Chrysostom's interpretation, "As there is nothing which
tends to elate a Christian evangelist so much as the enjoyment of
spiritual experiences," so "there is nothing so calculated to de-
flate the spiritual pride which may follow them as the opposition
he encounters while preaching the Word."[163]

The most common conjecture as to the nature of Paul's **thorn
in the flesh,** however, remains that of a bodily infirmity. There
are indications in his letters that his physical condition gave him
difficulty at times. To the Galatians he wrote: "You know that it
was because of a bodily illness [*asthenia tes sarkos*] that I preached
the gospel to you the first time; and that which was a trial to
you in my bodily condition [*en te sarki mou*] you did not despise

---

[160]*Op. cit.*, p. 325, fn. 1.   [161]*Op. cit.*, p. 109.

[162]This is not to deny that Satan is also portrayed in Scripture as the
agent of physical affliction: Job 2:5; Luke 13:16.

[163]*Op. cit.*, p. 176.

or loathe, but you received me as an angel of God, as Christ Jesus *Himself*" (4:13-14, NASB; cf. 1:8; I Cor. 2:3). Of Paul's attitude toward his ministry he has already written in this letter: "No wonder we do not lose heart! Though our outward humanity is in decay, yet day by day we are inwardly renewed" (4:16, NEB). The precise identification of such a physical infirmity has ranged from an earache or headache[164] to epilepsy[165] (Gal. 4:14), eye trouble (Gal. 4:15; 5:11), and a recurrent malarial fever. The last perhaps is the most plausible, for it is accompanied by a peculiar headache which has been described as "a red-hot bar thrust through the forehead," a description similar to Paul's **thorn in the flesh**.[166] Ramsay writes that malarial fever in some constitutions recurs "in very distressing and prostrating paroxysms, whenever one's energies are taxed for a great effort. Such an attack is for the time absolutely incapacitating: the sufferer can only lie and feel himself a shaking and helpless weakling, when he ought to be at work. He feels a contempt and loathing for self, and believes that others feel equal contempt and loathing."[167]

Such is the range of the best guesses. We do not and cannot know precisely to what the apostle was referring by his **thorn in the flesh**. It is no doubt best that he did not speak plainly enough for us to know. As it is, all of us possess inspired guidance for our particular "thorn for the flesh." We have a perspective from which to handle that which plagues our outward nature, whether it is a physical affliction, the actions of other people, or specific circumstances that humiliate us. Lenski insists that not only is it not known to us, but that even the Corinthians could not understand Paul's figurative language: "Paul tells about this thorn for the flesh just as he tells about his *raptus* into Paradise for the first time. In both he bares intimate secrets of his personal life which were never bared to the Corinthians before and are now bared only under compulsion."[168]

---

[164]Tertullian, *De Pudis.*, xiii, 16.

[165]Joseph Klausner, *From Jesus to Paul* (New York: The Macmillan Co., 1943), pp. 325-30.

[166]W. M. Ramsay, *St. Paul the Traveller and the Roman Citizen*, 7th ed. (London: Hodder and Stoughton, 1903), p. 97.

[167]*Ibid.*, pp. 95 ff. Allo, *op. cit.*, pp. 316 ff., espouses the fever theory. Barclay, *op. cit.*, pp. 288 ff., also appears to favor it.

[168]*Op. cit.*, p. 1301.

Whatever the identity of the humbling thorn, the apostle prayed earnestly that it **might depart from** him (8). The **Lord** to whom Paul directed his prayer is Christ (9), indicating that Paul equated Christ with God as the Recipient of prayer. Like his Lord in the Garden of Gethsemane (Matt. 26:44), Paul brought his petition for release three times. Even the result is similar: "Not as I will, but as thou wilt" (Matt. 26:39). Paul knew the experience of not having his prayers answered according to his human desires.

The response is definitive. **He said** (*eireken*) is the perfect tense, indicating that the decision continues to stand: **My grace is sufficient for thee: for my**[169] **strength is made perfect in weakness** (9). Paul's suffering is revealed as necessary because the divine power belongs with human weakness; it is finished (*teleitai*) or fulfills its purpose (*telos*) when man has reached the point of utter weakness. Only then is he a fit instrument for the Lord's hands: "Power comes to its full strength in weakness" (NEB).

The **grace** (8-9) that is sufficient (cf. 3:5) for the apostle is not only the favor of God manifested in the life, death, and resurrection of Christ, but also the **power of Christ** (cf. I Cor. 15:10). Thus Paul is not merely resigned to his **infirmities;** he accepts God's will as his own. He joyfully boasts in his weaknesses in order **that the power of Christ may rest upon me** (i.e., spread its tent, *episkenose;* cf. Luke 9:34). The verb may contain an allusion to the Shekinah of divine glory which rested on the ancient Tabernacle in the wilderness (cf. John 1:14).[170]

We are confronted now with a quite different revelation than in 12:1-4, where it was a matter of a vision of paradise and inexpressible words. Here it is the word of grace in personal encounter that gives in one word the meaning of suffering and aid for the sufferer. As the life of the apostle was bound up with the heavenly world in a special way, so was he involved in a special way with the Satanic power at work in his sufferings. This is the paradox of his existence. His ministry as a true servant of Christ necessarily partakes of that of his Lord.[171]

The pinnacle of the letter has now been reached. Paul has related the account of his thorn in the flesh in order that the basic

---

[169]The earlier Greek MSS omit **my.** That it is Christ's **strength,** however, is plain from the context.

[170]See Hughes, *op. cit.,* p. 452, fn. 141. Lenski, *op. cit.,* p. 1307, denies this.

[171]Wendland, *op. cit.,* p. 223.

principle of his ministry might be clearly revealed. From the perspective of the Lord's word, "My strength finds its full scope in thy weakness" (Knox), the apostle looks out on his life and brings it all into focus—human inadequacy makes way for the adequacy of the grace and power of God in Christ. **Therefore** he can **take pleasure in** (is "well content with," NASB) his state of weakness **for Christ's sake: for,** as he says, **when I am weak, then am I strong** (10). His ministry is secure in the strength of Another. This is his relaxed assurance.

His **infirmities,** rather than hindering, actually make room for the strength of the risen Christ to be revealed in his ministry (4:7-10; 6:4-10). He describes his **infirmities** by the four **in** phrases which follow their mention: Paul has had to endure **reproaches** and mistreatments from his enemies; he has not been able to rise above **necessities** and hardships; he has had to flee from **persecutions;** and suffered in the **distresses** (tight places from which he could not escape). All of this he bears gladly **for Christ's sake!** The direct opposite of the power of the world is the power of the Kingdom.

As the apostle concludes the boast that he has been forced to make, he reveals two essential principles which apply to Christian testimony, 12:1-10. The first is that we must be extremely modest when we speak of our extraordinary spiritual experiences: (1) lest we attract more attention to ourselves than to Christ, 1-5; and (2) lest we speak beyond that which can be clearly corroborated in our conduct, 6. The second is that, when we must call attention to ourselves in the course of our witness, (1) it should relate to our condition of weakness in the world, 5, 7; in order that (2) it might be clearly evident that our weakness is really our strength "in Christ," 8-10.

As an apostle, 11:21b—12:10, (1) Paul's credentials consist in his often humiliating sufferings endured for others in the cause of Christ, 11:21b-33; and (2) any boast he has focuses in his weaknesses, that his adequacy as a minister of the gospel might reside in the power of Christ alone, 12:1-10.

5. *Paul's Behavior in Corinth* (12:11-13)

With these verses Paul's boasting has come to an end. He wraps it up with a reiteration of its foolishness and a reemphasis on the authenticity of his ministry among the Corinthians.

In a moment of reflection, looking back over all that he has said, the apostle declares that he has been and is a **fool** (11; cf.

11:1, 16). The perfect (*gegona*) indicates a completed state. The phrase **in glorying** is omitted by the oldest MSS, but **I am become a fool** communicates even more forcefully without it.

While Paul does not excuse himself, he makes it plain that the Corinthians **compelled** him to indulge in self-vindication. For he **ought to have been commended** by them. After all, it was they who constituted his apostolic credentials. They were his letter of commendation (3:2; I Cor. 9:1). In contradiction to the inward witness of their transformed lives they had tragically failed their natural obligation to the apostle. He had been hurt deeply by their ungratefulness and disloyalty. In fact their commendation had gone rather to his opponents, those "super-apostles,"[172] to whom **in nothing** was Paul inferior, even **though**, as he said, **I am nothing.** That which his opponents tried to make him out to be, **nothing,** he takes as his only boast (11:30; 12:9-10). It is this totally repentant appraisal of himself that is the secret of the evident manifestation of the power of the Resurrection in his ministry (cf. 4:10-12; I Cor. 2:2-5).

The fact that **the signs of an apostle** (12) were accomplished **among** the Corinthians through Paul's ministry spells out why he was "not at all inferior to these superlative apostles" (RSV). The passive **were wrought** (*kateirgasthe*) indicates that the apostle regarded himself only as the instrument of the power of God. The **signs** (insignia of apostleship) refer first to all manifestations of the power of Christ through Paul's labors, not least that of changed lives (3:2; I Cor. 9:1), including his own (1:22). Even the **all patience** ("constant fortitude," NEB; 11:23—12:10) with which he conducted his ministry in the face of opposition and hardship is just as much an indication of his genuineness as the more unusual **mighty deeds.**

Signs, and wonders, and mighty deeds do not refer to three kinds of miracles, but to a different aspect of all miracles. First, writes Calvin, "he calls them *signs,* because they are not empty shows, but are appointed for the instruction of mankind—*wonders,* because they ought by their novelty, to arouse men, and strike them with astonishment—and *powers* or *mighty deeds,* because they are more signal tokens of Divine power, than what we behold in the ordinary course of nature."[173]

---

[172]On this interpretation of **very chiefest apostles**, see comments on 11:5.
[173]*Op. cit.*, p. 383.

The ability to perform such acts characterized the ministry of Jesus (Acts 2:22), and was granted by Him to His disciples (Matt. 10:1; Mark 3:15; Luke 9:1; 10:17). It was continued in the ministry of men of the Early Church (Acts 3:1-9; 5:15-16; 8:13; 9:32-34). From this list Paul was not excluded (Acts 19: 11-12), but as he wrote later to the Romans: "I will not presume to speak of anything except what Christ has accomplished through me resulting in the obedience of the Gentiles by word and deed, in the power of signs and wonders, in the power of the Spirit; so that . . . I have fully preached the gospel of Christ" (Rom. 15:18-19, NASB; cf. Heb. 2:4).

In the true apostle the divine power of Jesus was at work. Paul saw in these signs the mark of the authenticity of his apostleship. He viewed them, not as the miracles of a man full of supernatural power, but as proof of the power of Christ graciously manifesting itself through his weakness. Suffering and the insignia of an apostle belong together.[174]

With a final touch of his irony Paul asks the Corinthians in 13 what more they could have wanted of him. In view of the signs that had attested the apostolicity of his ministry in their midst, in what way had he treated them as **inferior to other churches?** There was only one possible thing that he could think of—**except it be that I myself was not burdensome**[175] **to you** (cf. 11:7-10). The NEB paraphrases it: "except this, that I never sponged on you? How unfair of me!" The false apostles had asked for support, as the emphatic **I myself** implies. One of the most difficult things for Paul to endure was the way the Corinthians distorted his motives for taking no support from them. All he knows to say is, **Forgive me this wrong!** The irony is keen, but certainly affectionate, that of "a father cajoling his children into a right frame of mind."[176]

In vv. 11-13 we see a true minister of Christ: (1) His humble yet confident character, 11; (2) His certain yet paradoxical power, 12; and (3) His despairing yet infinite patience, 13.

Before leaving this section perhaps it would be of benefit to gather together the accusations made against Paul by his opponents in Corinth. The main charge was that he had no right to call himself an apostle (12:12; 3:2; cf. 11:5; 12:11). They criti-

[174]Wendland, *op. cit.*, p. 226.
[175]The same verb as in 11:9, "I was chargeable to no man."
[176]Hughes, *op. cit.*, p. 459.

cized him from every possible angle to support their slander. Although his letters were admittedly forceful, his personal presence was pitiably weak (10:1, 9-10). He had not the eloquence or other qualities necessary for a missionary (11:5-9; 12:11). His conduct aroused suspicion, for he always had some scheme in mind (1:12-13; 3:12-14; 4:1-6; 5:11). His incessant commendation of himself only indicated his uneasy efforts to stay in the churches' favor (3:1; 5:12; 12:19). When he refused to accept from the Corinthians the support that he received from other churches, he was revealing his lack of love for the church in Corinth (11:7-12; 12:13). His plans were often carelessly changed without regard for the promises he had made to the church (1:15-18). Some would even have called Paul dishonest in relation to his handling of the collection for Jerusalem. How much of it found its way into Paul's own pocket to compensate him for his so-called free labor for the churches (7:2; 8:20; 12:16-18)?[177]

It was the successful handling of such charges that here allows us to gaze so deeply into the heart of Paul.

C. Paul Plans for a Third Visit, 12:14—13:10

As Paul approaches the end of this letter to the Corinthians, the apostle prepares the way for his third visit: "I am ready to come to you" (12:14). To this end he expresses the nature of his future conduct in line with the basic principles of his ministry among them (12:14-18). But he is apprehensive as to the moral and spiritual condition in which he will find them (12:19-21). They may be certain that he will be as firm in his discipline as their situation demands (13:1-10).

1. *Paul's Proposed Behavior in Corinth* (12:14-18)

The question of money must have been a touchy one (as always!) in Paul's relation to the church at Corinth. It played a significant role in cc. 11—12 and now he returns to it. Paul insists that he will not change his method of operation at this point.

This last phase of the apostle's defense of his ministry is concerned with his approaching **third** visit (14). The first visit was at the time he first brought to them the gospel (Acts 18:1-18). The second was the painful visit (2:1) which followed the writing of I Corinthians.[178] As always, when he is with them he **will not**

---

[177]Munck, *op. cit.*, p. 173.   [178]See Introduction.

be burdensome.[179] Even though Paul had been misunderstood at this point before (11: 7-12), his principles stand firm. The reasons are two. First, his demand of them is far greater than money: **I seek not yours, but you.** He continually (*zeto*) asks of them the best they have to give—themselves, that he might present them to Christ as "a chaste virgin" (11:2), an acceptable offering of his ministry to God (cf. Rom. 12:1; 15:16). Second, it is the normal duty of **parents** to provide for their **children,** and not children for the parents. The apostle makes use of this analogy only as an illustration of why he does not take advantage of his right as a minister in the gospel (I Cor. 9:6-12b, 14). He does not mean by this that grown children have no obligation toward their elderly parents when they are in need (cf. Mark 7:10-13).

For the Corinthians the apostle is willing to go beyond (*de*) mere obligation: **I will very gladly spend and be spent for you** (15; lit., your souls; i.e., your spiritual welfare). The **I** (*ego*) is emphatic. His time, money, and strength are freely theirs, even at the possible impoverishment of his own health and years. In keeping with the analogy of Paul's imagery in Phil. 2:17 ("I am being poured out as a drink-offering upon the sacrifice and service of your faith," NASB), Wendland translates, "I, however, will most willingly offer a sacrifice, indeed I will allow myself to be completely offered up as a sacrifice for you."[180]

The last part of the verse following the earlier MSS should read, "If I love you overmuch, am I to be loved the less?" (NEB)[181] As Filson points out, this unhappy question answers the one in 11:11, and indicates how unnatural it would be for the Corinthians to respond with a decreasing love to the apostle's increasing manifestation of his affection for them.[182]

The fact that he **did not burden** them (16), Paul assumes as conceded by them: "Very well, you will say; granted that I did not live at your expense, but that was just my cunning, so that I might trap you all the more craftily" (Bruce). The charge whispered by his opponents was that the apostle's apparent sacrifice for them was just another trick of his fox-like nature[183] to deceive

---

[179]See comments on 13 and 11:9.   [180]*Op. cit.*, p. 227.

[181]Reading *ei . . . agapo* rather than *ei kai . . . agapon*.

[182]*Op. cit.*, p. 414.

[183]*Huparchon* is to be distinguished here from *einai* and carries the sense of "being by nature." On **crafty** (*panourgos*) see comments on 4:2 and 11:3, where Paul uses the cognate *panourgia* (see I Cor. 3:19; Eph. 4:14).

them. What he had refused in person he had pocketed through his agents whom he put in charge of the collection for Jerusalem. He had not really been out anything.

But who were the **crafty** ones (cf. 11:2-4, 13, 15)? As Calvin writes, "It is customary for the wicked impudently to impute to the servants of God, whatever they would themselves do, if they had it in their power."[184] The self-seeking intruders at Corinth would no doubt have liked nothing better than to get their own hands on the offering. But instead they had been put in an embarrassing light by Paul's refusal to accept personal support, so they resorted to crafty lies to undermine the confidence of the Corinthians in his apostolic authority.

These suspicions, trumped up against the apostle, he answers with a series of four questions (17-18). The basic issue, bluntly put by the NEB, is, "Who, of the men I have sent to you, was used by me to defraud you?" (17) It is supported by a second, **Did Titus** defraud you? (18) These first two questions are asked with the negative particle *me*, which implies "no" as the answer. **Gain** in both questions, as in 2:11, has the connotation of "take advantage of" (ASV). These questions, writes Plummer, are quite ludicrous.[185] The Corinthians have to admit when pressed that **Titus** and the **brother** whom Paul had **sent** with him had conducted themselves with an unquestionable integrity when they came to initiate the collection.[186]

Paul next assumed complete responsibility for the collection and united his integrity with that of his emissaries. As the one sent, so is the one who sent.[187] Have they not acted **in the same spirit?**[188] Have they not taken **the same steps?** This final pair of questions use *ou*, which would indicate that Paul expected a "yes" answer. Both Paul and his messengers were blameless in their motives and actions. The suspicions of the Corinthians are in contradiction to what their own eyes have seen.

The apostle is able to hold to and successfully defend the basic principle of his ministry among them in relation to money because (1) his motive is simply and sincerely the sacrifice of

---

[184]*Op. cit.*, p. 387.   [185]*Op. cit.*, p. 365.

[186]This is not the same as the intended visit of Titus mentioned in 8:18, but the one first mentioned in 8:6. The aorists in v. 18 are not to be considered epistolary, as in 8:18.

[187]See comments on 1:18-20.

[188]Not "Spirit," as NEB. See ASV, NASB.

himself for others; and (2) his handling of the delicate matter of the collection is able to pass the test of open inspection.

2. *Paul's Apprehensiveness* (12:19-21)

His defense finished, Paul's real reason for it is here stated. A series of warnings follow which understandably rise out of Paul's anxiety concerning his coming visit. Will his third visit be as painful as his second (1:23; 2:1)? It is in their hands.

The Corinthians are not the real judges of the foregoing defense. **Excuse** (19) is better "defend." Paul's judgment is not by them, but with them **before God in Christ** (cf. I Cor. 4:3). In contrast to what they may have been thinking "all this time"[189] he is not defending himself before them out of motives of self-esteem or self-protection.[190] Paul's stance, comments Hughes, "so far from being self-centered or self-sufficient, is vicariously Christocentric."[191] He speaks only **in Christ** (2:17; 12:2; cf. 5:17), "a bond that keeps him from pride, parade and crafty guile."[192] God is his only real Judge (1:18, 23; 4:2; 5:11; 7:12; 11:11, 31), and what he is **in Christ** is his only motivation (5:14). So the Corinthians, far from being his accusing judges, are his **dearly beloved**, an expression which he employs for them in the letter only here and in 7:1. All things that he speaks, "we speak in Christ . . . for your edifying" (ASV). It is his loving concern for their spiritual welfare (11:2) that has driven him to a procedure which they may misunderstand.

For (*gar*) introduces one long sentence (20-21) that explains Paul's concern. Upbuilding is a mild way of expressing *their* need! But what he has to say is spoken with the affectionate restraint of a father: **I fear, lest . . . lest . . . lest.**[193] He does not denounce but voices his apprehension. His fear of encountering ethically deficient behavior is put two ways. First that he might **find** them not as he wishes. Second that he will be **found** by them not as they wish;[194] that is, as one who will have to exercise

---

[189]**Again** (*palin*) is a less attested reading than *palai*.

[190]The first sentence is more apt to be a statement (ASV, NASB) than a question (KJV, RSV).

[191]*Op. cit.,* p. 470.   [192]Filson, *op. cit.,* p. 415.

[193]*Me pos* occurs twice and *me* the third time.

[194]The Greek form of the two statements is contrasting: *thelo euro . . . euretho . . . thelete.*

stern discipline. The reference is no doubt to only a minority in the church (2:5-6).

What Paul fears that he may find in Corinth he lists in four pairs. Lenski suggests that "four is used to designate ordinary rhetorical completeness, and the doubling of each of the four intensifies the completeness."[195] Each member of a pair would then shed light on the other. Following the rendering of the NASB the pairs would be (1) "strife, jealousy," (2) "angry tempers, disputes," (3) "slanders, gossip," and (4) "arrogance, disturbances."

As the apostle continues to express his misgivings about his coming visit, he puts it in an unusual way, that **my God will humble me among you** (21). The opposite would be expected, that the Corinthians should suffer humiliation and disgrace. However, Paul fears he will discover that there has not been a repentance for past sins. He would then be made to mourn in sorrow over them. He will have failed to bring about their repentance, which will be for him a defeat. If so, he will accept his humiliation as from **God**. This mourning over their ruin is indicative of his apostolic heart. The only remedy for such unrepentance will no doubt be exclusion from the church (13:2; cf. I Cor. 5:1-5). Their immoral conduct cannot forever be tolerated.

The blatant immorality of some members in the Corinthian church is described by Paul in three overlapping words. **Uncleanness** (*akatharsia*) is a general term for impurity and intemperance of life; **fornication** (*porneia*) refers to promiscuous sexual intercourse; and **lasciviousness** (*aselgia*) indicates the willful defiance of public decency. These sins are the very ones which gave occasion to the writing of I Corinthians.[196] The basic moral problem in the church at Corinth may not have been solved at the time Paul was writing. Nevertheless, the attitude of the majority was such that, if the minority did not repent and turn from their brazen behavior, the apostle could deal with them sternly without precipitating another "painful visit" (2:2).

Opened to us afresh in these verses is the heartbeat of an authentically Christian ministry. From (1) the divine perspective it is (*a*) open to God's judgment and (*b*) controlled by a transforming relationship to Christ, 19*ab*. From (2) the human perspective it consists of (*a*) a consuming concern for others (*b*) exercised so affectionately that humiliation and heartbreak may be its reward, 19*c*-21.

---

[195]*Op. cit.*, p. 1322.   [196]See I Cor. 1:11; 3:3; 5:2; 6:1-10.

3. *Paul's Determination to Be Firm* (13:1-10)

The apostle now gives his final warning to the Corinthians that when he comes the third time he will be as severe in his discipline as their moral and spiritual condition warrants. If that is what they want, they will have the proof that Christ is speaking in him! But he hopes that they will so correct their situation before he comes that he will not be required to employ his authority with such sternness.

With the emphasis of repetition (12:14, 20-21) Paul mentions again that he is **coming** to Corinth for the **third time** (1). Further, he is coming to execute justice in their midst. The charges will be examined and judged according to the Mosaic principle laid down in Deut. 19:15, namely, "At the mouth of two witnesses or three shall every word be established" (ASV). This procedure was approved by Christ for handling cases of discipline and disputes in the Church (cf. John 8:17; I Tim. 5:19; Heb. 10:28; I John 5:8).[197] The Christian Church carried on the OT principle that a man could not be condemned by the testimony of only one witness. Two at least and preferably three were necessary. Paul was going to abide by this principle, but he *was* going to make use of it.

The warning that the apostle had given them on his **second** visit is now repeated (2). The words **I write** make this verse as it stands in KJV difficult. A better translation would be: "I have previously said when present the second time, and though now absent I say in advance to those who have sinned in the past and to all the rest as well, that if I come again, I will not spare anyone" (NASB).[198] The mention again of those who **have sinned** (cf. 12:21) and the fact of their tolerance by the church remind us how difficult it was for Gentile Christians to break with the sexual laxity characteristic of their environment (cf. I Cor. 5:1-2; 6:12-20; I Thess. 4:3-7). The Christian standard of sexual purity came not from the Greeks, but from the OT and the Jews. Paul warns such people and **all** the rest of them that when he comes he **will not spare** those who refuse to repent (cf. 10; 10:6). He will

---

[197]Some have felt that Paul was in cryptic or perhaps rabbinic fashion referring to his visits as witnesses against them. So Plummer, *op. cit.*, pp. 372 ff. But with Hughes, *op. cit.*, pp. 474 ff., who discusses the matter fully, it seems best to take it literally.

[198]See also RSV, which clearly brings out the sense.

excommunicate them from the fellowship of the church if his hand is forced.

With a final reference to the interchange of weakness and strength in the apostle of Christ,[199] Paul gives the reason why he will not be lenient when he comes (3). He is now ready to give his opponents and all who have listened to them the **proof** of Christ's **speaking** in him. Possibly in view of their richness of spiritual gifts (I Corinthians 12 and 14) they have refused to perceive the power of Christ in Paul's presence with them (cf. 10:10). So now they are going to get the decisive sign that they want, though not in the way they want. Stern discipline will be a sure sign that through Paul's ministry Christ **is not weak** toward them, but rather **is mighty in** them (cf. Rom. 15:18). As Denney says, "In challenging Paul to come and exert his authority . . . in presuming on what they called his weakness, they were really challenging Christ."[200]

What the apostle is really getting at is that the pattern of his ministry is simply that of his Lord: **For though** (*kai gar*) **Christ was crucified through weakness, yet** (*alla*) **he liveth by the power of God** (4). Out of (*ex*) His condition of incarnate **weakness** Christ suffered "the death of the cross" (Phil. 2:8), the ultimate of humiliation and weakness. **Yet . . . by** (*ek*, out of) **the power of God** He now lives "by the resurrection from the dead" (Rom. 1:4). In Jesus' ministry on behalf of fallen men the extremity of His weakness became the point at which God by the resurrection of Jesus most convincingly revealed His power to lift men out of their sins (cf. Acts 2:22-36; Rom. 4:25; 5:10; I Cor. 15:16-17). Denney beautifully leads us to the point that Paul is after: "The cross does *not* exhaust Christ's relation to sin; He passed from the cross to the throne, and when He comes again it is as Judge."[201] So "when Christ comes again, *He* will not spare. The two things go together in Him: the infinite patience of the cross, the inexorable righteousness of the throne."[202]

The same is true of Christ's ministers: **For we also** (*kai gar*) **are weak in him, but** (*alla*)[203] **we shall live with him by the power of God toward you.** Since the resurrection life of Christ is at work in the ministry of Paul (4:10-14), he will be able to

---

[199]See comments on 1:3-7.   [200]*Op. cit.*, p. 806.

[201]*Ibid.*, p. 807.   [202]*Ibid.*

[203]Note the parallel construction of the two parts of this verse as indicated by the repetition of *kai gar* and *alla*.

come to them with the authority of the living Christ. Because of
the full-orbed nature of this power he will not and cannot spare
the unrepentant sinner. The power of God in the gospel of Christ
(Rom. 1:16) cuts both ways, "to the one an aroma from death
to death, to the other an aroma from life to life" (2:16, NASB).
Of this power Paul, as an apostle of Christ, is an instrument. And
toward the Corinthians it will be made manifest. Power, not
weakness, will mark his impending visit.

Wendland observes that these verses (3-4) precisely define
the foundation of all that Paul has said about his weakness and
suffering.[204] His power residing in his weakness is in the likeness
of his crucified and resurrected Lord. Therefore his weakness
can be his boast; therefore also Christ acts through His apostle
and the life of Christ flows out from him. The "another gospel"
(11:4) of his opponents is characterized by the fact that it does
not include this paradox, this oppositeness of Cross and Resurrection, of suffering and the power of God, which are yet one.
For that reason his opponents do not comprehend the weakness
of Paul; they are fools if they suppose that they have disposed of
his apostleship with the proof that he is "nothing" (12:11).

The tables are now turned. With the threat of judgment which
arises out of the certainty that Christ is acting in him, the apostle
exhorts the church members at Corinth to continually **examine**
themselves to see if they are **in the faith** (5). They are to **prove**[205]
themselves. **Yourselves** and **your own selves** receive the emphasis
by being placed first in the Greek. Paul hopes to get the desired
behavior from them by reminding them that they are Christians:
"Or do you not fully know your own selves, that Jesus Christ is
in you?—unless you, indeed, are disproved!" (Lenski) If they
are **reprobates,** they will not apply the test. Paul's question probes
them, for if they are truly believers they will not resent a real
test. The form of the question (*ei meti*) indicates that Paul believed them sound at heart. The expressions **in the faith** and
Jesus Christ . . . in you interpret each other: "Faith is the reality
of the presence of Christ, it is the life of Christ in those who believe . . . (cf. Gal. 2:20; Eph. 3:17)."[206] The test of the authen-

---

[204]*Op. cit.,* p. 231.

[205]This word and its cognates occur six times in vv. 3, 5-7; **proof, prove,
reprobates, approved, reprobates.** The basic idea involved is
that of having succeeded or failed to meet a test, e.g., the purity of metals
or the genuineness of coins.

[206]Wendland, *loc. cit.*

ticity of their relationship to Christ is the ethical quality of their behavior.

On the same basis that the Corinthians are able to detect the presence of Jesus Christ in themselves, Paul hopes that they will be able to recognize that he and his associates in the ministry are not **reprobates (6)**. **I trust** is literally "I hope" (*elipizo*). He hopes that in their own saving relationship to Christ they will find the "proof of Christ speaking" (3) in him that they desired. Perhaps then he will not have to come with severity.

In line with this hope he is praying **to God** that they will do nothing **evil (7)**. He trusts that they will do the **honest** (*kalon*, morally right) thing and not side with the impenitent sinners in Corinth. Such is the motive for his prayer, not merely that he **should appear approved**. In fact he and his companions would be willing to appear as **reprobates** if only the Corinthians will do what is right. He is willing to dispense with the opportunity to demonstrate by disciplinary action the "proof" (3) that Christ is speaking in him with God's power. Paul does not delight in the chastisement of his spiritual children.[207]

Even the apostle's right to a clear, personal vindication must give way before **the truth (8)**, i.e., before the progress of the gospel in Corinth. All self-interest is barred (5:14). He wants only the obedience, purity, and unity of the church. To exercise his authority for its own sake would be a prostitution of his apostleship. The proper reception of the gospel is the great aim of his life to which all else surrenders. Thus Paul, in whom is "the truth of Christ" (11:10), is able (*dynametha*) to **do nothing against the truth**.

Rather, he explains, he rejoices when he is **weak** and they **are strong (9)**. He is **glad** to lose the opportunity for the legitimate use of his power to punish and thus to prove his strength if it can be due to their moral and spiritual strength. Paul's **wish** is a prayer.[208] This prayer is for their **perfection** (*katartisis*), the restoration of all that has been out of order in their lives as mem-

---

[207]For an interpretation of 2-7 which sees the possibility here, not of severe church disciplines and exclusion from the church, but something far worse, see Munck, *op. cit.*, pp. 189 ff. The suggestion is some miraculous punishment such as that mentioned possibly in I Cor. 5:4, which he thinks is alluded to in 10:11, the deliverance of the church over to Satan. It would thus be separated from Christ and exposed to the sufferings which Satan controls.

[208]**Wish** is a weak translation; the word is *euchomai*, as in 7.

bers together in the body of Christ. The basic idea in the word is that of being properly equipped and ordered for harmonious and efficient functioning. Delling writes that here *katartisis* "denotes inner strength, whether of the community in its organic relationship, or of the character of its members, i.e., their maturity as Christians."[209] The concern is similar to that in 7:1. As Wesley comments, it is **perfection** "in the faith that worketh by love."[210] The prayer comprehends (1) the full acceptance of the grace and (2) the effective expression of the ethic of Christian holiness.

The apostle has written this letter to help the Corinthians (10). He concludes with his answer to the charge of being powerful in his letters but weak in his personal presence (10:10), which has been in view since 10:1. He writes as he has when **absent** so that when **present** he will not have to act with **sharpness**. This is not a denial of his authority, but its obedient exercise. The **power which the Lord** gave him was not for **destruction** but for **edification** (10:8; 12:19). His authority is "for upbuilding and not for wrecking" (Lenski). But severe he will be if they have not taken action. How he comes is their decision. He is hopeful.

The authority of the Apostle Paul as a minister of Christ (1) includes the power to discipline in the church when repentance is persistently refused, for (2) it is the power of the life of Christ, but (3) its use is always controlled by the ultimate purposes of the gospel (cf. Matt. 16:19; 18:15-18; John 20:23; Acts 5:1-6; I Cor. 5:5).

In the NT Church there is only one Source of authority, Jesus Christ. He confers His authority by His presence upon His apostles, ministers, teachers, administrators, etc., who exercise their authority in line with their various functions. Such authority is not merely officially delegated, but must authenticate itself in its exercise: "We shall live with Him because of the power of God *directed* toward you" (4, NASB).

In 12:14—13:10, Paul has confronted us with a ministry that is (1) Consistent in its motivating principles, 12:14-18; (2) Compassionate in its commitment to the welfare of the church, 12:19-21; and (3) Confirmed in its authority to uphold the integrity of the body of Christ, 13:1-10.

---

[209]"*Artios, ex-, katartizo, katartismos, katartisis,*" TDNT, I, 476. See Clarke's comment, *op. cit.*, p. 374.

[210]*Op. cit.*, p. 676.

D. PAUL CONCLUDES THE LETTER, 13:11-14

The apostle brings this difficult and costly letter spontaneously and affectionately to its close: "The grace of the Lord Jesus Christ . . . be with you all" (14). Exhortation (11), greetings (12-13), and benediction (14) follow rapidly on one another as if they belonged together.

1. *Exhortation and Greeting* (13:11-13)

With his words of **farewell** (11)[211] the apostle joins together the final admonitions which his Corinthian **brethren** are in need of (12:20). They consist of a rhetorical four in two pairs (cf. 11: 23). These admonitions are all present imperatives, implying continuity of action. But the first two may be either passive or middle voice. We interpret them with Lenski as permissive passives.[212] **Be perfect,** then, linking up with Paul's prayer for their "perfection" (9), would mean, "Let yourselves be steadily perfected"[213] in grace and ethic. **Be of good comfort** (cf. 1:3) probably should be translated in terms of the other meaning of *parakaleisthe,* "Let yourselves be exhorted."[214] The meaning is that of the RSV: "Heed my appeal." The Corinthians are asked to receive the admonitions that will lead them to the perfecting of their lives together as the body of Christ. Involved is the quality of their relationship to Christ and its increasing expression within the fellowship of the church.

The second pair of imperatives likewise go together. The first, **Be of one mind** ("keep minding the same things," Lenski; cf. Rom. 12:16; 15:5; Phil. 2:2; 4:2), has reference to a common commitment to the love and truth of the gospel of Christ. The second, **Live in peace,** urges them to work out in the fellowship of believers the preceding commitment. The same two exhortations are combined beautifully by Paul when he writes later to the Philippians (2:5), "Have the same thoughts among yourselves as you have in your communion with Christ Jesus."[215] If

---

[211]Hughes (*op. cit.,* p. 486) feels that *chairete* should be translated here in the stronger sense of "rejoice" (Phil. 3:1).

[212]*Op. cit.,* p. 1338.

[213]If middle, the force would be "keep perfecting yourselves."

[214]If middle, we could translate "keep exhorting [or encouraging] one another."

[215]Arndt and Gingrich, *op. cit.,* p. 874.

643

the preceding admonitions are constantly observed, the encouraging promise is that **the God of love and peace shall be with you.** The phrase **the God of love** is unique to this verse, but "the God of peace" occurs frequently.[216] Only by channeling the love and peace of God to others can the Corinthians continue to enjoy the blessing of the presence of **the God of love and peace** (cf. Acts 5:32). The continuity of the promise with the two preceding imperatives is highly suggestive. Perhaps also it could be said that the second pair of imperatives reveals the how of the first two. The verse could then be analyzed in order as presenting "Life in Christ": (1) The call; (2) The method; (3) The results.

The brotherly love to which the apostle exhorts them is to be sealed with the **holy kiss** (12).[217] This external symbol is not merely a token of affection. It is **holy** (*hagio*) because it was exchanged by Christian (*hagioi*) worshippers as a sign of their brotherhood in Christ. The practice was adopted by the Christian Church from the synagogues, where the sexes were separated in worship. In the Christian services only men would kiss men and women would kiss women, as a security that the **kiss** would be kept **holy.** In the light of the significance of this custom in early Christianity and Judaism, the treacherous nature of Judas' betrayal kiss is clearly evident (Mark 14:45).

All the saints (13),[218] that is, all the Christians in Macedonia, from where Paul was writing, sent their greetings to the Corinthians. The Macedonian[219] Christians, although most of them had never met the Corinthians, belonged together with them to the body of Christ, which is the Church universal. They are united in Christ. The apostle has pointed up the behavior required of the church, not only by direct appeal, but also by mention of a Christian custom, and by a reminder of the Church as a wider fellowship.

2. *The Threefold Blessing* (13:14)

Finally, what the apostle desired most of all for the Corinthians, the full salvation blessing of God with all its ethical implications, is expressed in his benediction: **The grace of the Lord**

---

[216]Rom. 14:20; 15:33; Phil. 4:9; I Thess. 5:23. The order of the two genitives which are formed into one unit by the article is no doubt suggested by the two preceding imperatives.

[217]Rom. 16:16; I Cor. 16:20; I Thess. 5:26; I Pet. 5:14.

[218]See comments on 1:1.   [219]Hanson, *op. cit.,* p. 74.

Jesus Christ, and the love of God, and the communion of the Holy Ghost, be with you all (14). Amen is added only by the later MSS. Paul's normal benediction contains only the first phrase (I Cor. 16:24; Gal. 6:18; Phil. 4:23; I Thess. 5:28; II Thess. 3:18; Philem. 25). The inclusion of the other expression in this particular instance was due no doubt to the condition of the Corinthian church.

The three-in-one prayer of the apostle is comprehensively expressed in terms of the experience and faith of the Early Church. This explains the fact that the order—Christ, God, Spirit—is not designedly Trinitarian. The order is that of salvation experience. It is important to note that when Paul wanted to sum up his gospel those words most naturally fell into his mind which, when logically developed, form the basis of the doctrine of the Trinity.[220] The fact that in a single sentence the name of Jesus, a mere 30 years after His death, is brought together with the Holy Spirit and the name of God in a prayer indicates that "the fully developed doctrine of the Trinity has its theological roots in adoration of Jesus Christ."[221] Partly from this short summary Cullmann observes that "early Christian theology is in reality almost exclusively Christology."[222] The men of the NT were primarily concerned with redemptive history, which for them was a "Christ-process."

Theologically the three phrases form a parallel and progressing symmetry. **The grace of the Lord Jesus Christ** in which **the love of God** is revealed, Paul experienced through "participation[223] in the Holy Spirit" (RSV, marg.). The first two genitives are subjective and the last objective.[224] The balance of the gift and the Giver of the first two expressions is carried on in the third when it is recognized that the Holy Spirit is himself both the Gift and the Giver. He is the Founder of this fellowship which is constituted by a common sharing in the Holy Spirit (cf. Acts 2:42; Phil. 2:1).

This "participation in the Holy Spirit" brings to subjective reality in the experience of the Church the saving activity of God, that objective redemptive reality resident in the person of Christ in virtue of His crucifixion, resurrection, and exaltation (cf. I Cor.

---

[220]*Ibid.*

[222]*Christology,* p. 2.

[221]Strachan, *op. cit.,* p. 146.

[223]Greek *koinonia.* See on 8:4.

[224]Some would keep the third also subjective, translating, "The fellowship created by the Holy Spirit."

1:9; I John 1:3). The identity between the two is thus a dynamic one of redemptive action, an identity rooted in the fact that the Spirit as the Life of the resurrected and exalted Lord (13:4; Rom. 1:4; 6:4; 8:11; I Cor. 6:14; 15:45) is likewise the Channel of the Lord's life in redemptive action (3:17; I Cor. 12:3).

The emphasis of the apostle's prayer is on the mutuality of the participation, the ethical difference it will make in the life of the church. The practical realization of **the grace of the Lord Jesus Christ, and the love of God,** as the Corinthians open their lives more and more to the Holy Spirit, will bring about the perfecting (9) that Paul desires for them. Their "fellowship in the Holy Spirit" (NEB) is the common sharing in the Spirit which allows Him as both Gift and Giver to effect the unity and mutual love which must permeate the ethical life of the Church as the body of Christ. In fact it is only their common experience of the one Spirit which constitutes them the body of Christ (I Cor. 12: 12-13).

Paul gives evidence in his own attitude of that for which he is praying, for his desire is the same for **all.** There are no reservations, no grudges held; only a love that transcends all human barriers and longs for the best that God has for them. Their highest good expressed in a breathtaking summary of the Christian faith is (1) the grace of Christ (2) revealing the love of God (3) by their fellowship in the Holy Spirit, which is able to transform the quality of their lives together. With his spiritual hands thus spread in benediction over the Corinthians, the apostle's voice sinks into silence.

Every facet of Paul's closing words has revealed his apostolic heart. (1) His closing advice, (2) his attention to the formalities of Christian courtesy, and (3) his benedictory blessing are all concerned with the progress of the gospel of Christ at Corinth.

Because this gospel is authentically at work in Corinth, Paul has confident hope. He believes the complete openness of his witness to the character of his ministry will have effectively countered the resistance to his apostolic authority, 10:1—12:14. His service to Christ (1) does not depend upon the methodology of a worldly power structure, 10:1-18; but rather (2) his boast is in the power of the living Christ which finds its occasion in that which the world calls weakness, 11:1—12:13; and (3) this is the manner in which he as always will continue to make himself known to the Corinthians, 12:14—13:14.

This letter has come to us from the agonizing, refining furnace of interpersonal conflict. At stake have been the integrity and authority of Paul's ministry among the Corinthians. An illuminating presentation of the Christian ministry is torn from his soul by the suspicions of his converts. It is a ministry (1) whose integrity is simply that of the gospel it proclaims, cc. 1—7; and (2) whose authority is only that of the presence of Christ, cc. 10—13. The focus is Christ crucified and risen—the weakness of His humiliation and the power of His resurrection.

These basic principles of Paul's apostolic ministry must also be those of everyone who would serve in the name of Christ. Our stewardship of the gospel is in direct continuity with that of Paul and his helpers. This most crucial letter for our understanding of the Christian ministry could be profitably read, studied, or even consecutively preached through asking the question, "Precisely how are Christians to relate Christ and the gospel to the world in which we live?" Throughout this letter, in a strangely relevant way, witness is powerfully borne "to the inescapable truth that the mission of the church as the body of Christ is the self-giving, sacrificial, suffering ministry of Jesus."[225]

"So death works in us, but life in you" (4:12, NASB).

---

[225]See Introduction.

Bibliography

I. COMMENTARIES

ALLO, P. E. B. *Seconde Epitre aux Corinthiens.* Second edition. "Etudes Bibliques." Paris: Librairio LeGoffre, 1956.

BARCLAY, WILLIAM. *The Letters to the Corinthians.* "The Daily Study Bible." Edinburgh: The Saint Andrew Press, 1954.

BEET, J. A. *A Commentary on St. Paul's Epistles to the Corinthians.* Fifth edition. London: Hodder and Stoughton, 1892.

BENGEL, JOHN ALBERT. *Gnomon of the New Testament.* Translated by ANDREW R. FAUSSET. Seventh edition. Edinburgh: T. & T. Clark, 1877.

BERNARD, J. H. "The Second Epistle to the Corinthians." *The Expositor's Greek Testament.* Edited by W. R. NICOLL. Grand Rapids: Wm. B. Eerdmans Publishing Co., 1951 (reprint).

BRUCE, F. F. *Paul and His Converts.* New York: Abingdon Press, 1962.

CALVIN, JOHN. *Commentary on the Epistles of Paul the Apostle to the Corinthians.* Translated by JOHN PRINGLE, Vol. II. Grand Rapids: Wm. B. Eerdmans Publishing Co., 1948 (reprint).

CLARKE, ADAM. *The New Testament of Our Lord and Saviour Jesus Christ, A Commentary and Critical Notes,* Vol. II. New York: Carlton & Phillips, 1854.

DENNEY, JAMES. "The Second Epistle to the Corinthians." *The Expositor's Bible.* Edited by W. R. NICOLL, Vol. V. Grand Rapids: Wm. B. Eerdmans Publishing Co., 1947 (reprint).

FILSON, FLOYD. "The Second Epistle to the Corinthians" (Exegesis). *The Interpreter's Bible.* Edited by GEORGE A. BUTTRICK, et al., Vol. X. New York: Abingdon-Cokesbury Press, 1953.

HANSON, R. P. C. *The Second Epistle to the Corinthians.* "Torch Bible Commentaries." London: SCM Press, 1954.

HERING, JEAN. *La Seconde Epitre de Saint Paul aux Corinthians.* "Commentaire du Nouveau Testament," Vol. VIII. Paris: Delachaux and Niestle, 1958.

HODGE, CHARLES. *An Exposition of the Second Epistle to the Corinthians.* New York: Robert Carter and Brothers, 1868.

HUGHES, PHILIP E. *Paul's Second Epistle to the Corinthians.* "The New International Commentary on the New Testament." Grand Rapids: Wm. B. Eerdmans Publishing Co., 1962.

KLING, CHRISTIAN FREIDRICH. "Corinthians" (Exegesis). *A Commentary on the Holy Scriptures.* Edited by JOHN PETER LANGE. Grand Rapids: Zondervan Publishing House (reprint of 1868 edition).

LENSKI, R. C. H. *The Interpretation of St. Paul's First and Second Epistle to the Corinthians.* Columbus: Wartburg Press, 1937.

LIGHTFOOT, J. B. *Notes on Epistles of St. Paul from Unpublished Commentaries.* New York: Macmillan and Co., 1895.

McFayden, John Edgar. *The Epistles to the Corinthians.* New York: Hodder and Stoughton, 1911.

Menzies, Allan. *The Second Epistle of the Apostle Paul to the Corinthians.* London: Macmillan and Co., 1912.

Morgan, G. Campbell. *The Corinthian Letters of Paul.* New York: Fleming H. Revell Co., 1946.

Plummer, Alfred. *A Critical and Exegetical Commentary on the Second Epistle of St. Paul to the Corinthians.* "The International Critical Commentary." Edinburgh: T. & T. Clark, 1915.

Redpath, Alan. *Blessings out of Buffetings: Studies in II Corinthians.* Westwood, N.J.: Fleming H. Revell Co., 1965.

Robertson, F. W. *Expository Lectures on St. Paul's Epistles to the Corinthians.* London: Smith, Elder and Co., 1859.

Schlatter, Adolf. *Paulus, Der Bote Jesus, Eine Deutung Seiner Briefe an die Korinther.* Second edition. Stuttgart: Calwer Verlag, 1956.

Strachan, R. H. *The Second Epistle of Paul to the Corinthians.* "The Moffatt New Testament Commentary." New York: Harper and Brothers, 1935.

Strack, Herman, and Billerbeck, Paul. *Die Briefe des Neuen Testaments und die Offenbarung Johannis.* "Kommentar zum Neuen Testament aus Talmud und Midrash," Vol. III. Munchen: C. H. Beck'sche Verlagsbuchhandlung (Oskar Beck), 1926.

Tasker, R. V. G. *The Second Epistle of Paul to the Corinthians.* "The Tyndale New Testament Commentaries." London: The Tyndale Press, 1958.

Thrall, Margaret E. *The First and Second Letters of Paul to the Corinthians.* "The Cambridge Bible Commentary." Cambridge: Cambridge University Press, 1965.

Wendland, Heinz-Dietrich. *Die Briefe an die Korinther.* "Das Neue Testament Deutsch." Edited by Paul Althaus, seventh edition, Vol. VII. Gottingen: Vandenhoeck and Ruprecht, 1954.

Wesley, John. *Explanatory Notes upon the New Testament.* London: The Epworth Press, 1950.

Windisch, Hans. *Der Zweite Korintherbrief.* "Kritischexegetischer Kommentar ueber das Neue Testament." Goettingen: Vandenhoeck and Ruprecht, 1924.

II. OTHER BOOKS

Arndt, William F., and Gingrich, F. Wilbur. *A Greek-English Lexicon of the New Testament and Other Early Christian Literature.* Chicago: The University of Chicago Press, 1957.

Baird, William. *The Corinthian Church: A Biblical Approach to Urban Culture.* New York: Abingdon Press, 1964.

———. *Paul's Message and Mission.* Nashville: Abingdon Press, 1960.

Barrett, C. K. *Christianity at Corinth.* Manchester: Rylands Library, 1964.

Beardslee, W. A. *Human Achievement and Divine Vocation in the Message of Paul.* Naperville, Ill.: Alec R. Allenson, 1961.

Best, Ernest. *One Body in Christ.* London: S.P.C.K., 1955.

Bouttier, Michel. *Christianity According to Paul.* Translated by Frank Clarke. London: SCM Press, 1966.

BRUCE, F. F. *The Letters of Paul: An Expanded Paraphrase*. Grand Rapids: Wm. B. Eerdmans Publishing Co., 1965.

BULTMANN, RUDOLF. *Theology of the New Testament*. Translated by KENDRICK GROBEL, Vol. I. London: SCM Press, 1952.

CAIRD, G. B. *Principalities and Powers: A Study in Pauline Theology*. Oxford: The Clarendon Press, 1956.

CULBERTSON, PAUL T. *More like the Master: How to Develop a Christlike Personality*. Kansas City: Beacon Hill Press, 1966.

CULLMANN, OSCAR. *Christology of the New Testament*. Translated by SHIRLEY C. GUTHRIE and CHARLES M. HALL. Philadelphia: The Westminster Press, 1939.

————. *Immortality of the Soul or Resurrection of the Dead?* London: The Epworth Press, 1958.

DAVIES, W. D. *Paul and Rabbinic Judaism: Some Rabbinic Elements in Pauline Theology*. London: S.P.C.K., 1948.

DEAN, J. T. *St. Paul and Corinth*. London: Lutterworth, 1947.

DEISSMANN, ADOLF. *Bible Studies*. Translated by A. GRIEVE. Edinburgh: T. & T. Clark, 1901.

————. *Light from the Ancient East*. Translated by L. R. M. STRACHAN. New York: Harper and Brothers, 1927.

DELLING, GERHARD. *Worship in the New Testament*. Translated by PERCY SCOTT. Philadelphia: The Westminster Press, 1962.

ELLIS, E. EARLE. *Paul and His Recent Interpreters*. Grand Rapids: Wm. B. Eerdmans Publishing Co., 1961.

————. *Paul's Use of the Old Testament*. Grand Rapids: Wm. B. Eerdmans Publishing Co., 1957.

FEINE, PAUL; BEHM, JOHANNES; and KUEMMEL, WERNER GEORG. *Introduction to the New Testament*. Fourteenth edition (revised). Translated by A. J. MATTILL, JR. New York: Abingdon Press, 1966.

GASTER, THEODORE. *The Dead Sea Scriptures*. New York: Doubleday and Co., 1957.

GEORGI, DIETER. *Die Gegner des Paulus Im. 2. Korintherbrief: Wissenschaftliche Monographien zum Alten und Neuen Testament*. Edited by GUENTHER BORNKAMM and GERHARD VON RAD. Neukirchen-Vluyn: Neukirchener Verlag, 1964.

GUTHRIE, DONALD. *New Testament Introduction: The Pauline Epistles*. London: The Tyndale Press, 1961.

HAHN, FERDINAND. *Mission in the New Testament*. Translated by FRANK CLARKE. London: SCM Press, 1965.

HAMILTON, NEILL Q. *The Holy Spirit and Eschatology in Paul*. "Scottish Journal of Theology Occasional Papers," No. 6. Edinburgh: Oliver and Boyd, Ltd., 1957.

HARPER, A. F. *Holiness and High Country*. Kansas City: Beacon Hill Press, 1964.

HARRISON, EVERETT F. *Introduction to the New Testament*. Grand Rapids: Wm. B. Eerdmans Publishing Co., 1964.

HARRISVILLE, ROY A. *The Concept of Newness in the New Testament*. Minneapolis: Augsburg Publishing House, 1960.

HUNTER, A. M. *Interpreting Paul's Gospel*. London: SCM Press, 1960.

———. *Paul and His Predecessors*. New revised edition. London: SCM Press, 1961.

JAMES, M. R. *The Apocryphal New Testament*. Oxford: The Clarendon Press, 1924.

JEREMIAS, JOACHIM. *The Central Message of the New Testament*. New York: Charles Scribner's Sons, 1965.

———. *Jesus' Promise to the Nations*. London: SCM Press, 1958.

KITTEL, GERHARD (ed.). *Theological Dictionary of the New Testament*. Translated and edited by GEOFFREY W. BROMILEY, Vol. I. Grand Rapids: Wm. B. Eerdmans Publishing Co., 1964.

KNOX, WILFRED L. *St. Paul and the Church of the Gentiles*. Cambridge: The University Press, 1939.

KUEMMEL, WERNER GEORG. *Man in the New Testament*. Translated by J. J. VINCENT. Philadelphia: The Westminster Press, 1963.

LONGENECKER, RICHARD. *Paul, Apostle of Liberty*. New York: Harper and Row, 1964.

MACKINTOSH, H. R. *The Christian Experience of Forgiveness*. Glasgow: William Collins Sons and Co., 1961.

MANSON, T. W. *On Paul and John*. Edited by MATTHEW BLACK. London: SCM Press, 1963.

METZGER, BRUCE M. *Index to Periodical Literature on the Apostle Paul*. Grand Rapids: Wm. B. Eerdmans Publishing Co., 1951.

MOORE, GEORGE FOOT. *Judaism in the First Centuries of the Christian Era, the Age of the Tannaim*. Cambridge, Mass.: Harvard University Press, 1944.

MOULE, C. F. D. *An Idiom-Book of New Testament Greek*. Cambridge: The University Press, 1959.

MOULTON, J. H., and MILLIGAN, G. *The Vocabulary of the Greek New Testament*. Grand Rapids: Wm. B. Eerdmans Publishing Co., 1949.

MUNCK, JOHANNES. *Paul and the Salvation of Mankind*. Translated by FRANK CLARKE. Richmond, Va.: John Knox Press, 1959.

NEUGEBAUER, FRITZ. *In Christus*. Goettingen: Vandenhoeck und Ruprecht, 1961.

NICKLE, KEITH. *The Collection: A Study of Paul's Strategy*. London: SCM Press, 1966.

PILLAI, K. G. *Light Through an Eastern Window*. New York: Robert Speeler and Sons, 1963.

RAMSAY, W. M. *St. Paul the Traveller and the Roman Citizen*. Seventh edition. London: Hodder and Stoughton, 1903.

RICHARDSON, ALAN. *An Introduction to the Theology of the New Testament*. London: SCM Press, 1958.

ROBINSON, J. A. T. *The Body: A Study in Pauline Theology*. Chicago: Alec R. Allenson, 1952.

SCHWEIZER, EDUARD. *The Church as the Body of Christ*. London: S.P.C.K., 1965.

———. *Lordship and Discipleship*. London: SCM Press, 1960.

SHEDD, RUSSELL PHILLIP. *Man in Community. A Study of St. Paul's Application of Old Testament and Early Jewish Conceptions of Human Solidarity.* Grand Rapids: Wm. B. Eerdmans Publishing Co., 1959.

STACEY, W. DAVID. *The Pauline View of Man in Relation to Its Judaic and Hellenistic Background.* London: Macmillan and Co., 1956.

STANLEY, DAVID MICHAEL. *Christ's Resurrection in Pauline Soteriology, Analecta Biblica Investigationes Scientificae in Res Biblicas.* Romae: E. Pontificio Instituto Biblico, 1961.

THORNTON, L. S. *The Common Life in the Body of Christ.* Third edition. London: Dacre Press, 1950.

TRENCH, RICHARD C. *Synonyms of the New Testament.* Grand Rapids: Wm. B. Eerdmans Publishing Co., 1953 (reprint of 1880 edition).

TURNER, GEORGE ALLEN. *The Vision Which Transforms: Is Christian Perfection Scriptural?* Kansas City: Beacon Hill Press, 1964.

TURNER, NIGEL, and MOULTON, JAMES HOPE. *A Grammar of New Testament Greek,* Vol. III. Edinburgh: T. & T. Clark, 1963.

VAN UNNICK. *Tarsus or Jerusalem, the City of Paul's Youth.* Translated by GEORGE OGG. London: The Epworth Press, 1962.

VOS, GEERHARDUS. *The Pauline Eschatology.* Grand Rapids: Wm. B. Eerdmans Publishing Co., 1930.

WINCHESTER, OLIVE M., and PRICE, ROSS. *Crisis Experiences in the Greek New Testament.* Kansas City: Beacon Hill Press, 1953.

III. ARTICLES

AHERN, BARNABAS MARY. "The Fellowship of His Sufferings (Phil. 3:10), A Study of St. Paul's Doctrine of Christian Suffering." *Catholic Biblical Quarterly,* XXII (January, 1960), 1-32.

BAIRD, WILLIAM. "Letters of Recommendation: A Study of II Cor. 3:1-3." *Journal of Biblical Literature,* LXXX (1961), 166-72.

BARTLING, WALTER. "The New Creation in Christ." *Concordia Theological Monthly* (June, 1950), pp. 401-18.

BORNKAMM, GUNTHER. "The History of the Origin of the So-called Second Letter to the Corinthians." *The Authorship and Integrity of the New Testament.* London, S.P.C.K., 1965.

CRANFIELD, C. E. B. "Fellowship, Communion." *A Theological Wordbook of the Bible.* Edited by ALAN RICHARDSON. London: SCM Press, 1957.

———. "Minister and Congregation in the Light of II Cor. 4:5-7." *Interpretation,* XIX (1965), 163-67.

FITZMYER, JOSEPH, A. S. J. "Qumran and the Interpolated Paragraph in II Cor. 6:14—7:1." *Catholic Biblical Quarterly,* XXIII (1961), 271-88.

GILMOUR, S. M. "Corinthians, Second Letter to the." *The Interpreter's Dictionary of the Bible.* Edited by GEORGE BUTTRICK, Vol. I. New York: Abingdon Press, 1962.

HISEY, ALAN, and BECK, JAMES S. "Paul's 'Thorn in the Flesh,' a Paragnosis." *Journal of Bible and Religion,* XXIX (January, 1961), 125-29.

KASEMANN, ERNST. "Die Legitimitaet des Apostels." *Zeitschrift zum Neuen Testament Wissenschaft,* Vol. XLI (1942).

McCASLAND, VERNON. " 'The Image of God' According to Paul." *Journal of Biblical Literature*, LXIX (June, 1950), 85-100.

MENOUD, PHILIPPE H. "Revelation and Tradition, The Influence of Paul's Conversion on His Theology." *Interpretation* (July, 1953), pp. 134-41.

SMITH, NEIL GREGOR. "The Thorn That Stayed, An Exposition of II Corinthians 12:7-9." *Interpretation* (October, 1959), pp. 409-16.

STANLEY, D. M. "The Theme of the Servant of Yahweh in Primitive Christian Soteriology, and Its Transposition by Saint Paul." *Catholic Biblical Quarterly*, XVI (1954), 385-425.

STEPHENSON, A. M. G. "A Defence of the Integrity of II Corinthians." *The Authorship and Integrity of the New Testament.* London: S.P.C.K., 1965.

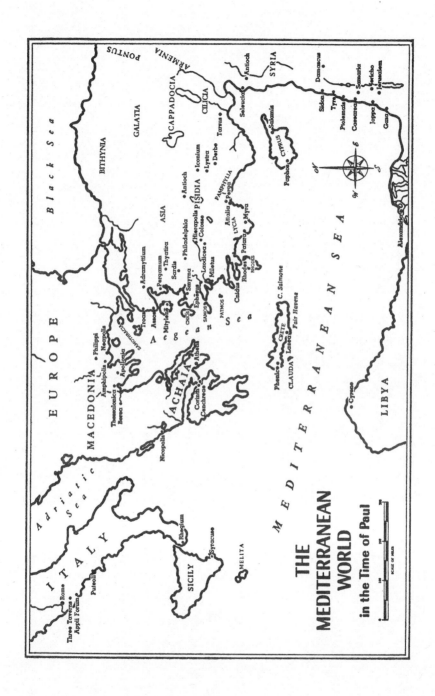

THE
MEDITERRANEAN
WORLD
in the Time of Paul